East Central & Eastern Europe
in the Early Middle Ages

East Central & Eastern Europe

IN THE

Early Middle Ages

FLORIN CURTA
Editor

THE UNIVERSITY OF MICHIGAN PRESS
Ann Arbor

In memory of Lucian Roşu
1932–98

Copyright © by the University of Michigan 2005
All rights reserved
Published in the United States of America by
The University of Michigan Press
Manufactured in the United States of America
♾ Printed on acid-free paper

2008   2007   2006   2005   4   3   2   1

A CIP catalog record for this book is available from the British Library.

Library of Congress Cataloging-in-Publication Data

East Central & Eastern Europe in the Early Middle Ages / Florin Curta, editor.
    p. cm.
    Includes revisions of papers presented at the International Congress on Medieval Studies
in Kalamazoo in 2000 and 2001.
    Includes bibliographical references and index.
    ISBN-13: 978-0-472-11498-6 (cloth : alk. paper)
    ISBN-10: 0-472-11498-0 (cloth : alk. paper)
    1. Europe, Eastern—History.   I. Title: East Central and Eastern Europe in the Early
Middle Ages.   II. Curta, Florin.

DJK46.E23   2005
909'.0491801—dc22

                                                                    2005048574

Preface

This book developed out of three sessions organized for the International Congress on Medieval Studies in Kalamazoo in 2000 and 2001. Several articles published here (Henning, Urbańczyk, Buko, Shepard, and Font) are expanded versions of the papers presented in Kalamazoo. Others (Kovalev, Barford, Petrov, Madgearu, and Stepanov) were later solicited by the editor for this publication.

The volume examines specific aspects of the early medieval history of Eastern Europe—with particular reference to society, state, and conversion to Christianity—and the diverse ways in which these aspects have been approached in the historiography of the region. Many previous studies have described developments in Eastern Europe as replicas of those known from Western Europe or as reactions to military and political encroachments from that same direction. This volume reconsiders such views and attempts to demonstrate that the processes of social integration, state formation, and conversion to Christianity were gradual and complex, displaying many specific variations at the regional and local level. A considerable amount of data is now available, and old questions can now be rephrased in the light of the new evidence. What forms of social organization existed in different regions of Eastern Europe in the early Middle Ages, and how different in that respect was Eastern from Western Europe? What were the implications of the contacts established with the world of the steppes or with early states founded by nomads in present-day Hungary (Avars) or Bulgaria (Bulgars)? How is the process of state formation reflected in the surviving material and documentary evidence? Above all, this volume's aim is to open up an interdisciplinary and comparative dialogue in the study of early medieval Europe, and the included chapters examine the documentary and archaeological evidence in an attempt to assess the relative importance of each in understanding the construction of cultural identity and the process of political mobilization responsible for the rise of states.

This collection of essays should also be viewed as an effort to provide a more theoretically sophisticated account of the early medieval history of Eastern Europe and to bring its study up to date in terms of developments in the regional schools of archaeology and history. The approach taken in this volume is both broader and more rigorously contextual than has been the case with previous English-language studies of the medieval history of this area.

Various authors seek to throw a new light on internal processes of economic and social differentiation, while at the same time moving on from the rigid model of Marxist inspiration, which has prevailed in the historiography of the region for the last five or six decades. A number of chapters demonstrate that the role of individuals, particularly in cases of early state formation, needs drastic reconsideration, while political goals of individual rulers, which have been the object of much discussion in earlier studies of conversion to Christianity, should be approached comparatively at a macroregional scale. The volume also emphasizes the building and rebuilding of local and regional identities and affinities, many of which point to both eastern and western regions of the European continent. What were the reasons for these cultural and political affinities? Are such connections just a construct of historiography, or do they reflect real differences in political choices? How do such developments differ from similar and contemporary developments in the West?

Although each contributor to this volume was allowed some freedom to develop his or her essay in a unique manner, each was asked to address at least some of the previously mentioned questions. Much greater efforts were made to bring uniformity to the spelling in proper names and transliteration of cited references. The preferred form of transliteration is a modified version of the Library of Congress system, but place-names, especially in the case of archaeological sites, generally follow the language in use today in a given area. The only exceptions are commonly accepted English equivalents, such as *Kiev* instead of *Kyïv, Cracow* instead of *Krakow,* or *Prague* instead of *Praha.* This is also true for such general terms as *qagan* (instead of *qağan, khagan, kagan,* and the like) and for such names as *Boleslav the Brave* (instead of *Bolesław Chrobry,* although the Polish epithet is sometimes used separately), *Cyril* (instead of *Kiril*), *Vladimir* (instead of *Volodymyr* or *Włodżimierz*), and *Stephen* (instead of *István*).

I am grateful to the Medieval Institute at the University of Notre Dame for a Mellon Fellowship in 2003/4 that allowed me to concentrate my efforts on finalizing this work and to the Medieval Institute at Western Michigan University, the organizer of the International Congress on Medieval Studies in Kalamazoo, for its continuous support of congress sessions dedicated to medieval Eastern Europe. I would like to express special appreciation to Maria Todorova, János Bak, Piotr Górecki, and the anonymous readers, for their comments, suggestions, and corrections. My thanks are also due to the staff of the University of Michigan Press for their support and cooperation.

Contents

Introduction

Florin Curta

Eastern Europe, East Central Europe: A Brief History of Words

A number of recent studies written after 1989 point to the distinction between Western and Eastern Europe as a product of the Cold War period and to the danger of anachronism inherent in applying such terms to the medieval history of the Continent.[1] Both Eastern and Western Europe became formal political and economic entities only after the Yalta and Potsdam agreements of 1945. Larry Wolff has shown, however, that the idea of "Eastern Europe" originated in the intellectual milieu of the Enlightenment: "The invention of Eastern Europe was a subtly self-promoting and sometimes overtly self-congratulatory event in intellectual history, whereby Western Europe also identified itself and affirmed its own precedence."[2] By contrast, the notion of "East Central Europe" has a much more recent history.

The phrase *East Central Europe* was first coined by Tomas Garrigue Masaryk, the first president of Czechoslovakia, as an alternative to the German word *Mitteleuropa* and its smack of German and Austrian imperialism. Masaryk defined East Central Europe as "the lands between East and West," that is, between Russia and Germany.[3] Oskar Halecki, a Polish historian specializing in the history of late medieval Poland, was the first to address the issue of a specific chronology and history of Eastern Europe, in a paper presented at the Fifth International Congress of Historical Sciences in Brussels (1923). At the Sixth International Congress, which took place in Oslo in 1928, another Polish historian, Każimierz Tymieniecki, first spoke of the medieval history of Eastern Europe, by which he meant the regions east of the Elbe River, excluding Scandinavia and the Balkans. At the Seventh International Congress, held in Warsaw in 1933, a special section for the history of Eastern Europe was formed on the basis of the already existing Federation of Historical Societies of Eastern Europe, founded by Marceli Handelsman in 1927.[4] Two years later, the first publication dedicated to the history of East Central Europe appeared in Budapest, the *Archivum Europae Centro-Orientalis*. By that time, the Institute of Southeast European Studies in Bucharest was already publishing the *Revue historique du sud-est européen*. Halecki, a refugee from occupied Poland, came to New York in 1940. By 1943, he began using Masaryk's phrase in historical studies. Like Masaryk, Halecki viewed East Central Europe as the region between the Holy Roman-German Empire and Kievan Rus'.[5]

Despite the fact that not all historians writing in English embraced Halecki's terminology,[6] the phrase *East Central Europe* is now commonly used in the historiography of the region in Masaryk's sense.[7] However, there is no consensus as to whether or not the phrase is more than a historiographical construct. What seems to be well understood, however, is that "East Central Europe" does not include (the European part of) Russia. By excluding Russia from East Central Europe, Halecki may have reacted to the political divisions of the early Cold War period. In doing so, his goal may have been to hint at a more recent past, namely, the independent development of the region during the decades before the Cold War, and to emphasize the historical roots of that independence. But during the early Middle Ages, that part of Europe had no sharp boundaries, especially to the east. As a consequence, any serious analysis of the medieval history of the region cannot leave out Kievan Rus'. Two papers included in this volume address this issue in strong terms. Petrov's examination of the interaction between state formation and the rise of hillforts and "service settlements" in northwestern Russia has some very important implications, with its challenges to the historical necessity for states and to the alleged difference between early medieval Russia and Poland. More to the point, Shepard compares most fruitfully and suggestively the involvement with Christianity of Boleslav the Brave in Poland and Vladimir Sviatoslavich in Rus'.

The phrases *East Central Europe* and *Eastern Europe* as used in this volume should thus be understood in a primarily and purely geographic sense and in no way as political divisions. If Europe is imagined as the entire area between the longitudinal boundaries of 10 degrees west and 60 degrees east, arbitrarily divided into three slightly unequal slices, East Central Europe is the middle third, between 10 and 35 degrees east,[8] and Eastern Europe is the easternmost one, from 35 to 60 degrees east.[9] However, in this volume, various authors use the phrase *Eastern Europe* as an umbrella term for both thirds, when either the region as a whole or the historiographic concept of the "other Europe" is at stake. The Baltic and the Aegean Seas mark the northern and southern boundaries of the area to which this volume is devoted, while the Black Sea may be considered as a more or less convenient way to separate the geography of early medieval Eastern Europe from that of the Byzantine Empire.

Some have rightly pointed out that medieval Europeans rarely, if ever, thought in terms of a West-East division of the Continent.[10] Prior to the mid-thirteenth century, the territories now defined as Eastern Europe have only episodically retained the attention of Western historians. It was only under the impact of the Mongol invasion that Westerners began to conceptualize the existence of an East European area.[11] Many historians, however, continue to view the distinction between West and East as rooted in the medieval history of the Continent, to the point of associating "the frontier dividing Charlemagne's Europe from the barbarian east" with "the line along which the Iron Curtain fell at the end of World War II."[12] Although much of what is now known as Eastern Europe was never part of the Roman Empire, many believe that the distinction dates back to the partitions of the Roman Empire in AD 285 and 395, later reinforced by the growing divergence and eventual schism between Eastern Orthodoxy and Western Catholicism.[13] Despite the fact that the region was beyond the effective reach of either the Frankish or the Byzantine powers in the ninth and tenth centuries, Eastern Europe is viewed as "a child of the West, who later married the East."[14] To many, the area first became "European" in the 900s, as a result of the conversion to Christianity. Political developments in this region replicated those in the Germanic-Frankish states of the sixth or seventh centuries, at a distance of two hundred years.[15] To the extent that Eastern Europe forms any entity worth studying, its distinctive feature is thus identified as the "consistent lateness of development, politically and culturally, as well as economically."[16]

However, as Jean W. Sedlar noted, the civilization of medieval East Central Europe, "while undoubtedly influenced by the examples of ancient Rome, Byzantium, and Western Europe, was by no means derivative and second-rate" and "does not deserve the historical obscurity to which it has been relegated."[17] Although the area now known as East Central Europe certainly became an area of colonization and expansion from the West during the late medieval period,[18] significant Western influences predating AD 1000 are hard to detect. In fact, much of what we know about the economic and social development in the West during the late sixth to early eighth centuries does not differ much from the picture drawn since the 1950s by generations of archaeologists in Eastern Europe.[19] Both the encroachment of forest and heath and the shrinking population have a direct match in the East. The shift of the settlements from plateaus and highlands to valleys is also a dominant feature in the East.[20] While peripheral areas in the West were left to lie fallow until the assarting (clearing) from waste during the first two centuries of the second millennium, the intensive agricultural system in such areas as Bohemia, Poland, and Hungary came into being only with the rural colonization of the twelfth and thirteenth centuries. Indeed, the three-field rotation, the heavy wheeled plow, and the shoulder collar—all key innovations in Georges Duby's and Lynn White's views of the eleventh-century "agricultural revolution"—were introduced from the West. Recent studies tend to move away from this idea of a technological breakthrough after AD 1000 and, while de-emphasizing the revolutionary aspect of the technological innovations discussed by Duby and White, propose a model of continuity between the early and the High Middle Ages.[21] The emphasis is now on the managerial powers of early medieval landlords and on social relations.

Paradoxically, for many decades now, a similar model is in use among East European scholars. In Eastern Europe, however, continuity between the early and the High Middle Ages has a very different meaning. In Poland, Czechoslovakia, and Hungary, stressing continuity represented a reaction to earlier claims that the rural colonization of the twelfth and thirteenth centuries had brought an abrupt change to a region economically different from the West.[22] While such claims were often viewed as nationalistically motivated (to the extent that the rural colonization was viewed as the work of outside forces), countering them was often done in works firmly grounded in a Marxist analysis of social relations of production. Without due consideration for the validity of conclusions drawn on such a basis, the significant body of literature produced on this subject in the last fifty years or so in certain East European countries was almost completely neglected in the West. The linguistic barrier can undoubtedly explain this "iron curtain," but most recent studies on the early medieval economy of Western Europe ignore even works published in West European languages, even though such studies come very close to, if not overlap, conclusions already drawn by East European scholars.[23]

The present volume rejects the old notion that there is a readily predictable and direct correlation between such factors as Western influence, its nature and impact, the development and expression of cultural identities, the social and political developments associated with the rise of the state, and the conversion to Christianity. It suggests that the available evidence has a lot more to reveal about the interaction between internal and external factors and about the diversity of the local responses to external stimuli. Its purpose is to demonstrate that there is a need to take into account regional variation as well as changes through time. More important, it raises the question of what, if anything, could account for the presumed "lateness of development" in the region, as compared to similar phenomena in the West. What are the differences between contemporary economic and social structures in the West and in the East? Can specific features in East Central Europe be explained in terms of lack of consistency in—or even absence of—structural developments as known from the West? Did Christianity, as an "imported ideology," contribute to the adjustment of social and political institutions in the East to a "Western model"? Were "Western structures" imported into Eastern Europe, and if so, what was the native response? Can the peculiarities of East European history in the early Middle Ages explain the late development of the region in subsequent centuries? Did Eastern Europe follow a *Sonderweg* (special path) responsible for its late incorporation into "Europe" and for the current lack of interest in its early medieval history?

Archaeology and History: European Developments and National "Schools"

If the scope for comparison is extended back into late antiquity, a yet more striking contrast emerges. An explosion of archaeological research in the last fifty years has dramatically changed the picture of East Central Europe during the two centuries or so following Emperor Aurelian's decision to abandon the Roman province of Dacia in 271.[24] Scholars in the West have occasionally noticed this change. But it took a number of recent books to reveal the full extent and the depth of the investigation to English-speaking audiences.[25] The situation remains difficult, however, for later centuries of early medieval history. For example, despite the extraordinary growth of Avar archaeology in recent years, there is still no work in English on that topic.[26] Such lack of interest may be the result of a perceived difference between the recent history of Western (especially American and British) archaeology and the national archaeological schools in Eastern Europe. To scholars aware of the significance of nationalism for recent political developments in the region, the association between history and archaeology seems too dangerous to open up this vast area of investigation.

An intriguing metaphor used in the recent literature to describe the problematic relation between history and archaeology is that of the centaur.[27] The Russian archaeologist Lev Klein argued that the result of the specific relations between the two disciplines in the Marxist system of knowledge was a hybrid product, something as aberrant as a centaur. Klein sarcastically described the typical Soviet archaeologist as completely ignorant about the limits of his own discipline. Instead of questioning the theoretical basis of his approach, "he undertakes raids into the other source-studying disciplines." Klein continued: "In these cases, he usually feels at full liberty and, not being tied and limited by strong rules, he plunders there as he can, shatters methodologies and violates facts. And after dragging his booty away he does not know how to integrate this information with his own. For he is not taught synthesis."[28] On the other hand, historians of the Middle Ages long maintained the view that history tells us a great deal about the past and that archaeology can only fill in the gaps, with some overlap. Even in cases (such as that of early medieval Eastern Europe) in which only a limited number of written sources is available, the practice of "text-hindered archaeology" (to use a recurrent phrase) shows that written information can impede the interpretation of material evidence. Indeed, physical remains can only rarely be linked with a high degree of certainty to a particular moment in history, exceptions like Pompeii being scanty.[29] Not only does the written evidence steer the archaeological interpretation toward conformity with traditional historiography; it also tells archaeologists what to find. For a long time, integration of archaeological and historical data was generally only at a detailed and trivial level, such as linking the phasing of a hillfort on the basis of archaeological analysis with the known historical sequence. To many archaeologists working in Eastern Europe in the early medieval period, written records were a substitute for a sound theoretical basis, to the extent that the need for theory disappears when a chronological narrative is all that scholars aim to obtain from their studies. Despite a long tradition of Marxist ideology, archaeology was often viewed as a servant of history—or as A. V. Arcikhovskii put it, as "history armed with a spade."[30]

Despite relatively recent attempts to move away from the view of archaeology as servant to history,[31] the dominant paradigm in archaeological interpretation in Eastern and East Central Europe remains culture history. The idea of labeling geographically and temporally restricted assemblages of archaeological material as cultures or civilizations is certainly not new. In Eastern and East Central Europe, it could be traced back to a fin de siècle preoccupation with and interest in tracing ethnic identities in the archaeological record.[32] The culture-historical approach in archaeology received its most exemplary expression in the work of a German archaeologist, Gustav Kossinna (1858–1931). Kossinna believed that "sharply defined archaeological culture areas corresponded unquestionably with the areas of particular peoples and tribes."[33] By means of the retrospective method, Kossinna applied his so-called settlement archaeology (*Siedlungsarchäologie*) to infer the situation in the past (prehistory or early Middle Ages) from the (ethnic) condition of the present. He made extensive use of maps to distinguish between distribution patterns, which he typically viewed as homogeneous and sharply bounded cultural provinces. These provinces he further equated with ethnic groups or tribes known from historical sources. Though not the first to attempt a correlation of archaeological cultures and ethnic groups,[34] Kossinna took to its extreme the Romantic idea of culture as reflecting the national soul (*Volksgeist*) in every one of its constitutive elements.[35] It is therefore no surprise that after World War II, despite the grotesque abuses of Kossinna's theories by the Nazi regime, his followers passed over in silence the fundamental issue of equating peoples (*Völker*) and cultures.

One of the most intriguing aspects of the postwar history of Kossinna's approach is its development in Eastern Europe.[36] In the aftermath of the Soviet occupation of the region at the end of World War II, the paradigm of archaeological interpretation favored by Soviet archaeologists was also imposed on "satellite" countries. Despite its veneer of Marxism, this model would have been nonetheless recognizable to Gustav Kossinna. During the years before and, especially, after World War II, Soviet archaeologists had successfully rehabilitated the culture-ethnic concept and were now focusing on isolating archaeological cultures and interpreting them in ethnic terms. The only tribute paid to the official ideology was the tendency to explain qualitative transformations in culture as the result of quantitative accumulations. As a consequence, although the interpretation favored by Soviet scholars became the norm, the first decades of the Communist regimes did not fully dislodge old concerns with finding ancient roots for modern nations and with using archaeology for writing ethnic history. Nor did the collapse of those regimes in 1989 change the value of archaeology for the construction of historical narratives designed to bolster national pride.[37] In Eastern Europe, archaeological cultures are still defined in monothetic terms, on the basis of the presence or absence of a list of traits or types either derived from assemblages and typical sites or intuitively considered the most appropriate attributes in the definition of culture. Archaeologists thus regard archaeological cultures as actors on the historical stage,[38] playing the role individuals or groups have in documentary history. Plotted on maps, archaeological cultures become ethnic groups, ready to be used for legitimizing claims of modern nation-states to territory and influence.

Besides facing the still pervasive influence of German archaeology, with its emphasis on drawing lists of cultural traits to be used for ethnic attribution, archaeologists working in the medieval history of Eastern Europe have done so under the double tyranny of the state and the written document. The study of archaeology as a discipline in the service of the state has only begun,[39] but the political implications of the archaeological work for the study of nationalism are already evident. Most authors represented in this volume focus on the tyranny of the written document. Some still feel the tyranny of the state, if only in much diluted and bizarre forms.[40] In each case, however, there is a clear tendency to give a new meaning to the idea of archaeology as a historical discipline. When dealing with the archaeological evidence pertaining to their specific topics, all of the authors emphasize that new archaeological studies have great potential to contribute to an understanding of early medieval history different from that based on just a few written sources.

Early Middle Ages: Problems of Chronology

A particularly strong emphasis on the archaeological evidence, especially for the period known as the Dark Ages (seventh to ninth centuries), also has considerable implications for chronology. In Eastern Europe, historians struggle with periodization when attempting to match the order of events in Western Europe and to find a place in the history of the Continent for their respective countries. Despite the predominantly Marxist inspiration of the national schools of historiography in the region during the last fifty years or so, such periodizations reflect the inherent contradictions of a predominantly nationalist historiography.

To many, the Danube, much like the Rhine, functioned as a "moral barrier" separating the civilized world of the Roman Empire from the savage barbarians.[41] As a consequence, much of what Halecki called East Central Europe was never a part of the Roman Empire. Nevertheless, following a practice originating in Germany, Czech and Polish archaeologists sometimes prefer to use the phrase *Roman period* instead of *Late Iron Age, La Tène III,* or the like, even for territories too far away from the closest point on the Roman frontier (*limes*) for the Roman army or administration to have had any influence on local developments.[42] With no real Rome to fall conveniently like a curtain at the end of antiquity, Austrian and Hungarian (but not Romanian or Slovak) historians chose AD 568, the year in which the Avars defeated the Gepids and the Lombards migrated to Italy, as the "dawn of the Dark Ages."[43] The "arrival of the Slavs" marks the beginning of the Middle Ages in Czech, Polish, Russian, Ukrainian, Serbian, Croatian, and Bulgarian history and archaeology, to such an extent that the adjectives *Slavic* and *medieval* are often used interchangeably.[44] In the archaeological jargon in use in Prague or Kiev, a hillfort is "Slavic" not necessarily because the Slavs built it but because it can be dated with some degree of certainty to the medieval period.

By 1950, as well as later, many historians and archaeologists were taking seriously the Marxist point of looking for the "feudal mode of production" as the main criterion for defining the Middle Ages. As a consequence, their periodizations tended to emphasize the lateness of local developments and thus differed substantially from previous (and subsequent) interpretations of national history. Given the problems associated with postulating an East European form of feudal society similar to that of Western Europe, especially for regions that were never part of the Roman Empire, great efforts were made during the 1950s and 1960s to demonstrate that, from a Marxist point of view, the early Middle Ages could not have ended before the early twelfth century.[45] Archaeologists and historians alike rushed to illustrate such postulates, and this desire to accommodate the ideological needs of the Communist regimes is largely responsible for the idiosyncratic use of such terms as *wczesnośredniowieczny* (early medieval) in Poland or *prefeudal* in Romania.[46] The underlying assumption, of course, was that at the time of Charlemagne's coronation, of Otto's victory over the Magyars at Lech, or of the First Crusade, the East was lagging behind—still not yet "feudal," not fully "developed," and, as a consequence, waiting for the "classical" form of feudalism to arrive eventually from the West.[47] Pál Engel explains: "twelfth-century Hungary was still archaic in both its culture and its social structure. At the end of the period, we can observe the rapid expansion of Western ideas, institutions, technology and customs. Its agents were foreign knights, merchants and peasants, who came to Hungary, but also Hungarians who had visited the West."[48]

The old chronological scheme following the Marxist stages of development naturally lost its popularity after the fall of the Communist regimes, but in the early 1990s, it was exposed to harsh criticism from yet another angle. A combination of factors ranging from the forceful imposition in many East European countries of Marxist ideology in the aftermath of the Soviet occupation in 1945 to Stalin's postwar policies of fostering a Soviet identity with a Russian makeup have turned the Slavic ethnogenesis into the major, if not the only, topic of archaeological and historiographical research on the early Middle Ages.[49] As a consequence, in Poland and East Germany, the postwar period witnessed massive investments in "Slavic archaeology," together with the imposition of a chronological system of Soviet inspiration. The "arrival of the Slavs" was dated to the sixth century (if not earlier), and all subsequent economic and social transformations, such as the rise of hillforts, were attributed to transformations taking place in local Slavic societies, according to the Marxist model of analysis. This is particularly evident in a number of works by East German scholars, such as Joachim Herrmann, in which there is a strong emphasis on early dates for anything pertaining to the presence of the Slavs in the northern part of Central and East Central Europe.[50] Beginning with the early 1990s, however, a series of dendrochronological dates obtained from early medieval sites, particularly hillforts in northeast Germany and northwest Poland, raised serious doubts about Herrmann's model of analysis.[51]

The now extensive series of dendrochronological dates indicate that the so-called Slavic culture in the region cannot be dated earlier than ca. AD 700. The "Slavic Middle Ages" begin much later than was assumed until now, and local societies did not develop at the pace described in previous research. More important, however, these dates suggest that the gradual changes in Herrmann's Marxist model of analysis were in fact quite abrupt, as illustrated, for example, in recent studies of tenth-century hillforts in Poland.[52] The value of dendrochronology, the science that uses tree rings for dating past events, has long been recognized in Eastern and East Central Europe.[53] Its application to medieval archaeological studies of northwestern Russia, for example, has become famous worldwide because of such sites as Staraia Ladoga and Novgorod.[54] Other areas of archaeological research on the early Middle Ages still rely on chronologies based on the traditional seriation of assemblages with metal artifacts. Most notably, and despite the significant quantity of wooden remains from both habitation units and burials, the precision of dendrochronological dating is much needed in Slavic and Avar archaeology. Remains of wooden beams (some of them recognized as of oak and with, presumably, sufficient tree rings for cross-dating) have already been signalized on various sites in Romania, Ukraine, and Moldova. Fully timber-chambered graves are rare, but more elaborate forms of burial include the use of coffins or bed burials (with one or several planks on the pit floor).[55] The use of this until now neglected body of evidence may certainly bring revolutionary changes similar to those introduced by the application of dendrochronology to the study of hillforts.

So when do the early Middle Ages end and the High Middle Ages begin in Eastern Europe? Generations of historians have been trained to pay attention to such key developments as the rise of states or the conversion to Christianity. A recent collection of studies on medieval Christianity in East Central Europe places great emphasis on the year 1000 and the successful conversion of several political leaders in Eastern Europe around that date.[56] While the significance of Emperor Otto III's visit to Gniezno in that year is viewed by many as a major development of the imperial plans for the expansion of Christendom,[57] the importance for the spread of Christianity of the personal conversion of King Stephen of Hungary has been recently downplayed in favor of earlier missions coming either from the West or from Constantinople.[58] Moreover, the conversion itself seems to have been a long drawn-out process, and recent studies insist on the significant presence of non-Christians (Muslims, Jews, and "pagans") in Hungary as late as the thirteenth century.[59]

Nevertheless, the year 1000 may indeed be a felicitous choice for a conventional end date of the early Middle Ages, particularly from a pan-European perspective. Indeed, AD 1000 appears to mark in some way a watershed in the history of Eastern Europe, as features "normally" associated with Byzantium or with the Carolingian and Ottonian regimes then appeared. With remunerative economic activities, networks of military elites, central locations with military, economic, and religious functions, and, last but not least, ideologies of Christian inspiration, there is little remaining difference between the polities emerging shortly before and after AD 1000 and those already in existence at that time in the West. In this book, without laying any special emphasis on that year in social, institutional, or cultural terms, various authors refer to the end of the first millennium AD as a chronological marker. Undoubtedly, it is one of many possibilities, and as such, this choice is exposed to criticism. But the alternative is equally unacceptable: to view the society of twelfth-century Poland, Hungary, or Bohemia as "early" is in fact a stereotypical view rooted in prejudice and misunderstanding. Janet Martin has argued in favor of treating the period between the death of Vladimir I (1015) and that of Vladimir Monomakh (1125) as different in the history of Kievan Rus' from the "final century" preceding the Mongol invasion of 1237–40.[60] Basil II's conquest also marks the end of independent Bulgaria, with multiple implications for the social and cultural history of the area.[61] In conclusion, the phrase *early Middle Ages* in this book should be understood as referring to the period between ca. 500 and ca. 1000.

Economic and Social Structures

Traditionally, in the Marxist historiography of the East European countries, far greater attention has been paid to economic and social infrastructure than to political leaders.[62] Paradoxically, the Marxist paradigm did not encourage much comparative work.[63] Such work is much needed in the context of the growing interest in "Dark Age economics."[64] Moreover, scholars studying the origins of the West-East distinction typically leave the issue of economic and social structures untouched. More attention to aspects of pastoralism and "mixed economy" is clearly required, and this will help elucidate not only how successful nomadic polities were established in Eastern Europe but also how elites emerged in a variety of political circumstances. The subject has already received some attention in recent years from students of the early medieval history of the region.[65] In an essay about Avars, Walter Pohl made a number of pertinent observations about the interaction within so-called barbarian societies between production of goods and the "predatory war machine," noting that unlike Germanic federates of previous centuries, the Avars never received supplies of food from the Romans, while everything indicates that they were capable of organizing a very successful economic infrastructure.[66] The same is true for eighth- and ninth-century Bulgaria, but the ways in which nomads and nonnomads interacted within the early medieval landscape is not simply an issue that hinges on social organization, because pastoralism and crop agriculture were not mutually exclusive modes of production.

With the notable exception of Hungary,[67] medieval (nomadic) pastoralism in Eastern Europe has often been treated as a marginal topic, despite the relatively large number of anthropological studies of transhumance systems in the Balkans[68] or the Carpathian Mountains.[69] There is a clear tendency to approach the subject almost exclusively in ethnic terms.[70] Transhumant pastoralism was an economic strategy associated with mountains, and old preconceptions about "primitive" or "backward" mountain communities of shepherds may be responsible for the current lack of archaeological studies of medieval pastoralists.[71] A lot more attention has been paid to transhumance in the Mediterranean area, with its typical traffic between upland and adjacent coastal plains. Here, again, comparative studies are much needed to answer fundamental questions. What was the impact of early medieval states on pastoralist practices? How did the introduction of nucleated settlements associated with intensive farming affect pastoralist communities, such as those using the grassy plains of central Hungary?

At any given time, the specific settlement pattern and distribution of elites within any region under the direct control of an early state depend on the exchange network and, ultimately, the economic profile of that region.[72] As a consequence, the archaeological evidence may be of utmost importance in understanding the mechanisms of economic adaptation of early medieval nomads. For example, one important factor in the choice of location for the earliest capital of medieval Bulgaria may have been the cyclical character of pastoralism and the seasonal shift from primarily pastoralist to primarily agricultural profiles in the economy of local communities in and around Pliska.

In chapter 1 of this book, Joachim Henning notes that Pliska was built without any concern for either the networks of roads or the existing settlement pattern in the region. The newly established "capital"—actually an enormous palatial compound—was not "served" by any preexisting or concomitantly established rural settlements. In fact, recent joint Bulgarian-German excavations in Pliska indicate that rural settlements were attached to the already existing palatial compound and formed a cluster of "service settlements" very similar to those known from tenth- and eleventh-century Poland, Hungary, and Bohemia. According to Henning, there is no Western parallel to such developments. The foundation of Pliska may first bring to mind King Godfred's decision to move the merchants of Reric to a new location at Hedeby.[73] But extensive excavations in Hedeby did not reveal any palatial compound comparable to that of Pliska. The shadow a ruthless ruler cast over his subjects seems to have been much longer in Bulgaria than in Denmark. Henning's conclusion also points to such differences: "Political power in early medieval Eastern Europe had very few limits: palaces could be built at various points, as desired, while entire communities of peasants and craftsmen could be moved around as needed." One is reminded of the Khazar capital at Itil, of Kiev, of Bribir in early medieval Croatia, or of Ostrów Lednicki in Poland.[74] More important, Henning's conclusion throws a new light on such archaeologically unexplained phenomena as the large seventh-century center of pottery production excavated in Ukraine at

Kancirka, which now looks very much like the settlement of a group of specialized craftsmen moved, perhaps forcefully, from the Caucasus region into the steppe north of the Black Sea, under the direct control of the Khazar ruler.[75]

Henning insists on the causal relation between the "more rigidly centralized forms of state organization typically associated with some form of despotism" and economic strategies. This is in sharp contrast with traditional interpretations of Marxist inspiration that prefer the opposite equation, from economic infrastructure to state formation. Recently, Paolo Squatriti has persuasively demonstrated that large economic investments in costly building programs can only be explained in terms of early medieval forms of power representation, and this is particularly true of ninth- and tenth-century Bulgaria.[76] Henning's conclusion seems to point to the same direction for future research.

By contrast, in chapter 2 of this book, Paul Barford stresses the importance of extensive agriculture—of a kind described for Bohemian and Moravian lands by Magdalena Beranová[77]—in the creation of loosely defined social and political structures ("tribes") that may have been responsible for the rise of the archaeological phenomenon known as the Sukow culture in northern Poland. The lack of centers of power of any kind until ca. 800, as well as the absence of material culture correlates of wealth and social differentiation, may explain the late process of state formation in that part of East Central Europe. When the first strongholds made their appearance, they were substantially different from such centers of power as Pliska, in that they emerged in the middle of already existing settlement networks. The interpretation of such sites is notoriously difficult. Barford points to the lack of evidence for supporting any interpretation based either on the idea of forts of primarily military use or on the assumption that strongholds were correlates of the burgeoning "feudal class." Being surrounded by earthen and wooden ramparts differentiated such settlements from other contemporary sites, but the significance of the rampart was certainly not military. Instead, Barford suggests that it may have been designed to express social prestige, not of the occupant of the site (the local lord or aristocratic group), but of the community as a whole.

More important for our discussion of economic and social structures, the archaeological evidence of early medieval strongholds in Poland clearly points to such sites being centers of redistribution of goods (including prestige goods, some of foreign origin) and perhaps nodal points in the regional economy, where accumulated valuables, such as furs, may have been brought as "tribute." Barford insists on the chronological (and one may surmise, causal) correlation between the rise of such strongholds and that of networks of long-distance trade signalized by *Seehandelsplatz*-type settlements on the southern coast of the Baltic Sea.[78] Judging from the evidence of associated burial grounds, the people responsible for the foundation of such ports of trade were settlers from across the sea, most likely Scandinavians and Frisians. That ports of trade seem to have emerged before the first wave of Islamic silver reached the south Baltic region raises questions about the exact nature of the relations between such sites and their immediate hinterland. Thomas Noonan's numismatic studies have brilliantly demonstrated that the coincidence in time of both the Viking presence in northwestern Russia and the beginnings of the Islamic silver flow into Eastern Europe was no historical accident.[79]

Missing at the moment is a comparison between the situation in northwestern Russia and that on the southern and eastern Baltic coasts. Noonan's numismatic studies have already begun to show the way.[80] The evidence from Poland seems to suggest that the flow of dirhams found Vikings already settled on the south Baltic coast. Others have suggested that the specific location of Truso (Janów Pomorski) and Grobin may have been associated with the revival of trade involving amber from the Prussian lands.[81] Baltic amber does indeed begin to show up on sites in Central Asia and the Far East at the same time as, or shortly after, the earliest ports of trade were established on the southeast and east coasts of the Baltic Sea.[82] Pace Michael McCormick, there was no comparable trade network moving amber from the Baltic region to central and Western Europe or to the Mediterranean along the old Amber Trail.[83] The study of relations between ports of trade on the south and southeast coasts of the Baltic Sea and those of northwest Russia still awaits its historian, but there are already hints of how much amber alone may change our image of East-West trade networks in the early Middle Ages.[84]

Barford's chapter also calls our attention to tenth-century strongholds associated with the beginnings of the Piast state, which seem to have triggered an explosion of rural settlements known as "service villages," whose exclusive role was to cater for the needs of the nearby strongholds and their garrisons and elites.[85] The term *service villages* is a somewhat awkward translation into English of a favorite phrase of several Polish and Czech medievalists, who use it frequently in reference to villages of specialized workers (peasants or craftsmen) serving the exclusive needs of neighboring fortresses (earthworks and, later, stone castles) under the leadership of the local duke or count. As Henning demonstrates in chapter 1, settlements associated with and certainly serving the Bulgar palatial compound at Pliska can also be categorized as service villages. Similarly, as Ryurik's Stronghold at Novgorod became the most important power center in the northwestern region of early medieval Rus', a number of settlements seem to have emerged solely for the purpose of serving the needs of the prince and his retinue of warriors.

There is more than one parallel between Bulgaria and ninth-century northwestern Rus'. According to Nikolai Petrov's study in chapter 4 of this book, the hoard of agricultural implements found at Kholopy Gorody suggests that, in the absence of any fortifications, the site must be interpreted as a "service settlement," very similar to those identified in Poland and discussed by Paul Barford. However, the hoard itself may be interpreted as something other than just a collection of tools. Its archaeological context and composition is different from contemporary hoards of implements in the regions further south or southeast but is reminiscent of hoards found in strongholds in Left-Bank Ukraine, such as Bitica.[86] Such hoards have been found in much greater numbers in Bulgaria and Moravia and have been interpreted as a ninth-century form of what Marcel Mauss identified as potlatch and what Arjun Appadurai called "tournaments of value"—competitions of conspicuous consumption or even destruction, participation in which was a privilege of those in power and an instrument of status contests.[87] Indeed, as Petrov notes in chapter 4, "hoards of Arab silver were a means not only of storing wealth but also of showing off." Kholopy Gorodok produced not just a hoard of agricultural implements but also one of dirhams. It is possible, therefore, that certain "service villages" were as much stages for elite competition as satellite settlements in the orbit of some nodal stronghold or palatial compound. Polish and Czech scholars have traditionally viewed service villages almost exclusively as subservient settlements. The evidence marshaled by both Barford and Petrov, however, suggests that elites may have resided in such settlements or at least used them as arenas for status competition and representation.

Alexandru Madgearu's study in chapter 3 of this book, examining how control was exercised over such important regional resources as salt, has much to contribute to the understanding of the military organization, as well as the distribution of settlements, in early medieval Transylvania. Gepids, Avars, Bulgarians, and Magyars were all interested in the rich salt mines of central and northern Transylvania. However, because all of these peoples established power centers outside that region, this may have created opportunities for the rise of local elites and for their military organization. Contrary to most recent statements on this matter,[88] Madgearu insists that very rarely, if ever, was local salt a matter of commerce during the early Middle Ages. Instead, the evidence points to salt being the cause of domination, control, and conquest. But, as Madgearu notes, "control over the rich salt resources of Transylvania also offered an opportunity for the rise of local forms of military organization." From local elites, the discussion of strategic resources thus moves on to a different topic, state formation.

The Rise of the State

Early medieval rulers in Eastern Europe have perhaps been most remembered for violent means of imposing their will. Rewriting the history of early states in the light of victorious political leaders has been the task of native historiography from its inception.[89] Yet, whatever glory is attached to the early Piasts, Přemyslids, or Arpadians, their political actions frequently did not follow any grand strategy. As Przemysław Urbańczyk observes in chapter 5 of this book, "no clear rules or recipes were available for how to organize a state, and in many cases, the victors were just survivors of a ruthless struggle for power in which the upper hand went to the claimant able to reorganize the economic system more effectively and to mobilize large numbers for military activities." Comparison between Poland, Bohemia, Hungary, and Kievan Rus' reveals that in all such cases, the state was not the "emanation" of the nation but the result of "private" ventures of the Piasts, Přemyslids, Arpadians, and Ryurikids, respectively. This view is in sharp contrast with the traditional approach of Polish historiography, epitomized by Henryk Łowmiański, who described the rise of the state as a "process of gradual aggregation of Slavic societies in structures of superior organization, from 'small tribes,' to 'large tribes' and 'states.'" Instead, state formation seems to have been the result of sudden and, in many cases, violent change.

Urbańczyk's chapter approaches, from an unexpected angle, a fundamental issue raised in some of the most recent historiographic debates. The recent literature on medieval Western Europe stresses the conceptual link between public order and privileged practice of violence,[90] as well as the religious response to social violence.[91] Violence is thus viewed as a major component of the transformation that some historians have dubbed "feudal revolution."[92] There is almost no evident interest in such problems among historians of early medieval Eastern and East Central Europe,[93] despite the considerable amount of evidence that points to ritualized violence as a major form of political representation in that region. Urbańczyk's conclusion suggests that a comparative approach may be particularly fruitful in this respect, as no historian has so far extended the conceptualization of the "feudal revolution" to East Central Europe.

In the meantime, revolution, rather than evolution, has become the favorite metaphor in use for describing how the Piasts came to power in Poland. To a great extent, the revolution that dendrochronology has caused in medieval archaeology is responsible for this change in terminology. In chapter 7 of this book, Andrzej Buko shows how archaeology confirms this new picture, as the "sudden, sometimes catastrophic, collapse of most, although not all, tribal strongholds" was soon followed by the appearance of "new centers arising at the behest of the Piast rulers." The exact chronology of these new fortifications nicely dovetails that of the political and military activities of Prince Mieszko, as in the case of the strongholds erected anew around Kalisz—perhaps, notes Buko, "in preparation for the annexation of Silesia in 990–91." The results of these new studies, however, bring to the fore, as Buko notes, "the personality of the first ruler of Poland, traditionally obscured by the towering figure of his son, Boleslav the Brave (Chrobry)."

Buko insists on the *early* "European dimension" of Piast political and organizational activities, which has long been associated only with the Act of Gniezno of 1000. However, the best analogies for the "Polish acceleration" ca. AD 1000 may be contemporary developments in Scandinavia, not on the Continent. There have been no attempts to compare late tenth- and eleventh-century Poland with early medieval Scandinavian polities, especially with Denmark under the Jelling dynasty. In both cases, the emphasis on strongholds placed at key points on the overlapping maps of power and trade networks is remarkable. To archaeologists preoccupied with the unique, (perfectly) circular strongholds of tenth-century Denmark, the so-called Trelleborg-type forts, Buko's comments on the use of forts to implement Piast power in late tenth-century Poland will no doubt raise some red flags. According to Buko, "in just two or three Piast generations, between 950 and 1000, Poland had moved from the periphery to the main scene of European developments." But the sharp contrast between Mieszko's beginnings and attempts to incorporate various territories into the Piast state, on one hand, and his son's bold interventions in both imperial politics and Kievan Rus', on the other hand, may suggest that there was nothing particularly unique about the political behavior of such kings as Sven Forkbeard or Canute.

By contrast, in chapter 6 in this book, Tsvetelin Stepanov suggests that the organization of the Bulgar state during the 800s was a reflection of Central Asian, "nomadic" political traditions otherwise illustrated by the Uighur state. In doing so, he expands on his earlier comparative work placing early medieval Bulgaria in the context of contemporary "steppe empires." In this case, however, his intention was less to focus on specific institutions or political ideas, such as the divine kingship, than to examine accommodation practices that enabled "steppe empires" to grow and flourish on the fringes of "sedentary empires."[94] There are striking similarities between the Byzantine-Bulgar relations, on one hand, and those opposing the Uighurs to the T'ang Empire, on the other. Khazanov's model of "trade-instead-of-raid" relations between nomads and neighboring empires can be applied both to treaties between Bulgar qagans and Byzantine emperors and to Uighur-Chinese contacts.[95] In that respect, the comparison between Bulgars and Uighurs is perhaps more illuminating than that between Bulgars and Avars in relation to the Byzantine Empire. Indeed, in comparison to its Avar counterpart, the Bulgar-Uighur nomadic pair was in a much closer relation to neighboring empires and used a much larger variety of methods to intervene in imperial politics.[96] It is important to move on from the traditional approach to nomadic polities (as fundamentally opposed to sedentary societies) and instead to examine them as elite creations within social and political contexts influenced by neighboring empires. The sudden appearance of the title *ek theou arkhon* (ruler by God's grace) in Omurtag's inscriptions dated to the years following the revolt of Thomas the Slav is perhaps to be associated with the military assistance offered by the Bulgar qagan to Emperor Michael II, a striking parallel to Uighur political developments following the An Lu-Shan revolt.[97]

Conversion to Christianity

Given the centrality of conversion to both Christianity as a whole and to the formation of East European society in particular, the considerable amount of literature devoted to analyzing and understanding the process of conversion is not surprising. Following A. D. Nock's influential distinction between "conversion" (as a fundamental reorientation of one's system of values and beliefs) and "adhesion" (as a public compliance with ritual and legislation without much knowledge or faith), scholars approached the conversion of Eastern Europe as a form of acculturation.[98] No student of conversion in East Central Europe, however, approached the phenomenon in polythetic terms, as a cultural adaptation involving the adoption of only "bits and pieces" under the stimulus of cultural contact.[99] The study in chapter 8 of this book demonstrates how, given that sixth-century missions operated under the aegis of the early Byzantine Empire, the problem of conversion of barbarians beyond the Danube frontier of the empire must be seen as a function of imperial policies in the region. That no evidence exists for missionary enterprises across the sixth-century Danube frontier may thus indicate that on that frontier, no political gains were expected to result from missions of evangelization. This conclusion seems to dovetail with the conclusions of earlier studies dealing with the rather puzzling absence of any evidence of sustained missionary efforts directed specifically toward the Slavs of ninth- and tenth-century Byzantine Greece.[100]

Much like the concept of mission, that of conversion is thus to be understood as a metaphor that historians use in reference to some momentous change in religious practice. As such, the term *conversion* brings to mind books, literacy, teaching, liturgical displays, and the fundamental alteration of daily and annual cycles of human life. It has only recently been noted that conversion may have had much deeper implications with long-term consequences. Conversions affected not just people but also landscapes that surrounded them and some of the material culture aspects around which their new life was centered.[101] In chapter 9 of this book, Roman Kovalev proposes a new way of approaching the history of medieval conversion in Eastern Europe. He turns the focus from religious practice to religious meanings attached to objects of more or less daily exchange, coins.

That coins served as media for political and religious messages is not a novel idea, given the long history of Roman political propaganda by means of coins.[102] Less known, however, is the role of coins in forging religious identities. From the portrait of Christ on Emperor Justinian II's coins to the iconography of saints on Middle Byzantine coins and lead seals, religious messages have been an important component of Byzantine coinage.[103] In the West, Charlemagne's coins bearing the inscription *Christiana Religio* contributed to his representation as the new Constantine.[104] The common message of coins minted in early Anglo-Saxon England was the promise of salvation, conveyed by means of such images as crosses, vine scrolls, or symbolic animals—a most typical aspect of a "culture that delighted in paradox and metaphor."[105] None of these examples truly matches Kovalev's extraordinary case study. He contends that the "special issue" imitation dirhams of 837/8 with the Arabic inscriptions *Arḍ al-Khazar* (Land of the Khazars) and *Mūsā rasūl Allāh* (Moses is the Messenger of God) "carried a specific and blatant message charged with political-religious ideology connected to Jewish, Khazar, and Turkic identity." These coins must have been minted at the time of the Khazar elites' conversion to Judaism initiated by Beg Bulan-Sabriel, who deprived the qagan of his powers and isolated him in the position of "sacral king." But, Kovalev insists, the coin reform of 837/8 was no more than "a venture that quickly proved to be futile." No coins with similar inscriptions were struck in the subsequent period, and the commemorative issues were soon withdrawn from circulation and hoarded outside Khazaria, in the remote regions of the northwestern Rus'. Kovalev insists that the main reason for the failure of this political initiative must have been that its message never reached the intended audience, the Khwarazmian mercenaries and viziers instrumental in Bulan-Sabriel's coup d'état. The message carried by the Arabic inscriptions of the 837/8 imitation dirhams was designed to "undo" inscriptions on "regular" dirhams referring to Allah and to affirm the tenets of Judaism.[106] A similar interpretation emphasizing resistance to Islam has been recently put forward for Thor's hammer or cross graffiti in Kufic coins that reached Scandinavia.[107]

Religious propaganda directed at rival religious or political groups is also apparent in the case of Boleslav the Brave's coins with Cyrillic inscriptions, most likely struck in response to the gold and silver coins that Vladimir of Kiev issued shortly after his own conversion.[108] Further exploring the parallel between these two rulers, Jonathan Shepard, in chapter 10 of this book, compares late tenth-century Poland and Kievan Rus' and points out that the Act of Gniezno must be seen not only as a display of power in the context of Boleslav's relations to the empire but also as a response to the political developments associated with the conversion of the Rus' under Vladimir. Shepard suggests that "Mieszko, Sviatoslav, and their respective sons had more in common with one another than they did with those rulers of rather longer-established dynastic regimes who combined personal baptism with the conversion of their subjects," but what Shepard identifies as an "emulation of the Rus'" raises a number of possible questions so far unexplored by historians. How did the Poles and the Rus' see each other? To what extent did the conflict between Boleslav and Vladimir over the so-called Cherven towns create an ethnic boundary? More important for Shepard's discussion of conversions, how and when did the religion embraced by the two rulers reach that ethnic boundary?

Márta Font's study in chapter 11 of this book suggests that in Hungary, both the missionary enterprise and the political decision of the ruler contributed to the integration into and the adaptation of the pre-Christian social and political structures. As Font emphasizes, the Hungarian case is a particularly useful example of rapid and "radical" conversion, for the documentary and archaeological evidence indicates that, just as in Bulgaria, resistance to conversion was relatively quickly and brutally crushed. In the light of Urbańczyk's remarks about violence, the use of force in such cases should be interpreted as politically motivated. The state-building potential of quelling pagan revolts in Eastern and East Central Europe is yet another subject awaiting its historian.

A reevaluation of the early medieval history of Eastern Europe is now possible on the basis of new data and new questions. The time has come to incorporate Eastern Europe into the early medieval history of the Continent. Eastern and East Central Europe represent both a challenge to medievalists interested in the early period and a region with unique social and political features. By bringing together a variety of specialists in a single volume, I hope to have taken the first step toward understanding this region not as a replica of the "classical" model known from Western history but on its own terms and with its own problems. If anything, this volume invites more careful and in-depth study of concepts used here that have no corresponding parallels in Western history, such as the concept of service villages. A number of terms originating in Western historiography and adapted to the study of the region need further scrutiny, given the new wave of revisionism that made problematic even such fundamental concepts as feudalism and mission. On the other hand, this volume raises a number of questions about issues requiring more comparison with similar phenomena in the early medieval history of Western Europe. From village communities in Bulgaria and ports of trade on the southern and eastern coasts of the Baltic Sea to the social and political use of violence in Poland and Hungary and the minting of coins in Khazaria to celebrate newly acquired religious identities, the studies collected in this volume offer a vast array of hypotheses and ideas to be tested against new theories and new evidence.

NOTES

1. Robin Okey, "Central Europe/Eastern Europe: Behind the definitions," *Past and Present* 137 (1992): 102–33; Piotr S. Wandycz, *The Price of Freedom: A History of East Central Europe from the Middle Ages to the Present* (London and New York, 1992); Larry Wolff, *Inventing Eastern Europe: The Map of Civilization on the Mind of the Enlightenment* (Stanford, 1994); Robert Bideleux and Ian Jeffries, *A History of Eastern Europe* (London and New York, 1998).

2. Wolff, *Inventing Eastern Europe,* 360.

3. Bideleux and Jeffries, *History of Eastern Europe,* 12.

4. Jerzy Kłoczowski, *East Central Europe in the Historiography of the Countries of the Region* (Lublin, 1995).

5. Oskar Halecki, *The Limits and Divisions of European History* (London and New York, 1950).

6. Francis Dvornik, *The Making of Central and Eastern Europe* (London, 1949); Bideleux and Jeffries, *History of Eastern Europe.*

7. Paul Robert Magocsi, *Historical Atlas of East Central Europe* (Seattle, 1993), ix–xiii.

8. In the context of this book, the central third between 10 and 35 degrees east cannot simply be called "central Europe," for as such it would imply the inclusion of such European regions as the Italian and Balkan Peninsulas and a good portion of the Scandinavian Peninsula. The term *East Central Europe* is therefore designed to mark a specific reference to the mainland part of central Europe, to the exclusion of Italy and Scandinavia but not of the Balkans.

9. Magocsi, *Historical Atlas,* xi.

10. Wandycz, *Price of Freedom,* 2.

11. Gian Andri Bezzola, *Die Mongolen in abendländischer Sicht, 1220–1270: Ein Beitrag zur Frage der Völkerbegegnungen* (Bern and Munich, 1974); Johannes Fried, "Auf der Suche nach der Wirklichkeit: Die Mongolen und die europäischen Erfahrungswissenschaften im 13. Jahrhundert," *Historische Zeitschrift* 243 (1986): 287–332; Felicitas Schmieder, "Der Einfall der Mongolen nach Polen und Schlesien: Schreckensmeldungen, Hilferufe und die Reaktionen des Westens," in *Wahlstatt 1241: Beiträge zur Mongolenschlacht bei Liegnitz und zu ihren Nachwirkungen,* ed. Ulrich Schmilewski (Würzburg, 1991), 77–86.

12. Philip Longworth, *The Making of Eastern Europe* (New York, 1992), 8. See also Jenő Szűcs, *Die drei historischen Regionen Europas* (Frankfurt am Main, 1990).

13. Longworth, *Making of Eastern Europe,* 265; Bideleux and Jeffries, *History of Eastern Europe,* 15. See also Andrzej Buko's contribution to this volume (chap. 7).

14. George H. Hodos, *The East-Central European Region: An Historical Outline* (Westport and London, 1999), 19.

15. Wandycz, *Price of Freedom,* 6, 19.

16. Longworth, *Making of Eastern Europe,* 301.

17. Jean W. Sedlar, *East Central Europe in the Middle Ages, 1000–1500* (Seattle, 1994), ix.

18. Robert Bartlett, *The Making of Europe: Conquest, Colonization, and Cultural Change, 950–1350* (Princeton, 1993), 7–9.

19. For an excellent, recent survey of the Western developments, see Jean-Pierre Devroey, "The economy," in *The Early Middles Ages: Europe, 400–1000,* ed. Rosamond McKitterick (Oxford, 2001), 97–129. For good introductions to the archaeology of the early Middle Ages in some parts of Eastern Europe, see Günter Mangelsdorf, "Zur Lage der Mittelalterarchäologie in Ostdeutschland, Polen und Tschechien," *Zeitschrift für Archäologie des Mittelalters* 25–26 (1997–98): 39–47; Sebastian Brather, *Archäologie der westlichen Slawen: Siedlung, Wirtschaft und Gesellschaft im früh- und hochmittelalterlichen Ostmitteleuropa* (Berlin and New York, 2001).

20. See, e.g., P. Meduna and E. Cerna, "Settlement structure of the early Middle Ages in northwest Bohemia: Investigations of the Petipsy basin area," *Antiquity* 65 (1991): 388–95; Michał Parczewski, "Rekonstruktionsversuch der Besiedlungsgeschichte der frühmittelalterlichen Slowakei," *Acta Archaeologica Carpathica* 15 (1990): 31–55; B. A. Timoshchuk, "Ob issledovanii vostochnoslavianskikh poselenii VI–IX vv.," in *Problemy izucheniia drevnikh poselenii v arkheologii (sociologicheskii aspekt),* ed. V. I. Guliaev and G. F. Afanas'ev (Moscow, 1990), 128–49; Zbigniew Kobyliński, "Settlement structures in central Europe at the beginning of the Middle Ages," in *Origins of Central Europe,* ed. Przemysław Urbańczyk (Warsaw, 1997), 97–114; Gheorghe Postică, "Evoluția așezărilor din spațiul pruto-nistrean în epoca migrațiilor (sec. V–XIII)," *Thraco-Dacica* 20 (1999): 7–12.

21. See Georges Comet, *Le paysan et son outil: Essai d'histoire technique des céréales (France, VIIIe–XVe siècles)* (Rome, 1992); Karl Brunner, "Continuity and discontinuity of Roman agricultural knowledge in the early Middle Ages," in *Agriculture in the Middle Ages: Technology, Practice, and Representation,* ed. Del Sweeney (Philadelphia, 1995), 21–40.

22. This underlying debate is most notably evident in the works of Magdalena Beranová and Joachim Henning: Beranová, "Počátek pluhu na československém území," *Archeologické rozhledy* 10 (1958): 324–30, and *Zemedelská vyroba v 11.–14. století na území Československa* (Prague, 1975); Henning, *Südosteuropa zwischen Antike und Mittelalter: Archäologische Beiträge zur Landwirtschaft des I. Jahrtausends u.Z.* (Berlin, 1987), and "Eisenverarbeitungswerkstätten in unteren Donaugebiet zwischen Spätantike und Frühmittelalter," *Zeitschrift für Archäologie* 21 (1987): 59–73. For similar conclusions, see Zofia Podwinska, "L'agriculture en territoire polonais pendant le haut moyen âge," *Studia historiae oeconomicae* 7 (1972): 3–21; Iu. A. Krasnov, *Drevnie i srednevekovye pakhotnye orudiia Vostochnoi Evropy* (Moscow, 1987); Dušan Čaplovič and Alojz Habovštiak, "The situation of the archaeological research of Middle Age agricultural settlement in the territory of Slovakia," *Ruralia* 1 (1996): 269–76.

23. There is no mention of such studies in any of the most prominent contributions to this debate, namely, Philippe Contamine, *L'économie médiévale* (Paris, 1993); Norman J. G. Pounds, *An Economic History of Medieval Europe,* 2nd ed. (London and New York, 1994); Michael McCormick, *The Origins of the European Economy: Communications and*

Commerce, A.D. 300–900 (Cambridge and New York, 2001); and Adriaan Verhulst, *The Carolingian Economy* (New York, 2002). Both Pounds and McCormick ignore Henning's *Südosteuropa zwischen Antike und Mittelalter,* a pioneering study of technological continuity between late antiquity and the Middle Ages.

24. Unrivaled and still fundamental for any discussion of the archaeological evidence is Kazimierz Godłowski's *The Chronology of the Late Roman and Early Migration Periods in Central Europe* (Cracow, 1970). See also A. K. Ambroz, "Problemy rannesrednevekovoi khronologii Vostochnoi Evropy," *Sovetskaia Arkheologiia* 2 (1971): 96–123; 3 (1971): 106–34. More recent works tend to focus on specific regions. See, e.g., Jaroslav Tejral, *Grundzüge der Völkerwanderungszeit in Mähren* (Prague, 1976); Andrzej Kokowski, *Grupa masłomęcka: Z badań nad przemianami kultury Gotów w młodszym okresie rzymskim* (Lublin, 1995); Radu Harhoiu, *Das frühe Völkerwanderungszeit in Rumänien* (Bucharest, 1997). There is only limited, and sometimes erroneous, reference to the eastern regions of the continent in the much cited work of Klavs Randsborg, *The First Millenium A.D. in Europe and the Mediterranean: An Archaeological Essay* (Cambridge, 1991).

25. The standard readings remain Malcolm Todd's *The Early Germans* (Oxford and Cambridge, 1992) and the works of Peter Heather: *Goths and Romans, 332–489* (Oxford and New York, 1991) and especially *The Goths* (Oxford and Cambridge, 1996).

26. There is also no English translation of Walter Pohl's excellent book *Die Awaren: Ein Steppenvolk im Mitteleuropa 567–822 n. Chr.* (Munich, 1988). The only survey available in English—Samuel Szádeczky-Kardoss's "The Avars," in *The Cambridge History of Early Inner Asia,* ed. Denis Sinor (Cambridge and New York, 1990), 206–28—is both too short and largely ignorant of the enormous mass of archaeological evidence available. Equally absent is a monograph on early medieval Bulgaria, to update—if not replace— Robert Browning's *Byzantium and Bulgaria: A Comparative Study across the Early Medieval Frontier* (Berkeley, 1975). For the time being, the best introduction available in English remains Jonathan Shepard's "Bulgaria: The other Balkan 'empire'," in *The New Cambridge Medieval History,* ed. Timothy Reuter, vol. 3 (Cambridge, 1999), 567–85. The only area in early medieval East Central Europe that received (perhaps too much) attention in recent studies written in English is Moravia, largely because of the still debated issue of its exact location. See Charles R. Bowlus, *Franks, Moravians, and Magyars: The Struggle for the Middle Danube 788–907* (Philadelphia, 1995). By contrast, the history of Kievan Rus' does not occupy such a central position in recent developments in American or British medieval studies, despite the existence of two excellent books, Simon Franklin and Jonathan Shepard's *The Emergence of Rus, 750–1200* (London and New York, 1995) and Janet Martin's *Medieval Russia, 980–1584* (Cambridge, 1995).

27. Lev S. Klein, "To separate a *centaur.* On the relationship of archaeology and history in Soviet tradition," *Antiquity* 67 (1993): 339–48. Cf. the much more optimistic tone of C. J. Arnold's "Archaeology and history: The Shades of confrontation and cooperation," in *Archaeology at the Interface: Studies in Archaeology's Relationships with History, Geography, Biology, and Physical Science,* ed. J. L. Bintliff and G. F. Gaffney (Oxford, 1986), 32–39. See also Timothy C. Champion, "Medieval archaeology and the tyranny of the historical record," in *From the Baltic to the Black Sea: Studies in Medieval Archaeology,* ed. David Austin and Leslie Alcock (London, 1990), 79–95; Bailey K. Young, "Text aided or text misled? Reflections on the uses of archaeology in medieval history," in *Text-Aided Archaeology,* ed. Barbara J. Little (Boca Raton, Ann Arbor, and London,

1992), 135–47; Florin Curta, "Archaeology and history: A centaur or an interface?" *Revue Roumaine d'Histoire* 33 (1994): 401–16; Slawomir Kadrow, "The 'Pompeii premise' and archaeological investigations in Poland: Selected aspects," in *Theory and Practice of Archaeological Research,* ed. Witold Hensel, Stanisław Tabaczyński, and Przemysław Urbańczyk, vol. 3 (Warsaw, 1998), 285–301.

28. Klein, "To separate a *centaur,*" 345.

29. J. A. Lloyd, "Why should historians take archaeology seriously?" in *Archaeology at the Interface: Studies in Archaeology's Relationships with History, Geography, Biology, and Physical Science,* ed. J. L. Bintliff and G. F. Gaffney (Oxford, 1986), 51.

30. A. V. Arcikhovskii, *Vvdenie v arkheologiiu* (Moscow, 1940), 3. A lively debate is currently taking place in Poland on the influence and significance of Marxism in archaeology, but the relation between history and archaeology in that intellectual tradition is only marginally discussed. See Paul Barford, "Paradigms lost: Polish archaeology and post-war politics," *Archaeologia Polona* 31 (1993): 257–70; Jacek Lech, "Malowierni spór wokól marksizmu w archeologii Polskiej lat 1945–1975," *Archeologia Polski* 42 (1997): 175–232, and "Between captivity and freedom: Polish archaeology in the 20th century," *Archaeologia Polona* 35–36 (1997–98), 25–222; Sarunas Milisauskas, "Observations on Polish archaeology, 1945–1995," *Archaeologia Polona* 35–36 (1997–98), 223–36; Przemysław Urbańczyk, "Political circumstances reflected in post-war Polish archaeology," *Public Archaeology* 1 (2000): 49–56; Zbigniew Kobyliński, "Theoretical orientations in archaeology in Poland (1945–1995)," in *Theory and Practice of Archaeological Research,* ed. Witold Hensel, Stanisław Tabaczyński, and Przemysław Urbańczyk, vol. 3 (Warsaw, 1998), 225–58. For Marxism in Bulgarian archaeology, see Douglass W. Bailey, "Bulgarian archaeology: Ideology, sociopolitics and the exotic," in *Archaeology under Fire: Nationalism, Politics, and Heritage in the Eastern Mediterranean and Middle East,* ed. Lynn Meskell (London and New York, 1998), 87–110. For a survey of Hungarian archaeology under Communism, see J. Lászlovsky and Cs. Siklódi, "Archaeological theory in Hungary since 1960: Theories without theoretical archaeology," in *Archaeological Theory in Europe: The Last Three Decades,* ed. Ian Hodder (London and New York, 1991), 272–98. For Eastern Germany, see Werner Coblenz, "Archaeology under Communist control: The German Democratic Republic, 1945–1990," in *Archaeology, Ideology, and Society: The German Experience,* ed. Heinrich Härke (Frankfurt am Main, Berlin, and Bern, 2000), 304–38. For Moldova, see Valentin Dergacev, "Arheologia Republicii Moldova: Retrospectivă istorică," *Thraco-Dacica* 15 (1994): 7–18. The revolutionary changes associated with Soviet archaeology have only recently received scholarly attention. See L. A. Chernykh, "Khoziaistvenno-ekonomicheskie rekonstrukcii v rabotakh sovetskikh arkheologov 30-kh godov," in *Issledovanie social'no-istoricheskikh problem v arkheologii: Sbornik nauchnykh trudov,* ed. S. V. Smirnov and V. F. Gening (Kiev, 1987), 118–37; Bruce G. Trigger, *A History of Archaeological Thought* (Cambridge, 1989), 207–43; A. A. Formozov, "Arkheologiia i ideologiia (20–30-e gody)," *Voprosy filosofii* 2 (1990): 70–82; V. S. Bochkarev, "V. I. Ravdonikas i revoliuciia v sovetskoi arkheologii," in *Mezhdunarodnaia konferenciia k 100-letiiu V. I. Ravdonikasa: Tezisy dokladov,* ed. G. V. Vilinbakhov (St. Petersburg, 1994), 13–15; Lev S. Klein, *Das Phänomen der sowjetischen Archäologie: Geschichte, Schulen, Protagonisten* (Frankfurt am Main and New York, 1997).

31. See Evžen Neustupný, "The settlement area theory in Bohemian archaeology," in *25 Years of Archaeological Research in Bohemia,* ed. Jan Fridrich (Prague, 1994), 248–58; Mirjana Stevanović, "'Nova arkheologija': Da li ona ima buduchnost?" *Balcanica* 21

(1990): 185–200. Cf. the almost contemporary paper of Lewis R. Binford, "The 'New Archaeology,' then and now," in *Archaeological Thought in America*, ed. C. C. Lamberg-Karlovsky (Cambridge and New York, 1989), 50–62. For a survey of theoretical and methodological developments in contemporary medieval archaeology, see John Moreland, "Method and theory in medieval archaeology in the 1990s," *Archeologia medievale* 18 (1991): 7–42, and "The Middle Ages, theory, and post-modernism," *Acta Archaeologica* 68 (1997): 163–82. In Eastern Europe, there has so far been only limited reaction to relatively recent breakthroughs in excavation techniques. See, e.g., Przemysław Urbańczyk, "Stratygrafia archeologiczna w świetle pogladów E. C. Harrisa," *Przegląd Archeologiczny* 34 (1987): 253–76.

32. Karel Sklenář, *Archaeology in Central Europe: The First 500 Years* (Leicester and New York, 1983). See also Bruce G. Trigger, "Romanticism, nationalism, and archaeology," in *Nationalism, Politics, and the Practice of Archaeology*, ed. Philip Kohl and Clare Fawcett (Cambridge, 1995), 263–79; Zofia Kurnatowska and Stanisław Kurnatowski, "Der Einfluss nationalistischer Ideen auf die mitteleuropäische Urgeschichtsforschung," in *Deutsche Ostforschung und polnische Westforschung im Spannungsfeld von Wissenschaft und Politik: Disziplinen im Vergleich*, ed. Jan M. Piskorski, Jörg Hackmann, and Rudolf Jaworski (Osnabrück and Poznań, 2002), 93–103.

33. Gustaf Kossinna, *Die Herkunft der Germanen: Zur Methode der Siedlungsarchäologie* (Würzburg, 1911), 3. The English translation is that of Ulrich Veit, "Ethnic concepts of German prehistory: A case study on the relationship between cultural identity and archaeological objectivity," in *Archaeological Approaches to Cultural Identity*, ed. Stephen Shennan (London, Boston, and Sidney, 1989), 39. For Kossinna and the culture-historical approach in archaeology, see Lev S. Klein, "Kossinna im Abstand von vierzig Jahren," *Jahresschrift für mitteldeutsche Vorgeschichte* 58 (1974): 7–55; Günter Smolla, "Das Kossinna-Syndrom," *Fundberichte aus Hessen* 19–20 (1979–80), 1–9; Ulrich Veit, "Gustaf Kossinna and his concept of a national archaeology," in *Archaeology, Ideology, and Society: The German Experience*, ed. Heinrich Härke (Frankfurt am Main, Berlin, and Bern, 2000), 40–59; Sebastian Brather, "Kossinna, Gustaf," in *Reallexikon der germanischen Altertumskunde*, ed. Heinrich Beck, Dieter Geuenich, and Heiko Steuer, vol. 17 (Berlin and New York, 2001), 263–67.

34. See Trigger, *History of Archaeological Thought*, 161–63; Hans-Peter Wotzka, "Zum traditionellen Kulturbegriff in der prähistorischen Archäologie," *Paideuma* 39 (1993): 25–44.

35. Reinhard Wenskus, *Stammesbildung und Verfassung: Das Werden der frühmittelalterlichen Gentes* (Cologne, 1961), 137. See also Hansjürgen Brachmann, "Archäologische Kultur und Ethnos: Zu einigen methodischen Voraussetzungen der ethnischen Interpretation archäologischer Funde," in *Von der archäologischen Quelle zur historischen Aussage*, ed. Joachim Preuss (Berlin, 1979), 101–21.

36. For a detailed discussion of this development in the Soviet Union, see Florin Curta, "From Kossinna to Bromley: Ethnogenesis in Slavic archaeology," in *On Barbarian Identity: Critical Approaches to Ethnicity in the Early Middle Ages*, ed. Andrew Gillett (Turnhout, 2002), 201–18. For Kossinna's influence on later generations of archaeologists in Britain and Germany, see Ulrich Veit, "Gustaf Kossinna und V. Gordon Childe: Ansätze zu einer theoretischen Grundlegung der Vorgeschichte," *Saeculum* 35 (1984): 326–64; Sabine Wolfram, "'Vorsprung durch Technik' or 'Kossinna syndrome'? Archaeological theory and social context in post-war West Germany," in *Archaeology, Ideology,*

and Society: The German Experience, ed. Heinrich Härke (Frankfurt am Main, Berlin, and Bern, 2000), 180–201.

37. See, e.g., Valeri Kacunov, "Etnokulturen model na istoricheskoto săznanie prez bălgarskoto srednovekovie," *Istoricheski pregled* 47 (1991): 36–48; Ivan Mužić, *Podrijetlo i pravjera Hrvata: Autohtonost u hrvatskoj etnogenezi na tlu rimske provincije Dalmacije* (Split, 1991); Ioan Mitrea, "Realităţi arheologice şi etno-culturale în spaţiul carpato-nistrean în secolele VI–VII," *Carpica* 23 (1992): 209–21; Silvia Laul, "Viron varhaiskeski-aikaisen kaakkoisrajan muodostumisen etnisestä ja kultuuritaustasta," in *Suomen var-haishistoria: Tornion kongressi 14.–16.6.1991,* ed Kyösti Julku and Markus H. Korhonen (Rovaniemi, 1992), 295–303; Milan Hanuliak, "Charakter etnických premien na uzemí Slovenska v 10.–11. storocí," *Archaeologia historica* 18 (1993): 37–51; V. V. Sedov, "Iz etnich-eskoi istorii naseleniia srednei polosy Vostochnoi Evropy vo vtoroi polovine I tysi-acheletiia n.e.," *Rossiiskaia Arkheologiia* 2 (1994): 49–66; Petr Chárvat, "De Theutonicis uxoribusque eorum: Etnicita v archeologii stredovekých Čech," *Listy filologické* 117 (1994): 32–36. The most egregious example of the misuse of archaeology is a recent at-tempt to legitimize Serbian claims to territory in the context of the war in Bosnia, Đurđe Janković's *Srpske gromile* (Belgrade, 1998), esp. 111. At times, this preoccupation with ethnic history takes on a downright racist character, as in I. I. Salivon's "Etnois-toricheskie aspekty formirovaniia fizicheskogo tipa belorusov," in *Etnogenez i etnokul'-turnye kontakty slavian,* ed. V. V. Sedov (Moscow, 1997), 270–78. For cautionary tales, see Henryk Mamzer, "Problem etniczny w archeologii," *Slavia Antiqua* 40 (1999): 169–201; Przemysław Urbańczyk, "Archelogia etniczności: fikcja czy nadzieja?" in *Archeologia w teorii i w praktyce,* ed. Andrzej Buko and Przemysław Urbańczyk (Warsaw, 2000), 137–46; Florin Curta, "Consideraţii privind conceptul de caracter etnic (etnicitate) în arhe-ologia contemporană," *Arheologia medievală* 4 (2002): 5–25.

38. See, e.g., Witold Hensel, "The acting of Bijelo Brdo culture on Poland's lands," *Archaeologia Polona* 13 (1972): 307–12.

39. Philip Kohl and Clare Fawcett, "Archaeology in the service of the state: Theoret-ical considerations," in *Nationalism, Politics, and the Practice of Archaeology,* ed. Philip Kohl and Clare Fawcett (Cambridge, 1995), 3–18. See also Florin Curta, "The changing image of the early Slavs in the Rumanian historiography and archaeological literature: A critical survey," *Südost-Forschungen* 53 (1994): 225–310; Timothy Kaiser, "Archaeology and ideology in southeast Europe," in *Nationalism, Politics, and the Practice of Archaeol-ogy,* ed. Philip Kohl and Clare Fawcett (Cambridge, 1995), 99–119; Pavel M. Dolukhanov, "Archaeology and nationalism in totalitarian and post-totalitarian Russia," in *National-ism and Archaeology: Scottish Archaeological Forum,* ed. John A. Atkinson, Iain Banks, and Jerry O'Sullivan (Glasgow, 1996), 200–213; Giedrius Puodziunas and Algirdas Girininkas, "Nationalism doubly oppressed: Archaeology and nationalism in Lithua-nia," in *Nationalism and Archaeology in Europe,* ed. Margarita Díaz-Andreu and Timo-thy Champion (Boulder and San Francisco, 1996), 243–55.

40. Alexandru Madgearu (chap. 3 in the present volume) suggests that "a series of archaic cranial features within the restricted area of the Apuseni Mountains" could help identify the Romanians of the early Middle Ages. One is reminded of the position taken in this regard by Constantin Daicoviciu, Emil Petrovici, and Gheorghe Ştefan in "Zur Frage der Entstehung der rumänischen Sprache und des rumänischen Volks," *Nouvelles études d'histoire* 2 (1960): 91–134.

41. András Alföldi, "Die ethische Grenzscheide am römischen Limes," *Schweizer*

Beiträge zur allgemeinen Geschichte 8 (1950): 37–50, and "The moral barrier on Rhine and Danube," in *The Congress of Roman Frontier Studies, 1949* (Durham, 1952), 1–16. See now Magocsi, *Historical Atlas*, 5.

42. See, e.g., Jaroslav Tejral, *Die Probleme der späten römischen Kaiserzeit in Mähren* (Prague, 1975); Achim Leube, *Die römische Kaiserzeit im Oder-Spree-Gebiet* (Berlin, 1975); Wojciech Nowakowski, *Die Funde der römischen Kaiserzeit und der Völkerwanderungszeit aus Masuren* (Berlin, 1998).

43. István Bóna, *The Dawn of the Dark Ages: The Gepids and the Lombards in the Carpathian Basin* (Budapest, 1976), 105; Pohl, *Die Awaren*, 52–57; M. Iu. Braichevskii, "Periodyzaciia istorychnogo rozvytku Skhidnoi Evropy v I tys. n.e.," *Arkheolohiia* 3 (1994): 16. For AD 568 as an equally crucial date for Lombard archaeology in Italy, see Lars Jørgensen, "A.D. 568: A chronological analysis of Lombard graves in Italy," in *Chronological Studies of Anglo-Saxon England, Lombard Italy, and Vendel Period Sweden,* ed. Lars Jørgensen (Copenhague, 1992), 94–122. For similar ideas about the "beginnings of the Middle Ages," see Konrad Jażdzewski, "Problematyka i potrzeby badań nad V–VII wiekiem," *Archeologia Polski* 13 (1968): 277–98; Chavdar Bonev, "Za periodizaciiata na rannosrednovekovnata materialna kultura v Dobrudzha," *Arkheologiia* 23 (1981): 15–21; Michał Parczewski, "Stan i potrzeby badań nad początkami wczesnego średniowiecza w Polsce (VI—polowa VII w.)," *Stan i potrzeby badań nad wczesnym średniowieczem w Polsce: Materialy z konferencji Poznań 14–16 grudnia 1987 roku,* ed. Zofia Kurnatowska (Poznań, 1990), 9–22.

44. See, e.g., Darina Bialeková, "Slovanské obdobie," *Slovenská Archeológia* 28 (1980): 213–28; Miloš Šolle, *Staroslovanské hradisko* (Prague, 1984); Ivana Pleinerová, "Stopy halštatského a staroslovanského osídlení vysinné polohy v Opočne u Loun," *Archeologické rozhledy* 51 (1999): 532–36.

45. K. A. Sofronenko, *Obshchestvenno-politicheskii stroi Galicko-Volynskoi Rusi XI–XII vv.* (Moscow, 1957); L. V. Cherepnin, "Obshchestvenno-politicheskie otnosheniia v drevnei Rusi i Russkaia Pravda," in *Drevnerusskoe gosudarstvo i ego mezhdunarodnoe znachenie,* ed. V. T. Pashuto and L. V. Cherepnin (Moscow, 1965), 128–276; V. D. Koroliuk, "Rannefeodal'naia gosudarstvennost' i formirovanie feodal'noi sostvennosti u vostochnykh i zapadnykh slavian (do serediny XI v.)," in *V International Congress of Economic History, Leningrad, 10–14 August 1970* (Moscow, 1970), 27–42; A. A. Gorskii, "O perekhodnom periode ot doklassovo obshchestva k feodal'nomu u vostochnykh slavian," *Sovetskaia Arkheologiia* 2 (1988): 116–31. See now M. B. Sverdlov, *Stanovlenie feodalizma v slavianskikh stranakh* (St. Petersburg, 1997). For Bulgaria, see Dimităr Angelov, "Problemy predgosudarstvennogo perioda na territorii budushchego bolgarskogo gosudarstva," in *Etnosocial'naia i politicheskaia struktura rannefeodal'nykh slavianskikh gosudarstv i narodnostei,* ed. G. G. Litavrin (Moscow, 1987), 7–15, and *Obshchestvo i obshchestvena misăl v srednovekovna Bălgariia (IX–XIV v.)* (Sofia, 1988). For Yugoslavia, see Mirjana Ljubinković, "Periodizacija srednjovekovne arheologije od VI do kraja XI veka," in *Referati i koreferati sa VII kongresa arheologa Jugoslavije, Herceg-Novi, 1966,* ed. N. Tašić (Belgrade, 1967), 171–88. For Czechoslovakia, see Z. Fiala, "O vyjasnení pojmu v marxistickém vykladu starších českych dejin," *Československy Časopis Historicky* 20 (1972): 234–44; Peter Ratkoš, "O hospodárskom a sociálnom vyvoji Slovenska v 9–13. storocí," *Historický časopis* 24 (1976): 571–97. For Romania, see Mircea Petrescu-Dîmbovița, "Considérations sur le problème des périodes de la culture matérielle en Moldavie aux VI–X-e siècles," *Revue Roumaine d'Histoire* 6 (1967): 181–99; Maria

Comşa, "Sur le caractère de l'organisation sociale-économique et politique sur le territoire de la Roumanie durant la période de passage à la féodalité," in *Nouvelles études d'histoire*, vol. 4 (Bucharest, 1970), 31–46; Ştefan Olteanu, *Societatea carpato-danubiano-pontică în secolele IV–XI: Structuri demo-economice şi sociale* (Bucharest, 1997). For an excellent survey of the most important theories about feudalism that were in fashion in Eastern Europe in the 1970s, see Henri H. Stahl, *Studii de sociologie istorică* (Bucharest, 1972), 5–62. For the last major development in that direction before the fall of Communism, see Joachim Herrmann and Jens Köhn, eds., *Familie, Staat und Gesellschaftsformation: Grundprobleme vorkapitalistischer Epochen einhundert Jahren nach Friedrich Engels' Werk "Der Ursprung der Familie, des Privateigentums und des Staates"* (Berlin, 1988).

46. In Poland, the term was used even in cases in which the evidence clearly postdated the latest date advanced by orthodox Marxists for the end of the early Middle Ages. See, e.g., Jerzy Lodowski, "Uwagi o wczesnośredniowiecznej ceramice grafitowej z terenu Śląska," *Silesia antiqua* 8 (1966): 110–32; Teresa Dunin-Wasowicz, "Rzymskie kulty swietych w Polsce wczesnośredniowiecznej: Kult sw. Maurycego i legionu tebanskiego," *Roczniki Teologiczno-Kanoniczne* 20 (1973): 25–34; Elżbieta Kowałczyk, "Powracajacy temat: Sieciechow. Z problemów organizacji grodowej w Polsce wczesnośredniowiecznej," *Kwartalnik historii kultury materiałnej* 42 (1994): 69–85; Roman Michałowski, "Translacja Pieciu Braci Polskich do Gniezna: Przyczynek do dziejów kultu relikwii w Polsce wczesnośredniowiecznej," in *Peregrinationes: Pielgrzymki w kulturze dawnej Europy*, ed. H. Manikowska and H. Zaremska (Warsaw, 1995), 173–84. In Romania, the term *prefeudal* was coined and only used by archaeologists. See Mircea Rusu, "The prefeudal cemetery of Noşlac (VI–VIIth centuries)," *Dacia* 6 (1962): 269–92; Ioan Stanciu and Alexandru V. Matei, "Sondajele din aşezarea prefeudală de la Popeni-Cuceu, jud. Sălaj. Câteva consideraţii cu privire la ceramica prefeudală din Transilvania," *Acta Musei Porolissensis* 18 (1994): 135–63. Ioan Stanciu's recent criticism points to major problems that Romanian archaeologists face when coping with "residual Marxism." Stanciu specifically and rightly proposes that the term *prefeudal* be replaced with the term *medieval timpuriu* (early medieval), the Romanian translation of the Polish term *wczesnośredniowieczny*. See Ioan Stanciu, "Despre ceramica medievală timpurie de uz comun, lucrată la roata rapidă, în aşezările de pe teritoriul României (secolele VIII–X)," *Arheologia medievală* 3 (2000): 127 with n. 1. The use of the term *early medieval* for a period in history known elsewhere as the High Middle Ages is not restricted to Polish or Romanian archaeologists and historians. The term appears sporadically in that sense in Bulgarian and Slovenian archaeology. See, e.g., Jozo Kastelić, "Nekaj problemov zgodnjesrednjeveske arheologije v Sloveniji," in *VI Kongres arheologa Jugoslavije, Ljubljana, 1963* (Belgrade, 1964), 109–24; Georgi Atanasov, "Rannosrednovekovni olovni ikonki săs sv. Georgi-voin ot Iuzhna Dobrudzha," *Arkheologiia* 24 (1992): 35–44; Irena Mirnik Prezelj, "Slovenska zgodnjesrednjeveska arheologija med preteklostjo in sedanjostjo: pogled z 'Zahoda,'" *Arheološki vestnik* 49 (1998): 361–81.

47. This assumption is most evident in the (Czecho-)Slovak literature concerning Great Moravia. See Peter Ratkoš, "Počiatky feudalizmu na Slovensku (k problematike raného feudalizmu v našich krajinách)," *Historický časopis* 3 (1954): 252–76; Josef Poulík, "K otázce počatku feudalizmu na Morave," *Památky Archeologické* 52 (1961): 498–505; Ondrej Halaga, "Ekonomické oblasti Slovenska a európsky obchod (Vyvoj za feudalismu)," *Slovanské studie* 22 (1981): 111–31. For Poland, see Henryk Łowmiański, "Rozdrobnienie feudalne Polski w historiografii naukowej," in *Polska w okresie rozdrobnienia*

feudalnego, ed. H. Łowmiański (Wrocław, 1973), 7–34, and "Przemiany feudalne wsi polski do 1138 r.," *Przegląd Historyczny* 65 (1974): 437–63. For an excellent overview of the most recent theories about feudalism in its Marxist definition, see Chris Wickham, "Le forme del feudalesimo," in *Il feudalesimo nell'alto medioevo, 8–12 aprile 1999* (Spoleto, 2000), 15–51.

48. Pál Engel, *The Realm of St. Stephen: A History of Medieval Hungary, 895–1526* (London and New York, 2001), 82. For more clear attempts to date the "feudalization" of the Hungarian society to the reign of Béla IV (1235–70), see Sándor Gyimesi, "IV. Béla és a feudalizálodás," *Budapesti Könyvszemle* 6 (1994): 334–37.

49. See Curta, "From Kossinna to Bromley," 207–13, and "Pots, Slavs, and 'imagined communities': Slavic archaeology and the history of the early Slavs," *European Journal of Archaeology* 4 (2001): 367–84. For Stalin's condemnation of Marxism and subsequent revival of "Slavic studies," see Stephen Velychenko, "The origins of the official Soviet interpretation of eastern Slavic history: A case study of policy formulation," in *Beiträge zur 6. internationalen Konferenz zur altrussischen Geschichte* (Wiesbaden, 1992), 231; E. P. Aksenova and M. A. Vasil'ev, "Problemy etnogonii slavianstva i ego vetvei v akademicheskikh diskussiakh rubezha 1930–1940-kh godov," *Slavianovedenie* 2 (1993): 86–104; V. A. Shnirel'man, "Zlokliucheniia odnoi nauki: Etnogeneticheskie issledovaniia is stalinskaia nacional'naia politika," *Etnograficheskoe obozrenie* 3 (1993): 52–68. For the role of the Soviet war propaganda, see Ewa Thompson, "Nationalist propaganda in the Soviet Russian press, 1939–1941," *Slavic Review* 50 (1991): 385–99.

50. See, e.g., Joachim Herrmann, *Siedlung, Wirtschaft und gesellschaftliche Verhältnisse der slawischen Stämme zwischen Elbe und Oder: Studien auf der Grundlage archäologischen Materials* (Berlin, 1968); "Probleme der Herausbildung der archäologischen Kulturen slawischer Stämme des 6.–9. Jhs.," in *Rapports du III-e Congrès international d'archéologie slave: Bratislava, 7–14 septembre 1975,* ed. B. Chropovský, vol. 1 (Bratislava, 1979), 49–75; "Probleme und Fragestellungen zur Westausbreitung slawischer Stämme und deren Burgenbau vom Ende des 6. bis zum Ende des 8. Jahrhunderts in Mitteleuropa," *Slavia Antiqua* 37 (1996): 55–71. For an early archaeological *mise au point,* see Hans-Jürgen Brachmann, "Die Funde der Gruppe des Prager Typs in der DDR und ihre Stellung im Rahmen der frühslawischen Besiedlung dieses Gebietes," *Slavia Antiqua* 29 (1993): 23–64. For a survey of German views of the early Slavs, see Christoph Kilger, "The Slavs yesterday and today: Different perspectives on Slavic ethnicity in German archaeology," *Current Swedish Archaeology* 6 (1998): 99–114.

51. Joachim Herrmann and Karl-Uwe Heußner, "Dendrochronologie, Archäologie und Frühgeschichte vom 6. bis 12. Jh. in den Gebieten zwischen Saale, Elbe und Oder," *Ausgrabungen und Funde* 36 (1991): 255–90. See especially Joachim Henning and Karl-Uwe Heußner, "Zur Burgengeschichte im 10. Jahrhundert: Neue archäologische und dendrochronologische Daten zu Anlagen vom Typ Tornow," *Ausgrabungen und Funde* 36 (1991): 314–424; Joachim Henning, "Neues zum Tornower Typ. Keramische Formen und Formenspektren des Frühmittelalters im Licht dendrochronologischer Daten zum westslawischen Siedlungsraum," in *Kraje słowiańskie w wiekach średnich: Profanum i sacrum,* ed. W. Łosiński, H. Kócka-Krenz, and Z. Hilczer-Kurnatowska (Poznań, 1998), 392–408. Henning's works are especially critical of Herrmann's *Tornow und Vorberg: Ein Beitrag zur Frühgeschichte der Lausitz* (Berlin, 1966). For a Polish use of dendrochronology and subsequent critique of Hermann's theories, see Marek Krąpiec, "Dendrochronological dating of early medieval fortified settlements in Poland," in *Frühmittelalterlicher Burgenbau*

in Mittel- und Osteuropa: Tagung, Nitra, vom 7. bis 10. Oktober 1996, ed. Joachim Henning and Alexander T. Ruttkay (Bonn, 1998), 257–67; Marek Dulinicz, *Kształtowanie sie Słowiańszczyzny Północno-Zachodniej* (Warsaw, 2001).

52. Marek Dulinicz, "The first dendrochronological dating of the strongholds of northern Mazovia," in *Origins of Central Europe*, ed. Przemysław Urbańczyk (Warsaw, 1997), 137–41.

53. For dendrochronology, in general, see Marvin A. Stokes and Terah L. Smiley, *An Introduction to Tree-Ring Dating* (Chicago, 1968); M. G. L. Baillie, *A Slice through Time: Dendrochronology and Precise Dating* (London, 1995); N. B. Chernykh, *Dendrokhronologiia i arkheologiia* (Moscow, 1996); Tomasz Ważny, *Dendrochronologia obiektów zabytkowych w Polsce* (Gdańsk, 2001). For an early plea for using dendrochronology in medieval archaeology in Poland, see Tadeusz Gorczyński, Bogusław Molski, and Władysław Golinowski, "Podstawy dendrochronologii w zastosowaniu do potrzeb archeologii," *Archeologia Polski* 9 (1965): 75–114. For its most recent applications in that country, see Marek Krąpiec and Tadeusz Ważny, "Dendrochronologia: Podstawy metodyczne i stan zaawansowania badań w Polsce," *Swiatowit* 39 (1994): 193–214.

54. Vsevolod M. Potin, "Numismatische Chronologie und Dendrochronologie im Licht der Novgoroder Ausgrabungen," *Hamburger Beiträge zur Numismatik* 27–29 (1973–75): 53–66; M. A. Sagaidak, "Dendrokhronologichni doslizhennia derev'iannikh budivel' Podolu," in *Arkheologiia Kieva: Doslidzhennia i materialy*, ed. P. P. Tolochko, Ia. E. Borovs'kii, S. O. Visoc'kii, and S. R. Kilievich (Kiev, 1979), 62–69; N. B. Chernykh, "Dendrokhronologiia drevneishikh gorizontov Ladogi (po materialam raskopok Zemlianogo gorodishcha)," in *Srednevekovaia Ladoga: Novye otkrytiia i issledovaniia*, ed. V. V. Sedov (Leningrad, 1985), 76–80; D. A. Avdusin and T. A. Pushkina, "Three chamber graves at Gniozdovo," *Fornvännen* 83 (1988): 20–33; N. B. Chernykh and A. A. Karpukhin, "Absoliutnaia dendrokhronologicheskaia shkala Tveri XII–XV vv. (po materialam iz raskopok v Tverskom kremle)," *Rossiiskaia Arkheologiia* 3 (2001): 46–54. In Russia, the early application of dendrochronology and building of an oak master chronology date back to the pioneering work of Boris A. Kolchin. See B. A. Kolchin, "Khronologiia novgorodskikh drevnostei," in *Novgorodskii sbornik: 50 let raskopok Novgoroda*, ed. B. A. Kolchin and V. L. Ianina (Moscow, 1982), 156–77, and *Wooden Artifacts from Medieval Novgorod* (Oxford, 1989).

55. Péter Ricz, "Timber constructions in Avar graves: Contributions to the resolving of problems linked with burial of the Avars in North Bačka," *Archaeologia Iugoslavica* 22–23 (1982–83): 96–112; Helena Zoll-Adamikowa, "Dereviannye konstrukcii v kurganakh s truposozhzheniem u vostochnykh i zapadnykh slavian," *Sovetskaia Arkheologiia* 4 (1982): 82–90. For other examples of burial wooden constructions, see Viktor S. Aksionov, "Dereviannye konstrukcii mogil'nika saltovskoi kul'tury Krasnaia Gorka," *Khazarskii almanakh* 1 (2002): 6–17.

56. Przemysław Urbańczyk, ed., *Early Christianity in Central and Eastern Europe* (Warsaw, 1997); see especially the essays by Przemysław Urbańczyk, Aleksander Gieysztor, and Marco Mostert.

57. For Otto's pilgrimage to Gniezno, see P. Bogdanowicz, "Zjazd gnieznienski w roku 1000," *Nasza przeszłość* 16 (1962): 5–151; Gerard Labuda, "Zjazd i synod gnieznienski w roku 1000," *Kwartalnik historyczny* 107 (2000): 107–22; Jonathan Shepard, "Otto III, Boleslaw Chrobry and the 'happening' at Gniezno, A.D. 1000: Some possible implications of Professor Poppe's thesis concerning the offspring of Anna Porphyrogenita," in *Byzantium and East Central Europe*, ed. Maciej Salamon, Günter Prinzing, and Paul

Stephenson (Cracow, 2001), 27–48; Przemysław Urbańczyk, "Zjazd Gnieznienski w polityce imperialnej Ottona III," in *Trakt cesarski: Ilawa-Gniezno-Magdeburg,* ed. Wojciech Dzieduszycki and Maciej Przybył (Poznań, 2002), 49–90.

58. Géza Érszegi, "The Christianisation of Hungary according to the sources," in *Europe's Centre around A.D. 1000,* ed. Alfried Wieczorek and Hans-Martin Hinz (Stuttgart, 2000), 394–98; Richard Marsina, "Christianization of the Magyars and Hungary between the East and the West," *Studia Historica Slovaca* 19 (1995): 37–52.

59. Nora Berend, *At the Gate of Christendom: Jews, Muslims, and "Pagans" in Medieval Hungary, c. 1000–c. 1300* (Cambridge, 2001), and "How many medieval Europes? The 'pagans' of Hungary and regional diversity in Christendom," in *The Medieval World,* ed. Peter Linehan and Janet L. Nelson (London and New York, 2001), 77–92.

60. Martin, *Medieval Russia,* 90. Martin's argument is, of course, political: following the death of Vladimir Monomakh, the political conditions in Rus' became too complex and very different from the arrangements that were previously typical between various members of the Riurikid family.

61. The conquest, however, is to be seen in a light very different from that of the fundamentally nationalist historiography of the conflict between Basil II and Samuel. See Paul Stephenson, "The legend of Basil the Bulgar-slayer," *Byzantine and Modern Greek Studies* 24 (2000): 102–32.

62. Maria Comşa, "Cu privire la caracterul organizării social-economice şi politice de pe teritoriul ţării noastre în epoca migraţiilor," *Studii şi cercetări de istorie veche* 18 (1967): 431–42; V. D. Koroliuk, "Pastushestvo u slavian v I tysiacheletii n.e. i peremeshchenie ikh v Podunav'e i na Balkany: Slaviane i volokhi (Popytka rekonstrukcii po pis'mennym istochnikam)," in *Slaviano-voloshskie sviazi (sbornik statei),* ed. N. A. Mokhov (Kishinew, 1978), 177–98; Victor Spinei, "Aspecte economice şi sociale ale evoluţiei comunităţilor locale din spaţiul est-carpatic în secolele X–XIII," *Hierasus* 1 (1979): 217–42; Vasil Giuzelev, "Economic development and forms of social and political organisation of the Proto-Bulgarians prior to the foundation of the Bulgarian state (4th–7th c.)," *Barukan Sho Ajia kenkyu* 6 (1980): 95–103; Magdalena Beranová, *Zemedelství starých slovanů* (Prague, 1980); Mircea Rusu, "Frühformen der Staatsentstehung in Rumänien: Betrachtungen zur sozialökonomische und politische Lage," *Zeitschrift für Archäologie* 18 (1984): 189–207; Henning, *Südosteuropa zwischen Antike und Mittelalter;* Aleksander Gieysztor, "Trade and industry in Eastern Europe before 1200," in *Cambridge Economic History of Europe,* ed. M. M. Postan and Edward Miller, vol. 2 (Cambridge, 1987), 474–524; E. A. Shmidt, "O zemledelii v verkhov'iakh Dnepra vo vtoroi polovine I tys. n. e.," in *Drevnie slaviane i Kievskaia Rus': Sbornik nauchnykh trudov,* ed. P. P. Tolochko (Kiev, 1989), 70–74. The emphasis on economic and social developments is a continuing trend in the post-Communist historiography of Eastern Europe: see Jadran Ferluga, "Mercati e mercanti fra Mar Nero e Adriatico: Il commercio nei Balcani dal VII al'XI secolo," in *Mercati e mercanti nell'alto medioevo: L'area euroasiatica e l'area mediterranea* (Spoleto, 1993), 443–98; Călin Cosma, "Consideraţii privind structura vieţii economice în spaţiul vestic şi nord-vestic românesc în secolele VIII–X d. H." *Crisia* 26–27 (1996–97), 67–78; Olteanu, *Societatea carpato-danubiano-pontică;* Alexander Ruttkay, "Großmähren: Anmerkungen zum gegenwärtigen Forschungsstand über die Siedlungs- und sozialökonomischen Strukturen," in *Origins of Central Europe,* ed. Przemysław Urbańczyk (Warsaw, 1997), 143–70; Stoian Vitlianov, "Arkheologicheski danni za ikonomicheskiia oblik na Pliska," *Pliska-Preslav* 8 (2000): 87–92.

63. See, however, László Makkai, "Les caractères originaux de l'histoire économique

et sociale de l'Europe orientale pendant le Moyen Age," *Acta Historica Academiae Scientiarum Hungaricae* 16 (1970): 261–87. The comparative approach is most clearly evident in the work of Joachim Henning: see "Unterscheide und Gemeinsamkeiten zwischen slawischer und fränkischer Landwirtschaft in Gebieten frühmittelalterlicher Stadtentwicklung," in *Trudy V Mezhdunarodnogo Kongressa arkheologov-slavistov: Kiev 18–25 sentiabria 1985 g.,* ed. P. P. Tolochko, Ia. E. Borovskii, A. A. Kozlovskii, and A. P. Mocia, vol. 2 (Kiev, 1988), 221–27; "Franken-Bulgaren-Byzantiner: Zur kulturellen Brückenfunktion Südosteuropas im Frühmittelalter im Lichte der neuesten Pliska-Grabungen," in *Zwischen Byzanz und Abendland: Pliska, der östliche Balkanraum und Europa im Spiegel der Frühmittelalterarchäologie,* ed. Joachim Henning (Frankfurt am Main, 1999), 19–21.

64. Richard Hodges, *Dark Age Economics: The Origins of Towns and Trade, A.D. 600–1000* (New York, 1982); Astill Grenville, "Archaeology, economics, and early medieval Europe," *Oxford Journal of Archaeology* 4 (1985): 215–32; John Haldon, *The State and the Tributary Mode of Production* (London and New York, 1993); Michael McCormick, *Origins of the European Economy: Communications and Commerce, A.D. 300–900* (Cambridge, 2001).

65. Joachim Henning, "Ostasiatische Einflüsse auf die landwirtschaftliche Produktion Ost- und Südosteuropas im frühen Mittelalter," in *Pliska-Preslav: Slaviani i nomadi VI–XII v.,* vol. 3 (Sofia, 1981), 66–70; Walter Pohl, "Herrschaft und Subsistenz: Zum Wandel der byzantinischen Randkulturen an der Donau vom 6.–8. Jahrhundert," in *Awarenforschungen,* ed. Falko Daim, vol. 1 (Vienna, 1992), 13–24; Florin Curta, "Iron and potlatch: Early medieval hoards of implements and weapons in Eastern Europe," *Archivum Eurasiae Medii Aevi* 10 (1998–99), 15–62. See also the important work of Thomas S. Noonan on the Khazars—e.g., "The Khazar economy," *Archivum Eurasiae Medii Aevi* 9 (1995–97), 253–314.

66. Walter Pohl, "Zur Dynamik barbarischer Gesellschaften: Das Beispiel der Awaren," *Klio* 73 (1991): 595–600.

67. Most illustrative in that respect is the work of the Hungarian historian György Györffy: "Système des résidences d'hiver et d'été chez les nomades et les chefs hongrois au X-e siècle," *Archivum Eurasiae Medii Aevi* 1 (1975): 45–153; *Wirtschaft und Gesellschaft der Ungarn um die Jahrtausendwende* (Vienna, Cologne, and Graz, 1983); "Nomades et seminomades: La naissance de l'état hongrois," in *Popoli delle stepe: Unni, Avari, Ungari 23–29 aprile 1987,* vol. 2 (Spoleto, 1988), 621–36. See also János Matolcsi, "A középkori nomád állattenyésztés kelet-európái jellegzetességei," in *Nomád társadalmak és államalakulatok,* ed. Ferenc Tökei (Budapest, 1983), 281–306. Research on nomads and pastoralism was very advanced in the Soviet Union, and the trend continued after 1991. See, e.g., Svetlana A. Pletneva, *Kochevniki srednevekov'ia: Poiski istoricheskikh zakonomernosti* (Moscow, 1982); A. O. Dobroliubskii, *Kochevniki Severo-Zapadnogo Prichernomor'ia v epokhu srednevekov'ia* (Kiev, 1986); G. N. Garustovich, A. I. Rakushin, and A. F. Iaminov, *Srednevekovye kochevniki Povolzh'ia (konca IX–nachala XV veka)* (Ufa, 1998).

68. Helle Jensen, *Sarakatsani: En diskussion af de afgraensede, etnografiske objekt* (Copenhague, 1989); Claudia Chang, *Pastoral Transhumance in the Southern Balkans as a Social Ideology: An Ethnoarchaeological Research in Northern Greece* (Washington, D.C., 1993).

69. C. Constantinescu-Mirceşti, *Păstoritul transhumant şi implicaţiile lui în Transilvania şi Ţara Românească în secolele XVIII–XIX* (Bucharest, 1976); Ján Podolák, *Tradicné ovciarstvo na Slovensku* (Bratislava, 1982).

70. This is primarily because of the thorny issue of the Balkan Vlachs, as well as the Romanian-Hungarian dispute over the historical presence of Romanians in Transylvania. See M. Gyóni, "La transhumance des Vlaques balkaniques au Moyen Age," *Byzantinoslavica* 12 (1952): 29–42; V. D. Koroliuk, "Slaviane, vlakhi, rumliane i rimskie pastukhi vengerskogo Anonima," in *Iugo-vostochnaia Evropa v srednie veka: Sbornik statei,* ed. Ia. S. Grosul (Kishinew, 1972), 139–58; V. Marinov, "Rasselenie pastukhov-kochevnikov vlakhov na Balkanskom poluostrove i za ego predelami," in *Slaviano-voloshskie sviazi: Sbornik statei,* ed. N. A. Mokhov (Kishinew, 1972), 162–77; Demetrius Dvoichenko-Markov, "The Vlachs: The Latin speaking population of Eastern Europe," *Byzantion* 54 (1984): 508–26.

71. But see Claudia Chang and Harold A. Koster, "Beyond bones: Toward an archaeology of pastoralism," *Advances in Archaeological Method and Theory* 9 (1986): 97–148.

72. Carol A. Smith, "Exchange systems and the spatial distribution of elites: The organization of stratification in agrarian societies," in *Regional Analysis,* ed. Carol A. Smith, vol. 2 (New York, 1976), 309–81; Carole L. Crumley, "Three locational models: An epistemological assessment for anthropology and archaeology," *Advances in Archaeological Method and Theory* 2 (1979): 141–71.

73. *Royal Frankish Annals,* s.a. 808, in Bernhard Walter Scholz and Barbara Rogers, eds., *Carolingian Chronicles, Royal Frankish Annals, and Nithard's Histories* (Ann Arbor, 1970), 88.

74. For Kiev, see Johan Callmer, "The archaeology of Kiev ca. AD 500–1000: A survey," in *Les pays du Nord et Byzance (Scandinavie et Byzance): Actes du colloque nordique et international de byzantinologie tenu à Upsal 20–22 avril 1979,* ed. R. Zeitler (Uppsala, 1981), 29–52. For Bribir, see *Bribir u srednjem vjeku,* ed. Tonci Burić (Split, 1987). For Ostrów Lednicki, see Zofia Kurnatowska, "Zum bisherigen Ausgrabungs- und Bearbeitungsstand der archäologischen Materialien aus Zentren des Piastenstaates am Beispiel von Ostrów Lednicki," in *Frühmittelalterliche Machtzentren in Mitteleuropa: Mehrjährige Grabungen und ihre Auswertung; Symposion Mikulčice, 5.–9. September 1994,* ed. Čenek Staňa and Lumír Poláček (Brno, 1996), 49–59.

75. A. T. Smilenko, *Slov'iani ta ikh susydi v stepovomu Podnyprov'i (II–XIII st.)* (Kiev, 1975), 118–60; and "Die Keramik der Töpferwerkstätten von Balka kancerka im Dneprgebiet," in *Die Keramik der Saltovo-Majaki Kultur und ihrer Varianten,* ed. Csanád Bálint (Budapest, 1990), 313–25.

76. Paolo Squatriti, "Digging ditches in early medieval Europe," *Past and Present* 176 (2002): 11–65, and "Moving earth and making difference: Dikes and frontiers in early medieval Bulgaria," in *Borders, Barriers, and Ethnogenesis: Frontiers in Late Antiquity and the Middle Ages,* ed. Florin Curta (forthcoming).

77. Magdalena Beranová, "Types of Slavic agricultural production in the 6th–12th centuries," *Ethnologia Slavica* 16 (1984): 7–48.

78. *Seehaudelsplatz* ("sea marketplace") or *Seehaudelszentrum* (sea trade center) is a phrase coined in the 1970s by Joachim Herrmann and quickly adopted by some German and Polish archaeologists. See Joachim Herrmann, "Nordwestslawische Seehandelsplätze des 9.–10. Jh. und Spuren ihrer Verbindungen zum Nordseegebiet," *Ethnographisch-archäologische Zeitschrift* 16 (1975): 429–42, and "Frühe Seehandelsplätze am 'äußersten Ende des westlichen Ozeans': Geschichtliche Grundlagen, siedlungstopographische Strukturen und ethnische Herkunft ihrer Bewohner," *Acta Praehistorica et Archaeologica* 26–27 (1994–95): 57–72; Władysław Filipowiak, "Wolin: Die Entwicklung

des Seehandelszentrums im 8.–12. Jh.," *Slavia Antiqua* 36 (1995): 93–104; H. Jöns, F. Lüth, and M. Müller-Wille, "Ausgrabungen auf dem frühgeschichtlichen Seehandelsplatz von Groß Strömkendorf, Kr. Nordwestmecklenburg," *Germania* 75 (1997): 193–221. *Seehandelszentren* are the German equivalent of what have been known in English ever since Richard Hodges's *Dark Age Economics* (1982) as "emporia" or "ports of trade," such as the sites of the Viking Age at Ribe, Dorestad, Hamwic, or Hedeby. See now John Moreland in *Medieval Archaeology: An Encyclopedia,* ed Pam J. Crabtree (New York and London, 2001), s.v. "Emporia."

79. Thomas S. Noonan, "When and how dirhams first reached Russia: A numismatic critique of the Pirenne theory," *Cahiers du monde russe et soviétique* 21 (1980): 401–69; "Why the Viking first came to Russia," *Jahrbücher für Geschichte Osteuropas* 34 (1986): 321–48; "The Vikings and Russia: Some new directions and approaches to an old problem," in *Social Approaches to Viking Studies,* ed. Ross Samson (Glasgow, 1991), 201–6; "The Vikings in the East: Coins and commerce," in *The Twelfth Viking Congress: Development around the Baltic and the North Sea in the Viking Age,* ed. Björn Ambrosiani and Helen Clarke (Stockholm, 1994), 215–36.

80. Thomas S. Noonan, "Ninth-century dirham hoards from northwestern Russia and the southeastern Baltic," *Journal of Baltic Studies* 13 (1982): 220–44; "The first major silver crisis in Russia and the Baltic, ca. 875–900," *Hikuin* 11 (1985): 41–51; "Dirham hoards from medieval Lithuania," *Journal of Baltic Studies* 23 (1992): 395–413.

81. V. I. Kulakov, *Prussy, V–XIII vv.* (Moscow, 1994), 118–20. For Truso, see Marek Jagodziński and Maria Kasprzycka, "The early medieval craft and commercial centre at Janów Pomorski near Elblag on the south Baltic coast," *Antiquity* 65 (1991): 696–715. For Grobin, see Birger Nerman, *Grobin-Seeburg: Ausgrabungen und Funde* (Stockholm, 1958); V. Petrenko, V. Ozere, and I. Ozere, "Novye dannye o balto-skandinavskikh otnosheniiakh po materialam pamiatnikov g. Grobina," in *Problemy etnicheskoi istorii baltov: Tezisy dokladov mezhrespublikanskoi nauchnoi konferencii,* ed. Aina Blinkena, R. Ia. Denisova, E. S. Mugurevich, et al. (Riga, 1985), 86–89.

82. Amber of Baltic origin appears in the Temple II hoard in Pendzhikent and the Shoshoin hoard from Nara (Japan), both dated to the eighth century. See M. A. Bubovna and I. A. Polovnikova, "Torgovye puti pribaltiiskogo iantaria v srednei Azii (drevnost', srednevekov'e)," in *Goroda i karavansarai na trassakh velikogo shelkovogo puti: Tezisy dokladov mezhdunarodnogo seminara UNESCO, Urgench, 2–3 maia 1991 g.* (Urganch, 1991), 26–27; "K voprosu o proiskhozhdenii izdelii iz iantaria naidennykh v Pendzhikente," in *50-let raskopok drevnego Pendzhikenta: Tezisy dokladov nauchnoi konferencii (15–20 avgusta 1997 god)* (Pendzhikent, 1997), 76–77. However, according to Etienne de la Vaissière (*Histoire des marchands sogdiens* [Paris, 2002], 248–49), those responsible for the easternmost leg of the amber trade route must have been Sogdian, not Viking, merchants.

83. Michael McCormick, *Origins of the European Economy: Communications and Commerce, A.D. 300–900* (Cambridge, 2001), 369–79. For the Amber Trail, see Jerzy Kolendo, "Naplyw bursztynu z polnocy na tereny imperium rzymskiego w I–VI w. n.e.," *Prace Muzeum Ziemi* 41 (1990): 91–100. In Bohemia, no medieval amber finds can be dated earlier than ca. AD 900. See Jan Frolík, Katerina Tomková, and Jaromír Žegklitz, "Vyzkum slovanského pohřebiště v jizním křídle jízdárny Pražského Hradu," *Památky Archeologické* 79 (1988): 437–38; Zdenka Krumphanzlová, "Amber: Its significance in the early Middle Ages," *Památky Archeologické* 83 (1992): 366. It has long been suggested that

the appearance of amber beads in tenth-century Bohemia is the result of accelerated exchange with early Piast Poland. See Jiří Sláma, "K česko-polským stykům v 10. a 11. století," *Vznik a počátky Slovanů* 4 (1963): 221–69.

84. E.g., the large residential unit known as House 2A at Staraia Ladoga, built in the 770s, produced 320 fragments of Baltic amber, in addition to one hundred glass beads. See E. A. Riabinin and N. V. Chernykh, "Stratigrafiia, zastroika i khronologiia nizhnego sloia Staroladozhskogo zemlianogo gorodishcha v svete novykh issledovanii," *Sovetskaia Arkheologiia* 1 (1988): 72–100; E. Mühle, *Die städtischen Handelszentren der nordwestlichen Rus': Aufzüge und frühe Entwicklung altrussischer Städte (bis gegen Ende des 12. Jahrhunderts)* (Stuttgart, 1991), 22. See also O. I. Davidan, "Iantar' Staroi Ladogi," *Arkheologicheskii sbornik Gosudarstvennogo Ermitazha* 25 (1984): 118–26.

85. See B. Krzemieńska and D. Třeštík, "Premyšlovská hradište a služebná organizace Premyšlovského státu," *Archeologické rozhledy* 17 (1965): 624–44, 649–55; Karol Modzelewski, "Grody i dwory w gospodarce polskiej monarchii wczesnofeudalnej: Cześc I. Osady służebne a dwory książece," *Kwartalnik historii kultury materiałnej* 21 (1973): 3–35; Leszek Pawel Słupecki, "Osady służebne pod Sandomierzem i Zawichostem," *Kwartalnik historii kultury materiałnej* 40 (1992): 153–66.

86. O. V. Sukhobokov, G. A. Voznesenskaia, and V. V. Priimak, "Klad orudii truda i ukrazhenii iz Bitickogo gorodishcha," in *Drevnie slaviane i Kievskaia Rus': Sbornik nauchnykh trudov,* ed. P. P. Tolochko (Kiev, 1989), 92–105. For other similar hoards, see A. V. Cirkin, "Kirzhemanovskii klad," *Sovetskaia Arkheologiia* 1 (1969): 237–42; L. I. Ashikhmina, "Klad s Buiskogo gorodishcha," in *Novye arkheologicheskie issledovaniia na territorii Urala: Mezhvuzovskii sbornik nauchnykh trudov,* ed. R. D. Goldina (Izhevsk, 1987), 103–20.

87. Marcel Mauss, "Essai sur le don: Forme et raison de l'échange dans les sociétés archaïques," *Année sociologique* (1923–24), reprinted in *Sociologie et anthropologie* (Paris, 1980), 153; Arjun Appadurai, "Introduction: Commodities and the politics of value," in *The Social Life of Things: Commodities in Cultural Perspective,* ed. Arjun Appadurai (Cambridge, 1986), 21. See Curta, "Iron and potlatch."

88. Paul Stephenson, *Byzantium's Balkan Frontier: A Political Study of the Northern Balkans, 900–1204* (Cambridge, 2000), 43–45. For a critique of this particular argument, see Alexandru Madgearu, "Rethinking the Byzantine Balkans: A recent book on the 10th–12th centuries," *Revue des études sud-est-européennes* 39 (2001): 203–12, as well as my review in *Balkan Academic Book Reviews* 22 (2000), available at http://groups.yahoo .com/group/balkans/message/923 (December 13, 2003).

89. Ludwilka Szczerbicka-Slek, "Mit Piastów w literaturze XVI–XVIII w.," in *Piastowie w dziejach Polski: Zbiór artykułów z okazji trzechsetnej rocznicy wygasniecia dynastii Piastów,* ed. Romana Hecka (Wrocław, 1975), 229–48; Adam Galos, "Piastowie w historiografii polskiej XIX–XX w.," in ibid., 249–68; Dušan Třeštík, "Mír a dobry rok: Státní ideologie raného přemyslovského státu mezi kreštanstvím a 'pohanstvím," *Folia historica bohemica* 12 (1988): 23–45; Jiří Sláma, "Počátky přemyslovského státu," *Historicky obzor* 3 (1991): 98–105; Gyula Kristó, *Die Arpaden-Dynastie: Geschichte Ungarns von 895 bis 1301* (Budapest, 1993); Gerard Labuda, "Polska piastowska X wieku w systemie państw i narodow europejskich wczesnego średniowiecza," in *Polska Mieszka I. w tysiącelecie smierci tworcy państwa i Kościoła polskiego 25.V.992–25.V.1992,* ed. Jan M. Piskorski (Poznań, 1993), 17–28; Roman Michalowski, "Ideologia monarchiczna Piastów wczesniejszego okresu," in *Imagines potestatis: Rytualy, symbole i konteksty fabularne władzy*

zwierzchniej; Polska X–XV w, ed. Jacek Banaszkiewicz (Warsaw, 1994), 185–205; Ryszard Grzesik, "Legitimierungsfunktion der ungarisch-polnischen Chronik," in *The Medieval Chronicle: Proceedings of the 1st International Conference on the Medieval Chronicle, Driebergen/Utrecht, 13–16 July 1996,* ed. Erik Kooper (Amsterdam and Atlanta, 1999), 144–54; Kornél Szovák, "Historiographie hongroise à l'époque arpadienne," in *Les Hongrois et l'Europe: Conquête et intégration,* ed. Sándor Csernus and Klára Korompay (Paris and Szeged, 1999), 375–84; Pál Engel, "The house of Arpád and its times," *Hungarian Quarterly* 41 (2000): 74–79.

90. This is most evident in some recent collections of essays: *La violence dans le monde médiéval* (Aix-en-Provence, 1994); Philippe Contamine and Olivier Guyotjeannin, eds., *La guerre, la violence et les gens au Moyen Age: Actes du 119e congrès des sociétés historiques et scientifiques, 26–30 octobre 1994, Amiens, section d'histoire médiévale et de philologie. Part I. Guerre et violence* (Paris, 1996); Guy Halsall, ed., *Violence and Society in the Early Medieval West* (Rochester, 1998); Richard W. Kauper, ed., *Violence in Medieval Society* (Woodbridge, 2000); Günther Mensching, Eckhard Homann, Heiner Lohl, and Michael Städtler, eds., *Gewalt und ihre Legitimation im Mittelalter: Symposion des Philosophischen Seminars der Universität Hannover vom 26. bis 28. Februar 2002* (Würzburg, 2003).

91. Thomas Head and Richard Allen Landes, *The Peace of God: Social Violence and Religious Response in France around the Year 1000* (Ithaca, 1992).

92. Thomas N. Bisson, "The 'feudal revolution,'" *Past and Present* 142 (1994): 6–42. For reactions to Bisson's theories, see Dominique Barthélemy and Stephen White, "Debate: The 'feudal revolution,'" *Past and Present* 152 (1996): 196–223; Timothy Reuter, Chris Wickham, and Thomas N. Bisson, "Debate: The 'feudal revolution,'" *Past and Present* 155 (1997): 176–225. For an early, "eastern" reaction to Georges Duby's ideas revived and continued by Bisson, see Iu. L. Bessmertnyi, "'Feodal'naia revoliuciia' X–XI vekov," *Voprosy istorii* 1 (1984): 52–67. For an elegant summary of the debate, see Wickham, "Forme del feudalesimo."

93. For a remarkable exception, see Piotr Górecki, "Violence and the social order in a medieval society: The evidence from the Henryków region, ca. 1150–ca. 1300," in ". . . *The Man of Many Devices, Who Wandered Full Many Ways . . .": Festschrift in Honor of János M. Bak,* ed. Balázs Nagy and Marcell Sebök (Budapest, 1999), 91–104.

94. Cvetelin Stepanov, "The Bulgar title ΚΑΝΑΣΥΒΙΓΙ: Reconstructing the notions of divine kingship in Bulgaria, AD 822–836," *Early Medieval Europe* 10 (2001): 1–19; "Razvitie na koncepciiata za sakralniia car u khazarite i bălgarite prez rannoto srednovekovie," in *Bălgari i khazari prez rannoto srednovekovie,* ed. Cvetelin Stepanov (Sofia, 2003), 219–32.

95. Anatolii M. Khazanov, *Nomads and the Outside World* (Madison and London, 1994).

96. Peter B. Golden, *Nomads and Sedentary Societies in Medieval Eurasia* (Washington, 1998).

97. Jonathan Karam Skaff, "Barbarians at the gate? The Tang frontier military and the An Lushan rebellion," *War and Society* 18 (2000): no. 2, 23–35.

98. A. D. Nock, *Conversion: The Old and the New in Religion from Alexander the Great to Augustine of Hippo* (Oxford, 1933); Karl F. Morrison, *Understanding Conversion* (Charlottesville, 1992); Riccardo Picchio, "From Boris to Volodimer: Some remarks on the emergence of proto-orthodox Slavdom," *Harvard Ukrainian Studies* 12–13 (1988–89):

200–213; Hans-Dietrich Kahl, "Das Fürstentum Karantanien und die Anfänge seiner Christianisierung," in *Karantanien und der Alpen-Adria-Raum im Frühmittelalter*, ed. Günther Hödl and Johannes Grabmayer (Vienna and Cologne, 1993), 37–99; Lynette Olson, "The conversion of the Visigoths and Bulgarians compared," in *Religious Change, Conversion, and Culture*, ed. Lynette Olson (Sydney, 1996), 22–32; Alain Besançon, "Les baptêmes de l'Europe de l'est," in *La France, l'Eglise, quinze siècles déjà: Actes du colloque organisé à la Sorbonne par l'Ecole pratique des Hautes Etudes, IVe Section et le Comité pour la commémoration des origines; De la Gaule à la France*, ed. Marceau Long and François Monnier (Geneva, 1997), 13–24; Teresa Dunin-Wasowicz, "Autour du baptême de Mieszko I-er de Pologne," in *Clovis, histoire et mémoire: Le baptême de Clovis, son écho à travers l'histoire*, ed. Michel Rouche (Paris, 1997), 369–85; Ryszard Grzesik, "Die Ungarnmission des Hl. Adalberts," in "*. . . The Man of Many Devices, Who Wandered Full Many Ways . . .*": *Festschrift in Honor of János M. Bak*, ed. Balázs Nagy and Marcell Sebök (Budapest, 1999), 230–40; Jerzy Kłoczowski, *A History of Polish Christianity* (Cambridge, 2000).

99. N. J. Higham, *The Convert Kings: Power and Religious Affiliation in Early Anglo-Saxon England* (Manchester, 1997), 20–23.

100. Marilyn Dunn, "Evangelism or repentance? The re-Christianisation of the Peloponnese in the ninth and tenth centuries," *Studies in Church History* 14 (1977): 71–86.

101. John M. Howe, "The conversion of the physical world: The creation of a Christian landscape," in *Varieties of Religious Conversion in the Middle Ages* (Gainesville, 1997), 63–78.

102. Walter Trillmich, *Familienpropaganda der Kaiser Caligula und Claudius: Agrippina Maior und Antonia Augusta auf Münzen* (Berlin, 1978); Lesław Morawiecki, *Political Propaganda in the Coinage of the Late Roman Republic (44–43 B.C.)* (Wrocław, 1983); Peter Hardetert, *Propaganda, Macht, Geschichte: Fünf Jahrhunderte römischer Geschichte von Caesar bis Theodosius in Münzen geprägt* (Gelsenkirchen, 1998).

103. James D. Breckenridge, "The iconoclasts' image of Christ," *Gesta* 11 (1972): 3–8; Andreass U. Sommer, "Die Heiligendarstellungen in der byzantinischen Münzprägung: Eine vergleichende Studie," *Numismatisches Nachrichtenblatt* 42 (1993): 62–70.

104. Renate Schumacher Wolfgarten, "XCTIANA RELIGIO: Zu einer Münzprägung Karls des Grossen," *Jahrbuch für Antike und Christentum* 37 (1994): 122–41.

105. Anna Gannon, *The Iconography of Early Anglo-Saxon Coinage, Sixth to Eighth Centuries* (Oxford, 2003), 185, 187.

106. The "special issue" of 837/8 thus sheds a new light on the religious disputation that, according to the *Vita Constantini*, was an important event in the history of St. Cyril's "Khazar mission." See T. Moriiasu, "Khazarskaia misiia Konstantina," *Starobălgarska literatura* 10 (1981): 39–51; Nikolai Kochev, "Khazarskata misiia na Konstantin Filosof-Kiril v svetlinata na Kembridzhskiia Anonim i izvestiiata na Iekhuda Alevi," *Kirilo-metodievski studii* 5 (1988): 91–97; Khristo Trendafilov, *Khazarskata polemika na Konstantin Kiril* (Sofia, 1999).

107. Egil Mikkelsen, "Islam and Scandinavia during the Viking age," in *Byzantium and Islam in Scandinavia: Acts of a Symposium at Uppsala University, June 15–16, 1996*, ed. Elisabeth Piltz (Jonsered, 1998), 48–50.

108. Kazimierz Szuda, "Niepublikowane denary Boleslawa Chrobregu z napisem cyrylicznym," *Wiadomości Numizmatyczne* 3 (1959): 62–63; Stanisław Suchodolski,

"Boleslaw Chrobry a-t-il émis des monnaies à Kiev?" in *Actes du 9ème Congrès international de numismatique, Berne, Septembre 1979,* ed. Tony Hackens and Raymond Weiller, vol. 2 (Louvain-la-Neuve and Luxembourg, 1982), 805–10. For Vladimir's coinage, see Tadeusz Wasilewski, "Chrystus Pantokrator na pięczeciach i monetach Włodżimierza i i jego nastepcow: Byzantynskie in bulgarskie wzorce," *Wiadomości Numizmatyczne* 32 (1988): 159–68; Jan L. Perkowski, "Linguistic history engraved in gold and silver: Legends on the coins of St. Vladimir," *Palaeoslavica* 8 (2000): 1–17.

PART ONE

Economic and Social Structures

Ways of Life in Eastern and Western Europe during the Early Middle Ages: Which Way Was "Normal"?

Joachim Henning

The solution to the problem of what constitutes "exceptional development" in history and what, by contrast, has to be seen as a "regular" or "normal" way depends on the cultural point of view of the observer. A Chinese scholar would most likely see the Carolingian civilization of Western Europe as *Sonderweg*.[1] Medievalists concerned solely with Western Europe insists on regarding early medieval Eastern Europe as diverging from Western "normality." Who is right? Is is possible at all to decide on this issue?

It is often stressed that East European societies developed more rigidly centralized forms of state organization typically associated with some form of despotism.[2] The *knyaz*, qagan, khan, or czar were, much like their Roman and Byzantine counterparts, at the top of a power pyramid, enabling them or their acolytes or officeholders (supported by the entire executive power of the state, including the infamous *agentes in rebus* of late antiquity)[3] to collect the agrarian surplus, more or less directly and in a simple manner, either as unified tax from each village or as tribute from an entire region.[4] The feudal disintegration of Western Europe, with the juridical sovereignty of private landlords and the extraordinarily complicated system of rent and revenue collection within the framework of the manorial economy, was undoubtedly the absolute opposite of the East European developments.[5] Eastern Europe seems to be closer in that respect to the eastern, southern, and western Mediterranean regions controlled by Byzantium and the caliphate, where the centralized state survived and flourished in the continuing tradition of late antiquity. Beyond Western Europe and its manorial system, probably no other world region in the second half of the first millennium had kings who, outside their own landed property, possessed so little jurisdiction at a local level. Was Western Europe's development a *Sonderweg*, the exception to a widespread "norm"? When and why did the dichotomy emerge between East and West?

In an attempt to offer plausible answers to these questions, a research project was recently established at the Johann Wolfgang Goethe University in Frankfurt am Main, which is now in its fifth year of activity.[6] The goal of this archaeological project is to compare two central places of regional settlement networks of particular political and religious importance in the 700s and 800s—one in the West, the other in the East. Excavations are currently taking place in Pliska,[7] the power center of early medieval Bulgaria and, later, the see of the first archbishop of Bulgaria, and in Büraburg-Fritzlar (north Hesse, Germany), a bishopric that was founded by St. Boniface and later became a royal *palatium*. The research project—including minute details of soil analysis and paleobotany, as well as macroregional comparative studies—is mainly supported by the Graduate School of Archaeology at the Johann Wolfgang Goethe University in Frankfurt am Main and sponsored by the Deutsche Forschungsgemeinschaft.[8] The remaining part of this chapter summarizes some of its preliminary results.

The Center and Settlement Pattern

The siting of the Büraberg center surely has much to do with the nearby crossroads of important long-distance routes and the Eder River waterway (fig. 1.1). While the Franks erected their fortified site of the eighth and ninth centuries on a hill, the Ottonian *palatium* emerged in the plain, near Fritzlar, much closer to both the crossroads and the waterway. The location of the surrounding rural settlements is equally determined by natural conditions and the road network. Almost the entire area suitable for agriculture had already been occupied by the time the Büraberg fort made its appearance. Three excavated villages (fig. 1.1, sites 1–3) have produced evidence of an early occupation going back to Roman times.[9] The rise of the fortified, central site on top of the Büraberg hill took place much later. It dates to the early Carolingian period.[10] It may be associated with the Frankish conquest and with the introduction of the manorial system. It has become clear, however, that the introduction and implementation of this system did not alter the settlement pattern. No major changes occurred in either the siting of rural settlements or their occupation.

The fortified palace complex at Pliska has been assumed to have its origins in the late 600s or the early 700s.[11] Its beginning would thus coincide in time with that of the Büraberg fort. Unlike Büraberg, however, its location was chosen irrespective of the ancient network of roads. Moreover, neither the "Outer Town" at Pliska (a huge area fortified by an earthen rampart) nor its immediate hinterland produced any rural settlements that could be dated to this early period. Todor Balabanov's investigations outside the outer earthen rampart at

Pliska have identified fifty-six sites dated between the second half of the eighth century and the tenth century.[12] In addition, only sites with ceramic types of the late eighth to tenth centuries are known from the area inside the great outer wall of Pliska (fig. 1.2).[13] Even if we suppose that the formation of the very first satellite settlements occurred immediately after the palace complex came into being, the number of such early sites inside the great rampart at Pliska must have been much smaller than previously thought.[14] The field research of the last five years has shown that the number of such settlements increased considerably from the late ninth and especially during the tenth and eleventh centuries. Even these developments resulted not in an expansive network of villages, covering the countryside in an equable pattern around the nucleus of the political center at Pliska, but in an enormous and amorphous agglomeration of sites, concentrated in a tight belt around the palatial compound (all surrounded by a gigantic rampart-and-ditch fortification, 6.5 km long and 3.9 km wide). Outside this belt region, called the "Outer Town" of Pliska, the density of sites is much smaller. Unlike Western Europe, the rise of a new power center took place without much regard to previous infrastructure and settlement. The majority of Bulgarian rural settlements were attached to the already existing palatial compound and formed a rather artificial pattern.

This pattern is reminiscent of the so-called service settlements of tenth- and eleventh-century Bohemia, Hungary, and Poland. For example, in Sandomierz (southeastern Poland), an older settlement pattern was radically altered by the conquering Piast rulers during the early eleventh century and turned into a service settlement pattern centered on its newly built stronghold.[15] In ninth- and tenth-century Great Poland, a radical change of settlement pattern around new power centers has been suggested for the hinterland of the Piast strongholds and has been associated with the settling of people deported from distant locations.[16] Another example of a service settlement pattern is the Nitra region (Slovakia) during the 800s.[17]

Crafts

To date, no substantial evidence of large-scale industrial activities has been found on the Büraberg site. Excavations carried out inside the fortified area by J. Vonderau in 1934,[18] by N. Wand in 1974,[19] and by the Johann Wolfgang Goethe University team in 1999 produced only two small pieces of iron slag, which, at most, could be interpreted as evidence of sporadic smithing. Starting in 1998, geomagnetic remote sensing discovered and mapped man-made features all over the nonfortified plateau at Büraberg—including sunken-featured buildings supposedly inhabited by craftsmen and traders, long thought to have been located there.[20] However, archaeological investigations in 2000 revealed them to be from a Neolithic settlement, not the *suburbium* of the center. The idea of a proto-urban settlement at Büraberg[21] is not supported by any archaeological evidence. In fact, the scarcity of signs of industrial activities is a feature most typical of contemporary forts in northern Hesse, judging from excavations at Kesterburg (on the Christenberg near Münchhausen)[22] and Glauberg (to the west from Büdingen).[23]

By contrast, industrial activities are well attested in contemporary settlements. At Neuental-Zimmersrode (fig. 1.1, site 5), a relatively long distance of 15 kilometers from Büraberg, but not far from the main local roads, a pottery production center with several kilns emerged in Carolingian times.[24] The production of bone or antler artifacts (especially combs), bronze and iron metalworking, and the production of textiles have also been documented in neighboring rural settlements.[25] All these industrial activities were well established in the countryside long before the imposition of the manorial economy. This is clearly indicated by the archaeological evidence of crafts and craftsmen on at least one of these sites, which dates back to Roman times but did function continuously.[26]

One of the most important discoveries of the joint German-Bulgarian excavations at Pliska is a large craft-working quarter of the eighth and ninth centuries, located next to the palatial compound.[27] Judging from the finds, this area not only served as a metalworking production center but also produced glass, both for vessels and for windows.[28] Undoubtedly, this center was designed to meet the needs of the palace. This is substantiated by the fact that the artisans' quarter was abandoned at the time of the transfer of the royal residence from Pliska to Preslav in the late 800s. During the tenth and eleventh centuries, the center disintegrated into several smaller workshops scattered over the entire area covered by satellite settlements.[29]

The conclusion seems obvious. While rural industries that predate the imposition of the manorial system were put to greater use under that system and continued more or less unchanged after that, specific circumstances in the East led to the establishment of large and, in the long run, often unstable artisan centers that depended on residences of rulers and exclusively served their needs.

The Structure of Rural Settlements

The pattern of excavated settlements in the hinterland of Büraburg (Geismar and Holzheim) matches the known picture of early medieval Western Europe. Some buildings were aboveground houses of large or medium size; others were sunken-floored huts. Documentary evidence and totally excavated villages in southern Germany (Kirchheim and Lauchheim) indicate the existence of farmsteads that normally included a relatively large number of buildings of different functions, used as dwellings, stables, storage buildings, and workshops (fig. 1.3).[30]

The building type attested in the satellite settlements at Pliska is well known to archaeologists working in Eastern Europe. It is a sunken-floored hut of relatively standard size, with a stone or clay oven in one corner. Larger auxiliary buildings, such as stables, are unknown, and no division of the settlement into farmsteads seems to have existed. Elsewhere, there are several examples of very large agglomerations of such houses, some without any recognizable organization (e.g., at Garvan, Popina-Dzhedzhovi Lozia, and Krivina, all in northeastern Bulgaria; see fig. 1.4),[31] some in loosely circular arrangements (e.g., at Ključ, in southwestern Bulgaria; see fig. 1.4),[32] and some in checkered arrangements (e.g., at Groß Raden, in northern Germany).[33]

In the sphere of rural forms of living, the structural differences between East and West are significant. In both cases, the different settlement patterns and the specific internal organization of the settlements long predate the rise of different forms of power in use by early medieval elites in the West and in the East. In each case, the different settlement patterns and building forms have a centuries-long tradition reaching back to prehistoric times. As a consequence, the different forms of power have to be explained as specific adaptations to preexisting different forms of rural settlement, that is, of rural forms of living and producing. In other words, one could not have exploited the manorial system and ruled over farmsteads unless developed farmsteads were already in existence in that area.

Agricultural Profile

Iron farming tools, botanical and faunal remains, and rural buildings suggest that during the late Roman period, the prevailing agricultural system in the West was based on advanced cattle-breeding techniques, such as stabling (documented by heavy iron forks)[34] and sophisticated fodder production for the winter months (documented by long-handled scythes).[35] Besides such intensive forms of production, crop agriculture seems to have developed in a much more extensive manner. The predominant crop was a simple spelt grain[36] associated with an extensive method of harvesting (the "combing-out" of the ears) known since prehistoric times and based on the so-called Gallic harvesting device, the *vallus*.[37] Judging from the distribution of pictorial references, this device's use was apparently linked to a large-scale organization of latifundia in the West. A widespread popularity of the reaping device may explain the absence of archaeological evidence for iron reaping sickles in the northwestern provinces of the empire, as opposed to the middle and lower Danube regions. Recent experiments with replicas of the Roman *vallus* suggest a considerable waste of grain during harvesting, which, unlike large latifundia, no small agrarian production unit (farmstead) could afford.[38]

Judging from the continuous use of a variety of stables,[39] iron forks (fig. 1.5, A6),[40] and long-handled scythes (fig. 1.5, A1),[41] high-standard cattle breeding remained an important component of the early medieval agriculture of the West. In addition, agriculture in the West now benefited from the introduction of new crops, such as rye and wheat; more intensive harvesting and thrashing techniques, such as those associated with the use of balanced curved sickles (fig. 1.5, A2)[42] and flails; and, last but not least, the adoption of the heavy wheeled plow and of the framed harrow.[43] Both were already known on some Roman villa sites on the Rhine and Danube rivers and in Dacia.[44] During the early Middle Ages, peasants in Western Europe developed a farmstead economy whose complex and advanced economic profile combined farming and cattle breeding (Kuchenbuch's *Verbundwirtschaft*)[45] and a communal organization of villages.

Since Roman times, cereal cultivation was far more important and intensive in the East than in the West. Unlike in the West, cattle breeding took on a more extensive development in the East. The high-tech long-handled scythe and the heavy three-pronged iron fork, two of the most important implements associated with stabling or livery as practiced in the West, were unknown in the eastern provinces of the Roman Empire.[46] By contrast, the East must have been responsible for the introduction of advanced plowing and harvesting techniques.[47] The migration of Germanic peoples from Eastern to Western Europe may have contributed to the diffusion of Eastern farming technology into the West.

Unlike the West, early medieval Eastern Europe had no qualitative balance between intensive forms of farming and cattle breeding. There seems to be no evidence of any exposure of East European farmers to the highly developed techniques of cattle breeding in the West. If they knew about them, such techniques definitely had no impact on the overall economic profile of the East. As a consequence, early medieval peasants in the East had no use for either the heavy three-pronged iron forks or for long scythes; they preferred more simple, short-handled scythes (fig. 1.5, B1).[48] These implements of prehistoric tradition were not suitable for high-quality meadow cultivation and for regular fodder production and harvesting, as practiced in the West by means of a long scythe (fig. 1.6). In the East, Roman traditions were evident mainly in implements for cereal cultivation. Balanced curved sickles continued to be used here from late antiquity throughout the early Middle Ages, while in the West, these implements seem to have no local Roman predecessors but were adopted in post-Roman times from the East. Early medieval households of the East adapted late Roman plowing techniques (originally connected with the heavy instruments) to lighter implements activated by the modest traction power of a few animals.[49] It comes as no surprise that, as a result of the shortage of fodder supply for traction animals, the plowshares found in Eastern Europe are much smaller than those in use in the West (fig. 1.5).[50] Finally, the absence of iron plow chains from the East suggests that the plowing implements there were typically light and without wheels. More often than not, small plowshares have traces of asymmetrical wear on the left side and are associated with coulters,[51] an indication that such light implements were nevertheless capable of turning the turf basically just like heavy plows. The number of traction animals available in East European farm households seems to have been limited. The absence of an elaborate inventory of buildings for cattle breeding (stables and storage facilities) explains the lack of functional divisions of buildings and hence the lack of farmsteads on East European rural sites.

The archaeological evidence throws new light on the much-debated problem of an East-West contrast in early medieval Europe. The borderline between East and West must be seen not as one separating different worldviews but as an economic boundary. This boundary did not emerge in the early Middle Ages but has its origins in antiquity—if not prehistory—and was determined by geographic factors and local economic conditions.

The small farms of Eastern European peasants specializing in the cultivation of cereals left little room for significant differentiation of wealth and made taxation of individual households pointless. Because of the stability of the rural landscape, there was no apparent need for structural changes in a ruling system whose formula was well tested in ancient societies—especially in the Near East—and thus closer to the "normal" path. Political power in early medieval Eastern Europe had very few limits: palaces could be built at various points, as desired, while entire communities of peasants and craftsmen could be moved around as needed.

By contrast, the manorial economy may be seen as a reaction to the high levels of productivity attained in the West during and shortly after the late Roman period by individual farmsteads engaged in both cereal production and cattle breeding by means of a well-balanced economic system. It was only logical that the manorial system would not displace such units of production but, instead, would maintain preexisting relations between them and interfere as little as possible in the production process, in order to tax individual farm-steads more effectively. The result of such circumspect economic behavior seems to have been substantial economic gains for landlords. Altering the de-veloped settlement pattern would have been not only impractical but alto-gether destructive for the implementation of the manorial economy.

Quite the opposite is true about East Central Europe, where the manorial system made its appearance much later, after the tenth century. Wherever the new system was introduced, it was accompanied by a radical, structural change of preexisting settlement patterns.[52] Nonfarmstead rural settlement structures were changed into farmstead or "true" villages, a process known as the farm-stead transformation of settlements (*Verhufung*). A similarly sharp contrast can be observed in the West during the fourth and fifth centures, between non-farmstead rural settlement structures of the region of late Roman villas in northeast Gaul and the expanding village on the one hand, and farmstead structures expanding into that area from outside the imperial borders, on the other.[53] This was the point of departure for a specific model of agrarian society in early medieval Western Europe. After AD 1000, because of its high produc-tivity, it was also "exported" to other areas of medieval Europe. The *Sonderweg* gradually became the "norm" of Europe and, in the end, the decisive basis for the rise of a new and ever-expanding town and commercial economy.[54]

NOTES

1. West European history since the early Middle Ages has been treated as *Sonderweg* (special path) in the Breuninger Foundation series *Der europäische Sonderweg: Ursachen und Faktoren*, ed. R. P. Sieferle and H. Breuninger (Stuttgart, 2001). In addition, the term *Sonderweg* has been used for rather different historical developments seemingly deviat-ing from "mainstream" European history, such as modern Germany (see *Deutscher Son-derweg: Mythos oder Realität?*, ed. K. D. Bracher et al. [Munich, 1982]) or Romania (see R. Wagner, *Sonderweg Rumänien* [Berlin, 1991]). The session "East Central Europe in the Early Middle Ages: A *Sonderweg?*" organized for the Thirty-Fifth International Congress on Medieval Studies in Kalamazoo (May 4–7, 2000) by Florin Curta (University of Florida) approached the *Sonderweg* problem from the point of view of special develop-ments in Eastern Europe during the second half of the first millennium AD.

2. For example, on Byzantium and its client states in southeast Europe, see B. Fer-jančić, *Despoti u Vizantiji i južnoslovenskim zemljama* (Belgrade, 1960).

3. W. Blum, Curiosi *und* regendarii: *Untersuchungen zur geheimen Staatspolizei der Spätantike* (Munich, 1969); M. Clauss, *Der magister officiorum in der Spätantike (4–6 Jh.)* (Munich, 1980). In what follows, I use the term *despotism* in a broader sense than Karl August Wittfogel. To me, despotism cannot be explained in terms of either a "hydraulic monopoly of the state" or a special "Asian mode of production." See K. A. Wittfogel, *Oriental Despotism* (New Haven, 1957). *Despots* and *despotates* are terms frequently em-

ployed in Byzantine sources to describe power structures, titles, and territories. See A. Kazhdan in *Oxford Dictionary of Byzantium*, vol. 1 (New York and Oxford, 1991), 614, s.v. "despotes." Despotism is therefore not a nineteenth-century Western label to be applied to Eastern political realities. Nevertheless, it is equally true that the concept of Oriental despotism prior to Wittfogel's book was often applied to justify the conquest and colonization of the Orient. I am grateful to Michael McCormick for the bibliographical references pertaining to this issue.

4. For the late antique taxation system, see W. Goffart, *Caput and Colonate: Towards a History of Late Roman Taxation* (Toronto, 1974). For tax collection in Slavonic lands, see P. Donat, "Zur Frage des Bodeneigentums bei den Westslawen," *Jahrbuch für Geschichte des Feudalismus* 4 (1980): 20–26. The limited productivity of such centralized systems has been described in C. M. Cipolla, ed., *The Economic Decline of Empires* (London, 1970).

5. For a detailed description of the West European system, see L. Kuchenbuch, *Bäuerliche Gesellschaft und Klosterherrschaft im 9. Jh: Studien zur Sozialstruktur der Familia der Abtei Prüm* (Wiesbaden, 1978). For a more general treatment of this problem, see J. P. Devroey, *Etudes sur le grand domaine carolingien* (Aldershot, 1993).

6. J. Henning et al., "Moderne Archäologie: Fortschritt durch Brückenschlag zwischen Geistes- und Naturwissenschaften," in *Spitzenforschung in Hessen*, vol. 1 (Wiesbaden, 1999), 54–60.

7. This is a joint project of the Archaeological Institute of the Bulgarian Academy of Science (Liudmila Doncheva-Petkova and Pavel Georgiev) and the Konstantin Preslavski University in Shumen (Stoian Vitlianov). See J. Henning, "Pliska: Machtzentrum zwischen Byzanz und Abendland; Neue Wege der Archäologie," *Forschung Frankfurt* 2 (2000): 6–15.

8. J. Henning et al., *Graduiertenkolleg "Archäologische Analytik"* (Frankfurt am Main, 1998), 1–44.

9. The site at Geismar was apparently occupied without interruption from Roman times to the eleventh and twelfth centuries. See R. Gensen, *Die chattische Großsiedlung von Fritzlar-Geismar, Schwalm-Eder Kreis,* (Wiesbaden, 1978). See however, N. Wand, The Roman, Merovingian, and Carolingian settlement features excavated at Holzheim have recently been published by N. Wand, Holzheim bei Fritzlar: Archdologie eines mittelalterlichen Dorfes (Kasseler Beitradge zur Vor- und Frühgeschichte 6) (Rhaden/Westf, 2002). See, however, N. Wand, "Holzheim bei Fritzlar in salischer Zeit: ein nordhessisches Dorf mit Herrensitz, Fronhof und Eigenkirche," in *Siedlungen und Landesausbau zur Salierzeit,* ed. H. W. Böhme, vol. 1 (Sigmaringen, 1992), 169–210. Johann-Heinrich Schotten, *Die Ausgrabungen von Büraburg und Wüstung Holzheim bei Fritzlar. An der Wende von der merowingischen zur karolingischen Zeit* (Arnstadt, 1998). Small excavations at Niedenstein-Kirchberg have produced features and artifacts of late Roman (assemblages dated by coins to the fourth century), Merovingian, and Carolingian dates. See R. Gensen, *Althessens Frühzeit: Frühgeschichtliche Fundstätten und Funde in Nordhessen* (Wiesbaden, 1979), 24.

10. There are, of course, a few Roman artifacts found on the Büraberg hill. See H. W. Böhme, "Völkerwanderungszeitliche Metallgegenstände vom Büraberg bei Fritzlar," *Archäologisches Korrespondenzblatt* 4 (1974): 165ff. Such finds were hastily interpreted as evidence of a Germanic fort. See G. Mildenberger, *Germanische Burgen* (Münster, 1978), 69 and maps 3–4. In reality, subsequent excavations (including the Johann Wolfgang Goethe-University excavations of 1999) demonstrated that no fortification on the

Büraberg hill could be dated earlier than ca. AD 750. See J. Vonderau, *Die Ausgrabungen am Büraburg bei Fritzlar 1926*, (Fulda, 1934); N. Wand, *Die Büraburg bei Fritzlar: Burg—"oppidum"—Bischofssitz in karolingischer Zeit*, Kasseler Beiträge zur Vor- und Frühgeschichte 4 (Marburg, 1974).

11. R. Rashev, "Nachaloto na Pliska i na bălgarskoto *Landnahmezeit*," in *Zwischen Byzanz und Abendland: Pliska, der östliche Balkanraum und Europa im Spiegel der Frühmittelalterarchäologie*, ed. J. Henning (Frankfurt am Main, 1999), 17–18.

12. The site at Pervomaiska Cheshma, located near the Stoian Mikhailovski village, produced wheel-made pottery and fragments of handmade pots further modeled on a *tournette* (slow wheel) and was dated by Todor Balabanov to the seventh and eighth centuries. See T. Balabanov, "Novootkriti rannosrednovekovni selishta v okolnostite na Pliska," in *Problemi na prabălgarskata istoriia i kultura*, ed. R. Rashev (Sofia, 1989), 281–82. The site became the object of a German-Bulgarian joint field survey in the summer of 2003. One of the most important conclusions of this survey was that the handmade pottery is in fact of prehistoric age. Todor Balabanov cites a similarly erroneous dating of pottery remains (long viewed as "early Slavic") from the site of the "aul of Omurtag" (near the present-day village of Khan Krum). See Todor Balabanov and Joachim Henning, "Eine Palisadenbefestigung des 8. Jahrhunderts unter den Resten des Steinpalastes des Chan Omurtag," *Archaeologia Bulgarica* (forthcoming).

13. Radoslav Vasilev, "Rannosrednovekovni selishta VIII–X v. v raiona na Pliska," in *Vtori mezhdunaroden kongres po bălgaristika, Sofiia, 23 mai–3 iuni 1986 g. Dokladi 6: Bălgarskite zemi v drevnostta Bălgariia prez srednovekovieto*, ed. Khr. Khristov et al. (Sofia, 1987), 400–406.

14. J. Henning, "Vom Herrschaftszentrum zur städtischen Großsiedlung mit agrarischer Komponente: Archäologische Nachweise der Landwirtschaft aus dem frühmittelalterlichen Pliska," *Pliska-Preslav* 8 (2000): 74–86.

15. L. P. Słupecki, "Osady służebne pod Sandomierzem i Zawichostem," *Kwartalnik historii kultury materialnej* 40 (1992): 153–66.

16. Zofia Kurnatowska, "Frühstädtische Entwicklung an den Zentren der Piasten in Großpolen," in *Burg, Burgstadt, Stadt: Zur Genese mittelalterlicher nichtagrarischer Zentren in Ostmitteleuropa*, ed. Hansjürgen Brachmann (Berlin, 1995), 133–47, esp. 135.

17. B. Chropovský, "Zur Entwicklung der spezialisierten Handwerksproduktion im 8.–9. Jh. auf dem Gebiet der Slowakei," in *La formation et le développement des métiers au Moyen Age (Ve–XIVe siècles): Colloque international*, ed. L. Gerevich and A. Salamon (Budapest, 1977), 47–54.

18. See n. 10.

19. See n. 10.

20. N. Wand, "Büraburg auf dem Büraberg," in *Hessen im Frühmittelalter*, ed. H. Roth and E. Wamers (Sigmaringen, 1984), 255.

21. N. Wand, "'Oppidum Büraburg: Der Beitrag der Büraburg bei Fritzlar zur frühen Stadt östlich des Rheins," in *Vor- und Frühformen der europäischen Stadt*, ed. H. Jankuhn, W. Schlesinger, and H. Steuer (Göttingen, 1973), 163–201.

22. R. Gensen, "Christenberg, Burgwald und Amöneburger Becken in der Merowinger- und Karolingerzeit," in *Althessen im Frankenreich*, ed. W. Schlesinger (Sigmaringen, 1975), 121–72.

23. Joachim Werner erroneously interpreted high medieval cellars found on this site as early medieval workshops, following the excavator's wishful thinking and obsession with finding a "truly Germanic" *Gauburg* (county fort). See Joachim Werner, "Zu den

alamannischen Burgen des 4. und 5. Jahrhunderts," in *Festiva lanx: Studien zum mittel-alterlichen Geistesleben: Johannes Spörl dargebracht aus Anlass seines 60. Geburtstags*, ed. Karl Schnith (Munich, 1966), 439ff.; G. Richter, "Der Glauberg," in *Volk und Scholle* 12 (1934): 289ff.

24. M. Mathias, "Ein karolingischer Töpferofen aus Neuental-Zimmersrode, Schwalm-Eder-Kreis," *Fundberichte aus Hessen* 27–28 (1987): 88ff.

25. Palaeobotanical analysis carried out at the Johann Wolfgang Goethe University in Frankfurt am Main on the site at Obervorschütz (fig. 1.1, site 4), which was occupied without interruption during most of the first millennium, seems to indicate the early medieval presence of water mills on the Elbe River (personal information from Dr. Schweitzer, Johann Wolfgang Goethe University in Frankfurt am Main).

26. The site at Geismar-Fritzlar produced a pit with associated crucibles, pottery, bronze slag, and iron ore, all dated to Roman times. Sunken-floored huts of the late Roman period found on the same site produced iron slag, bronze blanks, and bronze slag. Cultural layers dated to as late as the eighth century produced iron, bronz, and glass slag, bone and antler artifacts, and destroyed ovens. See R. Gensen, *Althessens Frühzeit: Frühgeschichtliche Fundstätten und Funde in Nordhessen*, Führer zur hessischen Vor- und Frühgeschichte 1 (Wiesbaden, 1979), 34, 84; H. Roth, "Bronzeherstellung und -verarbeitung während der späten römischen Kaiserzeit in Geismar bei Fritzlar, Schwalm-Eder-Kreis, und Altendorf bei Bamberg (Oberfranken)," *Fundberichte aus Hessen* 19–20 (1979–80): 795–806. For textile production in Geismar, see A. Tiedmann, "Die spätkarolingerzeitliche Tuchmacherei in der frühgeschichtlichen Siedlung von Fritzlar-Geismar im Schwalm-Eder-Kreis," in *Archäologisches Zellwerk: Beiträge zur Kulturgeschichte in Europa und Asien; Festschrift für Helmut Roth um 60. Geburtstag*, ed. Ernst Pohl, Udo Recker, and Claudia Theune (Rahden, 2001), 531–40.

27. J. Henning, "Pliska: Machtzentrum" (see n. 7).

28. K. H. Wedepohl, "Die Glasherstellung im 8./9. Jahrhundert am Asar-dere in Pliska im Vergleich mit karolingischem Glas des Frankenreiches," in *Zwischen Byzanz und Abendland: Pliska, der östliche Balkanraum und Europa im Spiegel der Frühmittel-alterarchäologie*, ed. J. Henning (Frankfurt am Main, 1999), 93–94.

29. T. Balabanov, "Zaniatchiiski proizvodstva v Pliska (VIII–XI v.)," Ph.D. diss., Institute of Archaeology of the Bulgarian Academy of Sciences (1983); St. Vitlianov, "Arkheologicheski danni za ikonomicheskiia oblik na Pliska," *Pliska-Preslav* 8 (2000): 87–92.

30. P. Donat, "Zur Entwicklung germanischer Siedlungen östlich des Rheins bis zum Ausgang der Karolingerzeit," *Zeitschrift für Archäologie* 25 (1991): 149–76 (with literature). For Kirchheim, see H. Geisler, *Studien zur Archäologie frühmittelalterlicher Siedlungen in Altbayern* (Straubing, 1993). For Lauchheim, see I. Storck, "Friedhof und Dorf, Herrenhof und Adelsgrab: Der einmalige Befund Lauchheim," in *Die Alamannen, Begleitband zur Ausstellung "Die Alamannen," 14. Juni 1997 bis 14. September 1997, Süd-westLB-Forum*, ed. K. Fuchs et al. (Stuttgart, 1997), 311–22.

31. For Garvan, see Zhivka Văzharova, *Srednovekovnoto selishte s. Garvän, Silistren-ski okrăg (VI–XI v.)* (Sofia, 1986). For Popina-Dzhedzhovi Lozia, see Zhivka Văzharova, *Slavianski i slavianobălgarski selishta v bălgarskite zemi ot kraia na VI–XI vek* (Sofia, 1965). For Krivina, see Michael Wendel, "Die mittelalterliche Siedlungen," in *Iatrus-Krivina: Spätantike Befestigung und frühmittelalterliche Siedlung an der unteren Donau*, vol. 3 (Berlin, 1986), 27–207.

32. D. Serafimova, *Nacionalen park-muzei "Samuilova krepost"* (Sofia, 1984), 6–7, 25

(fig.). An equally circular arrangement has been postulated for the multiphased settlement at Dessau-Mosigkau. See B. Krüger, *Dessau-Mosigkau: Ein frühslawischer Siedlungsplatz im mittleren Elbegebiet* (Berlin, 1967).

33. Phase I at Groß Raden features huts of post-and-wattle construction; phase II features aboveground houses built as log cabins. See E. Schuldt, *Groß Raden: Ein slawischer Tempelort des 9./10. Jahrhunderts in Mecklenburg* (Berlin, 1985), 34 fig. 29.

34. J. Henning, "Forke," in *Reallexikon der germanischen Altertumskunde*, ed. Heinrich Beck et al., vol. 9 (Berlin and New York, 1995), 324–26.

35. J. Henning, "Een zeis uit de Merovingische nederzetting te Kerkhove, deelgemeente Avelgem (W.VI.)," *Westvlaamse Archaeologica* 7 (1991): 90–96.

36. U. Körber-Grohne and U. Piening, "Verkohlte Nutz- und Wildpflanzen aus Bondorf, Kreis Böblingen," *Fundberichte aus Baden-Württemberg* 14 (1983): 17–88; K.-H. Knörzer, "Über den Wandel der angebauten Körnerfrüchte und ihrer Unkrautvegetation auf einer niederrheinischen Lößfläche seit dem Frühneolithikum," in *Festschrift Maria Hopf zum 65. Geburtstag am 14. September 1979*, ed. U. Körber-Grohne (Cologne, 1979), 147–63, 153 fig. 3.

37. Pliny *Nat. hist.* 18.30(72).296; Palladius, *De re rustica* 7.2.2–4. For the close association between spelt and the *vallus* reaping device, see F. Sigaut, "Les spécificités de l'épeautre et l'évolution des techniques," in *L'épeautre, histoire et technologie*, ed. J.-P. Devroey and J.-J. van Mol (Treignes, 1989), 29–49.

38. For such experiments, see P. J. Reynolds, *Iron Age Farm: The Butser Experiment* (London, 1979). The author also acknowledges a personal communication from E. Lange (Berlin).

39. H. Dölling, *Haus und Hof in westgermanischen Volksrechten* (Münster, 1958), 61ff.

40. For a Carolingian specimen found in Thèmes (Burgundy), see *Bourgogne médiévale: La mémoire du sol. 20 ans de recherches archéologiques* (Mâcon, 1987), 137 fig. 234.

41. A specimen was found in the "Alamannic" hoard of iron implements from Urach (Runder Berg). See U. Koch, "Ein Depotfund vom Runden Berg: Gerätschaften eines alamannischen Wirtschaftsbetriebes der Terrassensiedlung," *Archäologisches Korrespondenzblatt* 18 (1988): 205–8. For a similar hoard with six scythes, see J. Henning, "Zur Datierung von Werkzeug- und Agrargerätefunden im germanischen Landnahmegebiet zwischen Rhein und oberer Donau (der Hortfund von Osterburken)," *Jahrbuch des Römisch-Germanischen Zentralmuseums* 32 (1985): 570–94. For Roman-Germanic continuity of agricultural tool kits, see J. Henning, "Fortleben und Weiterentwicklung spätrömischer Agrargerätetraditionen in Nordgallien: Eine Mähsense der Merowingerzeit aus Kerkhove (Belgien)," *Acta Archaeologica Lovaniensia* 30 (1991): 49–59.

42. For a specimen from the Urach hoard, see Koch, "Depotfund vom Runden Berg."

43. A plowshare with two holes on the wings is an indication of a heavy "swivel plow." The carriage chain represented in fig. 1.5 (A5) indicates a heavy wheeled plow. Both artifacts were found in the fourth- to sixth-century hoard from Tarquimpol (France; see *Gallia* 11 [1953]: 143 fig. 3). A plow coulter with hole and stud is represented in fig. 1.5 (A3) and may have been a part of another heavy "swivel plow" of Merovingian date deposited in a grave found in Lausanne-Bel Air (Switzerland). For details regarding the heavy swivel plow and the harrow, see J. Henning, "Landwirtschaft der Franken," in *Die Franken: Wegbereiter Europas; Vor 1500 Jahren; König Chlodwig und seine Erben*, ed. Alfried Wieczorek (Mainz, 1996), 174–85.

44. For Roman plow chains in Romania, see I. Glodariu, A. Zrinyi, and P. Gyulai, "Le dépôt d'outils romains de Mărculeni," *Dacia* 14 (1970): 207–31. For Serbia, see I. Popović, *Antičko oruđe ot gvožđa u Srbiji* (Belgrade, 1988), 106–7. So far, no post-Roman hoards of agricultural implements containing plow chains have been found in Eastern Europe.

45. Kuchenbuch, *Bäuerliche Gesellschaft* (see n. 5 in the present chapter).

46. J. Henning, *Südosteuropa zwischen Antike und Mittelalter: Archäologische Beiträge zur Landwirtschaft des 1. Jahrtausends u.Z.* (Berlin, 1987), 91ff.

47. Balanced curved sickles were in use in southeastern Europe during the early Middle Ages, as evidenced by a specimen (fig. 1.5, B4) deposited in a burial of the seventh- and eighth-century cremation cemetery at Razdelna (Bulgaria). See Dimitär Il. Dimitrov, "Nekropolät pri gara Razdelna," *Izvestiia na Narodniia Muzei Varna* 14 (1978): 120–52 and fig. XVI.16.

48. Specimen from house 10 near the northern gate of the "Inner Town" at Pliska. See T. Balabanov, "Zhilishcha pokrai severnata i iztochnata krepostna stena v Pliska," *Pliska-Preslav* 5 (1992): 146–69, 159 fig. VII.X.1.

49. J. Henning, "Unterscheide und Gemeinsamkeiten zwischen slawischer und fränkischer Landwirtschaft in Gebieten frühmittelalterlicher Stadtentwicklung," in *Trudy V Mezhdunarodnogo Kongressa arkheologov-slavistov, Kiev 18–25 sentiabria 1985 g.,* ed. P. P. Tolochko et al., vol. 2 (Kiev, 1988), 221–27.

50. The specimen in fig. 1.5 (B3) is an assymetrical plowshare found during excavations near the eastern gate of the "Inner Town" at Pliska. See T. Balabanov, "Zemedelski orădiia ot Pliska (IX–XI v.)," *Bălgarska etnografiia* 10 (1985): 19–29. Early medieval plowshares found in the West are at least twice as long as those from the East. For a sixth-century specimen, see I. Stork, "Abschluß der Untersuchungen des fränkischen Friedhofs von Dittigheim, Stadt Tauberbischofsheim, Main-Tauber-Kreis," *Archäologische Ausgrabungen in Baden-Württemberg* (1985): 187–95.

51. The specimen in Fig. 1.5 (B2) was found in a tenth-century hoard from Pliska, which also contains aysmmetrical plowshares (publication by Stoian Vitlianov forthcoming). See *Pärvoprestolna Pliska,* ed. J. Henning and L. Doncheva-Petkova (Frankfurt am Main, 1999), 43 and fig. 7.77.

52. The settlement pattern in the Magdeburg region was primarily a creation of the Slavic immigrants of the 600s and 700s. It changed radically during the ninth and tenth centuries as a result of the Ottonian imposition of the manorial economy. See J. Henning, "Der slawische Siedlungsraum und die ottonische Expansion östlich der Elbe: Ereignisgeschichte, Archäologie, Dendrochronologie," in *Europa im 10. Jahrhundert: Archäologie einer Aufbruchszeit,* ed. J. Henning (Mainz, 2002), 137 and fig. 10.

53. J. Henning, "Germanisch-romanische Agrarkontinuität und -diskontinuität im nordalpinen Kontinentaleuropa: Teile eines Systemwandels? Beobachtungen aus archäologischer Sicht," in *Akkulturation: Probleme einer germanisch-romanischen Kultursynthese in Spätantike und frühem Mittelalter,* ed. Dieter Hägermann, Wolfgang Haubrichs, and Jörg Jarnut (Berlin-New York, 2004), 396–435. Recent archaeological surveys undertaken by a University of Durham team in northeast Gaul—though inspired by Chris Wickham's thesis of a continuation of the ancient world after the fall of Rome until ca. AD 1000 (see, e.g., Chris Wickham, "The other transition from the ancient world to feudalism," *Past and Present* 103 [1984]: 3–36)—have definitely shown that the decisive turning point in the history of local settlement patterns was that between the Roman villa and the post-Roman village around the middle of the first millennium,

with nearly 80 percent settlement discontinuity. Many French medievalists, following Marc Bloch (*La société féodale* [Paris, 1940]) and Georges Duby (*La société aux XIe et XIIe siècles dans la région mâconnaise* [Paris, 1953]), entertain hopes of detecting the signs for a fundamental change around the year 1000. See, e.g., Guy Bois, *La mutation de l'an mil: Lournand, village mâconnais, de l'antiquité au féodalisme* (Paris, 1989); Pierre Bonnassie, *Les sociétés de l'an mil: Un monde entre deux âges* (Brussels, 2001). Given that the University of Durham field survey project has shown more than 70 percent settlement continuity shortly before and after the year 1000, such hopes must now be abandoned. See Colin Haselgrove and Christopher Scull, "The changing structure of rural settlement in southern Picardy during the first millennium A.D.," in *Europe between Late Antiquity and the Middle Ages,* ed. John Bintilff and Helena Hamerow (Oxford, 1995), 58–70. A prevalent continuity of settlement before and after the year 1000 has also been revealed by several microregional studies in Germany. Information for northern Hesse is available from the project of the Johann Wolfgang Goethe University in Frankfurt am Main mentioned in n. 25 supra; for south Germany, see R. Schreg, "Archäologische Studien zur Genese des mittelalterlichen Dorfes in Südwestdeutschland: Eine Fallstudie: die mittelalterliche Besiedlung des Renninger Beckens," *Archäologisches Nachrichtenblatt* 7 (2002): 329–35. Thus, from an archaeological point of view, the critique leveled by Dominique Barthélemy ("La mutation féodale a-t-elle eu lieu?" *Annales E.S.C.* 47 [1992]: 367–77) at attempts to bring the "slavery system" to a close only at the end of the tenth century seems fully understandable. On attitudes toward rural "slavery" in the early Middle Ages, see also the important study of Jean-Pierre Devroey, "Men and women in early medieval serfdom: The ninth-century Frankish evidence," *Past and Present* 166 (2000): 3–30. Devroey's choice of the eighth century to mark the turning point is to be understood in the light of the written evidence for the rise of the manorial system. See Jean-Pierre Devroey, "The economy," in *The Early Middle Ages: Europe 400–1000,* ed. Rosamond McKitterick (Oxford, 2001), 97–129. This is also the opinion of some contributors to I. L. Hansen and C. Wickham, eds., *The Long Eighth Century: Production, Distribution, and Demand* (Leiden, Boston, and Cologne, 2000). However, archaeologists can look behind the curtain of written sources and show that the basic elements of the new system appear much earlier, more or less at the same time as the end of Roman power in the West.

54. Such an understanding of the rise and logic of European economy and ruling forms in the post-Roman West and East (including town development) stresses the fundamental factors of basic agricultural production. As such, it differs substantially from studies focusing primarily on power structures to explain the medieval economy as a whole. Richard Hodges's recent *Towns and Trade in the Age of Charlemagne* (London, 2000) tends to explain the development of a new type of medieval town and thus the expansion of exchange and commerce as a result of Charlemagne's or other elites' decisions to imitate Eastern standards (relayed by pilgrims returning from the East). What Hodges fails to explain is why the East did not produce an economic upturn similar to that visible in the West between AD 950 and 1100. For more details, see J. Henning, "Wandel eines Kontinents oder Wende der Geschichte? Das 10. Jahrhundert im Spiegel der Frühmittelalterarchäologie," in *Europa im 10. Jahrhundert: Archäologie einer Aufbruchszeit,* ed. J. Henning (Mainz, 2002), 11–17.

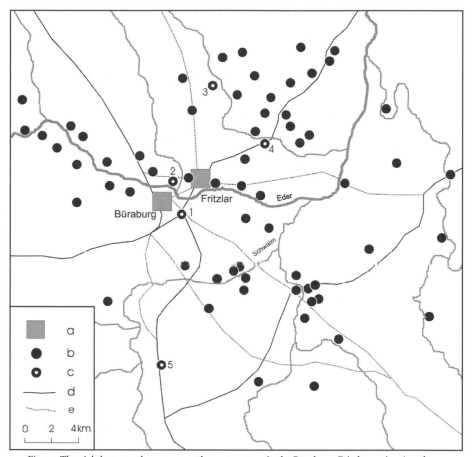

Fig. 1.1. The eighth- to tenth-century settlement pattern in the Büraburg-Fritzlar region (northern Hesse, Germany): (a) central place; (b) rural site (signalized by field surveys); (c) excavated rural site; (d) road (probable), (e) road (possible). (Data after N. Wand, with additions.)

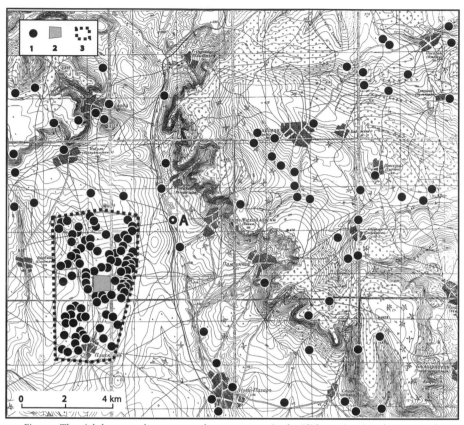

Fig. 1.2. The eighth- to tenth-century settlement pattern in the Pliska region (northeastern Bulgaria): (1) rural site (outside the earthen rampart; field survey, inside the rampart; field survey and excavations); (2) "Inner Town" with stone fortification and palace compound; (3) outside earthen rampart; (A) the site at Pervomaiska Cheshma. (Data after T. Balabanov, R. Vasilev, and Ia. Dimitrov, with additions.)

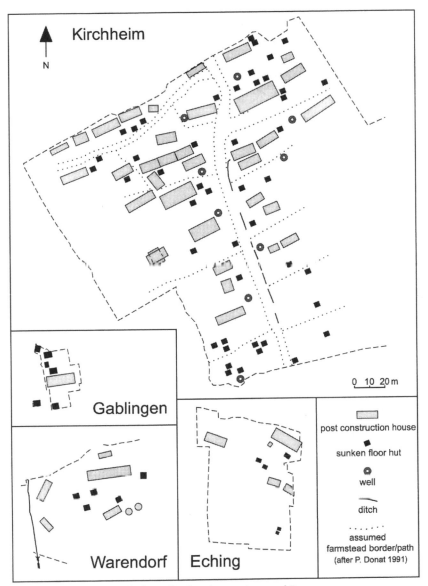

Fig. 1.3. Early medieval settlements in central Europe

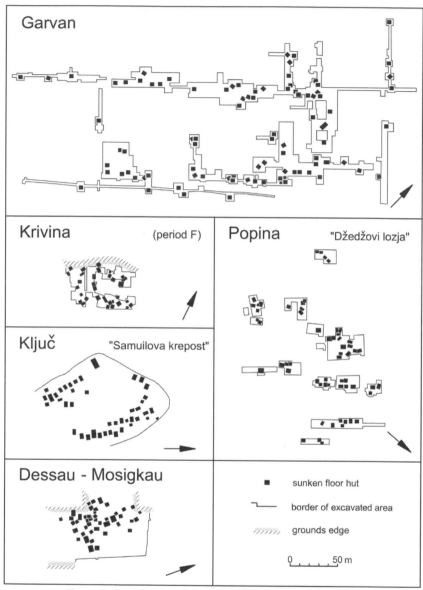

Fig. 1.4. Early medieval settlements in Bulgaria and eastern Germany

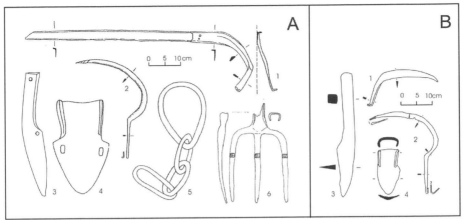

Fig. 1.5. Early medieval agricultural tools from Western Europe (A) and Eastern Europe (B): scythes (A1, B1), fork (A6), sickles (A2, B2), plowshares (A4, B4), coulters (A3, B3), plow chain (A5). Iron plow chains and three-pronged forks were unknown in the East, while the long scythe and the heavy wheeled plow in use in the West sharply contrast with the short scythe and the lighter plow with no wheels in the East. The find spots are (A1–2) Urach "Runder Berg" (see nn. 41–42); (A3) Lausanne-Bel Air (see n. 43); (A4–5) Tarquimpol (see n. 43); (A6) Thèmes (see n. 40); (B1, B3, B4) Pliska (see nn. 48, 50–51); (B2) Razdelna (see n. 47).

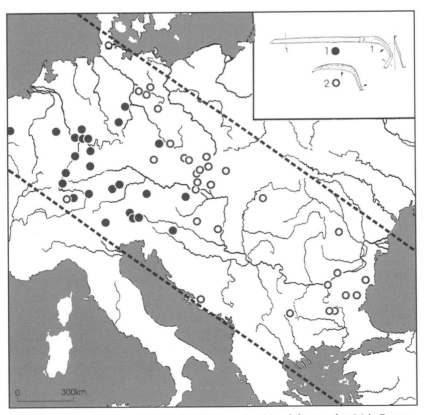

Fig. 1.6. Distribution map of early medieval long scythes (1) and short scythes (2) in Europe

CHAPTER TWO

Silent Centuries: The Society and Economy of the Northwestern Slavs

Paul M. Barford

*T*he past decade and a half have seen profound changes in the understanding of both the archaeological evidence for the societies that lived on the central segment of the North European Plain between the Elbe and the Western Bug (roughly the area of modern Poland and eastern Germany) and the dynamics of the changes that occurred between the fifth and the late tenth centuries. The purpose of this chapter is to summarize some aspects of the current knowledge of the economic and social structures of the early medieval societies of Polabia and the area of modern Poland (fig. 2.1).[1]

The area has been comparatively neglected in Western historiography. The relative lack of written sources has encouraged the air of otherness that prompts the Western historian more used to the rich variety of documents of the West to see the inhabitants of the area as peoples without a history on the periphery of Europe, recipients of influences from the mainstream of European (conceived as Western) history. Historians working in the nations of central and Eastern Europe have also acutely felt the paucity of native written sources for writing history.

Beginning with the 1930s, central European scholars turned to a different source of evidence about the past, for they realized that the archaeological methods previously used to shed light on the prehistoric periods could and should also be applied to the medieval period.[2] Archaeology was found to be capable of not just illustrating the scant written sources but producing new types of information. In 1948, in the aftermath of World War II, the development of central European historiography was given a new direction by two new phenomena: the inception of a series of long-term research projects to investigate the early medieval origins of modern states (Poland, eastern Germany, Czechoslovakia), which were clearly intended to play a political role and act as a platform for international cooperation within the Soviet Bloc;[3] and the stepping-up of attempts to reconstruct science and, especially, the humanities on a Marxist model.[4] The Marxist archaeology (called "progressive" by its practitioners), based on the principles of historical and dialectical materialism, represented a complete break with the traditional (culture-historical) manner of doing archaeology. Interest now shifted to the reconstruction of the socioeconomic foundations of early medieval society. The Marxist concept recognizing the fundamental significance of the development of forces and relations of production for social and cultural development encouraged attempts to create multivariate characterizations of the internal structure of the studied systems. However, the concept of a succession of socioeconomic formations turned out to be inhibiting to a useful application to archaeology of paradigms based on Marxism. Although the direct use of Marxist paradigms declined after 1956, the basic premises of "progressive" archaeology continued to exert some influence on several aspects of the study of the past.

Several important works on early medieval economy written in the 1950s reflect some of the theoretical concerns of the period. Among them are the programmatic statement of Marian Malowist and the seminal work of Henryk Łowmiański, which looks at the agricultural economy in different regions of Slav territory before passing on to a discussion of towns and trade.[5] Jan Brankačk did similar work in Polabia.[6] A seminal, highly original study by Karol Modzelewski broke away from the idea current in the 1950s of interpreting the Polish state as a strictly feudal one and produced a new characterization of the social system that emerged beyond the Carolingian sphere of influences in the tenth and eleventh centuries.[7] The maturing of the discipline of medieval archaeology is also reflected in the theoretical reflections contained in the work of Stanisław Tabaczyński.[8]

The air of the otherness of central Europe was instrumental in the area being treated by many as of somewhat marginal importance in studies of early medieval Europe. For example, the seminal work of Richard Hodges on the European economy, a book that has set the agenda for much of the discussion that has taken place in the field in the last twenty years, completely ignores this area.[9] The region is seen as irrelevant to the development of the economy of the "Europe" of the book's scope—that is, in essence, Carolingian Francia, England, and Scandinavia.[10] The area east of the Elbe and the southern and eastern shores of the Baltic—in short, everything north of Byzantium and the Mediterranean world—are omitted from the picture, as, according to Hodges, Slavic sites "such as Szcecin [sic] and Wollin [sic] in Poland, Grobin and Alt Ladoga in Russia [sic] belong to the Russian route southwards."[11] Nonetheless, the area was an integral part of the Baltic trade continuum with which the North Sea zone considered by Hodges was intimately linked, and incorporating these regions in the overall picture would require certain modifications to his proposals (discussed later in this chapter).

Similarly, Michael McCormick—although paying more attention, in his massive synthetic work,[12] to the situation on the routes between the Baltic and the Mediterranean world—deals with the area as a region through which run the routes that brought commodities to the south. Those commodities included not only oriental silver and amber but less archaeologically visible goods, such as forest products (furs and honey) and, potentially, a human cargo (slaves). The placement of these goods in the economic regimes along the "northern arc" (trade network from the Caspian to the Baltic Seas) is not considered in detail, however. These areas are thus treated merely as a periphery supplying raw materials to the economic core area.

The books I have mentioned are by no means isolated cases, and it seems that for a variety of reasons (by no means restricted to linguistic problems), the area east of Hamburg and the *limes Sorabicus* is seen by many scholars writing of the Middle Ages as somehow less relevant to a holistic picture of early medieval Europe. Nowhere is this less true than in the study of Dark Age economic systems.

Subsistence and Economy (Seventh to Tenth Centuries)

The early medieval communities of central Europe are presumed to represent the distant ancestors of the current Slav-speaking populations of the area, and few questions in central European historiography have involved so much discussion as those concerning how and when this situation came into being. This question cannot be fully discussed here,[13] but there are two main views. The first proposes that the archaeological remains classified as the Sukow culture developed in Polabia and in central and western Poland at the end of antiquity and that there is population and temporal continuity through the end of the period of Roman influences (late fourth and fifth centuries AD). By contrast, the opposing school of thought invokes a migration of the Slavs from the east of the Western Bug beginning in the migration period.[14] On the basis of dendrochronological evidence, a recent study of the Sukow culture[15] suggests that there is little evidence of a Slavic presence in Polabia or central and northwestern Poland before the end of the seventh or the early eighth century.[16] Indeed, over most of the area, there is only sparse settlement, which may be dated before the late 600s. In the subsequent century, we see a slow increase in settlement density and then a relatively rapid increase in the number of datable sites in the early part of the ninth century. In the tenth century, however, we again observe a sharp increase in the number of new settlement sites, perhaps reflecting a relatively rapid growth in overall population.

Society and Settlement: Rural Economies

If the arrangement of sites in the landscape may be regarded by archaeologists as the "material isomorph of the entire mode of production in its broadest sense, and of the core features of social and political organization,"[17] we may begin our inquiry here. The distribution of rural settlements in the area has been fairly well documented. The intensive field walking of the Polish AZP program[18] has produced a much closer definition of the dynamics of the development of the settlement network than would be available from less rigorous methods of creating a sites and monuments record. This allows us to study the spatial relationships between open settlements and enclosed ones (strongholds) and also to visualize the territory that produces no evidence of settlement. One of the areas where the settlement pattern has been particularly well examined is Great Poland, where sites can be clearly seen to form clusters separated by vast empty zones, presumably originally forested.[19] These settlement clusters are 10–15 kilometers across and generally consist of more localized settlement groups spread along river valleys, mostly situated at the junction between drier land and flood plains (fig. 2.2). It is tempting to regard these settlement clusters of different scales as the material traces of communities grouped in clans and "small tribes."[20] The latter may at some stage have been amalgamated into larger groups (tribal unions or states). The picture presented by detailed study of the evidence suggests very strongly that society in this area was relatively egalitarian. Before the rise of strongholds, there is little evidence of social differentiation between inhabitants of a single settlement or those living in neighboring settlements within the same microregion.

Settlements tend to be sited on good soils, near streams, rivers, or other bodies of water. They were typically small, from 1 to several hectares in size, and the excavated evidence consists usually of the lower parts of negative features. Residential structures are represented by sunken-floored huts,[21] although in the western part of the area, shallow irregular hollows may be the remains of sub-floor constructions of houses.[22] Ground-level structures of horizontal log (lofted or blockhouse) construction may also be presumed to have existed, but later soil processes (e.g., plowing) have on most sites removed such remains. Other features are scarce. There may be a number of pits of uncertain function (though some have been suggested to have been storage pits), but gullies and fence lines dividing the area of the settlement are rare. The settlement features may be scattered apparently randomly, they may form rows, or they may be arranged in a roughly circular manner around an open space.[23] When it is possible to determine phasing, these settlements are seen to consist of an agglomeration of successive phases of shifting homesteads built in the same general area; a typical example is Dessau-Mosigkau.[24] The difficulty of precise dating of the pottery that forms the primary dating evidence for such sites does not allow us to determine how long such a settlement and its adjacent fields were in use. It presumably would be measured in generations rather than years.

It is clear that arable farming played a considerable role in the early medieval economy of the area. We know nothing, however, about landownership. Łowmiański postulated the early existence of large landed estates, but this is more an assumption (primarily derived from the Marxist concept of feudalism) than concrete evidence. We may wonder whether the strongholds (discussed shortly) may have been estate centers. There is very little evidence about the siting or extent of the field systems that served such settlements. Some tentative models of their size and productivity have been created[25] but, as yet, cannot be tested in the field. Some interesting suggestions have been made as a result, for example, of the multisided consideration of the evidence from the site at Bruszczewo, where fields probably occupied a stretch of the slopes of the hill just above the site.[26]

Written sources (e.g., Ibrahim ibn Yakub's account) tell us that the west Slavs practiced winter sowing and were thus able to harvest their crops twice a year.[27] There has been some fairly inconclusive discussion in the literature on systems of rotation (the three-field system now appears to have been introduced only after ca. 1200). The relatively light density of occupation and ready availability of land would have allowed a shifting mode of soil regeneration, although manuring and fallowing seem also to have been practiced. Much has been made in past discussions of a reputed transition, supposedly in the migration period,[28] from slash-and-burn agriculture to a more intensive farming regime.[29] This ignores the fact that forest burning was one of the easiest ways to clear farming land and pasture (and was still practiced by some communities in the region until relatively recently). It should be remembered that the removal of a small homestead—together with all the livestock, stored fodder, and seed—that is implied by the shifting to fresh land was by no means an easy task and would not have been undertaken lightly.

The palynological and environmental evidence allows us to determine which crops were grown and, to some extent, their relative frequencies.[30] Three species of wheat, millet, rye, oats, and barley were grown. The quantities of remains of these cereals varies between soil samples taken from different sites within the same region (and even from different contexts on the same site), making interpretation of these figures difficult. Archaeologists once ascribed the high quantity of millet on some sites to its reputation as a crop characteristic in slash-and-burn agriculture, but this view is no longer accepted. The cereal is easy to grow (as long as the climate is suitable), can tolerate poor soils, and is also very nutritious. Its prevalence may even be due to the culinary preferences of its grower; it may be boiled and served as a dish in its own right (known in Poland as *kasza jaglana*). Rye, found in some quantities on some sites, is another crop that does not need good soils. Barley has a shorter growing period than the other crops, and oats are the least climatically demanding of the cereal crops grown. There was a high proportion of oats cultivated in Pomerania, one of the specific characteristics of the region. It was probably used there as livestock feed.

The early Slavs kept the usual domestic animals—cattle, pigs, sheep/goats—although horse bones are scarce.[31] The composition of herds is relatively easy to determine on the basis of the composition of bone assemblages. Apart from the mere counting of bones and determination of minimum numbers of individuals, more sophisticated analyses can be conducted, such as determining relative quantities (by weight) of meat and the age of slaughter of the animals to learn something of the herd management.[32] The relative importance of arable and livestock rearing to the economy of individual settlements is difficult to determine. There have been attempts to determine the relationship between arable land and pasture by comparing the ratios of cereal and plantain pollen, but it is not clear how reliable the results of this comparison can be.[33] It used to be thought that cattle rearing was more important in the economy of the early Slavs in the migration period than later on. This assumption, in turn, used as an explanation for their mobility,[34] was based in part on an uncritical application of information culled from early Byzantine sources about the Slavs in the Danube region, especially from Procopius and Menander the Guardsman. However, the extrapolation of such information to the completely different environment and cultural situation of the area north of the Carpathians is impossible. Beyond the immediate environs of settlements and fields, the forested environment of most of our region is evidenced by the pollen analysis. As such, it was not suitable for the development of extensive pastoralism.[35]

The forest and other natural resources also provided food resources from hunting and gathering. Fishing is attested by finds of tackle and fish remains. On most sites of the region, the ratio of hunted to domestic animal remains is relatively low, but in other areas, such as the forested terrain of the middle Havel and Spree Rivers, the remains of hunted animals make up as much as half of every bone assemblage.[36]

Finds of agricultural tools are relatively rare. The area discussed here lies outside the zone characterized by the deposition of iron hoards.[37] There is enough evidence to show that iron-shod plows were used—though probably alongside ards (the latter perhaps being more suitable for initially breaking up soil in new forest clearings). Cereal crops were harvested with sickles, of which a number have survived (scythes are thought to have been used for making hay for fodder for overwintering livestock).[38] Querns are evidence of cereal processing but are less common on Polish than on Polabian sites.[39] Flour was probably made by pounding in wooden mortars.

Craft activities were associated with the rural settlement, but the scale of such activities was commensurate with self-sufficiency. We find evidence of domestic and craft pottery manufacture, iron smelting and smithing, occasionally other metalworking, woodworking, weaving, and other crafts.[40] One important feature of the pottery of Tornow and Feldberg types of Polabia[41] and western Poland is the manner in which its form reflects that of pottery from the Frankish zones. For a long time, it had been assumed that this was due to Merovingian influences, and this concept was the basis of the early dating of sites producing this type of pottery. Now, the dendrochronological dating of this material has suggested that these stylistic influences must be Carolingian, if not Ottonian, in date.[42] Other evidence of contemporary contact is a number of Carolingian imports—principally of weapons and ornamented metalwork—into the same region.[43]

Early Central Places

After ca. 700, in much of the area discussed here, we find the construction of timber-framed earthwork enclosures with associated settlements in their immediate vicinity. The various types of these sites are known collectively as *Burgen* in German and *grody/grodziska* in Polish, two terms that we may translate into English (perhaps not entirely satisfactorily) as "strongholds." The varied typology of these sites belies a varied original function.[44] Not all settlement clusters contained a stronghold (neither does it seem that all early medieval strongholds were necessarily associated with a dense external settlement network).

The chronology of the construction of these sites has undergone some revision in recent years, with more critical assessment of the archaeological evidence and, especially, the application of dendrochronology. Instead of the general growth and consolidation of settlement and slow accumulation of power and change in settlement pattern suggested by the former chronological framework, we find several periods of intense stronghold building. There are apparently no strongholds associated with the earliest stages of settlement in the area.[45] Dendrochronology now suggests that the earliest strongholds should be assigned to the late eighth century, a period that marks a substantial cultural change in other spheres. In Schleswig-Holstein, there was some stronghold construction in the 720s and 730s, and more strongholds were built in the 820s and 830s. There were sharp peaks in construction rate in Brandenburg in 906–30 and in Mecklenburg in 928–40 and 980–88.[46] This pattern seems to be repeated further east in Great Poland. Although some sites were built at an earlier date (eighth and ninth centuries), the earliest horizon of stronghold construction dates to the period just after 900. While considerable changes in much of what is now Poland took place in the ninth and first part of the tenth centuries (fig. 2.1), these became more marked just before the middle of the tenth century, in connection with the rise of the Polish state. The most extensive program of stronghold construction dates to the 940s and 960s.

Over most of the western part of the area (Polabia and western Great Poland), the dominant stronghold type in the eighth to early tenth centuries is circular, usually 10 to 50 meters of internal diameter, with massive walls surrounding a fairly compact interior. This type of site is well illustrated by the typical stronghold in Tornow near Cottbus (eastern Germany).[47] The northeastern region of Polabia is characterized by large upland sites, sometimes with multiple enclosures.[48] These strongholds of the so-called Feldberg type appeared during the mid-eighth to the mid-ninth centuries.

While it may be true that much of what has been written in the past about changing patterns of frequency for such sites and chronological changes in their distribution was based on false premises, it seems still a little too early to attempt a definitive synthesis of the picture that is now emerging. Undoubtedly, a more critical approach to chronology and site typology, as well as mapping the results over the whole area, will produce important results in the next few years. Nevertheless, a few points may be made on the basis of the current picture.

The construction of a stronghold was clearly an enterprise that required the concentrated work of whole communities over a number of weeks or even months.[49] This implies either the imposition of some strong coercive power or the recognition that the construction of such a site fulfilled some general interest of the community as a whole. That some of these sites occur in the center of settlement zones encourages the view that they fulfilled the function of some kind of central place, but the interpretation of their function is far from clear. Past interpretations have been guided by extra-archaeological factors. In Poland, during the years leading up to and immediately after the traumas of World War II, these sites were seen almost exclusively as military outposts. During the 1960s, when the chief interest of Polish archaeologists was the process of the creation of the Polish state, they were regarded primarily as "prototowns." Marxist-inspired interpretations of such sites viewed them as epiphenomena linked to the rise of a class structure and social conflict developing at this time. During the 1970s and 1980s, no alternative interpretations were offered, a possible consequence of other developments taking place at that time in Polish archaeology. Only with the changes following the collapse of Communism in 1989 and the creation of a new social order do we see the rise of a new version of the past to fit the needs of a new society. In this version, the interpretation of strongholds became again linked with the processes of state formation but was also associated with the rise of personal power and the creation of social identities.

However well defended their ramparts make them appear, it is difficult to interpret the strongholds of the eighth to mid-tenth centuries as military strongholds. Finds of military equipment are rare. Very rarely do deposits associated with these sites produce evidence of arrowheads or spearheads. Such "strongholds" are rarely sited in defensive positions, most are low-lying, and some are even overlooked by nearby hills. It is difficult to see what military role they could fulfill. Most are too small to act as communal refuges or safe stores for produce—still less livestock. Many could not contain a sizable force ready to sally out against an invader. The ramparts were clearly defensive in character, but the difficulties of interpreting these sites in purely military terms induce us to suggest that this was not their primary purpose.

Archaeological assemblages from eighth- to mid-tenth-century strongholds rarely demonstrate their role as elite settlement units. Although the strongholds are richer in finds than contemporary open settlements, this is usually a reflection of the concentration of activity within the ramparts over a long time and the inability of finds to be scattered outside that area. The finds have the same general characteristics as those found on open settlements, giving the impression of a somewhat egalitarian society in which there were no specific differences in consumption. This may be illusory, as one must bear in mind the possibility that during this period, tribute collecting may have consisted of accumulation and redistribution of such perishable produce as grain. There is certainly evidence of differential consumption of meat on some sites, with different types (and cuts) of meat consumed by different parts of the community.[50] One or two luxury imports may also be found in find assemblages from these sites.

The excavation of some of these sites, in addition to the occasional residential buildings, has sometimes revealed lean-to structures along the inside of the wall face, which, judging from the absence of heating and cooking structures, do not seem to be permanent residences. The excavators of Tornow have suggested that they were stores for grain and other surplus agricultural produce, though other explanations cannot be ruled out. Such "casemates" are found on other sites of the prestate period, such as Podebłocie (fig. 2.3),[51] and would seem to be in some way connected with the function of these strongholds in the period.

Nevertheless, the very fact that being surrounded by earthen and wooden ramparts differentiated such settlement units is sufficient to set them apart from other contemporary sites. One possible significance of the rampart may have been to express social prestige, not necessarily of an occupant of the site, but (rather like nineteenth-century town halls of British towns) of the community as a whole. In several cases, such as Podebłocie, there is clear evidence that considerable effort has been spent on making the line of the ramparts imposingly symmetrical—carrying them across in-filled hollows in the ground, for example, instead of going around them.

In Poland, especially in Great Poland and the adjacent areas, early sites were apparently abandoned around the middle of the tenth century, perhaps in connection with social and political changes taking place during that time. It seems that they played a significant role in the maintenance of the "tribal" social system predating the rise of the Piast state. Despite much recent work done on this problem, we are still at a loss to explain the precise function of earlier sites. In the terminology of social anthropology, there is no difficulty in seeing the mid-tenth-century sites as the archaeological correlate of a so-called chiefdom heading toward statehood. What about the earlier sites? How could these social structures be categorized? While communal construction of monuments is generally regarded as an important criterion for the archaeological identification of chiefdoms, the archaeological evidence for this period lacks any of the other criteria. Are these sites, then, the reflection of undeveloped chiefdoms or developed big-man societies, or are they the traces of a society that is not classifiable in such simplistic evolutionary terms? There is no space here to go into all these issues. It is clear, however, that the sites in question represent some form of centralization of social organization and that this process created the necessary preconditions for the creation of a more complex and extensive polity by the assimilation of local units.

Revision of the chronology of stronghold sites, once thought to have been relatively evenly distributed across the area, has shown that there are in fact considerable differences in their regional distribution, especially for the prestate (so-called tribal) period. There is a considerable difference in density of strongholds of the ninth and early tenth centuries across Poland. Dense clusters exist in the settled areas of Upper and Lower Silesia, Great Poland, and Pomerania. There are very few strongholds of this date in central and eastern Poland, though there is a cluster in Little Poland (on the upper Vistula).[52] Unfortunately, we do not yet have a comparable picture for Polabia that incorporates the result of the chronological revision. The new picture we do have suggests that whatever the function of the strongholds may have been, there are differences in the socioeconomic processes leading to their construction across the region. Environmental factors must also have played a role. While the soil types across the region are very similar, the physical geography ensures that the maximum growing season is longer in western Poland than in the eastern part of the country, which may, at certain periods, have affected the relative ease of attaining an agricultural surplus, one of the factors underlying the ability to construct and make use of a stronghold.

Barter and Tribute Economies

The lack of units for monetary exchange suggests that a natural economy, of barter, was practiced. We have seen that the economy of these settlement clusters may have been simply geared to subsistence, and the majority of exchange probably took place within the cluster of adjacent sites. The rare imported goods tend to be found in the vicinity of strongholds. This is the case, for example, for the eighth-century Frisian antler comb from Santok.[53] This suggests that such sites may have fulfilled some role in the redistribution of goods (including prestige goods). We have seen that these sites may have been collection points and storage centers for the agricultural surplus and perhaps also sites where accumulated valuables, such as furs and other forest products, were brought as "tribute" and later redistributed according to various mechanisms.

The functioning of the barter economy is difficult to reconstruct, but anthropological and ethnographic analogies suggest that it would have involved the entire community in a series of face-to-face transactions at a personal level and may thus have played an important social and integrating role. Likewise, the mechanism of surplus redistribution through strongholds is poorly understood, as this does not seem to have been a fully developed tribute economy.[54]

Apart from metal coins, there may have been nonmonetary units (some of which would have an intrinsic wealth of their own) with the function of taking a debt or wealth beyond the bounds of the immediate community. Here, such objects may include skins of fur-bearing animals, tools, ornaments, or such commodities as honey and salt. For larger debts, cattle and horses might have served as well. There also are several classes of objects that seem likely to have had a more symbolic, rather than intrinsic, value, among them the iron bars (*griwny*) and the so-called Silesian bowls (slightly concave discs of iron), which seem to have functioned symbolically rather than being regarded as raw material.[55]

Long-Distance Exchange

The external written sources sometimes hint at the movement of goods across the territory of the northwestern Slavs, but the main source of our information for exchange is the distribution of certain types of objects. Coins, either stray or hoard finds, are the most informative archaeological source of this kind, because it is easy to establish their provenance and date.

The area beyond the Elbe did not participate in the circulation of gold issued by Merovingian mints. With the increasing importance of the silver standard, we see numismatic links between the northern part of central Europe and the area surrounding it. A great number of hoards of silver could be dated to the ninth century. During the subsequent period, the main component of these hoards were silver dirhams from Islamic—mostly Central Asian—mints. The distribution of finds of these hoards clearly shows that the coins in question came to the Baltic after traveling through the forests of northern Russia.[56] In earlier hoards, Carolingian and Western European coins are very rare, suggesting that contacts with Western Europe were more limited than those supplying the Islamic coins. In the region in question, ninth-century hoards tend to cluster along the Baltic coast,[57] in correlation with the location of contemporary *Seehandelsplatz* sites (discussed shortly). During the tenth century, hoard finds were more dispersed, with an important cluster in Great Poland that seems to indicate a concentration of wealth in that region. There is some debate about the significance of such deposits, their relationship to monetary exchanges,[58] owners, and reasons for burial. Whether these were hoards of merchants or not, the connection with long-distance exchange seems inescapable.

Islamic coins arrived in the area in four successive waves,[59] and this must have had an effect on or be an effect of the socioeconomic system of those peoples importing the silver. The earliest group of hoards in the area was dated to 800–825, though some scholars see the arrival of the first coins as early as the 770s and 780s. The first wave lasted until 830/33, when new coins began appearing with some regularity in Polish hoards.

The dates of the second wave have been much discussed. It seems clear that the wave began in 840 or 850 and lasted until 870 or 879, although some numismatists prefer an end date in the late ninth or early tenth century. During this period, a small number of newly minted coins were deposited together with larger quantities of late eighth- and early ninth-century dirhams. The second-wave hoards cluster on the southern coast of the Baltic Sea, in sharp contrast with the distribution of first-wave hoards. There is thus a clear shift westward, away from the former concentration around the early medieval port of trade at Truso.[60] The flow of silver stops abruptly with issues of the late 870s. It is also to this period that the majority of Eastern European hoards have been dated, a sign, perhaps, of social and or economic crisis.

The third wave, of the 890s, consists of a new flood of freshly minted dirhams. Tenth- and eleventh-century hoards contain mostly coins of the period 890–950. Most tenth-century hoards contain relatively few ninth-century coins, as the wave of previous decades of the century drowned out the earlier issues. The number of coins peaks in the early tenth century, but the flow was irregular, with regional fluctuations in the supply. However, by 970, the number of new coins declines sharply. The final wave, dated between 990 and 1010, was relatively weak and brought the last Islamic coins into the area. By 1030, the flow of Islamic coins ceased altogether.

Sture Bolin first drew attention to the possible connection between the economies of Sandinavia and the West, on one hand, and the flow of Islamic silver into the Baltic, on the other.[61] He suggested that Charlemagne's monetary reforms were influenced by this connection. Perhaps this was a major reason for the Carolingian interest in the Baltic trade and the motor for the drive to the East. But the relative lack of identifiable Western products (coins, luxury goods) in the area discussed here contradicts such views.

While the presence of many artifacts flowing into coastal trading posts may be explained in terms of their exotic nature, the material that was traded in exchange is less easy to trace. The existence of large trade *emporia* (ports of trade) suggests that long-distance exchange networks involved primarily the transport of goods for mass consumption, together with a few luxury goods.[62] The goods involved would probably have included agricultural produce, forest products (fur, honey, wax), and salt.[63]

We have suggested that strongholds might have been engaged in some way in the gathering of agricultural surplus. The ninth and tenth centuries were a climatic optimal period in central Europe, and this may have facilitated the generation of a surplus. The accumulation and then utilization of this surplus may have been one of the factors allowing political consolidation of the Slav tribes into larger and stronger units. This might have been one of the staple "exports" of these large coastal centers.

It is often suggested that other commodities that might have been "exported" would have included products of the forest beyond the settlement areas. The use of furs as a medium of exchange is amply attested in the written sources from several regions.[64]

Salt was a highly important commodity (used primarily for the preservation of foodstuffs). It could be produced from seawater by evaporation, and an important production site existed on the coast at Kołobrzeg (*wyspa solna*).[65]

Salt was also manufactured from saline springs. A tenth- to eleventh-century salt-extraction site has been excavated at Wieliczka near Cracow and consists of hearths, gullies, and tanks.[66]

Another high-demand commodity was slaves, which were probably largely "generated" by the taking of prisoners in intergroup conflict. Slaves are occasionally mentioned in written sources (particularly those concerning east Slav trade with the Islamic world), but they are difficult to detect in the archaeological material. It is thus difficult to assess the scale of the phenomenon and the role of slaves in the economy of different periods and different territories. McCormick's masterly survey of the historical, numismatic, and archaeological evidence for the development of the European economic system has led to the conclusion that a major element in the process was the development of the slave trade between north and south, particularly that transiting through Venice.[67] We have records of slavery in Moravia and Pannonia preserved in documents relating to the ninth-century Cyrillo-Methodian mission, in addition to a mention of a mysterious "Rugi" people (from the Rügen Island?) in the Raffelstetten Plea.[68] But there is very little evidence pertaining to the lands to the north of the Carpathian and Sudeten Mountains.[69] The only clue comes from the *Life of Methodius*, which tells us that the bishop threatened the powerful prince of the Vistulan tribe (in the upper Vistula region), "it would be good for you, my son, to be baptized in your own lands by your own will, otherwise you will be baptized in slavery in a foreign land." The account then notes that the prophecy came true. This suggests that at least the southern areas of what is now Poland were at some time within the range of Moravian slave catchers.[70]

Other objects that can be used to assess the major directions of movement accompanied the flow of all these goods across the region. We have already discussed the coins that entered the Baltic from across the eastern forests. Bone and antler combs,[71] like glass beads,[72] are not easy to use for this purpose; similar types were produced in the entire circum-Baltic area, so it is difficult to follow the products of any one center. One product of the coastal regions may be easier to detect. While there are deposits elsewhere, amber primarily comes from the southeast coast of the Baltic Sea, particularly from the region between the mouth of the Vistula and the Sambian Peninsula. Baltic amber traveled to the Roman world, but the evidence for the continuation of this "trade" is difficult to come by after ca. AD 500. Amber objects are found in ninth-century contexts at Dorestad and Truso, however, which suggests that amber was again being traded across the Baltic region by this time.[73]

One other artifact type that can be used to assess directions of contact is pottery. The so-called Baltic Ware, a pottery of typically Slav form and decoration, has turned up on a number of sites on the northern coasts of the Baltic

Sea.[74] From the style and fabric of this ceramic category, it is clear that while some pots may have been made locally, quite a lot of this material has come across the Baltic—presumably traded together with other goods, either to make up a load or as containers.

The overland routes by which goods were transported can be inferred only indirectly. There are many maps purporting to show medieval trade routes, some of them doing little better than "joining the dots" between known centers or hoard finds. Very few roadways have left any (recognized) field evidence (e.g., hollow ways), and some of the examples that have been claimed as such are dubious. It seems likely that rivers were used as transport systems—especially for bulky goods, such as agricultural produce. Some boats would have even been capable of going upriver. One example is the 8-meter dugout of the first half of the ninth century found under the vegetable market in Szczecin.[75] This boat had been used and repaired sixty years before being sunken.[76]

The Baltic Coast Emporia

Much work on the economy of barbarian Europe has concentrated on the North Sea coasts, the well studied Rhineland, and the adjacent areas. This system did not exist in isolation from the Baltic exchange network, and much attention has been concentrated on the well-known site at Hedeby, which served as a link between Western economies and the Baltic sphere (later supplemented by a number of Danish sites established shortly before AD 1000). Dendrochronological dating for the early spate of building at Hedeby suggests that it was founded by the Danish ruler Godfred at some point between 810 and 814 to replace the site at Reric in the territory of the Obodrites, somewhere farther to the southeast—a site he had destroyed in 808.[77] The site has been extensively excavated and well studied. Other Scandinavian sites (Ribe, Kaupang, Birka, Paviken) are also relatively well known. By contrast, the southern coasts of the Baltic have been relatively neglected in considerations of early medieval European trade networks, despite the fact that they are the obvious focus of attention for Scandinavian sites facing them. The evidence suggests that the Baltic was an area of maritime contact no less vibrant than the contemporary North Sea or Mediterranean.[78] An important factor in the creation of supraregional economic patterns was the rise of coastal emporia along the Baltic coast.[79] The interpretation of these sites involves a number of problems, not least the somewhat cavalier use that has previously been made of the archaeological evidence and especially of the radiocarbon dates.

The earliest (eighth- to ninth-century) sites dated by dendrochronology are Rostock-Dierkow and Gross Strömkendorf.[80] We have seen that the site at Reric was in use at the time of its destruction, known from the Frankish annals to have taken place in 808. Menzlin may also have begun in the middle of the eighth century. These settlements appear to have contained foreign merchants, possibly Frankish or Frisian in the beginning, but later Scandinavians as well.[81] There were also craftsmen's settlements and harbors near the strongholds at Oldenburg, Lübeck, and Mecklenburg. It is probably no coincidence that the earlier sites are situated to the west end of the south coast of the Baltic Sea, near the Frisian and Frankish territory.

Many of the sites further east are of later date, including Ralswiek on Rügen Island,[82] Menzlin on the Peene,[83] then Wolin[84] and Szczecin[85]—all four sites at the mouth of the Oder. Further along the coast was the complex of sites near Kołobrzeg, at the mouth of the Parsęta River: Budzistowo, Bardy, and Świelubie.[86] At the mouth of the Vistula was the site of Truso.[87] The date of Truso is still uncertain. The interim reports so far published contain conflicting evidence, though the site was visited in the 870s, 880s, or 890s by the English merchant (or emissary) Wulfstan. At the end of the tenth century, this site seems to have been superseded by the foundation of Gdańsk within Slav territory, on the opposite side of the lagoon at the mouth of the Vistula.

In several cases (Oldenburg, Lübeck, Mecklenburg, Szczecin, Kołobrzeg), the sites are organized around preexisting strongholds (probably tribal centers) situated near the coast, with craft settlements in and around them and with ports nearby. These seem to have developed within a preexisting settlement network (including the agricultural hinterland). A second type of sites (e.g., Gross Strömkendorf, Dierkow, Menzlin, Ralswiek, Truso) is commonly known as *Seehandelsplatz,* seems to have arisen as a result of the settlement of outsiders,[88] and consisted of extensive and apparently undefended clusters of permanent structures next to a harbor. These sites contain evidence of crafts of many types: specialist and general metalworking, amber working, the manufacture of glass objects, the production of antler combs, and so on.

Many of the *Seehandelsplatz* sites are situated well inland and could be reached on narrow inlets, presumably to protect them from casual raiding. Almost all of them are also sited near the mouths of important rivers,[89] which were presumably used for the transport of agricultural produce from the hinterland. Several sites—such as Truso, on the edge of Prussian territory—are located near the boundaries of major ethnic units. A notable feature of several such sites is the associated cemeteries containing graves with nonlocal burial rites (including boat burials and stone ship settings) and exotic grave goods.[90]

The precise mode of functioning of these sites is unclear. We may only surmise on the relationship between the different elements—the representatives of secular entities (authorities?), merchants, craftsmen, pirates, and others who frequented the sites and the items they used there (craft products, raw materials brought to the site [e.g., antler], mass agricultural products, luxury goods, silver coinage). It is difficult to see how the various hypotheses that have arisen to account for the nature of the assemblages from these sites may be tested.

It is possible that several other sites of the *Seehandelsplatz* type await discovery. Indeed, Marek Dulinicz points out certain regularities in the siting of these sites, and a model based on these regularities shows where other sites of this type may yet be found.[91] For example, the complex along the Parsęta River still requires further investigation. The rampart of the Budzistowo stronghold has produced a date of the turn of the ninth and tenth centuries (half a century later than originally thought).[92] The construction date of the adjacent stronghold at Bardy is unclear, but the entire complex may have acquired the attributes of a (not yet located) *Seehandelsplatz* at the turn of the eighth and ninth centuries.[93]

The complex at the mouth of the Oder is of special interest. Ralswiek has produced dendrochronological dates of 878 and after.[94] The earliest dates for Wolin seem to place its construction in the 880s or 890s.[95] The lowest layers at Szczecin lack dendrochronological dates, but Marek Rulewicz dates them to "the end of the ninth century."[96] These centers therefore seem to have experienced a floruit at about the same time, indicating a significant shift (or expansion) to the east of economic activities within the Baltic region.

The area seems to have maintained its importance even later. Zofia Kurnatowska has noted that a lot of the important centers of the early Piast state in Great Poland were situated on the Warta River (a tributary of the Oder) or its tributaries.[97] The famous document known as *Dagome iudex* refers to the Polish state as being *Schignesne civitas*,[98] which has received various interpretations. The phrase most likely refers to the hinterland supplying the port at *Schinesche* (Szczecin). Such an interpretation would give some idea of the importance attached to transmaritime trade by the first Piasts.

The development of these sites on the south coast of the Baltic raises several problems. The first concerns their appearance in the eighth century, as they seem to have been initiated before the first wave of Islamic silver came into the area.[99] Regardless of how they functioned at this time and of their purpose, the initiation of the flow of silver would have led to some changes taking place in their operation. It seems relatively clear, however, that far from reflecting the critical morphogenesis of Western economy ca. 830, as Richard Hodges proposed,[100] the south coast of the Baltic saw a flourishing of coastal emporia in the 880s and 890s. The mouth of the Oder seems to have been especially attractive for traders in the late ninth and early tenth centuries.[101]

Marek Dulinicz has also drawn attention to the fact that many of the *See-handelsplatz* sites on the southern coast of the Baltic were located in areas that, as the evidence suggests, had already seen relatively intense transmaritime contacts in late antiquity.[102] He raises the question of continuity, either of population or of traditions of certain locations for interethnic contacts. From such sites, we have some of the earliest dendrochronological dates for the presence of the Slavs in the region. Can this convergence simply be a matter of optimal locations for the functioning of long-distance trade? Since the evidence of continuity does not reach back beyond the fifth or the sixth century, this explanation seems more acceptable than the idea that the Slavs were new settlers drawn into an area of great economic resources derived from long-distance trade.

Systemic Change: The Tenth Century

In the tenth century, a number of significant changes took place in the region. Polabia experienced the expansion of the Ottonian Empire, which turned the area into several frontier marches. By contrast, in the Oder and Vistula basins, the tenth century was the period of crystallization of the Polish state under the Piast dynasty from Great Poland.

The Ottonian expansion into Polabia, which began in 928 and reached the Oder-Neisse line by 948,[103] was followed by a number of fundamental changes in the social organization of the region. This is evident from the construction of a network of new strongholds (there were sharp peaks in construction rate in Brandenburg in 906–30 and in Mecklenburg in 928–40),[104] the redistribution of lands among the new feudal elite, and the imposition of a modified version of the social organization in existence within the Ottonian Empire. Another important development was the attempt to convert the Slavs to Christianity. The archaeological evidence suggests that the Slavs were not entirely subsumed into this new state organism, though this aspect was perhaps overstressed by investigators of the former eastern Germany, in which the archaeological study of the Ottonian phase of Polabian history was de-emphasized in favor of a detailed study of Slavic continuity.[105] Indeed, some aspects of the Slavic settlement seem to have undergone a metamorphosis under Ottonian rule, reflecting, perhaps, the creation of new group identities in opposition to the "other." There were changes in the material culture, but perhaps not as marked as one would have expected. Recent work, for example, has shown that much of the ("Slavic") Tornow-type pottery was made at about the time of the Ottonian annexation, and one may presume that it was in use by both "Germans" and "Slavs."[106] Both the precise nature of the interactions between internal and external factors and the native response to Ottonian conquest require more future work.

Although Polabia was linked to the Ottonian economic system, there was no local production of coinage. However, beginning with the mid-tenth century, the exploitation of the silver mines in the Harz Mountains led to the strengthening of the economy of Saxony. As a consequence, coinage in Polabia was primarily Saxon, mostly of the Otto-Adeleide type, the early *Sachsenpfennige*.[107] While it is not yet clear to what extent the Polabian economy as a whole became monetarized, it seems likely that coinage in this area served as special-purpose money, while the barter economy probably continued to function alongside the monetary sphere. In any case, in contrast to areas farther west, Polabian hoards are rare before the eleventh century.

Many new central places (e.g., the bishoprics at Oldenburg, Havelburg, Brandenburg, Meissen, and Zaitz) are located in the western part of the region, leaving the area beyond that relatively weakly integrated with the system. This area witnessed the rise of a new tribal union, the Lutizi, and their violent uprising of 983, which led to the collapse of the Ottonian marches beyond the middle Elbe. A clearly visible peak in the dendrochronological dates from Mecklenburg between 980 and 988 apparently reflects these events.[108]

The situation in the period between the 980s and the German reconquest of the region in the twelfth century has been represented by the archaeologists of the former eastern Germany as "independence," but the significance of that label should not be overestimated, as both the Lutizi union and the Obodrites had, at times, very close political links with their western neighbors. It served as a detached buffer zone with its own leaders, perhaps in much the same way as Pannonia had done in the early decades of the eighth century.

In other respects, however, the portion of Polabia to the northeast of the middle Elbe, north of the Magdeburg-Frankfurt on the Oder line, remained outside the formal bounds of the Ottonian Empire. After ca. 980, this region shows many more features in common with the Slav territories further east, but unlike Poland, "independent Polabia" was more closely observed in the written records. Archaeological research has revealed a very high quality of material culture and the construction of a number of substantial and spectacular strongholds. In particular, the anaerobic conditions of preservation have led to the survival of many artifacts of organic material (including many wooden objects), giving us a very detailed picture of many aspects of daily life.[109] In many ways, however, the material culture of the area had been influenced by contact with its western neighbors,[110] and it is a mistake to extrapolate conclusions drawn on eleventh- and twelfth-century Polabia to other Slav regions.

The Evidence of Hoards

Something of the tenth-century economic developments in the area can be followed by looking at the numismatic evidence. The late ninth and tenth centuries had seen considerable fluctuation in the supply of oriental silver to the Baltic, the rhythms of which varied from region to region.[111] In the 920s, there was a slight reduction of the flow of the third wave of silver to the southern coast of the Baltic Sea. After the 930s, the flow of silver resumed, and Pomerania became one of the chief consumers of oriental silver, flowing first from Scandinavia and then, when these sources went into decline soon afterward, directly from northern Rus'. In subsequent decades, Pomerania was the main source of this silver for the neighboring regions (including Great Poland). At this time, Pomerania was part of the economic core area of the Baltic region.

In the 970s, the flow of Islamic silver into the Baltic diminished substantially and was supplemented by an increase of West European (English, Danish, and German) coins. A few decades later, they were followed by an increasing number of *Sachsenpfennige* deposited in hoards from Great Poland, Pomerania, and Silesia, an indication that such coins were apparently minted especially for trade with the Slavs. Tenth-century Polabian leaders did not mint their own coins and seem to have been content to use Western coins, much like the first Polish ruler. The first Polish coins were struck for Boleslav the Brave in the 990s, but they were special-purpose issues to be used alongside coinage from the outside. This situation persisted until the end of the eleventh century.[112] As was mentioned earlier, there was a relatively weak renewal of the inflow of Islamic silver into the region of the south coast of the Baltic in the last decade of the tenth century, but it was relatively short-lived.[113]

While a number of ninth-century hoards including only Islamic silver coins are known from the coastal area, it is the tenth century that witnessed an increase in Polabia and Poland of hoarded silver in the form of complete and fragmentary coins and jewelry. These hoards were deposited in some quantities in Pomerania from the last decades of the ninth century, in Polabia and in Great Poland after 940, and in Silesia after 960 (hoard finds in Mazovia and Little Poland are too scanty and chronologically scattered to constitute any significant pattern). It is not entirely clear, among several possibilities, who exactly was accumulating and then burying these hoards and what the reasons might have been for them not being retrieved at a later time.

The use of fine jewelry, often fragmented and thus treated merely as weighed bullion (hacksilver), is characteristic of certain groups of these hoards. It would seem that a mechanism was in operation whereby once elaborate and presumably highly prized prestige objects of high artistic value (the production of which had consumed much skilled work) were turned into mere scrap metal of unitary value. Perhaps this was due to piracy (e.g., stealing and division of the finery of captured women who were to join the slave trade) or to ritual prohibitions of passing down a deceased woman's jewelry to her daughters or successors. Whatever the reason behind this phenomenon, there are considerable quantities of broken and whole pieces of filigree silver jewelry in Great Poland in hoards dated to 940–60, as well as in those of the 980s. In Pomerania, where there is a spate of the use of this hacksilver in the 960s, the greatest peak of jewelry occurs between ca. 1010 and 1060. In most areas, the use of hacksilver was in decline in the 1070s, when the local numismatic evidence indicates that the Polish economy had become largely monetarized. Fluctuations in the frequency of hacksilver are difficult to explain. Some hoards contain ingots (both flat "spills" of metal and cast bars), and in Pomerania, Great Poland, and Silesia (regardless of other differences between the three areas), they occur mainly in hoards of about 1010 to 1040. That the early eleventh-century hoards of Great Poland consist mainly of ingots and contain less hacksilver of other types perhaps illustrates the drainage of wealth to the core of the state.[114]

It is possible that one reason for the delay in introducing a fully monetarized exchange system was that it would have meant a break with the social bonds created by the existence of the barter and tribute economies. This may have been one of the factors that led to the occurrence of hoards in which we find hacksilver alongside coinage. These hoards show that silver was clearly present in some quantity in Poland, but for some reason, it was preferred as a nonmonetary means of exchange and hoarding.

In Poland, we see several significant changes taking place ca. 940. There is an increase in the number of coins datable to this period in tenth-century hoards from Great Poland, a phenomenon interpreted as indicating the acceleration of the local economic growth. At the same time, new dendrochronological dates from major strongholds in the area—especially from Gniezno—show that there was some major investment in the defenses of these sites, which were soon to become the central places of the new state (as discussed shortly).[115] At about the same time, there is evidence of new connections between Great Poland and the Baltic coastal zone. In about the middle of the tenth century, we start to find antler and bone combs of the same types as were manufactured in coastal craft centers and also the first occurrences of amber products in the central places of Great Poland.[116] Such changes correspond to events recorded in the written sources. This is indeed the period when traces of a Polish state ruled by Mieszko I (of the Piast dynasty) first appear in chronicles of Poland's literate neighbors. Mieszko became a Christian in 966 and rapidly expanded his power base. By 967, he had conquered Pomerania, and new strongholds were established in the peripheral area to the north. A considerable expansion eastward followed these developments.[117] In the 980s, the Great Polish dynasty made a huge military effort to control the major east-west routes across the Carpathian forelands, formerly in Bohemian hands. This effort was again accompanied by the foundation of new strongholds in Silesia and Little Poland. In 965 or 966, a visitor from distant Spain, Ibrahim ibn Yakub, described the new state in the following terms: "The country of Mesco is the most extensive of theirs [i.e., the Slavs']. There is an abundance of food, meat, honey, and agricultural produce [or fish]. The taxes he collects are trade weights [meaning unclear]." The Spanish visitor also tells us what happened to some of the revenue and mentions the retinue that Mieszko supported from his own financial resources.[118]

We have already seen that the 970s and 980s saw the drying up of Islamic silver flowing through the Baltic region and the shift to the use of Western coinage in central Europe. Apart from these changes, it is quite clear that the conquest of these substantial territories by the leader of a tribal coalition from Great Poland (later named, possibly in retrospect, the Polanie) must have been accompanied by a substantial realignment of tribal economies. The destruction of the preexisting social and political organizations and the imposition of a state power would have had profound effects on the form of local and regional identities, now subsumed into an emerging state identity. One of Boleslav the Brave's titles appearing on coins most likely issued in 1000 is *princes Polonie*, although it is not clear whether all of those owing him allegiance would really have regarded themselves as in any way "Polish" by that date. We also know next to nothing about the dynamics of the process by which (through elite dominance) a certain language or dialect replaced preexisting languages and dialects as a lingua franca for mundane administrative, communicative, and cultural exchanges across the growing state. One other important change occurring at this time was the introduction of Christianity as the religion of the elite.[119]

Tenth-Century Central Places

The period between ca. 940 and 960 exhibits a number of changes in the distribution and typology of strongholds in Great Poland.[120] It is apparent that instead of being an incidental part of an existing settlement network, strongholds were now being constructed at points of strategic significance at river crossings, nodes on long-distance routes, and so on. In some cases, strongholds were now being constructed in areas where there had been relativley few, such as a dense cluster in the Kalisz region. Although there was continued occupation of some earlier strongholds, we more often see the abandonment (sometimes after their deliberate destruction) of sites that had fulfilled a role as central places in the prestate settlement network. They were replaced by sites built anew in the vicinity. This would suggest a deliberate attempt to slight these old central places in order to emphasize the introduction of a new social order.[121] In this period, we see much clearer signs of a connection with a social elite and the establishment of power by a dynasty. It is clear that the changes taking place on these sites after the 940s reflect altered perceptions of their main occupant's status and the way that strongholds were being used as a manifestation of centralized and personal, as opposed to communal, power and prestige.

In Great Poland and, later, further afield, a second type of site was also being constructed that emphasizes this point more forcefully. As a general rule, these sites are much larger and exhibit more complex layouts of ramparts and patterns of inner arrangements, which suggests that they were of more varied functions. In particular, we find elite residential and sacral structures in the interior of some of them (Poznań, Gniezno, Ostrów Lednicki, Giecz). These *palatia* consisted of long rectangular hall-like buildings (the ground floor sometimes subdivided into rooms), often with a chapel in the form of a rotunda attached to one end. The ruler moved between several royal centers (*sedes reges principales*) with his court and retinue of personal troops. Local administration seems to have been based on strongholds, with power in the hands of an elite hierarchy probably entrusted with wide military, administrative, judicial, and fiscal powers over the people residing in the neighborhood. The strongholds were probably also the centers where tribute was exacted. In addition to being built with stronger defenses and sited at militarily more strategic points, these mid-tenth century strongholds are often of much larger area than their predecessors, and excavations show that much of the interior was built up. We can see that they could have contained sizable temporary or permanent garrisons. A richer assortment of militaria are associated with these sites, which seems to demonstrate the presence of well-armed forces in and around at least some of these strongholds. Some of these finds (Kruszwica, Bnin, Ostów Lednicki) come from rich warrior burials in cemeteries excavated in the imemdiate vicinity, commonly interpreted as burials of princely retinue members.[122] There are also sites where graves of retinue members are not sited in sufficiently small distance from the major strongholds to show that such military forces were based in those sites. In such cases, the most probable explanation is that these cemeteries mark the centers of landed estates held by retinue members.

The internal arrangement of these strongholds seems to differ from those of an earlier period: the casemate type of construction in the lee of the rampart seems to disappear in favor of a more or less regularly built-up interior. These may take the form of sunken-floored construction or surface-built structures of log construction. These seem to be residential structures, but in some cases (to judge from the nature of the deposits that lap around their bases), the surface-built structures seem to have been there for considerable numbers of livestock. If the "casemate" structures of the earlier sites were indeed stores for other types of agricultural surplus, their absence in later structures (and the absence of any other obvious storage structures) would suggest that if these strongholds were connected with the gathering of surplus, it was no longer being accumulated in the strongholds but was being redistributed in some other manner.

Changes are seen in other spheres; in this period, settlement clusters (e.g., in Great Poland) tend to become denser but also of greater extent. Some evidence seems to suggest that the rise of the state was also accompanied by resettlement of entire groups of population, as, for example, in the settlement cluster at Piaski in the southern part of Great Poland. On the basis of certain "foreign" elements in nearby barrows, the excavator of the site interpreted the sudden appearance of settlements around a newly founded stronghold as representing the resettlement of a population from one region.[123] While this may simply be the imposition of coercive power accompanied by some deliberate policies of resettlement to break up preexisting social systems and create new ones, the motives for settling populations in previously sparsely inhabited territory may also have been economic, to increase revenues from these lands.

The social system established by these first leaders was probably based on a system of reciprocal obligations according to the so-called *ius ducale*. This system, as far as the limited evidence allows us to reconstruct it, was probably somewhat different from what was long thought to be the classic model of feudalism of Western Europe.[124] The Polish archaeologist Lech Leciejewicz calls the system "early feudalism," as it preceded the feudal society of the High and the late Middle Ages.[125] He sees in it the consequence of economic growth giving rise to "social forces" that led to social change, the result of which was the emergence of states. The most important consequences of the development and functioning of the new social order were class differentiation and integration, as well as the emergence of new identities.[126] One of the mechanisms of integration was the involvement of the whole society in the economic system. Leciejewicz presents an interesting model of evolutionary changes taking place in the systemic relationships between different social categories with time (fig. 2.4). He postulates the existence of three social classes in the seventh and eighth centuries: (1) duke and tribal elders, (2) members of community (farmers, warriors, craftsmen), and (3) slaves. These classes split and merge into five classes by the end of the tenth century: (1) dukes; (2) the wealthy, priests, and merchants; (3) free villagers, common knights, and craftsmen; (4) clients/dependents; and (4) slaves. In Leciejewicz's model, boundaries between classes are still fluid, but with the emergence of feudalism in the twelfth century, they have become more rigid. A broadly similar scheme by Herrmann has more obvious links to Marxist concepts, but the same themes are present in both models.[127]

The altering social and economic relations are revealed in changes in production. Archaeological evidence shows the increase of craft specialization and consequent technical improvement from the mid-tenth century in a number of crafts. This is observed, for example, in ceramic assemblages; it seems changes in the organization of pottery production gave rise to technological change.[128] Similar changes may be observed in other spheres of production, such as shoemaking and other leatherwork, bone and antler work, and fine metalworking—the tendency continuing well into the eleventh century.[129]

One feature of interest is the existence in Poland of so-called service villages, which, according to some written sources, were supposed to supply the strongholds with goods produced as "services," in order to make use of and spur rural production.[130] In this way, the Piast monarchy controlled, in a planned manner, the output of craftsmen specializing in certain branches of production. Village names that reflect responsibility for providing certain services or personnel are evidenced in the written sources; examples that have survived in Poland to the present day are *Sokolniki* (Falconers), *Piekary* (Bakers), *Skotniki* (Cattle herders), and *Winiary* (Vintners). The system operated until the end of the eleventh century, when it was replaced by local exchange of products from a variety of workshops.

The Problem of Urbanism

The question of differences in economic development across Europe took on an additional political meaning with the claims of German scholars concerning the civilizing influences of the Ottonian penetration into the region east of the Elbe River. In particular, the adoption of a narrow legalistic definition of a town emphasizing the existence of a charter allowed these scholars to insist that the Slavs came to benefit from the urban civilization very late and only under German influence. Such statements were vehemently rejected by scholars of Slav origin, who instead relied on different definitions of a town.

Much has been written on the definition of towns in both Western European and central European historiography, and it would seem that a detailed definition of what does and does not constitute a town or so-called prototown is still a long way off.[131] Indeed, we may need to consider whether such a thing is achievable at all across an area so diverse as Europe, with the Western towns being a continuation of the concepts of late antiquity, while those in central Europe arose under completely different circumstances to fulfill different social needs and developed under different conditions in subsequent centuries.

Three types of sites may be considered. The first is the *Seehandelsplatz*. While their main function seems to be connected with long-distance trade, such sites achieved this by acting as central places and were presumably integrated in some way into larger regional administrative and economic systems. The existence of inland sites of an apparently related type on nodes of major river routes in northern Russia[132] suggests that it is conceivable that similar sites may be found (near territorial boundaries?) among the western Slavs as well.

The second type of site are the strongholds of the centralized state, which apparently functioned as central places and concentrated political and military power along with administrative and economic functions. They also functioned as nodal points in exchange networks. That they were inhabited and frequented by an elite and by sizable military garrisons led to a growing demand for consumer goods. These demands were satisfied by a growing luxury trade and also stimulated local production. Some of these sites never developed beyond mere strongholds with associated production settlements and a local market; others grew into full-fledged medieval towns. The ambiguity of the situation is typified by the Polish term *gród,* which—like its Russian counterpart, *gorod*—means both "town" and "stronghold."

The third type is represented by sites that the modern observer would have no trouble in categorizing as urban, because they display most of the features of whatever criteria bundle the historian may wish to apply. It would be difficult, however, to point to an unequivocal example of such an urban complex in the area before the beginning of the eleventh century (outside it, Prague might be one example, Cracow perhaps a second).

Between these three types, there may of course be a whole range of intermediate stages. In central European historiography, attention has been drawn to the importance of settlements adjacent to the strongholds, the *podgrodzie,* which became the focus for the economic development of the late eleventh century.[133] Some of them had been surrounded by earthen and timber ramparts, much like the strongholds themselves, though they each performed a different function. The *podgrodzie,* relatively small built-up areas (which sometimes had a regular plan and wooden streets), housed a motley population—members of the elite, members of the military garrison, merchants, innkeepers, artisans, and servants, as well as fishermen or peasants. Although we know little about the social conditions of life and work of these people, it seems likely that they were settled by the will of the lords of the stronghold or gathered there of their own accord. In either case, part of their output was presumably due to the lords of the stronghold. Written sources mention markets adjacent to many *podgrodzie* (Ibrahim Ibn Yakub has left a vivid description of the one in Prague), but we have little information on how these operated before the eleventh century.[134] Not until the formation of local exchange networks in the late eleventh century did such centers take on most of the characteristics of medieval towns.

Changing Patterns of Long-Distance Exchange

The new states apparently saw the advantages of controlling long-distance trade routes. After the conquest of Pomerania, Gdańsk was founded at the mouth of the Vistula in the late decades of the tenth century, in an attempt to capture some of the Baltic trade from other centers on the Baltic coast. We have seen that at about the same time, sites like Szczecin and Wolin, at the mouth of the Oder, fulfilled a similar role in the utilization of the revenues from the agricultural hinterland to generate wealth by external exchange. These sites were no doubt linked with each other and their hinterland by a network of contacts and economic interactions. These are of course very difficult to reconstruct from the archaeological evidence, though some of the patterns visible in the numismatic evidence from the region may be interpreted as symptoms of other processes not so easily visible.

At about the time that these centers and the routes they fed were becoming established, the Baltic was experiencing the drying up of Islamic silver sources. Coin hoards in the hinterland of trading centers with last coins minted in ca. 980 include many West European coins. Such coins are evidence of a drastic shift in the directions and scale of trade in the 970s and 980s. Besides the maritime routes, central Europe was served by overland routes through southern Rus', and we have already seen that the patterns of deposition of *Sachsenpfennige* suggests they arrived in Poland by overland contact.

The numismatic and other evidence can only be understood by looking at the complexities of interaction between the various regions in the whole Baltic area and neighboring territories. Such a study must not neglect the processes occurring in the part of the system developing in the areas to the south of the Baltic. In particular, this evidence shows clearly how simplistic the picture presented by Hodges in his seminal study appears to be. That picture was based primarily on the Western European and Scandinavian evidence and ignored that from the southern coast of the Baltic. Hodges only highlights some aspects of the problem of the "origins of towns and trade" in Europe—even though the events of the last decade of the tenth century fall within the time span covered by his book.[135] We have seen that several distinct changes in the economic patterns revealed by the archaeological evidence have to be taken into account in any study of the development of the early medieval economy of Europe. These include the rise of the first coastal emporia in the Western regions, apparently in the mid-eighth century; the development of several major coastal sites in the 880s and 890s, especially at the mouth of the Oder; the shift in the economic core area from Pomerania in the 930s to Great Poland in the 940s to 960s (a phenomenon accompanying an extensive economic realignment in the area); and the systemic changes occurring in the 970s. Only a more complete study of the evidence from all regions around an area of complex interactions, such as the Baltic, will produce a more holistic picture of the changes taking place in the economy of Europe in the half millennium before AD 1000.

Conclusion

This necessarily summary and exploratory overview has attempted to bring together different threads to examine some of the relationships between the economies of a portion of the North European Plain and the adjacent areas and to illustrate the potential contribution that the evidence from central Europe can make to a fuller understanding of the European past. The "otherness" of the development of central and Eastern Europe, far from disqualifying these areas as of significance for serious academic study, render them of special interest: in their social organization, they offer innovative alternatives to the systemic resolutions of the West. Eastern and central European historiography arose from different regional traditions and developed in conditions different from their Western counterparts. The inevitable exchange between the various schools of thought as part of the integration accompanying cultural globalization and European unification will undoubtedly enrich our discipline. Development of electronic media of communication (in particular, of a new generation of translation programs) will soon ease communication between the so-called East and West and access to previously arcane data. This will leave only the other, mental barrier to be crossed.

NOTES

I would like to thank Florin Curta for asking me to put this account together, for help with some of the references, and for his patience. Various parts of this chapter resulted from discussions with Professors Stanisław Tabazcyński, Przemysław Urbańczyk, and

Andrzej Buko and with Marek Dulinicz. However, I alone am responsible for the way the material has been used and presented here.

1. Polabia is understood here as the area of Slav settlement on the middle Elbe River roughly corresponding to the territory of the former German Democratic Republic. Great Poland, the area of west central Poland around Poznań, is also the core area of the medieval state. This chapter has had to omit a consideration of the developments in the area of Baltic settlement to the east of the lower Vistula and, for reasons of space, some of the more specific problems of Silesia and Little Poland (the region in southeastern Poland around the later medieval capital at Cracow). See Paul Barford, *The Early Slavs: Culture and Society in Early Medieval Eastern Europe* (London, 2001).

2. For the history of archaeological research in East Central Europe, see Karel Sklenař, *Archaeology in Central Europe: The First 500 Years* (Leicester and New York, 1983).

3. Barford, *The Early Slavs*, 277–79.

4. Paul M. Barford, "Marksizm w archeologii polskiej w latach 1945–1975," *Archeologia Polski* 40 (1995): 7–78. See also Sarunas Milisauskas, "Observations on Polish archaeology, 1945–1995," *Archaeologia Polona* 35–36 (1997–98): 223–36; Jacek Lech, "Between captivity and freedom: Polish archaeology in the 20th century," *Archaeologia Polona* 35–36 (1997–98): 25–222.

5. Marian Malowist, "Problematyka gospodarcza badań wczesnośrednoiowiecznych," *Studia wczesnośredniowieczne* 1 (1952): 18–24; Henryk Łowmiański, *Podstawy gospodarcze formowanie się państw słowiańskich* (Warsaw, 1953).

6. Jan Brankačk, *Studien zur Wirtschaft und Sozialstruktur der Westslawen zwischen Elbe, Saale und Oder aus dem Zeit vom 9. bis zum 12. Jahrhundert* (Bautzen, 1964).

7. Karol Modzelewski, *Organizacja gospodarcza państwa piastowskiego* (Warsaw, 1975).

8. Stanislaw Tabaczyński, *Archeologia średniowieczna: Problemy, źródła, metody, cele badawcze* (Wrocław, 1987).

9. Richard Hodges, *Dark Age Economics: The Origins of Towns and Trade, AD 600–1000* (London, 1982); see also Richard Hodges and David Whitehouse, *Mohammed, Charlemagne, and the Origins of Europe: Archaeology and the Pirenne Thesis* (London, 1983).

10. Both books cited in the preceding note exhibit, almost to the point of caricature, a typically Anglophone archaeological picture of the Continent, from the peripheral "sunshine and pizza" area of activity of the British schools through France and Germany and the Low Countries to the English-speaking Scandinavian countries in the north.

11. Hodges, *Dark Age Economics*, 66. The concentration of spelling mistakes and geographical errors in this single statement is telling. On a later page of the same book (226), Grobin, now in Latvia, is even mistakenly placed in Poland. Of course, Szczecin, Wolin, and Grobin played no part in any sixth- to ninth-century "Russian" trade routes to the south.

12. Michael McCormick, *Origins of the European Economy: Communications and Commerce, AD 300–900* (Cambridge, 2001).

13. See Barford, *The Early Slavs*, for a summary.

14. This model lies at the basis of the disagreement between the chronology current until 1989 and the much later one now emerging from more recent work. This means that much of what has been written before the 1990s on the dating of phenomena connected with the Polabian Slavs and Poland should be treated with utmost caution.

15. Marek Dulinicz, *Kształtowanie się Słowiańszczyzny Północno-Zachodniej: Studium archeologiczne* (Warsaw, 2001).

16. It should be borne in mind that this method only dates the construction of the type of object that is capable of being dated. There is no guarantee that the earliest dates for strongholds and wells in the area are also the dates of the first Slavic settlement in the area, since there may be several reasons why Slavs did without wells and built no strongholds until later in the early medieval period.

17. B. J. Price, "Secondary state formation: An explanatory model," in *The Origins of the State*, ed. R. Cohen and E. Service (Philadelphia, 1978), 165.

18. *AZP* is the Polish abbreviation of the *Polish Archaeological Map*, the national archaeological record of archaeological sites. See Danuta Jaskanis, "La Carte Archéologique Polonaise: Théorie et pratique," *Nouvelles de l'archéologie* 28 (1987): 42–52; Jaskanis, "Polish national record of archaeological sites: General outline," in *Sites and Monuments: National Archaeological Records*, ed. C. Larsen (Copenhague, 1992), 81–87; A. Prinke, "Can developing countries afford national archaeological records? The Polish answer," in *Our Fragile Heritage*, ed. H. J. Hansen and G. Quine (Copenhague, 1999), 147–54.

19. Zofia Kurnatowska, "Wielkopolska w X wieku i formowanie się państwa polskiego," in *Ziemie Polskie w X wieku i ich znaczenie w kształtowaniu się nowej mapy Europy*, ed. Henryk Samsonowicz (Warsaw, 2000), 99–117, esp. figs. 1–2 and 8–9.

20. Zofia Hilczerówna, "Małe plemiona wczesnego średniowiecza i archeologiczne sposoby ich badania," *Slavia Antiqua* 12 (1965): 83–126; *Dorzecze górnej i środkowej Obry od VI do początków XI wieku* (Wrocław, 1967), 23–33.

21. Peter Donat, *Haus, Hof und Dorf in Mitteleuropa vom 7. bis 12. Jahrhundert: Archäologische Beiträge zur Entwicklung der bäuerlichen Siedlungen* (Berlin, 1980); Martin Gojda, *The Ancient Slavs: Settlement and Society* (Edinburgh, 1991). See also Peter Šalkovský, *Häuser in der frühmittelalterlichen slawischen Welt* (Nitra, 2001).

22. Barford, *The Early Slavs*, 65 and 339 fig. 15. See also Peter Donat, "Die unregelmässigen Gruben und der Hausbau bei den Nordwestslawen," *Slavia Antiqua* 24 (1977): 119–40.

23. Gojda, *The Ancient Slavs*.

24. Bruno Krüger, *Dessau-Mosigkau: Ein frühslawischer Siedlungsplatz im mittleren Elbegebiet* (Berlin, 1967).

25. Łowmiański, *Podstawy gospodarcze*, 155–59.

26. Michał Brzostowicz, *Bruszczewski zespół osadniczy we wczesnym średniowieczu* (Poznań, 2002), 165–93.

27. Zofia Podwińska, *Technika uprawy roli w Polsce średniowiecznej* (Wrocław, 1962); Lech Leciejewicz, *Słowianie zachodni: Z dziejów tworzenie się średniowiecznej Europy* (Wrocław, 1989), 69. For ibn Yakub's account, see Tadeusz Kowalski, ed., *Relacja Ibrahima ibn Jakuba z podróży do krajów słowiańskich w przekazie al-Bekriego*, Monumenta Poloniae Historiae 1 (Cracow, 1946); Georg Jakob, ed., *Arabische Berichte von Gesandten an germanische Fürstenhofe aus dem 9. und 10. Jahrhundert* (Berlin and Leipzig, 1927). See also the essays collected in Petr Charvát and Jirí Prosecký, eds., *Ibrahim ibn Yakub at-Turtushi: Christianity, Islam, and Judaism Meet in East-Central Europe, c. 800–1300 A.D.; Proceedings of the International Colloquy, 25–29 April 1994* (Prague, 1996).

28. The improved manner of production was of course used to bolster the argument for a massive demographic explosion required to fuel the "migrations."

29. Łowmiański, *Podstawy gospodarcze,* 138–59.

30. Magdalena Beranová, *Zemedělstvi starých slovanů* (Prague, 1980); Beranová, "Types of Slavic agricultural production in the 6th–12th centuries," *Ethnologia Slavica* 16: 7–48; Leciejewicz, *Słowianie zachodni,* 66–72; Joachim Herrmann, ed., *Die Slawen in Deutschland: Geschichte und Kultur der slawische Stämme westlich von Oder und Neisse vom 6. bis 12. Jahrhundert* (Berlin, 1985), 68–80. For the neighboring regions, see also Bazyli Czeczuga, Wieslawa Kossacka, and Edward Klyszejko, "Szczatki roślinne z badań grodziska w Hackach koło Bielska Podlaskiego (VI, XI–XII w.)," *Rocznik Białostocki* 13 (1976): 493–500; Maria Litynska, "Szczatki roślin z II–III i VI–VII wieku n.e. znalezione na stanowisku I w Wyszemborku koło Mrągowa," *Światowit* 37 (1993): 137–46; Z. Tempír, "Zemedelské plodiny a plevele z archeologických nálezu v Březne u Loun," *Vedecké práce Československého zemedelského muzea* 22 (1982): 121–95; Helena Svoboda, "Vegetace jižní Moravy v druhé polovine prvého tisíceletí," *Archeologické rozhledy* 42 (1990): 170–205.

31. Herrmann, *Slawen in Deutschland,* 81–92; Leciejewicz, *Słowianie zachodni,* 72–75.

32. See, e.g., H. Makowiecki, "Zaplecze gospodarcza Ostrowa Lednieckiego w świetle badan archeologicznych," in *Centrum i zaplecze we wczesnośredniowieczne Europie środkowej,* ed. Slawomir Możdzioch (Wrocław, 1999), 241–56.

33. P. Donat and E. Lange, "Botanische Quellen und Probleme der Landwirtschaftsentwicklung im ersten Jahrtausend," *Zeitschrift für Archäologie* 17 (1983): 223–47.

34. Władysław Łosiński, "Z badań nad strukturą gospodarstwa wiejskiego w późnej starożytności i na początku wczesnego średniowiecza," *Archeologia Polski* 15 (1970): 519–35; E. Lange, *Botanische Beiträge zur mitteleuropäischen Siedlungsgeschichte* (Berlin, 1971), 45; Lange, "Grundlagen und Entwicklungstendenzen der frühgeschichtlichen Agrarproduktion aus botanischer Sicht," *Zeitschrift für Archäologie* 10 (1976): 81.

35. There was only limited and indirect contact between the communities of this region and the pastoralists in the Carpathian Basin. There are very few finds of Avar metalwork north of the Carpathians, and only a few horsemen with ornament and weaponry of Magyar type made it far north of the Carpathians. For a survey of Polish finds of Avar provenance, see Helena Zoll-Adamikowa, "Zur Chronologie der awarenzeitlichen Funde aus Polen," in *Probleme der relativen und absoluten Chronologie ab Latènezeit bis zum Frühmittelalter: Materialien des III internationalen Symposiums, Grundprobleme der frügeschichtlichen Entwicklung im nördlichen Mitteldonaugebiet, Kraków-Karniowice 3.–7. Dezember 1990,* ed. Kazimierz Godłowski and Renata Madyda-Legutko (Cracow, 1992), 297–315; Nad'a Profantová, "Awarische Funde aus den Gebieten nördlich der awarischen Siedlungsgrenzen," in *Awarenforschungen,* ed. Falko Daim, vol. 2 (Vienna, 1992), 605–801.

36. Herrmann, *Slawen in Deutschland,* 92–98 and fig. 26.

37. Florin Curta, "Iron and potlatch: Early medieval hoards of implements and weapons in Eastern Europe," *Archivum Eurasiae Medii Aevi* 10 (1998–99), 15–62.

38. Beranová, *Zemĕdĕlstvi,* 236.

39. Herrmann, *Slawen in Deutschland,* 138 with fig. 55. For Bohemian and Moravian finds, see Magdalena Beranová, "Manual rotation grain mills on Czechoslovak territory up to the incipient 2nd millenium A.D.," *Ethnologia Slavica* 19 (1987): 15–43. For some interesting results of ethnoarchaeological research pertaining to the use of quern stones, see Raiko Krauss and Gerson H. Jeute, "Traditionelle Getreideverarbeitung in Bulgar-

ien: Ethnoarchäologische Beobachtungen im Vergleich zu Befunden der Slawen in frühen Mittelalter zwischen Elbe und Oder," *Ethnographisch-archäologische Zeitschrift* 39 (1998): 498–528.

40. Herrmann, *Slawen in Deutschland*, 100–126.

41. Barford, *The Early Slavs*, 104–5.

42. Marek Dulnicz, "Problem datowania grodzisk typu Tornow i grupy Tornow-Klenica," *Archeologia Polski* 39 (1994): 31–49; Sebastian Brather, "Feldberger Keramik und frühe Slawen: Studien zur nordwestslawischen Keramik der Karolingerzeit," *Ethnographisch-archäologische Zeitschrift* 35 (1994): 613–29; Brather, "Nordwestslawische Siedlungskeramik der Karolingerzeit-fränkische Ware als Vorbild?" *Germania* 73 (1995): 403–20; Brather, *Feldberger Keramik und frühe Slawen: Studien zur nordwestslawischen Keramik der Karolingerzeit* (Bonn, 1996).

43. Krzysztof Wachowski, *Kultura Karolinska a Słowiańszczyzna Zachodnia* (Wrocław, 1992), and *Śląsk w dobie przedpiastowskiej* (Wrocław, 1997); Sebastian Brather, "Merowinger- und karolingerzeitliches 'Fremdgut' bei den Nordwestslawen: Gebrauchsgut und Elitenkultur im südwestlichen Ostseeraum," *Prähistorische Zeitschrift* 71 (1996): 46–84.

44. P. Grimm, *Die vor- und frühgeschichtlichen Burgwälle der Bezirke Halle und Magdeburg* (Berlin, 1958); Hansjürgen Brachmann, *Der frühmittelalterliche Befestigungsbau in Mitteleuropa: Untersuchungen zu einer Entwicklung und Funktion im germanisch-deutschen Bereich* (Berlin, 1993); Herrmann, *Slawen in Deutschland*, 186–232.

45. In this statement lies the assumption that the earliest dendrochronological dates (necessarily largely from the timbers preserved in the anaerobic conditions of the ramparts of strongholds) do not necessarily date the very earliest settlement in the area.

46. Dulinicz, *Kształtowanie*, 27–35; K.-U. Heussner and T. Westphal, "Dendrochronologische Untersuchungen an Holzfunden aus frühmittelalterlichen Burgwällen zwischen Elbe und Oder," in *Frühmittelalterliche Burgenbau in Mittel- und Osteuropa: Tagung, Nitra, vom 7. bis 10. Oktober 1996*, ed. Joachim Henning and Alexander T. Ruttkay (Bonn, 1998), 223–34; Joachim Henning, "Archäologische Forschungen an Ringwällen in Niederungslage: Die Niederlausitz als Burgenlandschaft des östlichen Mitteleuropas im frühen Mittelalter," in ibid., 9–29.

47. Joachim Herrmann, *Tornow und Vorberg: Ein Beitrag zur Frühgeschichte der Lausitz* (Berlin, 1966); Dulinicz, "Problem datowania grodzisk."

48. Sebastian Brather, "Karolingerzeitlicher Befestungsbau im wilzisch-abodritischen Raum: Die sogenannten Felberger Hohenburgen," in *Frühmittelalterliche Burgenbau in Mittel- und Osteuropa: Tagung, Nitra, vom 7. bis 10. Oktober 1996*, ed. Joachim Henning and Alexander T. Ruttkay (Bonn, 1998), 115–47.

49. The author estimates that the construction of a smallish stronghold 30 meters across would take about fifty to sixty people about five weeks of Stakhanite work to build (not including cutting and hauling the wood or the construction of internal buildings).

50. Slawomir Możdzioch, *Castrum munitissimum Bytom: Lokalny ośrodek władzy w państwie wczesnopiastowskim* (Warsaw, 2002).

51. Paul M. Barford and E. Marczak, "The settlement complex at Podebłocie, gm. Trojanow: An interim report of investigations, 1981–1992," *Światowit* 37 (1993): 150–51 with fig. 3.

52. This revision has been carried out in the past two decades primarily by Poznań-based scholars, as an ongoing process that has generated a considerable amount of

detailed and synthetic literature. See, e.g., Zofia Kurnatowska, "Forschungen zu früh-mittelalterlichen Burgen in Großpolen," in *Frühmittelalterliche Burgenbau in Mittel-und Osteuropa: Tagung, Nitra, vom 7. bis 10. Oktober 1996*, ed. Joachim Henning and Alexander T. Ruttkay (Bonn, 1998), 31–36; "Wielkopolskie badania w ramach projektu 'Polska w dobie zjazdu gnieznieńskiego,'" in *Osadnictwa i architektura ziem polskich w dobie zjazdu gnieznieńskiego*, ed. A. Buko and Z. Świechowski (Warsaw, 2001), 43–54.

53. Eugeniusz Cnotliwy, *Rzemiosło rogownicze na Pomorzu wczesnośredniowiecznym* (Wrocław, 1973), 100–102.

54. See John Haldon, *The State and the Tributary Mode of Production* (London and New York, 1993).

55. Barford, *The Early Slavs*, 174–75 with fig. 51. For the iron bars (*griwny*), see Radomír Pleiner, "Slovanské sekerovite hrivny," *Slovenská Archeológia* 9 (1961): 405–50; Pleiner, "K otazce funce a rozsireni sekerovitých hriven," *Slovenská Numizmatika* 10 (1989): 81–86; Darina Bialeková and Anna Tirpaková, "K otazke funkcnosti sekerovitých hrivien z Pobedima z hl'adiska ich metrologickych hodnot," *Slovenská Numizmatika* 10 (1989): 89–96. For the "Silesian bowls," see Josef Bubeník, "K problematice železne misky tzv. sležského typu," *Archeologické rozhledy* 23 (1972): 542–67; "K otázce funkce železne misky tzv. sležského typu," in *Sborník referátu ze sympozia "Slované 6.–10. století," Břeclav-Pohansko, 1978*, ed. Bořivoj Dostál and Jana Vignatiová (Brno, 1978), 49–54.

56. Władysław Łosiński, "Chronologia napływu najstarszej monety arabskiej na terytorium Europy," *Slavia Antiqua* 31 (1988): 93–181; "Chronologia, skala i drogi napływu monet arabskich do krajów Europejskich u schyłku IX i w X w.," *Slavia Antiqua* 34 (1993): 1–42. See also Csanád Bálint, "Einige Fragen des Dirhem-Verkehrs in Europa," *Acta Archaeologica Academiae Scientiarum Hungaricae* 33 (1981): 105–31; Sebastian Brather, "Frühmittelalterliche Dirham-Schatzfunde in Europa: Probleme ihrer wirt-schaftsgeschichtlichen Interpretation aus archäologischer Perspektive," *Zeitschrift für Archäologie des Mittelalters* 23–24 (1995–96): 73–153; Andrzej Bartczak, "Finds of dir-hams in central Europe prior to the beginning of the 10th century A.D.," in *Origins of Central Europe*, ed. Przemysław Urbańczy (Warsaw, 1997), 227–38; Andrzej Bartczak and Dorota Malarczyk, "Dirhams of some early medieval finds from the area of Great Poland," *Wiadomości Numizmatyczne* 44 (2000): 39–54. These coins are one of the main markers of McCormick's "northern arc" (McCormick, *Origins*, 562–64).

57. Barford, *The Early Slavs*, 178 fig. 54.

58. Władysław Łosiński, "Chronologia napływu najstarszej monety"; "W sprawie rozwoju gospodarki towarowo-pieniężnej na ziemiach polskich we wczesnym śred-niowieczu w kontekście dziejów obrotu pieniężnego w strefie nadbałtyckiej. Cz. I," *Archeologia Polski* 35 (1990): 287–309; "Miejsce Pomorza i Wielkopolska w kształtowaniu się gospodarki towarowo-pieniężnej w Polsce wczesnofeudalnej," *Slavia Antiqua* 37 (1996): 163–80.

59. Łosiński, "Chronologia napływu najstarszej monety"; Barford, *The Early Slavs*, 178–81 with figs. 54–56.

60. For a quick overview, see Marek F. Jagodzinski, "Truso: A settlement and port of the Slav-Aesti borderland," in *Europe's Center around A.D. 1000*, ed. Alfried Wieczorek and Hans-Martin Hinz (Stuttgart, 2000), 111–12.

61. Sture Bolin, "Mohammed, Charlemagne, and Ruric," *Scandinavian Economic History Review* 1 (1952): 5–39.

62. Władysław Łosiński, "Pomorze: Bardziej slowianskie czy bardziej 'baltyckie'?" in

Ziemie polskie w X wieku i ich znaczenie w kształtowaniu się nowej mapy Europy, ed. Henryk Samsonowicz (Cracow, 2000), 124.

63. Lech Leciejewicz, "Słowianie zachodni i Normanowie we wzajemnych stosunkach kulturowych we wczesnym średniowieczu," *Pomerania Antiqua* 10 (1981): 164–65; "Normanowie nad Odrą i Wisła w IX–XI wieku," *Kwartalnik Historyczny* 100 (1993): 50. The Raffelstetten Plea (McCormick, *Origins,* 555, 604, 646–48) tells us that salt, foodstuffs, wax, slaves, and horses were being taken through the upper Danube region ca. 900, some apparently from Bohemia.

64. McCormick, *Origins,* 730–32.

65. Władysław Łosiński, *Początki wczesnośredniowiecznego osadnictwa grodowego w dorzeczu dolnej Parsęty (VII–X/XI w.)* (Wrocław, 1972), 35, 332.

66. H. Burchard, "Wyniki badań wykopaliskowych w Wieliczce, pow. Kraków w latach 1960–1962," *Sprawozdanie Archeologiczne* 16 (1964): 318–25.

67. McCormick, *Origins,* 733–77.

68. The *Life of Constantine* tells of the freeing of slaves by the Moravian mission, while the *Life of Naum* speaks of the enslavement of Moravian priests. McCormick (*Origins,* 190) links these references to an early medieval continuation or revival of the old Amber Trail. For Rugi, see McCormick, *Origins,* 763.

69. McCormick's suggestion (*Origins,* 744) that Slav strongholds were perhaps used for stockading slaves cannot be applied to the typical form of these sites, which have defenses clearly intended to keep somebody out rather than for penning anybody in.

70. Barford, *The Early Slavs,* 110.

71. Cnotliwy, *Rzemiosło rogownicze.*

72. Johan Callmer, *Trade Beads and Bead Trade in Scandinavia ca. 800–1000 A.D.* (Lund, 1977); "Pragmatic notes on the early medieval bead material in Scandinavia and the Baltic region ca. A.D. 600–1000," in *Studią nad etnogeneza słowian i kultura Europy wczesno-średniowieczej,* ed. G. Labuda and S. Tabaczyński, vol. 1 (Warsaw, 1987), 217–26; "Beads as a criterion of shifting trade and exchange conditions," *Studien zur Sachsenforschung* 7 (1991): 25–38.

73. For Dorestad, see W. A. van Es and W. J. H. Verwers, *Excavations at Dorestad 1: The Harbour; Hoogstraat 1* (Amersfoort, 1980), 169. For Truso, see Marek Jagodziński and Maria Kasprzycka, "Zarys problematyki badawczej osady rzemeslniczo-haudlowej w Janowie Pomorskim (gmina Elbląg)," *Pomorania Antiqua* 14 (1990): 18 22, figs. 11–12; "The early medieval craft and commercial center at Janów Pomorski near Elbląg on the south Baltic coast," *Antiquity* 65 (1991): 696–715. See also Marek Jagodziński, "Truso: A settlement and port of the Slav-Aesti borderland," in *Europe's Center around A.D. 1000,* ed. Alfried Wieczorek and Hans-Martin Hinz (Stuttgart, 2000), 111–12; McCormick, *Origins,* 610.

74. D. Selling, *Wikingerzeitliche und frühmittelalterliche Keramik in Schweden* (Stockholm, 1955); Johan Callmer, "Slawisch-skandinavische Kontakte am Beispiel der slawischen Keramik in Skandinavien während des 8. und 9. Jahrhunderts," *Bericht der römisch-germanischen Kommission* 69 (1988): 654–74; Mats Roslund, "Baltic Ware: A black hole in the cultural history of early medieval Scandinavia," in *Contacts across the Baltic Sea during the Late Iron Age (5th–12th Centuries): Baltic Sea Conference, Lund, October 25–27, 1991,* ed. Brigitte Hårdh and Bożena Wyszomirska-Werbart (Lund, 1992), 159–75. See also Mats Roslund, *Gäster i huset: Kulturell overföring mellan slaver och scandinaver 900 till 1300* (Lund, 2001); M. Andersen, "Westslawischer Import in Dänemark etwa 950 bis 1200: Eine Übersicht," *Zeitschrift für Archäologie* 18 (1984): 145–61.

75. Władysław Łosiński, "W sprawie lokalizacji portu wczesnośredniowiecznego Szczecina," in *Słowiańszczyzna w Europie średniowiecznej,* ed. Zofia Kurnatowska (Wrocław, 1996), 67–78; Marek Rulewicz, "Wrak szczecińskiego łodzi z IX wieku," in *Słowiańszczyzna w Europie średniowiecznej,* ed. Zofia Kurnatowska (Wrocław, 1996), 79–90. See also George Indruszewski, "Wczesnośredniowieczne łodzie klepkowe z południowiej strefy Bałtyku w świetle analizy porównawczej," *Materiały Zachodnio-Pomorskie* 42 (1996): 61–76.

76. Władysław Filipowiak, "'Żywot' statku wczesnośredniowiecznego," in *Słowiańszczyzna w Europie średniowiecznej,* ed. Zofia Kurnatowska, vol. 2 (Wrocław, 1996), 91–96. See also his "Shipbuilding at the mouth of the river Odra (Oder)," in *Crossroads in Ancient Shipbuilding: Proceedings of the Sixth International Symposium on Boat and Ship Archaeology, Roskilde 1991,* ed. Christer Westerdahl (Oxford, 1994), 83–96.

77. *Royal Frankish Annals,* s.a. 808, in Bernhard Walter Scholz and Barbara Rogers, eds., *Carolingian Chronicles, Royal Frankish Annals, and Nithard's Histories* (Ann Arbor, 1970), 88.

78. See the studies collected in *Contacts across the Baltic Sea during the Late Iron Age (5th–12th Centuries): Baltic Sea Conference, Lund, October 25–27, 1991,* ed. Brigitte Hårdh and Bożena Wyszomirska-Werbart (Lund, 1992); Łosiński, "Pomorze-bardziej slowiańskie," 122–23.

79. As noted earlier, Richard Hodges (*Dark Age Economics,* 47–86) mentions only a few of them. See Joachim Herrmann, ed., *Wikinger und Slawen: Zur Frühgeschichte der Ostseevölker* (Neumünster, 1982); Herrmann, *Slawen in Deutschland,* 232–42; Joachim Herrmann, "Zur Struktur von Handel und Handelsplätze im südwestlichen Ostseegebiet vom 8.–10. Jahrhundert," *Bericht der römisch-germanischen Kommission* 69 (1988): 720–39; Władysław Łosiński, "Rola kontaktów ze Skandynawią w dziejach gospodarczych Słowian nadbałtyckich," *Przegląd Archeologiczny* 45 (1995): 73–86; Łosiński, "Pomorze-bardziej slowianskie"; Marek Dulinicz, "Uwagi o początkach ośrodków handlowych na południowym brzegu Bałtyku w VIII–IX w.," in *Centrum i zaplecze we wczesnośredniowiecznej Europie środkowej,* ed. Slawomir Możdzioch (Wrocław, 1999), 97–110.

80. Dulinicz, *Kształtowanie,* 30–31, 281–82, 285–86; H. Jöns, F. Lüth, and M. Müller-Wille, "Ausgrabungen auf dem frühgeschichtlichen Seehandelsplatz von Gross Strömkendorf, Kr. Nordwestmecklenburg," *Germania* 75 (1997): 193–221.

81. Władysław Łosiński, "Rola kontaktów ze Skandynawia w dziejach gospodarczych Słowian nadbałtyckich," *Przegląd Archeologiczne* 45 (1997): 73–86. Władysław Duczko, "Scandinavians in the southern Baltic between the 5th and the 10th centuries A.D.," in *Origins of Central Europe,* ed. Przemysław Urbańczyk (Warsaw, 1997), 191–211.

82. Joachim Herrmann, "Ralswiek um 850. Lebensweise, Gewerbe und Kaufleute in einem Handelsplatz an der südlichen Ostseeküste," in *Słowiańszczyzna w Europie średniowiecznej,* ed. Zofia Kurnatowska, vol. 2 (Wrocław, 1996), 51–60; *Ralswiek auf Rügen: Die slawisch-wikingischen Siedlungen und deren Hinterland,* vol. 1, (Lübstorf, 1997). The site dates to after the 870s, see Dulinicz, *Kształtowanie,* 284.

83. Ulrich Schoknecht, *Menzlin: Ein frühgeschichtlicher Handelsplatz an der Peene* (Berlin, 1976). The chronology of this site is unclear. After a phase dated to the last decades of the eighth century, there are mid-ninth-century dendrodates from a causeway probably associated with the coastal trading site, but finds from the associated cemetery are of the late ninth century (Dulinicz, *Kształtowanie,* 283–84).

84. Władysław Filipowiak, "Die Bedeutung Wolins im Ostseehandel," in *Society and Trade in the Baltic during the Viking Age: Papers of the VIIth Visby Symposium Held at Gotlands Fornsal, Gotland's Historical Museum, Visby, August 15th–19th, 1983,* ed. Sven-Olof Lindquist (Visby, 1985), 120–38; *Wolin-Vineta: Ausgrabungen in einer versunkenen Stadt* (Stralsund and Rostock, 1986); "Wolin: Die Entwicklung des Seehandelszentrums im 8.–12. Jh.," *Slavia Antiqua* 36 (1995): 93–104. See also Władysław Filipowiak and Heinz Gundlach, *Wolin-Vineta: Die tatsächliche Legende vom Untergang und Aufstieg der Stadt* (Rostock, 1992).

85. Lech Leciejewicz, Marian Rulewicz, Stefan Weselowski, and Tadeusz Wieczorowski, *La ville de Szczecin des IX-e–XIII-e siècles* (Wrocław, 1972); Lech Leciejewicz, "Die Entstehung der Stadt Szczecin im Rahmen der frühen Stadtentwicklung an der südlichen Ostseeküste," in *Vor- und Frühformen der europäischen Stadt im Mittelalter: Bericht über ein Symposium in Reinhausen bei Göttingen vom 18. bis 24. April 1972,* ed. Herbert Jahnkuhn, Walter Schlesinger, and Heiko Steuer (Göttingen, 1975), 209–30; Leciejewicz, "Czy był Szczecin 'najstarszym miastem Pomorza'?" in *Zródłoznawstwo i studia historyczne,* ed. Kazimierz Bobowski (Wrocław, 1989), 41–50; Leciejewicz, "Les origines de la ville de Szczecin: Questions historiques et réalité archéologique," *Przegląd Archeologiczne* 37 (1990): 181–94; Łosiński, "W sprawie lokalizacji"; Eugeniusz Cnotliwy and Władysław Łosiński, "Szeczin/Stettin: Vom frühstädtischen Zentrum zur Lokationsstadt," *Slavia Antiqua* 36 (1995): 73–92; Cnotliwy and Łosiński, "Szczecin," in *Europe's Center around A.D. 1000,* ed. Alfried Wieczorek and Hans-Martin Hinz (Stuttgart, 2000), 105–6.

86. Władysław Łosiński, "Die Burgbesiedlung im mittleren und unteren Parsęta-Flussgebiet in den ältesten Phasen des frühen Mittelalters," *Archaeologia Polona* 11 (1969): 59–89; "Wczesnośredniowieczny zespół osadniczy w Bardach i Świelubiu pod Kołobrzegiem," *Koszalinskie Zeszyty Muzealne* 3 (1973): 102–19; "Bardy-Świelubie, ein Siedlungskomplex im unteren Parsęta-Flussgebiet," *Archaeologia Polona* 16 (1975): 199–219. For a barrow cemetery containing objects of Scandinavian origin dating to the end of the eighth century (?) and to the first half of the ninth century, see Helena Zoll-Adamikowa, *Wczesnośredniowieczne cmentarzyska ciałopalne Słowian na terenie Polski. Cz. I. Źródła* (Wrocław, Warsaw, Cracow, and Gdańsk, 1975), 226–35.

87. Jagodziński and Kasprzycka, "Zarys problematyki badawczej osady," 9–49; "Early medieval craft and commercial center," 696–715. See also Jagodziński, "Truso," 111–12.

88. See Łosiński, "Szeczin/Stettin."

89. Dulinicz, "Uwagi o początkach ośrodków," 99.

90. Władysław Łosiński, "Groby typu Alt Käbelich w świetlo badan prowadzonych na cmentarzysku wczesnośredniowiecznym w Swielubie pod Kołobrzegiem," *Przegląd Archeologiczne* 41 (1993): 17–34.

91. Dulinicz, "Uwagi o początkach ośrodków," 104–6. See also Johan Callmer, "Interaction between ethnical groups in the Baltic region in the late Iron Age," in *Contacts across the Baltic Sea during the Late Iron Age (5th–12th Centuries): Baltic Sea Conference, Lund, October 25–27, 1991,* ed. Brigitte Hårdh and Bożena Wyszomirska-Werbart (Lund, 1992), 99–107.

92. Dulinicz, "Uwagi o początkach ośrodków," 104; Lech Leciejewicz, "Pomorze zachodnie w projekcie badawczym poswieconym Polsce w dobie zjazdu gnieznieńskiego," in *Osadnictwa i architektura ziem polskich w dobie zjazdu gnieznieńskiego,* ed. A. Buko and Z. Świechowski (Warsaw, 2001), 139–44.

93. Łosiński, "Szeczin/Stettin," 104–6.

94. Joachim Herrmann and Karl-Uwe Heußner, "Dendrochronologie, Archäologie und Frühgeschichte vom 6. bis 12. Jh. in den Gebieten zwischen Saale, Elbe und Oder," *Ausgrabungen und Funde* 36 (1991): 268–69.

95. Tomasz Ważny and Dieter Eckstein, "Dendrochronologiczne datowanie wczesnośredniowiecznej słowiańskiej osady Wolin," *Materiały Zachodnio-Pomorskie* 33 (1987): 147–64.

96. Rulewicz, "Wrak szczecińskiego łodzi," 89.

97. Zofia Kurnatowska, "Centrum a zaplecze: Model wielkopolski," in *Centrum i zaplecze we wczesnośredniowieczne Europie środkowej,* ed. Sławomir Możdzioch (Wrocław, 1999), 54.

98. Brygida Kürbis, "*Dagome iudex:* Studium krytyczne," in *Początki państwa polskiego: Księga tysiąclecia,* ed. Kazimierz Tymieniecki (Poznań, 1962), 363–424.

99. However, the first settlement of Staraia Ladoga and the initial penetration of Scandinavians into the northern Russian forests date from about the eighth century. See Simon Franklin and Jonathan Shepard, *The Emergence of Rus, 750–1200* (London, 1996), 12–33.

100. Hodges, *Dark Age Economics,* 151.

101. Dulinicz, "Uwagi o początkach ośrodków," 101–5 with fig. 2.

102. Dulinicz, "Uwagi o początkach ośrodków," 106.

103. See Herbert Ludat, *An Elbe und Oder um das Jahr 1000: Skizzen zur Politik des Ottonenreiches und der slavischen Mächte in Mitteleuropa,* 2nd ed. (Weimar, Cologne, and Vienna, 1995); Herrmann, *Slawen in Deutschland,* 326–55; Peter Heather, "Frankish imperialism and Slavic society," in *Origins of Central Europe,* ed. Przemysław Urbańczyk (Warsaw, 1997), 171–90; Lutz E. von Padberg, "Consolidation and expansion of Latin Christianity: The Ottonian mission to the western Slavs and Hungarians," in *Europe's Center around A.D. 1000,* ed. Alfried Wieczorek and Hans-Martin Hinz (Stuttgart, 2000), 439–42.

104. Dulinicz, *Kształtowanie,* 27–35; Heussner and Westphal, "Dendrochronologische Untersuchungen," 223–34; Henning, "Archäologische Forschungen," 9–29.

105. Most typical in that respect is Herrmann's *Slawen in Deutschland.*

106. Joachim Henning, "Neues zum Tornower Typ. Keramische Formen und Formenaspekten des Frühmittelalters im Licht dendrochronologischer Daten zum westslawischen Siedlungsraum," in *Kraje Słowiańskie w wiekach średnich: Profanum i sacrum,* ed. Hanna Kóčka-Krenz and Władysław Łosiński (Poznań, 2000), 392–408.

107. See Peter Ilisch, "Polnische Otto-Adelheid-Pfennige," *Wiadomości Numizmatyczne* 34 (1990): 160–63; "Regensburg- und Otto-Adelheid-Imitationen aus Polen?" *Wiadomości Numizmatyczne* 38 (1994): 65–70.

108. For dates of construction of strongholds, see Heussner and Westphal, "Dendrochronologische Untersuchungen," 223–34; Henning, "Archäologische Forschungen," 9–29.

109. The results of this research are summarized in Herrmann, *Slawen in Deutschland.*

110. See Leszek Paweł Słupecki, *Slavonic Pagan Sanctuaries* (Warsaw, 1994).

111. Ryszard Kiersnowski, *Pieniądz kruszcowy w Polsce wczesnośrednioweiecznej* (Warsaw, 1960); Łosiński, "Chronologia, skala i drogi napływu." See also Jacek Slaski and Stanisław Tabaczyński, *Wczesnośredniowieczne skarby srebrne Wielkopolski* (Warsaw and Wrocław, 1959).

112. Stanisław Suchodolski, *Początki mennictwa w Europie środkowej, wschodniej i*

północnej (Wrocław, 1971); "The earliest coinage of Poland," in *Europe's Center around A.D. 1000*, ed. Alfried Wieczorek and Hans-Martin Hinz (Stuttgart, 2000), 124. For an interesting parallel with similar developments in Scandinavia, see Stanislaw Suchodolski, "Die Anfänge der Münzprägung in Skandinavien und Polen," *Nordisk Numismatisk Årsskrifter*, 1971, 20–37.

113. There are few single coins of late ninth- and tenth-century Anglo-Saxon kings in tenth-century hoards but considerable quantities of Anglo-Saxon coins in hoards deposited after 990. The latter derive from the Danegeld paid by English kings to Scandinavian leaders. These coins made a considerable contribution to the functioning of the economy of several regions around the Baltic Sea. In Polabia and Poland, they constitute a major component of hoards from 990 to well into the eleventh century. See Kiersnowski, *Pieniądz kruszcowy*, 158–72. For German coins in Poland, see Stanislaw Suchodolski, "Die Münzen des 10. und 11. Jahrhunderts aus Mainz, Speyer und Worms in Polen: Ein Beitrag zur Datierung, zu den Einstromwegen und zum Umlauf," in *Fernhandel und Geldwirtschaft: Beiträge zum deutschen Münzwesen in sächsicher und salischer Zeit; Ergebnisse des Dannenberg-Kolloquiums 1990*, ed. Bernd Kluge (Sigmaringen, 1993), 301–13.

114. For the changing characteristics of the Polish hoards, see Tabaczyński, *Archeologia średniowieczna*, 196–207; 204 fig. 55. See also Stanislaw Suchodolski, "Le problème de la circulation de l'argent sous la forme de bijoux, de lingots et de monnaies fragmentées dans la zone de la Baltique, du IXe au XIe siècle," *Rivista italiana di numismatica e scienze affini* 95 (1993): 577–84.

115. Marek Krąpiec, "Dendrochronological dating of early medieval fortified settlements in Poland," in *Frühmittelalterlicher Burgenbau in Mittel- und Osteuropa: Tagung, Nitra, vom 7. bis 10. Oktober 1996*, ed. Joachim Henning and Alexander T. Ruttkay (Bonn, 1998), 257–67; Zofia Kurnatowska, "Wielkopolskie badania w ramach projektu badawczego 'Polska w dobie zjazdu gnieźnieńskiego," in *Osadnictwo i architektura ziem polskich w dobie zjazdu gnieźnieńskiego*, ed. A. Buko and Z. Świechowski (Warsaw, 2001), 43–54; Michał Kara, "Stan badań dendrochronologicznych wczesnośredniowiecznych grodzisk z terenu wielkopolski," in ibid., 55–68.

116. See Cnotliwy, *Rzemiosło rogownicze*.

117. Barford, *The Early Slavs*, fig. 70.

118. Barford, *The Early Slavs*, 144.

119. See Jonathan Shepard's contribution to the present volume (chap. 10).

120. Zofia Kurnatowska, "Tworzenie się państwa pierwszych Piastów w aspekcie archeologicznym," in *Od plemienia do państwa: Śląsk na tle wczesnośredniowiecznej słowiańszczyzny zachodniej*, ed. Lech Leciejewicz (Wrocław, 1991), 77–98; "Territorial structures in West Poland prior to the founding of the state organization of Mieszko I," in *Origins of Central Europe*, ed. Przemysław Urbańczyk (Warsaw, 1997), 125–35; "Forschungen zu frühmittelalterlichen Burgen in Grosspolen," in *Frühmittelalterlicher Burgenbau in Mittel- und Osteuropa: Tagung, Nitra, vom 7. bis 10. Oktober 1996*, ed. Joachim Henning and Alexander T. Ruttkay (Bonn, 1998), 31–36; "Centrum a zaplecze"; "Wielkopolska w X wieku"; "Wielkopolskie badania."

121. See Andrzej Buko's contribution to the present volume (chap. 7).

122. Michał Kara, "Z badań nad wczenośredniowiecznymi grobami z uzbrojeniem z terenu Wielkopolski," in *Od plemiania do państwa: Śląsk na tle wczesnośredniowiecznej Słowiańszczyzny Zachodniej*, ed. Lech Leciejewicz (Wrocław, 1991), 99–118.

123. D. Kosiński, "Osada przygrodowa w Piaskach gmina Zduny," in *Słowiań-szczyzna w Europie średniowiecznej*, ed. Zofia Kurnatowska (Wrocław, 1996), 251–56.

124. Kazimierz Modzelewski, *Organizacja gospodarcza państwa piastowskiego X–XIII wiek* (Wrocław, 1975); Leciejewicz, "Słowianie zachodni," 160–68. For the "classical model of feudalism," see F. L. Ganshof, *Feudalism*, trans. Philip Grierson (Toronto, 1996). This model is currently under heavy criticism, primarily following the publication of Susan Reynolds, *Fiefs and Vassals: The Medieval Evidence Reinterpreted* (Oxford, 1996). For an excellent survey of the recent debate, see Chris Wickham, "Le forme del feudalesimo," in *Il feudalesimo nell'alto medioevo, 8–12 aprile 1999* (Spoleto, 2000), 15–51.

125. Leciejewicz, "Słowianie zachodni," 124.

126. Leciejewicz, "Słowianie zachodni," 168–98.

127. Leciejewicz, "Słowianie zachodni," 161–64 with fig. 82; Herrmann, *Slawen in Deutschland*, 252–61.

128. Witold Hensel, *Polska przed tysiącem lat* (Wrocław, 1960), 98–108.

129. See Slawomir Możdzioch, *Organizacja gospodarcza państwa wczesnopiastowskiego na Śląsku: Studium archeologiczny* (Wrocław, 1990).

130. Modzelewski, *Organizacja gospodarcza*; Leciejewicz, "Słowianie zachodni," 165–66. See also Joachim Henning's contribution to the present volume (chap. 1).

131. See Hodges, *Dark Age Economics*, 20–25; Leciejewicz, "Słowianie zachodni," pp. 138–48, 264–80; Herrmann, *Slawen in Deutschland*, 232–51. The literature on medieval cities and towns in Eastern Europe is enormous. For a quick orientation, see Herbert Ludat, *Vorstufen und Entstehung des Städtewesens in Osteuropa: Zur Frage der vorkolonialen Wirtschaftszentren im slavisch-baltischen Raum* (Cologne and Braunsfeld, 1955); Anton Gutkind, *Urban Development in East-Central Europe: Poland, Czechoslovakia, and Hungary* (New York, 1972); Hugo Weczerka, "Neuere Forschungen zur Geschichte des Städtewesens in Ostmitteleuropa," *Zeitschrift für Ostmitteleuropa-Forschung* 37 (1988): 443–78; Márta Font, "Grundriß der osteuropäischen Städte im Frühmittelalter," in *Mittelalterliche Häuser und Straßen in Mitteleuropa*, ed. M. Font and M. Sándor (Budapest, 2000), 191–201. See also the studies collected in Hansjürgen Brachmann, ed., *Burg, Burgstadt, Stadt: Zur Genese mittelalterlicher nichtagrarischer Zentren in Ostmitteleuropa* (Berlin, 1995); Przemysław Urbańczyk, ed., "Origins of Medieval Towns in Temperate Europe," *Archaeologia Polona* 32 (1994): 5–196; Jerzy Piekalski, "Uwagi o problemie definicji miasta średniowiecznego: Struktury wczesnomiejskie i późnośredniowieczny model osadnictwa miejskiego," in *Kraje Słowiańskie w wiekach średnich: Profanum i sacrum*, ed. Hanna Kóćka-Krenz and Władysław Łosiński (Poznań, 1998), 349–56.

132. Łosiński, "Chronologia napływu," 104. See also E. Mühle, *Die städtischen Handelszentren der nordwestlichen Rus': Aufzüge und frühe Entwicklung altrussischer Städte (bis gegen Ende des 12. Jahrhunderts)* (Stuttgart, 1991).

133. Leciejewicz, "Słowianie zachodni," 264–80.

134. Tadeusz Lalik, "Targ," in *Słownik Starożytności Słowiańskich*, ed. W. Kowalenko, vol. 6 (Wrocław, 1977), 25–32. For Prague in the tenth century, see Ivan Borkovský, *Die Prager Burg zur Zeit der Přemyslidenfürsten* (Prague, 1972); Vaclav Huml, "Research in Prague: An historical and archaeological view of the development of Prague from the 9th century to the middle of the 14th century," in *From the Baltic to the Black Sea: Studies in Medieval Archaeology*, ed. David Austin and Leslie Alcock (London, 1990), 267–84; Dušan Třeštík, "Die Gründung Prags," in *Burg, Burgstadt, Stadt: Zur Genese mittelalterlicher nichtagrarischer Zentren in Ostmitteleuropa*, ed. Hansjürgen Brachmann (Berlin,

1995), 229–40; K. Tomková, "Noch einmal zu den Anfängen der Prager Burg," in *Život v archeologii středoveku: Sborník příspevku,* ed. Jana Kubková (Prague, 1997), 630–38; Jarmila Čiháková, "Prague around the year 1000: Infrastructure and communications," in *Europe's Center around A.D. 1000,* ed. Alfried Wieczorek and Hans-Martin Hinz (Stuttgart, 2000), 113–14.

135. Hodges (*Dark Age Economics,* 162–84, 192–98) covers the tenth-century developments (mainly in Britain, Viking Scandinavia, and Ottonian Germany), but apparently mainly as a sequel to the more fundamental changes he saw taking place in the Carolingian early ninth century (ibid., 151–61).

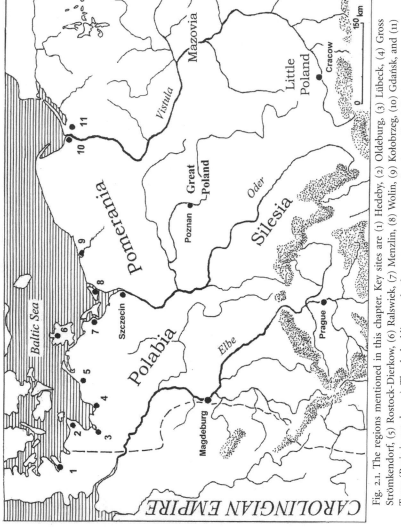

Fig. 2.1. The regions mentioned in this chapter. Key sites are (1) Hedeby, (2) Oldeburg, (3) Lübeck, (4) Gross Strömkendorf, (5) Rostock-Dierkow, (6) Ralswiek, (7) Menzlin, (8) Wolin, (9) Kołobrzeg, (10) Gdańsk, and (11) Truso (Reric is not shown). The dashed line marks the easternmost extent of early medieval Slavic toponyms.

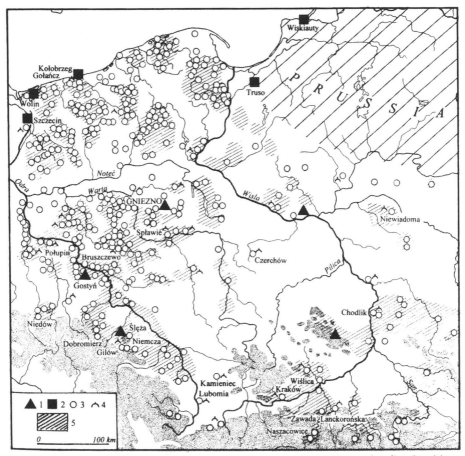

Fig. 2.2. Map of Poland in the prestate period: (1) cult sites on hilltops, (2) coastal trading sites, (3) strongholds, (4) prestige objects, (5) settlement clusters. (Drawn by J. Sawicka after Kurnatowska.)

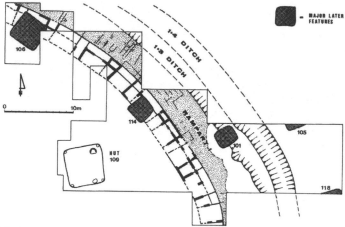

Fig. 2.3. The inner (earlier) rampart at Podebłocie, with internal "casemate" constructions on its interior face (Drawn by M. Różycka after Barford and Marczak.)

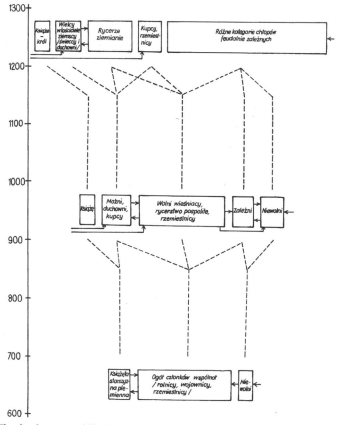

Fig. 2.4. The development of "feudal" relationships among the western Slavs from the seventh to thirteenth centuries (Drawn by H. Grocholski after Leciejewicz.)

Salt Trade and Warfare:
The Rise of the Romanian-Slavic
Military Organization in Early
Medieval Transylvania

Alexandru Madgearu

S alt was a strategic resource in the Middle Ages, as important as iron and gold. Control over salt resources and trade was an important aspect of medieval politics and warfare, particularly in the case of nomadic horsemen. Transylvania has the richest salt resources in central Europe. Its salt mines were exploited at least since the Roman times.[1] The most important are Sic, Turda, Cojocna, Ocna Dejului (Cluj district), Uioara-Ocna Mureș, Ocnișoara (Alba district), Ocna Sibiului (Sibiu district), Praid, Ocland, Ocna (Harghita district), and Ocnița (Bistrița-Năsăud district).[2]

Two major salt trade routes were in use in medieval Transylvania. The most important one was along the Mureș River. Salt was shipped on small boats or rafts to the Tisza River and then to the Danube. Slankamen, at the mouth of the Tisza, was an important trade center. The salt from the northern mines around Cluj moved along the second route, following the Someș River through the pass at Porțile Meseșului.[3] The names *Slankamen* and *Sălacea* are both derived from the Slavic word for salt.[4]

It has long been noted that Avar and Magyar cemeteries in Transylvania cluster around the salt mines (fig. 3.1).[5] This is no coincidence. In addition, a few Magyar cemeteries, such as Gâmbaș and Lopadea Nouă, were found on the exact spot of earlier Avar cemeteries. The distribution of these cemeteries suggests that both Avars and Magyars controlled the salt mine district.

It is important to note that the Avars did not conquer the salt mine district from the very beginning. The Gepids had controlled the area ever since the late fifth century. Although defeated by Avars in 567, they seem to have remained in place until ca. 630.[6] When plotted on the map, Gepidic cemeteries, too, cluster around major salt mines (fig. 3.2).

The Avars established a power center near present-day Aiud, in the middle of the salt mine district and next to the Mureș, the river on which salt moved on small boats. From that point, they were able to control the Mureş valley and had access to the Someş valley. Both rivers connected the salt mine district to Pannonia. Several other Avar finds in Transylvania cluster around strategic points along the salt routes—around the Mureş-Tisza confluence and near Sălacea (Căuaş, Dindeşti, Săcuieni, Valea lui Mihai).[7]

The same is true for the Magyar conquest of the tenth century. First, two strategic points were occupied, one on the Someş River (Cluj), the other on the Mureş (Alba Iulia). Both sites produced some of the earliest Magyar finds in Transylvania.[8] Transylvania seems to have been a distinct territory. It was somewhat separated from the main Avar center of power between the Tisza and the Danube. Similarly, in the tenth century, the Magyar tribe that settled in Transylvania remained independent from the main center of power in Pannonia during the 900s, until its conquest by King Stephen I in the early eleventh century.

The leading position of the salt mine district is also evident from the distribution of sixth- and seventh-century gold coins in Transylvania. They all cluster in the salt mine district (fig. 3.3). These coins were minted for early Byzantine emperors, from Justinian to Heraclius. With the exception of a solidus minted for Constantine IV, there are no coins postdating Heraclius's reign.[9] The gold coins arrived in Transylvania from Byzantium at the same time as Christian artifacts of clearly Eastern origin (clay and bronze lamps) dated to the sixth and early seventh centuries.[10] Gold coins indicate payments of some kind or, perhaps, gifts, but not trade. Nonetheless, they point to the possible location of the power center that received such payments. It is therefore not surprising that all coins were found within the salt mine district controlled by the Gepids.

Salt production implies the existence of a subject sedentary population, most probably Slavs and Romanians. They had the necessary skills and knowledge and provided labor for the extraction and transport of salt on behalf of their nomadic rulers. The involvement of the Slavs in salt extraction and trade is documented by several Romanian words and place-names of Slavic origin, such as ocnă (salt mine), Slănic, and Slatina.

The existence of a Slavic population in early medieval Transylvania is indisputable. The Slavs came to this region in the late 500s as subjects of the Avars and remained there as a distinct population group surviving well into the eleventh century. The archaeological evidence pertaining to this group consists of settlements and cemeteries, such as Bezid, Sălaşuri, Mediaş, and Cluj-Someşeni.

The presence of Romanians in Transylvania poses somewhat different problems. Several Romanian words of Latin origin, such as păcurar (shepherd), *arină* (sand), *nea* (snow), *june* (young man), or *ai* (garlic), are in use only within the territory of the former Roman province of Dacia, particularly in Transylvania. This suggests an early occupation of this region by speakers of the Romance dialect from which Romanian derives, as Transylvania was undoubtedly the Romanian territory that received the strongest and most durable Roman influence. Many of these words are of the basic vocabulary, and it is unlikely that they were borrowed from medieval Latin. Moreover, linguistic studies suggest that a number of dialectal features spread outside Transylvania at a later date.[11] In Transylvania proper, many river names are of Slavic origin, but in some cases, the Slavic name is in fact a translation of the Latin or Romanian one. For example, the upper course of the river bearing the Slavic name *Bistriţa* goes by the Romanian name *Repedea*. The meaning of both names is "swift river," but the former is most likely a translation of the latter. Other names, such as *Criş* and *Gălpâia,* have no Slavic intermediary, since their pre-Slavic forms are documented in Jordanes' *Getica* (*Grisia* and *Gilpil*). The same is true for *Ampoi,* a name derived from that of the Roman city Ampelum.[12] The distribution of these river names coincides with that of a series of archaic cranial features within the restricted area of the Apuseni Mountains.[13] Linguistic data thus suggest the existence of speakers of Romanian in the vicinity of the salt mine district.

This is indeed important, for it is very difficult to distinguish between "Slavic" and "Romanian" pottery or dress accessories. In most cases, archaeology can only identify cultural groups that, unlike Avars or Magyars, were not of nomadic origin. The wheel-made pottery produced on the fast wheel (as opposed to the tournette), which was found in several settlements of the eighth, ninth, and tenth centuries, may indicate the continuation of Roman traditions. Such pottery has been identified in Iernut, Popeni-Cuceu, Sighişoara-Albeşti, Eliseni, Şimoneşti, Ocniţa, and Comana de Jos but was also found in considerable quantities in northwestern Romania (Crişana).[14]

It is much more difficult to ascertain the archaeological evidence of burials. An important group of seventh- to ninth-century cremation and biritual cemeteries known as the Mediaş group (fig. 3.4) has been attributed to the Slavs, but the presence of Romanians in this context should not be ruled out. In any case, a number of such cemeteries cluster near the salt mines.[15] This is the case, for example, of the cemetery of Ocna Sibiului, with 120 cremation and fifteen inhumation burials. Double cremation burials with male and female remains (the so-called suttee burials), as well as East European cranial features, have been interpreted as indicating a Slavic population. At any rate, the deceased buried in this cemetery may have been workers in the salt mine of Ocna Sibiului during the eighth and early ninth centuries.[16]

Eighth-century spurs are a particularly interesting category of artifacts. Two specimens were found in settlements at Şura Mică and Medişoru Mare.[17] Both sites have salt mines nearby—at Ocna Sibiului and Praid, respectively. Since spurs have clear military connotations, they suggest the existence of a non-Avar military organization of the local population, for no evidence exists that Avars or any other nomads had or used spurs. Moreover, the chronology of the Transylvanian spurs suggests the existence of cavalry troops of Slavs and, perhaps, Romanians in Avar service.[18] The Avar qaganate was in fact a multiethnic polity, in which non-Avar chiefs ruled over various regions in the name of the qagan. Cooperation between Avars and Slavs is clearly documented for Moravia and Slovakia. Transylvania may have been another such region, under the direct rule of local chiefs of Slavic origin. They may have mediated between the local population and the Avar elite, which was interested primarily in controlling the production and distribution of salt.[19]

There are very few spurs in contemporary assemblages in neighboring regions, such as Bulgaria.[20] There are no spurs in hoards of iron implements and weapons found in Walachia or Moldavia.[21] A small settlement excavated at Dodeşti (Vaslui district) produced a single *Hakensporn* (hook-spur), but its association with a Byzantine buckle of the tenth or eleventh century suggests a much later date.[22]

Spurs were very popular in East Central Europe among the western Slavs, who seem to have imitated the military equipment of their Frankish neighbors. The Transylvanian spurs may thus document a Western influence across the Avar qaganate. The use of spurs of Western type continued in Transylvania during the ninth century under different circumstances. So far, Transylvania has produced no remains of strongholds,[23] but the existence of a local military organization under Avar control (as early as the eighth century) should not be excluded.

The local military forces may have been subdued in the ninth century by Bulgarians. Following the collapse of the Avar qaganate, Bulgaria expanded into the lower Tisza region and along the Mureş River, into the salt mine district of Transylvania.[24] In the early 800s, the middle Danube area was disputed between Bulgaria and the Frankish Empire. At the peace of 832, the regions to the east of the Tisza River, including present-day Banat, remained under Bulgarian control and were organized as marches, much like the area in present-day Walachia known in contemporary sources as "Bulgaria beyond the Danube."[25] In both cases, the Bulgarian qagan extracted tribute from local rulers, who otherwise enjoyed considerable autonomy. Tiles, bricks, and other building materials of Byzantine origin have been found near the confluence of the Danube and the Argeş and Siret Rivers and along the routes leading to the salt mines in northeastern Walachia (Slănic and Telega). It is possible, therefore, that "Bulgaria beyond the Danube" was in some way associated with the Bulgarian control over these mines. The stronghold excavated at Slon (Prahova district) may have defended one of the mountain passes securing access from this area to Transylvania.[26]

The Bulgarian presence in southern Transylvania is documented by a small group of settlements and cemeteries around present-day Alba Iulia, all dated to the second half of the ninth century. The ceramic assemblages found there have clear analogies on many sites in the lower Danube area. Fine, grey pottery with lustered decoration (the so-called Dridu B Ware) was found in burial and settlement assemblages in Alba Iulia,[27] Blandiana,[28] Câlnic,[29] Sânbenedic,[30] and Sebeș.[31] Two settlements in southeastern Transylvania (Covasna district), Poian and Cernat (fig. 3.5),[32] also produced Dridu B wares that both Romanian and Hungarian archaeologists associate with the Bulgarian control of southern Transylvania.[33]

Alba Iulia may have been the center of this Bulgarian march in southern Transylvania. The site produced a number of very interesting finds, including a small rotunda, which may have been built in the 800s.[34] The traditional interpretation advocates a date for this monument in the mid-tenth century. The only basis for this dating was the presumed association with the mission of the bishop Hierotheos mentioned in the Byzantine sources as having been sent from Constantinople, together with the Magyar chieftain who received baptism there in 953.[35] But Hierotheos did not come to Transylvania, for this was not the territory controlled by the Magyar chieftain. By contrast, finds of Byzantine coins and crosses dated to the tenth century suggest that the territory in question was the region between the Mureș, Criș, and Tisza Rivers. No such finds are known from Transylvania.[36] It seems more likely, therefore, that the Alba Iulia rotunda was erected by a local ruler in the 800s.

Another controversial site is Ciumbrud (Alba district), where Romanian archaeologists excavated a cemetery with thirty-two inhumation burials.[37] Associated grave goods include several types of earrings typically found on ninth-century sites in Moravia (fig. 3.6). As a consequence, the excavators of the site proposed that those buried in Ciumbrud came from Moravia. Many scholars endorsed this interpretation, on the basis of which they began entertaining the idea of Great Moravian colonies in Transylvania.[38] In reality, the Ciumbrud earrings have good parallels in ninth- and tenth-century burial assemblages in the lower Danube region (e.g., Sultana). Such earrings were also found on other Transylvanian sites, such as Alba Iulia-Statia de Salvare and Orăștie.[39] The same is true about the circular lead pendant found in grave 7 at Ciumbrud, for which good analogies are known from the lower Danube area.[40] In addition, the Mediterranean cranial features of the Ciumbrud skeletons do not match the series identified on Moravian sites.[41]

Another cemetery has been recently excavated in Orăştie. All ten inhumation burials were associated with earrings and other dress accessories similar to those found in Ciumbrud. Under the influence of the prevailing interpretation of that cemetery, the excavators of the Orăştie graves suggested the presence of a group of Moravian origin (an anthropological analysis has not yet been carried out).[42]

By contrast, István Bóna argued that the Ciumbrud burial assemblages belong to the same cultural group with strong influences from the lower Danube area.[43] Besides Ciumbrud and Orăştie, four other cemeteries (Alba Iulia–Staţia de Salvare, Blandiana A, Ghirbom, and Sebeş) produced evidence of similar funerary rites (particularly the west-east orientation of the graves) and grave goods.[44] Despite the absence of Dridu B wares from burial assemblages in Ciumbrud and Orăştie, this group of cemeteries (which we may call, for the sake of brevity, the Alba Iulia-Ciumbrud group) is in many ways linked to the so-called Dridu culture. Given that the majority of graves were aligned roughly west-east, with the head to the west, and given the symbolism of some of the associated grave goods, the people buried in cemeteries of the Alba Iulia-Ciumbrud group were most likely Christians.

An episode of 892 may illuminate the question of the Bulgarian control of the Transylvanian salt. During the war against Sventopluk, King Arnulf of Carinthia asked the Bulgarians to prevent shipments of salt to Moravia.[45] This episode shows that the Bulgarians controlled the salt trade routes from Transylvania to Moravia. If Ciumbrud was a Moravian cemetery, the neighboring salt mine in Aiud, located just a few kilometers away from Ciumbrud, must have been in Moravian hands. If so, however, Arnulf's request to Bulgaria would make no sense whatsoever. It is more likely, therefore, that the Bulgarians, not the Moravians, were in control of the salt mines, including the one in Aiud, which is located just thirty kilometers to the northeast from Alba Iulia, on the Mureş River. If Moravians settled in Transylvania, we would expect to find Moravian artifacts in the region between Moravia and Transylvania as well, especially in the area of the Criş rivers, between the Apuseni Mountains and the Tisza River. But so far, no such artifacts were found in that region. If we can ascertain that trade relations existed in the 800s between Transylvania and Moravia, such relations are sufficient for explaining the presence of "Moravian" earrings in burial assemblages from Ciumbrud and Orăştie. We thus need no Moravian presence to account for such artifacts found in the salt mine district of Transylvania.

The Transylvanian salt reached not only Bulgaria but also Pannonia and

Moravia. This Western connection may explain the presence in Transylvania and Banat of several artifacts of Frankish origin. Two spurs of Frankish type were accidentally found in an inhumation burial in Tărtăria (Alba district). They belong to Ruttkay's class A3, dated to the first half of the ninth century.[46] The Tărtăria horseman was buried at about the same time as most of the deceased interred in cemetery A in nearby Blandiana. A third ninth-century spur was found in a Dacian tower from Breaza (Braşov district), which was restored and reused during the early Middle Ages.[47] Four other specimens come from the tenth-century habitation phase of the Dăbâca hillfort (Cluj district),[48] a phase postdating the first Magyar raid into Transylvania. This suggests that the Magyars subjected but did not destroy the previously existing Slavic and Romanian military organization. This seems to be confirmed by the evidence of the *Gesta Hungarorum*, to which I will return later. Finally, three spurs of Frankish type were recently found in an eighth- and ninth-century settlement in Iernut (Mureş district). The settlement also produced horse gear and weapons, as well as wheel-made pottery.[49] Three stray finds from an unknown location between Alba Iulia and Orăştie are also of Frankish origin. The sword, the spear, and the lance head can all be dated to the ninth century and, according to Zeno Pinter, may have been artifacts associated with the Tărtăria horseman burial already mentioned.[50] Contacts with territories under Frankish influence are also documented for the late 800s by earrings of Köttlach type, such as found in Sălacea, Zalău, Deta (Romania), and Tápé (Hungary).[51] With the exception of Deta, all these sites are located outside Transylvania proper, along the salt routes. By contrast, a Frankish denier from a private collection in Orşova, which was minted between 855 and 875,[52] does not indicate any contacts with the Frankish Empire. Nothing is known about the circumstances in which the coin was found, and there is a good chance it may have been acquired from someplace else. The same is true about the so-called Frankish coins from Jamu Mare. In reality, these are commemorative medals minted in nineteenth-century France, not genuine evidence of trading relations with the Frankish Empire.[53]

The Bulgarian control never expanded into northwestern Transylvania. Instead, according to the *Gesta Hungarorum*, a small duchy emerged in the early 900s in this region, along the Someşul Mic River. Since the northern salt route crossed this region, it is quite possible that the Romanian-Slavic duchy emerged in connection with the salt production and trade. Magyars conquered the duchy at some point during the first half of the tenth century. Transylvania was not incorporated into the territory under the direct control of the nomads but became a distinct polity, to be (re)conquered later by King Stephen I. The political developments of tenth-century Transylvania are described in the

Gesta Hungarorum. The version given by the unknown author of this chronicle in chapters 24–27 is in sharp contrast with that of Simon of Keza and of other fourteenth-century chronicles. But it would be a mistake to treat the *Gesta* as a forgery, for nothing indicates that its author had any reason to forge anything. On the contrary, the main goal of his account of Tuhutum's conquest of Transylvania seems to have been to support Arpadian claims to power and legitimacy. The author of the *Gesta* made the Romanian (*Blacus*) duke Gelou a *dominus* (lord) with his own *dominium* (domain), in order to have the Magyar chieftain Tuhutum take both titles from him as a symbol of military prowess. In other words, the account of Tuhutum's conquest of Transylvania is an important narrative strategy that the author of the *Gesta* used to bolster Arpadian claims to territories not included within the Hungarian kingdom. Indeed, Transylvania became an important component of the Arpadian domain only after Stephen I. Despite being a piece of royal propaganda, the *Gesta Hungarorum* is not entirely a work of fiction. There was no reason for its author to "make up" Romanians (*Blaci*) and insert them into his narrative, because Arpadian claims to Transylvania were based on military conquest, not on nineteenth-century historical and demographic arguments.[54] It is therefore a mistake to treat Gelou as a purely fictional character whose name derived from that of the Transylvanian town Gilău. In reality, there are many examples in medieval Hungary of toponyms derived from person names. This seems to have been the case for *Gilău,* a place-name derived from the name of the Romanian duke Gelou, who died there while confronting the Magyars.[55]

That Tuhutum's attack was clearly targeted toward the salt mine district is evident from the *Gesta:* "Quod terra illa irrigaretur optimis fluviis [...] et quod in arenis eorum aurum colligerent, et aurum terre illius optimum esset, et ut ibi foderetur sal et salgenia . . ."[56] By the same token, the attempt of Achtum, who ruled in the early eleventh century in Banat, to take over the salt trade route along the Mureș River brought him into conflict with the king: "usurpabat sibi potestatem super sales regis descendentes in Morisio, constituens in portibus ejusdem fluminis usque ad Ticiam tributarios et custodes, conclusitque omnia suo tributo."[57]

Despite claims to the contrary,[58] there is no evidence of Hungarian shipments of salt to Byzantium during the tenth century. Transporting salt over land routes across Bulgaria would have been extremely difficult, while no ships could have sailed down the Danube River beyond the Iron Gates Gorge. Sviatoslav's famous letter to his mother, Olga, recorded in the *Russian Primary Chronicle* mentions a number of important goods traded in the lower Danube region, but there is no word about salt.[59] Moreover, the scarcity of Byzantine coins or artifacts from Transylvanian assemblages makes the idea of trade with

Transylvanian salt between Hungary and Byzantium very unlikely. The only tenth-century Byzantine artifact found in the salt mine district is the pectoral reliquary cross from Dăbâca. The cross may be associated with the presence of Christians of the Eastern rite, but is no indication of trade with Byzantium.[60]

The distribution of the earliest Magyar finds in Transylvania has been interpreted as indicating that the Magyar raids came from the northwest, through the Porțile Meseșului pass. Finds from Alba Iulia and Blandiana have been explained in terms of another raid, beginning in Cluj and moving along the middle course of the Mureș River, during a second phase of conquest, in which the main target may have been the Bulgarian march in southern Transylvania.

Gepids, Avars, Bulgarians, and Magyars were all interested in the rich salt mines of Transylvania. All established power centers outside the region but expanded into Transylvania because of the need to control shipments of salt for Western regions. Control, however, was established only at a few strategic points, not over the entire region. At all times, the garrisons left in Transylvania maintained contacts with the main centers of power in Pannonia, along the Mureș and Someș Rivers. Only Bulgarians seem to have used the passes across the Transylvanian Alps (southern Carpathian Mountains) to establish contacts with the lower Danube region. Control over the rich salt resources of Transylvania also offered an opportunity for the rise of local forms of military organization, most probably established by small Romanian and Slavic forces during the ninth century in the northwest. The first medieval polities in Transylvania thus emerged in reaction to specific economic and military circumstances.[61]

NOTES

This chapter is a much expanded version of a preliminary essay published in *Ephemeris Napocensis* 11 (2001): 271–84 under the title "Salt trade and warfare in early medieval Transylvania."

1. Géza Kovach, "Date cu privire la transportul sării pe Mureș în secolele X–XIII," *Ziridava* 12 (1980): 193; Cornelia Măluțan, "Drumurile sării din nord-vestul Transilvaniei," *Acta Musei Porolissensis* 8 (1984): 249–50. The Roman civilian settlements from Turda (*Potaissa*), Sic, Cojocna, Ocna Mureșului (*Salinae*), and Ocna Sibiului developed in relation to the extraction of salt.

2. For a map of salt resources in Transylvania, see Mircea Rusu, "Avars, Slavs, Romanic population in the 6th–8th centuries," in *Relations between the Autochthonous Population and the Migratory Populations on the Territory of Romania*, ed. Miron Constantinescu, Ștefan Pascu, and Petre Diaconu (Bucharest, 1975), 146 fig. 4.

3. Kovach, "Date cu privire la transportul sării," 193–98; Petre Iambor, "Drumuri și vămi ale sării din Transilvania în perioada feudalismului timpuriu," *Acta Musei Napocensis* 19 (1982): 75–85; Măluțan, "Drumurile sării," 249–55; Victor Spinei, "Migrația

ungurilor în spaţiul carpato-dunărean şi contactele lor cu românii în secolele IX–X," *Arheologia Moldovei* 13 (1990): 144.

4. Nicolae Drăganu, *Românii în veacurile IX–XIV pe baza toponimiei şi onomasticei* (Bucharest, 1933), 445.

5. Rusu, "Avars, Slavs," 145; Spinei, "Migraţia ungurilor," 145.

6. Kurt Horedt, "The Gepidae, the Avars, and the Romanic population in Transylvania," in *Relations between the Autochthonous Population and the Migratory Populations on the Territory of Romania*, ed. Miron Constantinescu, Ştefan Pascu, and Petre Diaconu (Bucharest, 1975), 119–20; Kurt Horedt, *Siebenbürgen im Frühmittelalter* (Bonn, 1986), 29–36, 66–72; Walter Pohl, *Die Awaren: Ein Steppenvolk im Mitteleuropa 567–822 n. Chr.* (Munich, 1988), 230. The Ocna Sibiului cemetery has not yet been published (personal communication from Radu Harhoiu).

7. Ioan Stanciu, "Teritoriul nord-vestic al României şi khaganatul avar," *Acta Musei Porolissensis* 23 (2000): 403–51; Călin Cosma, *Vestul şi nord-vestul României în secolele VIII–X d. H.* (Cluj-Napoca, 2002), 57–80.

8. Horedt, *Siebenbürgen*, 76–87; István Bóna, "Siebenbürgen im mittelalterlichen Königreich Ungarn: Zeit des ungarischen-slawischen Zusammenlebens (895–1172)," in *Kurze Geschichte Siebenbürgens*, ed. Béla Köpeczi (Budapest, 1990), 127–36; Radu Heitel, "Die Archäologie der ersten und zweiten Phase des Eindringens der Ungarn in das innerkarpatische Transilvanien," *Dacia* 38–39 (1994–95), 411–27.

9. A hoard with the last coin minted for Emperor Heraclius was long believed to have been found at Vădaş (Mureş County). Attila Kiss, in "Goldfunde des Karpatenbeckens vom 5–10. Jahrhundert (Angaben zu den Vergleichsmöglichkeiten der schriftlichen und archäologischen Quellen)," *Acta Archaeologica Academiae Scientiarum Hungaricae* 38 (1986): 121, has shown that the information about this hoard has been wrongly published and that the hoard in question included only Republican denarii. For the solidus minted for Constantine IV and found in Odorheiul Secuiesc, see Péter Somogyi, *Byzantinische Fundmünzen der Awarenzeit* (Innsbruck, 1997), 68.

10. A. Diaconescu, "Lămpi romane târzii şi paleobizantine din fosta provincie Dacia," *Ephemeris Napocensis* 5 (1995): 255–99; Alexandru Madgearu, *Rolul creştinismului în formarea poporului român* (Bucharest, 2001), 78–79; V. Moga, "Observaţii asupra unor piese paleocreştine inedite," *Apulum* 37 (2000): 429–35.

11. Simion Mehedinţi, *Ce este Transilvania?* (Bucharest, 1940), 26–31; Emil Petrovici, "Transilvania, vatră lingvistică a românismului nord-dunărean," *Transilvania* 72, no. 2 (1941): 102–6; Georg Reichenkron, "Die Entstehung des Rumänentums nach den neuesten Forschungen," *Südost-Forschungen* 22 (1963): 61–77.

12. Constantin Cihodaru, "Vechi toponime din Transilvania: Reflexe ale continuităţii populaţiei băştinaşe romanizate în regiunile nord-dunărene," *Analele ştiinţifice ale Universităţii "Al. I. Cuza"* 34 (1988): 41–42; Alexandru Madgearu, *Românii în opera Notarului Anonim* (Cluj-Napoca, 2001), 196–97.

13. C. Rişcuţia, "Etnoantropologie prin investigarea complementară a populaţiilor vechi şi actuale (Aplicare în cercetarea antropologică a românilor din Munţii Apuseni)," *Ziridava* 12 (1980): 63–69.

14. Ioan Stanciu, "Despre ceramica medievală timpurie de uz comun, lucrată la roata rapidă, în aşezările de pe teritoriul României (secolele VIII–X)," *Arheologia medievală* 3 (2000): 127–91. See also Zoltán Székely, "Aşezări din secolele VII–VIII în bazinul superior al Tîrnavei Mari," *Studii şi cercetări de istorie veche şi arheologie* 39 (1988): 171–78, 183–88;

Gheorghe Baltag, "Așezarea de la Albești-Sighișoara: Elemente inedite în cultura materială din sec. IX–X," *Revista Bistriței* 8 (1994): 76–77; Ioan Stanciu and Alexandru V. Matei, "Sondajele din așezarea prefeudală de la Popeni-Cuceu, jud. Sălaj: Câteva considerații cu privire la ceramica prefeudală din Transilvania," *Acta Musei Porolissensis* 18 (1994): 142–46; Mihai Bărbulescu, *Potaissa: Studiu monografic* (Turda, 1994), 183.

15. Mircea Rusu, "Notes sur les relations culturelles entre les Slaves et la population romane de Transylvanie (VI-e–X-e siècles)," in *Slavianite i sredizemnomorskiiat sviat VI–XI vek. Mezhdunaroden simpozium po slavianska arkheologiia, Sofiia, 23–29 april 1970,* ed. Stamen Mikhailov, Sonia Georgieva, and Penka Gakeva (Sofia, 1973), 196–97; Horedt, *Siebenbürgen,* 60–66; Vasile Moga and Horia Ciugudean, *Repertoriul arheologic al județului Alba* (Alba Iulia, 1995), 56, 100, 193, 196; Gheorghe Anghel, "Necropola birituală prefeudală de la Ghirbom (Gruiul Fierului)," *Apulum* 34 (1997): 270; Mihai Blăjan and Dan Botezatu, "Studiul arheologic și antropologic al mormintelor de incinerație prefeudale (secolul VIII) de la Alba Iulia-'Stația de salvare,'" *Apulum* 37 (2000): 453–70.

16. Dardu Nicolaescu-Plopșor and Wanda Wolska, *Elemente de demografie și ritual funerar la populațiile vechi din România* (Bucharest, 1975), 165–248; Dumitru Protase and Mihai Blăjan, "Ocna Sibiului," in *Cronica cercetărilor arheologice: Campania 1998* (Vaslui, 1999), 74–75; Wanda Wolska, "Die biologische Dynamik der Bevölkerungen des 8.–10. Jhs. auf dem Gebiet des heutigen Rumäniens," in *Transsilvanica: Archäologische Untersuchungen zur älteren Geschichte des südöstlichen Mitteleuropa; Gedenkschrift für Kurt Horedt,* ed. Nikolaus G. O. Boroffka and Tudor Soroceanu (Rahden, 1999), 349.

17. Ioan Paul, Ion Glodariu, Eugen Iaroslavschi, et al., "Șantierul arheologic Șura Mică (jud. Sibiu): Raport preliminar (1976–1978)," *Studii și comunicări (Sibiu)* 21 (1981): 46; Székely, "Așezări din secolele VII–VIII," 171; Alexandru Madgearu, "Pinteni datați în secolele VIII–IX descoperiți în jumătatea de sud a Transilvaniei," *Mousaios* 4 (1994): 155; Zeno Pinter, "Im Miereschtal entdeckte Bewaffnungsstücke und Teile militärischen Ausrüstung karolingischer Herkunft," *Arheologia medievală* 2 (1998): 151. However, it is also possible that the Medișoru Mare specimen belongs to the Dacian (Iron Age) phase of occupation identified on the same site, not to the seventh- or eighth-century settlement.

18. Madgearu, "Pinteni datați," 156–57.

19. See Rusu, "Notes sur les relations culturelles," 196.

20. Two settlement finds are known from Stärmen and Odărtsi; another was found in a mass burial in Kiulevcha. See Madgearu, "Pinteni datați," 153.

21. See Adrian Canache and Florin Curta, "Depozite de unelte și arme medievale timpurii de pe teritoriul României," *Mousaios* 4 (1994): 179–221.

22. Dan Gh. Teodor, *Continuitatea populației autohtone la est de Carpați: Așezările din secolele VI–XI e.n. de la Dodești-Vaslui* (Iași, 1984), 108, 114, 116, and fig. 62.2.

23. There are no signs of post-Roman habitation in Alba Iulia, on the site of the Roman camp of Apulum. The camp was reused for military purposes at a much later date. See Moga and Ciugudean, *Repertoriul arheologic,* 36–43.

24. Horedt, *Siebenbürgen,* 75–76, 185; Pohl, *Die Awaren,* 327; István Bóna, "Völkerwanderung und Frühmittelalter (271–895)," in *Kurze Geschichte Siebenbürgens,* ed. Béla Köpeczi (Budapest, 1990), 102–6.

25. The prisoners taken from Adrianople in 813 were moved into this region. They were able to escape in 839 with the assistance of the Byzantine fleet, but under their own appointed leaders.

26. A. Grecu, "Bulgaria în nordul Dunării în veacurile IX şi X," *Studii şi cercetări de istorie medie* 1 (1950): 226–28; Maria Comşa, "Die bulgarische Herrschaft nördlich der Donau während des IX. und X. Jhs. im Lichte der archäologische Forschung," *Dacia* 4 (1960): 401–2; Maria Comsa, "Contribuţii arheologice privind existenţa unor cnezate şi stabilirea unui drum comercial între Carpaţi şi Dunăre în sec. IX–X," *Muzeul Naţional* 6 (1982): 143–46; Stelian Brezeanu, "'La Bulgarie d'au-delà de l'Ister' à la lumière des sources écrites," *Etudes Balkaniques* 20 (1984): 121–28; Maria Comşa, "Un drum care lega ţinutul Vrancei de Dunăre şi existenţa unui cnezat pe valea Putnei în secolele IX–X," *Studii şi comunicări (Focşani)* 5–7 (1987): 39–44; Dan Gh. Teodor, "Quelques aspects concernant les relations entre Roumains, Byzantins et Bulgares au IX-e–X-e siècles," *Anuarul Institutului de Istorie şi Arheologie* 24 (1987): 9–15; Florin Curta, "Blacksmiths, warriors, and tournaments of value: Dating and interpreting early medieval hoards of iron implements in Eastern Europe," *Ephemeris Napocensis* 7 (1997): 250.

27. Mihai Blăjan and Al. Popa, "Cercetări arheologice de la Alba Iulia 'Staţia de salvare,'" *Materiale şi cercetări arheologice* 15 (1983): 375–80; Radu Heitel, "Unele consideraţii privind civilizaţia din bazinul carpatic în cursul celei de a doua jumătăţi a sec. IX în lumina izvoarelor arheologice," *Studii şi cercetări de istorie veche şi arheologie* 34 (1983): 100–113; Horedt, *Siebenbürgen*, 75, 78; Moga and Ciugudean, *Repertoriul arheologic*, 37, 43; Heitel, "Die Archäologie der ersten und zweiten Phase," 407–8.

28. Kurt Horedt, "Ceramica slavă din Transilvania," *Studii şi cercetări de istorie veche* 2 (1951): 192–94; Ioan Al. Aldea and Horia Ciugudean, "Noi descoperiri feudale timpurii la Blandiana (jud. Alba)," *Apulum* 19 (1981): 145–49; Horedt, *Siebenbürgen*, 75–76; Gheorghe Anghel and Horia Ciugudean, "Cimitirul feudal timpuriu de la Blandiana (judeţul Alba)," *Apulum* 24 (1987): 179–96; Moga and Ciugudean, *Repertoriul arheologic*, 60; Heitel, "Die Archäologie der ersten und zweiten Phase," 407.

29. Heitel, "Unele consideraţii," 104; Heitel, "Die Archäologie der ersten und zweiten Phase," 415; Moga and Ciugudean, *Repertoriul arheologic*, 80–81.

30. Comşa, "Die bulgarische Herrschaft," 411; Bóna, "Völkerwanderung und Frühmittelalter," 103–4; Moga and Ciugudean, *Repertoriul arheologic*, 173.

31. Horedt, "Ceramica slavă," 202–3; Heitel, "Unele consideraţii," 105; Horedt, *Siebenbürgen*, 75; Moga and Ciugudean, *Repertoriul arheologic*, 167; N. M. Simina, "Consideraţii asupra mormintelor medievale timpurii descoperite în anul 1865 la Sebeş (jud. Alba)," *Arheologia Medievală* 4 (2002): 47–58.

32. Zoltán Székely, "L'aspect de la culture materielle des VIII-e–X-e siècles dans le sud-est de la Transylvanie," *Mitteilungen des archäologischen Instituts der ungarischen Akademie der Wissenschaften* 1 (1972): 127–28; "Aşezări din secolele VI–XI p. Ch. în bazinul Oltului superior," *Studii şi cercetări de istorie veche şi arheologie* 43 (1992): 271, 278, 290, 294.

33. Comşa, "Die bulgarische Herrschaft," 408–15; Rusu, "Notes sur les relations culturelles," 198; Horedt, *Siebenbürgen*, 75–76, 185; Bóna, "Völkerwanderung und Frühmittelalter," 102–6; Csanád Bálint, *Südungarn im 10. Jahrhundert* (Budapest, 1991), 100.

34. Heitel, "Unele consideraţii," 100–103; Heitel, "Die Archäologie der ersten und zweiten Phase," 407; Moga and Ciugudean, *Repertoriul arheologic*, 36–38, 43.

35. For instance, see Heitel, "Unele consideraţii," 102; Heitel, "Die Archäologie der ersten und zweiten Phase," 417, 427; Horia Ciugudean, *Catalogul expoziţiei Anul 1000 la Alba Iulia: Între istorie şi arheologie* (Alba Iulia, 1996), 3. See also Márta Font's contribution to the present volume (chap. 11).

36. Bálint, *Südungarn,* 120; Madgearu, *Românii,* 132–33. The only apparent exception is the pectoral cross from Dăbâca, which may well be dated to the eleventh century. See Nicolae Gudea and C. Cosma, "Crucea-relicvar descoperită la Dăbîca: Considerații privind tipologia și cronologia crucilor-relicvar bizantine din bronz, cu figuri în relief, descoperite pe teritoriul României," *Ephemeris Napocensis* 8 (1998): 273–303.

37. A. Dankanits and István Ferenczi, "Săpăturile arheologice de la Ciumbrud (r. Aiud, reg. Cluj)," *Materiale și cercetări arheologice* 6 (1960): 605–15.

38. Comșa, "Die bulgarische Herrschaft," 419; Rusu, "Notes sur les relations culturelles," 200; Heitel, "Unele considerații," 106, 113; Horedt, *Siebenbürgen,* 78, 80; Uwe Fiedler, *Studien zu Gräberfeldern des 6. bis 9. Jahrhunderts an der unteren Donau* (Bonn, 1992), 180; Heitel, "Die Archäologie der ersten und zweiten Phase," 408, 427; Zeno Pinter and Nikolaus Boroffka, "Neue mittelalterliche Gräber der Ciumbrud Gruppe aus Broos/Orăștie, Fundstelle Böhmerberg/Dealul Pemilor X8." In *Transsilvanica: Archäologische Untersuchungen zur älteren Geschichte des südöstlichen Mitteleuropa: Gedenkschrift für Kurt Horedt,* ed. Nikolaus G. O. Boroffka and Tudor Soroceanu (Rahden, 1999), 327; Stanciu, "Despre ceramica medievală timpurie," 148. In this context, "Moravia" should be understood as the region along the Morava River in present-day Slovakia.

39. Ciugudean, *Catalogul expoziției,* 8; Sabin Adrian Luca and Zeno-Karl Pinter, *Der Bömerberg bei Broos/Orăștie: Eine archäologische Monographie* (Sibiu, 2001), 107 and pl. 65.2, 3, 6–8.

40. Oana Damian, "Despre un atelier de confecționat piese de plumb de la Păcuiul lui Soare," *Pontica* 25 (1992): 309–21. Two other specimens were found in grave 26 of the Alba Iulia-Stația de Salvare cemetery (Ciugudean, *Catalogul expoziției,* 12, no. 17) and in Orăștie (Pinter and Boroffka, "Neue mittelalterliche Gräber," 326 and fig. 7.7), respectively.

41. I. G. Russu and I. Ferenczi, "Cimitirul de la Ciumbrud (sec. X)," *Articole și lucrări științifice,* 1959, 3–16.

42. Pinter and Boroffka, "Neue mittelalterliche Gräber," 313–30; Luca and Pinter, *Der Bömerberg,* 98–114.

43. Bóna, "Völkerwanderung und Frühmittelalter," 104–6.

44. Eugen Stoicovici and Mihai Blajan, "Cercetări arheologice în cimitirul din sec. VIII e.n. de la Ghirbom-'Gruiul Măciuliilor' (jud. Alba)," *Apulum* 20 (1982): 139–54; Moga and Ciugudean, *Repertoriul arheologic,* 100; Heitel, "Die Archäologie der ersten und zweiten Phase," 410; Anghel, "Necropola birituală prefeudală," 270.

45. *Annales Fuldenses,* ed. by G. H. Pertz (Hannover, 1826; reprint Stuttgart and New York, 1963) 1:408. See also Grecu, "Bulgaria în nordul Dunării," 229–30; Peter Ratkoš, "Die großmährische Slawen und Magyaren," *Studijné zvesti* 16 (1968): 196–98; Teodor, "Quelques aspects," 4; Pinter, "Im Miereschtal entdeckte Bewaffnungsstücke," 150.

46. Horedt, *Siebenbürgen,* 74, 80, 185; Madgearu, "Pinteni datați," 154; Pinter, "Im Miereschtal entdeckte Bewaffnungsstücke," 150.

47. Thomas Nägler, "Cercetările din cetatea de la Breaza (Făgăraș)," *Studii și comunicări (Sibiu)* 14 (1969): 100–101; Madgearu, "Pinteni datați," 154.

48. Ștefan Pascu, Mircea Rusu, Petre Iambor, et al., "Cetatea Dăbîca," *Acta Musei Napocensis* 5 (1968): 177–78 and figs. 4.6, 4.9, 5.4–5.

49. Stanciu, "Despre ceramica medievală timpurie," 137, 155, and pl. IX.4–7.

50. Pinter, "Im Miereschtal entdeckte Bewaffnungsstücke," 145–50. It is unlikely that this was the grave of a Moravian horseman.

51. Bálint, *Südungarn,* 192, 208, and pls. LIII.b (16, 218, 235, 258), LXI.b (7–8); Călin

Cosma, "Morminte din secolele IX–X p.Ch. descoperite la Zalău (jud. Sălaj)," *Ephemeris Napocensis* 4 (1994): 323–29; Madgearu, "Pinteni dataţi," 160; Cosma, *Vestul,* 89–90.

52. László Kovács, *Münzen aus der ungarischen Landnahmezeit: Archäologische Untersuchungen der arabischen, byzantinischen, westeuropäischen und römischen Münzen aus dem Karpatenbecken des 10. Jahrhunderts* (Budapest, 1989), 51; Bálint, *Südungarn,* 102, 245, 265; Madgearu, "Pinteni dataţi," 159.

53. Kovács, *Münzen,* 47, 169.

54. Madgearu, *Românii,* 117–205.

55. Drăganu, *Românii în veacurile IX–XIV,* 427; Virgil Ciocâltan, "Observaţii referitoare la românii din Cronica Notarului Anonim al regelui Bela," *Revista de istorie* 40 (1987): 450; Madgearu, *Românii,* 135–40.

56. E. Szenpétery, ed., *Scriptores Rerum Hungaricarum,* vol. 1 (Budapest, 1937), 66. See also Gabriel Silagi, ed., *Die 'Gesta Hungarorum' des anonymen Notars: Die älteste Darstellung der ungarischen Geschichte* (Sigmaringen, 1991). For the ideology of *Gesta Hungarorum,* see László Veszprémy, "Gesta Hungarorum: The origins of national chronicles in the Middle Ages," in *Europe's Centre around A.D. 1000,* ed. Alfried Wieczorek and Hans-Martin Hinz (Stuttgart, 2000), 576–77. See also Spinei, "Migraţia ungurilor," 144.

57. E. Szenpétery, ed., *Scriptores Rerum Hungaricarum,* vol. 2 (Budapest, 1938), 489 (*Vita Sancti Gerardi,* chap. 10). Achtum's capital, Morisena (whose name is derived from that of the Mureş River and reflects the Romanian form *Morişana*), was located in a region of strategic importance for the salt trade, namely, the confluence of the Mureş and Tisza Rivers. Martin Eggers (*Das "Großmährische Reich": Realität oder Fiktion? Eine Neuinterpretation der Quellen zur Geschichte des mittleren Donauraumes im 9. Jahrhundert* [Stuttgart, 1995], 153–55) has advanced the idea that Morisena was the "city of Morava" mentioned in some ninth-century annals. However, this interpretation is unacceptable on several grounds. First—leaving aside the question of how much we can trust the Boba-Bowlus-Eggers theory about the exact location of Great Moravia—the difference between the names *Morisena* and *Morava* is just too important to be explained away by some scribal error or such. Second, the former name is clearly related to the name of the Mureş River (Maros), not the Morava. Recent research has identified the remains of the Greek monastery founded by Achtum within a fortress built on top of an old Roman camp and using its ramparts. See Petre Iambor, "Archaeological contributions to the study of the early medieval town of Cenad (Timiş County)," *Transylvanian Review* 10, no. 2 (2001): 98–111.

58. Paul Stephenson, *Byzantium's Balkan Frontier: A Political Study of the Northern Balkans, 900–1204* (Cambridge, 2000), 43–45.

59. S. Hazzard Cross and O. P. Sherbowitz-Wetzer, eds., *The Russian Primary Chronicle* (Cambridge, 1953), 86.

60. Gudea and Cosma, "Crucea-relicvar descoperită la Dăbîca," 273–83. Another pectoral cross was recently found in a tenth-century burial assemblage in Alba Iulia. It remains unclear whether this artifact is of Byzantine origin or of local production. See Mihai Blăjan, "Alba Iulia," in *Cronica cercetărilor arheologice: Campania 2001* (Buziaş, 2002), 33.

61. The archaeological and historical context of the interaction between these polities and the Hungarians has been recently examined by Florin Curta: see "Transylvania around A.D. 1000," in *Europe around the Year 1000,* ed. Przemysław Urbańczyk (Warsaw, 2001), 141–65.

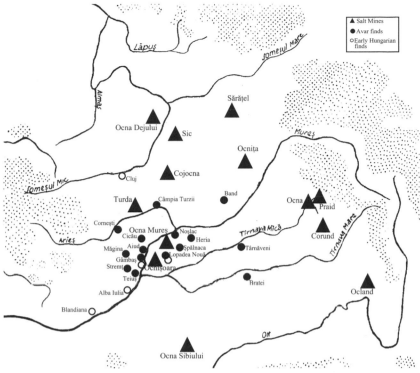

Fig. 3.1. Distribution of Avar and Magyar cemeteries in Transylvania

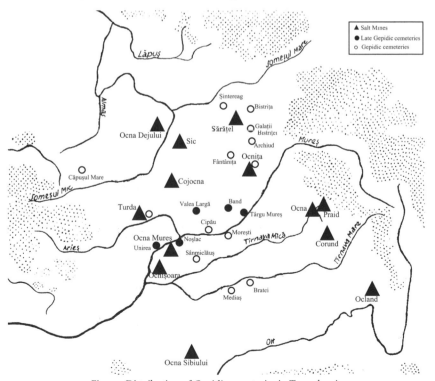

Fig. 3.2. Distribution of Gepidic cemeteries in Transylvania

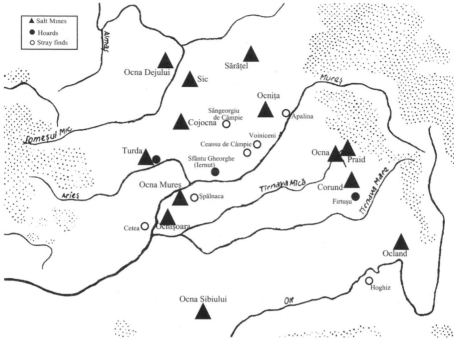

Fig. 3.3. Distribution of sixth- and seventh-century hoards (full circles) and single finds (circles) of gold coins in Transylvania: (1) Firtuşu (Harghita County; about three hundred coins, the latest being a solidus minted between 616 and 625); (2) Iernut (Mureş County; only two solidi preserved, minted in 527–65 and 602–10, respectively); (3) Turda (Cluj County; only two solidi preserved, both minted between 527 and 565); (4) Apalina-Reghin (Mureş County; solidus minted between 527 and 538, now lost); (5) Ceuaşu de Câmpie (Mureş County; solidus minted between 545 and 565); (6) Cetea (Alba County; solidus minted between 537 and 565); (7) Hoghiz (Braşov County; solidus minted between 582 and 602); (8) Sângeorgiu de Câmpie (Mureş County; solidus minted between 527 and 565); (9) Şomcuta Mare (Maramureş County; solidus minted between 555 and 565); (10) Şpălnaca (Alba County; solidus minted between 565 and 578 and found in grave 10, together with a knife and a spearhead); (11) Veţel (Hunedoara County; solidus minted between 527 and 565); (12) Voiniceni (Mureş County; solidus minted between 602 and 610); (13 and 14) unknown locations (Mureş County; two solidi minted in 545–65 and 582–602, respectively. Triangles represent salt mines

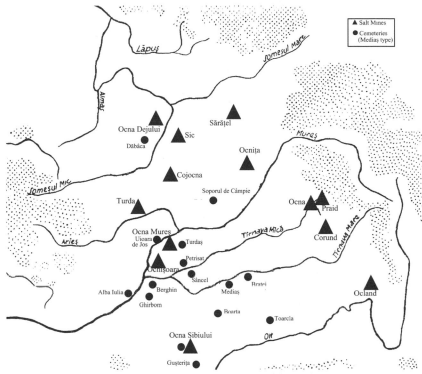

Fig. 3.4. Distribution of burial assemblages of the Mediaş group

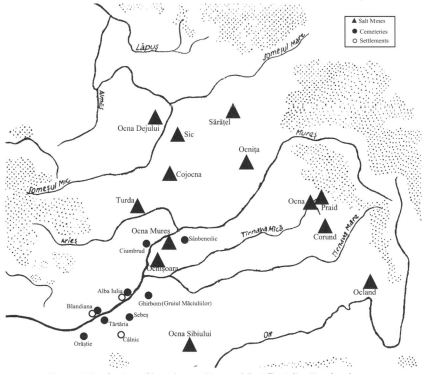

Fig. 3.5. Distribution of burial assemblages of the Alba Iulia-Ciumbrud group

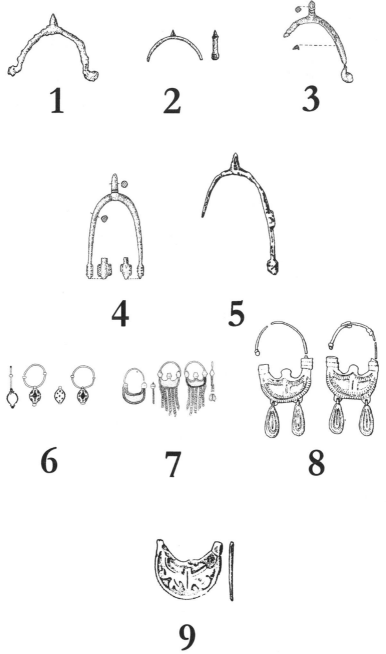

Fig. 3.6. Examples of ninth-century artifacts from Transylvania: spurs (1–5) and earrings (6–9). The find spots are (1) Medişoru Mare; (2) Şura Mică; (3) Breaza; (4) Tărtăria; (5) Iernut; (6) Ghirbom-Gruiul Fierului; (7) Ciumbrud; (8) Orăştie; (9) Zalău

Ladoga, Ryurik's Stronghold, and Novgorod: Fortifications and Power in Early Medieval Russia

Nikolai I. Petrov

There is very little information in medieval Russian chronicles[1] on Ryurik, the Scandinavian prince who came to northwestern Russia in 862 responding to the call of local tribes, or on his successor, Oleg. The archaeological record associated with this period and region cannot throw any light on these rulers, because it is typically anonymous. Archaeological excavations in the last ten years, however, added a significant amount of evidence directly pertaining to princely power in early Kievan Rus'. This is particularly true for excavations of forts and fortifications, or strongholds (*goroda*).

According to the entries in the Radzivil and Hypatian Chronicles under the years 862–64,[2] Ryurik's first residence was in Ladoga. Only later did he move his seat of power to Novgorod, a fort built not far from the source of the Volkhov River (fig. 4.1). The meaning of the place-name *Novgorod* in medieval Russian is "new fortifications";[3] the current meaning, "new town," appeared only later. As Evgenii Nosov persuasively demonstrated, Ryurik's Stronghold (so called only since the nineteenth century), a site located not far from modern-day Novgorod, was in fact the Novgorod known from chronicles as having been the scene of the ninth- and tenth-century history of northwestern Rus'.[4]

This general interpretation of the sequence of events is substantiated by the results of recent excavations. In the light of these investigations, the forts on the Volkhov River appear to mirror the development of princely power. In addition, the early medieval strongholds on the banks of the Volkhov were part of a larger network of settlements controlling the most important river segment of the trade route linking Scandinavia to the caliphate and to Byzantium. Along this waterway, strongholds were erected at key points, such as rapids or points of confluence.[5] Excavated fortifications also reflect different building techniques. The assumption that the most effective defenses in the region were associated with the power of the prince may assist us in identifying his residence.

Staraia Ladoga and Novgorod are mentioned in the chronicles as the princely residences. But what archaeological data can we consider to indicate the presence of social elites there? Scandinavian artifacts themselves may in any case signalize long-distance relations and even the presence of foreigners. However, "Viking" weapons or other artifacts of Scandinavian origin not only were incorporated into the so-called warrior retinue culture of Kievan Rus' but were viewed by the Rus' themselves as markers of high social status. A further indicator of the presence of elites is hoards of dirhams, such as those unearthed near Staraia Ladoga and Ryurik's Stronghold. Hoards of Arab silver were a means not only of storing wealth but also of showing off. A hoard of dirhams is known to have been found near the stronghold at Kholopy Gorodok (discussed later in this chapter),[6] a site without significant artifacts of Scandinavian origin. Ultimately, the most important indicator of the presence of elites are the strongholds themselves, as symbols of the political authority that mobilized the local population into building such fortifications and that controlled these nodal points at the crossroads of major trade routes.

According to the most recent interpretation of the stratigraphy at Staraia Ladoga, building phase VI, dated to 860–90 by means of dendrochronological analysis, coincides in time with Ryurik's alleged presence on the site.[7] This phase produced a number of Scandinavian artifacts, but Ryurik is to be associated only with the remains of one manor, for the site had no fortifications at that point in time (fig. 4.2). The ordinary character of this residence nicely dovetails with the idea that Ryurik stayed only briefly at Ladoga before moving to Novgorod in 864.

Ryurik's Stronghold is a much more sophisticated residence (fig. 4.3).[8] The central area enclosed by ramparts abounds in artifacts of Scandinavian origin (fig. 4.4).[9] Remains of fortifications surrounding this area came to light only during Evgenii Nosov's recent excavations.[10] In all probability, they can be dated to the second half of the ninth century and may thus be associated with either Ryurik or Oleg.[11] The remains consist of timber structures (fig. 4.5), evidently the rectangular timber frames forming the basis of the earthen rampart. Some of these timber remains may also represent traces of a palisade once surmounting the rampart or parts of a reinforcing structure built on the outside face of the rampart. The rampart itself seems to have been destroyed some time later, perhaps by dumping the soil into the adjacent ditch found next to the timber remains.

The existing evidence is difficult to interpret, but the timber framework may be viewed as supporting the earthen rampart at its base, a building technique most typical for early medieval fortifications in the Baltic region, especially in northern Germany and Poland (fig. 4.6).[12] The other, capelike part of the site is located outside the rampart and, like the fort itself, produced artifacts of Scandinavian origin, though not in quantities as significant as those for agricultural and craft tools (fig. 4.7.).[13] It is thus possible that this site operated as a production center and service settlement, perhaps inhabited by native Slavs.

It would be a gross mistake, however, to treat the fort's population (the princely retinue of warriors or his officials) a priori as Scandinavian and the population of the capelike part of the settlement as Slavic and exclusively dedicated to agriculture. The circumstances surrounding the arrival of Ryurik to northwestern Russia at the invitation of local chieftains suggests that local Slavs may well have been members of the princely retinue of warriors.

This situation is best illustrated by Evgenii Nosov's excavations at Kholopy Gorodok (the "slave stronghold").[14] The site was dated to the ninth century and is situated on a promontory separating Lake Kholop'ie from the Volkhov River. There are no fortifications and no artifacts of Scandinavian origin at Kholopy Gorodok. The presence of the local population, perhaps Slavs, is signalized by a hoard of agricultural implements (fig. 4.8). The pit in which the hoard was found may have served as a cellar to a timber house. If so, it may be interesting to note that the tools are represented in the hoard only by their metal parts, which seem to have been packed in a compact pile.[15]

Despite the absence of fortifications, Kholopy Gorodok coexisted with Ryurik's Stronghold, as part of the same settlement network controlling the valley of the Volkhov River. While Ryurik's Stronghold was designed to control the access to the point where the river splits into two branches (Volkhov proper and Volkhovec), Kholopy Gorodok was strategically located next to their point of confluence.

Evidence of another aspect of the ninth-century building techniques in use in northwestern Russia comes from recent excavations of the Liubsha stronghold near Ladoga. A drystone wall was found on the site, under the rampart (fig. 4.9).[16] The wall must have been used for defense at some point during the ninth century. Judging from the absence of wheel-made pottery remains from the rampart[17] (in sharp contrast to the presence of hand made pottery), the stone wall was no longer in use during the tenth century.

The evidence seems to suggest that the erection of the stone wall coincides in time with the presence of Scandinavians, an indication that the inspiration for this building technique may have originated in central or Western Europe. However, an important detail at this point is that the wall was already in disuse by the end of the ninth or the beginning of the tenth century, when it was completely covered with earth. The intention seems to have been to disable an effective fortification rampart and replace it with an earthen one. The precise reasons for this conversion remain obscure. It may be that returning to an earthen rampart had something to do with the presumed presence of native Slavs within the prince's retinue of warriors. The change may also signalize a difference of opinion between those who initially built the fort and those who ended up using it. The latter rebuilt the fort according to their idea of a most effective and, more important, habitual defense.

The end of the ninth century was an important period for the process of elaboration of local building techniques. In 882, after seizing Kiev, Prince Oleg began building strongholds throughout Rus'.[18] There is, however, very little archaeological evidence to confirm what we know from chronicles. To be sure, Anatolii Kirpichnikov hastily interpreted the drystone wall found in Staraia Ladoga (fig. 4.10) as the remains of one of Oleg's fortresses.[19] However, Nadezhda Stecenko has demonstrated that layers found near the rubble and containing fragments of handmade pottery of the ninth and tenth century were in secondary position, after being moved from much deeper deposition. This means that the drystone wall is that of the fortress erected in 1114, not that built in the 880s.[20]

In any case, fortifications erected presumably at the prince's initiative in northwestern Russia after 882 illustrate the development of building techniques in the region. If we are to believe the chroniclers, the Kievan princes between 882 and 947 paid very little attention to the northwestern region. In 947, Princess Olga launched a punitive expedition against the tribal elites between the Luga and the Msta Rivers.[21] Following this successful campaign, a number of forts were erected at Olga's orders. One of them is Gorodec in the Luga region (fig. 4.11), a fortification dated to the middle of the tenth century.[22] Because of its isolated location, Gorodec does not seem to have been in any way associated with the preexisting settlement pattern. Moreover, the fort produced another example of square timber frames designed to consolidate the rampart, like those at Ryurik's Stronghold. The same building technique was in use a century later in the Novgorod fortifications.

Novgorod ceased to be just the seat of princely power and began growing to the stature of a full-fledged town at the end of the tenth and in the early eleventh centuries. Following the conversion to Christianity in 989, a timber church dedicated to St. Sophia was built not at Ryurik's Stronghold but on the nearby territory, close to the manors of the local nobility erected in the early 900s. This foundation marks the beginning of a process of gradual transfer of political function from the prince's stronghold to the manors of the local elites. In the early eleventh century, during the reign of Yaroslav the Wise, the prince's residence was also moved into this area. At that same time, the rampart of Ryurik's Stronghold was dismantled and moved into the adjacent ditch. By 1044, a new fortification appeared at Detinec, on the opposite bank of the Volkhov River, on territory controlled by the local elites. In connection with this event, the name *Novgorod* (meaning "new stronghold") was transferred to the new location.[23]

Judging from the results of Sergei Troianovskii's recent excavations, the Detinec fort employed the same building techniques that had been used at Ryurik's Stronghold (fig. 4.12). Just as there, timber frameworks formed the base of the rampart, but it is also possible that they served as an independent fortification, much like the later timber defense walls.[24]

The way in which earthen and timber fortification techniques developed from the ninth to the eleventh centuries may indicate a "cultural compromise" between all parties involved in the construction of these forts—namely, customers, builders, and users. Initially, such buildings signalized the adaptation of the Scandinavian newcomers to the local conditions of the 800s. During the eleventh century, such forts were already symbols of the power of the Rus' state over the northwestern region.

It is perhaps revealing in this respect that the Detinec was built not on the site of the new seat of princely power but on the opposite bank of the Volkhov River. The process of moving the stronghold of Novgorod is in itself indicative of the process that led to the rise of a specific Novgorodian medieval state, one in which the prince had only executive authority, his power being checked by the assembly of patrimonial aristocrats, the *veche*. When Detinec was founded in 1044, another page had already turned in the history of medieval Novgorod.

NOTES

1. Most references in this chapter are to the critical editions of the Russian chronicles. To this day, only one of them was translated into English: see S. H. Cross and O. P. Shebowitz-Wetzor, trans., *The Russian Primary Chronicle: Laurentian Text* (Cambridge, Mass., 1953).

2. M. N. Tikhomirov, ed., *Polnoe sobranie russkikh letopisei*, vol. 2 (Moscow, 1962), 14; vol. 38 (Moscow, 1989), 16.

3. S. G. Bakhudarov, F. P. Filin, and D. N. Shmelev, *Slovar' russkogo iazyka XI–XVII vv.*, vol. 4 (Moscow, 1977), 90–91.

4. E. N. Nosov, *Novgorodskoe (Riurikovo) gorodishche* (Leningrad, 1990).

5. G. S. Lebedev, "On the early date of the way 'from the Varangians to the Greeks,'" in *Fenno-Ugri et Slavi*, ed. Edgren Torsten (Helsinki, 1980), 90–101; E. N. Nosov, "International trade routes and early urban centres in the North of Ancient Russia," in ibid., 49–62.

6. E. N. Nosov and A. V. Plokhov, "Kholopy Gorodok na Volkhove," in *Drevnosti Povolkhov'ia*, ed. A. N. Kirpichnikov and E. N. Nosov (St. Petersburg, 1997), 132.

7. S. L. Ku'zmin, "Iarusnaia stratigrafiia nizhnykh sloiov Staroladozhskogo gorodishcha," *Pamiatniki starini: Koncepcii, otkrytiia, versii* 1 (1997): 343–58; "Ladoga, le premier centre proto-urbain russe," in *Les centres proto-urbains russes entre Scandinavie, Byzance et Orient*, ed. M. Kazanski, A. Nercessian, and C. Zuckerman (Paris, 2000), 123–42.

8. E. N. Nosov, "Ryurik Gorodishche and the settlements to the north of Lake Ilmen," in *The Archaeology of Novgorod, Russia: Recent Results from the Town and Its Hinterland*, ed. Mark A. Brisbane (Lincoln, 1992), 5–66; "Rjurikovo gorodišče et Novgorod," in *Les centres proto-urbains russes entre Scandinavie, Byzance et Orient*, ed. M. Kazanski, A. Nercessian, and C. Zuckerman (Paris, 2000), 143–72.

9. See also E. N. Nosov, *Novgorodskoe (Riurikovo) gorodishche* (Leningrad, 1990), 90–146, 155–63.

10. My thanks to Professor Evgenii Nosov for a very useful discussion regarding the results of his 2000/1 excavations at Ryurik's Stronghold. I would also like to thank him for the permission to include in this chapter a photograph (fig. 4.5) from his still unpublished report on these excavations.

11. Nosov, *Novgorodskoe (Riurikovo) gorodishche*, 151–53; E. N. Nosov, T. S. Dorofeieva, K. A. Mikhailov, and I. Iansson, "Itogi izucheniia Riurikova gorodishcha v 1999 g.," *Novgorod i novgorodskaia zemlia: Istoriia i arkheologiia* 14 (2000): 38.

12. Joachim Herrmann and Werner Coblenz, "Burgen und Befestigungen," in *Die Slawen in Deutschland: Geschichte und Kultur der slawischen Stämme westlich von Oder und Neiße vom 6. bis 12. Jahrhundert*, ed. H. H. Bielfeldt and J. Herrmann (Berlin, 1985), 186–232.

13. Nosov, *Novgorodskoe (Riurikovo) gorodishche*, 37–89.

14. See Nosov and Plokhov, "Kholopy Gorodok na Volkhove," 129–52.

15. N. I. Petrov, "O kharaktere kontaktov etnosocial'nykh grupp naseleniia Povolkhoviia i Priil'men'ia v konce I tys. n. e.: Klad khoziaistvennykh orudii na gorodishche Kholopy Gorodok," in *Kul'turnye vzaimodeistviia v usloviiakh kontaktnykh zon. Tezisy konferencii molodykh uchenykh Sankt-Peterburga i SNG*, ed. V. N. Masson and D. G. Savvinov (St. Petersburg, 1997), 62–64.

16. E. A. Riabinin, "Otchet ob arkheologicheskikh issledovaniiakh v 1997 godu," (Institute for the History of Material Culture, Russian Academy of Sciences, St. Petersburg).

17. E. A. Riabinin, "Novye otkrytiia v Staroi Ladoge (itogi raskopok na Zemlianom gorodishche 1973–1975 gg.)," in *Srednevekovaia Ladoga: Novye otkrytiia i issledovaniia*, ed. V. V. Sedov (Leningrad, 1985), 37.

18. *Lavrent'ievskaia letopis'* (= *Laurentian Chronicle*), in *Polnoe sobranie russkikh letopisei*, ed. A. D. Koshelev, vol. 1 (Moscow, 1997), 23–24.

19. Anatolii N. Kirpichnikov, "Novootkrytaia Ladozhskaia kamennaia krepost' IX–X vv.," *Pamiatniki kul'tury: Novye otkrytiia* (1980): 441–55.

20. Nadezhda K. Stecenko, "Istoriia Ladozhskoi kreposti i problemi ee izucheniia," in *Divinec' Staroladozhskii: Mezhdisciplinarnye issledovaniia*, ed. Gleb S. Lebedev (St. Petersburg, 1997), 168–76.

21. *Lavrent'ievskaia letopis'*, 60.

22. Gleb S. Lebedev, "Der slawische Burgwall Gorodec bei Luga: Zum Problem der west- und ostslawischen Beziehungen," in *Beiträge zur Ur- und Frühgeschichte*, ed. Hans Kaufmann and Klaus Simon, vol. 2 (Berlin, 1982), 225–38; N. I. Zalevskaia, "K voprosu o vozniknovenii pogostov na Verkhnei Luge," in *Severnaia Rus' i ee sosedi v epokhu rannego srednevekov'ia: Mezhvuzovskii sbornik*, ed. A. D. Stoliar (Leningrad, 1982), 49–54.

23. Evgenii N. Nosov, "Novgorodskii detinec i gorodishche (k voprosu o rannykh ukrepleniiakh i stanovlenii goroda)," *Novgorodskii istoricheskii sbornik* 5 (1995): 5–17; N. I. Petrov, *Povolkhovye i il'menskoe poozer'e v IX–X vv. Uchebnoe posobie* (St. Petersburg, 1996), 74–81.

24. Sergei V. Troianovskii, "Istoriia izucheniia Novgorodskogo kremlia," *Novgorodskii istoricheskii sbornik* 5 (1995): 89–111; "O nekotorykh rezul'tatakh raskopok v Novgorodskom kremle v 1992–96 gg.," *Novgorod i novgorodskaia zemlia: Istoriia i arkheologiia* 12 (1998): 58–70. For the timber framework as the basis of the rampart, see also M. Kh. Aleshkovskii, "Novgorodskii detinec 1044–1430 gg. (po materialam novykh issledovanii)," *Arkhitekturnoe nasledstvo* 14 (1962): 3–26.

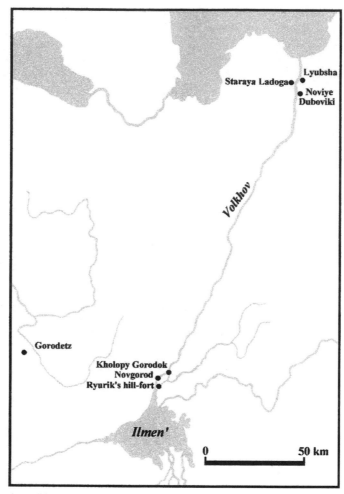

Fig. 4.1. The Volkhov region in the ninth and tenth century: strongholds and other important settlements

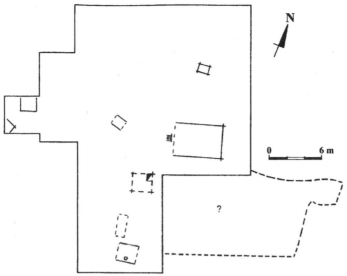

Fig. 4.2. Buildings of phase VI at Staraia Ladoga, ca. 860–90. (After Ku'zmin, "Iarusnaia strati-grafiia," 351.)

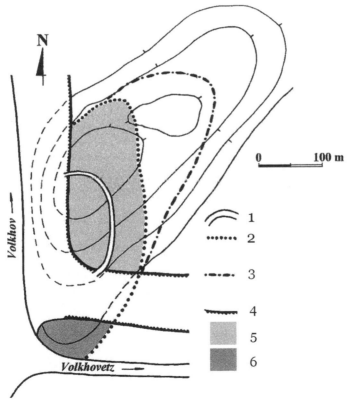

Fig. 4.3. Ryurik's Stronghold: (1) ditch; (2) boundary of the ninth- and tenth-century cultural layer; (3) probable extension of the ninth- and tenth-century occupation; (4) steep slopes of the present-day riverbank; (5) central section; (6) cape section. (After Nosov, *Novgorodskoe (Riurikovo) gorodishche*, 152.)

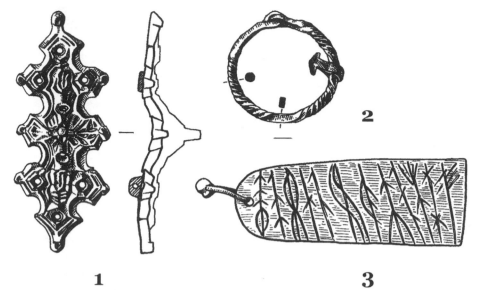

1 **2** **3**

Fig. 4.4. Artifacts of Scandinavian origin from Ryurik's Stronghold: (1) equal-armed brooch, copper-alloy; (2) torc with "Thor's hammer" pendant, iron; (3) pendant with Runic inscription, copper-alloy. (After Nosov, *Novgorodskoe (Riurikovo) gorodishche*, 122–24.)

Fig. 4.5. Timber fortification structures from Ryurik's Stronghold. (Source: Evgenii N. Nosov, "Otchet o polevykh arkheologicheskikh rabotakh Novgorodskoi oblastnoi ekspedicii v 2000 godu: KP-5304," [Institute for the History of Material Culture, Russian Academy of Sciences, St. Petersburg, 2001], fig. 44.)

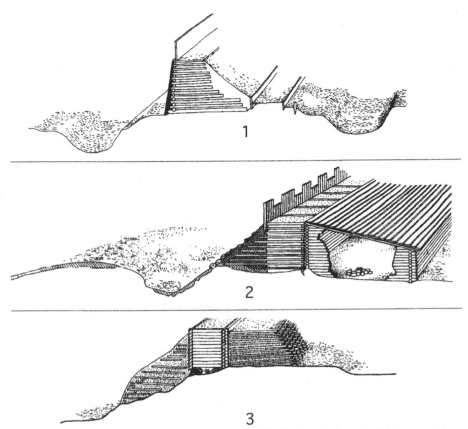

Fig. 4.6. Examples of timber and earth early medieval fortifications in the south Baltic region: (1) Brandenbrug (seventh century); (2) Schlossberg (seventh to eighth century); (3) Teterow (late tenth century). (After Herrmann and Coblenz, "Burgen und Befestigungen," 200, 202, 225.)

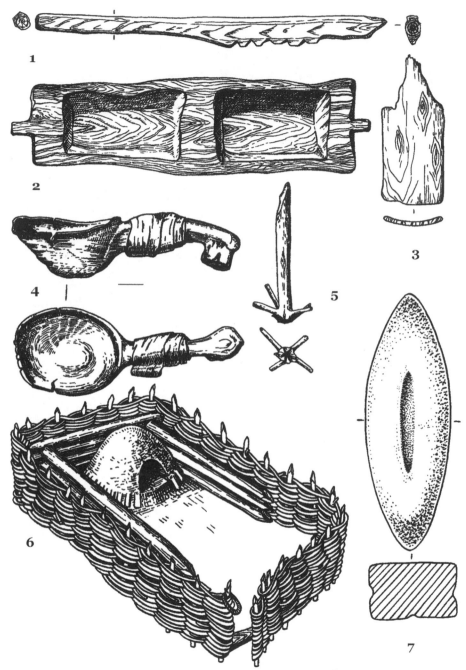

Fig. 4.7. Artifacts from the cape section of Ryurik's Stronghold: (1) wooden tool for the processing of flax; (2) wooden trough; (3) wooden shovel (for grain?); (4) wooden scoop; (5) wooden whisk; (6) reconstruction of the bread oven; (7) strike-a-light. (After Nosov, *Novgorodskoe (Riurikovo) gorodishche*, 56, 64–65, 67–68, 79.)

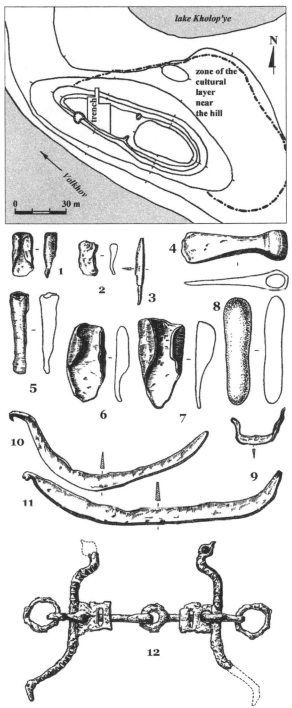

Fig. 4.8. Settlement plan of Kholopy Gorodok and hoard of iron implements found there: (1) mattock; (2) wedge; (3) knife; (4) axe; (5) adze (?); (6 and 7) plowshares (?); (8) whetstone; (9) scraper; (10 and 11) scythes; (12) bridle bit with damascened side bars. (After Nosov, *Novgorodskoe (Riurikovo) gorodishche*, 179–81.)

Fig. 4.9. Drystone wall under the earth rampart at Liubsha

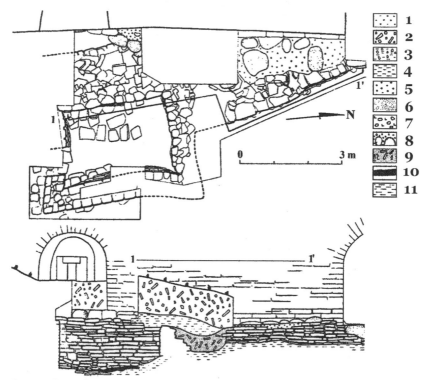

Fig. 4.10. Plan and section profile of the drystone wall at Staraia Ladoga: (1–8) twelfth- to nineteenth-century layers; (9) ruins of the late ninth- or tenth-century wall; (10) late ninth- and tenth-century cultural layer; (11) clay bed. (After Kirpichnikov, "Novootkrytaia Ladozhskaia kamennaia krepost'," 444.)

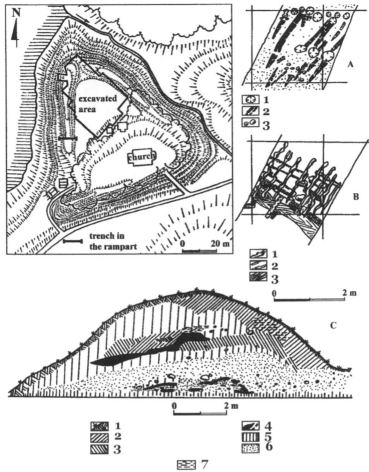

Fig. 4.11. General plan of Gorodec: (A) plan detail (1—pit; 2—charred wood; 3—stones); (B) timber framework under the rampart (1—upper level; 2—middle level; 3—lower level of logs); (C) rampart, section profile (1—turf; 2–cultural layer mixed with sand, 3—cultural layer; 4—charred wood; 5—clayey layer; 6—sand); 6—ashes.

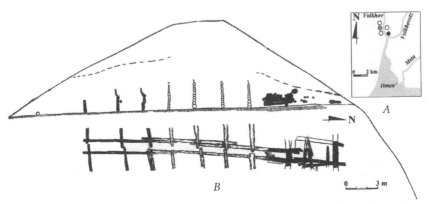

Fig. 4.12. (A) Distribution of sites in the Novgorod region (○ = manors of the tribal nobility; ● = Ryurik's Stronghold; ⊕ = Detinec). (B) Plan and section profile of the eleventh-century rampart with timber framework at Detinec.

PART TWO

The Rise of the State

CHAPTER FIVE

Early State Formation in East Central Europe

Przemysław Urbańczyk

*P*opular representations of state origin and formation are often shaped by works of vulgarization and by school textbooks. As myths of national origins, these representations are important elements of group identity. This makes any attempt at their deconstruction or correction a rather tedious endeavor—with little, if any, rewards. Mythologized representations use political history as heroic epics, while placing ancient rulers in the pantheon of national heroes. Origin narratives and heroic deeds are particularly useful propaganda tools during periods of crisis, such as threats to or loss of statehood or proclamation of independence. Recalling ancient glory and stressing original ethnic unity—always defined in contrast with neighbors—can legitimize current political needs. Such phenomena are common in the history of modern Europe, especially in cases of sudden collapse of multinational states, such as Austria-Hungary, the Soviet Union, or Yugoslavia. In all these cases, the construction of the national past follows similar paths, despite local variation due to different geopolitical circumstances.

The national past was and still is an important source of arguments for political discourse and negotiation. Recalling the mythologized representation of the past embedded in collective consciousness can be a very effective means of mobilization in the name of contemporary political concerns. Since it is not the subject of direct and critical judgment, the past can thus be easily manipulated to reach political goals. This may explain the dynamics of the process of continuous imagining of the national past. Ever-changing ideas about how past events must have happened have a direct influence on the constant reinterpretation of the past, at least as important as that of the intellectual traditions within the disciplines dedicated to its study. Both the distant and the recent past are continually reimagined, as each generation seeks its own explanations and justifications for the conditions of the present.

In this chapter, I will examine changes in the representation of the past that are the direct result of changing historiographical premises—determinism versus chaotic developments, reason versus contingency, linear developments versus repetitions, continuity versus fragmentation, the decisive roles of individuals versus populations, symbols and ideological factors versus material infrastructure, and so on. Such polarized positions underpin the broad range of possible interpretations of the same set of historical data. This is particularly true for the interpretation of early medieval state formation, the topic of this chapter.

For over three decades, Polish historiography has been dominated by the version of events promoted by the late Henryk Łowmiański in his monumental work *Początki Polski* (The Origins of Poland), published between 1963 and 1985. Despite the several decades that have already passed, his concepts still dominate Polish historiography. The appealing power of his vision overwhelmingly influenced the way of thinking of the next generation of historians studying the origin of the state. Łowmiański described the historical process in broad strokes, using centuries as minimal units of analysis and emphasizing the "natural" sequence of changes deriving from one another. According to him, "better types of economy and intensification of production, changes in methods and forms of social and political organization, resulted in the rise of many Slavic states between the second half of the eighth and the late tenth centuries, covering a vast area between the Baltic Sea and the Ladoga River to the north to the Adriatic and Aegean Seas and the south Russian steppes to the south."[1] Łowmiański's main assumption was the "constructive reference to the achievement of positivist science"; his goals were to discover the "objective foundations and directions of social development"[2] and to describe the process of the gradual aggregation of Slavic societies in structures of superior organization, from "small tribes" to "large tribes" and "states."

There is much inconsistency in Łowmiański's line of reasoning. On one hand, he argued that the process of state formation was a direct result of "group social and political factors, themselves determined by suitable economic circumstances that made possible the rise of state bureaucracies and mobilized certain social forces."[3] On the other hand, he maintained that the ruler and the supporting political elites played the most important role in state formation.[4] Such uncertainties reflect Łowmiański's efforts to reach a compromise between two conflicting traditions within Polish historiography. One has its roots in the work of Joachim Lelewel, who emphasized the gradual disappearance of community powers, as a result of internal transformations.[5] The other, associated with Michał Bobrzyński, stressed the decisive role of internal conquest in enabling a prince "to gain unlimited power."[6] Łowmiański attempted to combine these contrasting interpretations and to give equal weight to the gradual and inevitable process leading to higher stages of political organization, on one hand, and the decisive role of political elites, on the other. The result lacked both coherence and consistency.

Polish historians have always treated the rise of the medieval state in "national" terms. Indeed, Łowmiański viewed the nation as "the constitutive power of the state and the decisive factor in political life, as well as the emanation of society in its politically conscious categories." In his estimation, the "nation" was formed on the basis of the ethnic group acting as a figurehead of the state, ready "to defend the state and to suffer for its prosperity."[7] The national-democratic ideology derived from the nineteenth-century idea of the "nation-state" is easily recognizable in such statements. An independent state was viewed as a sine qua non for the existence of a nation defined in political, not ethnic, terms. The state emerged from the nation and warranted its survival. It comes as no surprise, then, that Łowmiański focused on the "national" aspects of the state formation process and celebrated the "victory of the national idea over tribal feelings."[8] Despite many changes in geopolitical circumstances and internal situations, the patriotic-nationalistic sentiments are still present in discussions of the early medieval history in East Central Europe—especially in the new states of Belarus, Lithuania,[9] Slovakia,[10] and Ukraine. Moreover, this old attitude is still to be found in Czech,[11] Hungarian, or Polish historiography.[12]

The integration of the historical and archaeological evidence currently available requires a very different approach to changes taking place in the early Middle Ages in East Central Europe. More important, such an approach will have to incorporate recent developments in historical anthropology and sociology that de-emphasize the historical necessity of states and will have to shift the emphasis to sudden attempts at reorganizing society and the role of ideology for establishing new forms of political power. Indeed, the origins of East Central European medieval states, as institutionalized systems of centralized power within defined political borders, cannot be explained in terms of "objective" mechanisms of social development gradually leading to higher forms of social organization. The political activities of specific individuals directed toward the consolidation and stabilization of their own social position played a much more important role. Their political and organizational decisions triggered the process of state formation. Their intelligence and charisma, as well as favorable circumstances, secured the success of the political entities they created. At the same time, their success secured their place in history, for "losers" had no appeal to medieval chroniclers and their "linear" narratives of events leading directly to early states. Such narratives are particularly useful for establishing historical traditions of national consciousness, because they provide powerful explanations for group identity and origins. Historians, however, took such narrative strategies at face value, without questioning the inevitability of the events narrated.

Any historian dealing with the rise of the medieval state in Poland will be confronted with a dearth of written sources and with problematic archaeological evidence, which often lacks the chronological precision needed for historical reconstruction. To understand the process of state formation, historians need a much broader chronological perspective and a much wider geographical scope. Although particular states emerged at different times and in different circumstances, a comparative approach will no doubt bring to the fore the general factors leading to political reorganization in East Central Europe in the late 900s.

One may start with the extraordinary expansion of the early Slavic culture over vast areas of Europe during the sixth and seventh centuries. No unequivocal judgment is possible on the agelong controversy between advocates of the idea that the Slavs were native to the region between the Oder and the Dnieper River,[13] on one hand, and supporters of a migrationist model, on the other, the latter of whom place the Slavic homeland within a relatively small region between the Carpathian Mountains and the Dnieper River.[14] The former group of scholars stresses continuity in material culture and toponymy but often ignores the dramatic changes in population, particularly migrations. By focusing on the dissolution of the social and political structures in the central European regions of *barbaricum,* scholars of the other group tend to exaggerate the "demographic explosion" leading to the Slavic "colonization of an amazingly large part of the Continent."[15] The fierce opposition between these two interpretive models—based on settlement continuity and colonization, respectively—is ultimately the result of both a naive representation of the historical process and the inability to acknowledge continuity at a continental scale and radical demographic changes at the local level. The sudden expansion of the Slavic world cannot be explained on either cultural or demographic terms alone, because both forces may have been at work.[16] The analysis of historical, archaeological, and linguistic evidence indicates that the spread of the Slavic culture was much more extensive than the range of actual migration. The two phenomena, however, were intertwined, and their respective impact may have varied regionally.[17]

An explanation is needed, however, not only for how the Slavic culture spread but also for why such a simple, almost "primitive" culture was so successful. What made communities living so apart from each other within the vast region between the Dnieper, the Alps, the Baltic, and the Adriatic Sea accept an egalitarian model of social relations, a simple system of nonspecialized economy, and a new language? How can we explain the cultural uniformity that both archaeologists and linguists observed in areas of considerable cultural variation in earlier times? What was the reason for departure from the "Germanic" model of hierarchical organization, with its strong emphasis on military activities?

In my view, the collapse of Attila's multiethnic Hunnic Empire, which maintained some degree of political order beyond the northern frontier of the
Roman Empire, played an important role in this respect. Following the death of
that charismatic leader, many Germanic petty kings used the political vacuum
to create their own political niches that would enable them to reach their political ambitions. With their close followers organized as "migrating armies," they
crossed the Continent, fighting against each other and against Roman armies, as
well as looking for territories that would offer relative military safety and that
would support their retinues and hierarchical power structures. In the alliances
that were then formed (and easily broken), purely political goals were much
more important aspects than ethnic origin, religion, or previous political affiliation. The Slavs emerged in the sixth century as an important component of
this system of political entities, for they appear as taking part in the struggle between various Germanic rulers or in their conflicts with the Roman Empire.[18]

Continuous warfare, political instability, and interruption of economically
vital contacts with the Roman world proved to be an unbearable burden for the
settled, agricultural populations and resulted in an economic crisis, the signs of
which are clearly visible in archaeology. Prompted by the Lombard migration
to Italy, the Avars entered this complicated network in 568.[19] This new power
had not been previously engaged in local conflicts. It quickly subjugated almost
all communities in East Central Europe and imposed a new political and military peace. From the nomads' point of view, a key aspect of this policy was
gaining the support of the local population involved in the production of food
and the provision of military recruits. The survival of the Avar "empire" depended on such locally bound communities with loose political organization.
It is possible that the need to consolidate the economic infrastructure of this
"empire" was responsible for the sudden "promotion" of the Slavs, since they
may have already cooperated with the Avars during their stay north of the
Black Sea. Otherwise, it is hard to explain the fact that the Slavic expansion coincided in time with the years of Avar domination. Unlike the Huns, for whom
booty and the support of the military Germanic elites were the most important
elements of political control, the stable political organization of the Avar qaganate was based on the domination of the Slavic majority. The Hunnic Empire was a confederation of multiethnic retinues of warriors depending on nomadic elite to guarantee military victories and political privilege. By contrast,
the Avar qaganate was an Avaro-Slavic commonwealth politically dominated
by the nomads but economically reliant on the subjugated agriculturists. Both
ethnic groups depended on each other.[20]

A successful military expansion is a function of considerable military resources. Without some degree of cooperation of the subjects, however, stability

cannot be attained within a polity established by such means. It is possible that in both cases under consideration here, the Slavs played a decisive role, first as soldiers, then as farmers. Their relatively egalitarian social structure made it easier to accept "foreign" leaders,[21] and their flexible economic system could be adapted to practically any ecological niche. The Slavs thus appear as important partners for the Avars, who could not maintain their political control without the Slavs. The nomads controlled the ecological niche of the steppelike Hungarian Plain (Alföld), which was crucial for their predominantly pastoralist economy. Surrounding this niche was a zone of Slavic settlements, from which the Avars extracted tribute and military recruits. This zone was organized militarily, with new Slavic settlers being occasionally brought in; and a relatively uniform Slavic model of social and economic organization was imposed everywhere. Avar domination did not imply absolute control, which was logistically impossible. The Avar qaganate had no clearly defined borders, for it consisted of a nomadic core surrounded by a tributary zone, where political order was maintained by military means by the Avar elite. A permanent Avar presence in this zone was neither necessary nor possible, but the military control of the nomads may explain the relative scarcity of finds of weapons in Slavic areas.

The Avaro-Slavic commonwealth turned out to be a great success for both parties involved, despite their apparent conflict of interests. In the long term, however, this cooperation was more profitable to the Slavs, who managed to survive politically the collapse of the qaganate in the late 700s. Peter Brown concludes: "Solidly indifferent to imperial pretensions, . . . [the Slavs] signaled the end of an imperial order. . . . If they identified with an imperial system at all, it was the new nomad confederacy of the Avars."[22] The remarkable adaptation of the Slavs to almost any ecological niche made it possible for them to fill in the buffer zone between powers in conflict.[23] Culturally, the Slavs absorbed the Bulgars, who conquered the lower Danube region in 680/1 but underwent a process of Slavicization during the subsequent two centuries. Ambitious Slavic leaders raised armies that supported the Avars, the Byzantines, and even the Arabs.

It is possible that the Slavs were also responsible, at least in part, for the eventual collapse of the qaganate of the Avars. That the latter also underwent gradual Slavicization is indicated by finds of the so-called Avaro-Slavic culture on the northern border of the Carpathian Basin. This is most likely the area in which Samo, a Frankish merchant, organized the "sons born to the Huns [i.e., Avars] by the Slavs' wives and daughters"[24] into an army capable of defeating, between 631 and 636, both the Avars and the Franks. In this particular area, the Avars abandoned both their mobility and their capability of immediate military action. Soon after their defeat in 803, the Avars completely disappeared from the European stage, only to be replaced by Slavic polities that filled the political vacuum created between the two early medieval superpowers, the Frankish and Byzantine Empires.

The defeat of the Avars also removed the main source of political control within surrounding Slavic societies, which had used and contributed to its profoundly "egalitarian" organization imposed to prevent the concentration of power in the hands of Slavic leaders. Although initially profitable for both sides, the Avar political and military system precluded the social and economic development of Slavic communities in the late eighth century. Therefore, it is possible that the Avars had no Slavic allies in their last and decisive confrontation with the Franks, because the Slavs may have seen this as a good opportunity to gain the political control they did not have within the qaganate.[25] Indeed, a process of internal stratification of Slavic society rapidly followed the collapse of the Avar qaganate, which caused the rise of local polities. This process is clearly visible in those areas of mixed Avar and Slavic traditions, in which, most likely, elites were more accustomed to mechanisms of political control inherited from the Avars. Such elites are recognizable in archaeological finds of the so-called Blatnica-Mikulčice group. These elites may have been responsible for Charlemagne's failure to reorganize the qaganate as a Christian state.[26]

By 822, Frankish sources speak of the existence of "princes" in Moravia.[27] Their number and relative importance remain unknown, for the annals only record the final victory of one of them, Moimir (Moimarus), against Pribina. The former expelled the latter form Nitra in 833[28] and thus laid the foundations of the Great Moravian state. Moimir's successor, Rostislav (Rastic, 846–70), took advantage of the increasing tensions between his neighbors. Although he had come to power with the support of Emperor Louis the German,[29] Rostislav eventually turned to the Byzantine emperor Michael III, demanding "a bishop and a teacher" to be sent to Moravia. This remarkable example of negotiating a position of power between powerful neighbors came to a sharp end in 906, as Great Moravia was destroyed by the Magyars.

The process of state formation in Bohemia, an area closer to the Carolingian Empire, was somewhat longer. Charlemagne had invaded the region in 805, when he killed "their duke named Lech."[30] Such interventions, however, did not prevent the concentration of power, stimulated, as it was, by similar developments in neighboring regions. The exact sequence of events is unclear, but the number of claimants to supreme power mentioned in written sources diminishes drastically after the middle of the ninth century. In 845, fourteen Bohemian "princes" received baptism.[31] In 872, only five princes are mentioned as opposing Carloman's invasion.[32] One of them, Bořivoj, a member of the founding Přemyslid family, accepted baptism from St. Methodius in 874 or 884.[33] By 895, there were only two princes left.[34] Finally, in 921, Wenceslas alone assumed supreme power, which had been kept until then by one dynasty—the Přemyslids.

Very little is known about the situation north of the Carpathian Mountains, in present-day Poland. This territory was beyond the range of interest of early medieval chroniclers. The earliest source available, the work of the so-called Bavarian Geographer, written at the court of Emperor Louis the German in ca. 848, exhibits only limited knowledge of the area beyond the eastern frontiers of the empire. However, this source suggests that the centralization of power had already begun in this region, as confirmed by the archaeological evidence of strongholds built since the mid-ninth century. Large mounds erected in southeastern Poland (Sandomierz, Cracow, Przemyśl) also indicate the presence of elites eager to represent symbolically their position of power.[35] No burials were found within these mounds, which may imply that they functioned as a material representation of the ability to mobilize labor forces. The probable date for this phenomenon is the late eighth or early ninth century, which coincides with the collapse of Avar power in the south.[36]

Similarly, strongholds that appear in great numbers after ca. 850 indicate a drastic reorganization of the social space, since open settlements now tended to cluster around the fortified residences of the new elites. As a material reflection of their power to mobilize society, these strongholds functioned as nodal points of social geography and as administrative centers that broke the uniform network of settlements into "cells."[37] The building of any such stronghold was a direct expression of the economic and demographic potential of the area and may have been an important reason for the mobilization of the local population. The traditional interpretation of these centers is therefore to be abandoned: the mid-ninth-century strongholds were not just residences of despotic leaders ruthlessly exploiting their subjects. Social developments seem to have been much more complex than that. Local leaders may indeed have been responsible for the building of these strongholds, but they also engaged in fierce political competition. With little economic resources and no fiscal instruments, such small political entities could not provide the necessary surplus for maintaining control at the center and acquiring enough "exotic" status symbols from the outside. Much more could be obtained by means of petty warfare and plundering raids or by forcing weaker neighbors into paying tribute. The war economy, however, encouraged competition, which in turn seems to have drastically reduced the number of competitors able to control large areas. Unfortunately, archaeology can do little to illuminate the exact sequence of events, since a change in power within any single stronghold cannot usually be observed archaeologically.

The first piece of evidence for this process is the *Life of St. Methodius*. According to its unknown author, "the powerful prince of Vislech" used to "harass Christians" (i.e., Moravians), before being defeated and forced to convert at some point between 874 and 880. The traditional interpretation of this account assumes the existence of a polity of the Vistulans, but no evidence supports such an assumption. The "prince" in question was probably one of many regional leaders on the northern or northeastern frontier of Great Moravia. Successful plundering raids were organized across that frontier, which advanced the leaders' positions of power both locally and at a regional scale. Most likely, violent competition for power was a common phenomenon for the entire area between the Baltic Sea and the Carpathian Mountains, and there is clear evidence of similar developments in the early 900s in different regions of Poland (Little Poland, Silesia, Great Poland, Mazovia, and Pomerania). At that time, the number of strongholds increased considerably, as such fortified settlements now clustered regionally. This suggests that within each region, the process of power centralization was on its way, with several kin groups in positions of considerable power that would enable them to submit the entire area between the sea, the mountains, and the Oder and Bug Rivers. Paradoxically, the region in which the earliest efforts toward unification were made produced no signs of extraordinary prosperity. The settlement network in Great Poland is no different from other regions, and no rich cemeteries have so far been found there.[38] Great Poland, however, had a particularly favorable position in geopolitical and military terms. Silesia provided the shield against any direct interventions from the Carolingian or Eastern Frankish Empires, Little Poland protected the region against any Rus' attacks, Pomerania absorbed much of the Scandinavian activity on the southern Baltic shore, and Mazovia blocked the access from Prussia. The elites in Great Poland thus succeeded because of geography, and the Piasts soon became a serious threat to all their neighbors.

As winners, the Piasts were presented from the onset as the rightful rulers, as suggested by the dynastic legend narrated by the early twelfth-century chronicler known as Gallus Anonymus. The story cannot be taken as a genuine *origo gentis,* but it offers a good description of the process of state formation. According to Gallus, at a time when "the Polish principality was not yet so large," Gniezno was ruled by a Prince Popiel, who had "very many noble men and friends." As he failed to provide for "the needs of his guests" (most probably in beer and meat), the obligation of generosity so typical for any successful leader was accomplished by a simple farmer named Piast. Therefore, Piast's son Semovit was elected prince of Poland ("after common approval"), and Popiel was expelled "together with his kin." Semovit "enlarged the borders of his principality" by military means, as did his successors Lestek and Semomysl. The latter, who used to gather his "earls and dukes" for sumptuous feasts and sought the advice of "elderly and wise men," ruled unchallenged for many years. His successor,

Mieszko, "invaded with great energy the lands of this neighbors" and eventually demanded the hand of "one good Christian woman from Bohemia." With her assistance, he "renounced the mistakes of paganism."[39]

This account is an excellent description of how military activities not only led to territorial expansion but also helped mobilize large numbers of people and provided the economic means for maintaining the political control of one single family. The Piasts, brought to the paramount position by disenchanted people, managed to stay in power by means of successful expeditions that produced both booty and the expansion of their domain. They still consulted with the members of the social elite, who were in no position, however, to check the power of the Piasts. Mieszko further consolidated his power when converting to Christianity in 966, as the new religion located the source of legitimacy for his regime outside the sphere of influence of the local elites. Mieszko's state was not yet "Poland." It was a Piast state, whose main goal was to promote Piast interests, with the assistance of the military aristocracy, taking advantage of the military success of the rulers. The need to gain acceptance for territorial expansion and geopolitical position became evident only during the reign of Mieszko's son Boleslav the Brave, who introduced the first attributes of an independent state as commonly accepted at that time in Christian Europe: an archbishopric (1000), separate coinage (late tenth century), a territorial name (early eleventh century), and a royal crown (1025).

A somewhat different course of events led to state formation in Rus', as different political traditions merged there during the ninth century. The local Slavs then accepted foreign Scandinavian leaders who applied elements of the nomadic political system and organized an alternative route of contacts between Western Europe and Byzantium, because direct contacts through the Mediterranean area were blocked at that time by Muslim expansion. The collapse of the Avar qaganate had important consequences for the political reorganization in present-day Ukraine. The geopolitical vacuum created between Great Moravia to the west and the Khazar qaganate and the Volga Bulghars to the east offered new opportunities to Scandinavian chiefs moving into the interior from the Baltic coast.[40] Already in 860, the Rus' attacked Constantinople. That sudden surge of military power took both empires by surprise, as evidenced by the correspondence between Emperors Basil I and Louis II in 871. The phrase *chaganus Northmannorum* (the qagan of the Norsemen), used in reference to the leader of the fierce warriors of the East, suggests serious difficulties in defining the new political and military phenomenon emerging between the Baltic and Black Seas. The Rurikids, established by Oleg in Kiev in 879, ruled over a world of Slavic farmers formerly under the domination of the nomads.[41] Imposing their model of effective political-military organization, the Scandinavians underwent a relatively rapid process of Slavicization. In 945, however, Olga harshly punished the Slavic tribe of the Drevlians for the assassination of her son. To consolidate the domination of her family, she accepted baptism from the Byzantine emperor Constantine VII Porphyrogenitus, while at the same time asking Emperor Otto I for a mission from Germany. Olga's policies continued under the rule of her son Vladimir, who crushed all opposition to the dynasty in ca. 978. To gain the support of the Slavs, he promoted their god, Perun, as the supreme god worshiped in the pagan sanctuary in Kiev. Soon, however, he switched to Christianity, in an attempt to consolidate his multiethnic state.[42]

The last to enter the historical stage of East Central Europe were the Magyars, who made their first appearance on the eastern frontier of the East Frankish Empire in 862. They were a loose confederacy of seven tribes, who, much like their nomadic predecessors, settled the steppelike region of present-day Hungary. Like the Huns and the Avars, the Magyars raided deep into Western Europe, before being defeated at Lechfeld by Emperor Otto I (955). This blow to the nomadic war economy forced tribal elites to concentrate on local resources and triggered competition for political hegemony. As a result of these political changes, a process of gradual sedentization took place, during which the emphasis shifted from pastoralism to agriculture.[43] This coincided in time with the rise to power of the Arpadian dynasty. Like many other "barbarian" leaders on the fringes of the Christian world, Prince Géza converted in 975 in an attempt to consolidate his power and gain legitimacy. These were also the political goals of his son Vajk, who became king as Stephen I and established the Hungarian archbishopric in AD 1000.[44]

This sweeping survey of the processes of early medieval state formation in East Central Europe shows that different leaders applied similar strategies to promote dynastic interests and establish firm political control. However, no clear rules or recipes were available for how to organize a state, and in many cases, the victors were just survivors of a ruthless struggle for power in which the upper hand went to the claimant able to reorganize the economic system more effectively and mobilize large numbers for military activities. No such claimant had a full understanding of the situation or anticipated the long-term results of his actions. Ability to raise a broad support and means to sustain power, determination in applying force, and just good luck were the main factors at work in bringing to political success those leaders whose names we associate with the rise of the medieval states in East Central Europe. In many ways, Bohemia, Poland, Rus', and Hungary emerged as "private" ventures of the Přemyslids, Piasts, Rurikids, and Arpadians, respectively. Medieval states were thus the direct result of the ability of such leaders to overcome political challenges, curb the ambitions of their neighbors, impose an ideological system that would provide a permanent source of legitimacy, organize the effective exploitation of conquered territories, and achieve geopolitical acceptance. Such states were in no way "emanations" of already existing nations. In fact, quite the opposite is true: nations came into being as a result of successful states.

NOTES

1. Henryk Łowmiański, *Początki Polski,* vol. 6, part 1 (Warsaw, 1985), 5.
2. Henryk Łowmiański, *Początki Polski,* vol. 5 (Warsaw, 1973), 363.
3. Henryk Łowmiański, *Początki Polski,* vol. 4 (Warsaw, 1970), 115.
4. Łowmiański, *Początki Polski,* 4:109.
5. Joachim Lelewel, *Polska, dzieje i rzeczy jej* (Poznań, 1855), 33–34.
6. Michał Bobrzyński, *Dzieja Polskie w zarysie* (Warsaw, 1879), 60–65.
7. Łowmiański, *Początki Polski,* 6.1:6.
8. Łowmiański, *Początki Polski,* vol. 5, p. 415.
9. See Aleksiejus Luchtanas, "The Balts during the 10th century," in *The Neighbours of Poland in the 10th Century,* ed. P. Urbańczyk (Warsaw, 2000), 199–204.
10. See Dušan Čaplovič, "The area of Slovakia in the 10th century: Development of settlement, interethnic, and acculturation processes," in *The Neighbours of Poland in the 10th Century,* ed. P. Urbańczyk (Warsaw, 2000), 147–56.
11. See Dušan Třeštik, *Počátky Přemyslovců* (Prague, 1997).
12. This was well shown during the international workshop on "Slavic origins" organized in Vienna on January 17–18, 2003.
13. Gerard Labuda, *Słowiańszczyzna starożytna i wczesnośredniowieczna* (Poznań, 1999), 11–19.
14. Michał Parczewski, "U źródeł Słowisńszczyzny," in *Słowianie w Europie wcześniejszego średniowiecza,* ed. M. Miśkiewicz (Warsaw, 1998), 33–49.
15. Parczewski, "U zródeł Słowisańszczyzny," 44.
16. Przemysław Urbańczyk, "Obcy wśród Słowian," in *Słowianie w Europie wcześniejszego średniowiecza,* ed. M. Miśkiewicz (Warsaw, 1998), 66–67, 71–72; "Foreign leaders in early Slavic societies," in *Integration und Herrschaft: Ethnische Identitäten und soziale Organisation im Frühmittelalter,* ed. W. Pohl and M. Diesenberger (Vienna, 2002), 257–68.
17. In the future, extensive DNA analysis may become, at least in theory, an extraordinary tool for tracing migrations.
18. Urbańczyk, "Obcy wśród Słowian," 68–69.
19. Walter Pohl, *Die Awaren: Ein Steppenvolk in Mitteleuropa, 567–822 n. Chr.* (Munich, 1981).
20. Florin Curta, *The Making of the Slavs: History and Archaeology of the Lower Danube Region, c. 500–700 A.D.* (Cambridge, 2001).
21. Przemysław Urbańczyk, "Struktury władzy na ziemiach polskich w I tysięcleciu n.e.," *Kwartalnik Historyczny* 53, no. 4 (1996): 3–22.
22. Peter Brown, *The Rise of Western Christendom* (Cambridge, 1996), 126.
23. For the situation in Lower Austria, see Falko Daim, *Das awarische Gräberfeld von Loebersdorf, NÖ* (Vienna, 1987), 179.

24. Fredegar *Chronicon* 4.48, ed. and trans. J. M. Wallace-Hadrill (London, 1960), 39–40.

25. In 803, some Slavs surrendered to Charlemagne without resistance and "with everything that they had" (*Annals of Metz*, s.a. 803, ed. B. v. Simson, MGH Scriptores, 10:90). Two years later, some Avar leader was seeking protection from the emperor against Slavic "oppression" (*Royal Frankish Annals*, s.a. 805, ed. F. Kurze, MGH Scriptores, 6:112).

26. Třeštík, *Počatky Přemyslovců*, 267.

27. *Royal Frankish Annals*, s.a. 822, MGH Scriptores, 6:159.

28. *Conversio Bagoariorum et Carantanorum*, chap. 10, ed. Fritz Lošek (Hannover, 1997), 50.

29. *Annals of Fulda*, s.a. 846, ed. F. Kurze (Hannover, 1911), MGH Scriptores, 7:36.

30. *Frankish Annals*, s.a. 805, MGH Scriptores, 6:120.

31. *Frankish Annals*, s.a. 845.

32. *Frankish Annals*, s.a. 872.

33. *Cosmas of Prague Chronica Bohemorum* 1.14, ed. E. Bretholz (Berlin, 1923).

34. *Frankish Annals*, s.a. 895.

35. Lotte Hedeager, "Kingdoms, ethnicity, and material culture: Denmark in a European perspective," in *The Age of Sutton Hoo: The Seventh Century in Northwestern Europe*, ed. Martin O. H. Carver (Woodbridge and Rochester, 1992), 291; Leszek Pawel Słupecki, "Monumentalna kopce Kakusa i Wandy pod Krakowem," in *Studia z dziejów cywilizacji: Studia ofiarowane Profesorowi Jerzemu Gassowskiemu w piecdziesiata rocznice pracy naukowej*, ed. A. Buko (Warsaw, 1998), 57–72.

36. For a different opinion, see Leszek Pawel Słupecki, "Tempel und Standbilder: Hochentwickelte Heiligtumsformen bei den Slawen in der Zeit des späten Heidentums," in *Istoriia i kul'tura drevnikh i srednevekovykh slavian*, ed. V. V. Sedov (Moscow, 1999), 196–209.

37. See Martin O. H. Carver, "Town and anti-town in first millenium Europe," in *Archeologia w teorii i w praktyce*, ed. Andrzej Buko and Przemysław Urbańczyk (Warsaw, 2000), 373–98.

38. Zofia Kurnatowska, "Wielkopolska w X wieku I formowanie się państwa polskiego," in *Ziemie polskie w X wieku i ich znaczenie w kształtowaniu się nowej mapy Europy*, ed. H. Samsonowicz (Cracow, 2000), 99–118.

39. Gallus Anonymus *Kronika Polska* 1.1–5, ed. Roman Grodecki and Marian Plezia (Wrocław, 1996). For an English translation of the relevant passages, see Michael J. Miklós, *Medieval Literature of Poland: An Anthology* (New York and London, 1992), 3–15.

40. Oleksiy Tolochko, "Kievan Rus' around the year 1000," in *Europe around the year 1000*, ed. P. Urbańczyk (Warsaw, 2001), 123–39.

41. Simon Franklin and Jonathan Shepard, *The Emergence of Rus, 750–1200* (London, 1996), 83–84.

42. Vladimir Rychka, "La Russie de Kiev au Xème siècle," in *The Neighbours of Poland in the 10th Century*, ed. P. Urbańczyk (Warsaw, 2000), 193–98.

43. Miklós Takács, "Die Lebensweise der Ungarn im 10. Jahrhundert im Spiegel der verschiedenen Quellen," in *The Neighbours of Poland in the 10th Century*, ed. P. Urbańczyk (Warsaw, 2000), 157–91.

44. Mariane Sághy, "The making of the Christian kingdom in Hungary," in *Europe around the year 1000*, ed. P. Urbańczyk (Warsaw, 2001), 451–64.

CHAPTER SIX

Ruler and Political Ideology in *Pax Nomadica:* Early Medieval Bulgaria and the Uighur Qaganate

Tsvetelin Stepanov

*B*etween the mid-eighth and the mid-ninth century, the Bulgars and the Uighurs played unique roles in the history of Eurasia. Their respective neighbors to the south were two powerful empires, Byzantium and China, that were traditionally associated with sedentary societies. To the extent that the Bulgar and Uighur polities were based on a mixed economy, both agriculturist and pastoralist (although this may apply more to the Uighurs than to the Bulgars), they may be characterized as seminomadic and, as such, had a strong influence on their neighbors to the south. For example, after 756, T'ang China almost completely depended on the military assistance of the Uighur qaganate for crushing internal opposition and repelling the attacks of the Tibetan state, which grew to considerable power during this period.[1]

In the course of many centuries and especially until the mid-ninth century, the Bulgars and the Uighurs were indeed the two most powerful states at both ends of what René Grousset (more than half a century ago) called "the empire of the steppes."[2] For much of the ninth century, the Bulgars were its westernmost manifestation, while the Uighurs represented the core of its eastern region between ca. 750 and ca. 830. By 800, the Bulgars could hardly have been an example of typical nomadism, if only because the soil types and the climate of medieval Bulgaria are not very good for nomadic pastoralism (with the exception of the soil and climate of Dobrudja, a small area between the Danube and the Black Sea, now divided between Romania and Bulgaria). Such conditions presuppose the existence of a primarily sedentary population and the economic preeminence of crop cultivation. Nonetheless, certain details of the social and political life of early medieval Bulgaria are reminiscent of steppe societies in the East and may therefore be called *steppe reflexes.* Particularly important in this context is the ability to extort revenue from neighboring sedentary societies—in this case, Byzantium.

The trade-or-raid policy[3] that the Bulgars systematically applied, under various guises, during the eighth and ninth centuries can easily be recognized in several stipulations of the treaties between Byzantium and Bulgaria, such as those of 716 and 815. On both occasions, frontier lines and the regulation of trade were given almost equal attention.[4] There were also special custom posts at various points along the Bulgaro-Byzantine frontier. The two most important outposts were Develtos (Develt, near Burgas) and Mesembria (modern Nesebăr), and finds of Byzantine lead seals indicate the existence of local *kommerkiarioi* (trade tax collectors) in both of them.[5] Moreover, archaeological excavations near Develt demonstrated that the Bulgar and Byzantine frontier outposts were located no more than 1 kilometer from each other, on two opposite hills on each side of the Sredecka River valley.[6] The frontier was most likely on the river itself, after both Develtos and Mesembria were conquered by Khan Krum in 812. At least that much can be gleaned from the stipulations of the treaty of 815, especially from the first paragraph: ". . . and [. . .] made peace for thirty years. The first from the eleven stipulated paragraphs refers to the territory. It should be from Develtos to the Potamokastel [the River Fort]."[7] Similarly, as Sechin Jagchid has pointed out, besides such types of exchange between nomads and China as court-to-court intermarriage or nomadic "tribute" in exchange for Chinese court titles, relations between the two parties were also mediated by frontier markets, the most regular form of exchange and the most effective measure of maintaining peace.[8]

During the second half of the eighth century and especially during the ninth century, both Bulgars and Uighurs built fortified centers that would later turn into large cities. In both cases, local rulers and elites made extensive use of experts, such as engineers and builders, from China, Byzantium, and Sogdiana.[9] Life in these centers must have been organized around the seasonal cycle of nomadism, which suggests that, at least initially, these must have been well-maintained winter residences for the khans and their retinues, as well as central places where tribute was collected and where raid booty was stored and distributed. More important, these must have also been the places where large armies gathered in times of war.[10] Another striking parallel between the two polities is the preoccupation with erecting earthworks and digging ditches on the frontier. Between the seventh and ninth centuries, such earthworks were erected on the southeastern, northwestern, and northeastern frontiers of Bulgaria, with its Byzantine, Avar, and Khazar neighbors, respectively; Uighur earthworks were built on the qaganate's northern frontier, with the Khakassians.[11]

The steppe reflexes are evident in the Bulgarian case as late as the early 900s. The so-called *Name List of Bulgar Rulers*, written most likely at the order of Symeon (893–927),[12] refers to the first five Bulgar khans as ruling "on the other side of the Danube"—that is, in the steppes north and northwest of the

Black Sea. The list reports that Asparuch (d. 701) crossed the river and conquered some of the lands of the Byzantine West, which remained in Bulgar hands "until now." It seems very likely that this text, placed immediately after the book of Kings in the compilation known as the *Greek-Roman Chronicle* (*Letopisec Elinski i Rimski*), had the important role of justifying the double legitimization of Bulgarian fortunes and destiny in the eyes of King Symeon. The king was in any case viewed as "half-Greek" in certain circles in Constantinople, because of his knowledge of Greek and the education he had received in the empire's capital city. In Symeon's eyes, his fellow Bulgarians, who had been recently converted to Christianity, were the heirs of the empire of the steppes and the next Chosen People, for they had succeeded in conquering the western part of the Christian empire, the Byzantine West. It is no surprise, therefore, that the unknown author of the text used the Danube as a special marker: the river had always represented a stereotypical barrier separating (Christian) Romans from the Other, often defined as barbarian, nomad, and "Scythian."[13]

Because the Byzantines were looking upon Bulgars as usurpers and upon their lands in the Balkans as temporarily handed over by the emperor, Bulgaria never became as strong an ally of Byzantium as the Uighurs were for T'ang China. Between 756 and ca. 830, T'ang rulers managed to stay in power and to defeat their enemies—both inside and outside the empire—only with the assistance of Uighur horsemen. This may give to the Uighur-Chinese alliance a strategic twist, but the rapprochement was based not just on circumstances but also on doctrinal issues. Unlike Byzantine attitudes toward Balkan lands, Chinese rulers never claimed the lands beyond the Great Wall as Chinese par excellence. All nomads of some significance for the empire of the steppes, from Huns to Turks and Uighurs, were located precisely in those lands.[14] In contrast to eighth- and ninth-century Bulgars, the Uighurs were thus in a different position in regard to the T'ang Empire, from which they were separated by an unproblematic frontier. To be sure, there was not much difference between Byzantine views of the Bulgars and Chinese attitudes toward Uighurs. Both Bulgars and Uighurs were regarded as barbarian and alien. Nonetheless, both Bulgar and Uighur rulers strove to obtain recognition of their independent power from the neighboring empires.

This obsessive concern with legitimacy may also explain yet another striking parallel between Uighurs and Bulgars. In both cases, rulers made political claims through stone inscriptions of great memorial value for both cultures.[15] The Bulgars used Byzantine prisoners of war to carve texts of various kinds into stone. The language of these inscriptions is Greek, while Uighur inscriptions are written in Turkic runes and only sporadically in Chinese ideograms carved by Chinese craftsmen. In both cases, the audience that the authors of these inscription texts had in mind was the rulers of the neighboring empires and their subjects. This is particularly true in the case of the Bulgar inscriptions written in Greek.

Besides similarities between Bulgaria and Byzantium, on one hand, and the Uighur qaganate and T'ang China, on the other, one other commonality prompts us to compare the political behavior of ruling elites within the two steppe empires. The An Lu-shan revolt broke out in 755 in T'ang China and was suppressed eight years later through the active intervention of the Uighurs.[16] In 821, Thomas the Slav rose in rebellion against the Byzantine emperor Michael II (820–29) in a revolt that was crushed in 823 with the decisive contribution of the Bulgar khan Omurtag (814–31).[17] Such events raise the question of why Bulgars and Uighurs would offer assistance to their traditional enemies. What were the reasons for their interference in Byzantine and Chinese domestic affairs, and what did they expect to gain from battling usurpers on behalf of foreign emperors?

Before attempting to provide some plausible answers to such questions, it might be useful to summarize the main historical events. Within a few months, An Lu-shan, the leader of the revolt against the T'ang dynasty, succeeded in conquering the eastern capital of the empire, Lo-yang, and quickly proclaimed himself emperor and founder of a new dynasty, with new titles and ministers.[18] Su-tsung (756–62), the ruling T'ang emperor, asked for assistance from both Tibetans and Uighurs, to take back not just Lo-yang but also Chang-an, the second and most important capital, which had meanwhile been conquered by the rebels. A special embassy was prepared to go to the qagan of the Uighurs in September 756 and obtain his military assistance against the rebels. The qagan agreed to help and, in exchange, asked for the hand of any one of the emperor's daughters. In diplomatic terms, his request indicates that the qagan either was or viewed himself as equal in status to the ruler of the Heavenly Empire. The Chinese, too, were fully aware of the unusual character of this request; until then, several "barbarian" leaders had married imperial princesses, but never daughters of the ruling emperor.[19]

During the following year, the two capitals were taken back by Su-tsung and his Uighur allies. As for the T'ang emperor, he kept his promise and gave one of his younger daughters, the princess of Ning-kuo, to Qagan Mo-yen-ch'o (or Bayanchor), but a special edict was needed to institute a new title for Su-tsung's son-in-law. The decree bestowed on Mo-yen-ch'o the lofty title "Ying-wu Wei-yüan [brave and bellicose, inspiring states/peoples with fear] P'i chia qagan of the Uighurs."[20] In 762, the qagan again offered his assistance to his "brother," the T'ang emperor, against the rebels. This time, his intervention was instrumental for the final defeat of the revolt in 763.

Mutual understanding and support was thus established as a basis for future relations between the two courts, to the advantage of both, although perhaps at a much higher political cost for the Chinese emperor than for the qagan
of the Uighurs. Such special relations were further consolidated in 788 and 821,
respectively, when two Chinese princesses of the highest known rank married
Uighur qagans.[21] During the T'ang dynasty (618–907), more than twenty imperial women married barbarian rulers. Three of them were imperial daughters,
and all three married qagans of the Uighurs.

Several decades later and several thousands of kilometers away, Thomas the
Slav revolted against the Byzantine emperor. According to Joseph Genesius, the
rebel had reached an agreement with the Arabs against Michael II. He was
crowned emperor by the patriarch of Antioch and soon put Constantinople
under siege by land and sea, after gaining control over most of Asia Minor. The
siege, however, dragged on for several months, thus giving Emperor Michael II
sufficient time to look for powerful allies.[22]

It is not altogether clear who had the idea of calling Omurtag: Genesius and
Theophanes Continuatus claim that Omurtag offered himself for assistance,
while George the Monk, who lived at the time of these events, openly blames
the emperor for having called the Bulgars.[23] It is clear, however, that Omurtag
"obeyed the oaths" taken at the time of the peace treaty of 815 or 816 with Emperor Leo V (813–20). Veselin Beshevliev suggested that in 821 (or perhaps in
820) a treaty was signed between Michael II and Omurtag,[24] which may have
confirmed the terms of the thirty-year peace treaty of 815. It is also possible that
Omurtag offered his assistance in exchange for political concessions. Just what
concessions he had in mind is not mentioned in any existing source. However,
the evidence available suggests that it is precisely during these years that
Omurtag began using the title *ek theou arkhon* (ruler from God). Moreover,
Theophanes Continuatus refers to the Bulgar khan as *basileus* (emperor) (not
arkhon) of the Bulgars.[25] The same title appears twice in the Madrid manuscript of John Scylitzes' *History.*[26] In both cases, this choice of words is in sharp
contrast with what we know about Byzantine views of the Bulgar ruler and of
Bulgars in general.

Possibly in connection with his victory over Thomas in the late autumn of
822 (or the early spring of 823),[27] Omurtag began striking gold commemorative
medallions on which he was represented with Byzantine imperial insignia, although the inscription identified him as *kanasybigi* (Bulgar phrase for "ruler
from God").[28] Theophanes Continuatus explicitly noted that following the victory over Thomas, Omurtag returned to Bulgaria "showing pride and boasting"
and carrying much booty taken during the campaign.[29] Unlike the Uighur
qagan, Omurtag could not have any hopes of marrying an imperial daughter, re-

gardless of whether or not Emperor Michael II had any available, because as a barbarian and pagan, he was not eligible to marry a princess "born in the purple." He could, however, ask for recognition of his right to rule over the western territories of Byzantium in the name of God rather than in the name of the ruling emperor. This must be the explanation for his assuming the title "*arkhon* [in the name] of God."

The title is first attested in the so-called Chatalar inscription of 822. The text of this inscription refers to Omurtag's threats, perhaps addressed to Thomas, that he (the khan) will trample the enemy under his feet, together with his Slavic allies, against whom Omurtag is said to have recently erected a stronghold on the Ticha River.[30] This was by no means the first time a Bulgar ruler provided military assistance to his powerful neighbor in the south in exchange for political concessions. In 705, Emperor Justinian II (685–95, 705–11) bestowed the title *Caesar*—in addition to gifts of gold and rich garments—upon the Bulgar ruler Tervel. In Byzantium, the title designated the heir apparent, but in this particular case, it referred to Tervel ruling Bulgaria in the emperor's name. By contrast, the title "ruler (in the name) of God" bestowed on Omurtag by Emperor Michael II allowed the former to assert his independence. The inscriptions surrounding the Madara Horseman relief clearly demonstrate the importance of such events for Bulgar rulers.[31] Two of these inscriptions explicitly refer to Tervel and Omurtag.

Uighur qagans behaved similarly: they offered military assistance to Chinese emperors, in exchange for gold, silk, lofty titles, and dynastic marriages. Gifts from the Chinese and Byzantine emperors elevated the status and confirmed the prestige of Uighur and Bulgar rulers and ruling clans and also enabled them to dominate and secure the support of subordinate elites. Loyalty in such cases was a function of royal generosity, as gifts obtained from distant monarchs were redistributed to close friends and political allies. Such political manipulation of relations with sedentary neighbors has long been recognized as typical for nomadic societies in which elites rely for their stability and social reproduction on extra-economic means of exploitation.[32]

Given that the T'ang emperor found himself in a comparatively more difficult position (as both his capitals had been taken by the rebels), it comes as no surprise that he showed more generosity toward his Uighur ally and broke with T'ang traditional policies toward the northern "barbarians," even if his concessions may have first appeared as damaging the image of the emperor. Such concessions secured the continuity of the dynasty, which remained in power for almost seven decades after the defeat of the Uighurs and the collapse of their qaganate. By contrast, the Byzantine emperor strictly followed the Byzantine practice of keeping barbarians—even barbarian allies—at an arm's distance.

He was undoubtedly in a much different position than the T'ang emperor, because he always had Constantinople under his control. Concessions made to Omurtag, therefore, were much smaller than those granted to the qagan of the Uighurs.

These two similar episodes illustrate similarities in political behavior, ambitions, and goals between rulers of early medieval states in general and of steppe empires in particular. Their strategy was aimed at achieving two main goals: (1) diplomatic recognition of their independent power or even of status equal to that of the rulers of sedentary empires and (2) regular flow of gifts and bribes in the form of rich garments, gold, and so on from elites in sedentary empires. Goods acquired by such means were redistributed within the nomadic polity and used by its elites in various feasts and potlatchlike ceremonies, most typical for the "prestige economy" of nomadic and semisedentary societies.[33] The unstable polities of such societies were thus strengthened economically and ideologically. In other words, steppe societies permanently needed long-term relations with their sedentary neighbors.[34] This may explain the frequency of long-term treaties between China and the Uighurs or Byzantium and the Bulgars, whereby "barbarian" rulers offered military assistance for the maintenance of political stability within empires on the southern borders of their respective polities. Tervel's 717/8 campaign against the Arabs may thus be viewed as an attempt to defend a status quo established by the Byzantine-Bulgar treaty previously signed by Emperor Theodosius III with the Bulgars.[35]

The flow of regular revenues, regarded as tribute by nomads and as gifts by neighboring empires, reduced the need of permanent warfare for the acquisition of riches and slaves to be redistributed by rulers to subordinate elites. There was now a regular flow of rich garments, luxurious goods, jewels, silk, and so on coming from the neighboring sedentary societies. This explains the similarities between Bulgars and Uighurs, as well as the political behavior of their rulers, despite the considerable distance separating their polities.

NOTES

1. For the struggle between T'ang China and Tibet, see A. Maliavkin, *Bor'ba Tibeta s Tanskim gosudarstvom za Kashgariiu* (Novosibirsk, 1992); Mu Shun-ying and Wang Yao, "The Western regions (Hsi-yü) under the T'ang Empire and the kingdom of Tibet," in *History of Civilizations of Central Asia*, vol. 3, ed. B. Litvinsky, Z. Guang-da, R. S. Samghabadi (Paris, 1996), 362–63.

2. René Grousset, *L'empire des steppes: Attila, Gengis-Khan, Tamerlan* (Paris, 1939).

3. For a general model for this policy applied to the "empire of the steppes," see

Anatolii Khazanov, *Nomads and the Outside World* (Madison, 1994), 84, 222–27. See also N. di Cosmo, "Ancient inner Asian nomads: Their economic basis and its significance in Chinese history," *Journal of Asian Studies* 4 (1994): 1092–1126.

4. For the specific stipulations of these treaties, see Veselin Beshevliev, *Părvobălgarski nadpisi,* 2nd ed. (Sofia, 1992), 164–75; Ivan Duichev, Mikhail Voinov, and Borislav Svetozarov Primov, eds., *Latinski izvori za bălgarskata istoriia,* vol. 2 (Sofia, 1960), 272.

5. I. Iordanov, *Pechatite na komerkiariiata Develt* (Sofia, 1992), 22–23.

6. Iordanov, *Pechatite,* 17.

7. Beshevliev, *Părvobălgarski nadpisi,* 164–65.

8. Sechin Jagchid, "The historical interaction between the nomadic people in Mongolia and the sedentary Chinese," in *Rulers from the Steppe: State Formation on the Eurasian Periphery,* ed. G. Seaman and D. Marks (Los Angeles, 1991), 66–68.

9. D. Sinor, G. Shimin, and Y. Kychanov, "The Uighurs in Mongolia and the Kyrgyz," in *History of Civilizations of Central Asia,* vol. 4, part 1, ed. M. Asimov and C. Bosworth (Paris, 1998), 191–214, esp. 191–200; V. Minorsky, *The Turks, Iran, and the Caucasus in the Middle Ages* (London, 1978), essay I; A. von Gabain, "Irano-Turkish relations in the late Sassanian period," in *The Cambridge History of Iran,* vol. 3, part 1, ed. E. Yarshater (Cambridge, 1983), 623.

10. Pliska is specifically called a "camp" (*kanpon*) in one of Omurtag's inscriptions. See Beshevliev, *Părvobălgarski nadpisi,* 216 and no. 57. For the Uighurs and their centers, see Iurii Khudiakov, "Pamiatniki uigurskogo kul'tury v Mongolii," in *Central'naia Aziia i sosednie territorii v srednie veka: Sbornik nauchnykh trudov,* ed. V. E. Larichev (Novosibirsk, 1990), 84–86.

11. Tsvetelin Stepanov, "Notions of the Other in the Pax Nomadica, 6th–9th centuries (Bulgars, Khazars, ancient Turks, and Uighurs)," in *Civitas divino-humana. V chest na profesor Georgi Bakalov,* ed. Ts. Stepanov and V. Vachkova (Sofia, 2004), 609–24. For Uighur earthworks, see *Stepi Evrazii v epokhu srednevekov'ia,* ed. S. A. Pletneva (Moscow, 1981), 53.

12. Liudmila Gorina, "*Imennik bolgarskikh khanov* v sostave Ellinskogo letopisca," *Bulgarian Historical Review* 19 (1991): 93–97; "Problemy *Imennika bolgarskikh khanov* kak chasti Ellinskogo letopisca," *Bulgarian Historical Review* 23 (1995): 10–29; "Bălgarskiiat khronograf," *Istorichesko bădeshte* 1–2 (2002): 148–77. For the image of Symeon as wise, as a new Moses, as resembling David, and so on, see also Rasho Rashev, "Car Simeon, prorok Moisei i bălgarskiiat zlaten vek," in *1100 godini Veliki Preslav,* ed. Totiu Totev, Ivan Iordanov, Rasho Rashev, et al., vol. 1 (Shumen, 1995), 55–73; S. Paskalevski, "Nabliudeniia za lichnostniia i izobrazitelniia ipostas na car Simeon," *Preslavska knizhovna shkola* 5 (2002): 243–56; Angel Nikolov, "Cariat-bogopodrozhatel: Edin prenebregnat aspekt ot politicheskata koncepciia na Simeon I," *Godishnik na Sofiiskiia Universitet: Centăr za slaviano-vizantiiski prouchvaniia "Ivan Duichev"* 91 (2001): 109–22; Jonathan Shepard, "The ruler as instructor, pastor, and wise: Leo VI of Byzantium and Symeon of Bulgaria," in *Alfred the Great: Papers from the Eleventh-Centenary Conferences,* ed. T. Reuther (Aldershot and Burlington, 2003), 339–58.

13. Bulgars and "Scythians" are explicitly associated with each other in the letters sent by Patriarch Nicholas Mystikos to King Symeon. See Paul Stephenson, "Byzantine conceptions of otherness after the annexation of Bulgaria (1018)," in *Strangers to Themselves: The Byzantine Outsider,* ed. D. Smythe (Aldershot and Burlington, 2000), 245–46. For later references to the Danube as a frontier in a Bulgarian cultural context, see Tsvetelin Stepanov,

"Aleksandăr Makedonski, Kavkaz i problemăt za granicata: Osmisliane na prostranstvoto na civilizaciiata u volzhkite i dunavskite bălgari," *Khazarskii almanakh* 1 (2002): 131–39.

14. For Chinese policies and attitudes toward northern barbarians, see Alastair Johnston, *Cultural Realism: Strategic Culture and Grand Strategy in Chinese History* (Princeton, 1995).

15. Beshevliev, *Părvobălgarski nadpisi;* S. Klyashtorny, "The Tes inscription of the Uighur Bögü Qaghan," *Acta Orientalia Academiae Scientiarum Hungaricae* 39 (1985): 137–56; T. Tekin, "Nine notes on the Tes inscription," *Acta Orientalia Academiae Scientiarum Hungaricae* 42 (1988): 111–18; S. Kliashtornyi and V. Livshic, "Sevreiskii kamen," *Sovetskaia turkologiia* 3 (1971): 106–12; S. Klyashtorny, "The Terkhin inscription," *Acta Orientalia Academiae Scientiarum Hungaricae* 37 (1982): 335–36; T. Tekin, "The Tariat (Terkhin) inscription," *Acta Orientalia Academiae Scientiarum Hungaricae* 37 (1982): 43–68.

16. D. C. Twichett and J. K. Fairbank, eds., *The Cambridge History of China,* vol. 3 (Cambridge, 1979), 455–58, 472–84, 561–63; E. Pulleybank, *The Background of the Rebellion of An Lu-shan* (London, New York, and Toronto, 1955); C. Mackerras, "The Uighurs," in *The Cambridge History of Early Inner Asia,* ed. D. Sinor (Cambridge, 1990), 317–18.

17. Paul Lemerle, "Thomas le Slave," *Travaux et Mémoires du Centre de recherches d'histoire et civilization byzantines* 1 (1965): 255–97.

18. C. Mackerras, *The Uighur Empire (744–840) according to the T'ang Dynastic Histories* (Canberra, 1968); Twichett and Fairbank, *Cambridge History of China,* 455, 472–84; Mackerras, "The Uighurs," 317, 330.

19. Mackerras, *The Uighur Empire,* 4–6, 15–20.

20. Mackerras, *The Uighur Empire,* 15–17 and n. 35.

21. Twichett and Fairbank, *Cambridge History of China,* 677–78; Mackerras, "The Uighurs," 325–26.

22. Joseph Genesius, *Reges,* in *Grăcki izvori za bălgarskata istoriia,* ed. I. Duichev and G. Cankova-Petkova, vol. 4 (Sofia, 1961), 325.

23. Genesius, *Reges,* 331; Theophanes Continuatus, *Chronographia,* in *Grăcki izvori za bălgarskata istoriia,* ed. I. Duichev and G. Cankova-Petkova, vol. 5 (Sofia, 1964), 114; Georgius Monachus, *Chronicon,* in *Grăckii izvori za bălgarskata istoriia,* ed. I. Duichev and G. Cankova-Petkova, vol. 4 (Sofia, 1961), 56.

24. Veselin Beshevliev, *Părvobălgari: Istoriia* (Sofia, 1984), 147.

25. Theophanes Continuatus, *Chronographia,* in *Grăcki izvori za bălgarskata istoriia,* ed. I. Duichev and G. Cankova-Petkova, vol. 4 (Sofia, 1961), 114.

26. A. Bozhkov, *Miniaturi ot Madridskiia răkopis na Ioan Skilica* (Sofia, 1972), 37, 39.

27. For the chronology of events, see Lemerle, "Thomas le Slave," 291; Beshevliev, *Părvobălgari,* 145.

28. Iordan Iordanov, "Ednostranni zlatni moneti-medalioni s imeto na Khan Omurtag," *Numizmatika* 10 (1976): 18–34; Iordanka Iurukova and Vladimir Penchev, *Bălgarski srednovekovni moneti i pechati* (Sofia, 1990), 22 and fig. I.3; Georgi Atanasov, *Insigniite na srednovekovnite bălgarski vladeteli: Koroni, skiptri, sferi, orăzhiia, kostiumi, nakiti* (Pleven, 1999), 49–50. For the title of *kanasybigi,* see Georgi Bakalov, *Srednovekovniiat bălgarski vladetel: Titulatura i insignii* (Sofia, 1985), 88–89; Beshevliev, *Părvobălgarski nadpisi,* 72–74; Tsvetelin Stepanov, *Vlast i avtoritet v rannosrednovekovna Bălgariia (VII–sr. IX v.)* (Sofia, 1999); Stepanov, "The Bulgar title ΚΑΝΑΣΥΒΙΓΙ: Re-

constructing the notions of divine kingship in Bulgaria, AD 822–836," *Early Medieval Europe* 10 (2001): 1–19.

29. Theophanes Continuatus, *Chronographia*, in *Grăcki izvori za bălgarskata istoriia*, ed. I. Duichev and G. Cankova-Petkova, vol. 4 (Sofia, 1961), 115.

30. Beshevliev, *Părvobălgarski nadpisi*, 215–24 (no. 57).

31. The literature on the Madara Horseman is enormous. For a good survey, see S. P. Dimitrova, "Istoriia na prouchvaniiata na Madarskiia relef i nadpisite okolo nego," *Minalo* 1 (1994): 21–33; Rasho Rashev, "Madarskiiat konnik, stari i novi văprosi," *Istorich-eski pregled* 3–4 (1998): 192–204. See also Krăstiiu Miiatev, "Madarskiiat konnik," *Izvestiia na Bălgarskiia arkheologicheski institut* 5 (1928–29), 90–126; B. Filov, "Madarskiiat kon-nik," in *Madara: Razkopki i prouchvaniia*, vol. 1 (Sofia, 1934), 255–68; Dimităr Ovcharov, "Za săshtnostta na ezicheskiia kultov centăr Madara," in *Madara*, vol. 3 (Shumen, 1992), 99–108. For inscriptions, see Géza Fehér, *Nadpisătă na Madarskiia konnikă* (Sofia, 1928); Veselin Beshevliev, "Zu der Inschrift des Reiterreliefs von Madara," *Byzantinisch-neu-griechische Jahrbücher* 9 (1930–32), 1–35; Beshevliev, "Zur Deutung und Datierung der protobulgarischen Inschrift vor dem Reiterrelief von Madara, Bulgarien," *Byzantinische Zeitschrift* 47 (1954): 117–22; Beshevliev, "Les inscriptions du relief de Madara (nouvelle lecture, compléments et interprétation)," *Byzantinoslavica* 16 (1955): 212–54; Beshevliev, "Nadpisite okolo Madarskiia konnik," in *Madarskiiat konnik (prouchvaniia vărkhu nad-pisite i relefa)* (Sofia, 1956), 51–114; T. Smiadovski, "Krumesis ot Madarskata skala i Ko-rmisosh ot Imennika edno i sashto lice li sa?" *Vekove* 10 (1981): 29–35; M. Grigoriou-Ioannidou, "He epigrafe ton Madaron: Paratereseis kai problemata," *Vyzantiaka* 17 (1997): 139–90; Grigoriou-Ioannidou, *The Inscription of the "Madara Horseman": Re-marks and Problems* (Athens, 1997).

32. For a detailed discussion, see Owen Lattimore, *Inner Asian Frontiers of China* (Boston, 1967); Thomas J. Barfield, *The Perilous Frontier: Nomadic Empires and China* (Oxford, 1989); Khazanov, *Nomads;* N. Kradin, "Obshchestvennyi stroi kochevnikov: Diskussii i problemy," *Voprosy istorii* 4 (2001): 21–32.

33. Kradin, "Obshchestvennyi stroi," 30.

34. Especially for Central Asian nomads and China, see Barfield, *The Perilous Fron-tier*, 24.

35. For both the treaty and the campaign, see Vassil Zlatarski, *Istoriia na bălgarskata dărzhava prez srednite vekove* (Sofia, 1970), 239–52.

CHAPTER SEVEN

Unknown Revolution: Archaeology and the Beginnings of the Polish State

Andrzej Buko

According to the legend of the Piast dynasty recorded in the first Polish chronicle, that of the twelfth-century monk known as Gallus Anonymus, the origins of the Polish state could be traced back to the ancestors of Mieszko, the first Polish ruler known from historical sources. Many historians regard as particularly important "those matters which were recorded by faithful memory," as the chronicler himself put it.[1]

As a consequence, despite the lack of any written sources concerning Poland prior to the conversion to Christianity in 966, the period between the late eighth and the early tenth centuries was traditionally viewed as the last formative stage leading to the rise of the Polish medieval state.[2] According to such views, the development of early urban centers and the rise of the state followed the same evolutionary scheme. The state was the end result of internal social, economic, and cultural changes, as well as of a process of political consolidation of regional tribal communities between the seventh and the ninth centuries. Similarly, urban centers grew from tribal centers into strongholds and administrative centers of the early Piast state.

There was, however, little support for the idea that the rise of both the Piast state and the early urban centers coincided with the earliest Piast rulers known from historical sources. Such coincidences recalled the event history condemned by Braudel's *longue durée* (long-term history), in itself an outgrowth of the structuralist approach to history.[3]

Archaeological research of the last decade produced a significant body of evidence pertaining to the rise of the Polish medieval state. The use of such dating techniques as dendrochronology allowed much refinement of previous textbook conclusions. This has raised new questions about the history of the early Piast state. In this chapter, I intend to summarize the discussion opened by this body of archaeological evidence and to suggest some possible solutions.

The Tribal Period: Consolidation or Decline?

Despite unquestionable progress made in the last few years, the study of the early Slav and tribal period (sixth to early tenth centuries) has left many unanswered questions. One of the key problems requiring resolution is that of when and how strongholds emerged in medieval Poland. Are such fortified settlements to be associated with different regions at different times, as it was often thought, or did they appear only at the end of the tribal period, that is, during the ninth century? The latter suggestion is now substantiated by an increasing number of dates obtained by the analysis of tree rings. This raises new questions regarding the interpretation of the historical record. For example, it is not clear why the Polanians, the tribe that was to give rise to the Polish state under the Piast dynasty, do not appear in the list of a ninth-century source known as the Bavarian Geographer. The list does mention the tribe of the Glopeans, with no less than 400 *civitates,* but the name of this tribe does not appear in any other source. Are the Glopeans and the Polanians one and the same tribe, and if so, under what circumstances did the change of name take place? What happened to the ninth-century Glopeans—one of the largest groups listed by the Bavarian Geographer, if we are to judge by the listed number of *civitates?* How did the name *Polanians* emerge—the name from which the name of the Polish state derives (fig. 7.1)? Do the *civitates* of the Bavarian Geographer represent strongholds, or was this a general term for settlement clusters?

Little is known about the sudden growth of religious centers in ninth-century Poland, and no satisfactory explanation has so far been advanced for their dramatic decline. Should their construction be interpreted as an attempt to organize pantribal centers, the precursors of statehood? What caused their collapse, and under what circumstances were they abandoned? The latter question is particularly important, given that some of the oldest monasteries in Poland were established on or near such sites (fig. 7.2). Further questions concern the likelihood of a migration into southern Poland (or Poland in general) of Christian communities from south of the Carpathian Mountains. Indeed, it remains unclear whether or not Christian communities existed on Polish territory before the conversion to Christianity of the Polanian elite.[4]

Recent research on early medieval strongholds in Mazovia, many of which have been redated by means of dendrochronology, provides answers to some of these questions. Many strongholds seem to have been built in the late 800s or early 900s, just before the Piast "revolution" in Great Poland. In addition, they were in use for a brief period, perhaps no more than a generation.[5] Why was their appearance so late and their destruction so quick? It is possible that such strongholds were built as means of defense against the threat of the neigh-boring Polanians. If so, the archaeological evidence suggests that attempts to contain that threat were not very successful, which may explain the short occu-pation of such sites.

The issue of when inhumation began to replace other burial rites in Poland is still controversial. The traditional explanation dated the shift to the second half of the tenth century, in connection with the conversion to Chris-tianity, but some archaeologists recently argued for a much earlier date.[6] Equally controversial are the questions of the mission from Moravia and the use of Slavic liturgy in Poland before Mieszko's conversion. These questions were raised by a number of postwar excavations in southern Poland, as well as by recent finds from Podebłocie that were interpreted by some as tablets with inscriptions (fig. 7.3).[7] According to the *Life of St. Methodius,* the Vistulans in southern Poland were ruled by a mighty pagan prince "who did much harm to the Christians."[8] It has been suggested that the polity of the Vistulans may have been in an advanced process of power centralization.[9] If so, what was the function of strongholds found in that region, which, unlike any other similar sites in Poland, have earthen ramparts of considerable size but only few re-mains of internal structures?

Despite extensive work in the last few decades, it has not been possible to locate the main center of the Vistulan polity. Many believe that the center must have been in Cracow, the capital of the Polish state from the eleventh century onward. However, detailed excavations on the Wawel Hill produced no traces of what might have been the oldest fortifications of the alleged central place, and the earliest fortifications are no earlier than the early eleventh century.[10]

A number of large burial mounds in southern Poland constitute a separate problem. Many share the same features and may have been inspired by the same set of symbols and beliefs or associated with similar attributes of power.[11] Are barrows in southern Poland to be seen as princely burials, perhaps similar to many such monuments in contemporary Europe, especially in Scandinavia (fig. 7.4)? If so and if such barrows are to be associated with the evidence of strongholds, those for whom they were both erected were not state founders. According to the recent dendrochronological analysis, all strongholds, with few exceptions, were built at the same time and ended in destruction by fire at about the same time as the Polanian state is known to have emerged.

The archaeological evidence thus points to a very complex picture of polit-ical developments in Poland prior to the rise of the Piast state. It also indicates that the Piast state had no traditions in the tribal period that may have been reflected in the material culture. The archaeological record suggests, therefore, that the account of Gallus Anonymus about Dukes Siemowit, Lestek, and

Siemomysł, all predecessors of Mieszko, should be treated as nothing more than a dynastic legend. Such stories were often associated with powerful rulers, eager to present themselves and their family as capable of providing good fortune to their subjects and country. Such legends appearing independently in different regions of Europe had a narrative structure very similar to the Piast legend of Poland.[12]

The Rise of the Medieval State: Revolutionary Origins and Rapid Growth

Recent archaeological research produced a radically different picture of how medieval state emerged in Poland.[13] An important aspect in this respect is the evidence of wholesale destruction (often by fire) and abandonment of many tribal centers in various regions, most markedly in Great Poland, Little Poland, and Mazovia. In Great Poland, where the state formation process seems to have been most advanced, fortified settlements appeared at different locations in the northeast, away from the old, now abandoned centers in the southwest.[14] The northwest was indeed the region with the two main centers of the early Piast state, Gniezno and Poznań. The destruction of the earlier tribal centers and their final abandonment coincided in time with a sustained settlement of the central areas under Piast control (fig. 7.5). Since this sudden growth of settlement in some areas was accompanied by depopulation in others, it is possible that the process involved massive and perhaps forced movements of population. A similar process seems to have been at work in other regions, such as Mazovia, Little Poland, and Silesia. In all such cases, new strongholds came into being in the late 900s and became important regional centers during the following centuries. They were built anew and characteristically in locations different and away from earlier tribal centers. In some cases, such as Lublin, earlier centers destroyed by fire were abandoned for a long time before new towns were erected on their ruins.[15] In other cases, such as Złota near Sandomierz, the change was even more dramatic, as the existence of such centers came to an abrupt end after a long period of relative prosperity.[16] So far, a new phase of fortification and habitation on the site of an earlier tribal town has been evidenced only in Cracow, Kalisz, Szczecin, and Kołobrzeg.

The new dendrochronological data show that the ramparts of Gniezno, the first capital of the Polish state, were built not in the 700s, as previously thought, but between 940 and 1026, under the first Piast rulers.[17] The beginnings of many Polish towns are equally to be placed within the second half of the tenth century. Some of the dates obtained by dendrochronological analysis surprisingly match the written evidence. Kołobrzeg was rebuilt in 980, while the rampart of the Castrum Minus in Wrocław was erected in ca. 985. The former must be a consequence of Mieszko I's conquest of Pomerania, while the latter may be associated with the incorporation of Silesia within the Piast state. These strongholds thus appear as the direct result of political decisions that turned them into political and administrative centers for the new power.

In Little Poland, Sandomierz, one of the *sedes regni principales* (the main seats of the kingdom), offers the best example of association between political decisions and regional centers. No settlement preceded the stronghold erected in the 970s or shortly thereafter, as Sandomierz became a provincial capital (fig. 7.6). Recent archaeological research indicates that the erection of this stronghold was accompanied by the resettlement of a substantial group of population from Great Poland.[18]

But this interpretation does not apply to all known strongholds. So far, three centers on the coast (Wolin, Szczecin and Kołobrzeg) and two centers in the interior (Kalisz and Cracow) produced evidence of a substantially different history. The coastal centers emerged as ports of trade in connection with the Baltic trade, as indicated by numerous finds of silver hoards. As paradoxical as it may seem and despite the current debate surrounding its Viking origins, Wolin was economically more closely associated with Scandinavia and northwest Europe in the ninth century than with its hinterland in Great Poland.[19] This may explain both the relatively early beginnings of this center and its rapid decline following the rise of the Polish state. By the late tenth century, the Piast strongholds of Szczecin and Kołobrzeg were successfully competing with Wolin for the control of the Baltic trade. The same is true for eastern Pomerania, particularly for Gdańsk, a center built in the late 970s that rapidly eliminated Truso, a previously important emporium in neighboring Prussia.[20] The written evidence indicates that, after its incorporation into the Přemyslid state, Cracow remained under Bohemian control until the late 900s. However, the architecture of the early medieval monuments excavated on the Wawel Hill (fig. 7.7) suggests a significant Piast presence.[21] Finally, the case of Kalisz is particularly interesting and is examined in the next section of this chapter in the broader context of the origins of the first Polish dynasty.

The Piasts: A Dynasty of Polanians or of Foreign Origin?

The sudden expansion of the early medieval state by means of military annexation of neighboring regions raises the question of the identity of its founders. The dynastic legend to be found in the chronicle of Gallus Anonymus makes it quite clear that the Piasts were of local—that is, Great Polish—origin. However, some have claimed a foreign origin for this dynasty on the basis of the famous document known as *Dagome iudex,* whereby the papacy received Poland as a fief. A Scandinavian origin has been ascribed to the name *Dago* that appears in this document, and early medieval Poland was consequently compared with Kievan Rus', with the Piasts mirroring the Varangian Rurikids as state builders.

Despite a considerable number of studies dedicated to this problem, no evidence exists to substantiate this interpretation. It is indeed likely that Mieszko I's retinue of bodyguards included at least some warriors recruited from abroad, as indicated by the tenth-century Andalusian Jewish traveler Ibrahim ibn Yakub.[22] Finds of weapons of Scandinavian origin around the royal residence at Ostrów Lednicki and burials of Scandinavian warriors in cemeteries excavated in Great Poland and Pomerania confirm the literary evidence.[23] A retinue of professional warriors (*druzhina*) secured Mieszko's successful policies of conquest and integration into the new state.

The revolution that led to the creation of the medieval Polish state originated in Great Poland. This region of Poland supplies the best evidence for dramatic change at the end of the tribal period, as well as for the shift of fortified settlement locations. The earliest princely residences were also found in Great Poland—on the island Ostrów Lednicki; in Poznań, the seat of the missionary bishop Jordan; and in Gniezno, the first capital of the Polish state. There is, however, an apparent contradiction: if the Piast state began in Great Poland, why were tribal strongholds in this area equally destroyed, and over what area in Great Poland did the Piasts rule before becoming rulers of Poland?

In Great Poland, just one old tribal stronghold escaped destruction, Kalisz. Unlike several other cases in Poland, the Piast stronghold in Kalisz was built on top of the earlier tribal center (fig. 7.8). Whether this was just a restoration and rebuilding phase (due to the rising water level of the nearby Prosna River) or the archaeological evidence should be interpreted in some other terms, the issue is beyond the scope of this chapter. The most important point is that Kalisz played a crucial role under the first Piasts. The site produced the unique remains of the earliest wooden church excavated in Poland, which has been dated to the early eleventh century. The presence of this building suggests that this was the site of an important mission and ecclesiastical center. Indeed, during the late twelfth century, Kalisz became the residence of Mieszko III the Old (1177–79, 1190–91, 1198–1201), who was also buried there.[24] In the late 900s, the region witnessed an impressive building program, as a great number of strongholds were erected anew all around Kalisz. Were these strongholds erected in preparation for the annexation of Silesia in 990–91 or some sort of long-term investment in the area initially ruled by the Piasts? In other words, is it possible that the southeastern region of Great Poland was the home duchy of the Piasts, the area from which they began building the medieval state of Poland? If so, moving the capital from Kalisz to Gniezno may have been an attempt to reach a compromise between conqueror and conquered. At any rate, recent excavations have shown that prior to the Piast takeover, Gniezno was the site of a pagan sanctuary, the function of which was later transferred to the archbishop established there after the conversion to Christianity.

The "Polish Acceleration" One Thousand Years Ago

The process of state formation is still poorly understood in all its details, with many questions still unanswered. However, there is a sharp contrast between Poland ca. 1000 and the image we have of that country for the mid-tenth century. By 950, Poland was still in the making, with a number of strongholds built anew, mainly in Great Poland. At the time of the Act of Gniezno (1000), Poland had changed dramatically. Instead of a single region, *Gnezdun civitas,* it now comprised all regions included in the present-day state, with the exception of the Prussian territory in the northeast. It had a number of developing urban centers, a new administrative structure, new churches, and an independent ecclesiastical organization in the form of five bishoprics—in Poznań, Gniezno, Cracow, Kołobrzeg, and Wrocław (fig. 7.9). It was also a very different society, one with many more foreigners, including clergy, warriors, merchants, and craftsmen. In just two or three Piast generations, between 950 and 1000, Poland had moved from the periphery to the main scene of European developments. Poland had taken a major step on the road to Europe.

How Poland Came into Being: A Possible Scenario

The developments taking place in Poland in the early tenth century can be reconstructed on the basis of archaeological excavations carried out in different regions of the country. Their outcome was a sudden, sometimes catastrophic collapse of most—although not all—tribal strongholds, which were replaced by new centers arising at the behest of the Piast rulers.

The tribal entities had little chance to survive the political changes taking place at that time in the neighboring regions of Europe, particularly the rise of the Holy Roman Empire and of other Christian states. Their military weakness was the lack of a professional army or retinue of warriors. Such entities were often at odds, if not war, with each other, and perpetual rivalry invited military intervention from militarily powerful neighbors, such as the Franks, who usually took advantage of such conflicts. Tribal leaders relied almost exclusively on the old religious system and could not break with tradition without the risk of losing face and power. More important, tribal entities lacked an efficient economic system similar to the so-called stronghold organization of the early Piast period.

It is possible that the foundations of medieval urban life in Poland were already laid within the first generation of Piast rulers. The building of such a great number of strongholds was not without consequences, particularly in terms of changes in the landscape, such as massive deforestation. Recent studies have shown that a large-scale building campaign was responsible in the 960s for the cutting of a great number of trees (mostly oaks), for the construction of stronghold ramparts and amenities. The impact of this campaign can only be measured if we take into consideration that in the late 900s, many regions of Poland experienced the first crisis in wood supply. At that time, enlargement and repair of already existing strongholds had to be done not with trunks of hundred-year-old oaks but with those of young trees of various species that were no more than thirty years old. The available data indicate that in Great Poland, this crisis reached its apex between 960 and 1039.[25]

What, then, were the developments leading to the formation of the medieval state of Poland? On the basis of recent studies, I propose the following scenario (fig. 7.10).

1. By the late ninth or early tenth century, the first attempts were made to restructure some of the old tribal confederacies, in response to the aggressive policies promoted by neighboring states. This may explain the erection of an important number of strongholds and the establishment of regional, intertribal centers of pagan cult. The political entity of the Vistulans was incorporated into Bohemia (after being part of Moravia as well), which coincided in time with the rise to political prominence of the Polanians of Great Poland.

2. Stage I (ca. 920–ca. 925). Intertribal confrontations in Great Poland pushed the Piasts to the fore of the political scene, as leaders of a powerful Polanian state. Mieszko I accepted baptism in 966 and began the process of radical transformation of the Polanian state. By 950, he had incorporated Mazovia, as suggested by the well-documented destruction of most tribal strongholds in the region.

3. Stage II (970–80). Mieszko reached Little Poland as far as Przemyśl. The tribal territory of the Lendizi in southeastern Poland was also conquered and annexed. New provincial centers emerged: San-

domierz in Little Poland. Przemyśl, Lublin, and the Czerwień strongholds were built on the eastern frontier.[26] During the same decade, Mieszko attacked Pomerania. He seems to have encountered difficulties in western Pomerania but succeeded in incorporating the eastern region near the mouth of the Vistula River, where Gdańsk was founded—followed by Kruszwica in Kuyavia, which may have been viewed as a basis for the future conversion of Pomerania.

4. Stage III (980–ca. 989). The center of military activity shifted to western Pomerania and to Silesia. Wolin, Kolobrzeg, and Szczecin— the main tribal centers on the Baltic coast—were conquered and re-built by the Piast rulers. Following the war with Boleslav II of Bo-hemia, Silesia was brought under Polish control, and the main Silesian towns were founded in Opole and Wrocław.

5. Stage IV (ca. 989–92). Cracow and its hinterland were taken from the Bohemians. In sharp contrast with the other main centers of Little Poland already discussed, there is no archaeological evidence of military activity that could be associated with the incorporation of Cracow into the Piast state. It is quite possible that western Little Poland was taken over without any violence. According to the ar-chaeological data, Cracow and other tribal centers in the region had been growing steadily without interruption since the 800s.

Conclusion

This chapter presents one of many possible scenarios for the tenth-century developments in Poland. The interpretation of the archaeological evidence offered here not only sheds a new light on the process of state formation but also brings to the fore the personality of the first ruler of Poland, traditionally obscured by the towering figure of his son, Boleslav the Brave (Chrobry). A careful examination of Mieszko's reign shows the European dimension of his political and organizational capabilities.

During the period of political consolidation in Eastern Francia under the successive rulers of the Ottonian dynasty, the policies promoted by the Polan-ian prince proved to be successful. The rise of the state centered in Gniezno and the conversion to Christianity in 966 brought the political acceptance of Chris-tian Europe and legitimacy for the newly united state. This was possible pri-marily because no conflict separated Mieszko's state from Ottonian interests. The Ottonians were torn between long-term political interests in Italy and the internal problems of the empire. Under such circumstances, the Polanian ruler felt encouraged and protected, as he could rely on the support of the empire. In his conflict with Boleslav II of Bohemia over Silesia, Mieszko received military support from Empress Theophano. He in turn provided military support for Otto III's efforts to convert the pagans.

The peculiar association between church and state created a neutral curtain between Poland and the Roman Catholic West, on one hand, and the Byzantine cultural influence from Kievan Rus', on the other. Despite temporary political and dynastic alliances, Poland and Rus' formed two distinct worlds, separated by different cultural and religious options. In contrast, the Holy Roman Empire was a political organism based on the idea of a universal empire encompassing all territories under Roman obedience, regardless of linguistic affiliation. Mieszko came to play an important role in the plans of this empire. Through his policies of conquest and annexation, he created Poland but also laid the foundations for a united Europe, an idea continued by Boleslav the Brave and Otto III and epitomized by the Act of Gniezno in AD 1000.

NOTES

1. K. Maleczyński, ed., *Anonima tzw. Galla Kronika czyli dzieje książąt i władców polskich*, No. 1.1 Pomniki dziejowe Polski, series 2, vol. 2 (Cracow, 1952); for the English translation, see Michael J. Mikós, *Medieval Literature of Poland: An Anthology* (New York and London, 1992), 6. See also Henryk Łowmiański, *Początki Polski*, vol. 3 (Warsaw, 1973), 441–43.

2. Witold Hensel, *Archeologia o początkach miast słowiańskich* (Wrocław, 1963); B. Miśkiewicz, "Monarchia wczesnych Piastów (IX w.–1138)," in *Dzieje Polski*, ed. Jerzy Topolski (Warsaw, 1977), 88–90.

3. Fernand Braudel, *Historia i trwanie* (Warsaw, 1971).

4. Jerzy Gąssowski, "Archeologia o schyłku pogaństwa," *Archeologia Polski* 37 (1992): 137–57.

5. Marek Dulinicz, "The first dendrochronological dating of the strongholds of northern Mazovia," in *Origins of Central Europe*, ed. Przemysław Urbańczyk (Warsaw, 1997), 137–41.

6. Gąssowski, "Archeologia o schyłku pogaństwa," 137–58.

7. Ewa Marczak, "Tabliczki z Podebłocia: Nie rozwiązana zagadka," in *Studia z dziejów cywilizacji: Studia ofiarowane Profesorowi Jerzemu Gąssowskiemu w pięćdziesiątą rocznicę pracy naukowej*, ed. Andrzej Buko (Warsaw, 1998), 93–102.

8. *Life of Methodius II*, in *Monumenta Poloniae Historica*, ed. A. Bielowski, vol. 1 (Lwów, 1864), 107; English translation from Marvin Kantor, *Medieval Slavic Lives of Saints and Princes* (Ann Arbor, 1983), 121.

9. Premysław Urbańczyk, "Procesy centralizacji władzy w okresie przechodzenia do organizacji wczesnopaństwowych," in *Centrum i zaplecze we wczesnośredniowiecznej Europie środkowej, Spotkania Bytomskie III*, ed. Sławomir Możdzioch (Wrocław, 1999), 661–67.

10. Andrzej Kukliński, "Wczesnośredniowieczne warstwy osadnicze Krakowa-Wawelu (odkryte w wykopie I C, rejon IX), a relikty jego walu datowanego dendrochronologicznie na okres po 1016 roku," *Sprawozdania Archeologiczne* 50 (1998): 277–92.

11. Leszek Pawel Słupecki, "Monumentalne kopce Kakusa i Wandy pod Krakowem," in *Studia z dziejów cywilizacji: Studia ofiarowane Profesorowi Jerzemu Gąssowskiemu w pięćdziesiątą rocznicę pracy naukowej*, ed. Andrzej Buko (Warsaw, 1998), 57–72.

12. Georges Dumézil, *Mythe et épopée. L'idéologie des trois functions dans les épopées des peoples indo-européens* (Paris, 1968). See Jacek Banaszkiewicz, *Podanie o Piaście Popielu: Studium porównawcze nad wczesnośredniowiecznymi tradycjami dynastycznymi* (Warsaw, 1986).

13. Andrzej Buko, "Początki państwa polskiego: Pytania-problemy-hipotezy," *Świątowit* 42 (1999): 32–45; Zofia Kurnatowska, *Początki Polski* (Poznań, 2002).

14. Zofia Kurnatowska, "Początki państwa i chrześcijaństwa w Polsce w świetle źródeł archeologicznych," in *Archeologia Wielkopolska: Osiągnięcia i problemy ochrony zabytków*, ed. Hanna Kočka-Krenz (Poznań, 1998), 91–101.

15. Andrzej Rozwałka, *Lubelskie Wzgórze Staromiejskie w procesie formowania średniowiecznego miasta* (Lublin, 1997).

16. Andrzej Buko, *Początki Sandomierza* (Warsaw, 1999), 17.

17. Tomasz Sawicki, "Gnieźnieński zespół grodowy w świetle najnowszych badań," in *Studia z dziejów cywilizacji: Studia ofiarowane Profesorowi Jerzemu Gąssowskiemu w pięćdziesiątą rocznię pracy naukowej*, ed. Andrzej Buko (Warsaw, 1998), 207–16.

18. Buko, *Początki Sandomierza*, 56.

19. Władysław Łosiński, "Miejsce Pomorza i Wielkopolski w kształtowaniu się gospodarki towarowo-pieniężnej w Polsce wczesnofeudalnej," *Slavia Antiqua* 37 (1996): 163–80; "Rola kontaktów ze Skandynawią w dziejach gospodarczych Słowian nadbałtyckich," *Przegląd Archeologiczny* 45 (1997): 73–86.

20. Andrzej Zbierski, "Rozwój przestrzenny Gdańska w IX–XIII w.," in *Historia Gdańska*, ed. Eugeniusz Cieślak (Gdańsk, 1978), 71–259.

21. Zbigniew Pianowski, "*Sedes regni principales": Wawel i inne rezydencje piastowskie do połowy XIII wieku na tle europejskim* (Cracow, 1994).

22. T. Kowalski, ed., *Relacja Ibrāhīma ibn Ja'kūba z podróży do krajów słowiańskich w przekazie al-Bekrīego* (Cracow, 1946), 48–50.

23. Michał Kara, "Z badań nad wczesnośredniowiecznymi grobami z uzbrojeniem z terenu Wielkopolski," in *Od plemiania do państwa: Śląsk na tle wczesnośredniowiecznej Słowiańszczyzny Zachodniej*, ed. Lech Leciejewicz (Wrocław, 1991), 99–118.

24. Tadeusz Baranowski, "Gród w Kaliszu: Badania, odkrycia, interpretacje," in *Kalisz wczesnośredniowieczny*, ed. Tadeusz Baranowski (Kalisz, 1998), 39–64.

25. Marek Krąpiec, "Dendrochronological dating of early medieval fortified settlements in Poland," in *Frühmittelalterlicher Burgenbau in Mittel- und Osteuropa: Tagung, Nitra, vom. 7. bis 10. Oktober 1996*, ed. Joachim Henning and Alexander T. Ruttkay (Bonn, 1998), 257–67.

26. Andrzej Buko, "From Great Poland to the Little Poland: The ruling Piast dynasty and the processes of creating the regions," in *Centre, Region, Periphery: Medieval Europe, Basel 2002*, ed. Guido Helmig, Barbara Scholkmann, Matthias Untermann, vol. 1 (Hertingen and Basel, 2002), 468–73.

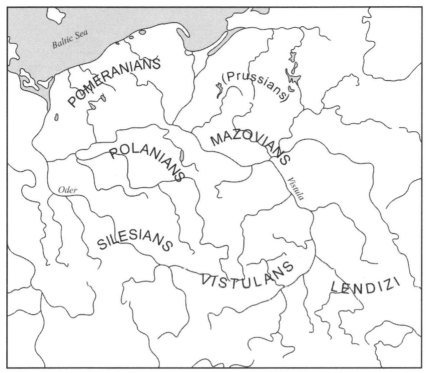

Fig. 7.1. Distribution of the main tribes in Poland, ca. 900. (Drawn by M. Trzeciecki.)

Fig. 7.2. The Holy Cross Benedictine monastery established in the early 1100s on Lysiec Mountain (Holy Cross Mountain in southern Poland), on the site of an old pagan center of cult. (Photography courtesy of A. Buko.)

Fig. 7.3. Ninth-century ceramic "tablet" from Podebłocie (eastern Poland), with incised signs purported to be Christ's monograph. (Photography courtesy of M. Gmur.)

Fig. 7.4. The Krak large barrow in Cracow, the alleged symbol of power from eighth-century southern Poland. (Photography courtesy of A. Buko.)

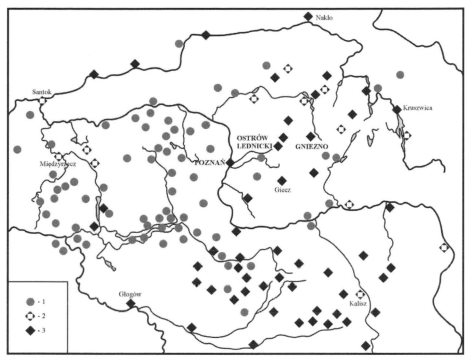

Fig. 7.5. Distribution of strongholds in Great Poland: (1) tribal strongholds, (2) strongholds that were restored and reused under the first Piast rulers, (3) Piast strongholds. (Drawn by M. Trzeciecki after Kurnatowska, "Początki państwa.")

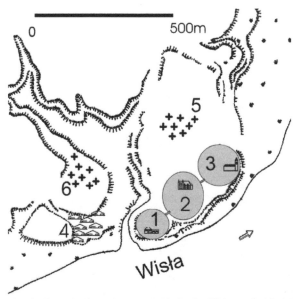

Fig. 7.6. Sandomierz in the early eleventh century: (1) Castle Hill (stronghold), (2) Cathedral Hill (fortified suburb), (3) Gostomianum Hill (fortified suburb), (4) St. James Hill (nonfortified suburb), (5–6) cemeteries. (Source: Buko, "From Great Poland.")

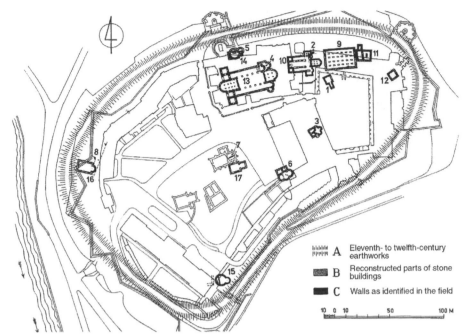

Fig. 7.7. Tenth- to eleventh-century architectural remains on Wawel Hill in Cracow: (1) the so-called rectangular building (early eleventh century); (2) chapel (early eleventh century); (3) the rotunda of Saints Feliks and Adaukt (ca. 1000); (4) remains of an apse (early eleventh century); (5) single-apsed rotunda with baptismal font (early eleventh century); (6) the so-called Pre-Romanesque rotunda B (early eleventh century); (7) fragment of a Pre-Romanesque wall inside the St. Michael Church; (8) corner of Pre-Romanesque building (early eleventh century); (9) the so-called room with twenty-four posts, the Romanesque palace (mid-eleventh century?); (10) Romanesque basilica of St. Gereon (late eleventh century); (11) annex on the eastern side of the palace (twelfth or early thirteenth century); (12) tower (twelfth century?); (13) the Cathedral of Prince Herman (ca. 1090–1142); (14) Romanesque chapel (thirteenth century?); (15) Romanesque rotunda (eleventh or twelfth century); (17) remains of the Romanesque Church of St. Michael. (Drawn by M. Trzeciecki after Pianowski, "*Sedes regni principales*.")

Fig. 7.8. The early eleventh-century stronghold and remains of the St. Paul cathedral built in Kalisz-Zawodzie in the 1100s, on top of an early eleventh-century wooden church. (Source: Institute of Archaeology and Ethnography of the Polish Academy of Sciences, Warsaw.)

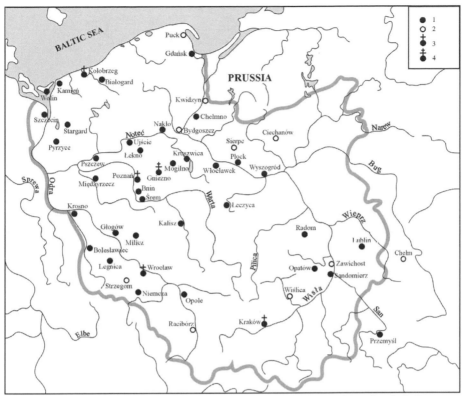

Fig. 7.9. Distribution of more important strongholds in Poland, ca. 1000: (1) archaeologically secured date, (2) uncertain date, (3) bishoprics, (4) archbishoprics. Also shown are the borders of
Poland, ca. 990. (Drawn by M. Auch.)

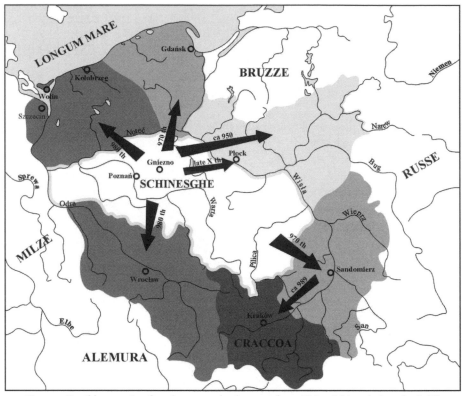

Fig. 7.10. Possible scenario of tenth-century development from *Civitas Schinesghe* into the Polish state. (Drawn by M. Auch after the author's sketch.)

PART THREE

Conversion

Before Cyril and Methodius: Christianity and Barbarians beyond the Sixth- and Seventh-Century Danube Frontier

Florin Curta

N̲o other concept in use among medievalists is more ambiguous, yet more potent, than conversion. The word *conversion* conjures a picture of dramatic transformation, something of the nature of St. Paul's blinding vision on the road to Damascus. Textbooks of medieval history use the "Christianization of the barbarians" conveniently illustrated by Clovis's conversion to mark the transition from late antiquity to the Middle Ages. St. Augustine, however, viewed conversion as a turning to God, not to Christianity or to the church. To him, conversion was not simply about accepting Christianity, submitting to church authority, or changing from one way of life to another. Conversion was a matter of divine intervention, not of human rationalization.[1] Moreover, it was a matter of personal choice, not one of collective enthusiasm. As such, conversion was to be understood as a profound, gradual, and, especially, personal change in values, beliefs, identity, and behavior.[2]

Early medieval sources rarely, if ever, speak of the conversion of an entire *gens*. It is unknown where and how the Lombards adopted Christianity, and Paul the Deacon, at least, had no need to explain that. Nothing is known about the beginnings of Christianity among the Ostrogoths or the Gepids.[3] In such cases, it is not possible to operate with a concept of conversion defined as an individual's change of mind and behavior introduced by a single, significant event in history, such as baptism. Instead, historians prefer A. D. Nock's distinction between "the reorientation of the soul of an individual" and the institutional adhesion to or "acceptance of new worships as useful supplements and not as substitutes" for older forms of worship.[4] It is assumed that by such means, "true converts" may be easily distinguished from the uncommitted. However, neither the individual's claims of religious affiliation nor his or her participation in rituals can be treated as accurate indicators of large-scale conversion.

Even greater complications arise when the object of study is conversion in

the past: "What is called conversion is a thing felt, evaporating with its dura-
tion. What we have as historical evidence is a text, a thing made."[5] Conversion
is thus a metaphor, not an event. As a metaphor, it can help us understand the
horizon shift in traditional societies from the microcosm of the local community populated by lesser spirits to a higher order reflected in new ideas regarding a supreme being and rituals developed for mediating contact with that
figure and harnessing its influence.[6] According to such views, early medieval
rulers adopted Christianity mainly because of new ideas about organization,
hierarchy, and authority that were now readily available through the agency of
missionaries.[7] Thus, the success of the mission of Cyril and Methodius to
Moravia may be interpreted as the result both of Byzantine plans to convert the
Slavs and of Rostislav's use of the new religion to achieve his own political
goals. Conversely, the failure to convert the Avars in the aftermath of the Carolingian destruction of their qaganate in the late eighth century may indicate
that no political force in the area was strong enough to protect missions and to
support a sustained effort of propagating Christianity. However, bishops par-
ticipating in the synod of 796 *ad ripas Danubii* (on the bank of the Danube)
knew that there were "uneducated priests" within the former qaganate, who
wrongly performed baptisms without reciting the baptismal formula.[8]

As for the Slavs, the earliest attempts to convert them are described in
Western, not Byzantine, sources. In his *Life of St. Columbanus*, Jonas of Bobbio,
speaking of Columbanus's missionary goals, claimed that the saint had once
thought to go preaching to the "Wends who were called Slavs." He eventually
gave up this mission of evangelization, for "the eyes of the Slavs were not yet
open for the light of the Scriptures."[9] However, one of his disciples, Bishop
Amandus, did preach to the Slavs at some point around 630. His *Life*, written
a century later, describes his journey across the Danube to the Slavs, who, "sunk
in great error, were caught in the devil's snares."[10] Some sixty years after Bishop
Amandus's visit, St. Marinus was burned at the stake by "Vandals" (most likely,
Carantanian Slavs) somewhere in the borderlands of Bavaria.[11] St. Rupert of
Salzburg was comparatively luckier when converting a king of the Carantanian
Slavs in the late 600s.[12] Perhaps as a result of such efforts, at the Sixth Ecumenical Council in Constantinople (November 680), the Slavs were known to have
welcomed Christian missionaries.[13] It was in Constantinople that the "Slavic
problem" first appeared and attempts were made to deal with it. It was in Constantinople that the name of the Slavs was first used and Avar hairstyles were
first noticed.[14]

Ever since the 500s, the early Byzantine Empire has maintained a close contact with both Slavs and Avars, more so than any missionary centers in the
West.[15] Why, then, was there a lack of interest in the progress of Christianity

among Slavs and Avars before 680? If the Slavs were regarded as already won for the cause of Christianity in the late seventh century, why was it necessary to reinvent the Slavic mission in the ninth? How can we explain such indifference toward territories across the sixth-century frontier on the Danube during a period of extraordinary initiatives in the administration, economy, and religious organization of the Balkan provinces of the empire? In this chapter, I intend to explore some of these issues and provide some plausible answers. I will argue that the specific circumstances in which Emperor Justinian's impressive building program in the Balkans came into being, especially the sharp decline of the rural population in the Balkans, may explain the striking absence of major monastic sites in the Balkans. This may in turn explain the lack of information about missions across the frontier, despite the growing power of local bishops.[16] The archaeological and historical evidence suggests that Christian artifacts and practices were known to barbarians north of the Danube. However, missions in the sixth century often operated under the aegis of the state, for they were harnessed for the political purposes of the empire. That no evidence exists for missionary enterprises across the sixth-century Danube frontier, which could be compared with the process of conversion elsewhere, may indicate that on the northern frontier of the empire, no political gains were expected to result from missions of evangelization.

The Archaeology of Slavic and Avar Christianity

The archaeological evidence that comes from north of the Danube and bears overtly Christian symbolism is not easy to interpret. Unlike the situation on the *limes* in Transcaucasia, where churches appear relatively far from the territories under the direct control of the Romans, almost no Christian monuments were found beyond the Danube frontier.[17] The only puzzling exception is the basilica at Fenékpuszta, on the western shore of Lake Balaton (Hungary). In the mid-500s, just before the arrival of the Avars, the fourth-century fort built there under Constantine the Great or his successors was reoccupied. At some time during the second half of the sixth century, the three-aisled basilica was erected in the northwestern corner of the fort. This church was restored sometime around 600 and then destroyed, together with the adjacent settlement, around 630.[18]

In all its architectural details, as well as in its location, the basilica at Fenékpuszta is unique. It has nothing in common with architectural types established since the early fourth century in the neighboring, eastern Alpine region or in Dalmatia. Christian congregations there used box churches, without apses; the altar was pushed forward into the nave, and a semicircular bench be-hind the altar served the clergy.[19] With its three apses, the church at Fenékpuszta is more likely to have been inspired by the architecture of Constantinople.[20] Similar churches were built during Justinian's reign in Scythia Minor,[21] Moe-sia,[22] Thrace,[23] Epirus Nova,[24] and Dacia Mediterranea.[25] The same plan was also popular on the *limes* in Transcaucasia.[26] These were very large basilicas in at least two cases.[27] In other cases, the presence of a residential complex built nearby suggests the existence of an episcopal residence.[28] It is possible, there-fore, that the church at Fenékpuszta was an episcopal basilica.[29] There is no in-dication of a Christian community at Fenékpuszta before ca. 550,[30] but both the choice of plan for the three-aisled basilica and its elevation suggest that de-spite its location relatively closer to the north Italian bishoprics, members of the Fenékpuszta community maintained strong ties with the empire and looked to the Balkan provinces as a source of inspiration for their church.

Long-distance relations are also illustrated by finds of Menas flasks.[31] Such vessels were produced in Egypt and were used by pilgrims to carry home miracle-working *eulogia* water, which was dispensed from cisterns at the fa-mous shrine of St. Menas at Abu Mina. At least two specimens (from Szombat-hely and Moigrad), can be dated to the early seventh century (i.e., to the Avar period) on the basis of recent chronological studies on Menas flasks found at Kom el-Dikka, near Alexandria.[32] Such a late date also corresponds to disc brooches with religious scenes, which occasionally appear in burials of the Early Avar period[33] found in southwest Hungary.[34] A stray find from Nagy-harsány (near Pécs) was decorated with the portrait of an archangel (Gabriel?) and an inscription in Greek ("Archangel have mercy [upon me]"). Three other specimens from Keszthely and Pécs have images of Christ surrounded by an-gels.[35] All this evidence clearly points to the existence of a relatively large, well-organized group of Christians in the region south and west of Lake Balaton, around Fenékpuszta. By year 600, these Christians, although undoubtedly sub-jects of the qagan of the Avars, maintained long-distance relations with Pales-tine, Egypt, and Italy. Whether they were recruited from Avars or from the local population the Avars had found in Pannonia after the defeat of the Gepids is difficult, if not impossible, to decide. In any case, both the basilica at Fenék-puszta and the burial assemblages attributed to this group (known as the "Keszthely culture") suggest that its identity derived, at least in part, from a strong sense of belonging to the Christian world.

The evidence of crosses worn as pectorals or brooches and imitating the imperial costume raises different questions.[36] Late fifth- or early sixth-century Latin crosses of various sizes and degrees of elaboration were often found in remarkably wealthy funerary assemblages,[37] settlement contexts,[38] or hoards[39] in the Balkans, all associated in some way with local elites (figs. 8.1–2). Crosses of this kind often display sophisticated ornamental patterns in cloisonné,[40] granulation,[41] and filigree,[42] which suggest that these artifacts were procured from distant production centers, perhaps from Constantinople or other major cities. They were replicated in less ornamented, cheaper versions in silver[43] or antimony.[44] Only a few crosses of this kind were found in the otherwise considerable number of settlement or funerary assemblages excavated so far across the Danube.[45] This is also true for slender stick crosses[46] or crosses moline,[47] which were worn as pectorals attached to lavishly adorned necklaces of gold (figs. 8.3–4).

By contrast, Maltese crosses worn (especially by women) either as pectorals[48] or attached to dress pins[49] and earrings[50] were found in much humbler contexts, often in association with ordinary effects, such as glass beads or crossbow brooches (figs. 8.5–8). Molds found in sixth-century forts[51] demonstrate that such crosses were produced locally. Identical molds were found, however, on contemporary sites north of the Danube,[52] and there is also evidence of crosses produced there.[53] In addition, the distribution of Maltese crosses overlaps that of ceramic artifacts (pots and spindle whorls) with incised crosses,[54] sometimes followed by wavy lines,[55] or swastikas (fig. 8.9).[56] There are also images of fish[57] and even short inscriptions.[58] That such signs carried a Christian symbolism was already proposed by many authors.[59] Very similar, if not identical, signs were found on various sites located far from each other. Handmade pots with such decoration are indisputably of local production. This suggests the existence of a cross-regional set of symbols shared by potters and/or users of pottery, despite an arguably localized production.

Finally, late sixth-century, luxury pectoral crosses with rounded ends, such as that from the Mersin hoard,[60] seem to have been imitated in the 600s by crosses found in Middle Avar archaeological assemblages.[61] Such crosses have no Balkan analogies and were perhaps inspired by artifacts obtained from the empire through either plundering or, more likely, gift giving.[62] Their distribution strikingly coincides with that of *phylacteria*, small pendants with enclosed relics or biblical verses (figs. 8.10–11).[63]

The different chronology and the distribution of these types of crosses suggest the existence of a pattern. Early pectoral crosses of the Latin type were not imitated north of the Danube. Judging from the existing evidence, access to such artifacts was restricted to local Balkan elites, either military or religious. By contrast, Maltese crosses produced locally on a large scale for soldiers in the garrisons of forts or for their wives were quickly replicated on contemporary sites north of the Danube. Pectoral crosses and *phylacteria* were still popular in mid- and late seventh-century Avaria, as high-status individuals, particularly women, were occasionally buried with such artifacts. Although at the time, many, if not all, early Byzantine sites in the Balkans had been abandoned, crosses and *phylacteria* produced in Byzantium or imitating artifacts from the empire, perhaps from outside the Balkans, continued to be in demand among upper-class members of Avar society. The existence of this distribution pattern points to a phenomenon known as *imitatio imperii,* which has been also documented for other areas of *barbaricum.*[64]

Not all artifacts with Christian associations seem to have enjoyed the same popularity. For example, humbler signs of Christian devotion, such as mold-made clay lamps with cross-shaped handles, are rare on sixth- to seventh-century sites in Romania, Moldova, and Ukraine.[65] But the ceramic decoration with crosslike signs seems to have been inspired by incised and painted (*dipinti*) crosslike signs and inscriptions, which appear in great numbers on sixth-century amphorae.[66] Such amphorae, carrying olive oil, wine, or *garum* (fish-sauce),[67] were particularly common on the Danube frontier and may have served for state distributions to the Roman troops stationed there.[68]

Limes and Mission

Judging from the intrasite distribution of artifacts on sixth- and seventh-century sites north of the Danube River, amphorae or, more likely, their contents were viewed and used as prestige goods by local elites. Access to such goods may have been a key strategy for imitating the military lifestyle of fort garrisons in the Balkans. They are rare north of the Danube frontier and may have been viewed as trophies and prestige goods.

The evidence of crosses, cross molds, *phylacteria,* and crosslike signs on ceramic artifacts found in *barbaricum* was often interpreted as a result of missions, in connection with the implementation, in the mid-500s, of Justinian's fortified frontier and the area controlled by Romans on the left bank through a number of bridgeheads.[69] There is, however, no indication of missions on the Danube frontier in the 500s. This may well be just because of our relatively poor knowledge of developments on the Danube frontier of the empire in the 500s. But it may equally be the result of the absence of a significant monastic movement in the Balkans, for many monasteries were also centers of missionary activity.[70] In all known cases, missions were directed toward protecting the empire's frontiers through building alliances with neighboring polities. The Pax Romana was equated with the Pax Christiana, and the empire's foreign policy became intimately associated with the missionary work of the church.[71]

This is particularly clear in cases in which the emperor himself was involved in the conversion of individual political leaders. For example, in the early years of Justinian's reign, Gord, a chieftain ruling over the Huns near the Crimean Bosporus, came in person to Constantinople to receive baptism. He returned home carrying gifts from the emperor and accompanied by Roman troops to be stationed in Bosporus, but he ended up being assassinated when he attempted to turn his fellow tribesmen to Christianity by destroying the idols they worshiped.[72] Another Hunnic chieftain came to Constantinople during the reign of Heraclius, was baptized, and received gifts and the dignity of *patricius* from the emperor.[73] According to the Syriac chronicle attributed to Zacharias of Mitylene, there were two other attempts in the 500s to convert the Huns living north of the Caucasus range. The first was undertaken by a monk of the monastery Beth Aishaquni near Amida, the other by Kardutsat (Theodetos), bishop of Albania, and Maku (Makarios), bishop of Armenia. Kardutsat's mission took place at some point during the second quarter of the sixth century and may have coincided in time with the Gord episode.[74] This mission was initially directed toward providing religious services to Roman prisoners but ended up baptizing a considerable number of Huns and translating the Gospels into their language. Bishop Makarios also erected a church in Hunnic territory.

There is nothing remotely similar to these relations in the region of the Danube frontier, and there is no parallel to the conversion of King Ethelbert of Kent by Augustine and forty other monks who landed at Thanet in 597 bearing an icon of Christ and a silver cross and chanting the Roman liturgy.[75] The absence of any information regarding sixth-century missions on the Danube frontier is puzzling, particularly in contrast with the 300s, when attempts were made to convert the Goths on the Danube frontier to the mainstream imperial Christianity of Bishop Ulfila's days.[76] In the early 400s, Theotimos, bishop of Tomis, was well known to the Huns living north of the Danube, who called him "the god of the Romans" (*theon Rhomaion*).[77] No sixth-century bishop, however, is known to have conducted such missions beyond that frontier, despite the increasingly prominent position bishops now occupied in the administration of the northern Balkans. To be sure, some of the groups living beyond the Danube frontier were already Christian. The Gepids were of Arian faith ever since, perhaps, their early contacts with the Goths converted by Ulfila.[78] By 528, Grepes, the king of the Herules settled by Emperor Anastasius in western Moesia and Dacia Ripensis, received baptism in Constantinople, together with his family and chief warriors.[79] However, no attempts are known to have been made for the conversion of any sixth-century group living north of the Danube. There is no indication of missions targeted at either Avars or Slavs.[80]

The presence of Christians among the "barbarians" of the Danube region is clearly attested in written sources. In 593, as Priscus's troops were chasing the Sclavenes deep into their own territory, one of their prisoners was a Gepid, who happened to be a friend and subject of the Sclavene "king" Musocius. He betrayed his "king," however, and revealed the location of Musocius's village to the Romans, because the prisoner "had once long before been of the Christian religion."[81] The *Miracles of St. Demetrius* described in detail the story of a group of Roman prisoners brought to Pannonia in the early 600s by Avar warriors. They maintained their language and Christian faith for more than sixty years and remained, even under their Avar masters, a "Christian tribe."[82] The author of the *Strategikon* knew that there were many Romans living among Sclavenes and that some of those Romans may have been Christians. He recommended caution in dealing with them, however, for they "have given in to the times, forget their own people, and prefer to gain the good will of the enemy" (i.e., of the Sclavenes).[83]

Despite the presence of many Christian prisoners, their proselytism can hardly explain the presence of artifacts with Christian symbolism on sixth- and seventh-century sites north of the Danube. In addition, the association, in some cases, of such artifacts with clearly non-Christian practices suggests another explanation.[84] Adoption by barbarian elites of Christian artifacts does not necessarily imply adoption of Christianity, although it certainly presupposes some knowledge of the underlying ideology. In many cases, the political use of this ideology, particularly its association with imperial power, seems to have been more attractive than its content.

According to Michael the Syrian, during a raid into Greece in the 580s, the Sclavenes carried off on carts the holy vessels and ciboria from devastated churches. In Corinth, however, one of their leaders took the great ciborium and, using it as a tent, made it his dwelling.[85] The Sclavene chief seems to have clearly grasped the symbolic potential of the otherwise useless stone ciborium, shaped as it was like a canopy over a throne. The same is true for the ruler of the Avars. Following the conquest of Anchialos in 584, the qagan proclaimed himself "king" by putting on a cloth of imperial purple from a local church, to which it had been donated by Empress Anastasia, the wife of Tiberius II.[86] That the qagan of the Avars was familiar with Christian practices and ideology is demonstrated by another episode. Theophylact Simocatta narrates that the Avars and the Romans met in Scythia Minor, under the walls of Tomis, at Easter in 598. At the time, "famine was pressing hard on the Romans." "With strange providence," the qagan sent an embassy to Priscus, the general of the Roman army, and revealed his intention not only to establish a five-day truce, in order to allow Romans to celebrate their Christian festival, but also to provide plenty of food for the occasion.[87] Whatever the exact intentions of the qagan, this episode shows that he was aware of the importance of Easter for his Christian enemies. In 579, Bayan even agreed to take an oath on the Gospels that, by building a bridge over the Sava River, he had no intentions to attack Singidunum. This did not make him either Christian or less treacherous in the eyes of Menander the Guardsman, who covered the story. The qagan was a master of deceit: when the archbishop of Singidunum brought the Gospels, Bayan "stood up from his throne, pretended to receive the books with great fear and reverence, threw himself on the ground and most fervently swore by the God who had spoken the words on the holy parchment that nothing of what he had said was a lie."[88] Unlike other similar cases, the Christian oaths taken by Bayan in 579 were not preceded by his baptism. Nevertheless, if, in 579, he had not left the impression of a pagan soul truly terrified by the word of the Christian God, it would have been impossible for him to dupe the emperor himself and, in the end, to surround, besiege, and conquer both Sirmium (582) and Singidunum (584). Perhaps the archbishop of Singidunum believed Bayan was sincere and hoped that he would eventually accept baptism. But when Sirmium fell in 582, all illusions quickly dissipated. During the last moments of the city, one of its desperate inhabitants scratched on a tile with a shaking hand, "God Jesus Christ, save our city, smash the Avars, and protect the Romans and the one who wrote this."[89]

Conclusion

The comparison between the archaeological evidence from Fenékpuszta and the pectoral crosses, cross molds, *phylacteria,* and ceramic artifacts with incised crosses, symbols, and inscriptions found north of the lower Danube shows how complex the situation was beyond the *limes.* Do the artifacts found on sixth- to seventh-century sites north of the Danube indicate a Christian identity?[90] As suggested in the previous section of this chapter, in the absence of any evidence of a well-organized congregation similar to that signaled by the basilica at Fenékpuszta, the artifacts with Christian symbolism found on "barbarian" sites can hardly be interpreted as evidence of conversion. By contrast, both the basilica and the burial assemblages in Fenékpuszta or on neighboring, contemporary sites point to the existence of a relatively strong Christian community in Pannonia.

How can this contrast be explained? It is tempting to associate the basilica and the intramural cemetery at Fenékpuszta with Justinian's increasing involvement, in the early 550s, in the conflict between Lombards and Gepids.[91]

Indeed, by the mid-sixth century, Justinian seems to have been able, by means of payments of large sums of money, to contain the threat to the Danube frontier. He allied himself with Lombards and Antes against Gepids and Huns, respectively. It is against this background that the sudden appearance of the Christian congregation at Fenékpuszta should be seen. The plan of the church built there shortly after ca. 550 was clearly inspired by contemporary churches in the Balkans, not by those in the neighboring regions of Dalmatia or north Italy. It is possible, therefore, that the existence of the Christian community at Fenékpuszta was in some way associated with imperial policies in *barbaricum*. If, as has been suggested, the church at Fenékpuszta was an Episcopal basilica, we have good reasons to associate this congregation with contemporary developments in the Balkans, where bishops were undertaking administrative responsibilities and baptisteries were multiplying in response to an increasing demand for religious services. No evidence exists, however, that the Fenékpuszta community was designed to be a mission in barbarian territory.[92]

The situation north of the lower Danube is somewhat different. After Chilbudius's death in 533, there was a drastic change in Justinian's agenda in the Balkans. From this moment until Maurice's campaigns of the 590s, no offensive strategy underpinned imperial policies in the area. Instead, Justinian began an impressive plan of fortification, of a size and quality the Balkans had never witnessed before. The project, or at least the most important part of it, was probably completed when Procopius finished book 4 of his *Buildings*. In addition, Justinian remodeled the administrative structure of the Balkans and created the *quaestura exercitus* to support, both financially and militarily, the frontier provinces most affected by his building program.[93] These measures were not taken in response to any major threat, for Roman troops continued to control the left bank of the Danube, possibly through bridgeheads such as those of Drobeta and Sucidava. In addition, the Danube fleet, which was under the command of the *quaestor exercitus*, continued to operate throughout the sixth century.[94]

In addition to military and administrative measures, Justinian offered his alliance to the Antes (*foedus* of 545)[95] and began recruiting mercenaries from among both Sclavenes and Antes for his wars in Italy and Transcaucasia. Unlike Antes, however, the Sclavenes never became Justinian's allies. In his *Wars*, Procopius reserved the longest ethnographic excursus for the Sclavenes but viewed them as newcomers and nomads.[96] They were unpredictable and disorderly barbarians. In the late 500s or early 600s, the author of the *Strategikon* described the Sclavenes as completely faithless and having "no regard for treaties, which they agree to more out of fear than by gifts."[97] The reluctance to view the Sclavenes as potential allies seems to have been based on the fact that "there are many kings among them always at odds with one another."[98]

Instead of building alliances, Justinian's response to the problems of the Danube *limes*, particularly to Slavic raids, was the building and fortification program. During the last fifteen years of his reign, no Slavic raid crossed the Danube. In addition, the implementation of the program seems to have been accompanied by an economic closure of the frontier. No coins of either copper or gold dated between 545 and 565 were found north of the Danube, in either stray finds or hoards.[99] This halt in coin circulation seems to have been accompanied by a strong crisis in trading activities across the Danube and a subsequent scarcity of goods of Roman provenance. Relative scarcity turned these goods into trophies. Soon after 565, however, the quantity of both coins and prestige goods of Roman provenance increased dramatically, as Slavic raiding resumed on a much larger scale. The evidence of amphoras found on sites north of the Danube frontier, many of which date from after ca. 550, is a case in point. Olive oil, wine, and *garum* seem to have been on a demand as high as gold, silver, horses, and weapons, which, according to John of Ephesus, now caught the attention of Sclavene warriors raiding the Balkan provinces of the empire.[100] Artifacts with Christian symbolism first appear on sites north of the Danube frontier during this period. Their locally produced replicas soon became part of many archaeological assemblages associated with local elites. With no apparent mission in sight, however, the Christianization of the Danube *limes* encouraged imitation but produced no conversion.

NOTES

1. F. H. Russell, "Augustine: Conversion by the Book," in *Varieties of Religious Conversion in the Middle Ages,* ed. J. Muldoon (Gainesville, 1997), 13–30.

2. N. J. Higham, *The Convert Kings: Power and Religious Affiliation in Anglo-Saxon England* (Manchester and New York, 1997), 14.

3. W. Pohl, "'Das sanfte Joch Christi': Zum Christentum als gestaltende Kraft im Mitteleuropa des Frühmittelalters," in *Karantanien und der Alpen-Adria-Raum im Frühmittelalter,* ed. G. Hödl and J. Grabmayer (Vienna, Cologne, and Weimar, 1993), 260.

4. A. D. Nock, *Conversion: The Old and the New in Religion from Alexander the Great to Augustine of Hippo* (Oxford, 1933; reprint, 1961), 7.

5. K. F. Morrison, *Understanding Conversion* (Charlottesville, 1992), 5.

6. R. Horton, "On the rationality of conversion," *Africa* 45 (1975): 219–35, 373–99; Higham, *The Convert Kings,* 20–21.

7. Higham, *The Convert Kings,* 27.

8. A. Werminghoff, ed., *Concilia aevi Karolini,* vol. 2 (Hanover, 1906), 175. For these *clerici inlitterati* as local priests, whom the Frankish mission may have found in place, see R. Bratož, "Der Einfluß Aquileias auf den Alpenraum und das Alpenvorland (Von den Anfängen bis um 700)," in *Das Christentum im bairischen Raum von den Anfängen*

bis ins 11. Jahrhundert, ed. E. Boshof and H. Wolff (Cologne, Weimar, and Vienna, 1994), 56–57. In the *Life of Constantine,* the "apostle of the Slavs" lists Avars among "numerous peoples who . . . render glory unto God, each in its own language." See *Vita Constantini* 16; English translation in M. Kantor, *Medieval Slavic Lives of Saints and Princes* (Ann Arbor, 1983), 71. See also I. Duichev, "Il problema delle lingue nazionali nel Medio Evo e gli Slavi," *Ricerche slavistiche* 8 (1960): 57.

9. H. Wolfram, A. Kusternig, and H. Haupt, eds., *Quellen zur Geschichte des 7. und 8. Jahrhunderts* (Darmstadt, 1982), 488. Written sometime between 639 and 643, the *Life* describes events of the late sixth century. See V. K. Ronin, "'Zhitie Sv. abbata Kolumbana i ego uchenikov' Iony iz Bobb'o," in *Svod drevneishikh pis'mennykh izvestii o slavianakh,* ed. S. A. Ivanov, G. G. Litavrin, and V. K. Ronin, vol. 2 (Moscow, 1995), 359–63. For Columbanus as a *peregrinus pro Christo,* not a true missionary, see I. Wood, *The Missionary Life: Saints and the Evangelisation of Europe, 400–1500* (Harlow, 2001), 31, and 34. In addition to his lack of commitment to mission goals, Columbanus's failure to evangelize the Slavs may have been caused by the growing Avar threats on the eastern Merovingian borders.

10. *Vita Amandi,* ed. B. Krusch, MGH Scriptores Rerum Merovingicarum, vol. 5 (Hanover, 1910), 440. On Amandus and his notion of mission to all nations, see Wood, *Missionary Life,* 39. The episode of Amandus's failed mission to the Slavs is also mentioned in a newly discovered fragment of the *Life of Amandus* preserved in an eighth-century manuscript in the Tiroler Landesmuseum Ferdinandeum in Innsbruck: see A. Verhulst and G. Declercq, "L'action et le souvenir de saint Amand en Europe centrale: A propos de la découverte d'une *Vita Amandi antiqua,*" in *Aevum inter utrumque: Mélanges offerts à Gabriel Sanders, professeur émérite à l'Université de Gand,* ed. M. van Uytfanghe and R. Demeulenaere (Steenbrugis, and The Hague, 1991), 502–26.

11. B. Sepp, ed., *Vita Sancti Marini* (Regensburg, 1892), 170. For Vandals as Slavs, see L. Steinberger, "Wandalen=Wenden," *Archiv für slavische Philologie* 37 (1920): 116–22. For Carantanian Slavs, see A. Pleterski, "Die karantanische Slawen und die Nichtslawen," in *Interaktionen der mitteleuropäischen Slawen und anderer Ethnika im 6.–10. Jahrhundert: Symposium Nové Vozokany 3.–7. Oktober 1983,* ed. P. Šalkovský (Nitra, 1984), 199–204; K. Bertels, "Carantania: Beobachtungen zur politisch-geographischen Terminologie und zur Geschichte des Landes und seiner Bevölkerung im frühen Mittelalter," *Carinthia* 177 (1987): 87–190; H.-D. Kahl, "Das Fürstentum Karantanien und die Anfänge seiner Christianisierung," in *Karantanien und der Alpen-Adria-Raum im Frühmittelalter,* ed. G. Hödl and J. Grabmayer (Vienna, Cologne, and Weimar, 1993), 37–99; H. Wolfram, "Les Carantaniens, le premier peuple slave baptisé," in *Clovis: Histoire et mémoire; Le baptême de Clovis, son écho à travers l'histoire,* ed. Michel Rouche (Paris, 1997), 279–87.

12. *Gesta Hrodberti,* ed. W. Levinson (MGH Scriptores Rerum Merovingicarum, vol. 6 (Hanover, 1913), 15. On Rupert of Salzburg and his representation in the late eighth-century *Gesta,* most likely based on an earlier *Life* of the saint, see Wood, *Missionary Life,* 146–50.

13. G. G. Litavrin, "Iz aktov shestogo vselenskogo sobora," in *Svod drevneishikh pis'-mennykh izvestii o slavianakh,* ed. S. A. Ivanov, G. G. Litavrin, and V. K. Ronin, vol. 2 (Moscow, 1995), 212. The Slavs in question must have been in the "West," not in the "East." Indeed, their name (*Sclabi*) first appears in the acts of the synod of Rome that took place on March 27, 680, in preparation for the ecumenical council. Along with Lombards, Franks, Goths, and others, the Slavs are cited as a gens with its own bishops.

This may well refer to then current events in Carantania. See R. Bratož, "Aquileia und der Alpen-Adria-Raum (von der Mitte des 6. Jahrhunderts bis 811)," in *Karantanien und der Alpen-Adria Raum im Frühmittelalter*, ed. Günther Hödl and Johannes Grabmeyer (Vienna, Cologne, and Weimar, 1993), 162–63; "Die römische Synode 680 und die Frage der Kirchenorganisation 'in gentibus' im 7. Jahrhundert," in *Radovi XIII. Međunarodnog Kongresa za starokršćansku arheologiju, Split-Poreč (25.9.–1.10. 1994)*, ed. N. Cambi and E. Marin, vol. 2 (Vatican and Split, 1998), 590–97.

14. F. Curta, *The Making of the Slavs: History and Archaeology of the Lower Danube Region, c. 500–700* (Cambridge and New York, 2001), 45–46. For Avar hairstyles, see Agathias 1.3.4, ed. R. Keydell (Berlin, 1967). See also S. Szádeczky-Kardoss, "Az avar történelem forrásai I. Közép-Azsiától az al-Dunáig," *Archaeologiai Értesitö* 105 (1979): 85; W. Pohl, *Die Awaren: Ein Steppenvolk im Mitteleuropa 567–822 n. Chr.* (Munich, 1988), 54.

15. See L. Waldmüller, *Die ersten Begegnungen der Slawen mit dem Christentum und den christlichen Völkern vom VI. bis VIII. Jahrhundert* (Amsterdam, 1976).

16. For sixth-century Eastern bishops and their role in the imperial administration, see J. H. W. G. Liebeschuetz, *The Decline and Fall of the Roman City* (Oxford, 2001), 145–55.

17. For sixth-century Christianity in the Caucasus region, see S. Patoura, "To Vyzantio kai ho ekkhristianismos ton laon tou Kaukasou kai tes Krimaias (6ou ai.)," *Symmeikta* 8 (1989): 405–21. For early Byzantine churches in the region, see L. G. Khrushkova, "Pitiunt et le littoral oriental de la Mer Noire à l'époque paléochrétienne," in *Actes du XI-e Congrès international d'archéologie chrétienne: Lyon, Vienne, Grenoble, Genève et Aoste (21–28 septembre 1986)*, vol. 3 (Rome, 1989), 2657–86.

18. See E. Tóth, "Bemerkungen zur Kontinuität der römischen Provinzialbevölkerung in Transdanubien (Nordpannonien)," in *Die Völker Südosteuropas im 6. bis 8. Jahrhundert*, ed. B. Hänsel (Berlin, 1987), 260–61; G. Kiss, "Funde der Awarenzeit aus Ungarn in Wiener Museen," part 1, "Funde aus der Umgebung von Keszthely," *Archaeologia Austriaca* 68 (1984): 166–68; R. Müller, "Die spätrömische Festung Valcum am Plattensee," in *Germanen, Hunnen und Awaren: Schätze der Völkerwanderungszeit*, ed. G. Bott and W. Meier-Arendt (Nuremberg, 1987), 270–72; R. Müller, "Ein Nebenschauplatz, die Befestigung von Fenékpuszta," in *Frühmittelalterliche Machtzentren in Mitteleuropa: Mehrjährige Grabungen und ihre Auswertung; Symposion Mikulčice, 5.–9. September 1994*, ed. Č. Staňa and L. Poláček (Brno, 1996), 131. The basilica at Fenékpuszta was first published by Károlyi Sági, who wrongly dated it to the fourth century. See K. Sági, "Die zweite altchristliche Basilika von Fenékpuszta," *Acta Antiqua Academiae Scientiarum Hungaricae* 9 (1961): 397–440. For the so-called Keszthely culture, see I. Kovrig, "Megjegyzések a keszthely-kultúra kérdéséhez," *Archaeologiai Értesitö* 85 (1958): 66–74; A. Kiss, "A Keszthely-kultúra helye a pannóniai római kontinuitás kérdésében," *Archaeologiai Értesitö* 95 (1968): 93–101; G. Kiss, "Adatok a Keszthely-kultura kutatástörténetéhez," *A Nyíregyházi Jósa András Múzeum Evkönyve* 30–32 (1992): 246–47; R. Müller, "La cultura di Keszthely," in *Gli Avari: Un popolo d'Europa*, ed. G. C. Menis (Udine, 1995), 165–72; R. Müller, "Über die Herkunft und das Ethnikum der Keszthely-Kultur," in *Ethnische und kulturelle Verhältnisse an der mittleren Donau vom 6. bis zum 11. Jahrhundert: Symposium Nitra 6. bis 10. November 1994*, ed. D. Bialeková and J. Zábojník (Bratislava, 1996), 75–82. The destruction of the basilica at Fenékpuszta may have taken place at the time of the "civil war" that broke within the Avar qaganate shortly after the 626 siege of Constantinople. See Pohl, *Die Awaren*, 268–69.

19. R. Krautheimer, *Early Christian and Byzantine Architecture* (London and New York, 1986), 179; R. Bratož, "The development of the early Christian research in Slovenia and Istria between 1976 and 1986," in *Actes du Xi-e Congrès international d'archéologie chrétienne: Lyon, Vienne, Grenoble, Genève et Aoste (21–28 septembre 1986)*, vol. 3 (Rome, 1989), 2355 (Rifnik), 2360 (Ajdna). For another example at Vranje, see S. Ciglenečki, *Höhenbefestigungen aus der Zeit vom 3. bis 6. Jh. im Ostalpenraum* (Ljubljana, 1987), 65. See also N. Duval, "Quelques remarques sur les églises-halles," *Antichità altoadriatiche* 22 (1982): 409–10.

20. T. Bogyay advances inspiration by Syrian architecture: see "Eine Grenzprovinz byzantinischer Kunst im Donauraum?" in *XVI. internationaler Byzantinistenkongreß. Akten. II,* ed. W. Hörandner, C. Cupane, and E. Kislinger, vol. 5 (Vienna, 1982), 150–51.

21. For Slava Rusă, see I. Barnea and R. Vulpe, *Romanii la Dunărea de Jos* (Bucharest, 1968), 476; I. Barnea, in *Enciclopedia arheologiei și istoriei vechi a Românei,* ed. C. Preda, vol. 1 (Bucharest, 1994), s.v. "absidă."

22. For the Episcopal basilica at Novae, see A. B. Biernacki, "Remarks on the basilica and Episcopal residence at Novae," *Balcanica* 2 (1990): 201; S. Parnicki-Pudelko, "The early Christian Episcopal basilica in Novae," *Archaeologia Polona* 21–22 (1983): 268. The three-aisled basilica with one apse was built in the late 400s. During the first half of the sixth century, the plan was modified with the addition of two other apses and two ancillary rooms flanking the presbytery (probably a *prothesis* and a *diakonikon,* respectively).

23. For Karanovo, near Nova Zagora, see B. D. Borisov, "Starokhristianskite baziliki (IV–VI v.) krai s. Karanovo, Burgaska oblast," *Arkheologiia* 30, no. 3 (1988): 38–46. The Karanovo basilica was built in the fourth century and modified in the sixth.

24. S. Anamali, "La basilique de Ballshi," *Bulletin de la Société Nationale des Antiquaires de France* (Paris, 1988), 131–35.

25. For Goliamo Belovo, in western Bulgaria, see R. F. Hoddinott, *Bulgaria in Antiquity: An Archaeological Introduction* (New York, 1975), 299; Krautheimer, *Early Christian and Byzantine Architecture,* 275. The trefoiled baptistery added during the last building phase indicates a date in the sixth century; see N. Chaneva-Dechevska, "Rannekhristianskie baptisterii v Bolgarii," in *Actes du XIV-e Congrès international des études byzantines, Bucarest, 6–12 septembre 1971,* ed. M. Berza and E. Stănescu, vol. 3 (Bucharest, 1976), 306–9. In two other cases, the central apse is not round but polygonal. For the episcopal basilica at Caričin Grad (basilica A), see N. Duval, "L'architecture religieuse de Tsaritchin Grad dans le cadre de l'Illyricum oriental au VIe siècle," in *Villes et peuplement dans l'Illyricum protobyzantin: Actes du colloque organisé par l'Ecole française de Rome (Rome, 12–14 mai 1982)* (Rome, 1984), 407. For Pirdop, see Krautheimer, *Early Christian and Byzantine Architecture,* 251; N. Chaneva-Dechevska, "Die frühchristliche Architektur in Bulgarien," in *Actes du X-e Congrès international d'archéologie chrétienne, Thessalonique, 28 septembre–4 octobre 1980,* vol. 2 (Vatican and Thessaloniki, 1984), 619. The episcopal basilica at Caričin Grad was probably built in the early 500s, at the time of the city's foundation.

26. Khrushkova, "Pitiunt," 2667, 2679; V. A. Lekvinadze, "O postroikakh Iustiniana v zapadnom Gruzii," *Vizantiiskii Vremennik* 34 (1973): 186.

27. The Novae basilica is the largest so far found in Bulgaria (24.30 m × 46.26 m). See Biernacki, "Remarks," 188. The Alakhadzy basilica is the largest in the eastern Black Sea area (28 m × 50 m). See Khrushkova, "Pitiunt," 2679.

28. For Novae, see Biernacki, "Remarks," 206. For Caričin Grad, see W. Müller-

Wiener, "Bischofsresidenzen des 4.–7. Jhs. im östlichen Mittelmeer-Raum," in *Actes du XI-e Congrès international d'archéologie chrétienne: Lyon, Vienne, Grenoble, Genève et Aoste (21–28 septembre 1986)*, vol. 1 (Rome, 1989), 659. The interpretation of the episcopal residence at Caričin Grad has been disputed by Duval, "L'architecture religieuse," 417.

29. A Pannonian bishop, "Vigilius episcopus Scaravansiensis," attended two church councils in Grado, 572/577 and 579, respectively. See E. Tóth, "Vigilius episcopus Scaravaciensis," *Acta Archaeologica Academiae Scientiarum Hungaricae* 26 (1974): 274. Scarabantia/Sopron was located to the north from Fenékpuszta, on the western shore of Neusiedler Lake, not far from modern Vienna. See N. Christie, "The survival of Roman settlement along the middle Danube: Pannonia from the fourth to the tenth century AD," *Oxford Journal of Archaeology* 11 (1992): 317–39. It has been argued that Vigilius, although a bishop of Scarabantia, resided in Italy. He would have left Pannonia in 568, together with the Lombards led by King Alboin. See K. Reindel, "Die Bistumsorganisation im Alpen-Donau-Raum in der Spätantike und im Frühmittelalter," *Mitteilungen des Instituts für österreichische Geschichtsforschung* 72 (1964): 288. There is no evidence to support this hypothesis. See H. Berg "Bischöfe und Bischofssitze im Ostalpen- und Donauraum vom 4. bis zum 8. Jahrhundert," in *Die Bayern und ihre Nachbarn: Berichte des Symposiums der Kommission für Frühmittelalterforschung 25. bis 28. Oktober 1982, Stift Zwettl, Niederösterreich*, ed. H. Wolfram and A. Schwarcz, vol. 1 (Vienna, 1985), 85.

30. Despite the existence of another, late fourth-century basilica at Fenékpuszta, there is no archaeological relationship between the sixth-century settlement and the one previously abandoned during the second half of the fifth century. The earliest burials in the intramural cemetery date from after ca. 550. See Müller, "Über die Herkunft," 76, 81. Cf. E. B. Thomas, "Die Romanität Pannoniens im 5. und 6. Jahrhundert," in *Germanen, Hunnen und Awaren: Schätze der Völkerwanderungszeit*, ed. G. Bott and W. Meier-Arendt (Nuremberg, 1987), 285.

31. For the specimens from Constanța, Orșova, Moigrad, and Capidava, see I. Barnea, "Menasampullen auf dem Gebiet Rumäniens," in *Akten des XII. internationalen Kongresses für christliche Archäologie, Bonn, 22.–28. September 1991*, ed. E. Dassmann, K. Thraede, and J. Engemann (Münster, 1995), 509–14. For the ampulla from Szombathely, see Z. Kádár, "Die Menasampulle von Szombathely (Steinamanger, Ungarn) in Beziehung zu anderen frühchristlichen Pilgerandenken," in ibid., 886. It is very likely that both the specimen from Moigrad and that from Szombathely came from Egypt through Dalmatia. The same may be true for the copper-alloy liturgical bowl found in Periam (western Romania). See D. Țeicu, "Căldarea de cult paleocreștină de la Periam," *Thraco-Dacica* 11 (1990): 153–56.

32. Z. Kiss, *Ampulki swietego Menasa z polskich wykopalisk na Kom el-Dikka (1961–1981)* (Warsaw, 1989).

33. *Early Avar* is a technical term going back to Ilona Kovrig's influential analysis of the cemetery at Alattyán. Kovrig divided the period between 568 (the foundation of the Avar qaganate) and 805 (the collapse of the Avar qaganate) into three phases: Early (ca. 570–650/660), Middle (650/660–700), and Late Avar (700–800). The archaeology of the Avars is still based on this chronology. See I. Kovrig, *Das awarenzeitliche Gräberfeld von Alattyán* (Budapest, 1963).

34. E. Garam, "Die awarenzeitlichen Scheibenfibeln," *Communicationes Archaeologicae Hungaricae* (Budapest, 1993), 99–134; *Funde byzantinischer Herkunft in der Awarenzeit vom Ende des 6. bis zum Ende des 7. Jahrhunderts* (Budapest, 2001), 51–54, 56, 55 fig.

5 (for a distribution map). According to Garam, the earliest disc brooches found in Keszthely-Fenépuszta must have been produced in some neighboring Roman province, perhaps in Sirmium. For other sixth-century Christian finds from Hungary, see E. Tóth, "Das Christentum in Pannonien bis zum 7. Jahrhundert nach den archäologischen Zeugnissen," in *Das Christentum im bairischen Raum: Von den Anfängen bis ins 11. Jahrhundert,* ed. E. Boshof and H. Wolff (Cologne, 1994), 241–72; T. Vida, "Neue Beiträge zur Forschung der frühchristlichen Funde der Awarenzeit," in *Radovi XIII. Međunarodnog Kongresa za starokršćansku arheologiju, Split-Poreč (25.9–1.10. 1994),* vol. 2, ed. N. Cambi and E. Marin (Vatican and Split, 1998), 529–40. For a remarkable piece of Ravennate sculpture, see E. B. Thomas, "Korabizánci köfaragvány Felsödörgicséröl," *Folia Archaeologica* 25 (1974): 161–65.

35. Garam, "Die awarenzeitlichen Scheibenfibeln," 101, 103; Garam, *Funde,* 52 (for a list of finds), 282 figs. 32.2 (the Nagyharsány brooch), 4, 6–7.

36. Imperial portraits with pectoral crosses appeared on solidi struck for Emperors Theodosius II, Arcadius, Honorius, and Justinian. They were also imitated on coins minted for the Ostrogothic kings Theodahat and Baduila, as well as Frankish and Visigothic tremisses of the 500s. See H. Vierck, "*Imitatio imperii* und *interpretatio Germanica* vor der Wikingerzeit," in *Les Pays du Nord de Byzance (Scandinavie et Byzance): Actes du colloque nordique et international de byzantinologie tenu à Upsal 20–22 avril 1979,* ed. R. Zeitler (Uppsala, 1981), 92.

37. For Gornje Turbe (Bosnia), see Z. Vinski, "Krstoliki nakit epohe seobe naroda u Jugoslaviji," *Vjesnik Arheološkog Muzeja u Zagrebu* 3 (1968): 105 with pl. I.4. For Cernavodă (Romania), see A. Rădulescu and V. Lungu, "Le christianisme en Scythie Mineure à la lumière des dernières découvertes archéologiques," in *Actes du XI-e Congrès international d'archéologie chrétienne: Lyon, Vienne, Grenoble, Genève et Aoste (21–28 septembre 1986),* vol. 3 (Rome, 1989), 2584–87, 2583 fig. 15. For Mangalia (Romania), see R. Pillinger, "Ein frühchristliches Grab mit Psalmzitaten in Mangalia/Kallatis (Rumänien)," in *Die Schwarzmeerküste in der Spätantike und im frühen Mittelalter,* ed. R. Pillinger, A. Pülz, and H. Vetters (Vienna, 1992), 99–102 with pl. 16.19. The Gornje Turbe cross was found in a Christian burial within a sixth-century basilica.

38. For Sadovsko Kale (Bulgaria), see S. Uenze, *Die spätantiken Befestigungen von Sadovec: Ergebnisse der deutsch-bulgarisch-österreichischen Ausgrabungen 1934–1937* (Munich, 1992), 527 and pls. 8.9, 126.2. For Golemannovo Kale (Bulgaria), see ibid., 116, 118–19, 302, 332–33, 403, 477–78, and pl. 126.1.

39. For Varna (Bulgaria), see D. I. Dimitrov, "Rannovizantiisko zlatno săkrovishte ot Varna," *Arkheologiia* 5, no. 2 (1963): 39 fig. 8. For Histria (Romania), see I. Barnea, O. Iliescu, and C. Nicolescu, *Cultura bizantină în România* (Bucharest, 1971), 139.

40. For Varna, see Dimitrov, "Rannovizantiisko zlatno săkrovishte," 35–40. For Gornje Turbe, see Vinski, "Krstoliki nakit," 105.

41. For Histria, see Barnea, Ilescu, and Nicolescu, *Cultura bizantină,* 139. For Mangalia, see Pillinger, "Ein frühchristliches Grab," 99–102. For Barbat (Croatia), see Vinski, "Krstoliki nakit," 105. See also J. Wolters, *Die Granulation: Geschichte und Technik einer alten Goldschmiedekunst* (Munich, 1983), 28, 162.

42. For Sadovsko Kale and Golemannovo Kale, see Uenze, *Die spätantiken Befestigungen,* 327, 332–33.

43. For Salona, see Vinski, "Krstoliki nakit," 107 and pl. V.12. For Viminacium, see L. Zotović, "Die gepidische Nekropole bei Viminacium," *Starinar* 43–44 (1992–93), 189 fig.

4. For Dicmo (Croatia), see Vinski, "Krstoliki nakit," 107 and pl. V.14. For Vid (Croatia), see ibid., 108 and pl. V.16. For Knin (Croatia), see ibid., 108 and pl. V.15. The Knin cross is unique for its niello decoration. The sixth-century cemetery at Gradina, near Duvno (Bosnia), produced a large number of such crosses, worn as brooches, not as pectorals. See N. Miletić, "Ranosrednjovekovna nekropola u Koritima kod Duvna," *Glasnik Zemaljskog Muzeja Bosne i Hercegovine u Sarajevu* 33 (1978): 145–51 and pls. I.16, II.24, II.37–38, III.52, and V.66, V.74; Z. Marić, "Kasnoantička nekropola na praistorijskoj Gradini u Kortima kod Duvna," in *Simpozijum "Predslavenski etnicki elementi na Balkanu u etnogenezi juznih Slovena," održan 24–26. oktobra 1968 u Mostaru,* ed. A. Benac (Sarajevo, 1969), 241 and fig. 2. Another cross brooch was found in an inhumation burial in the ruins of a late Roman villa at Lisičići, near Konjica (Herzegovina). See Vinski, "Krstoliki nakit," 106 with pl. IV.7. In the 500s, cross brooches were also popular in the Alpine region of northern Italy and in Spain. See R. Jurić, "Le fibule a forma di croce in Croazia," in *Radovi XIII. Međunarodnog Kongresa za starokršćansku arheologiju, Split-Poreč (25.9.–1.10. 1994),* ed. N. Cambi and E. Marin, vol. 2 (Vatican and Split, 1998), 1091–1106.

44. For Piatra Frecăţei (Romania), see A. Petre, *La romanité en Scythie mineure (IIe–VIIe siècles de notre ère): Recherches archéologiques* (Bucharest, 1987), 78 with pl. 143 figs. 237a–b.

45. A fragment of a silver cross with Greek inscription was found in an Early Avar burial assemblage of the so-called Keszthely culture in Balatonfüzfö-Szalmássy Telep, at the northeastern tip of Lake Balaton. The cross was associated with a silver *capsula* (reliquary box) bearing the image and the name of the apostle Peter. See G. László, "Die Awaren und das Christenum im Donauraum und im östlichen Mitteleuropa," in *Das heidnische und christliche Slaventum: Acta II Congressus internationalis historiae Slavicae Salisburgo-Ratisbonensis anno 1967 celebrati,* ed. F. Zagiba (Wiesbaden, 1969), 150; P. Tomka, "Il costume," in *Gli Avari, un popolo d'Europa,* ed. G. C. Menis (Udine, 1995), 88. The Balatonfüzfö-Szalmássy Telep cross is an exact replica, with Greek inscription (ZΩH ΦΩC, "life (and) light," in reference to John 8:12) identical to the one found in a sixth-century fort in Bezhanovo (Bulgaria); see D. Ovcharov and M. Vaklinova, *Rannovizantiiski pametnici ot Bălgariia IV–VII vek* (Sofia, 1978), 122. A bronze cross found in an Early Avar burial (no. 104) of the Závod cemetery in southern Hungary has an inscription hinting at contemporary controversies surrounding the Trisagion (ΑΓΙΟC ΑΓΙΟC ΑΓΙΟC Κ[ὺριο]C CΑΒΑΩΤ): see J. Hampel, *Alterthümer des frühen Mittelalters in Ungarn* (Braunschweig, 1905), 59 fig. 55 and pl. 252.1; A. Kollautz, *Denkmäler byzantinischen Christentums aus der Awarenzeit der Donauländer* (Amsterdam, 1970), 22–24. A distant parallel for both Hungarian finds is the silver cross with engraved images of the Lamb found at Izvoarele-Pârjoaia: see V. Culică, "Antichităţile creştine de la Izvoarele, jud. Constanţa," *Biserica Ortodoxă Română* 94 (1976): figs. 4.2, 7.21. For a bronze imitation from a mid-sixth-century cemetery in Hungary, see D. Csallány, *Archäologische Denkmäler der Gepiden im Mitteldonaubecken* (Budapest, 1961), 190, 274 with pl. CXXIV.12. For a silver Latin cross without inscription (grave 37 from the "G" cemetery in Deszk, Hungary), see G. László, "Újabb keresztény nyomok az avarkorból," *Dolgozátok az Erdélyi Nemzéti Múzeum érem- és régiség tárából* 16 (1940): 148 and pl. XX.1 (for the date of this assemblage, see Garam, *Funde,* 60). Similar crosses appear in contemporary Anglo-Saxon burial assemblages. See A. Meaney and S. C. Hawkes, *Two Anglo-Saxon Cemeteries at Winnall, Winchester, Hampshire* (London, 1970), 54–55.

46. For Budakalász, grave 1083 (Hungary), see Vida, "Neue Beiträge," 536 fig. 1.2. For

Kölked-Feketekapu, grave 207, see A. Kiss, *Das awarenzeitlich-gepidische Gräberfeld von Kölked-Feketekapu A* (Innsbruck, 1996), 64, 202, and pls. 48.2, 135.2. For Višnijca, near Belgrade, see M. Tatić-Đurić, "Zlatni nalaz iz Višnjice," *Zbornik Narodnog Muzeja* 4 (1964): 185–86 with pl. I.1–2. For Constanţa (Romania), see C. Cîrjan, "Un mormînt creştin descoperit la Tomis," *Pontica* 3 (1970): 383–85. All four crosses have a good analogy at Chufut Kale, in Crimea. See V. V. Kropotkin, "Iz istorii srednevekogo Kryma (Chufut Kale i vopros o lokalizacii goroda Fully)," *Sovetskaia arkheologiia* 28 (1958): 214 figs. 5.7–8. A slightly different cross of silver was found in an Early Avar female burial in Bečej near the Hungarian-Serbian border; see B. Mikić-Antonić, "Bečej-Pionirska ulica: Early medieval cemetery," *Arheološki pregled* (1988): 193–95.

47. For Prahovo (Serbia), see D. Janković, *Podunavski deo oblasti Akvisa u VI i početkom VII veka* (Belgrade, 1981), 213–314 with pl. XVIII.12. For Izvoarele-Pîrjoaia (Romania), see Culică, "Antichităţile creştine," figs. 6.5, 8.24. For Corinth, see G. R. Davidson, *The Minor Objects (Corinth XII)* (Princeton, 1952), pl. 110.2071. A grit stone mold for crosses moline was found in a mortuary assemblage at Suuk Su, in Crimea. See N. I. Repnikov, "Nekotorye mogil'niki oblasti krymskikh gotov," *Izvestiia imperatorskoi arkheologicheskoi kommisii* 19 (1906): 6, 72 fig. 51.

48. For Čipuljići (Bosnia), see Vinski, "Krstoliki nakit," 108 and pl. IV.19. For Mihaljevići, near Sarajevo, see N. Miletić, "Nekropola u selu Mihaljevićima kod Rajlovca," *Glasnik Zemaljskog Muzeja Bosne i Hercegovine u Sarajevu* 11 (1956): 13 and pls. II.2, III, VIII. For Ram (Serbia), see Vinski, "Krstoliki nakit," 110–11 and pl. VII.30. For Batočina (Serbia), see Vinski, "Krstoliki nakit," 108 and pl. VI.17. For Gornji Dolac (Croatia), see Vinski, "Krstoliki nakit," 110 and pl. VI.24. For Izvoarele-Pârjoaia (Romania), see V. Culică, "Obiecte cu caracter creştin din epoca romano-bizantină găsite la Pîrjoaia-Dobrogea," *Pontica* 2 (1969): 355–56, 358 fig. 1.3; Culică, "Antichităţile creştine," figs. 3.3, 7.18, 7.20, 8.28. For Golesh, see G. Atanasov, "Martyrium et *hagiasmon* dans le castel basbyzantin près du village de Golech, région de Silistra (communication préliminaire)," in *Von der Scythia zur Dobrudža*, ed. Khr. Kholiolchev, R. Pillinger, and R. Harreither (Vienna, 1997), 127–29, 138 fig. 5.10. For Piatra Frecăţei (Romania), see Petre, *La romanité*, 78 and pl. 143 figs. 236a–e. A bone specimen is known from the sixth-century fort of Balajnac, in Serbia: see M. Jeremić, "Balajnac, agglomération protobyzantine fortifiée," *Antiquité tardive* 3 (1995): 193–94, 206 fig. 27. A similar cross, but made of bronze, was found in a mortuary assemblage at Koreiz, in Crimea. See Repnikov, "Nekotorye mogil'niki," 37–38, 73 fig. 61. Maltese crosses were also worn as brooches: see Vinski, "Krstoliki nakit," 107 and pls. IV.9, V.10; K. Simony, "Funde aus der Völkerwanderungszeit in den Sammlungen des Archäologischen Museums in Zagreb," *Vjesnik Arheološkog Muzeja u Zagrebu* 22 (1989): 112 and pl. 4.4; F. Prendi, "Një varrezë e kulturës arbërore në Lezhë," *Iliria* 9–10 (1979–80): 128 and pl. IX.V.22.

49. For Golemanovo Kale, see Uenze, *Die spätantiken Befestigungen*, 501 and pl. 4.9. For Niš, see Vinski, "Krstoliki nakit," 109 and pl. VI.20. For Pernik, near Sofia, see V. Liubenova, "Selishteto ot rimskata i rannovizantiiskata epokha," in *Pernik I. Poselishten zhivotna khălma Krakra ot V khil. pr. n. e. do VI v. na n.e.*, ed. T. Ivanov (Sofia, 1981), 189 fig. 130. For Novi Banovci (Serbia), see Vinski, "Krstoliki nakit," 110 and pl. VI.29.

50. For Piatra Frecăţei, see Petre, *La romanité*, 78–79 and pl. 144 figs. 238a–g.

51. For Golemanovo Kale, see Uenze, *Die spätantiken Befestigungen*, 164 fig. 9.6. For Celei, see N. Dănilă, "Tipare de turnat cruci din secolele IV–VI, descoperite pe teritoriul României," *Biserica Ortodoxă Română* 101 (1983): 557–61.

52. For Olteni, see C. Preda, "Tipar pentru bijuterii din sec. VI e.n. descoperit la Olteni (r. Videle, reg. Bucureşti)," *Studii şi cercetări de istorie veche* 18 (1967): 513–15. For Bucharest, see V. Teodorescu, "Centre meşteşugăreşti din sec. V/VI în Bucureşti," *Bucureşti: Materiale de istorie şi muzeografie* 9 (1972): 95, 81 fig. 3.6. For Botoşana, see D. G. Teodor, *Civilizaţia romanică la est de Carpaţi în secolele V–VII (aşezarea de la Botoşana-Suceava)* (Bucharest, 1984), 40–41, 99 fig. 20.1. For other molds for casting crosses of unknown type, see A. Madgearu, *Rolul creştinismului în formarea poporului român* (Bucharest, 2001), 81.

53. For Davideni, see I. Mitrea, "Principalele rezultate ale cercetărilor arheologice din aşezarea de la Davideni (sec. V–VII e.n.)," *Memoria Antiquitatis* 6–8 (1974–76): 69 and fig. 14.1. For Ruginoasa, see D. G. Teodor, *Creştinismul la est de Carpaţi de la origini şi pînă în secolul al XVI-lea* (Iaşi, 1991), 165, 125 fig. 7.3. For Rashkov, see V. D. Baran, "Die frühslawische Siedlung von Raškov, Ukraine," *Beiträge zur allgemeinen und vergleichenden Archäologie* 8 (1986): 144, 91 fig. 7.7. By contrast, Avar assemblages in Hungary produced only one Maltese cross, that from Székkutas, grave 8. See K. B. Nagy, "Székkutas-Kápolnadűlői avar temető néhány 9. századi síregyűtese (Előzetes jelentés)," in *Az Alföld a 9. században (Az 1992. November 30 December 1 én elhangzott előadások írott változatai)*, ed. G. Lőrinczy (Szeged, 1993), 155–56 and fig. 3 (with crroncous dating); Vida, "Neue Beiträge," 534, 537 fig. 2.1; for its analogies and dating, see Garam, *Funde*, 61–62. A cross from an unknown location in Banat (now at the Museum in Timişoara) may well have been part of an Avar burial assemblage. See A. Bejan and P. Rogozea, "Descoperiri arheologice mai vechi şi mai recente prefeudale şi feudale timpurii din Banat," *Studii şi comunicări de istorie-etnografie* 4 (1982): 213 and pl. I.1.

54. For Bacău, see I. Mitrea and A. Artimon, "Descoperiri prefeudale la Curtea Domnească-Bacău," *Carpica* 4 (1971): 246 figs. 16.7–8, 247 figs. 17.1–2. For Borniş, see Teodor, *Creştinismul*, 133, 121 fig. 42.3. For Bratei, see I. Nestor and E. Zaharia, "Raport preliminar despre săpăturile de la Bratei, jud. Sibiu (1959–1972)," *Materiale şi cercetări arheologice* 10 (1973): 191–201. For several sites on the territory of the modern city of Bucharest (Băneasa, Soldat Ghivan Street, Străuleşti, and Tei), see M. Constantiniu, "Şantierul arheologic Băneasa-Străuleşti," *Cercetări arheologice în Bucureşti* 2 (1965): 93; S. Dolinescu-Ferche and M. Constantiniu, "Un établissement du VIe siècle à Bucarest," *Dacia* 25 (1981): 314 fig. 12.3; M. Constantiniu, "Săpăturile de la Străuleşti-Măicăneşti: Aşezarea feudală II," *Cercetări arheologice în Bucureşti* 2 (1965): 178 fig. 85.2; S. Morintz and D. V. Rosetti, "Din cele mai vechi timpuri şi pînă la formarea Bucureştilor," in *Bucureştii de odinioară în lumina săpăturilor arheologice*, ed. I. Ionaşcu (Bucharest, 1959), 11–47 with pl. XXXI.5. For Davideni, see Mitrea, "Principalele rezultate," fig. 5.3; I. Mitrea, "Aşezarea din secolele V–VII de la Davideni, jud. Neamţ. Cercetările arheologice din anii 1988–1991," *Memoria Antiquitatis* 19 (1994): 322 fig. 23.4. For Dodeşti, see D. G. Teodor, *Continuitatea populaţiei autohtone la est de Carpaţi: Aşezările din secolele VI–XI e.n. de la Dodeşti-Vaslui* (Iaşi, 1984), 47 fig. 19.7. For Dulceanca, see S. Dolinescu-Ferche, "Habitats du VIe et VIIe siècles de notre ère à Dulceanca IV," *Dacia* 36 (1992): 150 fig. 19.2, 143 fig. 12.10. For Gutinaş, see I. Mitrea, C. Eminovici, and V. Momanu, "Aşezarea din secolele V–VII de la Ştefan cel Mare, jud. Bacău," *Carpica* 18–19 (1986–87): 234 figs. 10.1, 10.4; 246 fig. 13.5. For Horga, see G. Coman, "Evoluţia culturii materiale din Moldova de sud în lumina cercetărilor arheologice cu privire la secolele V–XIII," *Memoria Antiquitatis* 3 (1971): 481 fig. 2.4. For Horodok, see B. O. Timoshchuk and O. M. Prikhodniuk, "Rann'oslov'iansky pam'iatki VI–VII st. v seredn'omu Podnystrov'i," in

Slov'iano-rus'ki starozhitnosti, ed. V. I. Bidzilya (Kiev, 1969), 77 figs. 4.3–4. For Izvoare-Bahna, see I. Mitrea, "Şantierul arheologic Izvoare-Bahna," *Materiale şi cercetări arheologice* 14 (1980): 444 fig. 11.2. For Kavetchina, see L. V. Vakulenko and O. M. Prikhodniuk, *Slavianskie poseleniia I tys. n.e. u s. Sokol na Srednem Dnestre* (Kiev, 1984), 46 fig. 21.15. For Lozna, see Teodor, *Creştinismul,* 133 figs. 15.5–6. For Murgeni, see Coman, "Evoluţia," 481 fig. 2.5. For Sighişoara, see G. Baltag, "Date pentru un studiu arheologic al zonei municipiului Sighişoara," *Marisia* 9 (1979): 75–106 with pl. XXXVIII.3. For Sălaşuri, see Z. Székely, "Aşezarea prefeudală de la Sălaşuri (com. Veţca, jud. Mureş)," *Marisia* 5 (1975): 71–80 with pl. XXXVI.1. For Selişte, see I. A. Rafalovich and V. L. Lapushnian, "Mogil'niki i ranneslavianskoe gorodishche u s. Selishte," in *Arkheologicheskie issledovaniia v Moldavii (1973 g.),* ed. V. I. Markevich (Kishinew, 1974), 132 fig. 11.6. For Suceava, see Teodor, *Creştinismul,* 133 figs. 15.1, 4. For crosses incised on clay rolls found on sixth- and seventh-century sites north of the Danube in association with—and often inside—clay ovens, see I. Stanciu, "Über frühslawische Tonklumpen und Tonklümpchen," *Ephemeris Napocensis* 8 (1998): 215–72.

55. For Dulceanca, see S. Dolinescu-Ferche, *Aşezări din secolele III şi VI e.n. în sudvestul Munteniei: Cercetările de la Dulceanca* (Bucharest, 1974), fig. 52.2. For Bucharest, see D. V. Rosetti, "Siedlungen der Kaiserzeit und der Völkerwanderungszeit bei Bukarest," *Germania* 18 (1934): 210 fig. 5.4. For Scoc, see Teodor, *Creştinismul,* 138 fig. 19.2.

56. For Bratei, see E. Zaharia, "La station no. 2 de Bratei, dép. de Sibiu (VIe–VIIIe siècle)," *Dacia* 38–39 (1994–95), 349 fig. 13.7. For Bucharest, see S. Dolinescu-Ferche, "Ciurel, habitat des VI–VIIe siècles d.n.è.," *Dacia* 23 (1979): 189 fig. 4.21; Dolinescu-Ferche and Constantiniu, "Un établissement du VIe siècle," 309 fig. 9.6. For Dănceni, see Teodor, *Creştinismul,* 125 fig. 7.8. For Dulceanca, see Dolinescu-Ferche, *Aşezări,* fig. 70.1. For Hansca, see Teodor, *Creştinismul,* 125 fig. 7.9. For Pen'kyvka, see D. T. Berezovec, "Poseleniia ulichei na r. Tiasmine," in *Slaviane nakanune obrazovaniia Kievskoi Rusi,* ed. B. A. Rybakov (Moscow, 1963), fig. 19.

57. For Botoşana, see Teodor, *Civilizaţia romanică,* 98 fig. 19.5. For Corlăteni, see Teodor, *Creştinismul,* 130 fig. 12.5.

58. For Târgşor, see Victor Teodorescu, "O nouă cultură arheologică recent precizată în ţara noastră: Cultura Ipoteşti-Cîndeşti (sec. V–VII)," in *Sesiunea de comunicări ştinţifice a muzeelor de istorie, dec. 1964,* vol. 2 (Bucharest, 1971), 109. For Hansca and Botoşana, see Teodor, *Creştinismul,* 137 figs. 19.1, 8.

59. See, e.g., G. Coman, "Mărturii arheologice privind creştinismul în Moldova secolelor VI–XII," *Danubius* 5 (1971): 75–100; I. Barnea, "Le christianisme des premiers six siècles au nord du Bas-Danube à la lumière des sources littéraires et des découvertes archéologiques," in *Das Christentum in Bulgarien und auf der übrigen Balkanhalbinsel in der Spätantike und im frühen Mittelalter,* ed. V. Giuzelev and R. Pillinge (Vienna, 1987), 39–50; I. Mitrea, "Secolul al VI-lea în istoria creştinismului la est de Carpaţi: Date arheologice şi concluzii istorice," *Carpica* 29 (2000): 27–38. Romanian archaeologists tend to treat this evidence in purely ethnic terms. Crosses and crosslike signs are viewed as indication of a Romanian population, since it is believed that the "barbarians" were unable to grasp the concepts of the Christian ideology. See Madgearu, *Rolul creştinismului,* 84.

60. A. V. Bank, *Byzantine Art in the Collections of Soviet Museums* (Leningrad, 1985), 287 and pl. 99.

61. For Ozora-Tótipuszta, see E. Garam, *Katalog der awarenzeitlichen Goldgegenstände und der Fundstücke aus den Fürstengräbern im Ungarischen Nationalmuseum*

(Budapest, 1993), 101 pl. 87.1. For Táp-Borbapuszta, see Tomka, "Il costume," 86. For Vaj-ska, see O. Bruckner, "The sixth-century necropolis at Vajska," in *Sirmium IV*, ed. N. Duval and V. Popović (Belgrade, 1982), 33 and pl. IV.8–9. For Valea Voievozilor, see L. Oancea, "Descoperiri arheologice la Valea Voievozilor (com. Răzvad), județul Dîm-bovița—1972," *Scripta Valachica* 4 (1973): 115–16, 113 fig. 27.7. For Băleni, see N. Dănilă, "Noi contribuții la repertoriul materialelor paleocreștine din Muntenia," *Glasul Bisericii* 45 (1986): 102. Such crosses also appear in contemporary and equally rich burial assemblages in the Dnieper region. See, e.g., the golden cross from Kelegeia in Oleg M. Prikhodniuk and Vladimir M. Khardaev, "Ein Edelmetallfund des 6.–7. Jahrhunderts aus Kelegej, Ukraine," *Eurasia antiqua* 7 (2001): 598, 599 figs. 7.1–3. Another cross with rounded ends was found in a burial assemblage at Koreiz, in Crimea. See Repnikov, "Nekotorye mogil'niki," 37–38, 73 fig. 63. In general, see E. Garam, "Über Halsketten, Halsschmucke mit Anhängern und Juwelenkragen byzantinischen Ursprungs aus der Awarenzeit," *Acta Archaeologica Academiae Scientiarum Hungaricae* 43 (1991): 163; *Funde*, 62–63.

62. Copper-alloy sheet crosses found in several burials of the Middle Avar cemetery at Káptalantóti (Hungary) point to the same direction. Their closest analogies are gold sheet crosses from burial assemblages in northern Italy. See A. Kiss, "Beiträge zur Ver breitung frühmittelalterlicher Folienkreuze im Karpatenbecken," *Archäologisches Korrespondenzblatt* 17 (1987): 235–43.

63. The most cited verse was Psalms 91:1 (King James Version): "He that dwelleth in the secret place of the most High shall abide under the shadow of the Almighty." See G. J. M. Bartelink, "Phylakterion-phylacterium," in *Mélanges Christine Mohrmann: Recueil nouveau offert par ses anciens élèves* (Utrecht, 1973), 30–31, 41, 43. One of the two *phylacteria* found in a female grave at Constanța (Romania) contained small fragments of human bones, presumably relics. See Cîrjan, "Un mormînt creștin," 384. The Ozora-Tótipuszta cross was found in association with a gold *phylacterium*. See Garam, "Über Halsketten," 160, 161 fig. 7. Three other specimens were attached to silver collars found in a female burial at Igar, dated to the Middle Avar period. See G. Fülöp, "New research on finds of Avar chieftains-burials at Igar, Hungary," in *From the Baltic to the Black Sea: Studies in Medieval Archaeology*, ed. D. Austin and L. A. Alcock (London, 1990), 141, 139 fig. 7.2. A bronze *phylacterium* attached to a bronze collar was also found in a Middle Avar burial at Bóly. See G. Fülöp, "Awarenzeitliche Fürstenfunde von Igar," *Acta Archaeologica Academiae Scientiarum Hungaricae* 40 (1988): 178 with n. 84. Two other *phylacteria* of bronze are known from the still unpublished cemetery at Bratei, which also produced a pectoral cross of unknown type. See I. Nestor and E. Zaharia, "Raport preliminar despre săpăturile de la Bratei, jud. Sibiu (1959–1972)," *Materiale și cercetări arheologice* 10 (1973): 198–99. *Phylacteria* were relatively common artifacts in Late Avar burials and contemporary mortuary assemblages in Crimea. See A. Točik, *Slawisch-awarisches Gräberfeld in Holiare* (Bratislava, 1968), 61, 67, 70, 85; A. Točik, *Slawisch-awarisches Gräberfeld in Štúrovo* (Bratislava, 1968), 30–31; A. Pásztor, "Adatok a közép-avarkori ékszerek kérdéséhez," *Archaeologiai Értesitö* 113 (1986): 129–33; E. V. Veimarn and A. I. Aibabin, *Skalistinskii mogil'nik* (Kiev, 1993), 51, 64, 51 fig. 31.27, 65 figs. 42.30–31 and 42.40. A cremation burial from the large sixth- and seventh-century cemetery at Sărata Monteoru (Romania) produced a gold *phylacterium* similar to that found on the nearby site at Izvoarele-Pârjoaia, on the right bank of the Danube. See Uwe Fiedler, *Studien zu Gräberfeldern des 6. bis 9. Jahrhunderts an der unteren Donau* (Bonn, 1992), 84;

Culică, "Obiecte cu caracter creştin," 355–56, 362 fig. 2. That the Sărata Monteoru *phylacterium* should be dated to the mid-600s is shown by its association with a crescent-shaped pendant very similar to that found—also associated with *phylacteria*—in the Middle Avar burial at Igar.

64. Vierck, "*Imitatio imperii*"; see also Garam, "Über Halsketten," 177. This conclusion is confirmed by rare finds of finger distaffs with dove-shaped ends. Such tools were used most likely by women of high status for fine-wool spinning. At the same time, these artifacts undoubtedly carried a Christian symbolism. Copper-alloy specimens were found on many early Byzantine sites (e.g., Sardis) but were particularly frequent on sixth-century military sites in the northern Balkans. See T. Völling, "'Der Vogel auf dem Kreuz': Ein frühchristliches Symbol aus Olympia," *Archäologischer Anzeiger* 80 (1996): 148, 153. For Balkan finds, see Janković, *Podunavski*, pl. XVIII.1–5, 8–13; Liubenova, "Selishteto," 191 fig. 132, 192 fig. 133; V. Liubenova, "Bronzovi predmeti ot kăsnoantichnata vila pri rudnik 'Bela voda', Pernik," *Arkheologiia* 37 (1995): 13 figs. 12a–d; Uenze, *Die spätantiken Befestigungen*, pl. 5.6; G. Gomolka-Fuchs, "Die Kleinfunde vom 4. bis 6. Jh. aus Iatrus," in *Iatrus-Krivina: Spätantike Befestigung und frühmittelalterliche Siedlung an der unteren Donau*, vol. 2 (Berlin, 1982), pl. 64.285–86; Atanasov, "Martyrium et *hagiasmon*," 138 figs. 5.11–12. Only a few specimens were found north of the Danube, one of which is from a sixth-century settlement. See G. Popilian and M. Nica, "Aşezarea prefeudală de la Craiova (Fîntîna Obedeanu)," *Symposia thracologica* 8 (1990): 231–32; Z. Vinski, "Arheološki spomenici velike seobe naroda u Srijemu," *Situla* 2 (1957): pl. XVII.56; O. Bozu, "Obiecte creştine inedite de uz casnic: Furcile de tors pentru deget datate în secolele IV–VI e.n.," *Analele Banatului* 2 (1993): 206, 208, 207 figs. 1.1–5. Some archaeologists associate finger distaffs with the Bonosian heresy documented for this period in the northern Balkans. Heresies, however, are rarely visible in the archaeological record, while the distribution of finger distaffs suggests a much different interpretation. See Janković, *Podunavski*, 229; Madgearu, *Rolul creştinismului*, 79; J. Werner, "Golemanovo Kale und Sadovsko Kale: Kritische Zusammenfassung der Grabungsergebnisse," in *Die spätantiken Befestigungen von Sadovec (Bulgarien): Ergebnisse der deutsch-bulgarisch-österreichischen Ausgrabungen 1934–1937*, ed. S. Uenze (Munich, 1992), 412.

65. For a few isolated finds of lamps, see Madgearu, *Rolul creştinismului*, 82. Clay lamps of the plain orange class were produced in large numbers in the Balkans, as indicated by molds, some signed in Greek, found in a fort near Kranevo (Bulgaria). Specimens with cross-shaped handles imitate bronze lamps. See N. Poulou-Papadimitriou, "Lampes paléochrétiennes de Samos," *Bulletin de Correspondance Hellénique* 110 (1986): 595; Z. Covacef and E. Corbu, "Consideraţii aspura unor categorii de opaiţe descoperite în sectorul V al cetăţii Capidava," *Pontica* 24 (1991): 291–92; G. Kuzmanov, "Die Lampen," in *Die spätantiken Befestigungen von Sadovec (Bulgarien): Ergebnisse der deutsch-bulgarisch-österreichischen Ausgrabungen 1934–1937*, ed. S. Uenze (Munich, 1992), 225–26. The Luciu specimen belongs to a rare series of bronze lamps (Kuzmanov's class LVIII) and may have been initially attached to a movable stand, such as that found, together with the accompanying lamp, in the filling of burial chamber no. 152 in Kerch (Crimea). See G. Kuzmanov, *Antichni lampi: Kolekciia na Nacionalniia Arkheologicheski Muzei* (Sofia, 1992), 55; I. P. Zaseckaia, "Datirovka i proiskhozhdenie pal'chatykh fibul bosporskogo nekropolia rannesrednevekovogo perioda," *Materialy po arkheologii, istorii i etnografii Tavrii* 6 (1997): 447–48, 473 pl. XVII.18. As such, the Luciu lamp may have

been taken from a Balkan church during a raid. The same may be true for the seventh-century bronze lamp from Tápiógyörgye: see Gy. László, "Kopt bronzlámpa tápiogyör-gyéröl," *Folia Archaeologica* 1–2 (1939): 110–15; Garam, *Funde*, 175–76.

66. N. Cheluță-Georgescu, "Complexe funerare din secolul VI e.n. la Tomis," *Pontica* 7 (1974): 363–76; D. Tudor, "Comunicări epigrafice. VII," *Studii și cercetări de istorie veche și arheologie* 26, no. 1 (1975): 132–35; D. Tudor, "Comunicări epigrafice (IX)," *Studii și cercetări de istorie veche și arheologie* 32, no. 3 (1981): 423–36; A. Opaiț, "O săpătură de sal-vare în orașul antic Ibida," *Studii și cercetări de istorie veche și arheologie* 41, no. 4 (1990): 19–54; A. Opaiț, "Ceramica din așezarea și cetatea de la Independența (Murighiol) sec-olele V î.e.n.–VII e.n.," *Peuce* 10 (1991): 133–82. See also Mabel Lang, *Athenian Agora 21: Graffiti and Dipinti* (Princeton, 1976); S. A. Beliaev, "Pozdneantichnye nadpisi na am-forakh iz raskopok Khersonesa 1961 g.," *Numizmatika i epigrafika* 7 (1968): 127–43. For a Maltese cross painted on a sixth-century amphora shard, see D. Tudor, "Sucidava III: Quatrième (1942), cinquième (1943) et sixième (1945) campagnes de fouilles et de recherches archéologiques dans la forteresse de Celei, département de Romanați," *Dacia* 11–12 (1945–47): 179 with fig. 29.6. The same site produced another shard with a painted inscription mentioning a certain priest named Loukonochos (ibid., 176–77, 176 fig. 27).

67. W. Hautumm, *Studien zu Amphoren der spätrömischen und frühbyzantinischen Zeit* (Fulda, 1981), 48, 64; F. H. van Doorninck, Jr., "The cargo amphoras on the 7th cen-tury Yassi Ada and 11th century Serçe Liman shipwrecks: Two examples of a reuse of Byzantine amphoras as transport jars," in *Recherches sur la céramique byzantine*, ed. V. Déroche and J.-M. Spieser (Athens and Paris, 1989), 252; B. Böttger, "Zur Lebensmit-telversorgungen des niedermösischen Kastells Iatrus (4.–6. Jh.)," in *Akten des 14. inter-nationalen Limeskongresses 1986 in Carnuntum*, ed. H. Vetters and M. Kandler (Vienna, 1990), 925–30; M. Mackensen, "Amphoren und Spatheia von Golemannovo Kale (Aus-grabung 1936/1937)," in *Die spätantiken Befestigungen von Sadovec (Bulgarien): Ergeb-nisse der deutsch-bulgarisch-österreichischen Ausgrabungen 1934–1937*, ed. S. Uenze (Mu-nich, 1992), 252.

68. See C. Abadie-Reynal, "Céramique et commerce dans le bassin égéen du IV-e au VII-e siècle," in *Hommes et richesses dans l'Empire byzantin*, ed. G. Dagron (Paris, 1989), 143–62; O. Karagiorgou, "LR2: A container for the military annona on the Danubian border?" in *Economy and Exchange in the East Mediterranean during Late Antiquity: Pro-ceedings of a Conference at Somerville College, Oxford, 29th May, 1999*, ed. Sean Kingsley and Michael Decker (Oxford, 2001), 129–66.

69. I. Mitrea, "Dovezi ale prezenței creștinismului în sec. VI în Moldova," *Mitropo-lia Moldovei și a Sucevei* 55 (1980): 400–403; Dănilă, "Noi contribuții," 557–61; M. Rusu, "Paleocreștinismul nord-dunărean și etnogeneza românilor," *Anuarul Institutului de Is-torie și Arheologie* 26 (1983–84): 35–84; I. Barnea, "Le christianisme sur le territoire de la RSR au III-e–XI-e siècles," *Etudes Balkaniques* 1 (1985): 92–106; Teodor, *Creștinismul*; N. Zugravu, *Geneza creștinismului popular al românilor* (Bucharest, 1997); Madgearu, *Rolul creștinismului*. For the association between mission and bow brooches, see D. G. Teodor, "Fibule 'digitate' din secolele VI–VII în spațiul carpato-dunăreano-pontic," *Arheologia Moldovei* 15 (1992): 124. For a radically different interpretation of cross molds, see M. Comșa, "Les formations politiques (cnézats de la vallée) du VIe siècle sur le territoire de la Roumanie," *Prace i materialy Muzeum Archeologicznego i Ethnograficznego w Łódźi* 25 (1978): 109–17. For "missionary" as a modern, not late antique or early medieval, cate-gory, see Wood, *Missionary Life*, 247.

70. The absence of monasteries may be explained in terms of the almost complete disappearance of nonfortified, rural settlements in the 500s. See F. Curta, "Peasants as 'makeshift soldiers for the occasion': Sixth-century settlement patterns in the Balkans," in *Urban Centers and Rural Contexts in Late Antiquity,* ed. T. S. Burns and J. W. Eadie (East Lansing, 2001), 199–217. *Contra:* S. Popović, "Prolegomena to early monasticism in the Balkans as documented in architecture," *Starinar* 49 (1998): 131–44.

71. I. Engelhardt, *Mission und Politik in Byzanz: Ein Beitrag zur Strukturanalyse byzantinischer Mission zur Zeit Justins und Justinians* (Munich, 1974), 179. All known missions operating without imperial control were Monophysite enterprises.

72. John Malalas, *Chronographia,* ed. L. Dindorf (Bonn, 1831), 431–32. Gord was replaced by his brother Mugel, and the Roman garrison of Bosporus was massacred. For the Gord episode, see S. Iordanov, "Epizod ot etnokulturnata istoriia na prabălgarite v severnoto Prichernomorie (khunskiiat vladetel Grod i khristianizaciiata na kutrigurite)," in *Bălgarite v severnoto Prichernomorie: Izsledvaniia i materiali,* ed. P. Todorov, vol. 3 (Veliko Tărnovo, 1994), 27–44; Ts. Stepanov, "Bălgarite ot nai-drevni vremena do vtorata polovina na VII vek," in *Istoriia na bălgarite,* ed. G. Bakalov, vol. 1 (Sofia, 2003), 69–70.

73. Nicephorus, *Short History,* ed. C. Mango (Washington, 1990), 48–51. Judging by the chronology of Nicephorus's narrative, the event must have taken place at some point between 619 and 623. The Hunnic chieftain arrived in the company of his noblemen, who brought their wives with them. According to Nicephorus, Roman aristocrats acted as sponsors at the baptism of the Hunnic noblemen and their wives. A late echo of this story is found in a fourteenth-century manuscript containing the fourteenth-century, Old Church Slavonic version of an encomium for St. Phokas. See I. Dobrev, "Novi vesti za prabălgarite v panegirichnata literatura," *Starobălgarska literatura* 11 (1982): 33–34. Following Vassil Zlatarski, almost all historians have assumed that Nicephorus's Hunnic leader was Kubrat, the founder of "Great Bulgaria" and Asparuch's father. But according to John of Nikiu (*Chronicle,* trans. R. Charles [London, 1916], 197), Kubrat (Kuernâkâ) was already "received in the Christian community in his childhood and has grown up in the imperial palace." See V. Beshevliev, "Zur Chronik des Johannes von Nikiu CXX 46–49," *Byzantinobulgarica* 5 (1978): 229–36. Ever since J. Werner's *Der Grabfund von Malaja Pereščepina und Kuvrat, Kagan der Bulgaren* (Munich, 1984), all Bulgarian historians believe that Kubrat's grave was in Malo Pereshchepino and that all the associated grave goods confirm Kubrat's conversion to Christianity. The assemblage contains a large silver plate bearing the name of its previous owner, Bishop Paternus of Tomis, and control stamps of Emperor Anastasius's reign (491–518): see I. Barnea, "Discul episcopului Paternus," *Analecta* (1944): 185–97; V. N. Zalesskaia, "Byzantinische Gegenstände im Komplex von Mala Pereščepina," in *Reitervölker aus dem Osten: Hunnen + Awaren; Burgenländische Landesausstellung 1996, Schloß Halbturn, 26. April–31. Oktober 1996,* ed. F. Daim, K. Kaus, and P. Tomka (Eisenstadt, 1996), 218. But in the context of the Malo Pereshchepino assemblage, Paternus's plate seems to have lost its liturgical function and may have been simply part of a functional set with drinking (amphora and goblets) and washing vesels (basin and ewer): see M. Mundell Mango, "Silver plate among the Romans and among the barbarians," in *La noblesse romaine et les chefs barbares du IIIe au VIIe siècle,* ed. F. Vallet and M. Kazanski (Saint-Germain-en-Laye, 1995), 81. However, artifacts with obvious Christian meaning are known from the lower Dnieper region. Gold pectoral crosses were found with the Glodosi and Kelegeia burial assemblages, while the middle Dnieper area produced such rare finds as a bronze

church-shaped candlestick: see A. T. Smilenko, *Glodos'ki skarbi* (Kiev, 1965), 10; A. Aibabin, "Kelegeiskoe pogrebenie voennogo vozhdia," *Problemi na prabălgarskata istoriia i kultura* 2 (1991): 31 fig. 3.12; G. F. Korzukhina, "Klady i sluchainye nakhodki veshchei kruga 'drevnosti antov' v srednem Podneprov'e: Katalog pamiatnikov," *Materialy po arkheologii, istorii i etnografii Tavrii* 5 (1996): 683 pl. 93.7.

74. F. J. Hamilton and E. W. Brooks, trans., *The Syriac Chronicle of Zachariah of Mitylene* (London, 1899), 329–31. See N. Pigulevskaia, "Note sur les relations de Byzance et des Huns au VI-e s.," *Revue des etudes sud-est-européennes* 7 (1969): 201; Patoura, "To Vyzantio," 422–24.

75. Bede *Ecclesiastical History* 1.25, ed. B. Colgrave and R. A. B. Mynors (Oxford, 1969). For the conversion of the Anglo-Saxons, see A. Angenendt, "The conversion of the Anglo-Saxons considered against the background of early medieval mission," in *Angli e Sassoni al di quà e al di là del mare, Spoleto, 26 aprile–1 maggio 1984,* vol. 2 (Spoleto, 1986), 747–81.

76. P. Heather, *The Goths* (Oxford, 1996), 60–61. For Ulfila's life and activity, see P. Heather and J. Matthews, *The Goths in the Fourth Century* (Liverpool, 1991), 133–54. For the problem of conversion as a mode of social and cultural integration, see J. Herrin, *The Formation of Christendom* (Princeton, 1987), 28–34. For early missionaries at work outside the empire, see also Wood, *Missionary Life,* 7–8.

77. Sozomen, *Ecclesiastical History* 7.26.6–9, ed. J. Bidez and G. C. Hansen (Berlin, 1960); trans. P. Schaff and H. Wace (Peabody, 1994). See Barnea and Vulpe, *Romanii,* 407. John Chrysostomos, the patriarch of Constantinople, is also known for having sent a mission to the "nomadic Scythians on the Ister River." At about the same time, another bishop, that of Margus, was organizing raids deep into the territory of the Huns, plundering their royal tombs (Priscus frag. 6).

78. Jordanes *Getica* 25, ed. Th. Mommsen, MGH Auctores Antiquissimi, vol. 5 (Berlin, 1882); trans. C. C. Mierow (New York, 1960). A sixth-century Arian bishop of the Gepids, Trasaricus, was known to John of Biclar (*Chronica,* ed. Th. Mommsen, MGH Auctores Antiquissimi, vol. 11 [Berlin, 1894], 212). See J. Zeiller, *Les origines chrétiennes dans les provinces danubiennes de l'Empire romain* (Paris, 1918), 538.

79. Procopius *Wars* 6.14.29–34, ed. J. Haury, trans. H. B. Dewing (Cambridge, 1914); John Malalas *Chronographia* 18.6, ed. L. Dindorf (Bonn, 1931); trans. E. Jeffreys, M. Jeffreys, and R. Scott (Melbourne, 1986). For the date of this event, see P. Lakatos, *Quellenbuch zur Geschichte der Heruler* (Szeged, 1978), 90; Patoura, "To Vyzantio," 427–29.

80. Unlike other cases in contemporary Europe, where the presence of missionaries was condoned by powerful kings whose political ambitions became closely bound up with the advancement of particular Christian cults or clerisies, missions to the Sclavenes had no potential target, for no rulers there were powerful enough to protect the missionaries. See Higham, *The Convert Kings,* 28–29; D. Obolensky, *The Byzantine Commonwealth: Eastern Europe, 500–1453* (New York and Washington, 1971), 281. For various strategies of mission, see Wood, *Missionary Life,* 256–58. For sixth- and seventh-century missions, see also S. Patoura, "La diffusion du christianisme dans le cadre de la politique etrangère de Byzance (IVe–VIIe siècles)," in *The 17th International Byzantine Congress, 1986: Abstracts of Short Papers* (Washington, 1986), 257. For the Sclavene "kings" and the nature of their power, see F. Curta, "Feasting with 'kings' in an ancient 'democracy': On the Slavic society of the early Middle Ages (sixth to seventh century)," *Essays in Medieval Studies* 15 (1999): 19–34.

81. Theophylact Simocatta 6.8.13, ed. C. de Boor and P. Wirth (Stuttgart, 1972); trans. M. Whitby and M. Whitby (Oxford, 1986), 171.

82. *Miracles of St. Demetrius* 2.284–85, ed. P. Lemerle (Paris, 1979).

83. *Strategikon* 11.4.31, ed. G. Dennis and E. Gamillscheg (Vienna, 1981); trans. G. Dennis (Philadelphia, 1984), 124. For this passage, see also A. Madgearu, "About Maurikios, Strategikon, XI.4.31," *Revue des études sud-est européennes* 35 (1997): 119–21.

84. An example is a *phylacterium* found in a cremation burial of the mid-seventh century at Sărata Monteoru. See Fiedler, *Studien,* 84. Even the association of Christian artifacts (such as pectoral crosses) with inhumation should always be treated with caution; see, in that respect, Gyula László's old, but still valid, remarks on burial 37 from Deszk that produced a lead pectoral cross of the Latin type ("Újabb keresztény nyomok," 145–58). For cremation and the conversion to Christianity, see V. Spinei, "Observaţii privind ritul incinerării în regiunile carpato-dunărene în a doua jumătate a mileniului I d. Hr.," in *Pe drumul credinţei,* ed. G. Ursache (Rives Junction, 1995), 82–100; B. Effross, "*De partibus Saxoniae* and the regulation of mortuary custom: A Carolingian campaign of Christianization or the suppression of Saxon identity?" *Revue belge de philologie et d'histoire* 75 (1997): 267–86.

85. Michael the Syrian *Chronicon* 10.21, ed. J. B. Chabot (Paris, 1963). In doing so, the Sclavene chief might have imitated the qagan of the Avars, who at one time had met the Byzantine embassy seating on a golden throne under a canopy. See Menander the Guardsman frag. 27, ed. R. C. Blockley (Liverpool, 1985), 238.

86. Michael the Syrian *Chronicon* 10.21. It is possible that this was the church of the martyr Alexander, which is mentioned by Theophylact Simocatta (6.5.2). For the date of this event and the identity of the qagan (Bayan's son), see Pohl, *Die Awaren,* 152–53; N. I. Serikov, "Ioann Efesskii," in *Svod drevneishikh pis'mennykh izvestii o slavianakh,* ed. L. A. Gindin, S. A. Ivanov, and G. G. Litavrin, vol. 1 (Moscow, 1991), 290.

87. Theophylact Simocatta 6.13.1–7, trans. Whitby and Whitby, 196–97. For the interpretation of this episode as a calculated display of generosity, see Pohl, *Die Awaren,* 152–53.

88. Menander the Guardsman frag. 25.1, trans. Blockley, 223. The earliest evidence of an oath taken by the Gospels dates back to the fourth century. By the mid-sixth century, it has become the rule. See M. Lemosse, "Recherches sur l'histoire du serment de *calumnia,*" *Revue de l'histoire du droit* 21 (1953): 48–50; L. Kolmer, *Promissorische Eide im Mittelalter* (Kallmünz, 1989), 238. For oaths taken from barbarians on the frontier, see Augustine Ep. 46 and 47, trans. W. Parsons (Washington, 1951), 220–21, 226–27.

89. R. Noll, "Ein Ziegel als sprechendes Zeugnis einer historischen Katastrophe (Zum Untergang Sirmiums 582 n. Chr.)," *Anzeiger der österreichischen Akademie der Wissenschaften* 126 (1989): 139–54. For the literary genre of this text and for the practice of calling God's protection on a city, see A. Kollautz, "Die *Inscriptio de Avaris von Sirmium* als Dokument einer byzantinischen Gebetsanrufung," in *Studia in honorem Veselini Beševliev,* ed. V. Georgiev, B. Gerov, V. Tăpkova-Zaimova, et al. (Sofia, 1978), 534–63.

90. For the problems associated with the interpretation of material culture, especially grave goods, as signalizing Christian identity, see A. Schülke, "Zeugnisse der 'Christianisierung' im Grabbefund? Eine Forschungsgeschichte mit Ausblick," *Ethnographisch-archäologische Zeitschrift* 38 (1997), 457–68; "On Christianization and grave finds," *European Journal of Archaeology* 2 (1999): 77–106.

91. W. Pohl, "Die Langobarden in Pannonien und Justinians Gotenkrieg," in *Ethnis-*

che und kulturelle Verhältnisse an der mittleren Donau vom 6. bis zum 11. Jahrhundert, ed. D. Bialeková and J. Zábojnik (Bratislava, 1996), 33. See also K. P. Christou, *Byzanz und die Langobarden: Von der Ansiedlung in Pannonien bis zur engültigen Anerkennung* (Athens, 1991), 91. For the policy of setting one group of barbarians against the other, as the fundamental principle of Justinian's policy on the northern frontier, see F. Wozniak, "Byzantine diplomacy and the Lombard-Gepidic wars," *Balkan Studies* 20 (1979): 156.

92. There is no indication that the "Keszthely culture" had any significant influence on contemporary Avar burial assemblages. By contrast, such artifacts as belt straps and plates of the Felnac type, buckles decorated in Animal Style II, or eye-shaped glass beads bespeak a strong influence of Early Avar fashions on the communities at Fenékpuszta and other related sites. See R. Müller, "Neue archäologische Funde der Keszthely-Kultur," in *Awarenforschungen*, ed. F. Daim, vol. 1 (Vienna, 1992), 278–79.

93. Novel 41 in *Corpus Iuris Civilis*, ed. P. Krüger, Th. Mommsen, R. Schöll, and W. Kroll, vol. 3 (Berlin, 1954), 262; John Lydus *On Powers* 2.28, ed. A. C. Bardy (Philadelphia, 1982). The new administration unit combined territories at a considerable distance from each other, such as Moesia Inferior, Scythia Minor, some islands in the Aegean Sea, Caria, and Cyprus, all ruled from Odessos/Varna by a prefect. The only link between all these provinces was the sea and the navigable Danube. Since Cyprus, the Aegean Islands, and Caria represented the most important naval bases of the empire but were also among the richest provinces, the rationale behind Justinian's measure must have been to secure, both militarily and financially, the efficient defense of the Danube frontier. For the *quaestura exercitus*, see S. Torbatov, "Quaestura exercitus: Moesia Secunda and Scythia under Justinian," *Archaeologia Bulgarica* 1 (1997): 78–87; F. Curta, "Quaestura exercitus Iustiniani: The evidence of seals," *Acta Byzantina Fennica* 1 (2002): 9–26.

94. See Menander the Guardsman frag. 21; Theophylact Simocatta 8.6.7. For the archaeological evidence, see D. Mitova-Dzhonova, "Stationen und Stützpunkte der römischen Kriegs- und Handelsflotte am Unterdonaulimes," in *Studien zu den Militärgrenzen Roms III: 13. internationaler Limeskongreß Aalen 1983; Vorträge* (Stuttgart, 1986), 504–9.

95. Procopius *Wars* 7.14.32–34. The Antes were *enspondoi* (i.e., *foederati*). For *enspondoi* as both military and political partners of the empire, see S. A. Ivanov, "Poniatiia 'soiuza' i 'podchineniia' u Prokopiia Kesariiskogo," in *Etnosocial'naia i politicheskaia struktura rannefeodal'nykh slavianskikh gosudarstv i narodnostei*, ed. G. G. Litavrin (Moscow, 1987), 28. Other examples of *enspondoi* in Procopius's *Wars* are the Lombards (7.33.12), the Gepids (7.34.10), the Saginae (8.2.18), the Goths (8.5.13), the Sabiri (8.11.24), and the Cutrigurs (8.19.5). Note that most of those allies were on the northern frontier of the empire. For Procopius's views of the Slavs, see S. A. Ivanov, "Psevdo-Kesarii, Prokopii i problemy informirovannosti o slavianakh v seredine VI v.," in *Etnogenez, ranniaia etnicheskaia istoriia i kul'tura slavian*, ed. N. I. Tolstoi (Moscow, 1985), 14–16; "Prokopii i predstavleniia drevnikh slavian o sud'be," *Byzantinobulgarica* 8 (1986): 175–82.

96. S. A. Ivanov, L. A. Gindin, and V. L. Cymburskii, "Prokopii Kesariiskii," in *Svod drevneishikh pis'mennykh izvestii o slavianakh*, ed. L. A. Gindin, S. A. Ivanov, and G. G. Litavrin, vol. 1 (Moscow, 1991), 219. Among all references to Sclavenes in Procopius's work, there is no use of the adverbs *palaion, palai, aei, es eme*, or *anekathen*, while all verbs used in reference to settlement (*oikeo, idryomai, nemonai*) appear in the present tense or in the medium voice. See L. A. Gindin, "Problema slavianizacii karpato-balkanskogo prostranstva v svete semanticheskogo analiza glagolov obitaniia u Prokopiia Kesariiskogo," *Vestnik Drevnei Istorii* 3 (1988): 178–81.

97. *Strategikon* 11.4.4, trans. Dennis, 122. Here and there, individual Sclavenes may appear as fighting for the Romans, as in the case of Souarounas, a Sclavene soldier in the Roman army operating in Transcaucasia (Agathias 4.20.4). Another Sclavene mercenary made himself useful to Belisarius during the siege of Auximum in 540 (Procopius *Wars* 6.26.16–22). But unlike Antes, these soldiers seem to have been hired on an individual basis, due to their special skills.

98. *Strategikon* 11.4.30, trans. Dennis, 123.

99. F. Curta, "Invasion or inflation? Sixth- to seventh-century Byzantine coin hoards in Eastern and Southeastern Europe," *Annali dell'Istituto Italiano di Numismatica* 43 (1996): 95–96. The economic closure was certainly not a deliberate effect, for it is likely that the strain on coin circulation, which is also visible in hoards found south of the Danube frontier, was caused by the very execution of Justinian's gigantic plan. Fewer coins were withdrawn from circulation, and even fewer found their way into hoards. See also E. Oberländer-Târnoveanu, "La monnaie byzantine des VIe–VIIIe siècles au-delà de la frontière du Bas-Danube: Entre politique, économie et diffusion culturelle," *Histoire et Mesure* 17 (2002): 155–96.

100. John of Ephesus *Ecclesiastical History* 6.6.25, ed. E. I. Brooks (Paris, 1935); trans. E. I. Brooks (Paris, 1936). For John's view of the Slavs, see A. D'iakonov, "Izvestiia Ioanna Efesskogo i siriiskikh khronik o slavianakh VI–VII vekov," *Vestnik Drevnei Istorii* 1 (1946): 20–34; Nina Pigulevskaia, "Une chronique syrienne du Vi-e siècle sur les tribus slaves," *Folia orientalia* 12 (1970): 211–14.

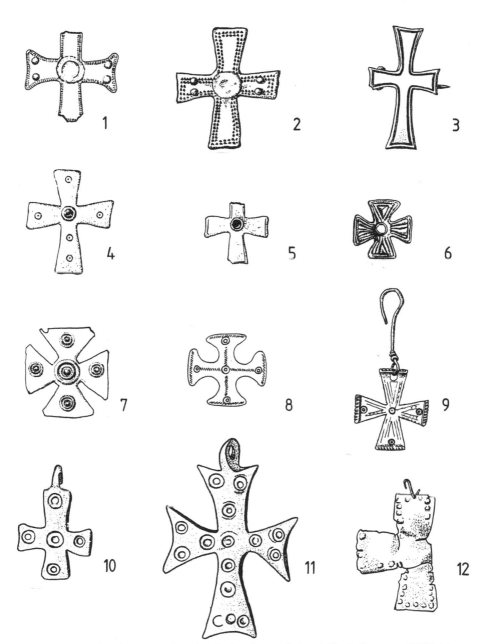

Fig. 8.1. Examples of Latin cross brooches (1–8) and pectorals (9–12). The find spots are (1) Vid; (2) Lišičići; (3) Knin; (4) Solin; (5) Dicmo; (6) Kranj, grave 104/1907; (7) Gračanica; (8) Batočina; (9) Čipuljići; (10) Ram; (11) unknown location in Serbia; and (12) unknown location in Croatia. The scales are different (Source: Vinski, "Krstoliki nakit.")

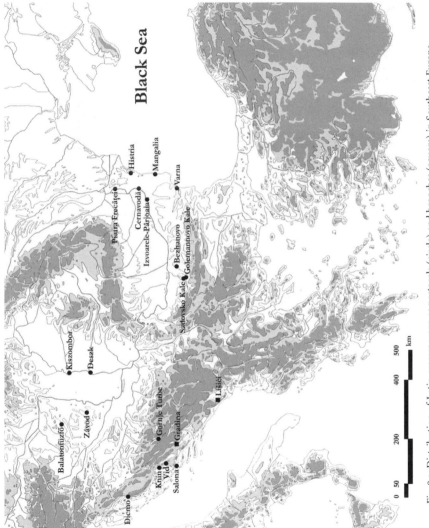

Fig. 8.2. Distribution of Latin crosses worn as pectorals (circle) and brooches (square) in Southeast Europe.

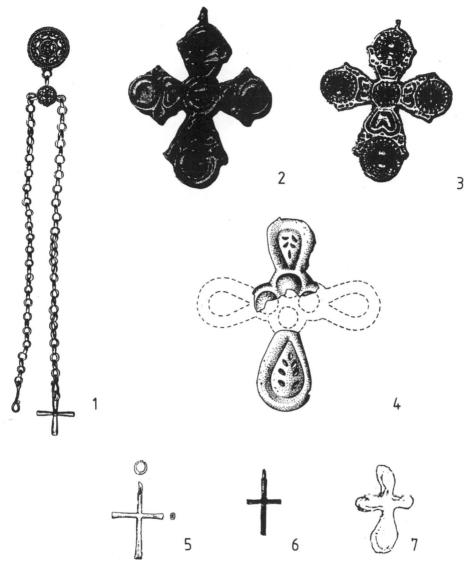

Fig. 8.3. Examples of slender stick crosses (1, 5–6) and crosses with rounded ends (2–4, 7). The find spots are (1) Višnjica; (2) Ozora; (3) Táp, grave 317; (4) Vajska, grave 5; (5) Constanţa; (6) Chufut Kale; and (7) Valea Voievozilor. The scales are different (Source: Various authors.)

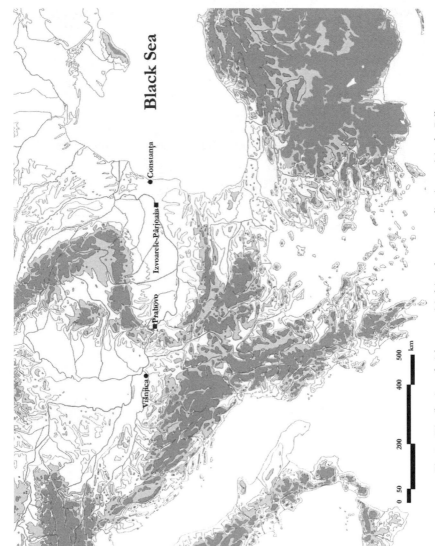

Fig. 8.4. Distribution of stick crosses (circle) and crosses moline (square) in the Balkans.

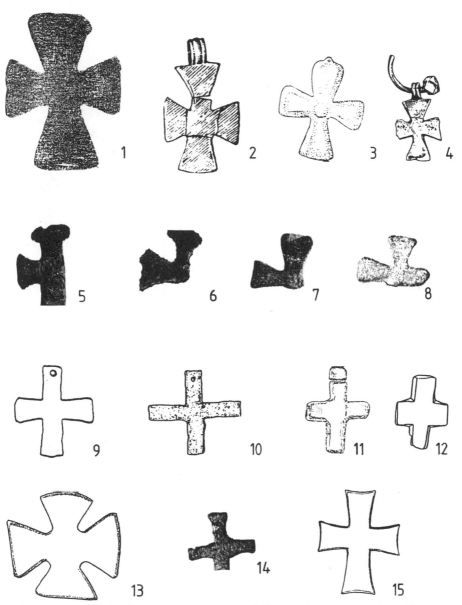

Fig. 8.5. Examples of Maltese crosses worn as pectorals (1–3, 13–15) or earring pendants (4). The find spots are (1) unknown location in Banat (Romania); (2) Piatra Frecăţei, grave D4; (3) Ruginoasa; (4) Piatra Frecăţei, grave A80; (5–8, 14) Izvoarele; (9) Celei; (10) Mijele, grave 7; (11) Lozna; (12) Golemannovo Kale; (13) Niš; and (15) Gornji Dolac. The scales are different. (Source: Various authors.)

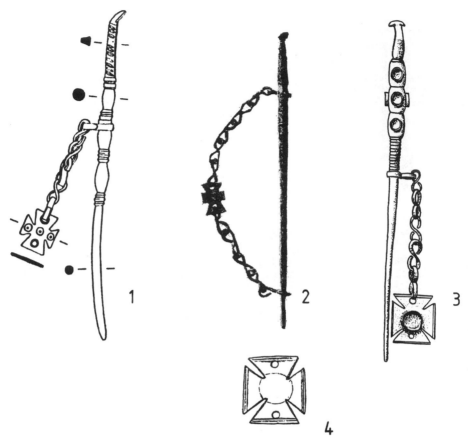

Fig. 8.6. Examples of dress pins with Maltese cross pendants. The find spots are (1) Golemannovo Kale; (2) Pernik; (3) Niš; and (4) Novi Banovci. The scales are different. (Source: Various authors.)

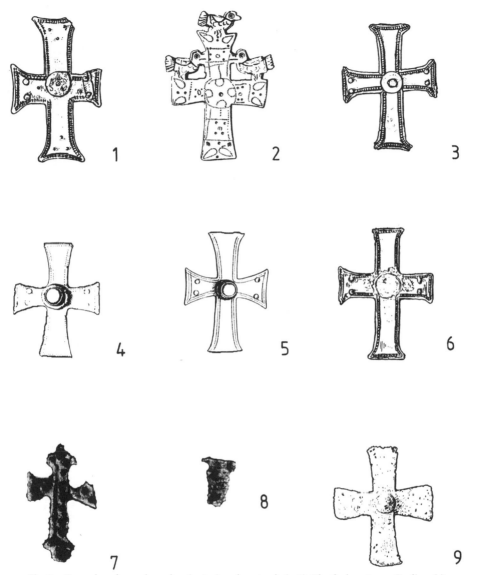

Fig. 8.7. Examples of cross brooches (1–6, 9) and pectorals (7, 8). The find spots are Gradina, (1) grave 37; (2) grave 74; (3) grave 24; (4) grave 66; (5) grave 52; (6) grave 16; (9) grave 38; and (7, 8) Izvoarele. The scales are different. (After Miletić, "Ranosrednjovekovna nekropola" and Culică, "Antichitățile creștine.")

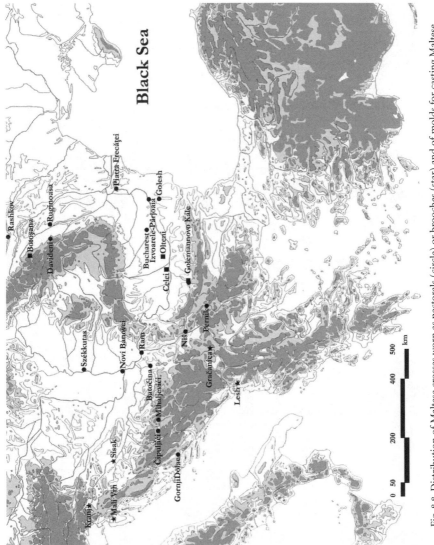

Fig. 8.8. Distribution of Maltese crosses worn as pectorals (circle) or brooches (star) and of molds for casting Maltese crosses (square) in the regions north and south of the Danube River.

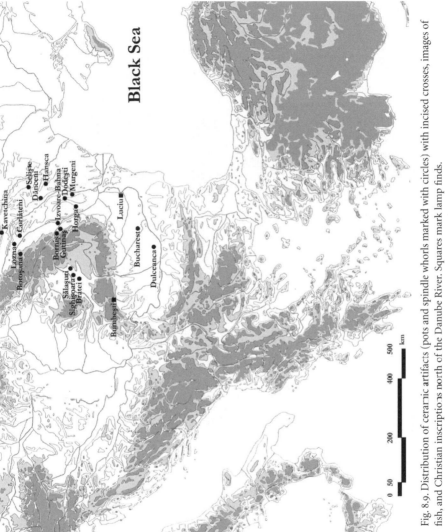

Fig. 8.9. Distribution of ceramic artifacts (pots and spindle whorls marked with circles) with incised crosses, images of fish, and Christian inscriptions north of the Danube River. Squares mark lamp finds.

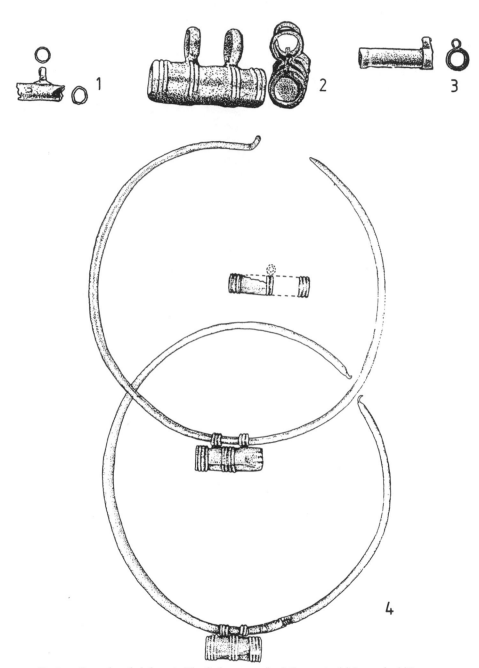

Fig. 8.10. Examples of *phylacteria*. The find spots are (1, 3) Constanța; (2) Izvoarele; (3) Igar, grave
1. The scales are different. (Source: Various authors.)

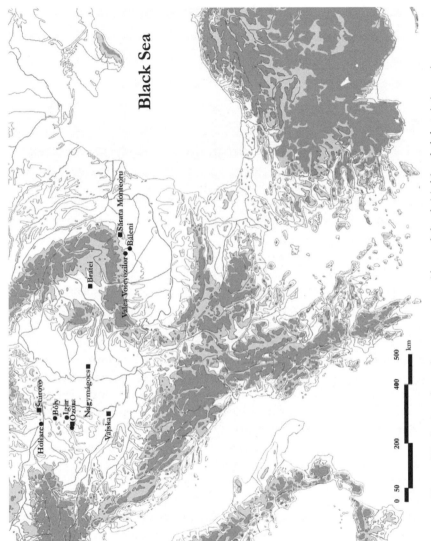

Fig. 8.11. Distribution of seventh-century crosses with rounded ends (circle) and *phylacteria* (square).

CHAPTER NINE

Creating Khazar Identity through Coins: The Special Issue Dirhams of 837/8

Roman K. Kovalev

The Kievan Rus' principality (ca. 853–ca. 1240), the Volga Bulghar emirate (ca. 800?–ca. 1236), and the Khazar qaganate (ca. 650–ca. 965) were the three states in existence during the early Middle Ages in the territories now included within the borders of European Russia, Belarus, and Ukraine. Established by pagan rulers, all three states adopted one of the three Abrahamic religions widely known in western Eurasia during the Middle Ages—Judaism in Khazaria, Christianity in Kievan Rus', and Islam in Volga Bulgharia. In all three cases, the decision to convert was made by the ruling elites, whose goal was to establish an official monotheistic state religion, one key ingredient for instituting a novel political ideology and formulating a new cultural identity.

As part of the conversion program and the establishment of the new religion, political legitimacy, and cultural identity, all three polities issued official state coins—the most prevalent (and at times the only) form of governmental mass media of the age. These coins, carrying blatant and sometimes subtle religious and political messages on their legends, were an indispensable venue for disseminating official state-sanctioned ideologies and the elites' views of government, religion, and identity. Sometime in the mid-tenth century, the earliest rulers of Kievan Rus'—probably Ol'ga in particular—made the first attempts at striking coins that were essentially imitations of Islamic coins but with a conspicuous addition of a small Christian cross to the legend.[1] This was a premature coin issue, since it marked Ol'ga's private conversion sometime between 954 and 957 but predated the formal state adoption of Christianity in 988/9.[2] Being essentially Islamic and clearly connected to a very different tradition, this coin emission was doomed to failure from the start. Soon after the official conversion to Byzantine Orthodoxy, however, the Rus' princes began to emit coins based on the Byzantine-Christian model. These issues not only carried the Byzantine imperial and Christian iconography but also included the important additions of Rus'-Rurikid dynastic insignias and the names of the rulers, inscribed on the legends in Cyrillic characters.[3] The Volga Bulghars, soon after converting to Islam in ca. 920, likewise established a state currency; while based on Islamic coins (with their Kufic characters), they were inscribed with the names of the Volga Bulghar emirs and official state mints, Bulghār and Suwār.[4] Like the pre-988/9 Rus' coins, the early Volga Bulghar issues were Islamic imitations. With conversion, however, both states began to strike official state currencies, based in part on the respective models of their superior coreligionists—the Byzantine emperors in Constantinople and the Abbasid caliphs in Baghdad—and on local political traditions. The rulers of Kievan Rus' and Volga Bulgharia hoped that their "reform," state coins, and religious conversion would provide their states and people with a sense of historical continuity, legitimacy, identity, and belonging to a larger Christian or Islamic world.

In adopting Judaism—a minority religion of the day—Khazaria differed from Kievan Rus' and Volga Bulgharia for many reasons, not least of which was its monetary history. With the official conversion to Judaism—a unique development in itself—Khazaria did not come to inherit a medieval Jewish tradition of state-issued coinage, since such a legacy had been lost in the ancient past.[5] Nonetheless, just as the Kievan Rus' grand prince who converted his principality to Christianity and the Volga Bulghar emir who converted his people to Islam and created an emirate, the Khazar *beg,* or "king," after converting to Judaism also desired to disseminate the new religious and political ideology and did so using the best means possible, namely, coins. As this study will show, the Khazars found a way to accomplish this goal—albeit very briefly—through imitating Islamic coins and through the incorporation of uniquely Khazar-Turkic-Jewish elements into their legends. These coins, in addition to providing great insight into Khazaria's attempts at state building, also offer an important new source for the dating of the official state conversion of Khazaria to Judaism—the best evidence yet available to historians to study this fundamental question. Before moving on to these coins, it would be of use to review some basic background information on the history of Khazaria, the main sources used for its study, and the earliest Khazar coinage.

Historical Overview of Khazaria

The Khazars, a nomadic Turkic-speaking tribal confederation and a western offshoot of the first Turk qaganate (552–630), established one of the earliest and most successful states situated within the territories of modern European Russia and Ukraine. Khazar history is divided into two stages, the Crimean–north Caucasus Phase (ca. 650–ca. 750) and the lower Volga Phase (ca. 750–ca. 965).

During the first phase, politically focused on the northern Black Sea region, the Khazars were locked in endless wars with the Arab Umayyad caliphate over the control of the Caucasus region. After a major Khazar defeat in 737, the Khazars relocated their political center to the north and established their capital of İtil/Atıl in the Volga delta, by the year 800.[6] The next one hundred years of Khazar history, known as the Pax Chazarica, brought security to the southern Russian and Ukrainian steppe and the surrounding regions, permitting cross-continental trade to flourish via Khazaria and providing it with the necessary stability for the formation of a unique material culture, known to archaeologists as Saltovo-Mayaki.[7]

Khazaria was an empire, or qaganate, the highest form of Turkic political organization. Khazar imperial pretensions seem to be underscored by their very name, for *Khazar* probably derives from *Caesar*.[8] The Khazar qagan, or leader, was apparently of Turkic origin and had supreme secular and sacred functions. Sometime in the first half of the ninth century, his secular-religious role was split: he retained his sacral function, while the governor or "king," known as the beg, qagan beg, *īša(d)*, *šad*, or *yilig*, ruled over the state.[9] Much more will be said about this issue later in this chapter.

At its height, in the early ninth century, the Khazar qaganate stretched from the Danube in the west to the Volga-Ural steppe in the east and from the middle Volga region in the north to Crimea and the north Caucasus region in the south.[10] It was populated by Turkic and Iranian pastoral nomads, Finno-Ugrian and Baltic foragers, Slavic and northern Caucasian agriculturalists, and urban Crimean Greeks, making the qaganate a multiethnic and multilingual state.[11] The Khazar economy was multifaceted, including animal husbandry, hunting and gathering, fishing, craft production, agriculture, viniculture, and developed domestic and international trade.[12] Khazars traded locally manufactured goods and the slaves, furs, honey, and wax they obtained as tribute from the east Slavic, Finno-Ugrian, and Baltic tribes of the north. From the late eighth or early ninth century, Khazaria also acted as an intermediary for Rus'-Arab trade and received a tithe (10 percent) from the passing merchants. Over the course of the ninth century, millions of Islamic silver coins or dirhams were exported from the Islamic world (mainly the Near East) through Khazaria (via the Caucasus/Caspian Sea route) and onto northern Russia (via the "Khazar Way," along the lower Volga, the Don, the Donec, the Oka, and the upper Volga),[13] in exchange for Rus' commodities, mainly furs and slaves.[14] In turn, about half of these dirhams were reexported into the Baltic area, either through trade (mostly via the town of Staraia Ladoga)[15] or through Viking raid activities in Russia.[16]

Most Khazars practiced the traditional Turkic shamanist-Tängri religion.

Christianity, Islam, Judaism, and many other religions—including the various pagan cults of the Slavs, Balts, Finno-Ugrians, Iranians, and other peoples inhabiting the core and the tributary territories—were found in the lands of Khazaria. The Islamic geographer al-Mas'ūdī (d. 956) reported that sometime during the reign of the Abbasid caliph Harun al-Rashid (786–809), the Khazars converted to Judaism.[17] Many questions remain concerning this conversion, its pervasiveness, and the actual date of the acceptance of Judaism.[18] What is clear is that religious tolerance and Khazaria's international commercial interests brought Christians, Muslims, Jews, pagans, and others to trade and live within the qaganate. Again, more will be said later about the Khazar religions—Judaism in particular.

The Pax Chazarica came to an end in the early tenth century. By the 890s, Pechenegs and Magyars (proto-Hungarians) had infiltrated Khazaria from the east and occupied a large part of the Khazarian steppe in the south, while the Rus' annexed Khazar territories in the forest region in the northwest, along with their tributary peoples.[19] Concurrently, the Khazar Way trade route declined because the Rus'-Islamic trade shifted from a Near Eastern–Khazar orientation to a Central Asian Samanid–Volga Bulghar direction, thereby bypassing Khazar toll collectors.[20] Greatly weakened, Khazaria was destroyed by the Rus' and their Torki/Oghuz allies in 965.

The Sources

Most of what is known about the Khazar qaganate comes from written records left behind not by the Khazars themselves but by outsiders, who preserved information in Arabic, Hebrew, Persian, Byzantine, east Slavic, Caucasian, and other sources.[21] The one exception is the so-called Hebrew-Khazar Correspondence of ca. 960, which consists of three letters. Two of these are different versions (long and short) of a reply of the Khazar King Joseph to Ḥasday ibn Šaprūṭ, the Jewish mayor of 'Abd al-Raḥmān III, the Umayyad caliph of Córdoba. The other is a letter from a Khazar Jew (possibly written to Ḥasday ibn Šaprūṭ) known as the Cairo Genizah Letter.[22] This correspondence preserves information of fundamental importance for the study of Khazaria. Aside from these letters, however, historians are left to consult documents written by non-Khazars. In addition to the traditional written sources, the many systematic archaeological excavations of sites in the former lands of Khazaria have unearthed numerous material remains that reveal a great deal of information about the history of the qaganate. These archeological discoveries often shed considerable light on many key questions that the standard written sources normally did not discuss in any detail (if at all), such as Khazar material culture, economy, ethnic makeup, and religious practices.[23] Alongside physical remains, archaeologists have also discovered and cataloged quite a sizable collection of graffiti inscribed on various items by the inhabitants of the qaganate.[24] As useful as the inscriptions and drawings may be for the study of Khazaria, this epigraphic evidence, even when adequately interpreted, very rarely provides enough information to reconstruct an entire episode in Khazar history.

Numismatic research has also revealed a great deal about many fundamental issues pertaining to the economic history of Khazaria. Close examination of the profiles of dirham hoards by their chronological, dynastic, and mint composition and of the hoards' topographic distribution has shed much new light on Khazaria's trade relations with the Islamic world, northern Russia, and the Baltic lands.[25] Some studies have used dirham hoards to analyze the regional commercial economy and monetary circulation of Khazaria.[26] Another branch of numismatic research has focused on the question of the existence of domestic coinage in Khazaria.

For over a century, numismatists have been at odds on the question of whether the Khazars minted their own coins. While this is not the place to discuss the historiography of this question, the arguments used by advocates[27] and opponents[28] of the idea of Khazar coinage have to be seriously revisited in light of recent findings made by Gert Rispling of the Numismatic Institute in Stockholm. His outstanding and meticulous die analysis of dirhams has shown the existence of a die link between several groups of suspected Khazar coins. Rispling was able to tie these coin issues with the Khazars conclusively by way of the so-called Moses dirhams, which are not only die-linked to other assumed Khazar coins but also connected with the Khazars by virtue of their religious message: their legends bear the invocation "Moses is the prophet of God," a statement that clearly binds these coins to the Jewish Khazars.[29] The Moses coins, first discovered in an Estonian dirham hoard of 1915, have never attracted the attention of numismatists. This situation changed, however, with the discovery of the Spillings 2 hoard in Gotland, Sweden, in 1999 and its close analysis by Rispling, who first brought this coin type to the attention of numismatists and historians.[30] It is now clear that the Khazars emitted their own currency.

Thanks to Rispling's invaluable research, historians now have an additional new source of evidence for the study of Khazaria.[31] The coins he has analyzed can be used in several ways as historical sources. Examination of the messages they carry is a particularly useful endeavor, since these coins are a primary source coming directly from the Khazars themselves. Unlike many traditional historical documents that deal with the Khazars, these coins can be dated to a very specific time period. Perhaps most important, the information carried on their legends has not been altered in any way and misinterpreted by later editors. These "unedited sources" speak of very specific events, in a clearly defined geographic area, within an exceptionally narrow time frame.

Among the different kinds of coins issued by the Khazars, three types are of particular interest in light of the messages they carry. This group of coins, which I will call special issue Khazar dirhams of 837/8, are the subject of the present study. Since Gert Rispling has already provided a detailed description of these coins and their die linkage in his study,[32] discussion of their attributes will be kept to a minimum here. However, it is necessary to consider here, in a very concise way, the history of the early Khazar coin emission.

Early Khazar Coinage

At the present state of research, it appears that the Khazars began to strike their own coins starting with the second quarter of the ninth century.[33] The earliest coins were essentially imitations of Islamic dirhams, but with numerous misspellings of Arabic words, mistakes in Kufic orthography, and erroneous mints, dates, rulers, and their combinations.[34] Khazar emission of local currency seems to be linked with the significant decline in the production of new dirhams in Islamic mints in the 820s, which in turn led to the diminishing volume of imports of these coins into Khazaria and northern Russia. The significant reduction in North African dirhams imported into European Russia beginning at the very same time (ca. 825) compounded the problem of diminishing availability of silver coins for trade with the north. Hence, the Khazars initiated an emission of local coins in ca. 825 to supplement the depleting coin stock in their lands, largely to entice Rus' merchants to trade in Khazaria, as well as to provide coins to the inhabitants and visitors of the qaganate.[35]

The decision to strike coins in full imitation of the Islamic dirham made perfect sense for the Khazars, and as noted earlier the Rus' and the Volga Bulghars made the same choice in the tenth century in issuing their earliest coinage. Because of its exceptionally high silver content, universal acceptance, and widespread circulation throughout much of medieval western and central Eurasia, the Islamic dirham was equivalent to the modern dollar in its worldwide recognition and utility in exchange. The dirham was well known in the lands of Khazaria because of the qaganate's intermediary role in trade relations between the Islamic world and northern Europe beginning ca. 800, and their Rus' trading partners were accustomed to receiving this high-quality Kufic silver coin. While there is no reason to presume that the Rus' could read the Arabic coin legends, they undoubtedly knew a good dirham when they saw one and accepted it in exchange for their merchandise, provided that it was within the same weight range and made of the same high-quality silver as the official Islamic dirham issue.

Indeed, the early Khazar imitation dirhams, aside from carrying legends with obvious errors (none of which would have been noticeable to the Rus'),[36] were not augmented in any way to carry specifically Khazar political or religious messages or symbolism. These imitations were simply made to look like Islamic dirhams. In fact, they are so well made and close to the originals that it takes the keen and trained eye of a modern numismatist to discern Khazar imitations from "official," caliphal dirhams.[37] Studies of the fineness of the silver content and weight of Khazar imitations have shown that these coins were just as heavy and just as pure as any of the contemporary "official" Islamic dirhams.[38] Thus, the Khazar imitation, "unofficial" dirhams would have been just as attractive and acceptable to the Rus' as any of the "official" Islamic dirhams. Based on the discovery of these coins in Baltic hoards beginning ca. 825, it appears that they fully served their function.[39]

The Special Issue Khazar Dirhams of 837/8

While the Khazar production of coins starting ca. 825 made perfect commercial sense, and the full adoption of the dirham model for the Khazar coinage was connected to economic as well as practical circumstances, the situation drastically changed in the year AH 223 (AD 837/8). That year, the Khazars issued three unique coins—Arḍ al-Khazar, Moses, and tamgha dirhams—which, while imitating much of the traditional features of the "official" caliphal dirhams, demonstrate subtle, profoundly important additions.

The Arḍ al-Khazar dirhams are unique in two main ways. First, they contain the name of the mint—*Arḍ al-Khazar,* meaning "Land of the Khazars." Second, they include the actual date of the emission of the coin—837/8 (AH 223). Both are placed in the standard mint-date formula found on regular caliphal dirhams. The Arḍ al-Khazar coins form a very tight-knit group chronologically, stylistically, and by die link—they all date to 837/8 and, according to Rispling, are part of die chain 108 (fig. 9.1).[40] To date, eighty-four Arḍ al-Khazar coins have been discovered in hoards dating to the ninth century, all found north of the Khazar lands (northern European Russia and the Baltic region).[41] The earliest hoards with Arḍ al-Khazar dirhams date to 837/8 (five hoards). Thus, most of these coins were exported north from Khazaria immediately after being struck.[42] In 837/8, instead of issuing imitations of Islamic dirhams with Islamic mints and fictitious dates, the Khazars considered it necessary to engrave a die carrying not only the actual date of the coin issue but also the official Khazar mint "Land of the Khazars," a clear reference to Khazaria's sovereignty and independence.

The Moses dirhams are unique in one key way: in the standard spot reserved for a quote of a part of a Sura, one of the chapters of the Qur'ān (found in a circle on the reverse of the coin on regular caliphal dirhams), the die engraver added an extra, unprecedented statement at the bottom, which reads in Arabic, *Mūsā rasūl Allāh*, or "Moses is the apostle/messenger of Allah/God." This reverse was almost certainly a copy of an official caliphal dirham minted in Basra in AH 160–63 (776/7–779/80), which contained the name of a certain "Muḥammad" who was at that time the governor of the city. In carving his die, the Khazar die cutter used that dirham as a model but intentionally substituted the statement *Mūsā rasūl Allāh* for the name of the governor (fig. 9.2).[43] Unlike the Arḍ al-Khazar dirhams, the Moses coins carry fictitious dates and mints, imitations of caliphal dirham legends. However, they belong to die chain 108—the same die used for striking some of the 837/8 Arḍ al-Khazar coins, with which they share many stylistic features.[44] The conclusion can only be that the Moses and the Arḍ al-Khazar dirhams were issued by the same workshop at roughly the same time. Since the Moses dirhams were discovered in hoards together with the Arḍ al-Khazar coins (some deposited as early as 837/8), the date of the Moses emission can be established with precision to 837/8. Thus far, five Moses coins have been discovered in four hoards, all found north of the Khazar lands (northern European Russia and the Baltic region). The earliest hoards with Moses dirhams date to 837/8 (two hoards). Hence, like the Arḍ al-Khazar dirhams, most of these coins were instantly transported north from Khazaria after they were issued.[45] The most obvious point of interest in regard to the Moses coin is its reference to the Old Testament prophet Moses, a well-recognized figure among all religious groups of the Abrahamic tradition—Jews, Christians, and Muslims. However, as Rispling noted, while Moses was a recognized prophet among Muslims, such an explicit reference to him on the coin seems "from an Islamic point of view . . . almost heretical, and certainly puzzling."[46] For reasons that will be discussed later in some detail, the Khazars considered it necessary in the late 830s to engrave a die that carried the statement "Moses is the apostle/messenger of Allah/God," which they used to strike their coins.

The tamgha dirhams are unique in one fundamental way—practically all of them carry the sign Υ, a tamgha symbol (a personal tribal/clan identity mark or symbol), located within the bottom section of the circle on the obverse or reverse side of the coin. Like the Moses dirhams, the tamgha coins were minted with fictitious dates and mints, imitating caliphal dirham legends. The tamgha dirhams are not only stylistically very close to the other two special issue Khazar coins but are also part of die chain 108.[47] Thus, they must have been issued by the same workshop at about the same time as the other two coins. Since the tamgha coins were discovered in the same hoards together with the Arḍ al-Khazar and Moses dirhams (some deposited as early as 837/8), we can conclude that these coins were issued at the same time, 837/8 (fig. 9.3). To date, seventy-seven tamgha coins of known provenance have been found, many of which come from hoards dating to the ninth century, all discovered north of the Khazar lands (in northern European Russia[48] and the Baltic region).[49] The earliest hoards with tamgha dirhams date to 837/8 (two hoards). Therefore, like the other two special issue Khazar dirhams of 837/8, most of these coins were instantly carried north from Khazaria after leaving the mint.[50]

The most interesting feature of the tamgha coins is the tamgha symbol Y and its significance. The location of the symbol on the coins sheds some light on its meaning. On official caliphal dirhams, the circle where the symbol Y appears is traditionally reserved for the *shahada* (or *kalima*), the Muslim profession of faith ("There is no Deity except God, alone He has no equal and Muhammad is his servant and messenger"). On the tamgha coins, the Y is situated just below the *shahada*, a space that was typically reserved for the names and titles of the various early Abbasid governors/administrators. Thus, the Y is strategically placed in an area of the coin where Islamic rulers traditionally placed their names and titles indicating their authority over the lands they governed.[51] It would stand to reason, therefore, that the Y must somehow be connected to Khazar ruling elite who desired to make a statement regarding their political independence and sovereignty over the lands of Khazaria, much like they did with the Arḍ al-Khazar dirhams.[52] They attempted to accomplish that based on the traditional Islamic model, on the one hand, and something local, on the other.

Thus far, a fully satisfactory explanation of this symbol has not been advanced. Recently, Omeljan Pritsak suggested an interesting and perhaps plausible interpretation of the so-called twig symbol.

The "twig"-sign can be easily recognized as the Old Norse rune R in the so-called Older Futhark alphabet—Y. As is well known, all Old Norse runes have their specific names. This particular rune R Y appears in the three lists of runic names from the ninth century (St. Gall, Brussels nos. 9565 and 9311) as *elux/elox/ilix*. In Old Norse the word had the meaning of "elk," and was pronounced as **ilig*-R ~ *elg*-R. Coincidentally, however, *ilig/elig* ~ *elg* was the Old Turkic royal title that sometime during the second half of the eighth century was usurped by the Khazarian majordomo. This decipherment of the rune R as a homonym for the Khazar royal title *ilg/ilig* resolves the mystery of the "strange" Devica *dirhams*. These, in fact, were produced by the Khazars—not by the kagan, but by the majordomo, the actual ruler after the Arab victory of 737.[53]

Aside from the dubious dating of the beg's takeover of the qaganal political functions to the second half of the eighth century,[54] Pritsak's interpretation seems quite tempting, in large part due to its obvious simplicity. Indeed, there are good linguistic reasons to believe that the name of the first Khazar beg, Bulan, has the meaning of "elk, deer" in Turkic.[55] Unfortunately, there is one problem—the absence of the character Υ in Old Futhark, which is no minor detail to be left unaddressed. In his analysis, Pritsak refers to the well-known runic character, Ψ, or R (*z*), hence everything else seems to fall into place. However, the symbol found on the Khazar coins almost always contains an extra line, extending downward from the left branch of the character. There is only one case when the extra branch is omitted and the character appears as Υ.[56] Thus far, the exact character Υ has not come to my attention from examining Old Norse runes. The literature Pritsak cites to substantiate his hypotheses also makes no mention and provides no illustration of such a character.[57] Aside from this fundamental problem, Pritsak also neglects to explain why the Khazars would choose to inscribe a Norse rune on their coins. While the relatively numerous discoveries of these dirhams in northern Europe indicates that the Norse-speaking Rus' did come to handle them, it is somewhat difficult to believe that the Khazars would strike their coins with a Norse runic character.

The Norse world was not unique in using runes similar to the symbol in question. While the sign Υ does not occur in the Old Futhark alphabet, it is encountered in early medieval Turkic graffiti (e.g., at Pliska in Balkan Bulgaria),[58] and the Turkic rune Υ (*č*) is widely known in the medieval nomadic steppe world from Mongolia to the north Pontic region, including in the Don-Kuban alphabet used in the lands of Khazaria.[59] The Turkic rune Υ has been found on numerous objects at Khazar sites, such as the Sarkel, Mayaki, and Khumarinskoe forts.[60] Thus, this symbol/character may well be of Turkic origin. Perhaps most interesting, however, is that both signs, Υ and Ψ, have been identified on a group of imitation dirhams dating to the first half of the tenth century. All of these coins were modeled on Samanid dirhams, but their legends were inscribed not in Kufic characters but in Turkic runes and tamghas. All known dirhams of this kind have been found in the Transcarpathian region of western Ukraine and, based on their topographic distribution, were linked to the Saltovo culture of Khazaria, where they must have been struck.[61] Thus, for reasons that are not clear, after the issue of the 837/8 dirhams with the symbol Y, the Khazars ceased to produce coins with such symbols until the first half of the tenth century. What is clear is that the tradition of emitting coins with such a symbol was known in the lands of Khazaria in the ninth century as well as the tenth.[62]

The emission of coins with Turkic tamghas was not unique to the Khazars. From the mid-sixth century, the qagans of the first Turk qaganate and later Toquz Oguz, Türgesh, and Qarluq khans, among others, issued coins with their royal insignias or tamghas in their Central Asian vassal states (e.g., Khwārazm, Soġdia, Chāch, Farghāna, and Tokharistān).[63] Interestingly, quite a good number of these were shaped in the form of a trident, and some look very similar to the Khazar tamgha but lack the extra branch.[64] Tridentlike tamghas also commonly occur on Chinggisid coins of the later Middle Ages.[65] While there is debate about the provenance of all of these tamghas (i.e., whether they are of Turkic-Mongolian, Chinese, Parthian, or some other origin),[66] it is clear that the Khazars followed a long-standing Turkic tradition of placing their royal family symbols on their coins. They continued this tradition into the tenth century. Whichever way one interprets the symbol Y—as a Norse rune or Turkic rune/tamgha—it is very likely that this symbol was somehow connected to Turkic political heritage, probably to the Khazar ruling house at the time the coins were issued.

In sum, all three special issue Khazar coins were struck by the same workshop somewhere in Khazaria in the year 837/8. While quantitatively insignificant, the minting of Arḍ al-Khazar, Moses, and tamgha dirhams is of tremendous historical value. All three coin types are unique and interesting individually and as a group, since they must have been struck in connection to some very special development that occurred in AH 223 (AD 837/8) in Khazaria. Each of the coin groups carries a specific and blatant message charged with political-religious ideology tied to Jewish, Khazar, and Turkic identity. Apparently, these coins were minted as part of a state program that was attempting to connect all three of these concepts and to unite them into one larger idea.

Why the Khazars Struck Special Issue Dirhams in 837/8

The Khazar emission of the special issue dirhams in 837/8 raises numerous questions, the most obvious of which concerns the event that prompted the striking of these "Khazar-Jewish-Turkic" coins. What motivated the Khazar rulers to issue coins that carry such loud and clear political-religious statements? Among

the most obvious and principal reasons for issuing coins with specific ideological messages is reorientation/restructuring in political-religious leadership of a
state or its structure. Indeed, the first four decades of the ninth century, particularly the 830s, proved to be momentous for Khazaria's political and religious
development. During this time, the military-political function of the Khazar
qagan was transferred to the beg, while the office of the qagan became sacral.
Concurrently, the Khazar state was officially converted to Judaism. To understand better how the emission of the special issue Khazar coins is connected to
these events, it is necessary to examine these developments more closely.

Sources are silent about a beg or dual kingship in Khazaria until the 830s.
This does not preclude the possibility of the existence of a beg and his sharing
of power with the qagan prior to the 830s. At the same time, it is unlikely that
the office of the beg was created much earlier than ca. 800. As late as the turn
of the ninth century, the qagan was still in charge of Khazar armies, as is attested in connection to the Khazar campaign against Arab-held Darband on
the Caspian in 798–99.[67] By the closing years of the 830s, circumstances had
clearly changed. When Khazar emissaries were given audience with Emperor
Theophilos (829–42) in Constantinople in late summer 839 to plead for Byzantine assistance with building the fortress of Sarkel on the lower Don, their letter came from the Khazar qagan as well as the beg.[68] Unfortunately, it cannot
be determined when this mission was dispatched from Khazaria or when it arrived in Constantinople. It can be safely assumed, however, that the emissaries
left the qaganate not much later than a year prior to their reception by
Theophilos in the Byzantine capital; they may have departed Khazaria sometime in 838, probably during the spring or summer months, when travel by
water was possible and travel by land easier.[69] Consequently, the envoys' letter
reflected the Khazar political reality of ca. 838. Thus, the office of the beg and
dual kingship probably came into existence sometime after 800 and no later
than 838.

Very soon after the Khazar embassy was sent to Constantinople, the positions of the beg and the qagan had changed yet again. In his official letter of 843
to the Khazars, the Abbasid caliph al-Wāthiq (842–47) only referred to the
"king of the Khazars" (*Ṭarkhān malik al-khazar*) or beg.[70] The qagan was
clearly no longer the active secular ruler of Khazaria at the time that letter was
written;[71] the beg was corresponding and dealing with heads of foreign states.
On the basis of available literary sources, there is no way to determine the precise date for this new political arrangement. At some point between 838 and
843, the beg took total control over the secular affairs of the qaganate, and the
qagan was made into a sacral Khazar leader.[72] In sum, sometime between the
turn of the ninth century and the time of the departure of Khazar envoys to

Constantinople in ca. 838, the institution of dual kingship came into being as the beg began to share power with the qagan. In the period of time between the departure of the emissaries from the Khazar lands in 838, on one hand, and the year 843, on the other, the political power of the qagan had totally eroded, becoming only sacral, while the beg came to act as the chief executive of all secular affairs in Khazaria.

The individual who succeeded in bringing the constitutional reforms to the qaganate was Beg Bulan-Sabriel—the first in the dynastic line of Khazar-Jewish begs. The short and long versions of King Joseph's reply in the "Hebrew-Khazar Correspondence" as well as Jahudah ben Barzillai (writing in ca. 1100) provide lists of Khazar begs.[73] All three sources agree that the name of the first beg was *Bulan*, equated with Sabriel (found in the conversion story of the Genizah Letter), who established a dynasty of the future begs.[74] In light of what we know about the chronology for the advent and development of the beg's office, it would be appropriate to date Bulan-Sabriel's rule in Khazaria to the first half of the ninth century.

The short version of King Joseph's reply (which is basically the same as the long version in this part) implies that the "lower king," or beg (Bulan), was already a convert to Judaism (i.e., had a private conversion) but needed approval from the "higher king," or qagan, to initiate the official conversion of the qaganate.[75] The text is clear in making the distinction between the lower and the higher kings but does so rather implicitly: the beg is portrayed as the actual ruler over the people ("the people, over whom I reign"), but the people also had "their chief prince" (i.e., the qagan), who needed to be convinced of the correctness of conversion before it could be fully carried out under the beg's auspices.[76] It is crucial to note that the document speaks of the existence of a dual kingship in the qaganate at the threshold of the official conversion and of the beg's subordination to the qagan. At the same time, the beg is clearly rendered as the factual ruler of the people "over whom" he reigns, while the qagan is a titular "chief prince" whose authority is honored by everyone, including the beg. The short version of King Joseph's reply thus shows the degree to which the secular powers of the qagan had degenerated to the benefit of the beg on the eve of the official conversion. The qagan nonetheless had to be consulted before any final decision on the conversion could be enacted. Clearly, the qagan was still in charge of the qaganate. As with King Joseph's reply, the Genizah Letter also implies that the beg (named Sabriel) was already a convert, but he had a religious "reawakening," since the "Lord took mercy and stirred the heart of the chief officer to repent" and also thanks to his wife, Serah, who reminded him that he was a Jew ("since he was circumcised") but was not actively practicing Judaism.[77] In all accounts, the beg succeeded in bringing Judaism to the

Khazars but required a Christian-Jewish-Islamic religious debate to be held at the Khazar court to make the conversion fully legitimate.[78]

The Genizah Letter provides one more critical detail about the conversion and directly links it with the constitutional reforms. It notes that from the time of the conversion, the qaganal office came to be known as šōp̄ēṭ,[79] which, as Dan Shapira observed, was the ancient Canaanite office of judge, but not in the modern English notion of judge, for it in fact meant that the qagan held "an ancient office overshadowed by kings."[80] As with the early Israelite monarchy of Saul and David (and probably with the religious reforms under David and Solomon), the office of the šōp̄ēṭ fell into disuse after having been superseded by kings, but it was still known in later centuries and was introduced into the political-religious structure of Khazaria with its conversion.[81] The Genizah Letter thus explicitly implies that after the conversion, the qagan's role in ruling the state took on aspects of an archaic Hebrew religious institution that placed him outside the performing of secular functions. The qagan's position as šōp̄ēṭ—in itself an archaism, but also an important historical-religious link to the Hebrew past—would doubtfully have interfered with his performing a sacral function. In fact, it may have enhanced it.

In light of all the evidence, it would stand to reason that the official conversion of the qaganate must have occurred sometime between 800 and 843. The latter date is established on the basis of what we know about the *terminus post quem* for the political power of the qagan. Of the four decades in question, the 830s seem the most likely choice for dating the conversion. The sources make clear that on the threshold of initiating the conversion, the qagan was acting more as a titular figurehead than as an actual ruler, while beg Bulan-Sabriel was in charge of the state as its de facto head. Such a condition existed only between 838 and 843. Perhaps the qagan's diminishing power gave the beg the necessary leverage over him to execute the conversion.

The beg's personal conversion must have taken place at an earlier date. While it cannot be determined with any degree of precision, the conversion must obviously be placed during Bulan-Sabriel's life span, that is, during the first half of the ninth century. It is possible to date his conversion to the first decade of that century, which would certainly corroborate al-Mas'ūdī's point about the Khazar conversion to Judaism taking place during the caliphate of Harun al-Rashid (786–809).[82]

The special issue Khazar coins of 837/8 substantiate this chronological hypothesis and allow us to zero in on more concrete dates for these developments. To begin, the very emission of these coins in 837/8 points to some spectacular and momentous event in Khazar history at that time. The messages carried on these coins seem to commemorate the entire episode of the official

Khazar conversion to Judaism and the beg's constitutional reforms. The issuer of these dirhams was clearly a convert to Judaism and also an executive of the highest rank in the qaganate, someone invested with the authority of minting official "Khazar-Jewish-Turkic" coins. Who could have had that position of authority in 837/8—or, more exactly, in the year AH 223 that spans the Christian calendar from December 3, 837, to November 22, 838? Was it the beg or the qagan?

On the one hand, it is unlikely that the beg, who had by that time already converted to Judaism, could authorize the striking of such coins prior to his full assumption of qaganal executive powers. The qagan, on the other hand, would not issue such coins until his own conversion; but once he was converted, the executive powers to make such political-fiscal decisions were already transferred to the beg. Therefore, these coins could only have been issued on the order of the beg, following the official conversion of the qaganate and his taking of all qaganal secular powers. Since the coins were minted sometime between December 3, 837, and November 22, 838, it can be deduced that the official conversion and the constitutional reforms must have occurred between these dates.

It is of interest to note an additional detail that seems to be of no minor consequence for the question of the official Khazar conversion to Judaism in 838. Under the year 839, the Carolingian *Annals of St. Bertin* report that a certain Bodo, an Alamanian noble and deacon at the court of the western emperor Louis the Pious (814–40), caused a major scandal because of his conversion to Judaism, a very unusual incident for that period. Through a ruse that involved persuading the court to provide him leave and money to travel to Rome on a pilgrimage, Bodo fled to a southern French city (probably to the Frankish Jewish princedom in Septimania), where he converted to Judaism on May 22, 838. He underwent circumcision, assumed the name Eleazar, and took a Jewish wife. A few months later, Bodo-Eleazar emigrated to Spain, first to Saragossa and soon after that to Córdoba, where he became a Jewish activist in the 840s and attempted to forcibly convert Christians to Judaism.[83] During this period, he also engaged in a written religious debate with Archbishop Paul Albar of Lyons, a Jewish convert to Christianity, but only a few lines of Bodo-Eleazar's letters remain, since his rival took great relish in destroying them.[84]

While many questions remain concerning Bodo's conversion and why it occurred when it did, it is likely that his knowledge of Hebrew and Judaism came through his contacts with Jewish merchants who were frequently present at the imperial Frankish court.[85] Indeed, Jewish merchants working in a "corporation" known in Arabic sources of the ninth and early tenth century as Rāḏānīya/Rāhdānīya, based in Iraq, operated from Firanja (France—probably Septimania) and al-Andalus (Spain) in Western Europe and as far east as China.[86] Among the key localities on their cross-continental itinerary was Khazaria, including Khamlīkh, the commercial sector of İtil/Atıl.[87] The role of the Rāḏānīya/Rāhdānīya merchants in Khazar conversion to Judaism has already been put forward.[88] As noted earlier, the same connections were suggested for Bodo's conversion. In light of the chronology of the conversions and Jewish missionary activities in Septimania-Spain and Khazaria, two key hubs of Jewish transcontinental commerce at the crossroads of Christian-Muslim trade and rivalry in Western Eurasia in the first half of the ninth century, it is perhaps time to suggest a link between these two extraordinary events.

With 838 established as the precise time of both the official conversion of the qaganate to Judaism and the beg's assumption of full secular powers, it is now possible to ponder the reason for these momentous turns of events. The 830s were very eventful years for Khazar relations with their neighbors. Among the most noteworthy of these was the westward migration of the Magyars (future Hungarians) from the lower Kama and Belaia river basins into Khazar territories, where they remained for the next half century.[89] While the precise location of those territories, which several sources call Lebedia, is still disputed, it does seem that the Magyars were stationed west of the Don River and probably came to control the north Black Sea steppe region from the Don to as far west as Pannonia.[90] Magyar migration into the Russian-Ukrainian steppe and the disruption it brought to the Khazar state almost certainly occurred in ca. 836,[91] prompting the Khazar qagan and beg to request assistance from the Byzantines with the building of Sarkel.[92] As discussed earlier, the Khazar embassy carrying that appeal was received in Constantinople in the late summer of 839.[93] Shortly thereafter (probably in 840 or 841),[94] the fortress was erected at a strategic location on the lower Don, no doubt for defense purposes, mainly aimed at protecting Khazar territories from Magyar incursions.[95]

Major unrest in the northern Black Sea steppe region in the late 830s is also recorded in the *Annals of St. Bertin*. From that source, we learn that on May 18, 839, two Rus' emissaries were received by the emperor in Ingelheim on the Rhine, along with a Byzantine embassy that Theophilos had sent to Louis the Pious. According to the *Annals*, the two Rus' envoys claimed that they had been sent to Constantinople by the Rus' qagan "for the sake of friendship" and that they were unable to return to their land by the same, usual route because the road had been blocked by "primitive tribes that were very fierce and savage, and Theophilus did not wish them to return that way in case some disaster befell them."[96] Evidently, Magyar penetration into territories west of the Don and occupation of the Russian-Ukrainian steppe in ca. 836 not only robbed the Khazars of all of their western steppe lands but also brought about a significant disturbance to the commercial routes that the Rus' had been using to trade between northern Europe, Byzantine Crimea, Khazaria, and the Islamic Near East since the turn of the ninth century. Both Byzantines and Khazars must have lost substantial income deriving from the Rus' commercial traffic, since, as noted by Ibn Khurdādhbeh (writing between 850 and 885), the Rus' used to pay a 10 percent toll to the Byzantines on all goods transported via Crimea and another 10 percent to the Khazars in the region of the lower Don (most likely the very area in which Sarkel was built).[97] The Rus', Khazars, and Byzantines must have been very concerned with the disturbances in the steppe. The joint Khazar-Byzantine venture to construct Sarkel, erected just a few years after the initial Khazar call, underscores their mutual interests in bringing stability to the key trade routes through this region.

Despite the building of Sarkel, the arrival of the Magyars in the steppes north of the Black Sea ca. 836 and their occupation of Lebedia during the subsequent decades (until ca. 889) represented a seriously diminished territory for the Khazars and the loss of control over the regions west of the Don River. Perhaps the new political arrangements were made in the circumstances surrounding this unprecedented catastrophe.[98] The qagan, the traditional military leader of the Khazars, was viewed as powerless and primarily ineffective in the military field, which undermined his *qut,* or heaven-granted political and military charisma.[99] The Khazar military must have been particularly disgruntled, especially the Khwārazmian heavy cavalry guard (Ors) and its viziers. The military may therefore have supported a radical change in the governmental structure of the qaganate. Indeed, in his most recent study dedicated to the question of the Khazar dual political institution, Peter B. Golden came to the conclusion that the Khwārazmian element in the Khazar military and government played a pivotal role in introducing the concept of Iranian-styled sacral kingship to Khazar rulers.[100] Perhaps not coincidentally, Beg Bulan-Sabriel was remembered in sources as a very active commander at arms. According to the Genizah Letter, this Khazar general "prevailed with his sword and put to flight the enemies come against Qazar."[101] The chronology of Bulan-Sabriel's rule in the first half of the ninth century—particularly his activities as beg in the 830s—make it possible to connect the unnamed Khazar enemies with the Magyars.[102] In fact, Bulan-Sabriel's active military service for the qaganate and his rank of general are strong indications that he was able to consolidate his power at the expense of the qagan and carry out the conversion and the constitutional reforms of 838.

The Function of the Special Issue Coins of 837/8

Besides serving an economic function as vehicles of exchange and means of accumulating and storing wealth, coins provided a first-rate form of governmental mass media in premodern societies. States quite often issued coins for the purpose of disseminating political-religious ideology or propaganda through images or inscriptions.[103] The Khazar imitation of Islamic dirhams to supplement the volume of available coin stock in their lands has already been discussed. It made much sense for the Khazars to copy the dirham. However, the wholesale imitation of the dirham, along with all the Muslim political and religious messages inscribed on the coin, proved to be an inadequate option in 838.

Bulan-Sabriel's constitutional reforms and official conversion of the state to Judaism necessitated a loud statement in regard to the new political and religious order. Coins provided one key avenue for the dissemination of the new state ideology. Adopting the dirham model by virtue of tradition, necessity, and practicality, Bulan-Sabriel took advantage of this opportunity to hint at something specifically "Khazar-Turkic-Jewish." At the same time, these additions were no mere trifles. The incorporation of the statement "Moses is the prophet of God," the name *Arḍ al-Khazar,* and the tamgha on the dirhams of 837/8 made these coins truly special—uniquely Khazar. By extension, these coins also made Khazaria unique. In striking them, the beg made a clear stance on Khazaria's religious neutrality and political independence from other polities of the day in western Eurasia, particularly the qaganate's two powerful and belligerent neighbors, the Islamic caliphate and the Christian Byzantine Empire.

In striking the three coin types at the same time, the beg was intentionally creating a state currency for his qaganate; it was clearly meant to proclaim its political and religious exclusivity and legitimacy to all external powers as well as to the inhabitants of Khazaria. Khazar religious uniqueness and the legitimacy of the Khazars as a people of a recognized world religion that came about as a result of the conversion to Judaism are particularly well reflected in the issue of the Moses coins. In this connection, it would be useful to quote a passage from the short version of King Joseph's reply in the "Hebrew-Khazar Correspondence," on the disputation that took place at the Khazar court between Jews, Christians, and Muslims.

On the third day he [the king] called all of them together and said to them in the presence of all his princes and slaves and his people: "I wish that you make for me the choice, which religion is the best and the truest." They began to dispute with one another without arriving to any

results until the king asked the priest: "If one compares the Israelite religion with that of the Ishmaelites, which is to be preferred?" The priest
answered and said: "The religion of the Israelites is better." Now he [the
king] asked al-Qāḍī (Muslim judges) and said: "If one compares the Israelite religion with that of the Edom which is to be preferred?" Al-
Qāḍī answered him and said: "The religion of the Israelites is better."
Upon this the king said, "Both of you admitted with your own lips that
the religion of the Israelites is the best and truest. Therefore I have chosen the religion of the Israelites, that is, the religion of Abraham . . ."[104]

In the Genizah Letter, the debate was resolved by consulting the "books of the
Torah of Moses": "the sages of Israel explained them according to the previous
words, which they had spoken. Then Israel with the people of Khazaria re-
pented completely."[105] As the preceding quotes demonstrate, the Moses coin,
proclaiming that "Moses is the messenger of God," was evoking the obvious—
namely, that Moses was recognized by all three factions of the People of the
Book (ahl al-kitāb) and that the Khazars were turning to the earliest historical
roots of the Abrahamic traditions common to all three biblical religions.
Through emitting the special issue coins, which clearly appealed to the Turkic
political heritage (tamgha), Judaism (Moses), and territorial/state sovereignty
(Arḍ al-Khazar or "Land of the Khazars"), it would almost seem as though
Bulan-Sabriel was also attempting to declare or perhaps even create a sense of
Khazar political-religious unity embodied in his state-issued coins. The Arḍ al-
Khazar dirham was of particular importance at a time when the qaganate was
experiencing major territorial losses and setbacks at the hands of the Magyars.
Perhaps, one can even go as far as to suggest that these coins represent an attempt by the beg to create a unique Khazar identity (ethnos). This may well
have been the reason behind Bulan-Sabriel's attempt to convert Khazaria to a
monotheistic world religion. But the great ethnic, cultural, linguistic, religious,
political, and economic diversity of the qaganate proved to be too complicated
to unite everyone inhabiting its vast lands into one Khazar ethnos.

    Just as Judaism remained a minority religion in the Khazar lands, Bulan-
Sabriel's coin reform of 837/8 failed immediately after its implementation. The
special issue coins of 837/8 were struck only for that year. While the Khazars
continued to emit coins in the later years of the ninth century, they were no
more than close imitations of Islamic dirhams, a complete reversion to the recent past.[106] Of course, it is possible that the special issue coins of 837/8 were
meant to be a commemorative set of coins, struck for only one year to mark
the earth-shattering political and religious developments of 837/8. Such a possibility cannot be ruled out. But if that were the case, one would have to explain

why the Khazars ceased to issue coins with any official state-religious markings in the following years. What could have stopped them from doing so?

To understand the reasons behind the failure of Bulan-Sabriel's coin reform, it is necessary to turn to the audience of dirham messages. Noteworthy is the use of Arabic on the coins (the tamgha of Turk origins presumably would have been understood by most in Khazaria as the symbol of the rulers). The Moses and Arḍ al-Khazar coins were aimed at those individuals capable of reading Arabic—in Khazaria, the visiting and permanent resident Islamic merchants and artisans, Muslim judges (qāḍī), the seven to twelve thousand Muslim Khwārazmian (al-Lārisiya/Ors) mercenaries and viziers employed by the qagan, and probably some Khazar elites.[107] It can even be suggested that these coins—or at least a number of them—were struck by Bulan-Sabriel to pay the Muslim mercenaries and the viziers employed in the Khazar bureaucratic apparatus. Writing in the first half of the tenth century, al-Mas'ūdī knew that "among the eastern kings of this region only the Khazar king has troops receiving stipends [murtaziqa?]."[108] Perhaps this was also the case for the first half of the ninth century. If so, one can wonder whether receiving their payments in coins carrying the message "Moses is the apostle/messenger of God" would resound well with the Muslim Khwārazmian mercenaries and viziers, who, incidentally, probably assisted Bulan-Sabriel with formulating and initiating his constitutional reforms.

The problem may not have been the questionable inscriptions on the legends of the coins. After all, it is unlikely that the tamgha or the Arḍ al-Khazar dirhams would have offended anyone in Khazaria. The answer probably rests with the matter of the utility of issuing messages on coins that practically never saw a day of circulation in the lands of Khazaria or in any of the regions that mattered, such as the caliphate. Almost immediately after they were struck, the coins must have been acquired by Rus' merchants, who carried them to northern Europe, where most of them ended up being collected in hoards and buried shortly thereafter.[109] The inhabitants of the qaganate who came to possess the coins, either through state payment or some commercial transaction, apparently traded them for Rus' goods the very same year they were minted. The Rus', unable to read the Arabic coin legends and with no concern for their linguistic deficiencies, accepted them as bullion in exchange for their merchandise. Thus, on one hand, the minting of the special issue coins of 837/8 by the Khazars may be seen as highly successful, for it served its immediate economic purpose—namely, to attract Rus' merchants to Khazar markets and to entice them to sell their goods in exchange for the Khazar coins. On the other hand, these special issue coins failed miserably as potential means for the dissemination of state ideology inside the qaganate or in Arab lands beyond the southern border. The intended audience rarely, if ever, had a chance to read the messages. When the dies used for the striking of these special issue dirhams wore out, there seems to have been no concern with cutting new ones with identical messages. Instead, the die cutters preferred to imitate the traditional caliphal dirhams that the Rus' knew so well and were more than happy to receive. The coin reform of Bulan-Sabriel was probably a trial run that quickly proved to be a futile venture.

Conclusion

The Khazar qaganate was one of the earliest and most enduring medieval states within the territories of modern European Russia and Ukraine, with a history spanning some three centuries. Despite its longevity and importance in western Eurasia, relatively few written sources preserve information about its history. Much of what is known about the qaganate comes from documents left behind not by the Khazars themselves but by outsiders, who often left only fragmentary and laconic accounts on its history. Written sources can be supplemented with the ever-increasing volume of Khazar artifacts and graffiti unearthed by archaeologists. Numismatics has also shed much light on the qaganate's commercial and monetary history, while die analysis of coins has shown that the Khazars emitted their own coinage.

Most recently, numismatic research has revealed an exclusive type of coins emitted by the Khazars in 837/8. Unlike many traditional documents pertaining to the history of the Khazars, these special issue coins are datable to a very specific time period, and the information they carry on their legends has not been altered by later editors. Thus, these "unedited sources" speak of very specific events, in a clearly defined geographic area, within an exceptionally narrow time frame. This coin emission offers a unique source for the study of several developments in Khazaria in the late 830s that proved to be of monumental importance for the qaganate's political and religious history.

Historical numismatics has shown that by 825 or so, the Khazars began to mint coins imitating Islamic dirhams. The decision to strike coins locally appears to have been an attempt to supplement the depleting coin stock available in the qaganate due to the decreasing coin inflow from the Arab lands in the same period. The choice of striking coins in full imitation of the dirham made perfect sense for the Khazars. Dirhams were widely accepted throughout much of western and central Eurasia and, most important, were indispensable for trade with the Rus', who had been visiting Khazaria for trade ever since ca. 800. The early Khazar imitation dirhams were not augmented in any way to carry specifically Khazar political or religious messages or symbolism. In the year AH 223 (AD 837/8), the situation had drastically changed, as the Khazars issued three unique coins: two with Arabic inscriptions—*Arḍ al-Khazar* (Land of the Khazars) and *Mūsā rasūl Allāh* (Moses is the apostle/messenger of God)—and one with the Turkic tamgha Y. All three special issue Khazar coins were struck by the same workshop somewhere in Khazaria in the year 837/8, and each carried a specific and blatant message charged with political-religious ideology connected to Jewish, Khazar, and Turkic identity. Apparently, these coins were minted in connection to some exceptional development that occurred that year.

Based on the available written sources, it can be gathered that sometime between 838 and 843, Khazaria experienced a profound political and religious transformation. During this time, the military-political function of the Khazar qagan was transferred to the beg, named Bulan-Sabriel, while the office of the qagan became sacral. At the same time, the qaganate adopted Judaism as the official state religion. The special issue Khazar coins of 837/8, minted at the beg's orders, were struck in connection to these religious and political changes. Thus, these coins permit us to confirm the chronology of the conversion and constitutional reforms and, in fact, to date them, with much greater accuracy, to the same year the coins were issued, a period spanning the Christian calendar from December 3, 837, to November 22, 838.

The Khazar conversion to Judaism was probably linked to the qaganate's intimate commercial relations with the Jewish Rāḏānīya/Rāhdānīya merchants, who operated from China in the east to France in the west, with two key hubs of trade in the Frankish Jewish princedom in Septimania and Khazaria—both situated at the crossroads of Christian-Muslim trade and rivalry in ninth-century western Eurasia. The conversion was intimately tied to the constitutional reforms in the qaganate. The political reforms apparently came about in connection with the qagan's loss of *qut*, or heaven-granted political-military charisma, because of his inability to protect the qaganate from the Magyar (proto-Hungarian) migration to the north Pontic steppe zone in ca. 836, which in turn led to the loss of the western half of the Khazar Empire stretching from the Don to the Danube Rivers.

The Khazars struck their special issue coins of 837/8 with legends that were clearly designed to disseminate the new political-religious ideology that came with the constitutional reform and official conversion of the state to Judaism. While these three types of coins were modeled on the Islamic dirham, the inclusion of the name *Arḍ al-Khazar*, the statement "Moses is the apostle/messenger of God," and the tamgha on their legends made these issues uniquely Khazar, truly "state" Khazar coins. In turn, these coins made Khazaria unique, since they evoked Khazaria's religious exclusivity, legitimacy, neutrality, and political independence from its powerful and rival states, the caliphate and Byzantium. Through emitting the special issue dirhams, the Khazar beg was also declaring and perhaps even creating a sense of Khazar political-religious unity and a unique Khazar identity for the qaganate's diverse population.

Despite their promising beginnings, the special issue coins of 837/8 were not struck for more than one year. In the following decades, the Khazars continued to strike dirhams, but as in the past, they were full imitations of Islamic dirhams, without any Khazar state-religious insignias or identity markings. While it is possible that the special issue dirhams of 837/8 were struck as a commemorative set of coins, issued to celebrate the momentous political and religious transformation of that year, it is most likely that the Khazars ceased to mint official state coins because they utterly failed in disseminating their ideological messages. Practically all of the special issue coins of 837/8 were shipped directly north of Khazaria by the Rus' merchants and ended up in hoards buried in northern Russia soon thereafter. Thus, the intended audience of the dirham legends, the inhabitants of the qaganate and the Muslim merchants visiting Khazaria, practically never had a chance to read them. It must have become quickly apparent that continuing to mint an official state coinage was pointless. The Khazar coin reform of 837/8 was probably an experimental trial run designed to establish a state Khazar currency, a venture that quickly proved to be futile, due to Khazaria's intense and close commercial relations with the Rus', which siphoned all of the official Khazar currency outside the qaganate.

NOTES

1. For Rus' imitations carrying Christian crosses and birds inside the Kufic dirham legends, see G. Rispling, "Coins with crosses and bird heads: Christian imitations of Islamic coins?" *Fornvännen* 82 (1987): 75–87; E. Lindberger, "The falcon, the raven, and the dove: Some bird motifs on medieval coins," in *Excavations in the Black Earth, 1990–1995: Eastern Connections, Part One; The Falcon Motif,* ed. B. Ambrosiani (Stockholm, 2001), 29–86.

2. For the basic arguments and literature on Ol'ga's conversion, see S. Franklin and J. Shepard, *The Emergence of Rus, 750–1200* (London and New York), 134–37.

3. The overwhelming majority of the coins struck by the Rus' were silver *srebreniki.* Out of about two hundred such coins that have been tested for their silver content, only twenty-three were made of relatively pure silver (960–600° to 375–300°), and about three-fourths of the coins had very little, if any, silver in their predominantly copper-base alloy. Therefore, it is very likely that Rus' princes struck their coins as political-religious propaganda rather than for economic reasons. It is no coincidence that these coins were issued immediately following the official Rus' conversion to Christianity in

988/9. See M. P. Sotnikova and I. G. Spasskii, *Russian Coins of the X–XI Centuries A.D.: Recent Research and a Corpus in Commemoration of the Millenary of the Earliest Russian Coinage* (Oxford, 1982); M. P. Sotnikova and I. G. Spasskii, *Tysiacheletie drevneishikh monet Rossii* (Leningrad, 1983); M. P. Sotnikova, *Drevneishie russkie monety X–XI vekov* (Moscow, 1995), 237 with table 3.

4. For the Volga Bulghar imitations ("unofficial") and later state ("official") dirhams, see R. R. Vasmer, "O monetakh Volzhskikh Bolgar X veka," *Izvestiia obshchestva arkheologii, istorii i etnografii pre Kazanskom universitete im. V.I. Ul'ianova-Lenina* 33, no. 1 (1926): 29–60; S. A. Ianina, "Novye dannye o monetnom chekane Volzhskoi Bolgarii X v.," in *Trudy Kuibyshevskoi arkheologicheskoi ekspedicii*, ed. A. P. Smirnov, vol. 4 (Moscow, 1962), 179–204; G. Rispling, "The Volga Bulgarian imitative coinage of al-Amir Yaltawar ('Barman') and Mikail b. Jafar," in *Sigtuna Papers: Proceedings of the Sigtuna Symposium on Viking-Age Coinage, 1–4 June 1989*, ed. K. Jonsson and B. Malmer (Stockholm and London, 1990), 275–82.

5. For Jewish coinage, see A. Reifenberg, *Ancient Jewish Coins*, 2nd ed. (Jerusalem, 1947); L. Kadman, *The Coins of the Jewish War of 66–73 C.E.* (Tel Aviv, 1960); Th. Reinach, *Jewish Coins* (Chicago, 1966); F. W. Madden, *History of Jewish Coinage and of Money in the Old and New Testament* (San Diego, 1967); Y. Meshorer, *Jewish Coins of the Second Temple Period* (Tel Aviv, 1967); L. Mildenberg, *The Coinage of the Bar Kokhba War* (Sauerländer, 1984).

6. For the fundamentals of Khazar history, see D. M. Dunlop's *The History of the Jewish Khazars* (Princeton, 1954; reprint New York, 1967) and several works by P. B. Golden: *Khazar Studies: An Historico-Philological Inquiry into the Origins of the Khazars*, 2 vols. (Budapest, 1980); "The peoples of the south Russian steppe," in *The Cambridge History of Early Inner Asia*, ed. D. Sinor (Cambridge, 1990), 263–70; and *An Introduction to the History of the Turkic Peoples* (Wiesbaden, 1992), 233–44. See also M. I. Artamonov, *Istoriia khazar* (Leningrad, 1962); M. G. Magomedov, *Obrazovanie khazarskogo kaganata* (Moscow, 1983); A. P. Novosel'cev, *Khazarskoe gosudarstvo i ego rol' v istorii Vostochnoi Evropy i Kavkaza* (Moscow, 1990).

7. On the Saltovo-Mayaki culture and other issues of Khazar archaeological studies, see S. A. Pletneva, *Ot kochevii k gorodam: Saltovo-maiackaia kul'tura* (Moscow, 1967); *Khazary* (Moscow, 1976); *Kochevniki srednevekov'ia* (Moscow, 1982); *Ocherki khazarskoi arkheologii* (Moscow and Jerusalem, 1999). See also S. A. Pletneva, ed., *Maiackoe gorodishche* (Moscow, 1984); A. Z. Vinnikov and S. A. Pletneva, *Na severnykh rubezhakh Khazarskogo kaganata: Maiackoe poselenie* (Voronezh, 1998).

8. Golden, *Introduction*, 134.

9. P. B. Golden, "The Khazar sacral kingship," in *Pre-Modern Russia and Its World*, ed. J. Tracy, K. Reyerson, and Th. Stavrou (Wiesbaden, in press). I would like to thank Peter B. Golden for kindly sharing with me this insightful article prior to its publication and for reviewing the present study.

10. For the historical geography of the Khazar qaganate, see S. A. Romashov, "Istoricheskaia geografiia Khazarskogo kaganata (V–XIII vv.)," *Archivum Eurasiae Medii Aevi* 11 (2000–2001), 219–338; 12 (2002–3), 81–222; 13 (2004): 185–264.

11. V. K. Mikheev, *Podon'e v sostave khazarskogo kaganata* (Kharkov, 1985); G. E. Afanas'ev, *Donskie Alany* (Moscow, 1993); A. Z. Vinnikov and G. E. Afanas'ev, *Kul'tovye kompleksy Maiackogo selishcha* (Voronezh, 1991); Pletneva, *Ocherki*; S. A. Pletneva, *Na slaviano-khazarskom pogranich'e: Dmitrievskii arkheologicheskii kompleks* (Moscow, 1989);

V. S. Flerov, *Pogrebal'nye obriady na severe Khazarskogo kaganata* (Volgograd, 1993); A. V. Gadlo, *Etnicheskaia istoriia Severnogo Kavkaza IV–X vv.* (Leningrad, 1979), 71–209.

12. Th. S. Noonan, "What can archaeology tell us about the economy of Khazaria?" in *The Archaeology of the Steppes: Methods and Strategies; Papers from the International Symposium Held in Naples, 9–12 September 1992,* ed. B. Genito (Naples, 1994), 331–45; "The Khazar Economy," *Archivum Eurasiae Medii Aevi* 9 (1995–97), 253–318.

13. For a ninth-century Arabic description of the route, see O. Pritsak, "An Arabic text on the trade route of the corporation of the ar-Rus in the second half of the ninth century," *Folia Orientalia* 12 (1970): 241–59. For the numismatic evidence pertaining to this route and its earliest use, see Th. S. Noonan, "When did Rūs/Rus' merchants first visit Khazaria and Baghdad?" *Archivum Eurasiae Medii Aevi* 7 (1987–91), 213–19; Th. S. Noonan and R. K. Kovalev, "Neizvestnyi klad nachala IX v. iz imeniia M. A. Obolenskogo Dmitrovskogo uezda Moskovskoi gubernii," *Arkheologicheskie vesti* 7 (2000): 206–17.

14. Th. S. Noonan, "When and how dirhams first reached Russia," *Cahiers du Monde russe et soviétique* 21, nos. 3–4 (1980): 401–69; "Why dirhams reached Russia: The role of Arab-Khazar relations in the development of the earliest Islamic trade with Eastern Europe," *Archivum Eurasiae Medii Aevi* 4 (1984): 151–282; "Khazaria as an intermediary between Islam and Eastern Europe in the second half of the ninth century: The numismatic perspective," *Archivum Eurasiae Medii Aevi* 5 (1985): 179–204; "Dirham exports to the Baltic in the Viking age: Some preliminary observations," in *Sigtuna Papers: Proceedings of the Sigtuna Symposium on Viking-Age Coinage, 1–4 June 1989,* ed. K. Jonsson and B. Malmer (Stockholm and London, 1990), 251–57.

15. For the main and most recent studies on Staraia (Old) Ladoga, see *Srednevekovaia Ladoga: Novye arkheologicheskie otkrytiia i issledovaniia,* ed. V. V. Sedov (Leningrad, 1985); A. N. Kirpichnikov, V. D. Sarab'ianov, *Staraia Ladoga: Drevniaia stolica Rusi* (St. Petersburg, 1996); S. L. Kuz'min, "Ladoga, le premier centre proto-urbain russe," in *Les centres proto-urbains russes entre Scandinavie, Byzance et Orient,* ed. M. Kazanski, A. Nercessian, and C. Zuckerman (Paris, 2000), 123–42. See also N. I. Petrov's study in the present volume (chap. 4).

16. Th. S. Noonan, "Ninth-century dirham hoards from northwestern Russia and the southeastern Baltic," *Journal of Baltic Studies* 13 (1982): 220–44; "Scandinavian-Russian-Islamic trade in the ninth century," *A Wosinszky Mór Múzeum Évkönyve* 15 (1990): 53–63; "Fluctuations in Islamic trade with Eastern Europe during the Viking age," *Harvard Ukrainian Studies* 16 (1992): 237–59; "The Vikings in the East: Coins and commerce," in *The Twelfth Viking Congress: Development around the Baltic and the North Sea in the Viking Age,* ed. B. Ambrosiani and H. Clarke (Stockholm, 1994), 215–36.

17. Mas'ūdī, *A History of Sharvān and Darband in the 10th–11th Centuries,* trans. V. Minorsky (Cambridge, 1958), 146.

18. O. Pritsak, "The Khazar kingdom's conversion to Judaism," *Harvard Ukrainian Studies* 2 (1978): 261–81; P. B. Golden, "Khazaria and Judaism," *Archivum Eurasiae Medii Aevi* 3 (1983): 127–56; C. Zuckerman, "On the date of the Khazars' conversion to Judaism and the chronology of the kings of the Rus Oleg and Igor: A study of the anonymous Khazar *Letter* from the Genizah of Cairo," *Revue des Études Byzantines* 53 (1995): 237–70; J. Shepard, "The Khazar's formal adoption of Judaism and Byzantium's northern policy," *Oxford Slavonic Papers* 31 (1998): 9–34.

19. C. A. Macartney, *The Magyars in the Ninth Century* (Cambridge, 1930; reprint, 1968); I. Boba, *Nomads, Northmen, and Slavs: Eastern Europe in the Ninth Century* (The

Hague and Wiesbaden, 1967); A. Bartha, *Hungarian Society in the 9th and 10th Centuries* (Budapest, 1975), 59–64; G. Kristó, *Hungarian History in the Ninth Century* (Szeged, 1996).

20. Th. S. Noonan, "Volga Bulghāria's tenth-century trade with Sāmānid Central Asia," *Archivum Eurasiae Medii Aevi* 11 (2000–2001): 140–218.

21. See Golden, *Khazar Studies*, for a thorough discussion of sources.

22. P. K. Kokovtsev, *Evreisko-khazarskaia perepiska v X veke* (Leningrad, 1932); N. Golb and O. Pritsak, *Khazarian Hebrew Documents of the Tenth Century* (Ithaca and New York, 1982).

23. See the references cited in n. 11 in connection to the archaeology of Khazaria.

24. I. Erdélyi, "Kabary (kavary) v karpatskom basseine," *Sovetskaia arkheologiia* 4 (1983): 174–81; I. L. Kyzlasov, *Runicheski pis'mennosti evraziiskikh stepei* (Moscow, 1994); V. E. Flërova, *Graffiti Khazarii* (Moscow, 1997); A. M. Shcherbak, *Turkskaia runika. Proiskhozhdenie drevneishei pis'mennosti turok* (St. Petersburg, 2001).

25. R. R. Fasmer (Vasmer), "Zavalishchenskii klad kuficheskikh monet VIII–IX v.," *Izvestiia Gosudarstvennoi Akademii istorii material'noi kul'tury imeni N. Ia. Marra 7*, no. 2 (1931): 1–20; R. R. Fasmer (Vasmer), "Ob izdanii novoi topografii nakhodok kuficheskikh monet v vostochnoi Evrope," *Izvestiia Akademii Nauk SSSR, Otdelenie obshch estvennykh nauk 6–7* (1933): 473–84; V. L. Ianin, *Denezhno-vesovye sistemy russkogo srednevekov'ia: Domongol'skii period* (Moscow, 1956), 79–118; Noonan, "When and how dirhams first reached Russia," 401–69; Noonan, "Why dirhams reached Russia," 151–282.

26. Th. S. Noonan, "Did the Khazars possess a monetary economy? An analysis of the numismatic evidence," *Archivum Eurasiae Medii Aevi* 2 (1982): 219–67; "What does historical numismatics suggest about the history of Khazaria in the ninth century?" *Archivum Eurasiae Medii Aevi* 3 (1983): 265–81; "Khazaria as an intermediary between Islam and Eastern Europe in the second half of the ninth century," *Archivum Eurasiae Medii Aevi 5* (1985): 179–204.

27. A. A. Bykov, "Devickii klad kuficheskikh monet," in *Tezisy dokladov nauchnoi sessii Gosudarstvennogo Ermitazha, Noiabr' 1967 g.* (Leningrad, 1967), 66–69; "O khazarskom chekane VIII–IX vv.: Doklad na III vsesoiuznoi konferentsii Arabistov," *Trudy Gosudarstvennogo Ermitazha, Numizmatika 4*, no. 12 (1971): 26–36; "Iz istorii denezhnogo obrashcheniia Khazarii v VIII i IX vv.," *Vostochnye istochniki po istorii narodov Iugo-Vostochnoi i Central'noi Evropy 3* (1974): 26–71; "Zagadochnye monety Devickogo klada: Iz zapisok starogo numismata," *Eesti NSV Teaduste Akadeemia Toimetised: Ühiskonnateaduste seeria 1 (1980): 79–86*.

28. M. Czapkiewicz, review of "O khazarskom chekane," by A. A. Bykov, *Folia Orientalia* 15 (1974): 306–10; M. Czapkiewicz, "Some remarks on the imitations of Arabic dirhams from the 8th to 10th century based on the examination of coin metal," *Proceedings of the International Numismatic Symposium*, ed. I. Gedai and K. Biró-Sey (Budapest, 1980), 101–7; Noonan, "Did the Khazars possess a monetary economy?" 219–67; Th. S. Noonan, "A ninth-century dirham hoard from Devitsa in southern Russia," *American Numismatic Society: Museum Notes* 27 (1982): 185–209; E. A. Pakhomov, *Monety Azerbaidzhana*, vol. 2 (Baku, 1963), 131.

29. G. Rispling, "A list of coin finds relevant to the study of early Islamic-type imitations," *Russian History* 28 (2001): 327–28, 332–38; "Khazar coins in the name of Moses and Muhammad," in manuscript. See also I. Hammarberg and G. Rispling, "The Spillings Viking coin hoards," *Minerva* 14, no. 2 (2003): 47–48.

30. Thus far, of the ca. 9,100 coins found in this hoard, about 3,000 have been

examined by Gert Rispling. It is certainly possible that more Khazar dirhams could be identified in the future.

31. I would like to express my gratitude to Gert Rispling for kindly sharing with me the manuscript of his article "Khazar Coins" prior to publication, for providing photographs of Khazar dirhams, and for invaluable assistance with this project, including a review of this study.

32. Rispling, "Khazar coins."

33. R. K. Kovalev, "What does historical numismatics suggest about the monetary history of Khazaria in the ninth century?—Question revisited," *Archivum Eurasiae Medii Aevi* 13 (2004): 107–12.

34. For a fundamental discussion of these issues, see Bykov, "Iz istorii denezhnogo obrashcheniia Khazarii," 26–71. A good English summary can be found in Noonan, "Did the Khazars possess a monetary economy?" 241–43.

35. Kovalev, "What does historical numismatics suggest."

36. Nothing indicates that the Rus' merchants could read Arabic. In fact, quite the opposite is true. Writing at some point between 850 and 885, Ibn Khurdādhbeh noted that when the Rus' traveled by camel from the shores of the Caspian Sea to trade in Baghdad, they needed *Ṣaqlab* (Slavic) eunuchs as interpreters. See Pritsak, "An Arabic text on the trade route," 257.

37. Rispling, "A list of coin finds," 327.

38. Bykov, "Iz istorii denezhnogo obrashcheniia Khazarii," 45–46.

39. Kovalev, "What does historical numismatics suggest."

40. Rispling, "Khazar coins."

41. The overwhelming majority of these dirhams (forty-two coins) come from the Kislaia hoard deposited in ca. 837/8 in Russia. See Kovalev, "What does historical numismatics suggest."

42. Kovalev, "What does historical numismatics suggest."

43. Rispling, "Khazar coins."

44. Rispling, "Khazar coins."

45. Kovalev, "What does historical numismatics suggest."

46. Rispling, "Khazar coins."

47. Rispling, "Khazar coins."

48. The overwhelming majority of these dirhams (forty-two coins) come from the Devica hoard deposited in ca. 837/8 in Russia. See Kovalev, "What does historical numismatics suggest."

49. Rispling, "Khazar coins."

50. Kovalev, "What does historical numismatics suggest."

51. M. Mitchiner, *The World of Islam: Oriental Coins and Their Values* (London, 1977), 68; O. Pritsak, *The Origins of the Rus' Weights and Monetary Systems* (Cambridge, Mass., 1998), 26.

52. The use of this space for declaration of independence was not unique to the Khazars. Beginning AH 196 (AD 811/12), the Idrīsids of North Africa, for instance, minted dirhams first with the six-pointed star (Solomon's seal) and later with the eight-pointed Polar Star. See M. Broome, *A Handbook of Islamic Coins* (London, 1985), 46 with fig. 71. In placing the tamgha in the *shahada/kalima* on their coins, the Khazars may have been inspired by the Idrīsids, whose coins were widely available in Eastern Europe.

53. Pritsak, *Origins*, 26–27.

54. Pritsak's "Khazarian majordomo" refers to the dynastic line of Khazar begs established by Bulan-Sabriel, discussed later in this chapter.

55. Golden, *Khazar Studies*, 1:171.

56. Bykov, "Iz istorii denezhnogo obrashcheniia Khazarii," fig. 11 (obverses of type 10).

57. L. Musset, *Introduction à la runologie* (Paris, 1965), 109; W. Krause, *Runen* (Berlin, 1970), 29.

58. L. Doncheva-Petkova, *Znaci vărkhu arkheologicheski pametnici ot srednovekovna Bălgariia VII–X vek* (Sofia, 1980), 64 nos. 10b and 16, table 3 nos. 10b and 16.

59. Kyzlasov, *Runicheskie pis'mennosti*, 15–35.

60. Flërova, *Graffiti*, table XXI cols. 1, 2, and 4.

61. A. V. Fomin, "Runicheskie znaki i tamgi na podrazhaniiakh kuficheskim monetam X v.," *Sovetskaia arkheologiia* 4 (1984): 189 with figs. 5A–V.1, 6A–B.1, 7A–V.1; 191 with fig. 8.7; 192; table 9.1–2, 1a–2a; 194.

62. Gert Rispling, who has closely examined the materials of the Maramaros ("Huszt") hoard in which many of these alleged Khazar dirhams were discovered, has noted to me in private correspondence that all imitation dirhams were Volga Bulghar in origin. Rispling also notes that the Volga Bulghars also struck coins with tamghas, such as the apparent "Christian" tamgha on the coins emitted at Suwār. Furthermore, Fomin's publications include coin photographs that are not clear enough to discern most of the legends (only some of the tamghas can be seen). See Fomin, "Runicheskie znaki i tamgi"; A. V. Fomin and L. Kovács, *The Tenth Century Maramaros ("Huszt") Dirham Hoard* (Budapest, 1987). In view of these problems, a more concrete statement about the origins of these dirhams and tamghas will have to await future study.

63. See, e.g., O. I. Smirnova, *Katalog monet s gorodishche Pendzhikent* (Moscow, 1963), 130–38; O. I. Smirnova, *Svodnyi katalog sogdiiskikh monet (bronza)* (Moscow, 1981), 311, 315, 338, 357–70, 397–412; B. I. Vainberg, *Monety drevnego Khorezma* (Moscow, 1977), 34–42.

64. Smirnova, *Katalog monet*, 32–33 with table XX, 747–76, 779, 782; *Svodnyi katalog*, 60 with figs. 35.1–2, 77 with fig. 36.2, 541 with table XCIII, 95–99, 101–6, 542 with table XCIV, 111–13, 126; Vainberg, *Monety*, table XI.12.

65. N. Ağat, *Altınordu (Cuçioğulları) paraları kataloğu, 1250–1502* (Istanbul, 1976), 51, 163.

66. Smirnova, *Svodnyi katalog*, 60–61; Vainberg, *Monety*, 41.

67. Al-Ya'qūbī, *Ta'rīkh*, ed. M. Th. Houtsma (Leiden, 1883), 120–25; al-Ṭabarī, *The History of al-Ṭabarī: An Annotated Translation*, trans. C. E. Bosworth, vol. 30 (New York, 1989), 170–71. See O. Pritsak, "Turkological remarks on Constantine's Khazarian mission in the *Vita Constantini*," in *Christianity among the Slavs: The Heritage of Saints Cyril and Methodius; Acts of the International Congress Held on the Eleventh Centenary of the Death of St. Methodius, Rome, October 8–11, 1985*, ed. E. G. Farrugia, R. F. Taft, and G. K. Piovesana (Rome, 1988), 297. See also Golden, *Khazar Studies*, 1:171, for discussion of a Georgian source that speaks of a Khazar qagan ca. 800.

68. Constantine Porphyrogenitus, *De administrando imperio*, trans. R. J. H. Jenkins, 2nd ed., vol. 1 (Washington, 1967), 182–83. For the dating of the Khazar embassy reception by Emperor Theophilos, see W. Treadgold, *The Byzantine Revival, 780–842* (Stanford, 1988), 297, 313; C. Zuckerman, "Two notes on the early history of the *thema* of Cherson," *Byzantine and Modern Greek Studies* 21 (1997): 212.

69. In the Genizah texts, the time of travel between "our land" (i.e., Khazaria) and Constantinople is given as nine days by sea and twenty-eight days by land. According to Hasdai, the distance of travel "between Constantinople and their [Khazar] land was a journey" of fifteen days by sea. See Golb and Pritsak, *Khazarian Hebrew Documents,* 82, 119–21. Unfortunately, in neither case is the starting point in Khazaria clear—that is, whether it was İtil/Atıl, Sarkel, Crimea, the eastern coast of the Black Sea, or some other Khazar locale. Constantine Porphyrogenitus (*De administrando imperio,* 1:184) noted that the voyage from the mouth of the Danube to Sarkel was sixty days long. When one adds to this journey the trip from the Danube to Constantinople in the west and from İtil/Atıl to Sarkel in the east, the period of travel would be significantly increased, perhaps by twofold or more. To the distance between İtil/Atıl and Constantinople covered by the envoys of the qagan and beg, one must also add all sorts of possible complications and delays en route, the most obvious of which at that time would have been the Magyars, who had migrated into the north Pontic area by 836 and had caused significant disturbances to the area and, hence, brought about the need to build Sarkel, the reason the envoys were dispatched to Constantinople in the first place. In connection to this chain of events, it must be noted that in early summer 838, the Rus' emissaries sent by the Rus' qagan to Constantinople had to return to northwestern Russia through Carolingian lands because the Magyars blocked off their route north via Khazaria. The Khazar envoys must also have been impeded and detained by the unstable conditions along their journey through Khazaria. (For the Magyars and the Rus' embassy, see the discussion later in this chapter.) In addition, Emperor Theophilos was away during much of the summer months of 839 on a stalemate campaign against the Arabs (see Zuckerman, "Two notes," 212). Therefore, the Khazar envoys, if they arrived by early summer 839, must have waited for several months to get an audience with the emperor, thereby extending the length of their stay by several additional months.

70. Ibn Khurdādhbeh, *Kitāb al-masālik wa'l-mamālik,* ed. M. J. de Goeje (Leiden, 1889), 191–211; Pritsak, "Turkological remarks," 297.

71. I agree with Pritsak ("Turkological remarks," 298) that the reference noted in the *Life of St. Constantine* to the qagan as the main decision maker and initiator of the religious debate between Christians, Jews and Muslims in Khazaria in 861 is an anachronism and a later addition to the account. For this reason, Zuckerman's suggestion ("On the date of the Khazars' conversion," 247–53) that the Khazar official conversion to Judaism should be dated to 861 cannot be accepted. Shepard ("The Khazar's formal adoption," 13–18) supports Zuckerman's thesis. Both also give much credence to Christian of Stablo (a monk at a monastery in Lorraine), who wrote in 864 of the Khazar adoption of Judaism as a "recent" (*iam*) event, which he associated with the Bulgar conversion to Christianity in ca. 864, thus suggesting that the two had occurred at about the same time. However, writing in ca. 903, Ibn al-Faqīh—another source Zuckerman and Shepard trust for dating the conversion to 861—also stated that the Khazars "recently" (*min qarīb*) converted to Judaism. *Recently* is a very relative term and may be applied in connection not to when the event occurred but to the time when the author became aware of what had happened. Some may regard twenty-six years as "recent," if we date the conversion to 838 (see the following discussion in text) and its mention by Christian of Stablo to 864. The mention of the Khazar conversion in context of the Balkan Bulgar conversion is also far from evidence for dating both to the 860s. It only shows that a learned monk living in a monastery in Lorraine saw a close connection between two Turkic

peoples of the Black Sea steppe zone, both of whom were "recent" converts to major world religions.

72. For the functions of the qagan as described in tenth-century and later sources, see Golden, "The Khazar sacral kingship."

73. For a comparative list and its discussion, see Zuckerman, "On the date of the Khazars' conversion," 249–50.

74. See the relevant passages in Pritsak, "The Khazar kingdom's conversion," 272–74; Golb and Pritsak, *Khazarian Hebrew Documents*, 107–13. For the discussion of these two names and their linkage with the first Khazar beg, see Dunlop, *History*, 168–69; D. Shapira, "Two names of the first Khazar Jewish beg," *Archivum Eurasiae Medii Aevi* 10 (1998–99): 231–41.

75. Pritsak, "The Khazar kingdom's conversion," 273.

76. Pritsak, "The Khazar kingdom's conversion," 273.

77. Golb and Pritsak, *Khazarian Hebrew Documents*, 107–9. For convincing discussions on why the account of the conversion depicted in the Genizah Letter downplays the role of the qagan in Khazar politics at the time of the conversion, see Dunlop, *History*, 158–61; Zuckerman, "On the date of the Khazars' conversion," 252; Shapira, "Two names," 236–37.

78. For this religious disputation, see Dunlop, *History*, 90–91, 154–58; Shapira, "Two names," 232–33 with n. 7.

79. Golb and Pritsak, *Khazarian Hebrew Documents*, 19, 110–11, 16.

80. Shapira, "Two names," 236.

81. Shapira, "Two names," 236.

82. Al-Masʿūdī, *History*, 146.

83. J. L. Nelson, trans., *The Annals of St-Bertin: Ninth-Century Histories*, vol. 1 (New York, 1991), 41–42, 47; A. J. Zuckerman, *A Jewish Princedom in Feudal France, 768–900* (New York, 1972), 204–5, 274–84.

84. For the Albar-Eleazar correspondence, see A. Cabaniss, "Bodo-Eleazar, a famous Jewish convert," *Jewish Quarterly Review* 43 (1952–53): 313–28; B. Blumerkranz, "De nouveau sur Bodo-Eleazar?" *Revue des Etudes Juives* 12 (1953): 35–42; B. Blumerkranz, *Juifs et chrétiens dans le monde occidental, 430–1096* (Paris and The Hague, 1960).

85. S. Schwarzfuchs, "France under the early Capets," in *The World History of the Jewish People: The Dark Ages, 711–1096*, ed. C. Roth (New Brunswick, 1966), 140. Also see B. S. Bachrach, *Jews in Barbarian Europe* (Lawrence, 1977); B. S. Bachrach, *Early Medieval Jewish Policy in Western Europe* (Minneapolis, 1977); E. Benbassa, *The Jews of France: A History from Antiquity to the Present* (Princeton, 1999).

86. Ibn Khurdādhbeh, *Kitāb*, 153–54. For an English translation of the Rādāniya routes recorded by Ibn Khurdādhbeh (writing between ca. 850–85), see R. S. Lopez and I. W. Raymond, *Medieval Trade in the Mediterranean World: Illustrative Documents, Translations with Introductions and Notes* (New York, 1955; reprint, 1990), 29–33. For these merchants, their goods, and their operations, see F. Kmietowicz, "The term ar-Rādānīya in the work of Ibn Ḥurdāḏbeh," *Folia Orientalia* 11 (1969): 163–73; M. Gil, "The Rādhānite merchants and the land of Rādhān," *Journal of the Economic and Social History of the Orient* 17, no. 3 (1974): 299–328.

87. For the identity of Khamlīkh with İtil/Atıl, see Romashov, "Istoricheskaia geografiia."

88. Pritsak, "The Khazar kingdom's conversion," 280–81; Golden, "Khazaria and Judaism," 138 with n. 29.

89. Constantine Porphyrogenitus, *De administrando imperio,* 1:182–85; C. Zuckerman, "Vengry v strane Levedii: Novaia derzhava na granicakh Vizantii i Khazarii ok. 836–889 g.," *Materialy po arkheologii, istorii i etnografii Tavrii* 6 (1998): 664–65.

90. Constantine Porphyrogenitus, *De administrando imperio,* 1:171–73; Zuckerman, "Vengry v strane Levedii," 659–64.

91. Zuckerman, "Vengry v strane Levedii," 659–65.

92. For a comprehensive and recent examination of Sarkel, see S. A. Pletneva, *Sarkel i "shelkovyi" put'* (Voronezh, 1996). See also my review of that work, in *Archivum Eurasiae Medii Aevi* 10 (1999): 245–54; Zuckerman, "Vengry v strane Levedii," 677–82.

93. Treadgold, *Byzantine Revival,* 297, 313; Zuckerman, "Two notes," 212.

94. Zuckerman, "Two notes," 214.

95. Zuckerman, "Vengry v strane levedii," 662, 665–66.

96. *Annals of St-Bertin,* 44.

97. Pritsak, "An Arabic text on the trade route," 257. Prior to the construction of Sarkel on the left bank of the Don, another fortified settlement, the so-called Cimliansk Gorodishche, existed on the opposite, right bank of the river. The Cimliansk fort may well have been the al-Baydā' mentioned in Arabic sources, but it was certainly destroyed at some point during the first two or three decades of the ninth century, most likely by Magyars. For the site, see Artamonov, *Istoriia khazar,* 298–302, 318; M. Goldelman, "On the location of the Khazarian city of al-Baydā," *Archivum Eurasiae Medii Aevi* 10 (1998–99): 63–71, esp. n. 45. Imitation Khazar dirhams, but not special issues of 837/8, have been discovered in a hoard found on the site; see Bykov, "Iz istorii denezhnogo obrashcheniia Khazarii," 57–59. It is quite possible that the Rus' paid their tolls to the Khazars at this location, as they traveled up and down the Don during the first three decades of the ninth century.

98. Zuckerman, "Vengry v strane Levedii," 670.

99. For the Khazar qaganal *qut,* see P. B. Golden, "Imperial ideology and the sources of political unity among the pre-Činggisid nomads of western Eurasia," *Archivum Eurasiae Medii Aevi* 2 (1982): 37–76. In relation to the potential loss of qaganal political and military "charisma," it may be of interest to note an additional reason that may have contributed to the decline of the qagan's position of secular power. Coinciding in time with the conversion of Khazaria and the constitutional reforms of the late 830s, the Uighur qaganate of eastern Eurasia was undergoing a process of rapid disintegration, followed by collapse ca. 840. The fall of the Uighur state has been explained in terms of loss of qaganal *qut,* or charisma, "preceded and perhaps brought on by famine, heavy snows, epidemics and epizootics with much loss of livestock in the Uighur lands" (Golden, *Introduction,* 162–63). Khazaria was not immune to the detrimental climate change that was apparently felt throughout Eurasia in the late 830s. This is directly evidenced by an entry in an Albanian-Armenian chronicle under the Armenian year 287 (AD 838): "In this year a locust came from the direction of the Khazars, an extraordinary thing larger than a sparrow, and it devoured part of the land of Albania. . . . After two years the winter was severe, and it affected and brought death upon many beasts and herdsmen." Previously, under the Armenian year 280 (AD 831), the chronicler had noted, "And the next year there were heavy rains for forty days and the river Kur filled to overflowing and flooding the land for fifteen parasangs beyond its estimated limits" (Movsēs Dasxurançi, *The History of the Caucasian Albanians,* trans. C. J. F. Dowsett [Oxford, 1961], 216–18). Quite clearly, the inclement weather and the locusts must have taken their toll

on neighboring Khazaria. Byzantine sources also report an invasion of locusts for the spring and then a severe winter in Asia Minor for the years 832 and 833. See Treadgold, *Byzantine Revival,* 279 n. 385, 435.

100. Golden, "The Khazar sacral kingship."

101. Golb and Pritsak, *Khazarian Hebrew Documents,* 107.

102. Zuckerman, "Vengry v strane Levedii," 670.

103. See, e.g., P. Grierson, *Numismatics* (London, 1975), 79–80; J. Casey, *Understanding Ancient Coins: An Introduction for Archaeologists and Historians* (Norman and London, 1986), 23–25; Ch. J. Howgero, "Why did ancient states strike coins?" *Numismatic Chronicle* 150 (1990): 20–21.

104. Pritsak, "The Khazar kingdom's conversion," 274.

105. Pritsak, "The Khazar kingdom's conversion," 276.

106. For more on Khazar coins, see Kovalev, "What does historical numismatics suggest."

107. See, e.g., al-Mas'ūdī, *History,* 146–47; James E. McKeithen, *The Risāla of Ibn Faḍlān: An Annotated Translation with Introduction,* (Ph.D. diss, Bloomington, 1979), 158–59.

108. Al-Mas'ūdī, *History,* 147.

109. Kovalev, "What does historical numismatics suggest."

Fig. 9.1. Arḍ al-Khazar dirham from the Stora Velinge hoard (Sweden). The obverse inscription (*A*) reads, "Arḍ al-Khazar, AH 223 [= AD 837/8]" (chain 108 2/R2). (Photography by Gabriel Hildebrand. Reproduced with the kind permission of Gert Rispling, Numismatic Institute in Stockholm.)

Fig. 9.2. Moses dirham from the Spillings 2 hoard (Sweden). The obverse inscription (*A*) reads, "Madīnat al-Salām, AH 149 (= AD 766/7)" (chain 108 obv. 6). The reverse inscription (*B*) reads, "Moses is the apostle/messenger of Allāh/God" (center, fourth line from top) (chain 108 R9 R2). (Photography by Gabriel Hildebrand. Reproduced with the kind permission of Gert Rispling, Numismatic Institute in Stockholm.) Below the photographs are drawings-cum-reconstructions of the worn-out coin. (Made by Gert Rispling.)

Fig. 9.3. Dirham no. 2658 from the Stora Velinge 1 hoard (Sweden). The obverse inscription (*A*) reads, "Muḥammadiyya, AH 150 (= AD 767/8)"; there is a tamgha (Υ) at the bottom (chain 38 obv. 2). The reverse inscription (*B*) reads, "By the command of/al-Mahdī Muḥammad/son of the Commander of the Faithful" (chain 38 rev. R1 R2). (Photography by Gabriel Hildebrand. Reproduced with the kind permission of Gert Rispling, Numismatic Institute in Stockholm.)

CHAPTER TEN

Conversions and Regimes Compared: The Rus' and the Poles, ca. 1000

Jonathan Shepard

From a twenty-first-century perspective, there may not appear to be room for useful comparison between the regimes of Boleslav the Brave of the Poles and Vladimir Sviatoslavich of Rus', and very little attention has been paid to this issue in modern historiography. Such disregard is understandable enough. Boleslav (who ruled over the Poles from 992 until 1025) was a second-generation Christian, not a convert to the faith. When he was seven years of age, his hair was sent by his father to Rome as a token of the family's devotion to the papacy and, most probably, in hopes of gaining the saint's protection for the boy.[1] In contrast, Vladimir ruled Rus' for ten years or so as a flamboyant and sometimes militant pagan, a "fornicator immensus et crudelis."[2] He then brought about the conversion of his people ca. 988 and ended his days, in 1015, as a "new Constantine"—in the words of the *Russian Primary Chronicle*.[3] More than twenty years before Vladimir's conversion, in the mid-960s, Boleslav's father, Mieszko, had received baptism "and then the Poles were baptized," as a much later set of annals put it.[4]

The best known of Mieszko's political contacts, kingship ties, and culturo-religious affinities were orientated not eastward or southeastward but southward to Bohemia and Rome, northward to the Baltic world—where his daughter married King Erik Segersäll of the Swedes and, later, the King Sven Forkbeard of the Danes—and, most conspicuously of all, westward to Ottonian Germany.[5] Mieszko and Boleslav were regarded by Saxon chroniclers, such as Thietmar of Merseburg, as being mere tributaries of the German ruler. Mieszko, according to Thietmar, would not presume to remain seated when the emperor stood up.[6] This representation is akin to the designation of Mieszko as a margrave (*marchio*) in the Abbey of Fulda's register of deaths.[7] Mieszko owed his rise partly to having enemies in common with Otto I—for example, the grouping known as the Veleti on the Oder River, whose mouth Mieszko wished to control.[8] He was of use to Otto as a client potentate, potentially troublesome in his own right but capable of intimidating the other Slav magnates who sought ascendancy in the new conditions created by the Hungarians' reverses at Otto's hands. One sign of the German leadership's close interest in the emerging Christian polity is the identity of the second bishop dispatched to evangelize among the Poles. This bishop, Unger, had probably been both a close associate of Otto II and the abbot of the monastery founded by Otto and Theophano at Memleben as a kind of mission center.[9]

Vladimir, in contrast, was not beholden to any external ruler after he seized control of Kiev ca. 978. The nearest major Christian power, Byzantium, was much further removed from the Rus' lands than were the Germans from the core territories of Mieszko and Boleslav. The axis of the Rus' celebrated in the *Russian Primary Chronicle* runs basically from north to south, along the "Way from Varangians to the Greeks." This would imply a separate "force line" from that of the Poles, whose only intersection or overlap was in the Baltic region.

The Rus' and Polish Polities

In the final third of the tenth century, the Rus' and Polish polities had in common the quality of "territorial amorphousness," that is, a lack of clear-cut, generally agreed borders of dominion. Neither of them could boast of a long-established sociopolitical hierarchy revolving round a central point beneath the ruler's patronage. Yet the rulers of both polities had lofty hegemonic aspirations, in terms of both personal status and the geographical sweep of their dominions.

This is shown clearly by the claim in the text known as the *Dagome iudex* (probably datable to 991 or 992) that Mieszko's possessions stretched along the Baltic coast to include the region of the Prussians "as far as the place which is called Rus' (*Russe*)," also encompassing Cracow and the territories as far west as the Oder River.[10] This was more of a wish list than a statement of the politico-administrative actuality of the late tenth century. Recent archaeologically based studies (especially those of Z. Kurnatowska) suggest that the core region of Mieszko was in fact more modest. It seems to have been located between the bend in the Warta River in the south and west and a line between Lake Goplo and the Notec River in the east and the Welna River in the north.[11] In making out to the papacy that more extensive tracts of lands belonged to him, Mieszko was not wholly falsifying matters. Undeniably, he did dispose of a formidable force majeure capable of breaking or cowing most individual rival potentates within the area outlined in the *Dagome iudex*. He had, according to Ibrahim ibn Yakub, "3,000 men in armor" at the ready and receiving monthly pay, "warriors of whom a hundred is equal to ten hundred of others."[12] This gave Mieszko formidable striking power but not the means for regular policing or governance of the area.

The position of the Rus' polity was not so very different, despite its rulers' formidable military reputation and record. Their principal base on the middle Dnieper in the mid- to later tenth century was quite modest in extent, and it was neither secure nor well enough connected to match the Rus' princes' aspirations. Around 970, Sviatoslav Igorevich made a serious bid to relocate to the lower Danube. He reportedly declared, "that shall be the center of my land, for there all good things flow." According to a contemporary Byzantine chronicle, he even ordered the Byzantine emperor to quit "Europe" altogether.[13]

This is not to say that Mieszko or Sviatoslav and their respective sons lacked substantial military clout, but one must emphasize that they had yet to convert military virtuosity into firmly rooted and extensive territorial holdings. There was a wide discrepancy between their hegemonic aspirations and their respective actual core areas. Equally, neither dynasty was very long established in those core areas. Boleslav's family had not constituted a ruling "dynasty" (overriding numerous other families of notables) for more than a generation or two. Mieszko seems virtually to have "risen without trace" in the middle years of the tenth century.[14] The ancestry of Vladimir goes back somewhat further, but his forebears had not been ensconced in the middle Dnieper for much longer than a generation at the time of his birth in the 950s, although they had probably been exercising princely authority somewhere in the north before making for Kiev. So neither family was particularly well established in the sense of having long-standing links with a particular location or with a clearly defined sizable grouping or "people." In this negative sense, I suggest, Mieszko, Sviatoslav, and their respective sons had more in common with one another than they did with those rulers of rather longer-established dynastic regimes who combined personal baptism with the conversion of their subjects—for example, Boris-Michael of the Bulgars or Vajk-Stephen of the Hungarians.

Vladimir Sviatoslavich and Boleslav within Their Dynasties

Legitimacy Deficit

Both Boleslav and Vladimir suffered from legitimacy deficit. There were question marks over their right to rule at all, let alone over their aspirations to rule in hegemonic mode, with rights of intervention and patronage over an extensive area. Because dynastic standing and the personal attributes of individual members of the dynasty determined, to a considerable extent, the shape, nature, and fate of political structures in this period, a legitimacy deficit was not a minor problem.

Boleslav could be deemed the "legitimate" son of Mieszko, having been borne to him by the woman who was his privileged partner or "wife" (Dobrava). However, Mieszko seems to have intended that the children by his second wife (Oda) should succeed to his authority and, apparently, rule collectively. After Mieszko's death in 992, Boleslav reportedly expelled his three half brothers and stepmother and blinded their leading supporters. In the words of a hostile contemporary, Thietmar, "[so] that [Boleslav] alone might have lordship, he set aside all right and justice."[15]

Vladimir's origins and road to power in Rus' were even more checkered than Boleslav's were among the Poles. While the reports of his gargantuan sexual appetites might be dismissed as a contrivance of Christian historiography, there is no pressing reason to reject them outright.[16] In any case, Vladimir's humble origins—the product of a liaison between the unfree "chief keyholder" of Sviatoslav's hall in Kiev and her master—were still remembered in the twelfth century. His road back from exile in the Scandinavian world in, most probably, the later 970s involved the killing of the prince of Polock. Vladimir also staged the murder in cold blood of his own brother, Iaropolk, when the latter arrived to parley with Vladimir in the family hall in Kiev.[17] Such outmaneuvering and ruthless elimination of a brother has something of the "wolfish cunning" attributed to Boleslav by Thietmar.[18]

Pressing "Religious" Needs

Both Vladimir (most conspicuously) and Boleslav used cults and public ritual to justify their regimes, associating their personal seizure of power with a more general notion of the extension of their territorial dominion. This rationale holds equally true of Vladimir the pagan and of Boleslav the Christian. Both had, after all, been usurpers and so stood in particular personal need of unique, or "religious," sanction for their regimes. To sustain a credible reputation for enjoying supernatural aid and access to heavenly powers was all the more important when these two potentates' hegemonic aspirations were at variance with their actual spheres of direct control.

The five idols set up outside Vladimir's hall in Kiev visibly proclaimed and amplified his special relationship with Perun, the mighty god of lightning and power. It is surely significant that Vladimir is described as turning the approaches to his hall into a place of public congregation and worship soon after his accession.[19] No less significantly, the sacrifices offered to the idols seem to have been closely linked with military successes and the cult of victory. Vladimir presumably regarded the sacrifices as being of practical effect, pleasing the gods and thus bringing him victory. They were also a means of involving Vladimir's subjects in his aggressive campaigns against other peoples. Quite early in his reign, after subjugating the Iatviagi, a people on Rus' western approaches, he ordered human sacrifices to be offered up to the gods in thanksgiving. Vladimir was, in effect, "bonding" with the Kievans by leading "the people" in person in performance of the sacrifices[20] and was thereby displaying his unique ability to gain not only the gods' favor but also the material riches that could follow from looting, the taking of prisoners, and extension of tribute-catchment areas.

Nothing so specifically linking religious worship with expansionism is attested for the very start of Boleslav's rule. But he, too, may have tried to link his regime with a throne city in sacred style soon after mounting the throne by violence. He struck coins (denarii) that portrayed him in profile, helmeted in armed ruler's guise. On the reverse is a Christian cross, and around the circumference runs the inscription *Gnezdun civitas,* thus giving in Latin the name of Boleslav's principal seat. Gniezno did not yet constitute a bishopric in the 990s, the dating that has been proposed for this type of Boleslav's denarii.[21] But presumably this would have been the usurper's way of displaying, in literal fashion, the cross at the center of his regime, besides intimating the extraordinary powers with which persons depicted on coins were often accredited in early medieval Western societies.[22] Gniezno seems to have had cult connotations well before the coming of Christianity, and it may even have housed a sanctuary that was used for incoming chieftains' inauguration rituals.[23] At any rate, in 997, within four years or so of ousting his half brothers, Boleslav was showing zeal for helping Adalbert and his fellow missionaries en route to evangelize among the Slavs and Prussians on the northeastern approaches of his dominions. He very probably regarded such patronage as an opportune means of gaining authority over these groupings as well as a form of collaboration with Emperor Otto III, himself an avid admirer and spiritual son of Adalbert.

Religious Opportunism

The previously mentioned démarches of Vladimir and Boleslav suffered serious setbacks. Remarkably, these two potentates succeeded in turning the episodes to positive advantage by means of adroit maneuvering.

Vladimir faced resistance to human sacrifices from Christian Scandinavians in Kiev, and at least one well-to-do "Varangian" paid for this with his life. More seriously still for Vladimir's prestige, a campaign against the Bulgars on the middle Volga, presumably aimed at bringing them, too, within the fold of tribute payers, ended inconclusively: Vladimir had to settle for a sworn peace agreement with the Bulgars, treating with them on more or less equal terms.[24] In other words, his victory cult was ceasing to deliver, and it may be no accident that directly after his Volga campaign, in the mid-980s, he embarked on his famous investigation of the faiths. For all the literary and exegetical features of the *Primary Chronicle*'s account of the investigation, there is no reason to doubt that Vladimir carried out some sort of inquiry into the various monotheist religions. He seems to have been preparing his subjects in a well-publicized—and perhaps consultative—manner before abandoning polytheism in favor of one form or another of monotheism. Kinsmen of Vladimir were dispatched to procure for Rus' an instructor in Islam—the religion to which the Volga Bulgars had long adhered.[25] But in the event, he adopted Christianity from the emperors of Byzantium, taking advantage of their domestic plight and, in effect, striking a deal with Basil II. As is well known, a sizable force of some six thousand warriors was sent to quash the military revolt that was threatening Basil's throne. In return, Vladimir took the emperors' sister as his bride, was baptized, and received a full-scale religious mission, headed by metropolitans. The effect was to introduce to Rus' a religious cult that was more expertly organized—and more sharply focused on the ruler's authority—than any cult over which Vladimir had previously presided.

Boleslav, for his part, turned the more or less instant debacle of Adalbert's mission to the Prussians to his political advantage. Adalbert was beheaded by pagans almost immediately, and Boleslav's prospects of employing him as a kind of roving senior churchman died with him. However, Boleslav's response was quickly to track down the remains of Adalbert and, "with a large amount of money," buy them from his killers.[26] Hagiographical accounts offer exclusively pious motives for his zeal to recover the remains of an evangelist who had been slain by the pagans.[27] However, Boleslav may well have been quick to perceive that Adalbert could be of even greater use to him dead than alive.[28] By installing the relics of a locally slain martyr in his own throne city, he could hope to make of *Gnezdun civitas* a sacral center with unimpeachably Christian credentials. There is evidence that he had already been entertaining such ambitions, if his denarii may be dated to the opening years of his reign;[29] and in any case, the *Dagome iudex* defined his father's polity as *civitas Schinesghe*. One likely effect would be to qualify Gniezno for precedence in ecclesiastical status over other towns, such as Poznań, where Bishop Unger may perhaps have had a see. Boleslav was probably also resolved to forestall any attempt on the part of Otto III to have all the relics transferred to Rome.

Sacral Centers of Authority

The two centers of Vladimir and Boleslav, Kiev and Gniezno, owed their sacredness partly to the installation in them of inherently holy objects, foremost among which were religious relics. In the case of Vladimir's throne city, the relics consisted of the martyred Pope Clement together with Phoebus, "his pupil."[30] As already noted, Boleslav was prompt to make himself chief custodian of the relics of a latter-day martyr for the faith. The Rus' and the Polish potentates were both effectively drawing attention to their own roles in what could very plausibly pass for sacred events, and they commemorated these unique roles by building monuments to the events and patronizing cults that enshrined the story. In the sacred episodes of, respectively, the conversion of Rus' and Adalbert's mission work and subsequent martyrdom, the potentates had, in their capacity as rulers, played a starring role. Obviously, the conversion of a people and the act of martyrdom for the faith were valued for their own sake, and each was of transcendent significance. But one may suggest that the relics had an important part to play in reifying these episodes. They constituted a still active, potent link with the actions carried out by the respective rulers in past time. The relics' new resting places constituted a focal point where the saints could be constantly venerated while their earthly protectors stood to benefit from lasting association with them—not least for their achievement in acquiring them, in itself a mark of favor from above and a pledge of further favors to come.

To substantiate these suggestions, it is worth looking a little closer at the ways in which Vladimir and Boleslav set about establishing their respective sacral centers. Vladimir built a lengthy, sumptuously ornamented church dedicated to the Mother of God—perhaps to the Feast of the Assumption—in Kiev. The church formed part of Vladimir's new palace complex, and the close proximity to his residence of a major place of worship bore the same message as the richly adorned idol of Perun had done outside his hall a decade earlier or as Mieszko's complex of stone palace with adjoining baptistery at Ostrów Lednicki did, if indeed the excavated remains will admit of such an interpretation.[31] In layout, function as "palace church," and overall dedication, Vladimir's church seems to have been modeled on the Pharos church of the Mother of God in Constantinople, with obvious overtones of imperial dignity.[32]

Vladimir expected his retainers and other notables to attend the Sunday feasts in his palace, which were held whether or not he was in Kiev himself. These gatherings gave Vladimir the opportunity to raise guests' hopes of reward through conspicuous display—"abundance in everything." An anecdote in the *Primary Chronicle* highlights his concern to maintain "consumer satisfaction," providing silver spoons when his retainers grumbled in their cups at having to eat with wooden ones.[33] One may reasonably suppose that their Sunday feasting followed hard upon worship in the nearby church of the Mother of God (or Tithe Church), and this amounted to a fairly patent attempt to establish a sacral center sustained by rites of worship and more immediate prospects of earthly satisfaction. What may be slightly less obvious to us is that the Tithe Church served literally to set in stone a particular series of events, some of them more profane than sacred—namely, Vladimir's victory over the Byzantines at Cherson, followed by his baptism there and the subsequent conversion of his subjects.

The Tithe Church and its precincts commemorated Vladimir's capture of Cherson and paraded his trophies seized there, high-class relics and ancient exotica. The bronze statues of four horses and two humans—"idols" (*kapishchi*)—set up outside the church on public view became a talking point, judging by the *Primary Chronicle*.[34] Inside the church, the relics of St. Clement were accorded great prominence, seeing that this "martyr of Christ and pope" was taken to be the church's dedicatee, at least by outsiders.[35] Clement's relics have fairly been termed "the first sacred object of significance throughout Christendom to appear in Rus."[36] Moreover, the entrusting of the palace church to Anastasius, who was reputed to bear responsibility for the fall of Cherson to the Rus', together with the appointment of other Chersonite priests to the church, served to recall military victory as well as events of unalloyed spiritual significance. The Tithe Church had, in other words, the attributes of a personal victory monument of Vladimir, whose sarcophagus was—together with that of Anna Porphyrogenita—"standing publicly in the middle of the church" soon after his death and very possibly well beforehand.[37] It set the seal on his ability to "inflict great violence upon the soft Greeks," hostilities still recollected around the time of his death[38] and not wholly incompatible with the epithet of "new Constantine" that later generations bestowed on him. The church may also, perhaps, have been intended to stake his claim, as builder of a great Temple, to be a new Solomon.[39]

In Gniezno, Boleslav greatly extended the fortified area, surrounding the city with an earthen rampart perhaps as broad as 30 meters and up to 12 meters in height.[40] Adalbert's relics were laid in the main church (dedicated to the Virgin Mary, Mother of God) and became the focal point for the cult of a latter-day saint and martyr, enjoying widespread recognition.[41] Almost overnight, Boleslav had succeeded in making his own power base a center of pilgrimage. Already in the early months of 1000, Otto III was approaching it "barefoot" and "for the sake of prayer,"[42] and within a few years, "a thousand miracles" were reportedly "shining forth" from the relics in "the great city of Gniezno."[43]

The cult of a martyred missionary and Boleslav's patronage of Adalbert (in both life and death) served to highlight and legitimize Boleslav's own special mandate to evangelize the pagans. In fact, Otto III formally granted him this mandate in 1000, according to Gallus Anonymus: Otto is said to have conceded to Boleslav and his successors "in ecclesiastical offices [*honores*] whatever pertained to the empire in the realm of the Poles or in other regions of the barbarians that had been conquered by him or would be conquered by him."[44] In effect, so far as the emperor was concerned, whichever "barbarians" (pagans) Boleslav subjugated would rightfully come beneath his sway, and their pastoral care would pertain to the church structure under Boleslav's supervision. Otto also saw to the installation of Adalbert's half brother, Gaudentius, as the senior churchman (archbishop) at the head of virtually all the other bishops in Boleslav's polity. In the early spring of 1000, Gaudentius was clearly expected to be based in Gniezno. A few months earlier, a charter of Otto III in Italy had designated him as "archbishop of St. Adalbert," implying a broad—if not wideopen—brief for his future pastoral and missionary activities performed in the footsteps of his half brother. Gaudentius had witnessed the martyrdom and probably supplied evidence for the first *Life*.[45] In this way, Boleslav's power base gained an additional attribute upon becoming the center of a church organization. As in the case of Vladimir, the new ecclesiastical role of Boleslav's throne city drew attention to specific happenings, sacred in their own right and yet wherein the ruler had played a central part.

Boleslav and Vladimir were far from being the first medieval potentates to try and define their spheres of dominion with the aid of sacral centers, but few of their precursors could plausibly lay claim to be "new Constantines" or the associates of latter-day martyrs.[46] An attempt may well have been made to obtain specific protection for Gniezno through positioning its key churches in an overall pattern forming the outline of a cross. The inauguration of this program cannot be ascribed to Boleslav with certainty. But already in the portentous year of 1000, there was probably a sense that Gniezno enjoyed extraordinary protection, not only through the intercession of the Virgin—dedicatee of its foremost church—but also through St. Adalbert's relics.[47] A few years after the relics of Adalbert were installed, Boleslav seems to have reinforced Gniezno with the relics of further new martyrs, this time of Polish stock.[48]

The Rus' and Polish Dominions as Christian Polities

Modest-sized Core "Christianized" Areas

For all the hegemonic ambitions that conversion and the patronage of missionaries would seem to have legitimized and fostered in the Rus' and Polish rulers, the core areas of both regimes were fairly modest. Undeniably, the potential reach of the Rus' prince's retainers—and thus the extent of his tribute-catchment areas—was enormous, and there were no real Polish counterparts to the huge population centers strewn along the northern Rus' riverways at intervals of hundreds of miles. Even so, the fixed points of the institutionalized church in Rus' would seem to have been concentrated in the middle Dnieper region, precisely the area where Vladimir supervised a massive program for the construction of earthworks, forts, and fortified settlements. The immediate aim of this new steppe frontier was mainly to enhance the protection of Kiev itself from the nomadic Pechenegs. A broad band of what had been their grazing grounds was appropriated to make room for Vladimir's forts and settlements.[49] Seemingly, a state of constant alert was necessary, and the major strongholds were interdependent, with beacon chains between them signaling nomad attacks and calling up reinforcements.

Vladimir is depicted by the *Primary Chronicle* as often campaigning in person against the nomads. His new religion provided a means of solemnizing this military activity and of associating particular episodes with the Christian cycle of liturgical ritual. Thus, he saw to the foundation of a church at Vasil'ev dedicated to the Feast of the Transfiguration, in thanksgiving for a narrow escape from the Pechenegs. While hiding under a bridge from the nomads on that day, he made a vow to build a church dedicated to the festival; and presumably because of this special association with the ruler, the fort came to be known by his Christian name, *Basil/Vasiliy.*[50] As this example suggests, Vladimir sought to imprint his personal achievements and victories on the new borderlands. It seems that the name *Cherson* was given, in its Rus' form (*Korsun*), to a settlement on the Ros River, most likely at the behest of the Greek town's captor.[51]

Location and Number of the Rus' Sees, ca. 990–ca. 1050

The precise location of the earliest sees in Rus' has yet to be established, and the number of sees is correspondingly uncertain. It may well be that some bishops were not initially attached to fixed sees. The Byzantine authorities may have provided for this, if one takes literally the statement of Yahya of Antioch that an unspecified number of "metropolitans [in the plural] and bishops" were sent to Rus' at the time of the conversion.[52] Moreover, the precise significance and practical role of sees created for a newly converted people is not wholly clear, and it may have been deliberately left flexible in the early years of a mission. At any rate, it is likely that the first episcopal sees instituted and endowed in Rus' were concentrated in or close to the middle Dnieper region. These were, most probably, Belgorod, Chernigov, Pereiaslavl', Iur'ev, and Turov, all located within about 150 miles of Kiev. The one place to have quite firmly attested episcopal status for the first half century or so after Vladimir's conversion is Novgorod, far removed from Kiev; Polock, too, may well have been a see from soon after the conversion.[53]

The literary and circumstantial evidence concerning the early existence of these sees matches the archaeological data fairly well. Such finds as have been made of ecclesiastical buildings, church furnishings, and other artifacts of unequivocally Christian significance occur mainly in or quite near the middle Dnieper zone or along the main riverways to Novgorod.[54] Their distribution pattern is largely congruent with that of the burial grounds having pronounced Christian traits—namely, pit burials orientated toward the east, with a few of the dead being accompanied by small crosses and other more or less Christian symbols. Some of these burial grounds consist of graves that are not marked by barrows at all.[55] Against this background may be viewed the account in the *Life of St. Theodosius* of Theodosius's childhood in the important frontier town of Kursk during (probably) the 1030s or 1040s. The boy is represented as being instructed in the Scriptures, daily attending church services, and being invited to wait at the town governor's table on a (presumably religious) feast day: "all the town's magnates" were to be there.[56] While the hagiographer drew extensively on orthodox literary models to fit Theodosius's early life into the framework of established sanctity, he is unlikely to have entirely invented conditions in Kursk little more than a generation before his own time. One may therefore accept his representation of the urban elite in this border region as constituting quite a tight-knit society, bonded by Christian ritual.

Polish Church Organization, ca. 1000–1050

The core Christian region in the early eleventh century lay between Gniezno and Poznań. These two places were instituted (or perhaps, in Poznań's case, confirmed) as sees at the meeting of Otto III, Boleslav the Brave, and the papal legate in March 1000, with Gniezno being accorded primacy. The three other sees were to be Wrocław, Colberg (Kołobrzeg), and Cracow. Of these sees, all but Cracow lay within 150 miles of Gniezno.[57] This core area was not, in fact, drastically smaller than that of Vladimir's Rus', while the number of Polish sees was about the same as the Rus' total.

In both polities, the distribution of known church buildings seems to have been roughly coterminous with the "hard points" of princely authority. Most of the early stone churches of the Poles were built at or very near the forts of the ruler. Kurnatowska has drawn attention to the distribution pattern of the earliest *Missions-Seelsorgezentren* (mission and religious centers). Six or seven were located in the core region of Gniezno, while most of the other known churches or monasteries were built on the outer reaches of Boleslaw's dominions—for example, in the west, at (probably) Santok as well as Międzyrzecz. At the latter place, Boleslav was the zealous patron of what developed into a monastery in honor of five hermit missionaries just after their martyrdom there in 1003. Boleslav had a stone basilica built over 'the bodies of the saints"—which reportedly worked miracles—and he was himself a lay member of the house's confraternity.[58] Relics of three of the martyrs—perhaps the three who were native Poles—were apparently translated to Gniezno and laid beneath an inscribed slab of gypsum, at Boleslav's behest.[59] Among the other early church centers were Włoclawek and Płock, located on the eastern approaches of Boleslav's core region. These two centers lay on the Vistula River, which itself provided natural defenses of a sort. The Polish ruler seems to have been using the church's organization as a means of firming up his borderlands and also as a springboard for further expansion.[60]

In contrast, according to Kurnatowska, some areas quite close to Gniezno show few signs of Christianization in the sense of containing early stone churches or in terms of burial ritual. There were similar zones of paganism—or at least, of only very partial Christianization of ritual—not far from the core regions of the Rus' princely regime. In the region between Turov and Kiev, the Derevlians continued to deposit their dead at ground level or inside barrows. Further afield, the Viatichi remained robustly pagan, sometimes even militantly so, well into the twelfth century.[61] Thus, there are grounds for supposing that both the Rus' and the Polish leaderships used Christianization as a means of strengthening the princely presence on the periphery, side by side with the new fortifications and garrisons established there. These activities were contemporaneous and, I suggest, carried out in conjunction with the establishment of sacral centers for both sets of regimes.

Transplants of Populations to Borders

The steps taken by Vladimir to stock the region of the middle Dnieper with people transplanted from the northern forest zones are recorded in the *Russian Primary Chronicle*. Vladimir is said to have announced, "Behold, it is not good that there are few towns around Kiev!" and to have set about founding towns along the river valleys to the south and east of Kiev. He supervised the stocking of them with "the best men" (and, one may assume, women) from the diverse peoples of the northern forests.

The fundamentally strategic significance of these settlements is spelled out explicitly by the *Primary Chronicle*: "for there was strife from the Pechenegs."[62] The nomad's militancy is unsurprising, seeing that the settlements were built on their former summer grazing lands. The chronicle's remark about the heterogeneity of their inhabitants is borne out by archaeological evidence. Many forts and settlements south of Kiev have now been excavated, and traces of Finnic jingling pendants and Radimichi-style silver earrings have been found in some of their burial grounds.[63] But in some ways more striking is the lack of finds of organized pagan rites in the burial grounds or elsewhere in the settle-ments. The combination of Christianity with allegiance to the prince was, one may suppose, much more easily inculcated into those who had been uprooted from their traditional kin groups and way of life and who were continually de-pendent on the prince and his agents for protection. The new religion was held up as a means of providing strong protection not only for the prince himself but also for his associates and subjects.

After his narrow escape from capture or death at Vasil'ev, Vladimir staged a feast lasting eight days, summoning to it "his nobles, governors, elders of all the towns and many other people," thereby bringing in many witnesses to celebrate his foundation of the newly built church dedicated to the Feast of the Transfigu-ration.[64] He then headed for Kiev for observance of the Feast of the Assumption of the Virgin with another round of feasting that was attended by "a countless multitude of the people." Vladimir thus aligned the commemoration of his per-sonal deliverance with the rhythms of sacred time. Such solemnities and social bonding with the leader formed part of what was most probably his conscious policy of creating "a new Christian people" in and around Kiev.

Boleslav's responsibility for constructing a frontier is not as clear-cut as Vladimir's, not least because there was no precise Polish equivalent of the Rus' steppe frontier and because much fortification work had been carried out before his time. The core region of the Piast family seems to have become studded with fortifications quite abruptly a couple of generations earlier, in the mid-tenth cen-tury.[65] But there are grounds for supposing that Boleslav acquired a reputation for personal solicitousness about the populations of his borderlands and that he actually carried out population transplants from one area to another.

Gallus Anonymus devoted a chapter to the subject of border defenses, aver-ring, "Boleslav was very often occupied with defending the limits of his territory [*finibus regionis*] from enemies."[66] He also made provision for feasts in "the towns and castles" there, but he reportedly preferred to send close associates to feast and perform gift giving, rather than going in person. According to Gallus Anonymus, he would say that the security of his borders—guarding the chicks of his subjects' hens—was of more account to him than doing the rounds of feasts: "For to be violently robbed of a chicken is by my reckoning to lose a fort or a town, not a chicken."[67] In other words, Boleslav made a name for himself as the vigilant guardian of all those settled on his borderlands. It appears that the organization of his progresses throughout his lands was cause for pride: "every-where he had his stopping places, and the services due had been worked out. He did not simply pitch camp anywhere using tents like the Numidian [*Numida*] or in the open fields; more often he would stay in forts and towns [*in civitatibus et castris*]."[68] Like the *Russian Primary Chronicle*, the *Chronica* of Gallus Anonymus lays quite heavy emphasis on the ruler's solicitousness for contested border settlements. Both works were composed in their present form in the early twelfth century—long after the events that they purport to recount—and were at least partly addressing contemporaneous, twelfth-century concerns, which inevitably raises questions as to their *Quellenwert* (source value). However, a different form of evidence provides indications that Boleslav took measures on his borders comparable to those of his Rus' neighbor.

Archaeological evidence points to at least one instance of population transfer around the turn of the tenth and eleventh centuries. People were transplanted from the wilder reaches of Boleslav's dominions to a frontier zone that was more directly under his control. In their new abode, they came to observe Christian burial ritual. Excavations at Piaski-Rochy (near modern Krotoszyn) have revealed a small fort and a large settlement together with a burial ground. Two types of burial ritual have been found, grouped essentially in two different sectors (if one may judge from the preliminary excavations of the site). Some of the barrows contained urnless cremations; in other barrows, the dead lay with their heads facing east, interred in Christian style. The use of cremation and styles of pottery decoration suggest that a number of the inhabitants had come from western Pomerania, whether voluntarily or as prisoners of war,[69] and one may surmise that the two types of burial ritual register a process of gradual Christianization. The fort and settlement at Piaski-Rochy were founded around 1000. Located on the main route from Gniezno to Wrocław, they were designed to hinder or deter incursions from Czechs and other outsiders. They formed part of a system of fortified settlements for which Boleslav may fairly be credited with prime—albeit not exclusive—responsibility.[70]

Presumably, Vladimir and Boleslav shared much the same rationale. They deliberately uprooted persons from remote areas, whether the more northerly forests of Rus' or the Baltic coast lands, and installed them in zones that were on the outer reaches of their dominion but that were fortified and under relatively tight supervision. Their aim was partly the practical one of garrisoning contested borderlands and providing logistical backup. But they probably also reckoned that as transplantees, the settlers would be more dependent on the ruler's agents and susceptible to the new cult providing for their own protection.

Reasons for the Resemblances between the Poles and Rus' Rulers' Stances and Measures

Whatever the reasons, there is quite a close chronological coincidence between the initiatives of the neophyte Vladimir and the second-generation Christian

Boleslav. The establishment of two Christian sacred centers owing their charisma in varying measure to their holy relics occurred within a decade of one another. Boleslav can scarcely have failed to observe the trappings of piety and established authority that came with the baptism of his erstwhile conspicuously pagan neighbor. Vladimir managed to acquire at a stroke a panoply of "metropolitans and bishops,"[71] and soon afterward (if one may take Ilarion's rhetoric literally), "priests and deacons and all the clergy adorned the churches . . . ; monasteries rose on the hills; monks appeared."[72] At the same time, the Rus' ruler saw to the construction of his Tithe church within his palace complex.

These initiatives occurred shortly before and at the time of Boleslav's self-identification with the cult of Adalbert and the installation of Gaudentius as archbishop in *Gnezdun civitas* in 1000. Modern historians paid almost no attention to this coincidence. The démarches of Vladimir and Boleslav tend to be viewed as prompted simply and solely by their respective internal circumstances. Their political agendas were indeed comparable, comprised of the need for personal legitimization and a common, unexceptionable desire to consolidate one's power base. Each potentate would answer well enough to the description of "upward mobile on the make," utilizing the Christian church to create a fixed, solemn, and sacral center for his regime and also to dominate outlying regions of greatest strategic concern to him. But I suggest that there was also a strong vein of mutual emulation in Vladimir's relationship with Boleslav, even though the *Primary Chronicle* expressly portrays it as peaceful.[73] The emulation certainly did not amount to formal imitation, but the two potentates were reacting to one another's moves, wittingly or unwittingly triggering responses from the other.

The relationship between these rulers should not, of course, be viewed in isolation. Around the turn of the tenth and eleventh centuries, Emperor Otto III was greatly concerned to elaborate on his preeminent status in the West. Not only did Otto conduct himself as a kind of "new Constantine," showing fervent support for Adalbert's missionary work and encouraging Gaudentius to continue it in his name. He also sought to match up to the Eastern emperor while repeatedly seeking the hand of a princess "born in the purple," the same outstanding mark of respect that Vladimir had been accorded.[74] The evident concern of Otto to be seen to belong to the same imperial league as his Eastern counterpart makes it the all more likely that Boleslav was anxious not to be outdone by his own opposite number to the east. He was, I suggest, well aware of the recent upgrade in Vladimir's status and of Kiev's rapid—and, for Boleslav, neither foreseeable nor particularly welcome—development as a *Schauplatz* (stage) of Christian rulership during the 990s. Issues of prestige and personal standing were reinforced and compounded by territorial rivalries.

It is noteworthy that one of Vladimir's earliest recorded expeditions after seizing Kiev involved the far western approaches of Rus', where he attacked the "Liachs."[75] Precisely which grouping is meant by this mention in the *Primary Chronicle* or who exercised authority over such towns as Cracow during the 980s is controversial. It was very possibly only around 988 that the Poles seized Cracow and gained a vantage point on the lucrative trade routes between Prague and Kiev. If that is so, Boleslav came to power as a new neighbor for Vladimir—and not a particularly welcome one.[76] At any rate, the Rus' and Polish rulers seem to have been drawn to the region of the so-called Cherven towns in hopes of controlling and tapping the trade routes converging there, rather than solely from strategic considerations. Competition for these towns was keen, and although there is scholarly controversy as to the exact location of "Cherven" and thus also of the "Cherven towns,"[77] there is no compelling reason to doubt that Przemyśl (the Peremyshl of the *Primary Chronicle*) could be included in this area. This border region remained a bone of contention between the two potentates. A year or two before Vladimir died, he suspected Boleslav of dabbling in Rus' affairs. One of Boleslav's daughters had been wedded to Sviatopolk, a senior son of Vladimir and prince of Turov, a key town on the route westward. Boleslav may well have been hoping that the match would eventually net for him the "Cherven towns" and other vantage points in the area. They remained potentially very lucrative, whether valuables, such as silver, flowed through them from the Muslim Orient or, increasingly from the late tenth century, from the European West.[78]

If the "Cherven towns" and the East-West trade routes provided material grounds for rivalry, they also supplied channels for news to reach the Rus' and Polish rulers about one another's feats and claims. The finds of enameled crosses and pectoral crosses in Eastern Christian style (Byzantine- or Rus'-made) in such princely centers as Gniezno and Poznań register the personal presence of traders or warriors of fortune, arrived from the lands to the east.[79] Moreover, a significant number of full-time warriors were in the employ of both the Rus' and Polish rulers. Their weaponry and martial skills were on hire to whoever could reward them best in the Baltic world or still further afield, and they constituted the sort of retainers whom the *Primary Chronicle* portrays as grumbling over the use of wooden spoons at Vladimir's feasts.[80] The implication of the tale is that they could do better elsewhere, and it is likely that such high-placed warriors brought to Vladimir's and Boleslav's courts a steady flow of updates on the military feats, sacral attributes, and construction projects of the other ruler.

Vladimir's employment of "Varangians" is quite well known, and the presence of "fast Danes" was one of the Kievan region's salient characteristics for

Thietmar, writing shortly after Vladimir's death.[81] Less well known are hints from a medley of sources that warriors with Scandinavian cultural character-istics—"Varagians"—were also in the Polish ruler's service. The *Jómsvikinga saga*'s account of a band of Vikings who entered the service of a certain "Burisleifr" is usually treated with skepticism by historians. But while its details are suspect, the saga may well reflect the vitality of links between Scandinavian "professional" warriors and a powerful "Wendish" ruler—and one such ruler was Boleslav the Brave.[82] That Polish rulers maintained a well-armed standing force was, after all, noted by Ibrahim ibn Yakub and Gallus Anonymus alike,[83] and one might infer from the successive marriages of Boleslav's sister, Sven-toslava, with the kings of the Swedes and the Danes that warriors could move freely between these potentates' courts. Furthermore, archaeological evidence suggests that a significant number of warriors well furnished with Scandina-vian-style weapons, riding-gear ornaments, buckets, and, occasionally, silver coins were laid to rest in burial grounds in the midst of Mieszko's and Bole-slav's dominions in the late tenth and earlier eleventh centuries—for example, in Sowinki, near the princely center of Poznań. These warriors belonged to the culture of the Nordic world, if they did not directly hail from Scandinavia it-self. Moreover, a group of Scandinavian warriors seems to have had a separate burial ground to themselves on the polity's southeastern approaches at Lu-tomiersk.[84] These finds register only such Scandinavians and other "Var-angians" as left their bones among the Poles. Others may well only have served Mieszko or Boleslav for a few years before seeking their fortune elsewhere, and some could easily have circulated between the Rus' and Polish courts. These itinerants between the two courts were active in quest of status and remuner-ation, rather than being neutral observers or idle drawers of comparisons. Competition for their services might a priori be expected to have accentuated tendencies toward emulation between the Rus' and Polish leaders, making it a matter of political self-interest—not just personal whim—for the one to avoid being seen to be outdone by the other.

Emulation of the Rus': The Neglected Dimension of the Events at Gniezno in 1000

Against this background, it is worth considering the spectacular events mounted at Gniezno shortly before the great Easter festival of the millennial year of 1000.[85] The occasion may appear somewhat less bizarre when viewed against a back-drop of emulation between Boleslav and his eastern neighbor, rather than exclu-sively in terms of Boleslav's western and southern affiliations. Undeniably, the latter affiliations prompted the encounter: Adalbert's death struck a chord among churchmen in central Europe and Italy, and there was mutual desire to reach an accommodation on the part of the regimes of Otto III and Boleslav. Each of them was, in effect, ritually acknowledging the other's right to rulership, albeit in conjunction with symbolic intimations of Otto's paramount, uniquely imperial status. Their public encounter conflated elements of religious devotion, status affirmation, and politico-military alliance, and the arrangements made for church organization and further mission work aligned their interests in close, though not absolute, harmony. Foundations for lasting collaboration were, at first sight paradoxically, being laid at the very time when the end of the world seems to have loomed large in the outlook of many clergymen and laypersons, not least Otto himself.[86] This was essentially an accommodation between two potentates, each with considerable capacity to do harm to the other's regime, not so much through invasion as by giving haven to one another's malcontents or succor to dissident peripheral elites and alternative power structures.

The grand concourse or "synod" at Gniezno brought together Boleslav, Otto III, Archbishop Gaudentius, the papal cardinal Robert and other senior churchmen, and many members of the diverse elites within the ambit of the two potentates. The progress of the imperator in full pomp through Slav territory well beyond his traditional confines and yet, near journey's end, "barefoot" was clearly designed to attract widespread attention, and Otto's dealings with Boleslav provoked diverse reactions from near-contemporaneous and subsequent writers.[87] Boleslav himself sought a large audience for his meeting with Otto, holding their formal encounter outdoors "in a spacious plain" before "warriors" and "magnates" stationed in "many kinds of rows," "as if they were choirs."[88] Reportedly, each row was differentiated from the others by the color of its members' precious vestments. If this really was the case, it implies considerable planning and a desire for ranking witnesses on Boleslav's part.

One may reasonably suspect that the salient features of the ceremonial were agreed in advance between the Western emperor and the leader of the nascent Slav polity, even if they meant slightly different things to the various parties involved.[89] Certain acts were clear-cut and intended to be legally binding, including the installation of Gaudentius as archbishop—though even this aspect of the settlement raised eyebrows among some contemporaries, such as Thietmar.[90] Other elements of the ritual were ambivalent or multivalent, as befitted the solemnizing of what was, in effect, a new politico-military axis, whether or not the Second Coming was at hand. Otto's setting of his own crown on Boleslav's head could be taken to be acknowledgment of the latter's kingly status, even if it simultaneously classified Boleslav's status as inferior to him who bestowed the crown. Such ritual, apparently taken by the Poles "to be a bond of friendship,"[91] might well have been acceptable to Boleslav, since it visibly raised his status from that of a mere marcher-lord or tributary, even while also declaring the emperor's upper hand in the partnership.

The bestowal of an imperial crown by the senior emperor upon a close associate or designated successor and, on occasion, the dispatch of a crown to external potentates were features of Byzantine inauguration ritual and diplomatic practice.[92] The Byzantine connotations of Otto's gesture with his crown may well have been known to at least some members of the elites swelling the crowds at Gniezno, whether "members of the Roman senate" and senior churchmen,[93] Saxon and other adherents of Otto, or the Slav "warriors," "magnates," and other notables who lined up before Boleslav. Overtones of Eastern imperial practices have been discerned in other facets of the proceedings at Gniezno: the hierarchical positioning of title- and office-holders by rank with corresponding costumes was a striking feature of the Byzantine court.[94] General evocations and ad hoc adaptations of familiar—or vaguely supposed—Eastern imperial ritual and authority symbols were not so unusual, on the part of Western potentates aspiring to Christian order in the grand style. They could confer dignity on diverse attempts at innovation. Their overtones of legitimate authority, at once unmistakably hegemonic and untrammeled by local or familial associations, imparted a certain sovereign impartiality to a ruler's stance.[95] This keys in with many facets of Otto III's conduct of policy and the iconography it inspired. One of his more abiding aspirations was to convince the medley of local worthies, senior churchmen, and peripheral elites in the West of his unique status as amicable overlord of them all.[96] Invocations of Constantine the Great, Charlemagne, and the contemporary Eastern Empire were alike grist to this mill.

The evocation of Eastern imperial ceremonial by Otto III and Boleslav, acting in concert at Gniezno, might be explained on these grounds alone. However, it had a more distinctive and targeted edge if, as has already been suggested, Boleslav and Vladimir were keenly aware of one another's doings and mutually competitive. It seems reasonable to make the further suggestion that the well-attended rites and junkets at Gniezno represented a joint response on the part of Otto and Boleslav to a decade of extraordinary development among the Rus'. As noted earlier in this chapter, Vladimir's lavishly adorned palace complex and Tithe Church turned Kiev into a *Schauplatz* for his personal achievements of piety and hegemonic status in little more than a decade. From soon after his conversion ca. 988, gold and silver coins portraying Vladimir in what might pass for imperial mode—albeit progressively more loosely and crudely—were struck in Kiev and circulated as far afield as Gotland, with exemplars very possibly reaching lands under Boleslav's dominion. Even if the denarii bearing the *Gnezdun civitas* legend cannot be ascribed with certainty to the very first years of Boleslav's rule, there does not seem to be any question that he had begun striking coins by the mid-990s. The new style of coins of the Danes and the beginning of minting by the Norwegian and Swedish kings around this time seem to register close mutual contacts, as do the abundance and status of the silver paid to Sven Forkbeard by the Anglo-Saxons as tribute.[97] But these aspirants to kingly status in the Baltic world, together with Boleslav, can scarcely have been unaware of the introduction of coin minting in Rus' by Vladimir, himself a former exile at a Scandinavian court, and they may have been anxious not to be outdone. The ability to make regular, monthly, payment to numerous warriors had been a distinguishing mark of the regime of Mieszko, and remuneration in the grand style was no less incumbent upon his son.

A thesis of Professor A. Poppe may have some bearing on the suggestion that the proceedings mounted by Otto and Boleslav at Gniezno served as a kind of symbolic riposte both to the emerging sacral center at Kiev and to the Byzantino-Rus' partnership embodied in the marriage of Vladimir to Anna Porphyrogenita. Poppe has adduced evidence pointing to a more active role for Anna in the cultural and political life of Rus' than has generally been supposed. There is reason to believe that Anna bore to Vladimir no less than three children, Boris-Romanus, Gleb-David, and Theophana.[98] By the time of the proceedings at Gniezno in 1000, Anna had given birth to the eldest, Boris, if not to the others, and the Christian name given Boris in honor of his maternal grandfather, Romanus II,[99] served as a reminder that the Rus' ruling family had been infused by an Eastern imperial bloodline. Even if Theophana was not yet born by 1000, the naming of her after her maternal grandmother is another indication of the imperial aura overhanging the Rus' court at the turn of the tenth and eleventh centuries. Bestowal of these names on the children of Vladimir's only Christian marriage implicitly placed them in the same league as the children of Otto II and Theophano, one of whose daughters was named Sophia in honor of her maternal grandmother. It is therefore noteworthy that at Gniezno, Otto III betrothed his closest available blood relative, his niece Richeza, to Boleslav's eldest son and presumed heir apparent, Mieszko. Seemingly at the same time, Otto stood as godfather to a son of Boleslav, who was named Otto after him.[100]

The ties of spiritual and dynastic significance affirmed at Gniezno were the product of Otto's initiative at least as much as Boleslav's and, in themselves, could be viewed as merely setting the seal on their settlement. But when taken together with other facets of the ceremonial and with the rhetoric of friendship,[101] the ensemble seems to amount to a conscious attempt to match the nexus crafted between the ruling houses on the Dnieper and the Bosporus.

This, too, was a complex relationship involving several wars and a victory for Vladimir actually highlighted by his sacral center (as discussed earlier in this chapter), but the birth of at least one male heir by Vladimir's Byzantine wife now bid fair to perpetuate amity. Both Otto and Boleslav had an interest in putting on a parallel show of a many-stranded partnership.[102] In so doing, they demonstrated that their ties of marriage and political cooperation would be not merely firm but pleasing to God—in fact, "sacred" and focused on mission work in fulfillment of God's plan for humankind. The intention was, of course, to strengthen the axes orientating Boleslav's new polity and church organization southward to Rome and westward to the Germanic lands. These could pose an alternative to the "force field" emerging not so far away to the east and probably well known to Boleslav's retainers and regional notables, the "warriors" and "magnates" paraded at Gniezno.

Immediately after the ceremonial encounter at Gniezno, Boleslav very probably accompanied Otto to Aachen, being there at the time of the opening of Charlemagne's tomb; he himself reportedly received the golden throne of Charlemagne.[103] This complemented the exchanges at Gniezno, where, in effect, Boleslav had given an arm of St. Adalbert and received a nail of the True Cross, attached to the blade of the lance of St. Maurice.[104] The symbolic message probably intended by these exchanges was that while Otto's gift of lance and throne were offered from the superior stance of imperator, his relationship with Boleslav was essentially one of fellowship in a sacred task. If, as has been suggested,[105] the opening of the tomb was intended to be preliminary to the declaration of Charlemagne as a saint, this would have underlined that a "holy empire" had been reestablished in the West, just as there was—on prominent Westerners' own avowal—a "holy empire" centered on the Bosporus.[106]

The proceedings at Gniezno and Aachen, a visible rallying of forces spiritual and temporal, were probably intended in a spirit of peaceful coexistence with the empire now putting forth spectacular shoots in the lands of the Rus'. Boleslav's outlook may well have been more earthbound than Otto's, although not devoid of respect for heavenly powers or of zeal for personal salvation.[107] But for Boleslav, too, the new state of affairs to the east probably loomed large as he performed the spectacular and newly concocted rites of partnership with the imperator at Gniezno. After all, his rivalry with Vladimir was more immediate than that between Otto and the Eastern *basileis* (emperors) and their Rus' brother-in-law. It rested on territorial disputes and on actual similarities between Boleslav's personal route to power and hegemonic aspirations and those of Vladimir. The two potentates were pursuing what were in many respects parallel courses, making shrines of their throne cities and linking them with their own doings—Vladimir's capture of Cherson, Constantine-like conversion, and installation of a martyr's relics in his church of the Mother of God at Kiev; Boleslav's well-attested reverence for Adalbert in his lifetime and installation of his relics in the church of Mary, Mother of God, at *Gnezdun civitas* just after the martyrdom. Each was trying to make a sacral center of his power base, and the solemnities at Gniezno in 1000 were partly intended to be a demonstrative—in fact, liturgical—response to what Vladimir was seen to be achieving with his new *Schauplatz*.

The prolix and largely fictitious accounts of military contests between Boleslav and the "king" (*rex*) of the Rus' in the *Chronica* of Gallus Anonymus refer—in distorted form—to campaigning that occurred after the death of Vladimir.[108] But they most probably also register the long-standing tensions between Vladimir and Boleslav, tensions that the happening at Gniezno in 1000 may partly have been designed to sublimate. This perspective, together with most of the other ramifications of the proceedings at Gniezno and Aachen, was effaced by the unexpected death of Otto III in January 1002 and the rapid deterioration in relations between Boleslav and Otto's successor, Henry II. But their ephemeral nature does not detract from the likely significance of Gniezno as a pious yet also competitive response to the Christian political culture then emerging to the east. The tableau of joint authority staged by Otto and Boleslav at Gniezno may well, after its fashion, verify the importance of drawing comparisons between the regimes of Boleslav the Brave and Vladimir Sviatoslavich.

NOTES

1. The dispatch of the hair is recorded by the epitaph on Boleslav's tombstone. Only a much later transcript survives, in several versions, but its factual data may well derive from an eleventh-century original. See A. Bielowski, ed., *Monumenta Poloniae Historica* vol. 1 (Lvov, 1864), 320; R. Gansiniec, "Nagrobek Boleslawa Wielkiego," *Przeglad Zachodni* 7, nos. 5–8 (1951): 359–537, esp. 421; B. Kürbis, "Epitafium Boleslawa Chrobrego: Analiza literacka i historyczna," *Roczniki Historyczne* 55–56 (1989–90): 95–132, esp. 124–32 (all recorded versions of the text and the most important reconstructions); J. Strzelczyk, "The first two historical Piasts: Opinions and interpretations," *Quaestiones Medii Aevi*, n.s., 5 (Warsaw, 2000): 99–143, esp. 114–16.

2. Thietmar of Merseburg, *Chronicon*, ed. R. Holtzmann, MGH Scriptores, n.s., vol. 9 (Berlin, 1935), 486.

3. V. P. Adrianova-Peretts and D. S. Likhachev, eds., *Povest' vremennykh let*, 2nd ed., rev. M. B. Sverdlov (St. Petersburg, 1996), 58.

4. G. H. Pertz, ed., *Annales Cracovienses Compilati, Annales Poloniae*, MGH Scriptores in usum schol. (Hanover, 1866), 36.

5. These axes are highlighted in the contributions to P. Urbańczyk, ed., *The Neighbours of Poland in the 10th Century* (Warsaw, 2000): e.g., P. Urbańczyk, "It is good to have

a neighbour," 1–5; W. Duczko, "Continuity and transformation: The tenth century AD in Sweden," 7–36, esp. 28–31; C. Lübke, "Die Elbslaven: Polens Nachbarn im Westen," 61–77, esp. 61–62 and 75–77; D. Třeštík, "Von Svatopluk zu Boleslav Chrobry," 111–45, esp. 130–45.

6. Thietmar, *Chronicon*, 232.

7. G. Waitz, ed., *Annales necrologici Fuldenses*, MGH, vol. 8 (Hanover, 1881), 206; Lübke, "Die Elbslaven," 76.

8. A. Gieysztor, "Medieval Poland," in *History of Poland*, ed. A. Gieysztor et al. (Warsaw, 1979), 23–141, esp. 50–51.

9. J. Fried, "Theophanu und die Slawen: Bemerkungen zur Ostpolitik der Kaiserin", in *Kaiserin Theophanu: Begegnung des Ostens und Westens um die Wende des ersten Jahrtausends*, ed. A. von Euw and P. Schreiner, vol. 2 (Cologne, 1991), 361–70, esp. 363–65 and 370. Objections were, however, raised by G. Labuda, "Der 'Akt vom Gnesen' von Jahre 1000: Bericht über die Forschungsvorhaben und-ergebnisse," *Quaestiones Medii Aevi*, n.s., 5 (2000): 145–88, esp. 157–58.

10. For a brief transcript of the original text of the *Dagome iudex*, see the reconstruction of B. Kürbis, "Dagome iudex: Studium krytyczne," in *Początki państwa polskiego: Księga tysiąclecia*, ed. K. Tymieniecki, vol. 1 (Poznań, 1962), 363–424, esp. 394–95; Ch. Warnke, "Ursachen und Voraussetzungen der Schenkung Polens an den Heiligen Petrus," in *Europa Slavica–Europa Orientalis: Festschrift für Herbert Ludat zum 70. Geburtstag*, ed. K.-D. Grothusen and K. Zernack (Berlin, 1980), 127–77, esp. 170–71 (text) and 163–64 (interpretation). See also G. Labuda, *Studia nad początkami państwa polskiego*, vol. 1 (Poznań, 1987), 81, 457–60, and vol. 2 (Poznań, 1988), 240–63; B. Sliwinski, "Pomorze w polityce i strukturze państwa wczesnopiastowskiego (X–XII w.)," *Kwartalnik historyczny* 107 (2000): 3–40, esp. 10–11.

11. Z. Kurnatowska, "Die Christianisierung Polens im Lichte der materiellen Quellen," in *Early Christianity in central and Eastern Europe*, ed. P. Urbańczyk (Warsaw, 1997), 101–21, esp. 108; "Frühstädtische Entwicklung an den Zentren der Piasten in Großpolen," in *Burg, Burgstadt, Stadt: Zur Genese mittelalterlicher nichtagrarischer Zentren in Ostmitteleuropa*, ed. H. Brachmann (Berlin, 1995), 133–47, esp. 135–39.

12. Ibrahim Ibn Yakub, *Relatio de itinere slavico, quae traditur apud al-Bekri*, ed. T. Kowalski, Monumenta Poloniae Historica, n.s., vol. 1 (Cracow, 1946), 147 (Latin translation) with nn. 69–70; 89–90.

13. Adrianova-Peretts and Likhachev, *Povest'*, 32; Leo the Deacon, *Historia*, ed. C. B. Hase (Bonn, 1829), 105.

14. See A. Buko's contribution to the present volume (chap. 7).

15. Thietmar, *Chronicon*, 198.

16. Thietmar's statement accords with the *Primary Chronicle*'s depiction of hundreds of girls kept for Vladimir's pleasure at Berestovo, Belgorod, and Vyshgorod (Adrianova-Peretts and Likhachev, *Povest'*, 37). These statements could be regarded as, respectively, sheer vilification and a literary device to underline the change in Vladimir following his baptism and to evoke the image of King Solomon. But the singling out of the settlements by name and the fact that a medley of unfree females bore him children weighs against such reasoning. See also A. Poppe, "Vladimir le chrétien," in *Le origini e lo sviluppo della christianità slavo-bizantina*, ed. S. W. Swierkosz-Lenart (Rome, 1992), 43–58, esp. 43–47; J. Korpela, "A new Christ, Holy Mother, and Judas in medieval Russia," *Acta Byzantina Fennica* 7 (1995–96), 9–36, esp. 15–17.

17. Adrianova-Peretts and Likhachev, *Povest'*, 36–37.

18. Thietmar, *Chronicon*, 198.

19. This sequence is clearly implied by the *Povest'* (Adrianova-Peretts and Likhachev, *Povest',* 37).

20. Adrianova-Peretts and Likhachev, *Provest',* 38.

21. See T. Sawicki, "Gniezno w X wieku: Na szlaku ku meczenstwu," in *Tropami Swietego Wojciecha,* ed. Z. Kurnatowska (Poznań, 1999), 111–31, esp. 111 and fig. 1. Skepticism as to a dating before ca. 1000 was expressed by S. Suchodolski: see "Początki rodzimego mennictwa," in *Ziemie polskie w X wieku i ich znaczenie w kształtowaniu sie nowej mapy Europy,* ed. H. Samsonowicz (Cracow, 2000), 351–60, esp. 356.

22. H. Maguire, "Magic and money in the early Middle Ages," *Speculum* 72 (1997): 1037–54, esp. 1040 and 1050–54.

23. T. Sawicki, "Z badań nad przemianami topografii i funkcji grodu książecego na Górze Lecha w Gnieznie," *Slavia Antiqua* 40 (1999): 9–29, esp. 18 and 20–22; Sawicki, "Gniezno w X wieku," 119; M. Kara, "Anfänge der Bildung des Piastenstaates im Lichte neuer archäologischer Ermittlungen," *Quaestiones Medii Aevi,* n.s., 5 (2000): 57–85, esp. 72–74.

24. Adrianova-Peretts and Likhachev, *Provest',* 39. See also, in the present volume, the contributions of A. Buko (chap. 7) and P. Urbańczyk (chap. 5).

25. Marwazi in V. Minorsky, trans., *Sharaf al-Zaman Tahir Marvazi on China, the Turks and India* (London, 1942), 36; J. Shepard "Some remarks on the sources for the conversion of Rus'," in *Le origini e lo sviluppo della christianità slavo-bizantina,* ed. S. W. Swierkosz-Lenart (Rome, 1992), 76–77. That inquiries of a sort could underlie the *Primary Chronicle*'s account is acknowledged by, e.g., V. I. Petrukhin, *Drevniaia Rus':* *Narod, kniaz'ia, religiia* (Moscow, 2000), 261–62, 266–69. See also A. Nazarenko, *Drevniaia Rus' na mezhdunarodnykh putiakh: Mezhdisciplinarnye ocherki kulturnykh, torgovykh, politicheskikh sviazei IX–XII vekov* (Moscow, 2001), 432–34.

26. Bruno of Querfurt, *Passio Sancti Adalberti,* ed. J. Karwasinska, Monumenta Poloniae Historica, n.s., vol. 4, part 2 (Warsaw, 1969), 40: "grandem pecuniam."

27. The two extant contemporary *Lives* of Adalbert are compared in detail in I. Wood, *The Missionary Life: Saints and the Evangelisation of Europe, 400–1050* (London, 2001), 211, 215–20.

28. A comparable observation was made by K. Potkański, "Swiety Wojciech," in *Pisma posmiertne,* vol. 2 (Cracow, 1924), 329, cited by G. Labuda, *Swiety Wojciech Biskup-Meczennik Patron Polski, Czech i Węgier* (Wrocław, 2000), 250.

29. Sawicki, "Gniezno w X wieku," 111.

30. Adrianova-Peretts and Likhachev, *Povest',* 52.

31. See Z. Kurnatowska, "Stan chrzystianizacji Polski w czasach sw. Wojciecha," in *Tropami Swietego Wojciecha,* ed. Z. Kurnatowska (Poznań, 1999), 97–110, esp. 99–101; T. Rodzińska-Chorazy, "Co nam mówi architektura murowana?" in *Ziemie polskie w X wieku i ich znaczenie w kształtowaniu sie nowej mapy Europy,* ed. H. Samsonowicz (Cracow, 2000), 361–87, esp. 365–68 and 374–75.

32. A. I. Komech, *Drevnerusskoe zodchestvo konca X-nachala XII v.: Vizantiiskoe nasledie i stanovlenie samostoiatel'noi tradicii* (Moscow, 1987), 76, 175–76.

33. Adrianova-Peretts and Likhachev, *Povest',* 56. It is probably no accident that, together with martial prowess, generous hospitality and the laying-on of feasts are integral to tales of the rise of Piast and his successors. See Urbańczyk's contribution in the present volume (chap. 5).

34. There was apparently controversy as to which materials they were made from: see Adrianova-Peretts and Likhachev, *Povest'*, 52.

35. Thietmar, *Chronicon*, 488; A. Poppe, "The building of the Church of St. Sofia in Kiev," *Journal of Medieval History* 7 (1981): 15–66, esp. 18 and 52 n. 13, reprinted in A. Poppe, *The Rise of Christian Russia* (London, 1982), no. 4. It seems likely that the relics of Clement and Phoebus were installed in the Tithe Church at the time of its dedication, rather than that they were the "saints" said by the *Primary Chronicle* to have been translated to the church several years later, ca. 1007: see Adrianova-Peretts and Likhachev, *Povest'*, 57.

36. E. V. Ukhanova, "Moshchi sv. Klimenta rimskogo i stanovlenie russkoi cerkvi v X–XI vekakh," in *Relikvii v iskusstve i kul'ture vostochnokhristianskogo mira*, ed. A. M. Lidov (Moscow, 2000), 67–68, esp. 67. See also G. Podskalsky, *Khristianstvo i bogoslavskaia literatura v Kievskoi Rusi (988–1237 gg.)*, 2nd ed. (St. Petersburg, 1996), 401–3, 520, 536.

37. Thietmar, *Chronicon*, 488; Poppe, "Building of the Church of St. Sophia," 18.

38. Thietmar's apparent reference to the fall of Cherson in these terms (*Chronicon*, ed. Holtzmann, 486) may well relay the impression that the Tithe Church had made on his chief informant for Rus' affairs, an eyewitness who had recently returned from Kiev.

39. Petrukhin, *Drevniaia Rus'* 277, 285–87.

40. Sawicki, "Gniezno w X wieku," 120–22 and fig. 6 (ground plan).

41. The original dedication seems to be clear: see K. Skwierczyński, "Custodia civitatis: Sakralny system ochrony miasta w Polsce wcześniejszego średniowiecza," *Kwartalnik Historyczny* 103, no. 3 (1996): 1–51, at 8 and n. 27; Labuda, "Der 'Akt von Gnesen,'" 186. However, the church's material remains have yet to be identified securely: see Kurnatowska, "Stan chrystianizacji," 101; Sawicki, "Gniezno w X wieku," 124–26; Rodzińska-Chorazy, "Co nam mówi architektura murowana?" 372–73.

42. Thietmar, *Chronicon*, 182, 184; English translation by David A. Warner (Manchester and New York, 2001) 183; Gallus Anonymus, *Chronicae et gesta ducum sive principum Polonorum*, ed. K. Maleczyński, Monumenta Poloniae Historica, n.s., vol. 2 (Cracow, 1952), 18.

43. Bruno of Querfurt, *Passio Sancti Adalberti*, 29–30.

44. Gallus Anonymus, *Chronicae et gesta*, 20.

45. M. Uhlirz, *Die Regesten des Kaiserreiches unter Otto III* (Graz and Cologne, 1957), 736–37 no. 1336; G. Labuda, "Zjazd i synod gnieznieński w roku 1000," *Kwartalnik Historyczny*, 107, no. 2 (2000): 107–22, at 112; Labuda, "Der 'Akt von Gnesen,'" 169–70; Labuda, *Swiety Wojciech*, 227–28.

46. D. Harrison, "Invisible boundaries and places of power: Notions of liminality and centrality in the early Middle Ages," in *The Transformation of Frontiers from Late Antiquity to the Carolingians*, ed. W. Pohl, I. Wood, and H. Reimitz (Leiden, 2001), 83–93, esp. 87–93. On Mieszko and Boleslav's use of Christianity to consolidate their rule, see Urbańczyk's contribution to the present volume (chap. 5).

47. Skwierczyński, "Custodia civitatis," 10, 12, 42–45.

48. See discussion later in this chapter.

49. S. Franklin and J. Shepard, *The Emergence of Rus', 750–1200* (London, 1996), 170–72.

50. Adrianova-Peretts and Likhachev, *Povest'*, 55–56.

51. Petrukhin, *Drevniaia Rus'*, 170 with n. 29.

52. Yahya ibn-Said of Antioch, *Histoire*, ed. and trans. I. Kratchovsky and A. Vasiliev (Paris, 1932; reprint, Turnhout, 1988), 423.

53. A. Poppe, "L'organisation diocésaine de la Russie aux XIe–XIIe siècles," *Byzan-*

tion 40 (1970): 165–217, esp. 188–89 and 206–7, reprinted in A. Poppe, *The Rise of Christian Russia* (London, 1982), no. 8; S. Senyk, *A History of the Church in Ukraine*, vol. 1 (Rome, 1993), 130–38; Y. N. Shchapov, *State and Church in Early Russia, 10th–13th Centuries* (New Rochelle, 1993), 34–45; Ch. Hannick, "Les nouvelles chrétientés du monde byzantin: Russes, Bulgares, Serbes," in *Évêques, moines et empereurs: 610–1054*, ed. G. Dagron, P. Riché, and A. Vauchez (Paris, 1993), 909–39, esp. 917–19; Franklin and Shepard, *The Emergence of Rus'*, 228.

54. V. V. Sedov, "Rasprostranenie khristiantsva v drevnei Rusi," *Kratkie Soobshcheniia Instituta Arkheologii* 208 (1992): 3–11, esp. 3–4, 7, and 5 fig. 1.

55. A. P. Mocia, *Pogrebal'nye pamiatniki iuzhnorusskikh zemel' IX–XIII vv.* (Kiev, 1990), 64–65, 70–71 with map 64, 76–77 with map 65, 84–85 with map 68; *Naselennia pivdenno-rus'kikh zemel' IX–XIII st.: Za materialamy nekropoliv* (Kiev, 1993), 83–87, 93, 101; Sedov, "Rasprostranenie khristianstva," 6–7.

56. Nestor, *Life of Theodosius*, in *Paterik*, ed. D. I. Abramovich (Kiev, 1930), reprinted, with an introduction by D. Tschiževskij, as *Das Paterikon des Kiever Höhlenklosters* (Munich, 1964), 23, 25, and 27; trans. M. Heppell as *The Paterik of the Kievan Caves Monastery* (Cambridge, Mass., 1989), 27, 29, 30–31.

57. Thietmar of Merseburg, *Chronicon*, 184. Strictly speaking, a total of seven sees were instituted or confirmed at the meeting in Gniezno, rather than the five specified by Thietmar: see Labuda, "Zjazd i synod gnieznienski," 111, 113; Labuda, "Der 'Akt von Gnesen,'" 153, 186; Labuda, *Swiety Wojciech*, 246–48.

58. Kurnatowska, "Christianisierung Polens," 111–12; A. Pleszczyński, "Boleslav the Brave konfratrem eremitow sw. Romualda w Miedzyrzeczu," *Kwartalnik Historyczny* 103, no. 1 (1996): 3–22, esp. 13–18; M. Derwich, "Studia nad początkami monastycyzmu na ziemiach polskich: Pierwsze opactwa i ich funkcje" *Kwartalnik Historyczny* 107, no. 2 (2000): 77–105, esp. 84–85 and 94–95.

59. Sawicki, "Gniezno w X wieku," 124–25; Kurnatowska, "Stan chrzystianizacji," 101.

60. Kurnatowska, "Christianisierung Polens," 112; Kurnatowska, "Stan chrzystianizacji," 104, 103 fig. 1.

61. Mocia, *Pogrebal'nye pamiatniki*, 95 with map 69, 97; Mocia, *Naselennia pivdenno-rus'kikh zemel'*, 88; D. A. Belen'kaia, "Kresty i ikonki iz kurganov Podmoskov'ia," *Sovetskaia Arkheologiia* 4 (1976): 88–99, esp. 96–98; Franklin and Shepard, *The Emergence of Rus'*, 179, 268, 336.

62. Adrianova-Peretts and Likhachev, *Povest'*, 54.

63. Franklin and Shepard, *The Emergence of Rus'*, 176.

64. Adrianova-Peretts and Likhachev, *Povest'*, 56.

65. Kara, "Anfänge der Bildung," 61–62, 68–71, 78–80; T. Jasiński, "Die Konsolidierung des ältesten polnischen Staates um 940," *Quaestiones Medii Aevi*, n.s., 5 (2000): 87–98, esp. 93–95.

66. Gallus Anonymus, *Chronicae et gesta*, 34.

67. Gallus Anonymus, *Chronicae et gesta*, 34–35.

68. Gallus Anonymus, *Chronicae et gesta*, 31–32.

69. D. Kosiński, "Wczesnośredniowieczny zespół osadniczy Piaski-Rochy," in *Studia lednickie*, ed. E. Dzieciolowski, vol. 2 (Lednica and Poznań, 1991), 87–99, esp. 88 fig. 1 (plan), 91–92, 94, 97; Kurnatowska, "Christianisierung Polens," 115. On indications of a population transplant at Sandomierz in the 970s or shortly thereafter, see A. Buko's contribution in the present volume (chap. 7).

70. Kosiński, "Piaski-Rochy," 97; J. Bardach, "L'état polonais aux X et XI siècles," in *L'Europe aux IXe–Xe siècles: Aux origines des Etats nationaux; Actes du colloque international sur les origines des états européens aux IXe–Xe siècles, tenu à Varsovie et Poznan du 7 au 13 septembre 1965*, ed. T. Manteuffel and A. Gieysztor (Warsaw, 1968), 279–319, esp. 299; Kara, "Anfänge der Bildung," 61–62. The dating of extant earthen ramparts in Poland is not uncontroversial, but there are grounds for ascribing the elongated ramparts on the right bank of the Warta, the Waly Zaniemyskie, to the late tenth century: see E. Kowalczyk, *Systemy obronne walow podlużnych we wczesnym średniowieczu na ziemiach polskich* (Wrocław, 1987), 176–90. The issue of whether the ramparts near Czermno (in the region of the "Cherven towns") were raised by the Polish or the Rus' regimes is open to debate, but there is no doubt that they were designed by the one against the other: see ibid., 201–10, 221–23.

71. Yahya ibn-Said of Antioch, *Histoire*, 423.

72. Ilarion, *Slovo o zakone i blagodati*, ed. L. Müller in *Des Metropoliten Ilarion Lobrede auf Vladimir den Heiligen* (Wiesbaden, 1962), 106; trans. S. Franklin in *Sermons and Rhetoric of Kievan Rus'* (Cambridge, Mass., 1991), 19.

73. Adrianova-Peretts and Likhachev, *Povest'*, 56.

74. See J. Shepard, "Byzantium and the West," in *New Cambridge Medieval History*, ed. T. Reuter, vol. 3 (Cambridge, 1999), 605–32, esp. 617–21.

75. Adrianova-Peretts and Likhachev, *Povest'*, 38.

76. Labuda, *Studia nad poczatkami*, 2:167–211, 264–93; G. Labuda, "Narodziny polsko-ukrainskiej granicy etnicznej w polskiej historiografii," in *Początki sasiędztwa: Pogranicze etniczne polsko-rusko-slowackie w średniowieczu; Materialy z konferencji, Rzeszów, 9–11 V 1995*, ed. M. Parczewski and S. Czopek (Rzeszów, 1996), 9–17; Třeštík, "Von Svatopluk," 138; A. Pleszczyński, "Poland as an ally of the Holy Ottonian Empire," in *Europe around the Year 1000*, ed. P. Urbańczyk (Warsaw, 2001), 409–25, esp. 415. Objections, primarily from an archaeological standpoint, were, however, raised by E. Kowalczyk, "Momenty geograficzne państwa Boleslawa Chrobrego. Na styku historii i archeologii," *Kwartalnik Historyczny* 107 (2000): 41–76, esp. 65–72.

77. Labuda, *Studia nad poczatkami*, 2:208–9; Labuda, "Narodziny," 16–17; Kowalczyk, "Momenty geograficzne," 55–65; Nazarenko, *Drevniaia Rus'*, 393–94.

78. On the routes linking Rus' with Cracow, Prague, and the middle Danube region and also with the Baltic world, see, e.g., Ibn Yakub, *Relatio de itinere slavico*, 49; Franklin and Shepard, *The Emergence of Rus'*, 157, 174, 180, 187; P. Charvát, "Bohemia, Moravia, and long-distance trade in the 10th–11th centuries," *Quaestiones Medii Aevi*, n.s., 5 (2000): 255–66, esp. 263–64; Nazarenko, *Drevniaia Rus'*, 89–94, 109–11. Indications concerning the routes are supplied by hoards uncovered inland, such as that of women's ornaments found at Zawada Lanckorońska, on the river Dunajec, about 70 kilometers east from Cracow. Some of these ornaments (e.g., half-moon pendants and earrings) have close analogies with examples from Gnezdovo or elsewhere in Rus' lands and were probably brought from there, quite likely by a trader, perhaps in the 970s or 980s: see H. Zoll-Adamikova, *The Early Mediaeval Hoard from Zawada Lanckorońska (Upper Vistula River)* (Warsaw, 1999), 96–100, 110–11, 114–15. See also A. V. Fomin, "Drevnerusskie denezhno-monetnye rynki v 70–80kh godakh X v.," in *Drevneishie gosudarstva vostochnoi Evropy: Materialy i issledovaniia 1992–1993 gody* (Moscow, 1995), 63–73, esp. 67, 68 with map; S. Suchodolski, "Change of transcontinental contacts as indicated by coins in the Baltic zone," in *Europe around the Year 1000*, ed. P. Urbańczyk (Warsaw, 2001), 85–100, esp. 86, 88–90, and 96–97.

79. M. Wołoszyn, "Die byzantinischen Fundstücke in Polen: Ausgewählte Probleme," in *Byzantium and East Central Europe*, ed. M. Salamon, G. Prinzing, and P. Stephenson (Cracow, 2001), 49–59, esp. 51, 53–55, and 53 n. 27.

80. Adrianova-Peretts and Likhachev, *Povest'*, 56.

81. Thietmar, *Chronicon*, 530.

82. L. P. Słupecki, "Jómsvikingalog, Jómsvikings, Jomsborg/Wolin and Danish circular strongholds," in *The Neighbours of Poland in the 10th Century*, ed. Urbańczyk (Warsaw, 2000), 49–59, esp. 53–56.

83. Strzelczyk, "The first two historical Piasts," 111 with n. 37.

84. M. Kara, "The graves of the armed Scandinavians from the middle and the younger Viking period from the territory of the first Piasts' state," in *Death and Burial: Pre-printed Papers, IV; Conference on Medieval Archaeology in Europe, 21–24 September 1992, at the University of York* (York, 1992), 167–77, esp. 177 fig. 1 (map); A. Krzyszowski, "Ein reiches Gräberfeld aus dem 10./11. Jh. in Sowinki bei Poznań," *Slavia Antiqua* 36 (1995): 49–71, esp. 53 and 64–71; H. Zoll-Adamikova, "Gräberfelder des 8./9.–10./11 Jhs. mit skandinavischen Komponenten im slawischen Ostseeraum," *Sprawozdania Archaeologiczne* 49 (1997): 9–19, esp. 14–15. I am most grateful to Marcin Wołoszyn for alerting me to these papers and furnishing me with copies of them. See also W. Panasiewicz and M. Wołoszyn, "Staroruskie minaturowe toporki z Gródka, pow. Hrubieszów," *Archaeologia Polski* 47 (2002): 269–70; A. Buko's contribution in the present volume (chap. 7).

85. The onset of the millennium of the goings-on prompted renewed scholarly efforts to account for them. See, e.g., G. Althoff, *Otto III* (Darmstadt, 1996), 126–52; R. Michałowski, "Początki arcybiskupstwa gnieznieńskiego," in *1000 lat Archidiecezji Gnieznieńskiej*, ed. J. Strzelczyk and J. Górny (Gniezno, 2000), 37–47; J. Strzelczyk, *Otton III* (Wrocław, 2000), 111–45; Strzelczyk, "The first two historical Piasts," 131–36, 140–42; Labuda, "Der 'Akt von Gnesen,'" 145–88; Labuda, "Zjazd i synod gnieźnienski," 107–22; Pleszczyński, "Poland as an ally of the Holy Ottonian Empire," 409–25; L. Körntgen, "The emperor and his friends: The Ottonian realm in the year 1000," in *Europe around the Year 1000*, ed. P. Urbańczyk (Warsaw, 2001), 465–88; J. Fried, *Otto III. und Boleslav Chrobry: Das Widmungsbild des Aachener Evangeliars, der Akt von Gnesen und das frühe polnische und ungarische Königtum; Eine Bildanalyse und ihre Folgen*, 2nd ed. (Stuttgart, 2001), 72–132, 171–78; J. Shepard, "Otto III, Boleslav Chrobry, and the 'happening' at Gniezno, A.D. 1000: Some possible implications of Professor Poppe's thesis concerning the offspring of Anna Porphyrogenita," in *Byzantium and East Central Europe*, ed. M. Salamon, G. Prinzing, and P. Stephenson (Cracow, 2001), 27–48.

86. H. Mayr-Harting, *Ottonian Book Illumination: An Historical Study*, vol. 2 (London, 1999), 11–20, 31–53; R. Landes, "The fear of an apocalyptic year 1000: Augustinian historiography," *Speculum* 75 (2000): 118–45; R. Landes, "Introduction: The *terribles espoirs* of 1000 and the tacit fears of 2000," in *The Apocalyptic Year 1000: Religious Expectation and Social Change, 950–1050*, ed. R. Landes et al. (Oxford, 2003), 3–15; S. Keynes, "Apocalypse then: England A.D. 1000," in *Europe around the Year 1000*, ed. P. Urbańczyk (Warsaw, 2001), 247–70, esp. 263–67; J. Shepard, "Marriages towards the millennium," *Byzantium in the Year 1000*, ed. P. Magdalino (Leiden, 2003), 29–31.

87. *Annales Quedlinburgenses*, ed. G. H. Pertz (Hanover, 1839), MGH Scriptores 3:77; Thietmar, *Chronicon*, 182, 184, 232; G. Waitz, ed., *Annales Hildesheimenses*, MGH *in usum schol.* (Hanover, 1878), 28; Gallus Anonymus, *Chronicae et gesta*, 18–21.

88. Gallus Anonymus, *Chronicae et gesta*, 18.

89. Shepard "Otto III," 46, 48. See also Labuda, "Der 'Akt von Gnesen,'" 187.

90. Thietmar, *Chronicon,* 184.

91. Galus Anonymus, *Chronicae et gesta,* 19.

92. T. Wasilewski, "Le couronnement de l'an 1000 à Gniezno et son modèle byzantin," in *L'Europe aux IXe–Xe siècles: Aux origines des Etats nationaux; Actes du colloque international sur les origines des états européens aux IXe–Xe siècles, tenu à Varsovie et Poznan du 7 au 13 septembre 1965,* ed. T. Manteuffel and A. Gieysztor (Warsaw, 1968), 461–72; T. Wasilewski, "La couronne royal: Symbole de dépendance à l'époque du haut Moyen Age," in *La Pologne au XV Congrès International des Sciences Historiques à Bucarest: Etudes sur l'histoire de la culture de l'Europe Centrale-Orientale,* ed S. Bylina (Wrocław, 1980), 25–50, esp. 25–36; Shepard, "Otto III," 44–45.

93. The senators mentioned as going north of the Alps with Otto could well have accompanied him as far as Gniezno: see *Annales Quedlinburgenses,* 77; Shepard, "Otto III," 38–39.

94. Shepard, "Otto III," 41–42.

95. J. Shepard, "Courts in East and West," in *The Medieval World,* ed. P. Linehan and J. L. Nelson (London, 2001), 14–36, esp. 25–26. See also L. E. Scales, "Identifying 'France' and 'Germany': Medieval nation-making in some recent publications," *Bulletin of International Medieval Research* 6 (2000): 21–46, esp. 36.

96. Althoff, *Otto III,* 197–207; Shepard, "Byzantium and the West," 617–20.

97. B. Malmer, "Från Olaf till Anund: Ur sigtunamyntningens historia," *Numismatiska Meddelanden* 40 (1995): 9–26, esp. 10, 14, and 24–25; B. Malmer, *The Anglo-Swedish Coinage c. 995–1020* (Stockholm, 1997), 14–15, 45, 53–56; Suchodolski, "Początki rodzimego mennictwa," 356–57; Duczko, "Continuity and transformation," 30–31.

98. A. Poppe, "Theophana von Novgorod," *Byzantinoslavica* 58 (1997): 131–58; "Feofana Novgorodskaia," *Novgorodskii istoricheskii sbornik* 6 (1997): 102–20; "'Losers on earth, winners from heaven': The assassinations of Boris and Gleb in the making of eleventh-century Rus," *Quaestiones Medii Aevi Novae,* 8 (2003), 138–39.

99. Poppe, "Theophana von Novgorod," 151; Poppe, "Feofana," 115; Shepard, "Otto III," 30–32.

100. Thietmar, *Chronicon,* 182–84, 198, 428, 492; Shepard, "Otto III," 37, 47 (with references to earlier secondary literature).

101. Gallus Anonymus, *Chronicae et gesta,* 20; Shepard, "Otto III," 43.

102. A comparable suggestion has been made by Fried, *Otto III. und Boleslav Chrobry,* 180, 148.

103. Ademar of Chabannes, *Chronicon,* ed. P. Bourgain, R. Landes, and G. Pon (Turnhout, 1999), 153–54; Althoff, *Otto III,* 148–49; K. Görich, "Otto III. öffnet das Karlsgrab in Aachen," in *Herrschaftsrepräsentation im ottonischen Sachsen,* ed. G. Althoff and E. Schubert (Sigmaringen, 1998), 381–430, esp. 417–18 with n. 141 and 424; Strzelczyk, "The first two historical Piasts," 139–40 with n. 93; Strzelczyk, *Otton III,* 140–45.

104. Shepard, "Otto III," 42; Körntgen, "The emperor and his friends," 476; Fried, *Otto III. und Boleslav the Brave,* 135–36, 143–49, 178–79.

105. Görich, "Otto III. öffnet das Karlsgrab in Aachen," 393–406, 429–30.

106. Gerbert d'Aurillac, *Correspondance,* ed. and trans. P. Riché and J. P. Callu, vol. 1 (Paris, 1993), 268–71.

107. Strzelczyk, "The first two historical Piasts," 136–37. See also n. 57 in the present chapter.

108. Gallus Anonymus, *Chronicae et gesta,* 21–25, 28–29.

CHAPTER ELEVEN

Missions, Conversions, and Power Legitimization in East Central Europe at the Turn of the First Millennium

Márta Font

*A*round the turn of the first millennium, a number of power centers emerged in the vicinity of the two Christian empires. As a consequence, many historians attribute the rise of the historical region now known as East Central Europe to those formative centuries. In my opinion, these centers of power must be treated as a whole, for no subdivisions existed in the region during the High Middle Ages (tenth to twelfth centuries).[1] The beginnings of the Přemyslid, Piast, Arpadian, and Ryurikid dynasties that ruled in these centers at the time of the conversion to Christianity in the late 900s go back to the tribal past. The rise of the ruling clans from among tribal aristocracies had taken place before conversion, but each one of these dynasties came to play a decisive role in the history of the region for the centuries to come. The Arpadian and Přemyslid lines died out in the early fourteenth century (1301 and 1305, respectively), followed by the Piasts (1372) and, much later, the Ryurikids (1598). With their power already established shortly before AD 1000 and continuing uninterrupted for several centuries, the beginnings of these dynasties are still obscure, as written sources only provide vague information about their tribal enemies and allies.

Concentrating Power

In the case of the Arpadians, we know very well who their opponents were and how they were eventually destroyed in the early eleventh century, as they clashed with the ruling Arpadian clan.[2] Constantine Porphyrogenitus knew that the Arpadians were leaders of a tribal alliance comprising no less than eight tribes, not just chiefs of a single tribe.[3] By 950, the tribal alliance seems to have broken apart; the power of the Arpadian clan weakened as a result of direct relations established with Constantinople by several tribal leaders who had accepted baptism. However, shortly after AD 1000, the Arpadians were back in a leading position within the newly formed Christian monarchy.

For a relatively long period of time, the main opponents of the Přemyslid dynasty were the Slavníks, the aristocratic family to which belonged the bishop of Prague, Adalbert/Wojtěch, who later died a martyr on the northeastern frontier of Poland.[4] Adalbert's death may have caused the chronicling of the power struggle between Přemyslids and Slavníks. As for the enemies of the Piast rulers, there is only an obscure hint in the chronicle of Gallus Anonymus to the fate of the Popelids.[5] The chronicler knew nothing about the aristocracy of the Vistulans, Lendizi, or other Slavic tribes in Poland. But he was definitely aware of oral traditions, as the Slavs "like all other barbarians preserve the memory of past heroic deeds."[6] All known rulers mentioned in the *Russian Primary Chronicle,* from the Kievan brothers Askold and Dir to Oleg, the ruler of Novgorod, were Varangians, not Slavs. The only exception is Mal, the prince of the Derevlians, whom Kievan princes had a hard time subduing.[7] A common element in all these cases is that the emerging dynasty began by attacking other tribes. The new power had then to be reckoned with by neighbors.

Establishing Power

Military organization played a key role in the emergence of tribal aristocracy. This is most evident in the Hungarian case, as the very organization of the tribes was rooted in the military traditions of "steppe societies."[8] The Arpadian organization of the army was facilitated both by gaining independence from the Khazars and by Arpad's rise to political prominence. According to Constantine Porphyrogenitus, Levedi, the paramount chief of the tribal union, "resigned," thus passing power into the hands of Arpad and his family. There is no reason to believe that this story is not genuine or that it did not originate in the Hungarian tradition, which may have shaped the narrative of Constantine's Hungarian informants.[9]

The tribal organization preceding the rise to power of both Přemyslids and Piasts was permanently challenged by the eastward expansion of the Eastern Frankish, later Ottonian, Empire.[10] Slavic tribal organization existed only at a small, microregional level, often around some important stronghold (*grad/gród/hrad*). The new power centers established in the late 900s were now responsible for the defense of such strongholds. The political and, later, military pressure from the empire must have triggered a process of power concentration, but Viking raids into Polish territories may have contributed to this process at least as much as the Hungarian raids elsewhere.[11] External impulses thus accelerated the process of military organization by powerful leaders, who then gave their names to the ruling dynasties. The same is certainly true about the Rus' princes, who strengthened their power by waging war against both Khazars and Pechenegs.[12] Seaborne raids against Byzantium were partially the result of this military organization. The legendary Ryurik who gave his name to the Ryurikid dynasty was undoubtedly just the lord of Novgorod, while the organization of the Novgorod-Kiev trade and political axis must have been the work of Oleg.[13]

The power of the dynasty emerging from among tribal elites was in practice based on retinues of warriors. Such retinues supplied the prince with most reliable and loyal troops.[14] The perspective of greater war spoils encouraged leaders to increase the size of their military retinues, which in turn contributed to the consolidation of dynastic power. For their part, retinues were generating new demands for further raiding and campaigning. In more than one way, maintaining a retinue of warriors was sufficient reason for going to war.[15] The retinue provided a formidable force, which the prince often used to bring the entire tribe under his authority. The unconditional loyalty of the retinue was secured by its heterogeneous composition and mixed origins. In Kievan Rus', the two dominant elements, Varangians and Slavs, were in all likelihood strengthened with recruits from the steppe. In the Hungarian case, although the existence of military auxiliaries with discretionary force was part of the steppe traditions, it is not altogether clear what relation, if any, existed between them and the grand prince.[16] Similarly, the existence of retinues in Přemyslid Bohemia and Piast Poland is well attested (e.g., during military campaigns),[17] but almost no evidence exists as to their ethnic composition. They perhaps consisted of members of tribal aristocracies and a few foreigners, mainly Scandinavians. The formidable force represented by such retinues of warriors, as well as the charismatic leadership most often shown during military campaigns, enabled the aforementioned dynasties to gain political prominence in their neighbors' eyes. Neighbors had to take these new developments into consideration for their own expansion, as well as for the possible use of such military potential now available on their borders. To do so, they had to recognize the newly formed centers of military power as independent de facto and to treat them as partners, if not equals.

Early Recognition of Power: Conversion to Christianity and Dynastic Policies

Conversions to Christianity joined dynastic relations as the first signs of recognition of the East Central European dynasties by such great powers as

Byzantium and the Eastern Frankish, later Ottonian, Empire. Byzantium had a long tradition of using conversion as a means of protecting and furthering the interests of the Christian empire. During the last third of the ninth century, Constantine/Cyril and Methodius, together with their disciples, brought Christianity to Moravia and Bulgaria, respectively.[18] However, with the collapse of Moravia in the early tenth century, the influence of this missionary tradition was lost. Much like Ryurik of Novgorod, Bořivoj of Bohemia was a ruler of almost legendary stature, who, if we are to believe the twelfth-century chronicle of Cosmas of Prague, was baptized by no other than Methodius.[19] Some accept Cosmas at face value; others treat this as nothing more than legend.[20] Missions from the West first reached the Přemyslids. The first converts were Wenceslas (921–29) and his mother, Ludmila, both bereft of power and assassinated by their pagan opponents. As a consequence, they became the first west Slavic martyrs.[21] Christianity received a new impetus with the establishment of the diocese of Prague in 973 and the beginnings of the cult of St. Wenceslas.[22] The bishop of Prague was a suffragan of the archbishop of Mainz and thus was under imperial control. The same is also true about Přemyslid policies.[23] Ottonians treated Bohemia as part of their empire, and there was no intermarriage between the two ruling houses.

The conversion of the Piasts took place under Duke Mieszko through Bohemian agency. Indeed, Mieszko's first wife was Dobrava, a Přemyslid princess.[24] After her death (around 977), Mieszko married the daughter of a Saxon (Nordmark) margrave, who ruled over modern-day Brandenburg.[25] The marriage established closer links with the empire. By 986, Otto II employed Polish troops for his campaign against Bohemia.[26] As indicated by their matrimonial alliances, the Bohemian and Polish princes differed in their attitudes and positions toward the empire.[27] Boleslav the Brave first married Rygdag, then a daughter of the Hungarian prince Géza. He abandoned both for political reasons. Following the death of his third wife, Emnilda, ca. 1018, he married Oda, the daughter of Margrave Ekkehard. The last marriage was meant to elevate Boleslav's status and allow him to assert his independence from the empire.[28]

The initial missions to the Hungarian tribes came from Byzantium and followed an established pattern of missionary activity.[29] While establishing links with tribal leaders, the emperor treated them as "friends." However, there is no evidence of either dynastic marriages or mass conversions, although enough is known to reconstruct the beginnings of the ecclesiastical organization. A Byzantine bishop, Hierotheos, was sent to the tribe of Gyula in Transylvania and to the Hungarian tribe in southern Hungary, where a monastery was later founded at Marosvár (later Cenad/Csanád).[30] The baptism of Termacsu remained, however, the only case of conversion to Byzantine Christianity among

Arpadians.[31] Historians often quote Thietmar of Merseburg in referring to Prince Géza's conversion as perfectly compatible not only with his marriage to a Christian (Princess Sarolt of Transylvania) but also with his continuing worship of the old tribal gods.[32] This, however, must have been true of all other chieftains recently converted to Christianity. Unlike them, Géza, after 973, supported especially missions from Salzburg, Passau, and St. Gall.[33] At the same time, he acknowledged the religious traditions of the local population in Pannonia. In 996, he founded Pannonhalma Abbey, dedicated to St. Martin, whose cult had local traditions.[34] Géza's activities thus show that the conversion of the Hungarians is not to be associated with King Stephen alone, as the latter must have been baptized by St. Adalbert during his sojourn in Hungary.[35] Moreover, under Stephen, an archdiocese was established in Esztergom (1000). As a consequence, dioceses must have already been in existence since the days of Géza. Besides Veszprém, the diocese of Győr may be an early foundation, as it was visited by Azo, the papal legate, in 1009.[36]

Christian missions thus came to Hungary from two geographic and political directions, but it would be wrong to assume tensions or conflicts, for there was no rivalry between Byzantium and the Ottonian Empire at the turn of the millennium. On the contrary, there seems to have been a growing consensus between the two powers.[37] King Stephen subdued the tribal chief who had converted to Byzantine Christianity, but he did so out of domestic and political, not religious, concerns. Byzantine Christianity continued to flourish in Hungary, albeit under Roman episcopal administration.[38] As far as marriages are concerned, Stephen was indeed the first Hungarian ruler to marry a Westerner, in the person of Gisella, the daughter of the Bavarian margrave. This marriage greatly contributed to the recognition of Stephen's coronation. Furthermore, Stephen's links with the empire were also strengthened with the rise of Emperor Henry II, a former duke of Bavaria (995–1004) and thus a relative of the Hungarian king.

The conversion of the Rus'[39] took a radical turn in 988, after several other attempts during the mid-900s. Cooperation between Byzantine emperors and the Kievan princes had begun at the time of wars in the steppe against the Pechenegs. In 988, however, the Rus' were instrumental in assisting Emperor Basil II's restoration of authority. After eliminating Skleros, the usurper Bardas Phokas gained control over most cities on the Black Sea coast and threatened Constantinople itself. In this situation, Prince Vladimir of Kiev offered his assistance to Basil and besieged Chersonesus, in Crimea, a city under Bardas Phokas's control. In exchange for his military assistance, Vladimir was given the hand of the emperor's sister Anna.[40] The marriage implied Vladimir's conversion, an episode covered by several contradictory sections in the *Russian*

Primary Chronicle. What is clear, however, is that Basil II needed a strong ally and the formidable power of the Rus' military retinue. To assess the importance of Vladimir's marriage with the emperor's sister, it is sufficient to consider that under different circumstances, Emperor Otto I's efforts to secure a princess "born in the purple" for his son, the future Otto II, were ultimately unsuccessful. Theophano was indeed a relative of the ruling Byzantine emperor (John Tzimiskes), but not a princess of the highest rank, like Anna.[41] Contemporary chroniclers understood this very well. They valued the marriage of Vladimir as a remarkable one, and some even argued that the princess who was to marry Otto never did so because of Vladimir.[42]

Missionary activities on the borders of the Christian world did not stop at the turn of the millennium. Nor did Europe split into Western and Eastern spheres of Christian influence. Bruno of Querfurt, for example, led missions to both Hungary and Rus'. However, in both cases, his missions failed: the region of Hungary known as Ungaria Nigra (Black Hungary) remained pagan, while in Kiev, Bruno was no match for the Byzantine mission.[43] By contrast, in Bohemia, the monks of the Eastern rite monastery of Sázava were expelled.[44] This marked the end of the Old Church Slavonic liturgy in the region. Traces of the Moravian tradition survived in Silesia,[45] while in Hungary, Orthodox monasteries were in use well into the twelfth century.[46]

International Recognition of Power: Crown and Sword

Coronation ceremonies marked a difference in quality in the eyes of many members of ruling dynasties. The ceremony developed from the ordination of bishops and was accordingly based on the idea that the power of the Christian monarch derived directly from God (*Dei gratia*). Coronation made the ruler *rex* and *sacerdos* at the same time, while the church ceremony underlined the special position the king held among laymen.[47] The idea of *rex et sacerdos* going back to the Old Testament contributed to the articulation of the concept of *renovatio imperii*. At the turn of the millennium, the Christian world was ruled by two emperors, the *basileus kai autokrator* (emperor and lord) and the *imperator Augustus Romanorum,* with spiritual power divided between the patriarch and the pope. According to the Byzantine political practice, the emperor always had a position higher than that of the patriarch. Given that he was raised in a political climate influenced by the Byzantine court, Otto III's political activity seems to have been inspired by a similar model. That he made Pope Sylvester II his tutor may be an indication of cooperation between the two emperors, but an initiative from Otto inspired by Byzantine political practice should not be excluded.[48]

The most important symbol of power illustrating the idea of divine grace, the crown, was to be obtained by princes from one of the two emperors. Receiving a crown was a sign of recognition by the emperor or the pope and was a way to outdo other dynasties. Emperor Otto III seems to have been aware of the meaning attached to coronations, when refusing to bestow crowns on any prince. Emperors used so-called closed crowns, combining an episcopal miter and a royal "open" crown.[49] Such a royal crown appears, for example, on King Stephen's coronation mantle. At the turn of the millennium, other symbols of power appeared alongside or instead of crowns. Swords and coins were two of the most important.

The first Piast to wear a crown was Boleslav the Brave (992–1025), during whose reign an archdiocese was established in Gniezno. When Emperor Otto III visited Gniezno in 1000, he handed over a sword to Boleslav, thereby acknowledging his position of power, but no crown was given to the Polish ruler. Boleslav's special relations to Otto, however, are revealed by his frequent visits to the imperial court.[50] The significance of these relations became apparent with the new change in policy following Otto III's death. Henry II did not endorse the Ottonian idea of *renovatio Imperii*. Instead, his main goal was to obtain acceptance for the imperial primacy from all rulers. A period of protracted war with Boleslav ended with the peace of 1013. It may have been in reaction to such hostility that, following Henry's death in 1024, Boleslav had himself crowned. The coronation probably took place at Christmas in 1024, but Boleslav died shortly after that, on July 17, 1025.[51] The new emperor did not recognize the crowning, and there is no evidence of any attempts to make the papacy accept it. Boleslav himself must have been aware of the arbitrary nature of this coronation. The timing had been well chosen, for no retaliation was to be expected from the empire during the interregnum.

The coronation of King Stephen of Hungary in 1000 also took place at Christmas. Hungarian historians have long debated whether Stephen's crown was from the emperor or the pope.[52] Since relations between the two were excellent at the turn of the century, this is in fact a moot point. At the time of Bishop Astrik's visit to Rome, Emperor Otto III was in the city. The crown could not have been sent to Hungary without his knowledge and agreement.[53] The episode is nevertheless important in that the Hungarian king thus received a double confirmation, from both emperor and pope. The coronation ceremony probably took place in Esztergom, for the Székesfehérvár basilica was not yet erected at that time. The high priest performing the ceremony was most likely Astrik, who had brought from Rome the crown, no doubt the same one that is depicted on Stephen's coronation mantle. Stephen's coronation was confirmed by Emperor Otto's successor, Henry II, who was the brother-in-law of the Hungarian king. During all of Henry's reign, relations between Hungary and the empire were peaceful, in sharp contrast to those between the empire, on one hand, and Bohemia and Poland, on the other.

The Byzantine emperor Michael VII (1071–78) sent a crown to the Hungarian king Géza I (1074–77) but not to the Kievan princes with whom he had much closer relations. There is no evidence that the latter ever asked for one. Moreover, there is no hint of a coronation ceremony in the early history of Kievan Rus'. The first such ceremony took place in 1497 and involved the Grand Prince of Moscow, Ivan III.[54] The examples already discussed indicate that the prince who wished to be crowned usually initiated the coronation process. However, this does not seem to have been the case in Kievan Rus', where rulers maintained relations to Byzantium that were very different from those between the Ottonian Empire and its eastern neighbors. Geography may also explain the absence of a military and political dependence of Rus' on Byzantium. In addition, Rus' was not a part of the old Roman Empire to be revived by Byzantine rulers. The only form of dependence linking Rus' to Byzantium was ecclesiastical. With few exceptions, all metropolitans of Kiev between 988 and 1241 were Greeks, despite Yaroslav the Wise's attempt of 1051 to put an end to this practice.[55]

The circumstances surrounding the first coronations of rulers belonging to dynasties in East Central Europe that became Christian around AD 1000 were substantially different. The Piast state was not part of the Ottonian Empire, but Piast rulers maintained special relations with the emperor, such as tax paying and attending imperial assemblies. As a consequence, they were never regarded as equal, and emperors did not bestow on them the sacred symbols of supreme power. During the eleventh century, Piast rulers organized their own coronation ceremonies, taking advantage of inner tensions within the empire. The independence of the Piasts, however, results from the fact that the archdiocese of Gniezno was not part of the imperial church. The same is not true about Přemyslid Bohemia, in which the bishop of Prague was a suffragan of the archbishop of Mainz. During the eleventh century, only one Přemyslid prince was crowned, and he, too, took advantage of the political conjuncture created by the Investiture Controversy. In Hungary, the independence of the church from the empire was underlined by the presence of not one but two archdioceses. Following the coronation of King Stephen in 1000, which was confirmed by both emperor and pope, coronations continued uninterrupted throughout the High Middle Ages. Almost none raised problems of legitimacy. The Arpadians made good use of the strategic position of their kingdom on the periphery of the other Christian empire, which enabled them to obtain recognition from both Byzantium and the Holy Roman Empire. After the coronation of King Coloman in 1095, however, there was no need of recognition diplomacy, as the issue was settled for good. In the case of Kievan Rus', the lack of coronation ceremonies points to a different source of legitimacy. Because Rus' was not threatened by Byzantine expansion, political independence did not need to be expressed by such symbolic means. This is particularly evident when comparing Rus' with Bulgaria, for which Byzantium was a permanent threat. Bulgarian princes always insisted on obtaining recognition from Byzantium for their rights to rule. Even without coronation, however, the German emperor was at times forced to acknowledge the considerable power of Bohemian or Polish rulers—albeit as princes, not as kings.

The new dynasties were eager to demonstrate their power to their subjects. They made extensive use of the imagery and symbolism of the sword and of ceremonies involving its manipulation. Other ceremonies, such as those involving sitting on the throne, grew in parallel with the rise of the new dynasties and played an important role in this process. Přemyslid rulers rising to power were often described in chronicles as being "enthroned."[56] The prince of Kiev "occupied the throne of his father and grandfather."[57] More often than not, the ceremony of enthronization may be linked to a specific throne. In Prague, the stone throne was still to be seen in 1142 in an open-air area near the castle, while the throne of the Kievan princes was located either at the court of Yaroslav or in the St. Sophia Cathedral.[58]

The rise to power took many symbolic forms. The ceremonies surrounding the coronation were phenomena most typically marking the transition from tribal to state organization, for which there were many parallels in contemporary Western and northern Europe. Details were different in different places. For instance, the custom of having the future ruler sit on a stone appeared in connection with a certain object designed for that purpose. This custom became absorbed in Christian traditions.[59] Even where no coronation existed, similar ceremonies developed to show the power of the new rulers. It is believed that the origins of such ceremonies could be traced back to old tribal customs, but they also borrowed symbols from neighboring empires.[60]

Conclusion

The tenth century witnessed a process of accelerated concentration of power, as dynasties in East Central Europe gradually eliminated their rivals. Indeed, no rulers came to power around AD 1000 who were not members of these powerful families. The dynasties themselves, however, lacked any principles of succession. Their claims to power were based on kinship, the structuring principle of pre-Christian tribal society, but the conversion to Christianity drastically altered this principle, as acceptable heirs to the throne were now only those children born of marriages that were legitimate from a Christian point of view. Converted or converting princes were thus coerced to live in and promote legitimate matrimonial bonds. This was particularly expected from a pagan prince choosing or receiving a Christian spouse from a foreign dynasty—for example, Mieszko (marrying Dobrava and then Ote), Vladimir (marrying Anna), Géza (marrying Sarolt), and especially Stephen (marrying Gisella). However, at least initially, sons born from previous marriages of formerly pagan princes were not automatically excluded from succession. It is particularly notable that Vladimir seems to have kept his previous wives and concubines even after conversion. The Rus' chronicler says nothing about the denial of claims of sons born from those marriages, despite the obvious hostility expressed by the Christian writer toward such lack of Christian moral standards.

Throughout the High Middle Ages (tenth to twelfth century), the region now known as East Central Europe was on the periphery of the great powers of the time, Byzantium and the Holy Roman Empire. As a periphery, this region was important to both empires for various military reasons and also because it was an area of missionary activity. Proximity to great powers was a threat to local elites, who were drawn into the "religious imperialism" of missions from both empires. The Bohemian and Polish lands were a target for missions from the Ottonian Empire, as the last traces of the missionary tradition established in the ninth century in the area by Cyril and Methodius disappeared shortly before or after AD 1000. By contrast, missions from the West (e.g., that of Bruno of Querfurt) had little success in those areas, such as Rus', where the Byzantine influence could not be ensconced. The Hungarians were a special case. On one hand, the *gyula* in southern Hungary and Prince Achtum in southwest Transylvania received the Byzantine form of Christianity. Other members of the Arpadian clan were even baptized in Constantinople or married Christians following the Eastern rite. On the other hand, western Hungary was already an area of lively contacts with the Church of Rome. For the Arpadians, who initially controlled this area, conversion meant strengthening already existing ties with missionary centers in Bavaria.

Christian missions targeted the princely families and dynasties, as conversion was understood as a transformation from "above." The tribal elites backing missions enjoyed imperial support and recognition. With such powerful allies, they quickly asserted their power over fellow tribesmen, but not without fierce resistance from "pagans." Another strategy employed by elites supporting missions was to establish matrimonial alliances with ruling dynasties from neighboring empires. Such marriages were in themselves a form of international recognition for the newly emerging powers. More often than not, Christian princes consolidated their domination over other tribes with imperial assistance and tacit approval. Boleslav the Brave occupied Little Poland, while Boleslav II of Bohemia incorporated Moravia into the Přemyslid state. The Kievan prince Vladimir subjected several other Slavic tribes to his authority, while the Arpadian prince Géza became the master of western Hungary during the years following his marriage to Sarolt.

A higher level of recognition for the newly established polities is indicated by coronation ceremonies. It was no accident that with the exception of the Rus', all rulers in the area seem to have been preoccupied with obtaining and using crowns. Being crowned undoubtedly elevated their status and improved their image in the Christian world. Hostility from German emperors for princes seeking recognition by such means can only be understood if the symbolism of the crown is taken into consideration. However, the absence of coronation ceremonies does not necessarily imply a lack of interest in rituals of power representation. Pre-Christian ceremonies involving the use of stone thrones became particularly popular throughout Europe during this period, as Christianity gave a new meaning to the act of enthronement.

NOTES

1. J. Szücs, *Vázlat Európa három történeti régiójáról* (Budapest, 1983), translated into German as *Die drei historischen Regionen* (Frankfurt am Main, 1990); M. Font, "On the question of European regions from the eleventh through the thirteenth centuries," *A Pécsi Janus Pannonius tudományegyetem történettudományi tánszékének évkönyve*, 1992, 171–78; M. Font, "Korona és/vagy kard," in *Ezredforduló, századforduló, hetvenedik évforduló: Ünnepi tanulmányok Zimányi Vera tiszteletére* (Piliscsaba, 2001), 15–46.

2. E. Szentpétery, ed., *Scriptores Rerum Hungaricarum*, vol. 1 (Budapest, 1937), 312–16; vol. 2 (Budapest, 1938), 489–92.

3. Constantine Porphyrogenitus, *De administrando imperio*, ed. Gy. Moravcsik (Budapest, 1950), 179.

4. Cosmas of Prague, *Chronicle*, ed. B. Bretholz and W. Weinberger, MGH Scriptores rerum Germanicarum, n.s., vol. 2 (Berlin, 1923; reprint, Munich, 1995), 34–35, 52–53.

5. Gallus Anonymus, *Chronicae et gesta ducum sive principum Polonorum*, ed. K. Maleczyński, Monumenta Poloniae Historica, n.s., vol. 2 (Cracow, 1952), 9–13. See J. Banaszkiewicz, *Podanie o Piascie i Popielu: Studium porównawcze nad wczesnośredniowiecznymi tradycjami dynastycznymi* (Warsaw, 1986).

6. Gallus Anonymus, *Chronicae et gesta*, 12. See E. O. Kossmann, *Polen in Mittelalter: Staat, Gesellschaft, Wirtschaft in Bannkreis des Westens* (Marburg, 1985), 182.

7. D. S. Likhachev and L. A. Dmitriev, eds., *Pamiatniki literatury Drevnei Rusi*, (Moscow, 1978), 36–39, 70–71.

8. I. Vásáry, "Nép és ország a türköknél," in *Nomád társadalmak és államalakulatok:*

Tanulmányok, ed. F. Tökei (Budapest, 1983), 189–213; G. Kristó, *Hungarian History in the Ninth Century* (Szeged, 1996), 68–70.

9. Constantine Porphyrogenitus, *De administrando imperio*, 173. See also G. Györffy, *Tanulmányok a magyar állam eredeteröl: A nemzetségtól a vármegyéik, a törzstol az országig Kurszán és Kurszán vára* (Budapest, 1959), 158–59; G. Kristó, *Levedi törzsszövétségétöl Szent István államaig* (Budapest, 1980), 11–150.

10. P. Heather, "Frankish imperialism and Slavic society," in *Origins of Central Europe*, ed. P. Urbańczyk (Warsaw, 1997), 171–90.

11. W. Pohl, "The role of the steppe peoples in Eastern and central Europe in the first millennium A.D.," in *Origins of Central Europe*, ed. P. Urbańczyk (Warsaw, 1997), 65–78.

12. Likhachev and Dmitriev, *Pamiatniki*, 38–41. See also M. Font, *Oroszország, Ukrajna, Rusz* (Budapest and Pécs, 1998), 26–31.

13. Likhachev and Dmitriev, *Pamiatniki*, 36–39. See also K. Zernack, "Fürst und Volk in der ostslavischen Frühzeit," *Forschungen zur osteuropäischen Geschichte* 18 (1973): 9–24.

14. O. Pritsak, *The Origin of Rus'* (Cambridge, Mass., 1981), 3–33.

15. Vásáry, "Nép és ország," 189–213.

16. Györffy, *Tanulmányok*, 44–77; G. Kristó, *A magyar állam megszületése* (Szeged, 1995), 287–97; S. L. Tóth, *Levediától a Kárpát-medencéig* (Szeged, 1998), 112–30.

17. K. Zernack, *Polen und Rußland: Zwei Wege in der europäischen Geschichte* (Berlin, 1994), 43–48.

18. I. H. Tóth, *Cirill-Konstantin élete és müködese* (Szeged, 1991); A. Avenarius, *Die byzantinische Kultur und die Slawen: Zum Problem der Rezeption und Transformation (6. bis 12. Jahrhundert)* (Vienna, 2000), 49–109, 150–76.

19. Cosmas of Prague, *Chronicle*, 22.

20. F. Grivec, *Konstantin und Method: Lehrer der Slaven* (Wiesbaden, 1960), 137–38; H. Birnbaum, "Zum (hoffentlich) letztenmal über den weitgereisten Method und die Lage Altmährens," *Byzantinoslavica* 57 (1996): 188–93; D. Třeštík, *Počatky Přemyslovců: Vstup čechu do dejin (530–935)* (Prague, 1997), 312–25.

21. Cosmas of Prague, *Chronicle*, 34–38. Thietmar of Merseburg places Wenceslas's death among the events of 937: "For the wicked Boleslav, having killed his brother Wenceslaus, Duke of the Bohemians and faithful to God and the king, remained full of pride for a long time. But afterwards, the king conquered him by force and placed him in the custody of his brother Henry, the Duke of the Bavarians." English translation by David A. Warner (Manchester and New York, 2001), 90. See Thietmar of Merseburg, *Chronicon*, ed. R. Holtzmann, MGH Scriptores, n.s., vol. 9 (Berlin, 1935; reprint, Munich, 1996), 39–40. The exact date of Wenceslas's martyrdom is September 28, 935.

22. Z. Fiala, "Die Organisation der Kirche im Přemyslidenstaat des 10.–13. Jh.," in *Siedlung und Verfassung Böhmens in der Frühzeit*, ed. F. Graus and H. Ludat (Wiesbaden, 1967), 133–43.

23. H. Mitteis, *The State in the Middle Ages: A Comparative Constitutional History of Feudal Europe* (New York, 1975), 365–66. R. Fletcher, *The Conversion of Europe: From Paganism to Christianity, 371–1386* (London, 1998), 323–25.

24. Cosmas of Prague, *Chronicle*, 49.

25. Thietmar of Merseburg, *Chronicon*, 196.

26. Lambert of Hersfeld, *Annales*, ed. O. Holder-Egger, MGH Scriptores rerum Germanicarum in usum scholarum, vol. 38 (Hanover, 1894; reprint, 1984), 46.

27. J. Fried, *Otto III. und Boleslaw Chrobry: Das Widmungsbild des Aachener Evangeliars, der Akt von Gnesen und das frühe polnische und ungarische Königtum; Eine Bildanalyse und ihre Folgen*, 2nd ed. (Stuttgart, 2001), 69–72.

28. K. Jasiński, *Rodowód pierwszych Piastów* (Warsaw and Wrocław, 1992), 82–94.

29. P. Schreiner, "Die byzantinische Missionierung als politische Aufgabe: Das Beispiel der Slaven," *Byzantinoslavica* 56 (1995): 525–33.

30. Szentpétery, *Scriptores Rerum Hungaricarum*, 2:473. See G. Moravcsik, "Byzance et le christianisme hongrois du Moyen Age," *Corso di cultura sull'arte ravennate e bizantina* 16 (1969): 313–41; G. Moravcsik, *Az Arpád-kori magyar történet bizánci forrásai* (Budapest, 1988), 85. For a different interpretation of this episode, see A. Madgearu's contribution in the present volume (chap. 3).

31. G. Györffy, *István király és müve* (Budapest, 1977) translated into English as *King Saint Stephen of Hungary* (Boulder, 1994), 61, 89; L. Koszta, "A kereszténység kezdetei Magyarországon," in *Az államalapitó*, ed. G. Kristó (Budapest, 1988), 153–207, esp. 167–68. See also L. Koszta, "A keresztény egyházszervezet kialakulása," in *Arpád elött és után: Tanulmányok a magyarság és hazája korai történetérol*, ed. G. Kristó and F. Makk (Szeged, 1996), 105–15.

32. Thietmar of Merseburg, *Chronicon*, 496–98. See Pohl, "The role of the steppe peoples," 74–75.

33. Györffy, *István király*, 67–81; Koszta, "A kereszténység kezdetei," 162.

34. For the history of Pannonhalma Abbey, see the studies published in I. Takács, ed., *Mons Sacer 996–1996 (Pannonhalma 1000 éve)*, vol. 1 (Pannonhalma, 1996).

35. Szentpétery, *Scriptores Rerum Hungaricarum*, 2:379. The wrong chronology appears in Pohl, "The role of the steppe peoples," 74–75.

36. G. Györffy, ed., *Diplomata Hungariae antiquissima, accedunt epistolae et acta ad Hungariae pertinentia* (Budapest, 1992), 52–53, 58, 60–61.

37. K. Görich, *Otto III., Romanus, Saxonicus et Italicus: Kaiserliche Rompolitik und sächsische Historiographie* (Sigmaringen, 1995).

38. I. H. Tóth, "A magyarok és szlávok a 9–11. században," in *Arpád elott és után: Tanulmányok a magyarság és hazája korai történetérol*, ed. G. Kristó and F. Makk (Szeged, 1996), 75–84, esp. 79–80; I. Baán, "'Turkia metropolitája': Ujabb adalék a bizánci egyház történetéhez a középkori Magyarországon," *Századok* 129 (1995): 1167–70. See also I. Baán, "The metropolitanate of Tourkia: The organization of the Byzantine church in Hungary in the Middle Ages," in *Byzanz und Ostmitteleuropa, 950–1453: Beiträge zu einer table-ronde des XIX Internationalen Congress of Byzantine Studies, Copenhagen 1996*, ed. G. Prinzing and M. Salamon (Wiesbaden, 1999), 45–53.

39. A. Poppe, *The Rise of Christian Russia* (London, 1982); L. Müller, *Die Taufe Russlands: Die Frühgeschichte des russischen Christentums bis zum Jahre 988* (Munich, 1987); V. Vodoff, *La naissance de la chrétienté russe: La conversion du prince Vladimir de Kiev (988) et ses conséquences (XIe–XIIIe siècles)* (Paris, 1988). See also John Fennell, *A History of the Russian Church to 1448* (London and New York, 1995).

40. Likhachev and Dmitriev, *Pamiatniki*, 124–37.

41. H. Keller, "Das Kaisertum Ottos des Grossen im Verständnis seiner Zeit," in *Otto der Grosse*, ed. H. Zimmermann (Darmstadt, 1976), 208, 277.

42. Thietmar of Merseburg, *Chronicon*, 476 (Thietmar calls Vladimir's wife "Helena").

43. F. A. Gombos, ed., *Catalogus fontium historiae Hungaricae aevo ducum et regum ex stirpe Arpad descendentium*, vol. 1 (Budapest, 1937), 429–30.

44. Třeštík, *Počatky Přemyslovců*, 137. For Sázava, see K. Reichertová, E. Bláhová, V. Dvoráková, and V. Hunácek, *Sázava: Památnik staroslovenské kultury v čechách* (Prague, 1988).

45. B. Stasiewski, "Zur Verbreitung des slavischen Ritus in Südpolen während des 10. Jh.," *Forschungen zur osteuropäischen Geschichte* 7 (1959): 7–25.

46. M. Font, "Magyarok és keleti szlávok: Adalékok a kapcsolatok egyháztörténeti hátteréhez," in *A magyar müvelödés és a kereszténység: A IV Nemzetközi Hungarológiai Kongresszus elöadásai, Róma-Nápolyi, 1996, szeptember 9–14*, ed. J. Jankovics (Budapest, 1998), 497–506.

47. E. P. Schramm, *Kaiser, Könige und Päpste: Gesammelte Aufsätze zur Geschichte des Mittelalters* (Stuttgart, 1971), 3:81–87, 175; 4:130–32.

48. Görich, *Otto III*, 187–261.

49. Schramm, *Kaiser, Könige und Päpste*, 3:166.

50. Thietmar of Merseburg, *Chronicon*, 184, 241.

51. Jasiński, *Rodowód*, 82–83.

52. G. Székely, "Koronaküldések és királykreálások a 10–11. századi Európában," *Századok* 116 (1984): 905–49, esp. 918–19.

53. Györffy, *István kiraly*, 150–51; J. Gerics and E. Ladanyi, "A Szentszék és a magyar állam a 11. században," in *Magyarország és a Szentszék kapcsolatának ezer éve*, ed. I. Zombori (Budapest, 1996), 9–20.

54. J. Martin, *Medieval Russia, 980–1584* (Cambridge, 1995), 247.

55. Likhachev and Dmitriev, *Pamiatniki*, 168–69.

56. Cosmas of Prague, *Chronicle*, 175, 185, 197.

57. M. N. Tikhomirov, ed., *Polnoe sobranie russkikh letopisei*, vol. 2 (Moscow, 1962), 321, 327, 478.

58. R. Schmidt, "Die Einsetzung der böhmischen Herzöge auf den Thron zu Prag," in *Aspekte der Nationenbildung im Mittelalter: Ergebnisse der Marburger Rundgespräche 1972–1975*, ed. H. Beumann and W. Schröder (Sigmaringen, 1978), 439–64, esp. 439.

59. W. Maisel, *Rechtsarchäologie Europas* (Vienna, 1992), 6–10; J. Peddie, *Alfred the Warrior King* (Stroud, 1999), 17; W. A. Chaney, *The Cult of Kingship in Anglo-Saxon England: The Transition from Paganism to Christianity* (Berkeley, 1970), 135–37; P. Gerber, *Stone of Destiny* (Edinburgh, 1997), 174–81.

60. Gerber, *Stone of Destiny*, 13, 22–27. In many cases, both traditions—tribal and imperial—were blended, as illustrated by Charlemagne's stone throne in Aachen or the Stone of Scone in Scotland.

The History and Archaeology of Early Medieval Eastern and East Central Europe (ca. 500–1000): A Bibliography

Florin Curta

*A*lmost all important works on early medieval Eastern and East Central Europe were written in languages other than English. But there is also a significant number of articles and chapters in collections of studies, often English translations of the same texts previously published in one East European language or another. Most authors preferred, however, to have their work translated into either German or French. The number of works originally published in English by authors based in Eastern Europe is comparatively smaller. The main goal of this bibliography, therefore, is to bring together works that appeared in various publications, some of which are not readily accessible to the English-speaking reader. The bibliography covers the period between 1900 and 2004.

HISTORIOGRAPHY AND BIBLIOGRAPHIES

Avenarius, Alexander. 1995. "Historiography in Slovakia: The pre-Hungarian period, first to ninth century." In *A Guide to Historiography in Slovakia*, ed. Elena Mannova and David P. Daniel, 45–58. Bratislava: Historicky ústav Slovenskej Akadémie Vied.

Bubeník, Josef. 1991. "The archaeology of the early Middle Ages (6th–12th centuries): On the present state of early medieval archaeology in Bohemia." In *Archaeology in Bohemia, 1986–1990*, ed. Pavel Vareka, 27–34. Prague: Institute of Archaeology of the Czechoslovak Academy of Sciences.

Čurčić, Slobodan. 1984. *Art and Architecture in the Balkans: An Annotated Bibliography.* Boston: G. K. Hall.

Klapšte, Jan. 1994. "The development of medieval archaeological research in the Prague Archaeological Institute (1969–1993)." In *25 Years of Archaeological Research in Bohemia*, ed. Jan Fridrich, 103–32. Prague: Institute of Achaeology of the Czechoslovak Academy of Sciences.

Marsina, Richard. 1995. "Slovak historiography on the Middle Ages: Early tenth to the early sixteenth century." In *A Guide to Historiography in Slovakia*, ed. Elena Mannova and David P. Daniel, 59–75. Bratislava: Historicky ústav Slovenskej Akadémie Vied.

Richter, Miroslav, and Zdeněk Smetánka. 1970. "Medieval archaeology in Bohemia: The concepts and results." In *Actes du VIIe Congrès international des sciences préhistoriques et protohistoriques*, ed. Jan Filip, 1:94–96. Prague: Academia.

———. 1991. "Medieval archaeology, 1986–1990 (traditions and a perspective)." In *Archaeology in Bohemia, 1986–1990*, ed. Pavel Vařeka, 44–55. Prague: Institute of Archaeology of the Czechoslovak Academy of Sciences.

Šekeli Ivančan, Tatiana. 1995. *Catalogue of Medieval Sites in Continental Croatia*. Oxford: Tempus Reparatum.

EXHIBITION CATALOGUES

Camber, Richard, ed. 1975. *Treasures from Romania*. London: Trustees of the British Museum.

Fodor, István, ed. 1996. *The Ancient Hungarians: Exhibition Catalogue*. Budapest: Hungarian National Museum.

Jaskanis, Danuta, and Marian Kachinski, eds. 1981. *The Balts: The Northern Neighbours of the Slavs*. Warsaw: Ministry of Art and Culture in the Polish People's Republic.

PRIMARY SOURCES IN ENGLISH TRANSLATION

Blockley, R. C., ed. and trans. 1985. *The History of Menander the Guardsman*. Liverpool: F. Cairns.

Butler, Thomas, ed. 1996. *Monumenta Bulgarica: A Bilingual Anthology of Bulgarian Texts from the 9th to the 19th Centuries*. Ann Arbor: Michigan Slavic Publications.

Cross, Samuel Hazzard, and Olgerd P. Sherbowitz-Wetzor, trans. 1953. *The Russian Primary Chronicle: Laurentian Text*. Cambridge, Mass.: Medieval Academy of America.

Dennis, George T., trans. 1984. *Maurice's Strategikon: Handbook of Byzantine Military Strategy*. Philadelphia: University of Philadelphia Press.

———. 1985. *Three Byzantine Military Treatises*. Washington D.C.: Dumbarton Oaks Research Library and Collection.

Dewey, Horace Williams, and Ann M. Kleimola, eds. and trans. 1977. *Zakon sudnyi liudem: Court Law for the People*. Ann Arbor: Department of Slavic Languages and Literatures, University of Michigan.

Duichev, Ivan. 1985. *Kiril and Methodius, Founders of Slavonic Writing: A Collection of Sources and Critical Studies*. Boulder and New York: Columbia University Press.

Foulke, William D., trans. 1974. *Paul the Deacon: "History of the Lombards."* Philadelphia: University of Pennsylvania Press.

Golb, Norman, and Omeljan Pritsak, eds. and trans. 1982. *Khazarian Hebrew Documents of the Tenth Century*. Ithaca: Cornell University Press.

Jenkins, Romilly J. H., trans. 1967. *Constantine Porphyrogenitus' "De Administrando Imperio."* Washington, D.C.: Dumbarton Oaks Center for Byzantine Studies.

Kaiser, Daniel H. 1992, ed. and trans. *The Laws of Rus', Tenth to Fifteenth Centuries*. Salt Lake City: C. Schlacks.

Kantor, Marvin, trans. 1983. *Medieval Slavic Lives of Saints and Princes*. Ann Arbor: Department of Slavic Languages and Literatures, University of Michigan.

————. 1990. *The Origins of Christianity in Bohemia: Sources and Commentary.* Evanston: Northwestern University Press.

Mango, Cyril, trans. 1958. *The Homilies of Photius, Patriarch of Constantinople.* Cambridge: Harvard University Press.

————. 1990. *Nikephoros, Patriarch of Constantinople: Short History.* Washington D.C.: Dumbarton Oaks Research Library and Collection.

————. 1997. *The Chronicle of Theophanes Confessor: Byzantine and Near Eastern History, AD 284–813.* Oxford: Clarendon Press.

McKeithen, James E. 1979. "The Risalah of Ibn Fadlan: An annotated translation with introduction." PhD diss., Indiana University.

Melovski, H., and N. Proeva. 1987. "Macedonia in the "De Thematibus" of Constantine VII Porphyrogenitus: A translation with commentary of selected passages." *Živa Antika* 37:19–37.

Nelson, Janet T., trans. 1991. *The Annals of St-Bertin.* Manchester: Manchester University Press.

Perfecky, George A. 1973. *The Hypatian Codex II: The Galician-Volynian Chronicle.* Munich: W. Fink.

Reuter, Timothy, trans. 1992. *The Annals of Fulda.* Manchester: Manchester University Press.

Rogers, Barbara, trans. 1970. *Carolingian Chronicles: Royal Frankish Annals and Nithard's Histories.* Ann Arbor: University of Michigan Press.

Scott, Stephen Neil. 1989. "The collapse of the Moravian mission of Saints Cyril and Methodius, the fate of their disciples, and the Christianization of the southern Slavs: Translations of five historical texts with notes and commentary." Ph.D. diss., University of California, Berkeley.

Thomson, Robert, et al., trans. 1999. *The American History Attributed to Sebeos.* Liverpool: Liverpool University Press.

Tsamakda, Vasiliki, ed. and trans. 2002. *The Illustrated Chronicle of Ioannes Skylitzes in Madrid.* Leiden: Alexandros Press.

Wallace-Hadrill, J. M., ed. and trans. 1960. *The Fourth Book of the Chronicle of Fredegar with its Continuations.* London and Edinburgh: Thomas Nelson and Sons.

Warner, David, trans. 2001. *Ottonian Germany: The Chronicon of Thietmar of Merseburg.* Manchester: Manchester University Press.

Westerink, L. G., trans. 1973. *Nicholas I, Patriarch of Constantinople: Letters.* Washington D.C.: Dumbarton Oaks Center for Byzantine Studies.

Whitby, Michael, and Mary Whitby. 1986. *The History of Theophylact Simocatta: An English Translation with Introduction and Notes.* Oxford: Clarendon Press.

————. 1989. *Chronicon Paschale, 284–628 AD.* Liverpool: Liverpool University Press.

GENERAL HISTORY

Alexander, Eugene M. 1994. "Early Slavic invasions and settlements in the area of the lower Danube in the sixth through the eighth centuries." Ph.D. diss., New York University.

Altankov, Nikolai G. 1992. "The Balkans in the seventh century: An ethnic approach." In *Scholar, Patriot, Mentor: Historical Essays in Honor of Dimitrije Djordjević,* ed. Richard B. Spence and Linda L. Nelson, 35–50. Boulder: East European Monographs.

Ančić, Mladen. 1997. "From the Carolingian official to the ruler of the Croats. Croats and the Carolingian Empire in the first half of the 9th century." *Hortium Artium Medievalium* 3:7–13.

———. 1998. "The waning of the Empire. The disintegration of Byzantine rule on the Eastern Adriatic in the 9th century." *Hortium Artium Medievalium* 4:15–24.

Angelov, Petăr D. 1994. "The Bulgarians through the eyes of the Byzantines." *Bulgarian Historical Review* 22:18–32.

Anna, Luigi de. 1992. "The peoples of Finland and early medieval sources: The characterization of 'alienness.'" In *Suomen varhaishistoria: Tornion kongressi 14.–16.6.1991*, ed. Kyösti Julku and Markus H. Korhonen, 11–22. Rovaniemi: Pohjois-Suomen Historiallinen Yhdistys.

Antoljak, Stjepan. 1986. "Military and administrative organization of the Macedonian Sclavenes." *Macedonian Review* 16:275–79.

———. 1988. "Internal conditions during Samuel's rule." *Macedonian Review* 18:213–32.

Antoniewicz, Jerzy. 1970. "Studies of the Balto-Slavonic contacts in the 6th–8th centuries in northern Poland." In *Studia archaeologica in memoriam Harri Moora*, ed. M. Schmiedehelm, L. Jaanits, and J. Selirand, 45–49. Tallinn: Kirjastus "Valgus."

Antonopoulos, P. T. 1993. "Byzantium, the Magyar raids, and their consequences." *Byzantinoslavica* 54:254–67.

Bačić, Jakov. 1983. "The emergence of Sklabenoi (Slavs), their arrival on the Balkan Peninsula, and the role of the Avars in these events: Revised concepts in a new perspective." Ph.D. diss., Columbia University, New York.

Bakay, Kornél. 1994. "Hungary in the tenth and eleventh centuries." In *Sacra Corona Hungariae*, ed. K. Bakay, 3–82. Köszeg: Városi Múzeum.

———. 1999. "Hungary." In *The New Cambridge Medieval History*, ed. Timothy Reuter, 3:536–52. Cambridge: Cambridge University Press.

Bakirtzis, Charalambos. 1994. "Byzantine Thrace (AD 330–1453)." In *Thrace*, ed. Vasiliki Papoulia, Michael Meraklis, Charalambos Symeonidis, et al., 151–210. Athens: General Secretariat of the Region of East Macedonia-Thrace.

Báko, Geza. 1975. "The relations of the principality of Banat with the Hungarians and the Petchenegs in the 10th century." In *Relations between the Autochthonous Population and the Migratory Populations on the Territory of Romania*, ed. Miron Constantinescu, Ştefan Pascu, and Petre Diaconu, 241–48. Bucharest: Editura Academiei Republic Socialiste România.

Bálint, Csanád. 1989. "Some ethnospecific features in central and Eastern European archaeology during the Middle Ages: The case of Avars and Hungarians." In *Archaeological Approaches to Cultural Identity*, ed. Stephen Shennan, 185–94. London: Unwin Hyman.

———. 2000. "The Carpathian Basin from the conquest to statehood." In *Europe's Centre around A.D. 1000*, ed. Alfried Wieczorek and Hans-Martin Hinz, 361–67. Stuttgart: Theiss.

Baran, Volodymyr. 1998. "The Veneti, Sclaveni, and Antae in the light of archaeology." *Ukrainian Review* 45:49–63.

Barford, Paul. 2001. *The Early Slavs: Culture and Society in Early Medieval Eastern Europe.* London: British Museum; Ithaca: Cornell University Press.

Bárkoczi, L., and A. Salamon. 1971. "Remarks on the 6th century history of 'Pannonia.'" *Acta Archaeologica Academiae Scientiarum Hungaricae* 23:139–53.

Bartha, Antál. 1975. *Hungarian Society in the 9th and 10th Centuries.* Budapest: Akademiai Kiadó.

Belke, K. 2002. "Roads and travel in Macedonia and Thrace in the middle and late Byzantine period." In *Travel in the Byzantine World: Papers from the Thirty-Fourth Spring Symposium of Byzantine Studies, Birmigham, April 2000,* ed. Ruth Macrides, 73–90. Aldershot and Burlington: Ashgate.

Beranová, M., Z. Váňa, and Z. Krumphanzlová. 1991. "Bohemia in the 6th–12th centuries." In *Archaeology in Bohemia, 1986–1990,* ed. Pavel Vaŕeka, 35–43. Prague: Institute of Archaeology of the Czechoslovak Academy of Sciences.

Bialeková, Darina. 1999. "Beginnings of contacts of Moravian Slavs with the Carolingian world." In *Thessaloniki Magna Moravia,* 133–48. Thessaloniki: SS. Cyril and Methodios Center for Cultural Studies.

Birnbaum, Henrik. 1989. "Was there a Slavic landtaking of the Balkans and, if so, along what routes did it proceed?" In *Migrations in Balkan History,* ed. Ivan Ninić, 47–60. Belgrade: Srpska Akademija Nauka i Umetnosti.

———. 1992. "The Slavic settlements in the Balkans and the Eastern Alps." In *Byzantine Studies: Essays on the Slavic World and the Eleventh Century,* ed. Spcros Jr. Vryonis, 1–13. New Rochelle, N.Y.: Aristide D. Caratzas.

———. 1993. "The location of the Moravian state—revisited." *Byzantinoslavica* 54:336–38.

———. 1993. "Where was the centre of the Moravian state?" In *American Contributions to the Eleventh International Congress of Slavists. Bratislava, August–September 1993. Literature, Linguistics, Poetics,* ed. Robert A. Maguire and Alan Timberlake, 11–24. Columbus, OH: Slavica.

———. 1995–96. "How did Glagolitic writing reach the coastal regions of Croatia." *Croatica* 42–44:69–79.

———. 1997–99. "Some remaining puzzles in Cyrillo-Methodian studies." *Slovo* 47–49:7–32.

———. 1999. "Where was the missionary field of SS. Cyril and Methodius?" In *Thessaloniki Magna Moravia,* 47–52. Thessaloniki: SS. Cyril and Methodios Center for Cultural Studies.

Blindheim, Ch. 1970. "Discussion continued from volume 2, Comments on Daniil Avdusin: Smolensk and the Varangians according to the archaeological data." *Norwegian Archaeological Review* 3:113–15.

Blum, Jerome. 1961. *Lord and Peasant in Russia from the Ninth to the Nineteenth Century.* Princeton: Princeton University Press.

Blumfeldt, Evald. 1954. "Estonian-Russian relations from the IX–XIII century." In *Charisteria Iohanni Kopp octogenario oblata,* ed. Arthur Voobus, 200–222. Holm: Estonian Theological Society in Exile.

Boba, Imre. 1967. *Nomads, Northmen, and Slavs: Eastern Europe in the Ninth Century.* The Hague: Mouton; Wiesbaden: Harrassowitz.

———. 1971. *Moravia's History Reconsidered. A Reinterpretation of Medieval Sources.* The Hague: Martinus Nijhoff.

———. 1971. "Payment of tribute and political structure of early Rus." In *Actes due VIIe Congrès international des sciences préhistoriques et protohistoriques, Prague, 21–27 août 1966,* ed. Jan Filip, 2:1076–78. Prague: Academia.

———. 1973. "Methodian and Moravian continuity and tradition in Poland." In *VII*

Międzynarodowy kongres sławistów, Warszawa, 21–27 VIII 1973: Streszczenia refer-atów i komunikatów, ed. Witold Doroszewski, 969–71. Warsaw: Państwowe Wydawnictwo Naukowe.

———. 1982. "'Caranthani Marahenses' and 'Moravi sive Karinthi.'" *Slovene Studies* 4:83–90.

———. 1982–83. "A twofold conquest of Hungary or 'secundus ingressus.'" *Ungarn-Jahrbuch* 12:23–41.

———. 1983. "The Pannonian Onogurs, Khan Krum, and the formation of the Bulgarian and Hungarian polities." *Bulgarian Historical Review* 11:73–76.

———. 1984. "'Abodriti quae vulgo Praedenecenti vocantur' or 'Marvani Praedenecenti'?" *Palaeobulgarica* 8:29–37.

———. 1987. "Moravia, Bulgaria, 'Messiani,' and 'Sclavi' in medieval Hungarian sources." In *Vtori mezhdunaroden kongres po bălgaristika, Sofiia, 23 mai–3 iuni 1986 g. Dokladi 6: Bălgarskite zemi v drevnostta Bălgariia prez srednovekovieto,* ed. Khristo Khristov, Pantelei Zarev, Vladimir Georgiev, et al., 709–26. Sofia: Izdatelstvo na Bălgarskata Akademiia na Naukite.

———. 1987. "Saint Methodius, Moesia, and the Moesiani in documents, vitae and in chronicles." *Kirilo-metodievski studii* 4:138–47.

———. 1987. "Transylvania and Hungary: From the times of Almos and Arpad to the times of King Stephen." *Forschungen über Siebenbürgen und seine Nachbarn* 1:17–32.

———. 1991. "The federal structure of the earliest Hungarian polity: The role of the 'Covenant of Blood.'" *Ural-altaische Jahrbücher* 63:99–122.

———. 1996. "Three papers to the prehistory of the Hungarians." *Eurasian Studies Yearbook* 68:189–202.

Bogdanova, N. M. 1996. "Cherson in the tenth–fifteenth centuries: History of a Byzantine provincial city." In *Acts. XVIIIth International Congress of Byzantine Studies: Selected papers,* ed. Ihor Ševčenko, Gennadi G. Litavrin, and Walter K. Hanak, 1:72–76. Shepherdstown, W.V.: Byzantine Studies Press.

Boldur, Alexandru V. 1968. "The enigma of the Ulichy-Tivertsy people." *Balkan Studies* 9:55–90.

Bóna, István. 1976. *The Dawn of the Dark Ages: The Gepids and the Lombards in the Carpathian Basin.* Budapest: Corvina.

———. 1990. "Byzantium and the Avars: The archaeology of the first 70 years of the Avar era." In *From the Baltic to the Black Sea: Studies in Medieval Archaeology,* ed. David Austin and Leslie Alcock, 113–18. London: Unwin Hyman.

———. 1994. "The Hungarian-Slav period (895–1172)." In *History of Transylvania,* ed. Béla Köpeczi, 109–77. Budapest: Akadémiai Kiadó.

———. 2000. "Hungarian military tactics in the raids on Europe." In *Europe's Centre around A.D. 1000,* ed. Alfried Wieczorek and Hans-Martin Hinz, 145–49. Stuttgart: Theiss.

———. 2001. "From Dacia to Erdöelve: Transylvania in the period of the Great Migrations (271–896)." In *History of Transylvania,* ed. László Makkai and András Mócsy. Vol. 1, 139–329. New York: Columbia University Press.

Bowlus, Charles R. 1985. "Prosopographical evidence concerning Moravia's location." *Medieval Prosopography* 6:1–21.

———. 1987. "Imre Boba's reconsiderations of Moravia's early history and Arnulf of Carinthia's Ostpolitik (887–892)." *Speculum* 62:552–74.

————. 1995. *Franks, Moravians, and Magyars: The Struggle for the Middle Danube, 788–907.* Philadelphia: University of Pennsylvania Press.

————. 1998. "Archbishop Theotmar of Salzburg's letter to Pope John IX: A forgery of Bishop Pilgrim of Passau?" *Südost-Froschungen* 57:1–11.

————. 1999. "Frankish-Moravian conflicts in the ninth century: A turning point in the history of the Carpathian Basin." In *Thessaloniki Magna Moravia,* 53–63. Thessaloniki: SS. Cyril and Methodios Center for Cultural Studies.

————. 2001. "Carolingian military hegemony in the Carpathian Basin, 791–907." In *Karl der Große und das Erbe der Kulturen: Akten des 8. Symposiums des Mediävistenverbandes, Leipzig, 15.–18. März 1999,* ed. Franz-Reiner Erkens, 153–58. Berlin: Akademie Verlag.

————. 2002. "Italia-Bavaria-Avaria: The grand strategy behind Charlemagne's *renovatio imperii* in the West." In *The Journal of Medieval Military History,* ed. Bernard Bachrach, Clifford J. Rogers, and Kelly DeVries, 1:43–60. Woodsworth: Boydell Press.

Boyle, Leonard E. 1988. "The site of the tomb of St. Cyril in the lower basilica of San Clemente, Rome." In *Christianity among the Slavs: The heritage of the Saints Cyril and Methodius; Acts of the International Congress Held on the Eleventh Centenary of the Death of St. Methodius, Rome, October 8–11, 1985,* ed. Edward G. Farrugia, Robert Taft, and Gino Piovesana, 75–82. Rome: Pontificium Institutum Studiorum Orientaliorum.

Bozhilov, Ivan. 1978. "Hase's Anonym and Ihor Ševčenko's hypothesis." *Byzantinobulgarica* 5:245–59.

Brachmann, Hansjürgen. 1997. "Tribal organizations in central Europe in the 6th–10th centuries A.D.: Reflections on the ethnic and political development in the second half of the first millenium." In *Origins of Central Europe,* ed. Przemysław Urbańczyk, 23–37. Warsaw: Scientific Society of Polish Archaeologists.

Browning, Robert. 1975. *Byzantium and Bulgaria: A Comparative Study across the Early Medieval Frontier.* Berkeley: University of California Press.

————. 1986. "Byzantine foreign policy and the Bulgarian state, seventh to tenth century." In *Studies in Honour of T. B. L. Webster,* ed. J. H. Betts, J. T. Hooker, and J. R. Green, 1:23–32. Bristol: Bristol Classical Press.

————. 1988. "Byzantines in Bulgaria (late 8th–early 9th c.)." In *Issledovaniia po slaviano-vizantiiskomu i zapadnoevropeiskomu srednevekov'iu: Posviashchaetsia pamiati Ivana Duicheva,* ed. Petar Dinekov, Aksinia Dzhurova, Georgi Bakalov, et al., 32–36. Sofia: Centăr dlia slaviano-vizantiiskikh issledovanii imeni Ivana Duicheva and Gosudarstvennoe izdatelstvo imeni D-ra Petra Berona.

Buko, Andrzej. 2002. "From Great Poland to the Little Poland: The Ruling Piast dynasty and the processes of creating the regions." In *Centre, Region, Periphery: Medieval Europe, Basel 2002,* ed. Guido Helmig, Barbara Scholkmann, and Matthias Untermann, 468–73. Hertingen: Folio Verlag Dr. G. Wesselkamp; Basel: Archäologische Bodenforschung Basel-Stadt.

Callmer, Johan. 1992. "Interaction between ethical groups in the Baltic region in the late Iron Age." In *Contacts across the Baltic Sea during the Late Iron Age (5th–12th Centuries): Baltic Sea Conference, Lund, October 25–27, 1991,* ed. Brigitte Hardh and Bozena Wyszomirska-Werbart, 99–107. Lund: Institute of Archaeology and Historical Museum.

————. 1996. "Oriental beads and Europe, A.D. 600–800." In *Rome and the North,* ed. Alvar Ellgård and Gunilla Åkerström-Hougen, 53–71. Jonsered: Paul Åströms Förlag.

Cankova-Petkova, Genoveva. 1963. "Bulgarians and Byzantium during the first decades after the foundation of the Bulgarian state." *Byzantinoslavica* 24:41–53.

Cansdale, Lena. 1997–98. "Vikings by boat to Byzantium." *Acta Byzantina Fennica* 9:9–20.

Čaplovič, Dušan. 1997. "Central Europe in the 8th–10th centuries (introductory remarks of the editor)." In *Central Europe in 8th–10th Centuries: International Scientific Conference, Bratislava October 2–4, 1995,* ed. Dušan Čaplovič and Ján Dorul'a, 7–14. Bratislava: Ministry of Culture in the Slovak Republic and Slovak Academy of Sciences.

————. 2000. "The area of Slovakia in the 10th century: Development of settlement, interethnic, and acculturation processes (focused on the area of northern Slovakia)." In *The Neighbors of Poland in the 10th Century,* ed. Przemysław Urbańczyk, 147–56. Warsaw: Institute of Archaeology and Ethnology.

Carile, Antonio. 1988–89. "Byzantine political ideology and the Rus' in the tenth–twelfth centuries." *Harvard Ukrainian Studies* 12–13:400–413.

Carne, Simon Roger. 1996. "Representing the migration period: Stories of the Hungarian conquest." Ph.D. diss., University of Southern California, San Diego.

Carter, F. W. 1998. "Central Dalmatia in Balkan historical geography: Evidence from a frontier region." In *Istorike geografia: Dromoi kai komboi tes Balkanikes apo ten Arkhaioteta sten eniaia Europe,* ed. E. P. Demetriades, A. Ph. Lagopoulos, and G. Tsotsos, 57–66. Thessaloniki: Tmema arkhitektonon, Aristoteleio Panepistemio Thessalonikes.

Charanis, Peter. 1970. "Kouver, the chronology of his activities, and their ethnic effects on the regions around Thessalonica." *Balkan Studies* 11:1–34.

————. 1976. "The Slavs, Byzantium, and the historical significance of the first Bulgarian kingdom." *Balkan Studies* 17:5–24.

Chekin, L. S. 1990. "The role of Jews in early Russian civilization in the light of a new discovery and new controversies." *Russian History* 17:379–94.

————. 1997. "Christian of Stavelot and the conversion of Gog and Magog: A study of the ninth-century reference to Judaism among the Khazars." *Russia mediaevalis* 9:13–34.

Cheshmedzhiev, Dimo. 1997. "On the question of the localization of the Slav tribe Smoljani." *Bulgarian Historical Review* 25:89–93.

Chodor, Joanna. 1993–96. "Queens in early medieval chronicles of East Central Europe." *East Central Europe* 20–23:9–50.

Chorovich, Vladimir. 1990. "The state of the Macedonian Slavs." *Macedonian Review* 20:5–18.

Christie, Neil. 1995. *The Lombards: The Ancient Longobards.* Oxford and Cambridge: Blackwell.

Chropovský, Bohuslav. 1989. *The Slavs: Their Significance; Political and Cultural History.* Prague: Orbis.

Čilinská, Zlata. 1983. "The development of the Slavs north of the Danube during the Avar empire and their social-cultural contribution to Great Moravia." *Slovenská Archeológia* 31:237–76.

Cross, Samuel Hazzard. 1948. *Slavic Civilization through the Ages.* Cambridge: Harvard University Press.

Curta, Florin. 1997. "Slavs in Fredegar and Paul the Deacon: Medieval 'gens' or 'scourge of God'?" *Early Medieval Europe* 6:141–67.

———. 1998. "Making an early medieval 'ethnie': The case of the early Slavs (sixth to seventh century A.D.)." Ph.D. diss., Western Michigan University, Kalamazoo.

———. 1999. "Hiding behind a piece of tapestry: Jordanes and the Slavic Venethi." *Jahrbücher für Geschichte Osteuropas* 47:1–18.

———. 2001. *The Making of the Slavs: History and Archaeology of the Lower Danube Region, c. 500–700.* Cambridge and New York: Cambridge University Press.

———. 2001. "Transylvania around A.D. 1000." In *Europe around the Year 1000,* ed. Przemysław Urbańczyk, 141–65. Warsaw: Wydawnictwo DiG.

———. 2004. "Barbarians in Dark-Age Greece: Slavs or Avars?" In *Civitas divino-humana. V chest na profesor Georgi Bakalov,* ed. Tsvetelin Stepanov and Veselina Vachkova, 513–50. Sofia: Centăr za izsledvaniia na bălgarite Tangra TanNakRa IK.

Daim, Falko. 1998. "Archaeology, ethnicity, and the structures of identification: The example of the Avars, Carantanians, and Moravians in the eighth century." In *Strategies of Distinction: The Construction of Ethnic Communities, 300–800,* ed. Walter Pohl and Helmut Reimitz, 71–94. Leyden, Boston, and Cologne: Brill.

Deievskii, N. I. 1977. "Novgorod: The origins of a Russian town." In *European Towns: Their Archaeology and Early History,* ed. M. W. Barley, 391–403. London, New York, and San Francisco: Academic Press for the Council for British Archaeology.

———. 1977. "Novgorod in the early Middle Ages: The rise and growth of an urban community." Ph.D. diss., University of Oxford.

———. 1977. "The Varangians in Soviet archaeology." *Mediaeval Scandinavia* 10:7–34.

Deletant, Dennis. 1991. *Studies in Romanian History.* Bucharest: Editura Enciclopedică.

Diaconu, Petre. 1975. "The Petchenegs on the lower Danube." In *Relations between the Autochthonous Population and the Migratory Populations on the Territory of Romania,* ed. Miron Constantinescu, Ştefan Pascu, and Petre Diaconu, 235–40. Bucharest: Editura Academiei Republicü Socialiste România.

Dimitrov, Hristo. 1986. "Bulgaria and the Magyars at the beginning of the 10th century." *Etudes Balkaniques* 22:61–77.

Dinekov, Petăr. 1981. "Bulgaria: Center of Old Slavic culture." *Southeastern Europe* 8:40–47.

Djilas, Aleksa. 1985. "The foundations of Croatian identity: A sketch for historical reinterpretation." *South Slav Journal* 8:1–12.

Dolukhanov, Pavel M. 1996. *The Early Slavs: Eastern Europe from the Initial Settlement to the Kievan Rus.* London and New York: Longman.

Donat, I. 1975. "The Romanians south of the Carpathians and the migratory peoples in the 10th–13th centuries." In *Relations between the Autochthonous Population and the Migratory Populations on the Territory of Romania,* ed. Miron Constantinescu, Ştefan Pascu, and Petre Diaconu, 277–98. Bucharest: Editura Academiei Republicü Socialiste România.

Dubov, I. V. 1984. "Finno-Ugrians and Slavs of the Yaroslavl area on the Volga: Exchange and cultural traditions." In *Fenno-Ugri e Slavi 1983: Papers Presented by the Participants in the Soviet-Finnish Symposium "Trade, Exchange, and Culture Relations of the Peoples of Fennoscandia and Eastern Europe," 9–13 May 1983, in the Hanasaari Congress Center,* ed. Torsten Edgren, 169–73. Helsinki: Vammala.

Duczko, Władysław. 1997. "Real and imaginary contributions of Poland and Rus to the conversion of Sweden." In *Early Christianity in Central and Eastern Europe,* ed. Przemysław Urbańczyk, 129–35. Warsaw: Semper.

———. 1997. "Scandinavians in the southern Baltic between the 5th and the 10th centuries A.D." In *Origins of Central Europe,* ed. Przemysław Urbańczyk, 191–211. Warsaw: Scientific Society of Polish Archaeologists.

Dusa, J. 1991. *The Medieval Dalmatian Episcopal Cities: Development and Transformation.* New York: Peter Lang.

Dvoichenko-Markov, Demetrius. 1984. "The Vlachs: The Latin speaking population of Eastern Europe." *Byzantion* 54:508–26.

Dvornik, Francis. 1949. *The Making of Central and Eastern Europe.* London: Polish Research Centre.

———. 1956. *The Slavs: Their Early History and Civilization.* Boston: American Academy of Arts and Sciences.

———. 1964. "Byzantium, Rome, the Franks, and the Christianization of the Southern Slavs." In *Cyrillo-Methodiana. Zur Frühgeschichte des Christentum bei den Slaven, 863–1963,* ed. Manfred Hellmann, R. Olesch, B. Stasiewski, and F. Zagiba, 85–125. Cologne and Graz: Böhlau.

Eggers, Martin. 1999. "The historical-geographical implications of the Cyrillo-Methodian mission among the Slavs." In *Thessaloniki Magna Moravia,* 65–86. Thessaloniki: SS. Cyril and Methodios Center for Cultural Studies.

Engel, Pál. 2000. "The house of Arpád and its times." *Hungarian Quarterly* 41:74–79.

———. 2001. *The Realm of St. Stephen: A History of Medieval Hungary, 895–1526.* London and New York: I. B. Tauris.

Featherstone, Michael. 1990. "Olga's visit to Constantinople." *Harvard Ukrainian Studies* 14:293–312.

———. 2003. "Olga's visit to Constantinople in *De Ceremoniis.*" *Revue des Etudes Byzantines* 61:241–51.

Ferluga, Jadran. 1976. *Byzantium on the Balkans: Studies on the Byzantine Administration and the Southern Slavs from the VIIth to the XIIth Centuries.* Amsterdam: Adolf M. Hakkert.

Fest, Sándor. 1938. "The sons of Eadmund Ironside, Anglo-Saxon king, at the court of Saint Stephen." *Archivum Europae Centro-Orientalis* 4:115–46.

Fine, John V. A. 1978. "A fresh look at Bulgaria under Tsar Peter (927–969)." *Byzantine Studies* 5:88–95.

———. 1983. *The Early Medieval Balkans: A Critical Survey from the Sixth to the Late Twelfth Century.* Ann Arbor: University of Michigan Press.

———. 1987. *The Late Medieval Balkans: A Critical Survey from the Late Twelfth Century to the Ottoman Conquest.* Ann Arbor: University of Michigan Press.

———. 2000. "Croats and Slavs: Theories about the historical circumstances of the Croats' appearance in the Balkans." *Byzantinische Forschungen* 26:205–18.

Fodor, István. 1979. "Archaeological traces of the Volga Bulgars in Hungary of the Arpád period." *Acta Orientalia Academiae Scientiarum Hungaricae* 33:315–25.

———. 1982. *In Search of a New Homeland: The Prehistory of the Hungarian People and the Conquest.* Budapest: Corvina.

———. 1998. "The culture of conquering Hungarians." In *Tender Meat under the Saddle: Customs of Eating, Drinking, and Hospitality among Conquering Hungarians and Nomadic Peoples; In Memory of Gyula László (1910–1998)*, ed. József Lászlovszky, 9–43. Krems: Medium Aevum Quotidianum.

Franklin, Simon. 1989. "Constantine Porphyrogenitus and Russia." In *Konstantinos Z' ho Porphyrogennetos kai he epokhe tou: B' diethnes Byzantinologike Synantese, Delphoi, 22–26 Iouliou 1987*, ed. A. Markopoulos, 57–68. Athens: Europaiko Polistiko Kentro Delphon.

———. 1992. "Greek in Kievan Rus'." *Dumbarton Oaks Papers* 46:69–81.

———. 2002. *Writing, Society, and Culture in Early Rus', ca. 950–1300.* Cambridge and New York: Cambridge University Press.

Franklin, Simon, and Jonathan Shepard. 1996. *The Emergence of Rus, 750–1200.* London and New York: Longman.

Frazee, Charles A. 1993. "The Balkans between Rome and Constantinople in the early Middle Ages, 600–900 A.D." *Balkan Studies* 2:213–28.

Frisnyák, Sándor. 2000. "The Carpathian Basin." In *Europe's Centre around A.D. 1000*, ed. Alfried Wieczorek and Hans-Martin Hinz, 52–53. Stuttgart: Theiss.

Galuška, Luděk. 1991. *Great Moravia.* Brno: Moravské Zemské Muzeum.

Genito, B. 1993. "Some evidence from Iran: On Some Iranian and Central-Asiatic connections with Eastern Europe." *Acta Archaeologica Academiae Scientiarum Hungaricae* 45:151–58.

Georgieva, Sashka. 1995. "The Byzantine princess in Bulgaria." *Byzantinobulgarica* 9: 163–201.

———. 1996. "The political activity of women during the period of the first Bulgarian kingdom." *Bulgarian Historical Review* 24:109–14.

Geremek, Bronislaw. 1982. "Poland and the cultural geography of medieval Europe." In *A Republic of Nobles: Studies in Polish History to 1864*, ed. J. K. Fedorowicz, Maria Bogucka, and Henryk Samsonowicz, 10–27. Cambridge: Cambridge University Press.

Gerics, József. 2000. "Centres of power and organisation of power." In *Europe's Centre around A.D. 1000*, ed. Alfried Wieczorek and Hans-Martin Hinz, 373–75. Stuttgart: Theiss.

———. 2000. "Poland and Hungary as Otto III's footholds in the East." In *Europe's Centre around A.D. 1000*, ed. Alfried Wieczorek and Hans-Martin Hinz, 514–15. Stuttgart: Theiss.

Gimbutas, Marija. 1971. *The Slavs.* New York and Washington, D.C.: Praeger.

Giuzelev, Vasil. 1979. *The Protobulgarians: A Pre-History of the Asparouhian Bulgaria.* Sofia: Izdatelstvo na Bălgarskata Akademiia Naukite.

———. 1981. "The Bulgarian medieval state: Seventh to fourteenth centuries." *Southeastern Europe* 8:19–39.

———. 1988. *Medieval Bulgaria, Byzantine Empire, Black Sea, Venice, Genoa.* Villach: Baier.

Gojda, Martin. 1991. *The Ancient Slavs: Settlement and Society.* Edinburgh: Edinburgh University Press.

Goldblatt, Harvey. 1986. "On 'rusăskymi pismeny' in the 'Vita Constantini' and Russian religious patriotism." In *Studia slavica mediaevalia et humanistica Riccardo Picchio dicata*, ed. Michele Colucci, Giuseppe Dell'Agata, and Harvey Goldblatt, 311–28. Rome: Edizioni dell'Ateneo.

Goldelman, M. 1998–99. "On the location of the Khazarian city of al-Bayda." *Archivum Eurasiae Medii Aevi* 10:63–71.

Golden, Peter B. 1980. *Khazar Studies: An Historico-Philological Inquiry into the Origins of the Khazars.* Budapest: Akadémiai Kiadó.

———. 1982. "Imperial ideology and the sources of political unity among the pre-Cinggisid nomads of western Eurasia." *Archivum Eurasiae Medii Aevi* 2:37–76.

———. 1982. "The question of the Rus' qaganate." *Archivum Eurasiae Medii Aevi* 2:77–97.

———. 1990. "The peoples of the Russian forest belt." In *The Cambridge History of Early Inner Asia,* ed. Denis Sinor, 229–55. Cambridge and New York: Cambridge University Press.

———. 1990. "The peoples of the south Russian steppes." In *The Cambridge History of Early Inner Asia,* ed. Denis Sinor, 256–84. Cambridge and New York: Cambridge University Press.

———. 1992. *An Introduction to the History of the Turkic Peoples: Ethnogenesis and State-Formation in Medieval and Early Modern Eurasia and the Middle East.* Wiesbaden: Otto Harrassowitz.

———. 1998. *Nomads and Sedentary Societies in Medieval Eurasia.* Washington, D.C.: American Historical Association.

———. 2003. *Nomads and their neighbors in the Russian steppe. Turks, Khazars, and Qipchaqs.* Aldershot/Burlington: Ashgate.

Goldstein, Ivo. 1996. "Byzantine presence on the eastern Adriatic coast, 6th–12th century." *Byzantinoslavica* 57:257–64.

———. 1999. "Between Byzantium, the Adriatic, and central Europe." In *Croatia in the Early Middle Ages: A Cultural Survey,* ed. Ivan Supičić, 169–78. London: Philip Wilson Publishers; Zagreb: AGM.

Gorsky, A. A. 1996. "On the origins of the institutions of zhupans among the Slavs." In *Acts. XVIIIth International Congress of Byzantine Studies: Selected Papers,* ed. Ihor Sevcenko, Gennadi G. Litavrin, and Walter K. Hanak, 1:232–41. Shepherdstown, W.V.: Byzantine Studies Press.

Graebner, Michael. 1975. "The role of the Slavs within the Byzantine Empire, 500–1018." Ph.D. diss., University of Michigan, Ann Arbor.

———. 1975. "The Slavs in Byzantine population transfers of the seventh and eighth centuries." *Etudes Balkaniques* 11:40–52.

———. 1978. "The Slavs in Byzantine Europe: Absorption, semi-autonomy, and the limits of Byzantinization." *Byzantinobulgarica* 5:41–55.

Grigoriou-Ioannidou, Martha. 1998. "Monoxyla, Slavs, Bulgars, and the coup organised by Artemios-Anastasios II (719)." *Balkan Studies* 39:181–95.

———. 2000. "The 'kath'emas glossa' in the Mauros and Kouber episode (*Miracula S. Demetrii* 291)." In *Byzantine Macedonia: Identity, Image, and History. Papers from the Melbourne Conference, July 1995,* ed. J. Burke and R. Scott, 89–101. Melbourne: Australian Association for Byzantine Studies.

Guldescu, Stjepan. 1964. *History of Medieval Croatia.* The Hague: Mouton.

Györffy, György. 1975. *The Original Landtaking of the Hungarians.* Budapest: Hungarian National Museum.

———. 1994. "Dual kingship and the seven chieftains of the Hungarians in the era of the conquest and the raids." *Acta Orientalia Academiae Scientiarum Hungaricae* 47: 87–104.

———. 1994. *King Saint Stephen of Hungary.* Boulder, Colo.: Social Science Monographs; Highland Lakes: Atlantic.

————. 2000. "St. Stephen and his influence." In *Europe's Centre around A.D. 1000*, ed. Alfried Wieczorek and Hans-Martin Hinz, 376–77. Stuttgart: Theiss.

Halperin, Ch. J. 1983. "Bulgars and Slavs in the first Bulgarian empire: A reconsideration of the historiography." *Archivum Eurasiae Medii Aevi* 3:183–200.

Hanak, Walter K. 1976. "Some conflicting aspects of Byzantine and Varangian political and religious thought in early Kievan Rus." *Byzantinoslavica* 37:46–55.

————. 1995. "The infamous Svjatoslav: Master of duplicity in war and peace?" In *Peace and War in Byzantium: Essays in Honor of George T. Dennis, S.J.*, ed. Timothy S. Miller and John Nesbitt, 138–51. Washington, D.C.: Catholic University of America.

————. 1996. "Photios and the Slavs, 855–867." In *Acts. XVIIIth International Congress of Byzantine Studies: Selected Papers*, ed. Ihor Sevcenko, G. G. Litavrin, and Walter K. Hanak, 1:248–58. Shephardstown, W.V.: Byzantine Studies Press.

————. 1998. "At the crossroads of cultural interaction: The Great Moravian Empire." *Byzantine Studies* 3:74–84.

Havlík, Lubomír E. 1965. "The relationship between the Great Moravian Empire and the papal court in the years 880–885 A.D." *Byzantinoslavica* 26:100–122.

————. 1972–73. "Roman universalism and 9th-century Moravia." *Cyrillomethodianum* 2:14–22.

————. 1979. "The Slavic Balkan states in the 9th century (the foreign political situation of Croatia and Bulgaria between Byzantium, the papacy, and the Franks)." In *Rapports, co-rapports, communications tchécoslovaques pour le IV-e Congrès de l'Association International d'études du Sud-Est européen*, ed. Karel Herman and Jozef Vladár, 93–105. Prague: Institut de l'historie tchécoslovaque et mondiale de l'Académie tchécoslovaque des sciences.

————. 1984. "Byzantium and the Slavs of the Danubian countries in the 9th century." In *Rapports, co-rapports, communications tchécoslovaques pour le V-e Congrès de l'Association internationale d'études sur le Sud-Est européen*, ed. Karel Herman and Jozef Vladár, 131–44. Prague: Ústav československých a svetových dejín Československé Akademie Ved.

————. 1989. "Bulgaria and Moravia between Byzantium, the Franks, and Rome." *Palaeobulgarica* 13:5–20.

————. 1989. "Great Moravia between the Franconians, Byzantium, and Rome." In *Centre and Periphery: Comparative Studies in Archaeology*, ed. Timothy C. Champion, 227–37. London and Boston: Unwin Hyman.

————. 1991. "King Sventopluk's of Moravia image in the Middle Ages." *Critica storica* 28:164–79.

Havlikova, L. 1991. "Slavic ships in 5th–12th centuries Byzantine historiography." *Byzantinoslavica* 52:89–104.

Heather, Peter. 1997. "Frankish imperialism and Slavic society." In *Origins of Central Europe*, ed. Przemysław Urbańczyk, 171–90. Warsaw: Scientific Society of Polish Archaeologists.

Hensel, Witold. 1969. "The origins of western and eastern Slav towns." *World Archaeology* 1:51–60.

————. 1972. "The acting of Bijelo Brdo culture on Poland's lands." *Archaeologia Polona* 13:307–12.

————. 1975. "From studies on the ethnogenesis of Slavs." *Ethnologia Slavica* 7:35–47.

————. 1975. "New discoveries of early medieval culture in Poland." *Archaeology* 28:84–91.

————. 1977. "The origins of Western and Eastern European Slav Towns." In *European Towns: Their Archaeology and Early History,* ed. M. W. Barley, 373–90. London, New York, and San Francisco: Academic Press for the Council for British Archaeology.

————. 1988. "The cultural unity of the Slavs in the early Middle Ages." *Archaeologia Polona* 27:201–8.

Hóman, Bálint. 1938. "King Stephen the Saint." *Archivum Europae Centro-Orientalis* 4:15–50.

Horedt, Kurt. 1975. "The Gepidae, the Avars, and the Romanic population in Transylvania." In *Relations between the Autochthonous Population and the Migratory Populations on the Territory of Romania,* ed. Miron Constantinescu, Ştefan Pascu, and Petre Diaconu, 111–22. Bucharest: Editura Academiei Republicü Socialiste Romănia.

Horváth, István. 2000. "Esztergom at the time of St Stephen." In *Europe's Centre around A.D. 1000,* ed. Alfried Wieczorek and Hans-Martin Hinz, 378–80. Stuttgart: Theiss.

Hosek, Radislav. 1965. "Antique traditions in Great Moravia." In *Magna Moravia: Sborník k 1100. vyrocí príchodů byzantské miše na Moravů,* ed. Josef Macurek, 71–84. Prague: Státní pedagogické nakladatelství.

Howard-Johnston, J. D. 1983. "Urban continuity in the Balkans in the early Middle Ages." In *Ancient Bulgaria: Papers presented to the International Symposium on the Ancient History and Archaeology of Bulgaria, University of Nottingham, 1981,* ed. A. G. Poulter, 242–54. Nottingham: University of Nottingham.

————. 1997. "Byzantium, Bulgaria, and the peoples of Ukraine in the 890s: A critical re-examination of the Logothete's account." In *Mezhdunarodnaia konferenciia "Vizantiia i Krym," Sevastopol', 6–11 iunia 1997 g. Tezisy dokladov,* 98. Simferopol': Nacional'naia Akademiia Nauk Ukrainy.

————. 2000. "Byzantium, Bulgaria and the peoples of Ukraine in the 890s." *Materialy po arkheologii, istorii i etnografii Tavrii* 7:342–56.

Hoydou, Gabor. 1996. "The Hungarian bow and other composite bows." In *Az öshazától Arpád honalapításáig,* ed. Kálmán Magyar, 203–14. Kaposvár: Magyar Nemzeti Történeti Társaság.

Huxley, George. 1984. "Steppe-peoples in Konstantinos Porphyrogennetos." *Jahrbuch der österreichischen Byzantinistik* 34:77–89.

————. 1990. "Byzantinochazarika (Byzantine texts concerned with Chazaria and adjacent territories)." *Hermathena* 148:69–87.

Ilyés, Elemer. 1992. *Ethnic continuity in the Carpatho-Danubian area.* Hamilton, Ontario: Hunyadi ocs., MK.

Jakobsson, Sverrir. 1994. "A research survey on scholarly works concerning the Varangians and their relations with the Byzantine Empire." In *Seriis Intendere: A Collection of Essays Celebrating the Twenty-Fifth Anniversary of the Centre for Medieval Studies,* ed. Sharon Abra Hanen, 59–64. Leeds.

Jakšić, Nikola. 1984. "Constantine Porphyrogenetus as the source for [the] destruction of Salona." *Vjesnik za arheologiju i historiju Dalmatinsku* 77:315–26.

Janković, Đorđe. 1995. "The Serbs in the Balkans in the light of archaeological findings." In *The Serbian Question in the Balkans,* ed. Jovan Ilić, Dušanka Hadži-Jovančić, and Ivanka Grdović, 125–46. Belgrade: Faculty of Geography, University of Belgrade.

Jansson, I. 1987. "Communications between Scandinavia and Eastern Europe in the Viking age." In *Untersuchungen zu Handel und Verkehr der vor- und frühgeschicht-*

lichen Zeit in Mittel- und Nordeuropa, ed. Klaus Düwel, Herbert Jahnkuhn, Harald Siems, and Dieter Timpe, 4:773–807. Göttingen: Vandenhoek und Ruprecht.

———. 1997. "Warfare, trade, or colonisation? Some general remarks on the eastern expansion of the Scandinavians in the Viking period." In *The Rural Viking in Russia and Sweden,* ed. P. Hansson, 9–64. Örebro: Gullers.

Jeleček, Leos, and Zdeněk Boháč. 1985. "Mountains, forests, rivers: Medieval Bohemia in the context of Central Europe." In *History and Society: Published on the Occasion of the XVI International Congress of Historical Sciences in Stuttgart,* ed. J. Purs and K. Herman, 305–33. Prague: Institute of Czechoslovak and World History of the Czechoslovak Academy of Sciences.

———. 1989. "Medieval Bohemia in the context of central Europe." In *Montagnes, fleuves, forêts dans l'histoire: Barrières ou lignes de convergence? Travaux présentés au XVIe Congrès international des Sciences historiques, Stuttgart, août 1985,* ed. Jean-François Bergier, 147–66. St. Katharinen: Scripta Mercaturae Verlag.

Jenkins, R. J. H. 1966. "The peace with Bulgaria (927) celebrated by Theodore Daphnopates." In *Polychronion: Festschrift Franz Dölger zum 75. Geburtstag,* ed. Peter Wirth, 287–303. Heidelberg: Carl Winter.

Kaczmarczyk, Zdisław. 1962. "One thousand years of the history of the Polish western frontier." *Acta Poloniae Historica* 5:79–109.

Karlin-Hayter, P. 1968. "The homily on the peace with Bulgaria of 927 and the 'coronation' of 913." *Jahrbuch der österreichischen byzantinischen Gesellschaft* 17:29–39.

Katičić, Radoslav. 1999. "On the origins of the Croats." In *Croatia in the Early Middle Ages: A Cultural Survey,* ed. Ivan Supičić, 149–67. London: Philip Wilson Publishers; Zagreb: AGM.

Kazanski, Michel. 1993. "The sedentary elite in the 'empire' of the Huns and its impact on material civilisation in southern Russia during the early Middle Ages (5th–7th centuries AD)." In *Cultural Transformations and Interactions in Eastern Europe,* ed. John Chapman and Pavel Dolukhanov, 211–35. Aldershot and Brookfield: Avebury.

Kazhdan, Alexander P. 1997. "Joseph the Hymnographer and the first Russian attack on Constantinople." In *From Byzantium to Iran: Armenian Studies in Honour of Nina G. Garsoian,* ed. Jean-Pierre Mahé and Robert W. Thomson, 187–96. Atlanta: Scholars Press.

Khvoshchinskaia, N. V. 1984. "Dress of the Finnish population of the early second millenium A.D. in the western areas of the Novgorod lands." In *Fenno-Ugri e Slavi 1983: Papers Presented by the Participants in the Soviet-Finnish Symposium "Trade, Exchange, and Culture Relations of the Peoples of Fennoscandia and Eastern Europe," 9–13 May 1983, in the Hanasaari Congress Center,* ed. Torsten Edgren, 174–78. Helsinki: Vammala.

Kiss, Lájos. 2000. "The linguistic, ethnic, and cultural make-up of the Hungarians." In *Europe's Centre around A.D. 1000,* ed. Alfred Wieczorek and Hans-Martin Hinz, 135–36. Stuttgart: Theiss.

Klaniczay, Gábor. 1993. "The paradoxes of royal sainthood as illustrated by central European examples." In *Kings and Kingship in Medieval Europe,* ed. Anne J. Duggan, 351–74. London: Centre for Late Antique and Medieval Studies, King's College London.

Klápště, Jan. 1991. "Bedřichův-Svetec and early feudal residences in NW Bohemia." In *Archaeology in Bohemia, 1986–1990,* ed. Pavel Varěka, 64–67. Prague: Institute of Archaeology of the Czechoslovak Academy of Sciences.

————. 2000. "Economy, settlement, and settlement areas of the western Slavs between the Ore Mountains and the Danube." In *Europe's Centre around A.D. 1000*, ed. Alfried Wieczorek and Hans-Martin Hinz, 69–72. Stuttgart: Theiss.

Klein, L. S. 1973. "Soviet archaeology and the role of the Vikings in the early history of the Slavs." *Norwegian Archaeological Review* 6:1–4.

Klindt-Jensen, O. L. E. 1970. "The evaluation of the archaeological evidence." In *Varangian Problems: Report on the First International Symposium on the Theme "The Eastern Connections of the Nordic Peoples in the Viking Period and Early Middle Ages," Moesgaard-University of Aarhus, October 7–11, 1968*, ed. Knud Hannestad, Knud Jordal, Ole Klindt-Jensen, et al., 39–49. Copenhague: Munksgaard.

Knific, Timotej. 1976. "Carniola in the early Middle Ages." *Balcanoslavica* 5:111–21.

————. 1999. "Carniola Sclavorum patria: Autochtons, invaders, neighbors." In *Istoriia i kul'tura drevnikh i srednevekovykh slavian*, ed. V. V. Sedov, 314–23. Moscow: Institut Arkheologii Rossüskoi Akademii Hauk.

Kobyliński, Zbigniew. 1989. "An ethnic change or a socio-economic one? The 5th and 6th centuries AD in the Polish lands." In *Archaeological Approaches to Cultural Identity*, ed. Stephen Shenna, 303–12. London, Boston, and Sydney: Unwin Hyman.

Kochev, N. 1995. "East and West relations and the matter of papal primacy up to the 10th century." *Etudes Balkaniques* 31:115–29.

Koleva, Rumiana. 1993. "Slavic settlement on the territory of Bulgaria." In *Actes du XII-e Congrès international des sciences préhistoriques et protohistoriques, Bratislava, 1–7 septembre 1991*, ed. J. Pavul, 4:17–19. Bratislava: Institut Archéologique de l'Académie Slovaque des Sciences.

Korpela, Jukka. 1995–96. "A new Christ, Holy Mother, and Judas in medieval Russia." *Acta Byzantina Fennica* 7:9–36.

Kosmenko, M. G. 1992. "Formation of the Iron Age archaeological cultures in Karelia." In *Suomen varhaishistoria: Tornion kongressi 14.–16.6.1991*, ed. Kyösti Julku and Markus H. Korhonen, 197–206. Rovaniemi: Pohjois-Suomen Historiallinen Yhdistys.

Kowalska, Maria. 1973. "Ibn Fadlan's account of his journey to the state of the Bulgars." *Folia orientalia* 14:219–30.

Kralovánszky, A. 1972. "The early history of Alba Regia (Székesfehérvár) in the light of archaeological excavations." *Alba Regia* 13:305.

Kramar, Y. 1988. "The question of prince Volodymyr's religious choice." *Ukrainian Review* 36:16–23, 30–40.

Kristó, Gyula. 1992. "Directions of orientation in the Carpathian Basin at the end of the first millenium." In *Mutual Dynamics of Organisational Levels in Evolution*, ed. Béla Lukács, 128–33. Budapest: Központi Fizikai Kutató Intézet.

————. 1996. *Hungarian History in the Ninth Century*. Szeged: Szegedi Középkorász Mühely.

————. 2000. "The Arpads and the Hungarians." In *Europe's Centre around A.D. 1000*, ed. Alfried Wieczorek and Hans-Martin Hinz, 370–72. Stuttgart: Theiss.

————. 2000. "The historical geography of the Hungarian lands." In *Europe's Centre around A.D. 1000*, ed. Alfried Wieczorek and Hans-Martin Hinz, 358–60. Stuttgart: Theiss.

————. 2000. "International routes through the Carpathian Basin." In *Europe's Centre around A.D. 1000*, ed. Alfried Wieczorek and Hans-Martin Hinz, 93–94. Stuttgart: Theiss.

Kroll, Helmut. 2000. "Diet and nutrition in Slav Eastern Central Europe around the year 1000." In *Europe's Centre around A.D. 1000*, ed. Alfried Wieczorek and Hans-Martin Hinz, 75–76. Stuttgart: Theiss.

Kucera, Matús. 2000. "Moravia Magna and Slovak history: From the genesis of Great Moravia to its fall in 907." In *Europe's Centre around A.D. 1000*, ed. Alfried Wieczorek and Hans-Martin Hinz, 578–80. Stuttgart: Theiss.

Kurelac, Miroslav. 1999. "Narrative sources." In *Croatia in the Early Middle Ages: A Cultural Survey*, ed. Ivan Supičić, 321–36. London: Philip Wilson Publishers; Zagreb: AGM.

Kurnatowska, Zofia. 1995. "Recent problems and research on the early Middle Ages in Poland." *Slavia Antiqua* 36:7–18.

———. 1997. "Territorial structures in west Poland prior to the founding of the state organization of Mieszko I." In *Origins of Central Europe*, ed. Przemysław Urbańczyk, 125–35. Warsaw: Scientific Society of Polish Archaeologists.

———. 2000. "Centres and structures of power of the state." In *Europe's Centre around A.D. 1000*, ed. Alfried Wieczorek and Hans-Martin Hinz, 295–98. Stuttgart: Theiss.

Labuda, Gerard. 1960. "Slavs in early mediaeval Pomerania and their relations with Scandinavians in the 9th and 10th centuries." In *Poland at the XIth International Congress of Historical Sciences in Stockholm*, 61–80. Warsaw: Panstwowe Wydawnictwo Naukowe.

Laourdas, Basil. 1954. "A new letter of Photius to Boris." *Hellenika* 13:263–65.

Lászlovszky, József. 1998. "Research possibilities into the history and material culture of eating, drinking, and hospitality during the period of Hungarian conquest." In *Tender Meat under the Saddle: Customs of Eating, Drinking, and Hospitality among Conquering Hungarians and Nomadic Peoples; In Memory of Gyula László (1910–1998)*, ed. József Lászlovszky, 44–60. Krems: Medium Aevum Quotidianum.

Lebedev, G. S. 1980. "On the early date of the way 'from the Varangians to the Greeks.'" In *Fenno-Ugri et Slavi*, 90–101. Helsinki: Suomen Muinaismuistoyhdistys.

Lebedev, G. S., and V. A. Nazarenko. 1973. "The connections between Russians and Scandinavians in the 9th–11th centuries." *Norwegian Archaeological Review* 6:5–9.

Leciejewicz, Lech. 1978. "Traditional and progressive patterns in the early Slavonic urban culture." *Slovenská Archeológia* 26:51–57.

———. 1985. "Polish archaeology and the medieval history of Polish towns." In *The Comparative History of Urban Origins in Non-Roman Europe: Ireland, Wales, Denmark, Germany, Poland, and Russia from the Ninth to the Thirteenth Century*, ed. H. B. Clarke and Anngret Simms, 1:335–51. Oxford: British Archaeological Reports.

———. 1990. "Ethnogenetic legends in the Slav world." *Quaestiones Medii Aevi* 4:29–43.

———. 1993. "The integration activities in the Baltic during the early Middle Ages." In *Actes du XII-e Congrès international des sciences préhistoriques et protohistoriques, Bratislava, 1–7 septembre 1991*, ed. J. Pavuj, 4:23–25. Bratislava: Institut Archéologique de l'Académie Slovaque des Sciences.

———. 1997. "Great Moravia and Venice in the 9th century." In *Central Europe in 8th–10th Centuries: International Scientific Conference, Bratislava October 2–4, 1995*, ed. Dušan Čaplović and Ján Dorul'a, 115–20. Bratislava: Ministry of Culture in the Slovak Republic and Slovak Academy of Sciences.

———. 2000. "The origin and divisions of the western Slavs." In *Europe's Centre around A.D. 1000*, ed. Alfried Wieczorek and Hans-Martin Hinz, 153–56. Stuttgart: Theiss.

Leitgeber, Boleslaw. 1989. "Multi-ethnic glimpses of Old Poland." *Slavonic and East European Review* 67:435–41.

Lencek, Rado. 1982. "At the roots of Slavic cultural history." In *Părvi mezhdunaroden kongres po bălgaristika, Sofiia 23 mai–3 iuni 1981: Dokladi; Plenarni dokladi,* ed. Pantelei Zarev, Dimităr Kosev, Vladimir Georgiev, et al., 29–53. Sofia: Izdatelstvo na Bălgarskata Akademiia na Naukite.

Levin, Eve. 1989. *Sex and Society in the World of the Orthodox Slavs, 900–1700.* Ithaca: Cornell University Press.

Lewicka-Rajewska, Urszula. 1997. "The Slavs of central Europe and the Muslim world until the beginning of the 10th century in the light of the Arab written sources." In *Origins of Central Europe,* ed. Przemysław Urbańczyk, 213–25. Warsaw: Scientific Society of Polish Archaeologists.

Lewis, A. R. 1975. "The Danube route and Byzantium, 802–1195." In *Actes du XIV-e Congrès international des études byzantines, Bucarest, 6–12 septembre 1971,* 2:359–68. Bucharest: Editura Academiei Republicü Socialiste România.

Leyser, K. 1965. "The battle at the Lech, 955: A study in tenth-century warfare." *History* 50:1–25.

Likhachev, D. S. 1970. "The legend of the calling-in of the Varangians, and political purposes in Russian chronicle-writing from the second half of the XIth to the beginning of the XIIIth century." In *Varangian Problems: Report on the First International Symposium on the Theme "The Eastern Connections of the Nordic Peoples in the Viking Period and Early Middle Ages," Moesgaard-University of Aarhus, October 7–11, 1968,* ed. Knud Hannestad, Knud Jordal, Ole Klindt-Jensen, et al., 170–87. Copenhague: Munksgaard.

Lind, J. H. 1984. "The Russo-Byzantine treaties and the early urban structure of Rus'." *Slavonic and East European Review* 62:362–70.

Lindstedt, Jouko. 1992. "Byzantium and the Slavs in the early Middle Ages." *Acta Byzantina Fennica* 6:35–49.

Louda, Jiří. 1975. "Good 'King' Wenceslas." *Coat of Arms* 1:106–7.

Lübke, Christian. 1997. "Forms of political organization of the Polabian Slavs (until the 10th century A.D.)." In *Origins of Central Europe,* ed. Przemysław Urbańczyk, 115–24. Warsaw: Scientific Society of Polish Archaeologists.

Luchtanas, Aleksiejus. 2000. "The Balts during the 10th century." In *The Neighbors of Poland in the 10th Century,* ed. Przemysław Urbańczyk, 199–204. Warsaw: Institute of Archaeology and Ethnology.

Ludvíkovský, Jaroslav. 1965. "The Great Moravian tradition in the 10th cent. Bohemia and Legenda Christiani." In *Magna Moravia: Sborník k 1100. vyrocí príchodů byzantské miše na Moravů,* ed. Josef Macůrek, 525–66. Prague: Státní pedagogické nakladatelství.

Lunt, Horace G. 1958. "Again the Rus'kijmi Pismenij." In *Mélanges linguistiques offerts à Emil Petrovici par ses amis étrangers à l'occasion de son soixantième anniversaire,* 323–26. Bucharest: Editura Academiei RPR.

———. 1995. "Skimpy evidence, nationalism, and closed minds: The case of Methodius, Morava, and the 'Moravian king.'" In *O RUS! Studia litteraria slavica in honorem Hugh McLean,* ed. Simon Karlinsky, J. L. Rice, and B. P. Scherr, 142–52. Berkeley: University of California Press.

———. 1998. "Cyril and Methodius with Rastislav, prince of Morava: Where were they?" *Russian History* 25:21–25.

————. 1999. "Cyril and Methodius with Rastislav, prince of Moravia: Where were they?" In *Thessaloniki Magna Moravia*, 87–112. Thessaloniki: SS. Cyril and Methodios Center for Cultural Studies.

Macartney, C. A. 1930. "The attack on 'Valandar.'" *Byzantinisch-neugriechische Jahrbücher* 8:20–31.

————. 1930. *The Magyars in the Ninth Century*. Cambridge: Cambridge University Press.

————. 1930. "On the Black Bulgars." *Byzantinisch-neugriechische Jahrbücher* 8:32–40.

————. 1930. "The Petchenegs." *Slavonic and East European Review* 8:41–54.

————. 1969. "The eastern auxiliaries of the Magyars." *Journal of the Royal Asiatic Society*:49–58.

————. 1999. *Studies on Early Hungarian and Pontic History*. Aldershot: Variorum; Brookfield: Ashgate.

Machula, Jan. 2002. "Foreign items and outside influences in the material culture of tenth-century Bohemia." *Annual of Medieval Studies at the CEU* 8:65–88.

Madgearu, Alexandru. 1992. "The placement of the fortress Turris." *Balkan Studies* 33: 203–8.

————. 1999. "The military organization of Paradunavon." *Byzantinoslavica* 60:421–46.

————. 1999–2000. "The restoration of the Byzantine rule on the Danube." *Revue des études sud-est-européennes* 37:5–23.

————. 2000. "Recent discussions about 'Onglos.'" In *Istro-Pontica: Muzeul tulcean la a 50-a aniversare 1950–2000; Omagiu lui Simion Gavrilă la 45 de ani de activitate, 1955–2000*, ed. Mihaela Iacob, Ernest Oberländer-Târnoveanu, and Florin Topoleanu, 343–48. Tulcea: Consiliul Județean Tulcea.

————. 2001. "Rethinking the Byzantine Balkans: A recent book on the 10th–12th centuries." *Revue des études sud-est-européennes* 39:203–12.

————. 2001. "Two mutinies against the center in the province of Scythia." *Revue des études sud-est-européennes* 39:5–17.

Magyar, Kálmán. 1996. "Who is the Hungarian? What is the Hungarian?" In *Az öshazától Arpád honalapításáig*, ed. Kálmán Magyar, 293–300. Budapest: Magyar Nemzeti Történeti Társaság.

Majeska, George P. 1997–98. "The Byzantines on the Slavs: On the problem of ethnic stereotyping." *Acta Byzantina Fennica* 9:70–86.

Makk, Ferenc. 2000. "The Magyar raids." In *Europe's Centre around A.D. 1000*, ed. Alfried Wieczorek and Hans-Martin Hinz, 143–44. Stuttgart: Theiss.

Makkai, László. 1990. "The foundation of the Hungarian Christian state, 950–1196." In *A History of Hungary*, ed. Peter F. Sugar, Péter Hanak, and Tibor Frank, 15–22. London: I. B. Tauris.

Maksimov, Sergei E. 1992. "Three towns of the Rus people (old hypotheses revisited)." *Ukrainian Review* 40:22–32.

Maleszka, Monika. 2002. "Forgotten partners: The role of the Slav in the Baltic Viking age." In *Centre, Region, Periphery: Medieval Europe Basel 2002*, ed. Guido Helmig, Barbara Scholkmann, and Matthias Untermann, 1:157–61. Basel: Dr. G. Wesselkamp.

Mandić, D. 1964. "Dalmatia in the exarchate of Ravenna from the middle of the VI until the middle of the VIII century." *Byzantion* 34:347–74.

Manteuffel, Tadeusz. 1982. *The Formation of the Polish State: The Period of Ducal Rule, 963–1194*. Detroit: Wayne State University.

Margetić, Lujo. 1999. "The Croatian state during the era of rulers from the Croatian national dynasty." In *Croatia in the Early Middle Ages: A Cultural Survey*, ed. Ivan Supičić, 197–214. London: Philip Wilson Publishers; Zagreb: AGM.

Marjanović-Vujović, Gordana. 1974. "Archaeological proving the presence of the Pechenegs in Beograd town." *Balcanoslavica* 3:183–88.

Markov, V. V. 1995. "Byzantium and the early Vlachs." *Macedonian Studies* 12:59–74.

Marović, Ivan. 1984. "Reflexions about the year of the destruction of Salona." *Vjesnik za arheologiju i historiju Dalmatinsku* 77:293–314.

Marsina, Richard. 2000. "The dukedom of Nitra and Hungary." In *Europe's Centre around A.D. 1000*, ed. Alfried Wieczorek and Hans-Martin Hinz, 381–82. Stuttgart: Theiss.

Marti, Roland. 1999. "Abecedaria: A key to the original Slavic alphabet; The contribution of the Abecedarium Sinaiticum Glagoliticum." In *Thessaloniki Magna Moravia*, 175–200. Thessaloniki: SS. Cyril and Methodios Center for Cultural Studies.

Martin, Janet. 1988. "Russian expansion in the far north; X to mid-XVI century." In *Russian Colonial Expansion to 1917*, ed. Michael Rywkin, 23–43. London: Mansell.

———. 1995. *Medieval Russia, 980–1584*. Cambridge: Cambridge University Press.

Matanov, Ch. 1992. "Bulgarian-Russian cultural relations in the early Middle Ages (historiographic aspects)." In *The Legacy of Saints Cyril and Methodiu to Kiev and Moscow: Proceedings of the International Congress on the Millenium of the Conversion of Rus' to Christianity, Thessaloniki, 26–28 November 1988*, ed. A. E. Tachiaos, 157–66. Thessaloniki: Hellenic Association for Slavic Studies.

Maurya, Abhai. 1987. "The humanism of Cyril and Methodius and their mission." *Kirilo-metodievski studii* 4:34–43.

McGrath, Stamatina. 1995. "The battles of Dorostolon (971): Rhetoric and reality." In *Peace and War in Byzantium: Essays in Honor of George T. Dennis, S.J.*, ed. Timothy S. Miller and John Nesbitt, 152–64. Washington, D.C.: Catholic University of America.

Melamed, Katia. 1997. "Scythia Minor-Dobrudža: An uncontrolled barbarian road." In *Von der Scythia zur Dobrudža*, ed. Khristo Kholiolchev, Renate Pillinger, and Reinhardt Harreither, 9–16. Vienna: Verein "Freunde des Hauses Wittgenstein."

Mel'nikova, E. A. 1995. "Ancient Rus' and Scandinavia and their relations to Byzantium." *Bysantinska sällskapet: Bulletin* 13:5–11.

———. 1996. *The Eastern World of the Vikings: Eight Essays about Scandinavia and Eastern Europe in the Early Middle Ages*. Göteborg: Litteraturvetenskapliga Institutionen, Göteborgs Universitet.

Mel'nikova, E. A., and V. I. Petrukhin. 1990–91. "The origin and evolution of the name Rus': The Scandinavians in Eastern-European ethno-political processes before the 11th century." *Tor* 23:203–34.

Meřínsky, Zdeněk, and Jaroslav Mezník. 1998. "The making of the Czech state: Bohemia and Moravia from the tenth to the fourteenth century." In *Bohemia in History*, ed. Mikulas Teich, 39–58. Cambridge and New York: Cambridge University Press.

Mihai, L. 1994. "From Thracians to Romanians and Slavs." *Macedonian Studies* 11:69–73.

Milich, Petar. 1995. "Cumulative Slavicity: Cultural interaction and language replacement in the north Balkans during the Slavic migration period, AD 500–900." Ph.D. diss., Ohio State University.

Miklas, H. 1989. "Litterae palaeoslovenice." *Saeculum* 40:253–71.

Mishin, Dmitrii. 1994–95. "Ibrahim ibn-Ya'qub at-Turtushi's account of the Slavs from the middle of the tenth century." *Annual of Medieval Studies at the CEU* 1:184–99.

Mladjov, I. 1998. "Trans-Danubian Bulgaria: Reality and fiction." *Byzantine Studies* 3: 85–128.

Montgomery, J. E. 2000. "Ibn Fadlān and the Rūsiyyah." *Journal of Arabic and Islamic Studies* 3:1–25.

Moravcsik, Gyula. 1966. "Hungary and Byzantium in the Middle Ages." In *The Cambridge Medieval History*, ed. J. M. Hussey, 4:566–92. Cambridge: Cambridge University Press.

———. 1970. *Byzantium and the Magyars*. Budapest: Akadémiai Kiadó.

Moshe, Gil. 1974. "The Radhanite merchants and the land of Radhan." *Journal of the Economic and Social History of the Orient* 17:299–328.

Nandriş, Grigore. 1939. "The earliest contacts between Slavs and Roumanians." *Slavonic and East European Review* 18:142–54.

Nechvátal, Bořivoj. 1991. "Studies on the ducal and royal centre at Vyšehrad." In *Archaeology in Bohemia, 1986–1990*, ed. Pavel Vaŕeka, 149–58. Prague: Institute of Archaeology of the Czechoslovak Academy of Sciences.

Nepper, M., and L. Révész. 1996. "The archaeological heritage of the ancient Hungarians." In *The Ancient Hungarians: Exhibition catalogue*, ed. István Fodor, 37–56. Budapest: Hungarian National Museum.

Nielsen, Jens Petter. 1992. "The troublesome Rjurik and his house: The Norman question in Soviet historiography under Stalin." *Acta Borealia* 9:19–37.

Nikolajević, Ivanka. 1973. "The redemption of captives in Dalmatia in the 6th and 7th century." *Balcanoslavica* 2:73–79.

Nikolov, Stephen. 1994–95. "The Latin bishops and the Balkan bishoprics." *Annual of Medieval Studies at the CEU* 1:200–217.

———. 1997. "The Magyar connection or Constantine and Methodius in the steppes." *Byzantine and Modern Greek Studies* 21:79–92.

———. 1999. "Building the Tower of Babel: Michael III, Photius, and Basil I and the Byzantine approval for the use of the Slavic liturgy and alphabet in the late ninth century." *Starobălgarska literatura* 31:41–53.

Noonan, Thomas S. 1986. "Why the Viking first came to Russia." *Jarhbücher für Geschichte Osteuropas* 34:321–48.

———. 1987–91. "When did Rus/Rus' merchants first visit Khazaria and Baghdad?" *Archivum Eurasiae Medii Aevi* 7:213–19.

———. 1991. "The Vikings and Russia: Some new directions and approaches to an old problem." In *Social Approaches to Viking Studies*, ed. Ross Samson, 201–6. Glasgow: Cruithne Press.

———. 1992. "Byzantium and the Khazars: A special relationship?" In *Byzantine Diplomacy: Papers from the Twenty-Fourth Spring Symposium of Byzantine Studies*, ed. J. Shepard and S. Franklin, 109–32. Aldershot: Variorum.

———. 1998–99. "The Khazar-Byzantine world of the Crimea in the early Middle Ages: The religious dimension." *Archivum Eurasiae Medii Aevi* 10:207–30.

———. 1999. "European Russia, c. 500–c. 1050." In *The New Cambridge Medieval History*, ed. Timothy Reuter, 3:487–513. Cambridge: Cambridge University Press.

———. 2000. "Dress and clothing along the Central Asian-Middle Volga caravan route, ca. 922: the evidence of Ibn Fadlan." In *Kul'tury stepei Evrazii vtoroi poloviny I tysiacheletiia n.e. (iz istorii kostiuma). Tezisy dokladov III Mezhdunarodnoi arkheologicheskoi konferencii 14–18 marta 2000 g*, ed. D. A. Stashenkov, 102–5. Samara: Samarskii oblastnoi istoriko-kraevedcheskii muzei im. P. A. Alabina.

Nosov, E. N. 1984. "Historical ties between the population of Novgorod land centre and the Baltic countries in the 9th–10th centuries." In *Fenno-Ugri e Slavi 1983: Papers Presented by the Participants in the Soviet-Finnish Symposium "Trade, Exchange, and Culture Relations of the Peoples of Fennoscandia and Eastern Europe," 9–13 May 1983, in the Hanasaari Congress Center,* ed. Torsten Edgren, 145–50. Helsinki: Vammala.

Obolensky, Dmitri. 1963. "Sts. Cyril and Methodius, apostles of the Slavs." *St. Vladimir's Seminary Quarterly* 7:3–13.

———. 1970. "The Byzantine sources on the Scandinavians in Eastern Europe." In *Varangian Problems: Report on the First International Symposium on the Theme "The Eastern Connections of the Nordic Peoples in the Viking Period and Early Middle Ages," Moesgaard-University of Aarhus, October 7–11, 1968,* ed. Knud Hannestad, Knud Jordal, Ole Klindt-Jensen, et al., 149–69. Copenhague: Munksgaard.

———. 1971. *The Byzantine Commonwealth: Eastern Europe, 500–1453.* New York and Washington: Praeger.

———. 1978. "The Crimea and the north before 1204." *Archeion Pontou* 35:123–33.

———. 1981. "The Varangian-Russian controversy: The first round." In *History and Imagination: Essays in Honour of H. R. Trevor-Roper,* ed. Hugh Lloyd-Jones, Valerie Pearl, and Blair Worder, 232–42. London: Duckworth.

———. 1986. "The Cyrillo-Methodian mission: The scriptural foundations." *St. Vladimir's Seminary Quarterly* 30:101—16.

———. 1988–89. "Ol'ga's conversion: The evidence reconsidered." *Harvard Ukrainian Studies* 12–13:145–58.

———. 1990. "Continuity and discontinuity in the Balkans: The ninth-century syndrome." *Etudes Balkaniques* 1:38–41.

———. 1993. "Byzantium, Kiev, and Cherson in the tenth century." *Byzantinoslavica* 54: 108–13.

———. 1994. *Byzantium and the Slavs.* Crestwood: St. Vladimir's Seminary Press.

———. 1999. "Great Moravia and the Byzantine Commonwealth." In *Thessaloniki Magna Moravia,* 9–15. Thessaloniki: SS. Cyril and Methodios Center for Cultural Studies.

Oikonomides, N. 1983. "Presthlavitza, the Little Preslav." *Südost-Forschungen* 42:1–9.

———. 1985. "Mesembria in the 9th century: Epigraphical evidence." In *Essays in the Area of Slavic Languages, Linguistic, and Byzantology: A Festschrift in Honor of Antonín Dostál on the Occasion of His Seventy-Fifth Birthday,* ed. Thomas G. Winner, 269–73. Irvine: Charles Schlacks Jr.

———. 1996. "The medieval Via Egnatia." In *Via Egnatia under Ottoman Rule (1380–1699),* ed. Elizabeth Zachariadou, 9–16. Rethymnon: Crete University Press.

Ostman, R. A. E. 1997. "'Our land is great and rich, but there is no order in it': Reevaluating the process of state formation in Russia." *Archaeological News* 21–22:73–91.

Pallua, Emilio. 1990. "A survey of the constitutional history of the kingdom of Dalmatia, Croatia, and Slavonia." *Canadian American Slavic Studies* 24:129–54.

Panov, Branko. 1987. "The early years of Cyril and Methodius and the initial stage of their work." *Macedonian Review* 17:97–106.

Panova, Rosica. 1996. "The capital city in the medieval Bulgarian culture." *Jahrbuch der österreichischen Byzantinistik* 46:437–40.

———. 1996. "Some reflexions on the khan's residences in early Bulgarian medieval history." *Bulgarian Historical Review* 24:105–8.

Pap, Livija. 1997. "A contribution to the solution of some Slavic migrations in the early Middle Ages according to the miracles of Demetrius of Thessalonica." In *Etnogenez i etnokul'turnye kontakty slavian,* ed. V. V. Sedov, 251–60. Moscow: Institut Arkheologii Rossüskoi Akademii Nauk.

Papastathis, Charalambos K. 1995. "On the 'Saint Constantine' of the *Zakon Sudnyi Liudem.*" *Byzantinoslavica* 56:557–59.

Parczewski, Michał. 1991. "Origins of early Slav culture in Poland." *Antiquity* 65:676–83.

———. 1997. "Beginnings of the Slavs' culture." In *Origins of Central Europe,* ed. Przemysław Urbańczyk, 75–90. Warsaw: Scientific Society of Polish Archaeologists.

Paszkiewicz, Henryk. 1954. *Origins of Russia.* New York: Philosophical Library.

———. 1963. *The Making of the Russian Nation.* London: Darton, Longman, and Todd.

Peisker, Jan. 1926. "The expansion of the Slavs." In *The Cambridge Medieval History,* ed. H. M. Gwatkin and J. P. Whitney, 418–58. New York: Macmillan; Cambridge: Cambridge University Press.

Penkov, Sava. 1981. "Bulgaro-Byzantine treaties during the early Middle Ages." *Palaeobulgarica* 5:40–52.

Pétrin, N. 1998. "Caranthani Marahenses: Philological notes on the early history of the Hungarians and Slavs." *Eurasian Studies Yearbook* 70:39–63.

Petrukhin, Vladimir Ia. 1992. "The Normans and the Khazars in the south of Rus' (The formation of the 'Russian land' in the middle Dnepr area)." *Russian History* 19: 393–400.

———. 2001. "The decline and legacy of Khazaria." In *Europe around the Year 1000,* ed. Przemysław Urbańczyk, 109–21. Warsaw: Wydawnictwo DiG.

———. 2002. "Khazaria and Russia: Sovereignty and territory in Eastern Europe in the 9th to the beginning of the 10th centuries." In *Centre, Region, Periphery: Medieval Europe Basel 2002,* ed. Guido Helmig, Barbara Scholkmann, and Matthias Untermann, 1:528–32. Basel: Dr. G. Wesselkamp.

Picchio, Riccardo. 1988–89. "From Boris to Volodimer: Some remarks on the emergence of proto-orthodox Slavdom." *Harvard Ukrainian Studies* 12–13:200–213.

Pleszczyński, Andrzej. 2001. "Poland as an ally of the Holy Ottonian Empire." In *Europe around the Year 1000,* ed. Przemysław Urbańczyk, 409–25. Warsaw: Wydawnictwo DiG.

Pliakov, Zdravko. 1995. "The city of Melnik." *Bulgarian Historial Review* 23:74–90.

Pohl, Walter. 1997. "The empire and the Lombards: Treaties and negotiations in the sixth century." In *Kingdoms of the Empire: The Integration of Barbarians in Late Antiquity,* ed. Walter Pohl, 75–133. Leiden, New York and Cologne: Brill.

———. 1997. "The role of the steppe peoples in Eastern and central Europe in the first millennium A.D." In *Origins of Central Europe,* ed. Przemysław Urbańczyk, 65–78. Warsaw: Scientific Society of Polish Archaeologists.

Polek, Krzysztof. 1997. "The political and military relations between the Charlemagne's Frankish Empire and Avarian Khanate." In *Central Europe in 8th–10th Centuries: International Scientific Conference, Bratislava October 2–4, 1995,* ed. Dušan Čaplovič and Ján Dorul'a, 46–52. Bratislava: Ministry of Culture in the Slovak Republic and Slovak Academy of Sciences.

Pope, Richard W. F. 1974. "Bulgaria: The third Christian kingdom in the Razumnik-Ukaz." *Slavia: časopis pro slovanskou filologii* 43:141–53.

Poppe, Alexander. 1982. *The Rise of Christian Russia.* London: Hammondsworth.

————. 1992. "Once again concerning the baptism of Olga, archontissa of Rus." *Dumbarton Oaks Papers* 46:271–77.

Primov, B. 1978. "Bulgaria in the eighth century: A general outline." *Byzantinobulgarica* 5:7–40.

Pritsak, Omeljan. 1967. "The name of the third king of Rus' and their city." *Journal of the Royal Asiatic Society,* 2–9.

————. 1975. "The Pechenegs: A case of social and economic transformation." *Archivum Eurasiae Medii Aevi* 1:211–35.

————. 1981. *The Origin of Rus'.* Cambridge: Harvard University Press.

————. 1982. *Viking Relations with the Southeastern Baltic/Northwestern Russia: The Perspective of the Slavs, Finns, and Balts.* Cambridge: Harvard Ukrainian Research Institute.

————. 1983. "The Slavs and the Avars." In *Gli Slavi occidentali e meridionali nell'alto Medioevo,* 353–435. Spoleto: Presso la sede del Centro.

————. 1984. "Where was Constantine's Inner Rus'?" In *Okeanos: Essays Presented to Ihor Ševčenko on His Sixtieth Birthday by His Colleagues and Students,* ed. Cyril Mango, Omeljan Pritsak, and Uliana M. Pasicznyk, 555–67. Cambridge: Ukrainian Research Institute.

————. 1988. "Pre-Ashkenazic Jews of Eastern Europe in relation to the Khazars, the Rus', and the Lithuanians." In *Ukrainian-Jewish Relations in Historical Perspective,* ed. Peter J. Potičnyj and Howard Aster, 3–21. Edmonton: Canadian Institute of Ukrainian Studies, University of Alberta.

————. 1988. "Turkological remarks on Constantine's Khazarian mission in the 'Vita Constantini.'" In *Christianity among the Slavs: The Heritage of Saints Cyril and Methodius; Acts of the Internaitonal Congress Held on the Eleventh Centenary of the Death of St. Methodius, Rome, October 8–11, 1985,* ed. Edward G. Farrugia, Robert F. Taft, and Gino K. Piovesana, 295–98. Rome: Pontificum Institutum Studiorum Orientalium.

————. 1995. "The system of government under Volodimer the Great and his foreign policy." *Harvard Ukrainian Studies* 19:573–93.

Procházka, Vladimír. 1966. "The problem of Slavonic law." *Vznik a počátky Slovanů* 6:53–86.

Provaznik, Adolf. 1979. "The British Isles and Great Moravia in the early Middle Ages." *Journal of Medieval History* 5:97–114, 149.

Putík, Alexander. 1996. "Notes on the name *GBLYM* in Hasdai's letter to the khaqan of Khazaria." In *Ibrahim ibn Yakub al-Turtushi: Christianity, Islam, and Judaism Meet in East-Central Europe, c. 800–1300 A.D.; Proceedings of the International Colloquy, 25–29 April 1994,* ed. Petr Charvát and Jiří Prosecký, 169–75. Prague: Oriental Institute, Academy of Sciences of the Czech Republic.

Rashev, Rasho. 1983. "Pliska: The first capital of Bulgaria." In *Ancient Bulgaria: Papers Presented to the International Symposium on the Ancient History and Archaeology of Bulgaria, University of Nottingham, 1981,* ed. A. G. Poulter, 255–67. Nottingham: Department of Classical and Archaeological Studies, University of Nottingham.

Ratkoš, Peter. 1988. "The territorial development of Great Moravia (fiction and reality)." *Studia Historica Slovaca* 16:121–55.

Raukar, Tomislav. 1999. "Land and society." In *Croatia in the Early Middle Ages: A Cultural Survey,* ed. Ivan Supičić, 181–95. London: Philip Wilson Publishers; Zagreb: AGM.

Reisman, Edward Steven. 1987. "Determinants of Collective Identity in Rus', 988–1505." Ph.D. diss., University of Chicago.

Riasanovsky, Alexander V. 1962. "The embassy of 838 revisited." *Jahrbücher für Geschichte Osteuropas* 10:1–12.

———. 1980. "Pseudo-Varangian origins of the Kievo-Pecherskii monastery: The 'finger in the pie' hypothesis." *Russian History* 7:265–82.

Richter, Miroslav, Petr Sommer, and Tomáš Durdík. 1994. "Towns, monasteries, and feudal residences." In *25 Years of Archaeological Research in Bohemia*, ed. Jan Fridrich, 201–20. Prague: Institute of Archaeology of the Czechoslovak Academy of Sciences.

Risos, A. 1990. "The Vlachs of Larissa in the 10th century." *Byzantinoslavica* 51:202–7.

Romanchuk, Alla I. 1996. "Medieval Cherson: Agreement and discrepancy between written and archaeological sources." In *Acts. XVIIIth International Congress of Byzantine Studies: Selected Papers; Moscow 1991*, ed. Ihor Ševčenko, G. G. Litavrin, and Walter Hanak, 2:265–71. Shepherdstown, W.V.: Byzantine Studies Press.

Róna-Tas, András. 1997. "The migration of the Hungarians and their settlement in the Carpathian Basin." In *Historical and Linguistic Interaction between Inner Asia and Europe: Proceedings of the 39th Permanent International Altaistic Conference (PIAC), Szeged, Hungary, June 16–21, 1996*, ed. A. Berta and E. Horváth, 243–53. Szeged: Department of Altaic Studies.

———. 1999. *Hungarians and Europe in the Early Middle Ages: An Introduction to Early Hungarian History*. Budapest: Central European University Press.

———. 2000. "Where was Khuvrat's Bulgharia?" *Acta Orientalia Academiae Scientiarum Hungaricae* 53:1–22.

Ronin, V. K. 1985. "The Franks on the Balkans in the early ninth century." *Etudes Balkaniques* 1:39–57.

Rothe, Hans. 1995. "Slavia Latina in the Middle Ages between Slavia Orthodoxa and the Roman Empire (the pope and the emperor)." *Ricerche slavistiche* 42:75–87.

Runciman, Steven. 1930. *A History of the First Bulgarian Empire*. London: G. Bell and Sons.

———. 1983. "The Bulgarian Princes' List." In *Ancient Bulgaria: Papers Presented to the International Symposium on the Ancient History and Archaeology of Bulgaria, University of Nottingham, 1981*, ed. A. G. Poulter, 322–41. Nottingham: Department of Classical and Archaeological Studies, University of Nottingham.

Rusu, Mircea. 1975. "The autochthonous population and the Hungarians on the territory of Transylvania in the 9th–11th centuries." In *Relations between the Autochthonous Population and the Migratory Populations on the Territory of Romania*, ed. Miron Constantinescu, Ştefan Pascu, and Petre Diaconu, 201–17. Bucharest: Editura Academiei Republicii Socialiste România.

———. 1975. "Avars, Slavs, Romanic population in the 6th–8th centuries." In *Relations between the Autochthonous Population and the Migratory Populations on the Territory of Romania*, ed. Miron Constantinescu, Ştefan Pascu, and Petre Diaconu, 123–53. Bucharest: Editura Academiei Republicii Socialiste România.

Ruttkay, Alexander. 1982. "The organization of troops, warfare, and arms in the period of the Great Moravian state." *Slovenská Archeológia* 30:165–98.

Sághy, Marianne. 2001. "The making of the Christian kingdom in Hungary." In *Europe around the Year 1000*, ed. Przemysław Urbańczyk, 451–64. Warsaw: Wydawnictwo DiG.

Schmidt, Knut Rahbek. 1970. "The Varangian problem: A brief history of the controversy." In *Varangian Problems: Report on the First International Symposium on the Theme "The Eastern Connections of the Nordic Peoples in the Viking Period and Early Middle Ages," Moesgaard-Univeristy of Aarhus, October 7–11, 1968*, ed. Knut Hannestad, Knut Jordal, Ole Klindt-Jensen, et al., 7–20. Copenhague: Munksgaard.

Sedlar, Jean W. 1993. *East Central Europe in the Middle Ages, 1000–1500*. Seattle: University of Washington Press.

Sedov, V. V. 1984. "Old Russia and southern Finland (finds of Old Russian origin in Finland)." In *Fenno-Ugri e Slavi 1983: Papers Presented by the Participants in the Soviet-Finnish Symposium "Trade, Exchange, and Culture Relations of the Peoples of Fennoscandia and Eastern Europe," 9–13 May 1983, in the Hanasaari Congress Center*, ed. Torsten Edgren, 16–25. Helsinki: Vammala.

Setton, Kenneth. 1950. "The Bulgars in the Balkans and the occupation of Corinth in the 7th century." *Speculum* 25:502–43.

Ševčenko, Ihor. 1987. "Byzantium and the Slavs." In *Byzantio kai Europe: A' diethnes Byzantinologike Synantese, Delphoi, 20–24 Iouliou 1985*, ed. A. Markopoulos, 101–13. Athens: Europaiko Polistiko Kentro Delphon.

———. 1991. *Byzantium and the Slavs in Letters and Culture*. Cambridge: Harvard Ukrainian Research Institute; Naples: Instituto Universitario Orientale.

Shaskol'skii, I. P. 1970. "Recent developments in the Normannist controversy." In *Varangian Problems: Report on the First International Symposium on the Theme "The Eastern Connections of the Nordic Peoples in the Viking Period and Early Middle Ages," Moesgaard-University of Aarhus, October 7–11, 1968*, ed. Knut Hannestad, Knut Jordal, Ole Klindt-Jensen, et al., 21–38. Copenhague: Munksgaard.

Shchukin, Mark B. 1986–90. "The Balto-Slavic forest direction in the archaeological study of the ethnogenesis of the Slavs." *Wiadomości Archeologiczne* 51:3–30.

Shepard, Jonathan. 1975. "Byzantinorussica." *Revue des études byzantines* 33:211–25.

———. 1978. "The Russian steppe-frontier and the Black Sea zone." *Archeion Pontou* 35:218–37.

———. 1989. "Symeon of Bulgaria—peacemaker." *Godishnik na Sofiiskiia Universitet "Kliment Ohridski": Istoricheski Fakultet* 83:9–48.

———. 1995. "A marriage too far? Maria Lekapena and Peter of Bulgaria." In *The Empress Theophano: Byzantium and the West at the Turn of the First Millenium*, ed. Adelbert Davids, 121–49. Cambridge: Cambridge University Press.

———. 1995. "The Rhos guests of Louis the Pious: Whence and wherefore?" *Early Medieval Europe* 4:41–60.

———. 1998. "Slavs and Bulgars." In *The New Cambridge Medieval History*, ed. Timothy Reuter, 2:228–48. Cambridge: Cambridge University Press.

———. 1999. "Bulgaria: The other Balkan 'empire.'" In *The New Cambridge Medieval History*, ed. Timothy Reuter, 3:567–85. Cambridge: Cambridge University Press.

———. 1999. "Constantine VII's doctrine of 'containment' of the Rus.'" In *Gennadios: 70-letiiu akademika G. G. Litavrina*, ed. B. N. Floria, 264–83. Moscow: Indrik.

———. 2002. "Spreading the Word: Byzantine missions." In *The Oxford History of Byzantium*, ed. Cyril Mango, 230–47. Oxford: Oxford University Press.

———. 2003. "The ruler as instructor, pastor, and wise: Leo VI of Byzantium and Symeon of Bulgaria." In *Alfred the Great: Papers from the Eleventh-Centenary Conferences*, ed. Timothy Reuter, 339–58. Aldershot: Ashgate.

————. 2004. "Byzantine writers on the Hungarians in the ninth and tenth centuries." *Annual of Medieval Studies at the CEU* 10:97–123.

Shevelov, George Y. 1990. "'Prosta Cadb' and 'Prostaja Mova.'" In *Proceedings of the International Congress Commemorating the Millenium of Christianity in Rus'-Ukraine*, ed. Omeljan Pritsak, Ihor Ševčenko, and Miroslav Labunka, 593–624. Cambridge: Harvard University Press.

Shuvalov, Piotr V. 1996. "Politics and society in the lower Danube in the sixth century." In *Acts. XVIIIth International Congress of Byzantine Studies: Selected Papers; Moscow 1991*, ed. Ihor Ševčenko, G. G. Litavrin, and Walter Hanak, 2:82–87. Shepherdstown, W.V.: Byzantine Studies Press.

Sidorenko, V. A. 1996. "Procopius of Caesarea concerning the Dory region and the Long Walls of Byzantine Cherson." In *Acts. XVIIIth International Congress of Byzantine Studies: Selected Papers; Moscow 1991*, ed. Ihor Ševčenko, G. G. Litavrin, and Walter Hanak, 2:88–95. Shepherdstown, W. V.: Byzantine Studies Press.

Simeonova, Liliana. 1991–92. "Preslav in the mirror of the Byzantine narrative sources and the idea of reconquista." *Vyzantinos Domos* 5–6:165–75.

————. 1993. "Power in Nicholas Mysticus' letters to Symeon of Bulgaria: Notes on the political vocabulary of a tenth-century Byzantine statesman." *Byzantinoslavica* 54:89–94.

Sindbaek, Soeren Michael. 1999. "A Magyar occurrence: Process, practice, and ethnicity between Europe and the steppes." *Acta Archaeologica* 70:149–64.

Sinor, Denis. 1990. "The establishment and dissolution of the Türk Empire." In *The Cambridge History of Early Inner Asia*, ed. Denis Sinor, 285–316. Cambridge and New York: Cambridge University Press.

Slabe, Marijan. 1976. "The Ljubljana area at the time of the arrival of the Slavs." *Archaeologia Iugoslavica* 17:50–53.

Sláma, Jiří. 2000. "Boleslav I, Boleslav II, and Boleslav III." In *Europe's Centre around A.D. 1000*, ed. Alfried Wieczorek and Hans-Martin Hinz, 278–81. Stuttgart: Theiss.

————. 2000. "Premyślids and Slavnikids." In *Europe's Centre around A.D. 1000*, ed. Alfried Wieczorek and Hans-Martin Hinz, 282–83. Stuttgart: Theiss.

Slaveva, Lidia. 1992. "Slavic literacy and culture and the ethnogenesis of the Macedonian people." *Macedonian Review* 22:258–68.

Smedley, John. 1978. "Archaeology and history of Cherson: A survey of some results and problems." *Archeion Pontou* 35:172–92.

Smyser, H. M. 1965. "Ibn Fadlan's account of the Rus, with some commentary and some allusions to Beowulf." In *Medieval and Linguistic Studies in Honour of Francis Peabody Magoun Jr.*, ed. Jess B. Bessinger and Robert P. Creed, 92–119. London: George Allen and Unwin.

Sokol, Vladimir. 1999. "The archaeological heritage of the early Croats." In *Croatia in the Early Middle Ages: A Cultural Survey*, ed. Ivan Supičić, 117–46. London: Philip Wilson Publishers; Zagreb: AGM.

Sørensen, Hans Christian. 1968. "The so-called Varangian-Russian problem." *Scando-Slavica* 14:141–48.

————. 1970. "The so-called Varangian-Russian problem." In *Varangian Problems: Report on the First International Symposium on the Theme "The Eastern Connections of the Nordic Peoples in the Viking Period and Early Middle Ages," Moesgaard-University of Aarhus, October 7–11, 1968*, ed. Knud Hannestad, Knud Jordal, Ole Klindt-Jensen, et al., 133–42. Copenhague: Munksgaard.

Spinei, Victor. 1975. "Relations of the local population of Moldavia with the nomad Turanian tribes in the 10–13th centuries." In *Relations between the Autochthonous Population and the Migratory Populations on the Territory of Romania*, ed. Miron Constantinescu, Ştefan Pascu, and Petre Diaconu, 265–76. Bucharest: Editura Academiei Republicü Socialiste România.

———. 1991. "The Turkish nomadic population in Romanian countries in the 10th–14th centuries." In *Kongreye sunulan bildiriler X. Türk Tarih Kongresi, Ankara 22–26 Eylül 1986*, 3:981–89. Ankara: Türk Tarih Kurumu Basimevi.

Stalsberg, Anne. 1982. "Scandinavian relations with northwestern Russia during the Viking age: The archaeological evidence." *Journal of Baltic Studies* 13:267–95.

———. 1988. "The Scandinavian Viking age finds in Rus'." *Bericht der römisch-germanischen Kommission* 69:418–71.

Stavridou-Zafraka, A. 2000. "The development of the theme organisation in Macedonia." In *Byzantine Macedonia: Identity, Image, and History; Papers from the Melbourne Conference, July 1995*, ed. J. Burke and R. Scott, 128–38. Melbourne.

Stefanovičová, Tatiana. 1997. "Slavic settlement of Greece in the light of archaeological sources." In *Etnogenez i etnokul'turnye kontakty slavian*, ed. V. V. Sedov, 352–61. Moscow: Institut Arkheologii Rossüskoi Akademii Nauk.

———. 1999. "Great Moravia and Byzantium." In *Thessaloniki Magna Moravia*, 273–84. Thessaloniki: SS. Cyril and Methodios Center for Cultural Studies.

———. 2000. "The Nitran principality in Great Moravia and Hungary." In *Europe's Centre around A.D. 1000*, ed. Alfried Wieczorek and Hans-Martin Hinz, 200–201. Stuttgart: Theiss.

Steinhübel, Ján. 1995. "Division of Pannonia among Franconian marches." *Studia Historica Slovaca* 19:7–36.

Stein-Wilkeshuis, Martina. 1991. "A Viking-age treaty between Constantinople and Northern merchants, with its provisions on theft and robbery." *Scando-Slavica* 37: 35–47.

———. 1998. "Scandinavian law in a tenth century Rus'-Greek commercial treaty?" In *The Community, the Family, and the Saint: Patterns of Power in Early Medieval Europe; Selected Proceedings of the International Medieval Congress, University of Leeds, 4–7 July 1994, 10–13 July 1995*, ed. Joyce Hill and Mary Swan, 311–22. Turnhout: Brepols.

Stepanov, Tsvetelin. 1999. "Avitohol: A historical personality or a mythical figure?" *Bulgarian Centuries* 1:50–60.

———. 2000. "Ruler and doctrines in pre-Christian Bulgaria (an attempt for "reading" and interpretation)." *Godishnik na Sofiiskiia universitet "Kliment Okhridski"* 90:357–66.

———. 2001. "The Bulgar title *KANASYBIGI*: Reconstructing the notions of divine kingship in Bulgaria, AD 822–836." *Early Medieval Europe* 10:1–19.

———. 2004. "Notions of the 'other' in Pax Nomadica, 6th–9th centuries (Bulgars, Khazars, ancient Turks, and Uighurs)." In *Civitas divino-humana. V chest na profesor Georgi Bakalov*, ed. Tsvetelin Stepanov and Veselina Vachkova, 609–24. Sofia: Centăr za izsledvaniia na bălgarite Tangra TanNakRa IK.

Stephenson, Paul. 1999. "The Byzantine frontier at the lower Danube in the late tenth and eleventh centuries." In *Frontiers in Question: Eurasian Borderlands, 700–1700*, ed. Daniel Power and Naomi Standen, 80–104. New York: St. Martin's Press.

———. 2000. "The Byzantine frontier in Macedonia." *Dialogos* 7:23–40.

———. 2000. *Byzantium's Balkan Frontier: A Political Study of the Northern Balkans, 900–1204*. Cambridge: Cambridge University Press.

———. 2001. "Early Medieval Hungary in English." *Early Medieval Europe* 10:95–112.

Stipišić, Jakov. 1999. "Croatia in diplomatic sources up to the end of the 11th century." In *Croatia in the Early Middle Ages: A Cultural Survey*, ed. Ivan Supičić, 285–318. London: Philip Wilson Publishers; Zagreb: AGM.

Stokes, A. D. 1961–62. "The background and chronology of the Balkan campaigns of Svyatoslav Igorevich." *Slavonic and East European Review* 40:44–57.

Strzelczyk, Jerzy. 1999. "Bohemia and Poland: Two examples of successful western Slavonic state-formation." In *The New Cambridge Medieval History*, ed. Timothy Reuter, 3:514–35. Cambridge: Cambridge University Press.

———. 2000. "The first two historical Piasts: Opinions and interpretations." *Quaestiones Medii Aevi* 5:99–143.

———. 2000. "The foreign relations of the first Piasts." In *Europe's Centre around A.D. 1000*, ed. Alfried Wieczorek and Hans-Martin Hinz, 345–47. Stuttgart: Theiss.

———. 2000. "The Gniezno assembly and the creation of the Gniezno archbishopric." In *Europe's Centre around A.D. 1000*, ed. Alfried Wieczorek and Hans-Martin Hinz, 319–21. Stuttgart: Theiss.

———. 2000. "The Piasts and Poland." In *Europe's Centre around A.D. 1000*, ed. Alfried Wieczorek and Hans-Martin Hinz, 342–44. Stuttgart: Theiss.

———. 2000. "Poland in the tenth century." In *Europe's Centre around A.D. 1000*, ed. Alfried Wieczorek and Hans-Martin Hinz, 287–94. Stuttgart: Theiss.

Szádeczky-Kardoss, Samuel. 1990. "The Avars." In *The Cambridge History of Early Inner Asia*, ed. Denis Sinor, 206–28. Cambridge and New York: Cambridge University Press.

Szőke, Béla Miklós. 1991. "The question of continuity in the Carpathain Basin of the 9th century." *Antaeus* 19–20:145–57.

———. 2000. "Political, cultural, and ethnic conditions in the Carpathian Basin at the time of the Magyar's conquest." In *Europe's Centre around A.D. 1000*, ed. Alfried Wieczorek and Hans-Martin Hinz, 137–39. Stuttgart: Theiss.

Szücs, Jenő. 1990. "The peoples of medieval Hungary." In *Ethnicity and Society in Hungary*, ed. Ferenc Glatz, 11–20. Budapest: Institute of History of the Hungarian Academy of Sciences.

Tachiaos, A. E. 1988–89. "The Greek metropolitans of Kievan Rus': An evaluation of their spiritual and cultural activity." *Harvard Ukrainian Studies* 12–13:433–42.

———. 1993–94. "Some controversial points relating to the life and activity of Cyril and Methodius." *Cyrillomethodianum* 17–18:41–72.

———. 2002. "Cyril and Methodius' visit to Rome in 868: Was it scheduled or fortuitous?" *Palaeoslavica* 10:210–21.

Takács, Miklós. 1998. "How did conquering Hungarians prepare and serve their food?" In *Tender Meat under the Saddle: Customs of Eating, Drinking, and Hospitality among Conquering Hungarians and Nomadic Peoples; In Memory of Gyula László (1910–1998)*, ed. József Lászlovszky, 98–119. Krems: Medium Aevum Quotidianum.

Tallgren, A. M. 1938. "The prehistory of Ingria." *Eurasia Septentrionalis Antiqua* 12:90–105.

Tăpkova-Zaimova, Vasilka, and Liliana Simeonova. 1987. "Aspects of the Byzantine cultural policy towards Bulgaria in the epoch of Photius." In *Byzantio kai Europe: A' diethnes Byzantinologike Synantese, Delphoi, 20–24 Iouliou 1985*, ed. A. Markopoulos, 153–63. Athens: Europaiko Polistiko Kentro Delphon.

Tashkovski, Dragan. 1973. "Samuel's empire." *Macedonian Review* 3:34–38.

Teodor, Dan Gh. 1975. "Natives and Slavs in the East-Carpathian region of Romania in the 6th–10th centuries." In *Relations between the Autochthonous Population and the Migratory Populations on the Territory of Romania*, ed. Miron Constantinescu, Ștefan Pascu, and Petre Diaconu, 155–70. Bucharest: Editura Academiei Republicii Socialiste România.

———. 1980. *The East-Carpathian Area of Romania in the V–XI Centuries A.D.* Oxford: B.A.R.

Terpilovskii, R. V. 1992. "The Slavs of the Dnieper basin in the Migration Period." In *Medieval Europe 1992: Death and burial*, 4:161–66. York: Medieval Europe.

Thomson, Francis J. 1978. "The nature of the reception of Christian Byzantine culture in Russia in the tenth to thirteenth centuries and its implications for Russian culture." *Slavica Gandensia* 5:107–39.

———. 1985. "Early Slavonic tradition: An Italo-Greek connection." *Slavica Gandensia* 12:221–34.

———. 1988–89. "The Bulgarian contribution to the reception of Byzantine culture in Kievan Rus': The myths and the enigma." *Harvard Ukrainian Studies* 12–13:214–61.

———. 1991. "John the Exarch's theological education and proficiency in Greek as revealed by his abridged translation of John of Damascus' 'De fide orthodoxa.'" *Palaeobulgarica* 15:35–58.

———. 1992. "SS. Cyril and Methodius and a mythical Western heresy: Trilinguism; A contribution to the study of patristic and medieval theories of sacred languages." *Analecta Bollandiana* 110:67–122.

Tirr, D. A. 1976. "The attitude of the West towards the Avars." *Acta Archaeologica Academiae Scientiarum Hungaricae* 28:111–21.

Tolochko, Oleksyi. 2001. "Kievan Rus' around the year 1000." In *Europe around the Year 1000*, ed. Przemysław Urbańczyk, 123–39. Warsaw: Wydawnictwo DiG.

Tomka, Peter. 1998. "Customs of eating and hospitality among nomadic peoples of the migration period." In *Tender Meat under the Saddle: Customs of Eating, Drinking, and Hospitality among Conquering Hungarians and Nomadic Peoples; In Memory of Gyula László (1910–1998)*, ed. József Lászlovszky, 75–97. Krems: Medium Aevum Quotidianum.

Tóth, Sándor László. 1994. "Hungarian-Bulgarian contacts in the ninth century." In *Hungaro-Bulgarica V. Szegedi Bolgarisztika*, ed. Samu Szádeczky-Kardoss, Téréz Olajos, I. H. Tóth, and István Ferincz, 71–78. Szeged: Kiadja a JATE-Press.

———. 1999. "The territories of the Hungarian tribal federation around 950 (some observations on Constantine VII's 'Tourkia')." In *Byzanz und Ostmitteleuropa, 950–1453: Beiträge zu einer table-ronde des XIX Internationalen Congress of Byzantine Studies, Copenhagen 1996*, ed. Günter Prinzing and Maciej Salamon, 23–33. Wiesbaden: Otto Harrassowitz.

Treadgold, Warren T. 1984. "The Bulgars' treaty with the Byzantines in 816." *Rivista di studi bizantini e slavi* 4:213–20.

———. 1988–89. "Three Byzantine provinces and the first Byzantine contacts with the Rus'." *Harvard Ukrainian Studies* 12–13:132–44.

Třeštík, Dušan. 2000. "Christian the Monk, brother of Boleslav II." In *Europe's Centre around A.D. 1000,* ed. Alfried Wieczorek and Hans-Martin Hinz, 270–71. Stuttgart: Theiss.

———. 2000. "The creation of a Slavic empire: The Great Moravian empire." In *Europe's Centre around A.D. 1000,* ed. Alfried Wieczorek and Hans-Martin Hinz, 193–95. Stuttgart: Theiss.

———. 2000. "The Czechs." In *Europe's Centre around A.D. 1000,* ed. Alfried Wieczorek and Hans-Martin Hinz, 227–34. Stuttgart: Theiss.

———. 2000. "Wenceslas, Ludmilla, and Adalbert." In *Europe's Centre around A.D. 1000,* ed. Alfried Wieczorek and Hans-Martin Hinz, 586–88. Stuttgart: Theiss.

———. 2001. "Bohemia's iron year." In *Europe around the Year 1000,* ed. Przemysław Urbańczyk, 427–50. Warsaw: Wydawnictwo DiG.

Třeštík, Dušan, and Anežka Merhautová. 2000. "The Czech insignia and the stone throne." In *Europe's Centre around A.D. 1000,* ed. Alfried Wieczorek and Hans-Martin Hinz, 600–601. Stuttgart: Theiss.

Tuma, Oldřich. 1996. "Contacts between central Europe and Byzantium in the ninth to the eleventh centuries." In *Acts. XVIIIth International Congress of Byzantine Studies: Selected Papers; Moscow 1991,* ed. Ihor Ševčenko, G. G. Litavrin, and Walter Hanak, 2:135–42. Shepherdstown, W.V.: Byzantine Studies Press.

Tyszkiewicz, Jan. 1975. "Cultural processes connected with expansion of the Rus' of Kiev towards Lithuania in the 9th–11th centuries." *Archaeologia Polona* 16:107–26.

Urbańczyk, Przemysław. 1997. "Changes of power structure during the first millenium A.D. in the northern part of central Europe." In *Origins of Central Europe,* ed. Przemysław Urbańczyk, 39–44. Warsaw: Scientific Society of Polish Archaeologists.

———. 2001. "The Lower Vistula areas as a 'region of power' and its continental contacts." In *Topographies of Power in the Early Middle Ages,* ed. Mayke de Jong, Frans Theuws, and Carine van Rhijn, 509–32. Leiden, Boston, and Cologne: Brill.

———. 2002. "Foreign leaders in early Slavic societies." In *Integration und Herrschaft: Ethnische Identitäten und soziale Organisation im Frühmittelalter,* ed. Walter Pohl and Max Diesenberger, 257–68. Vienna: Verlag der Österreichischen Akademie der Wissenschaften.

Váczy, P. 1990–91. "The Byzantine emperor Constantine VII Porphyrogenitus and the saga of the Hungarian conquest." *Antaeus* 19–20:251–56.

———. 1990–91. "Some questions of early Hungarian material culture." *Antaeus* 19–20: 257–329.

Valtonen, Irmeli. 1992. "A land beyond seas and mountains: A study of references to Finland in Anglo-Saxon sources." In *Suomen varhaishistoria: Tornion kongressi 14.– 16.6.1991,* ed. Kyösti Julku and Markus H. Korhonen, 641–51. Rovaniemi: Pohjois Suomen Historiallinen Yhdistys.

Vána, Zdeněk. 1983. *The World of the Ancient Slavs.* Detroit: Wayne State University Press.

Vasary, I. 1988. "Medieval theories concerning the primordial homeland of the Hungarians." In *Popoli delle stepe: Unni, Avari, Ungari,* 1:213–42. Spoleto: La pressa del Centro.

Vasiliev, Alexander Alexandrovich. 1936. *The Goths in the Crimea.* Cambridge: Medieval Academy of America.

———. 1946. *The Russian Attack on Constantinople in 860.* Cambridge: Medieval Academy of America.

Vavřínek, Vladimír. 1999. "Great Moravia between Byzantium and the Latin West." In *Gennadios: 70-letiiu akademika G. G. Litavrina*, ed. B. N. Floria, 39–55. Moscow: Indrik.

Vavřínek, Vladimír, and Bohůmila Zasterová. 1982. "Byzantium's role in the formation of Great Moravian culture." *Byzantinoslavica* 43:161–88.

Văzharova, Zhivka. 1970. "The Slavs south of the Danube." In *I. Międzynarodowy Kongres archeologii słowiańskiej, Warszawa 14–18 IX 1965*, ed. Witold Hensel, 3:96–120. Wrocław, Warsaw, and Cracow: Wydawnictwo Polskiej Akademii Nauk.

Vékony, Gábor. 1979. "The role of a march in ethnic political changes." *Acta Orientalia Academiae Scientiarum Hungaricae* 33:301–14.

———. 1998. "Feasting and hospitality among Eastern nomadic peoples." In *Tender Meat under the Saddle: Customs of Eating, Drinking, and Hospitality among Conquering Hungarians and Nomadic Peoples; In Memory of Gyula László (1910–1998)*, ed. József Lászlovszky, 61–74. Krems: Medium Aevum Quotidianum.

Vernadsky, George. 1938. "The Spali of Jordanis and the Spori of Procopius." *Byzantion* 13:263–66.

———. 1939. "Lebedia: Studies on the Magyar background of Kievan Russia." *Byzantion* 14:179–203.

———. 1939. "On the origins of Antae." *Journal of the American Oriental Society* 59:56–66.

———. 1940–41. "Byzantium and southern Russia: Two notes." *Byzantion* 15:67–86.

———. 1943. *Ancient Russia*. New Haven: Yale University Press.

———. 1946. "The Rus' in the Crimea and the Russo-Byzantine treaty of 945." *Byzantina-Metabyzantina* 1:249–60.

Veszprémy, Lászlo. 1995. "Mythical origins of the Hungarian medieval legislation." *Parliaments, Estates, and Representation* 15:67–72.

———. 2000. "Hungary: A historical overview." In *Europe's Centre around A. D. 1000*, ed. Alfried Wieczorek and Hans-Martin Hinz, 351–57. Stuttgart: Theiss.

———. 2000. "Stephen: King and saint." In *Europe's Centre around A.D. 1000*, ed. Alfried Wieczorek and Hans-Martin Hinz, 581–83. Stuttgart: Theiss.

Völling, Thomas. 2001. "The last Christian Greeks and the first pagan Slavs in Olympia." In *Hoi skoteinoi aiones tou Byzantiou (70s–90s ai.)*, ed. Eleonora Kountoura-Galake, 302–23. Athens: Ethniko Idryma Ereunon and Institouto Byzantinon Ereunon.

Weinfurter, Stefan. 2000. "New wars: Henry II and his policy in the East." In *Europe's Centre around A.D. 1000*, ed. Alfried Wieczorek and Hans-Martin Hinz, 536–39. Stuttgart: Theiss.

Werbart, B. 1996. "'Khazars' or 'Saltovo-Majaki-Culture'? Prejudices about archaeology and ethnicity." *Current Swedish Archaeology* 4:199–221.

Whitaker, I. 1983. "Late classical and early mediaeval accounts of the Lapps (Sami)." *Classica et Mediaevalia* 34:283–303.

Wilson, David M. 1970. "East and West: A comparison of Viking settlement." In *Varangian Problems: Report on the First International Symposium on the Theme "The Eastern Connections of the Nordic Peoples in the Viking Period and Early Middle Ages," Moesgaard-University of Aarhus, October 7–11, 1968*, ed. Knud Hannestad, Knud Jordal, Ole Klindt-Jensen, et al., 107–20. Copenhague: Munksgaard.

Wolfram, Herwig. 1989. "The image of Central Europe in Constantine VII Porphyrogenitus." In *Konstantinos ho Porphyrogennetos kai he epokhe tou: Diethnes Byzanti-*

nologike synantese Delphoi, 22–26 Iouliou 1986, ed. A. Markopoulos, 5–14. Athens: Eurapadko Politisko Kentro Delphon.

———. 1997. "The ethno-political entities in the region of the upper and middle Danube in the 6th–9th centuries A.D." In *Origins of Central Europe,* ed. Przemysław Urbańczyk, 45–57. Warsaw: Scientific Society of Polish Archaeologists.

———. 2000. "New states and peoples around the year 1000." In *Europe's Centre around A.D. 1000,* ed. Alfried Wieczorek and Hans-Martin Hinz, 217–23. Stuttgart: Theiss.

———. 2001. "New peoples around the year 1000." In *Europe around the Year 1000,* ed. Przemysław Urbańczyk, 391–408. Warsaw: Wydawnictwo DiG.

Wortley, John. 1980. "Legends of the Byzantine disaster of 811." *Byzantion* 50:533–62.

Wozniak, Frank E. 1975. "Byzantine policy on the Black Sea or Russian steppe in the late 830s." *Byzantine Studies* 2:56–62.

———. 1979. "Byzantine diplomacy and the Lombard-Gepidic wars." *Balkan Studies* 20:139–58.

———. 1984. "Byzantium, the Pechenegs and the Rus': The limitations of a great power's influence on its clients in the 10th century Eurasian steppe." *Archivum Eurasiae Medii Aevi* 4:299–316.

Wyszomirska-Werbart, Bożena. 1992. "Scandinavia and the Eastern Baltic during the Migration Period. The cultural interactions." In *Contacts Across the Baltic Sea During the Late Iron Age (5th–12th Centuries). Baltic Sea Conference, Lund October 25–27, 1991,* ed. Birgitta Hårdh and Bożena Wyszomirska-Werbart, 59–72. Lund: Institute of Archaeology and Historical Museum.

Zemlička, Josef. 2000. "Centres and the organisation of rule." In *Europe's Centre around A.D. 1000,* ed. Alfried Wieczorek and Hans-Martin Hinz, 235–38. Stuttgart: Theiss.

———. 2000. "The common traits of Central European states." In *Europe's Centre around A.D. 1000,* ed. Alfried Wieczorek and Hans-Martin Hinz, 545–47. Stuttgart: Theiss.

———. 2000. "The Premyslids and Bohemia." In *Europe's Centre around A.D. 1000,* ed. Alfried Wieczorek and Hans-Martin Hinz, 274–77. Stuttgart: Theiss.

Zientara, Benedykt. 1974. "Foreigners in Poland in the 10th–15th centuries: Their role in the opinion of the Polish medieval community." *Acta Poloniae Historica* 29:5–28.

Zimonyi, István. 1990. *Origins of the Volga Bulghars.* Szeged: Universitas Szegediensis de Attila József nominata.

———. 1997. "The concept of nomadic polity in the Hungarian chapter of Constantine 'Porphyrogenitus' De administrando imperio." In *Historical and Linguistic Interaction between Inner Asia and Europe: Proceedings of the 39th Permanent International Altaistic Conference (PIAC), Szeged, Hungary, June 16–21, 1996,* ed. A. Berta and E. Horváth, 459–71. Szeged: Department of Altaic Studies.

Zlatarski, V. N. 1925–26. "The making of the Bulgarian nation." *Slavonic and East European Review* 4:364–65.

Zuckerman, C. 1995. "A Gothia in the Hellespont in the early eighth century." *Byzantine and Modern Greek Studies* 19:234–41.

TECHNOLOGY, TRADE, AND ECONOMIC HISTORY

Beranová, Magdalena. 1966. "The raising of domestic animals among Slavs in early Middle Ages according to archaeological sources." *Vznik a počátky Slovanů* 6:153–96.

————. 1984. "Types of Slavic agricultural production in the 6th–12th centuries." *Ethnologia Slavica* 16:7–48.

————. 1987. "Manual rotation grain mills on Czechoslovak territory up to the incipient 2nd millenium A.D." *Ethnologia Slavica* 19:15–43.

Bialeková, Darina. 2000. "Iron currency bars." In *Europe's Centre around A.D. 1000,* ed. Alfried Wieczorek and Hans-Martin Hinz, 128–29. Stuttgart: Theiss.

Bliujiéne, Audrone. 2003. "Lithuanian amber artifacts from the Roman Iron Age to early medieval times." In *Amber in Archaeology. Proceedings of the Fourth International Conference on Amber in Archaeology, Talsi 2001,* ed. Curt W. Beck, Ilze B. Loze, and Joan M. Todd, 47–71. Riga: Institute of the History of Latvia.

Bökönyi, Sándor. 1995. "The development of stockbreeding and herding in medieval Europe." In *Agriculture in the Middle Ages: Technology, Practice, and Representation,* ed. Del Sweeney, 41–61. Philadelphia: University of Pennsylvania Press.

Bravermannová, Milena, Petr Charvát, Vlastimíl Novák, and Kateřina Tomková. 2000. "Trade between the West and the East." In *Europe's Centre around A.D. 1000,* ed. Alfried Wieczorek and Hans-Martin Hinz, 91–92. Stuttgart: Theiss.

Brutzkus, J. 1943. "Trade with Eastern Europe, 800–1200." *Economic History Review* 13:31–41.

Callmer, Johan. 1994. "Urbanization in Scandinavia and the Baltic region ca. AD 700–1100: Trading places, centres, and early urban sites." In *Developments around the Baltic Sea in the Viking Age: The Twelfth Viking Congress,* ed. Björn Ambrosiani and Helen Clarke, 50–90. Stockholm.

————. 1987. "Pragmatic notes on the early medieval beadmaterial in Scandinavia and the Baltic region, ca. A.D. 600–1000." In *Studia nad etnogeneza słowian i kultury Europy wczesnośredniowiecznej: Praca zbiorowa,* ed. Gerard Labuda and Stanisław Tabaczyński, 1:217–26. Wrocław, Warsaw, Cracow, Gdańsk, and Łódż: Zaklad Narodowy imeria Ossolińskich.

————. 1990. "The beginning of the Easteuropean trade connections of Scandinavia and the Baltic regions in the 8th and 9th centuries A.D." *A Wosinszky Mór Múzeum Evkönyve* 15:19–51.

————. 1997. "Beads and bead production in Scandinavia and the Baltic region c. AD 600–1100: A general outline." In *Perlen: Archäologie, Techniken, Analysen; Akten des Internationalen Perlensymposiums in Mannheim vom 11. bis 14. November 1994,* ed. Uta von Freeden and Alfried Wieczorek, 197–202. Bonn: Rudolf Habelt.

Charvát, Petr. 2000. "Bohemia, Moravia, and long-distance trade in the 10th–11th centuries." *Quaestiones Medii Aevi* 5:255–66.

Ciháková, Jarmila. 2000. "Prague around the year 1000: Infrastructure and communications." In *Europe's Centre around A.D. 1000,* ed. Alfried Wieczorek and Hans-Martin Hinz, 113–14. Stuttgart: Theiss.

Filipowiak, Władysław. 1994. "Shipbuilding at the mouth of the river Odra (Oder)." In *Crossroads in Ancient Shipbuilding: Proceedings of the Sixth International Symposium on Boat and Ship Archaeology, Roskilde 1991,* ed. Christer Westerdahl, 83–96. Oxford: Oxbow.

Gieysztor, Aleksander. 1987. "Trade and industry in Eastern Europe before 1200." In *Cambridge Economic History of Europe,* ed. M. M. Postan and Edward Miller, 2:474–524. Cambridge: Cambridge University Press.

Giuzelev, Vasil. 1980. "Economic development and forms of social and political organisation of the Proto-Bulgarians prior to the foundation of the Bulgarian state (4th–7th c.)." *Barukan Sho Ajia kenkyu* 6:95–103.

Golden, Peter B. 1991. "Aspects of the nomadic factor in the economic development of Kievan Rus." In *Ukrainian Economic History: Interpretive Essays*, ed. I. A. Koropeckyj, 58–101. Cambridge: Harvard University Press.

Indruszewski, George. 2003. "Early medieval ships as ethnic symbols and the construction of a historical paradigm in Northern and Central Europe." In *Inventing the Pasts in North Central Europe: the National Perception of Early Medieval History and Archaeology*, ed. Matthias Hardt, Christian Lübke, and Dittmar Schorkowitz, 69–95. Bern, etc.: Peter Lang.

Jagodzinski, Marek. 2000. "Truso: A settlement and port of the Slav-Aesti borderland." In *Europe's Centre around A.D. 1000*, ed. Alfried Wieczorek and Hans-Martin Hinz, 111–12. Stuttgart: Theiss

Jagodzinski, Marek, and Maria Kaśprzycka. 1991. "The early medieval craft and commercial centre at Janów Pomorski near Elblag on the south Baltic coast." *Antiquity* 65:696–715.

Krumphanzlová, Zdenka. 1992. "Amber: Its significance in the early Middle Ages." *Památky Archeologické* 83:350–71.

Kuleff, I., and R. Dzhingova. 2002. "Glass production during Roman and medieval times on the territory of Bulgaria." *Archaeologia Bulgarica* 6:101–8.

Kuleff, I., R. Dzhingova, and G. Dzhingov. 1985. "Provenience study of medieval Bulgarian glasses by NAA and cluster analysis." *Archaeometry* 27:185–93.

Madgearu, Alexandru. 2001. "Salt trade and warfare in early medieval Transylvania." *Ephemeris Napocensis* 11:271–84.

Mamzer, H. 1988. "Determinants of technical development in ferrous metallurgy in Central Europe in antiquity and the early Middle Ages." In *Trudy V Mezhdunarodnogo Kongressa arkheologov-slavistov, Kiev 18–25 sentiabria 1985 g.*, ed. P. P. Tolochko. 2:104–7. Kiev: Naukova Dumka.

Mugurevics, Evalds. 2003. "Viking Age and medieval finds of East Baltic amber in Latvia and the neighboring countries (9th–16th century)." In *Amber in Archaeology. Proceedings of the Fourth International Conference on Amber in Archaeology, Talsi 2001*, ed. Curt W. Beck, Ilze B. Loze, and Joan M. Todd, 90–95. Riga: Institute of the History of Latvia.

Noonan, Thomas S. 1965. "The Dnieper trade route in Kievan Russia (900–1240 A.D.)." Ph.D. diss., Indiana University, Bloomington.

———. 1982. "Khazaria as an intermediary between Islam and Eastern Europe in the second half of the ninth century." *Archivum Eurasiae Medii Aevi* 2:222–51.

———. 1990. "Scandinavian-Russian-Islamic trade in the ninth century." *A Wosinszky Mór Múzeum Evkönyve* 15:53–63.

———. 1992. "Fluctuations in Islamic trade with Eastern Europe during the Viking age." *Harvard Ukrainian Studies* 16:237–59.

———. 1992. "Rus', Pechenegs, and Polovtsy: Economic interaction along the steppe frontier in the pre-Mongol era." *Russian History* 19:301–26.

———. 1994. "The Vikings in the East: Coins and commerce." In *The Twelfth Viking Congress: Development around the Baltic and the North Sea in the Viking Age*, ed. Björn Ambrosiani and Helen Clarke, 215–36. Stockholm: Birka Project.

———. 1994. "What can archaeology tell us about the economy of Khazaria?" In *The*

Archaeology of the Steppes: Methods and Strategies; Papers from the International Symposium Held in Naples, 9–12 September 1992, ed. Bruno Genito, 331–45. Naples: Istituto universitario orientale.

————. 1995–97. "The Khazar economy." *Archivum Eurasiae Medii Aevi* 9:253–314.

————. 2000. "Coins, trade, and the origins of ninth-century Rus' towns." In *Akten-Proceedings-Actes. XII. Internationaler Numismatischer Kongress, Berlin 1997*, ed. B. Kluge and B. Weisser, 934–42. Berlin: Staatliche Museen zu Berlin and Gebrüder Mann Verlag.

————. 2000. "The fur road and the silk road: the relations between Central Asia and northern Russia in the early Middle Ages." In *Kontakte zwischen Iran, Byzanz und der Steppe im 6.–7. Jahrhundert*, ed. Csanád Bálint, 285–302. Budapest: Institut für Archäologie der Ungarischen Akademie der Wissenschaften.

————. 2000–2001. "Volga Bulgharia tenth-century trade with Samanid Central Asia." *Archivum Eurasiae Medii Aevi* 11:140–218.

Nosov, E. N. 1980. "International trade routes and early urban centres in the north of ancient Russia." In *Fenno-Ugri et Slavi*, 49–62. Helsinki: Suomen Muinaismuistoyhdistys.

Oikonomides, Nicholas. 1988. "Tribute or trade? The Byzantine-Bulgarian treaty of 716." In *Issledovaniia po slaviano-vizantiiskomu i zapadnoevropeiskomu srednevekov'iu: Posviashchaetsia pamiati Ivana Duicheva*, ed. Petar Dinekov, Aksinia Dzhurova, Georgi Bakalov, et al., 29–31. Sofia: Centăr dlia slaviano-vizantiiskikh issledovanii imeni Ivana Duicheva and Gosudarstvennoe izdatelstvo imeni D-ra Petra Berona.

Olczak, Jerzy. 1987. "The state and prospects of research into glassmaking in Poland in the early and late Middle Ages." *Archaeologia Polona* 25–26:107–19.

Paládi-Kovács, Attila. 1996. "Hungarian horse-keeping in the 9th–10th centuries." *Acta Ethnographica Hungarica* 41:55–66.

Pleiner, Radomír. 1960. "Experimental smelting of steel in early medieval furnaces." *Památky Archeologické* 60:458–87.

Pritsak, Omeljan. 1970. "An Arabic text on the trade route of the corporation of the ar-Rus in the second half of the ninth century." *Folia orientalia* 12:241–59.

Smedley, J. 1977–78. "Some aspects of trade in Cherson, 6th–10th centuries." *Archeion Pontou* 34:20–27.

————. 1980. "Trade in Cherson, 6th–10th centuries." In *Actes du XV-e Congrès international d'études byzantines, Athènes, septembre 1976*, ed. P. Zepos, 4:291–97. Athens: Association internationale des études byzantines.

Smolarek, Przemysław. 1994. "Aspects of early boatbuilding in the southern Baltic region." In *Crossroads in Ancient Shipbuilding: Proceedings of the Sixth International Symposium on Boat and Ship Archaeology, Roskilde 1991*, ed. Christer Westerdahl, 77–81. Oxford: Oxbow.

Souchopová, V., and R. Pleiner. 1979. "Excavations of Slav bloomeries at Olomucany, Moravia." *Archeologické rozhledy* 31:317.

Sprincz, Emma. 2003. "Amber artifacts of Hungary from the Middle Bronze Age to the Hungarian conquest (from 1600 BC to 896 AD)." In *Amber in Archaeology. Proceedings of the Fourth International Conference on Amber in Archaeology, Talsi 2001*, ed. Curt W. Beck, Ilze B. Loze, and Joan M. Todd, 203–12. Riga: Institute of the History of Latvia.

Takács, Miklós. 2000. "Economy and settlement in Hungary in the period of the foundation of the Hungarian state." In *Europe's Centre around A.D. 1000*, ed. Alfried Wieczorek and Hans-Martin Hinz, 80–83. Stuttgart: Theiss.

Tomková, Kateřina. 1992. "Exchange between Bohemia and other European countries." In *Medieval Europe 1992: Exchange and Trade*, 5:125–30. York: Medieval Europe.

Tuma, Oldřich. 1985. "Great Moravia's trade contacts with the eastern Mediterranean and the mediating role of Venice." *Byzantinoslavica* 46:67–77.

Vaitkunskienė, Laima. 1992. "Amber in the art and religion of the ancient Balts." In *Contacts Across the Baltic Sea During the Late Iron Age (5th–12th Centuries). Baltic Sea Conference, Lund October 25–27, 1991*, ed. by Birgitta Hårdh and Bożena Wyszomirska-Werbart, 49–57. Lund: Institute of Archaeology and Historical Museum.

SOCIAL HISTORY

Beshevliev, V. 1955. "What was the title *itzirgou (itzourgou) boilas* in the Protobulgarian inscriptions?" *Byzantinoslavica* 16:120–24.

Comşa, Maria. 1975. "Socio-economic organisation of the Dacoromanic and Slav population on the lower Danube during the 6th and 7th centuries." In *Relations between the Autochthonous Population and the Migratory Populations on the Territory of Romania*, ed. Miron Constantinescu, Ştefan Pascu, and Petre Diaconu, 171–200. Bucharest: Editura Academiei Republicü Socialiste Românâ.

Curta, Florin. 1999. "Feasting with 'kings' in an ancient democracy: On the Slavic society of the early Middle Ages (sixth to seventh century A.D.)." *Essays in Medieval Studies* 15:19–34.

Granberg, Antoaneta. 2004. "Observations on Bulgarian clan names in the 7th–9th centuries." In *Civitas divino-humana. V chest na profesor Georgi Bakalov*, ed. Tsvetelin Stepanov and Veselina Vachkova, 551–61. Sofia: Centăr za izsledvaniia na bălgarite Tangra TanNakRa IK.

Lászlovszky, József. 1991. "Social stratification and material culture in 10th–14th century Hungary." In *Alltag und materielle Kultur im mittelalterlichen Ungarn*, ed. András Kubinyi and József Lászlovszky, 32–67. Krems: Medium Aevum Quotidianum.

Nikolov, G. N. 2001. "The Bulgarian aristocracy in the war against the Byzantine Empire (971–1019)." In *Byzantium and East Central Europe*, ed. Maciej Salamon, Günter Prinzing, and Paul Stephenson, 141–58. Cracow: Secesja.

Profantová, Nad'a. 1997. "On the archaeological evidence for Bohemian elites of the 8th–9th century." In *Central Europe in 8th–10th Centuries: International Scientific Conference, Bratislava October 2–4, 1995*, ed. Dušan Čaplovič and Ján Dorul'a, 105–14. Bratislava: Ministry of Culture in the Slovak Republic and Slovak Academy of Sciences.

———. 2000. "Social elites." In *Europe's Centre around A.D. 1000*, ed. Alfried Wieczorek and Hans-Martin Hinz, 189–90. Stuttgart: Theiss.

Ševčenko, Ihor. 1971. "On the social background of Cyril and Methodius." In *Studia paleoslovenica*, ed. B. Havránek, 331–51. Prague: Academia.

Stalsberg, Anne. 2001. "Visible women made invisible: Interpreting Varangian women in Old Russia." In *Gender and the Archaeology of Death*, ed. by Bettina Arnold and Nancy L. Wicker, 65–79. Walnut Creek, Lanham, New York, and Oxford: Altamira Press.

Zemlička, Josef. 1994. "Origins of noble landed property in Premyslide Bohemia." In *Nobilities in Central and Eastern Europe: Kingship, Property, and Privilege*, ed. János M. Bak, 7–24. Krems: Medium Aevum Cotidianum.

PAGANISM, CONVERSION, CHURCH ORGANIZATION, AND HERESY

Ashanin, Charles B. 1991. "The Primary Chronicle and the conversion of Russia to Christianity in the 10th century." *Patristic and Byzantine Review* 10:57–64.

Atanasov, Georgi. 1996. "Influences ethno-culturelles dans l'ermitage rupestre près de Murfatlar." *Byzantinoslavica* 57:112–24.

Baán, István. 1997. "The foundation of the archbishopric of Kalocsa: The Byzantine origin of the second archdiocese in Hungary." In *Early Christianity in Central and Eastern Europe*, ed. Przemysław Urbańczyk, 67–73. Warsaw: Semper.

———. 1999. "The metropolitanate of Tourkia: The organization of the Byzantine church in Hungary in the Middle Ages." In *Byzanz und Ostmitteleuropa, 950–1453: Beiträge zu einer table-ronde des XIX Internationalen Congress of Byzantine Studies, Copenhagen 1996*, ed. Günter Prinzing and Maciej Salamon, 45–53. Wiesbaden: Harrassowitz.

Bakalova, E. 1996. "The role and importance of monasteries in the cultural history of Bulgaria." In *Taseis tou orthodoxou monakhismou, 90s–200s aiones: Praktika tou Diethnous Symposiou pou diorganotheke sta plaisia tou Programmatos "Hoi dromoi tou orthodoxou monakhismou: Poreuthentes mathete," Thessalonike, 28 Septembriou–2 Oktobriou 1994*, ed. K. Nikolaou, 115–24. Athens: Institouto Byzantinon Ereunon.

Birnbaum, Henrik. 1990. "When and how was Novgorod converted to Christianity?" In *Proceedings of the International Congress Commemorating the Millenium of Christianity in Rus'-Ukraine*, ed. Omeljan Pritsak, Ihor Ševčenko, and Miroslav Labunka, 505–30. Cambridge: Harvard University Press.

Boba, Imre. 1985. "The episcopacy of St. Methodius." *Die slawischen Sprachen* 8:21–33.

———. 1985. "The cathedral church of Sirmium and the grave of St. Methodius." *Die slawischen Sprachen* 8:5–19.

Borkowska, Urszula. 1995. "The Church and feudal society in central and Eastern Europe." In *Chiesa e mondo feudale nei secoli X–XII: Atti della dodicesima Settimana internazionale di studio, Mendola, 24–28 agosto 1992*, 257–74. Milan: Vita e Pensiero.

Čaplovič, Dušan. 1997. "Archaeology and the beginnings of Christianity in the territory of Slovakia." In *Early Christianity in Central and Eastern Europe*, ed. Przemysław Urbańczyk, 95–100. Warsaw: Semper.

Constantelos, D. J. 1970. "Canon 62 of the synod in Trullo and the Slavic problem." *Byzantina* 2:21–25.

———. 1989. "The Greek missionary background of the Christianization of Russia and the respect for its cultural identity." *Theologia* 60:654–71.

———. 1992. "Greek precursor missions to Russia's conversion to Christianity." In *The Legacy of Saints Cyril and Methodiu to Kiev and Moscow: Proceedings of the International Congress on the Millenium of the Conversion of Rus' to Christianity, Thessaloniki, 26–28 November 1988*, ed. A. E. Tachiaos, 247–56. Thessaloniki: Hellenic Association for Slavic Studies.

Diehl, Ernst-Dieter. 2000. "The foundation of the archbishopric of Gniezno from a canon law perspective." In *Europe's Centre around A.D. 1000*, ed. Alfried Wieczorek and Hans-Martin Hinz, 322–24. Stuttgart: Theiss.

Dimevski, Slavko. 1973. "The archbishopric of Ohrid." *Macedonian Review* 3:39–46.

Dittrich, Zdenek Radslav. 1962. *Christianity in Great Moravia*. Groningen: J. B. Wolters.

Dostál, Antonín. 1965. "The origins of the Slavonic liturgy." *Dumbarton Oaks Papers* 19: 67–87.

Dragojlović, Dragoljub. 1974. "The history of Paulicianism on the Balkan Peninsula." *Balcanica* 5:235–44.

Dunin-Wasowicz, Teresa. 2000. "New cults of saints in central Europe around the year 1000." In *Europe's Centre around A.D. 1000*, ed. Alfried Wieczorek and Hans-Martin Hinz, 548–50. Stuttgart: Theiss.

———. 2000. "St. Adalbert: Patron saint of the new Europe." In *Europe's Centre around A.D. 1000*, ed. Alfried Wieczorek and Hans-Martin Hinz, 551–52. Stuttgart: Theiss.

Dvornik, Francis. 1963. "Sts. Cyril and Methodius in Rome." *St. Vladimir's Seminary Quarterly* 7:20–30.

———. 1970. *Byzantine Mission among the Slavs: SS. Constantine-Cyril and Methodius.* New Brunswick: Rutgers University Press.

Dyggve, Ejnar. 1951. *History of Salonitan Christianity.* Oslo: H. Aschehoug.

Érszegi, Géza. 2000. "The Christianisation of Hungary according to the sources." In *Europe's Centre around A.D. 1000*, ed. Alfried Wieczorek and Hans-Martin Hinz, 394–98. Stuttgart: Theiss.

Fennell, John. 1995. *A History of the Russian Church to 1448.* London and New York: Longman.

Flor'ia, Boris N., and Gennadii G. Litavrin. 1988. "Christianization of the nations of central and southeast Europe and the conversion of Old Rus'." *Byzantinoslavica* 49: 185–99.

Galuška, Luděk. 1997. "The sacral area in Uherské Hradište-Sady and its significance to the beginning of the Moravian Slavs in the 9th century." In *Central Europe in 8th–10th Centuries: International Scientific Conference, Bratislava October 2–4, 1995*, ed. Dušan Čaplovič and Ján Dorul'a, 142–48. Bratislava: Ministry of Culture in the Slovak Republic and Slovak Academy of Sciences.

———. 1998. "Christianity in Great Moravia and its centre in Uherské Hradište-Sady." *Byzantinoslavica* 59:161–80.

———. 1999. "Archaeological sources for Christianity in Great Moravia." In *Thessaloniki Magna Moravia*, 273–84. Thessaloniki: SS. Cyril and Methodios Center for Cultural Studies.

Gąssowski, Jerzy. 1997. "Cult and authority in central Europe." In *Origins of Central Europe*, ed. Przemysław Urbańczyk, 59–64. Warsaw: Scientific Society of Polish Archaeologists.

Gervers-Molnár, Veronika. 1972. "Romanesque round churches of medieval Hungary." In *Evolution générale et développements régionaux en histoire de l'art*, ed. György Rózsa, 1:385–401. Budapest: Akadémiai Kiadó.

Giuzelev, Vasil. 1976. *The Adoption of Christianity in Bulgaria.* Sofia: Sofia Press.

Golden, Peter B. 1983. "Khazaria and Judaism." *Archivum Eurasiae Medii Aevi* 3:127–56.

Gregorios, Paulos Mar. 1988. "The foundation of the Russian people and the conversion of Russia to Christianity." In *Issledovaniia po slaviano-vizantiiskomu i zapadno-evropeiskomu srednevekov'iu. Posviashchaetsia pamiati Ivana Duicheva*, ed. Petar Dinekov, Aksinia Dzhurova, Georgi Bakalov, et al., 119–22. Sofia: Centăr dlia slaviano-vizantiiskikh issledovanii imeni Ivana Duicheva and Gosudarstvennoe izdatelstvo imeni D-ra Petra Berona.

Guzenko, Svitlana. 1997. "The development of Kiev as religious centre (5th c.–1240)." In *Early Christianity in Central and Eastern Europe*, ed. Przemysław Urbańczyk, 137–40. Warsaw: Semper.

Homza, Martin. 1997. "The role of Saint Ludmila, Doubravka, Saint Olga, and Adelaide in the conversion of their countries (the problem of 'mulieres suadentes,' persuading women)." In *Early Christianity in Central and Eastern Europe,* ed. Przemysław Urbańczyk, 187–202. Warsaw: Semper.

Karwasińska, Jadwiga. 1971. "Wojciech-Adalbert (c. 956–997), bishop of Prague." In *Hagiografia polska, II: Słownik bio-bibliograficzny (L-Z),* ed. O. Romuald Gustaw, 572–610. Poznań: Księgarnia Sw. Wojciecha.

Khandzhiiskii, Antonii. 1985. *Rock Monasteries.* Sofia: Septemvri.

Kłoczowski, Jerzy. 2000. *A History of Polish Christianity.* Cambridge University Press: Cambridge.

Koledarov, Petar. 1980. "On the initial hearth and centre of the Bogomil teaching." *Byzantinobulgarica* 6:237–42.

Kostova, Rosina. 1995. "Some aspects of the daily life of monks in an early medieval Bulgarian monastery." In *La vie quotidienne des moines et chanoines réguliers au Moyen Age et temps modernes: Actes du Premier Colloque International du L.A.R.H.C.O.R. Wroclaw-Ksiaz, 30. nov.–4. dec. 1994,* ed. Marek Derwich, 701–20. Wrocław: Institut d'histoire de l'Université de Wrocław.

———. 1998. "Topography of three early medieval monasteries in Bulgaria and the reasons for their foundation: A case of study." *Archaeologia Bulgarica* 6:108–25.

———. 2000. "Bulgarian monasteries, ninth to tenth centuries: Interpreting the archaeological evidence." *Pliska-Preslav* 8:190–202.

———. 2002. "Monasticism and monasteries in Bulgaria, ninth to tenth century: The interpretation of the archaeological evidence." Ph.D. diss., Central European University, Budapest.

Kralovánszky, Alán. 1983. "The earliest church of Alba civitas Alba regia." *Alba Regia* 20: 75–88.

Kurnatowska, Zofia. 2000. "The Christianisation of Poland as reflected in the archaeological record." In *Europe's Centre around A.D. 1000,* ed. Alfried Wieczorek and Hans-Martin Hinz, 317–18. Stuttgart: Theiss.

Kussef, M. 1950. "St. Nahum." *Slavonic and East European Review* 29:139–52.

Kútnik, J. 1982. "Benedictine missionaries in Slovakia in the 9th–11th centuries." *Slovak Studies* 22:79–131.

Labunka, Miroslav. 1988–89. "Religious centers and their missions to Kievan Rus': From Ol'ga to Volodimer." *Harvard Ukrainian Studies* 12–13:159–93.

Lacko, M. 1982. *The Popes and Great Moravia in the Light of Roman Documents.* Cleveland and Rome: Slovak Institute.

Lamm, Jan Peder. 1987. "On the cult of multiple-headed gods in England and the Baltic area." *Przegląd Archeologiczny* 34:219–31.

Loos, Milan. 1974. *Dualist Heresy in the Middle Ages.* Prague: Academia.

Lübke, Christian. 2001. "The Polabian alternative: Paganism between Christian kingdoms." In *Europe around the Year 1000,* ed. Przemysław Urbańczyk, 379–89. Warsaw: Wydawnictwo DiG.

Macháček, Jiří. 2000. "The sacral area of Pohansko near Břeclav: A contribution to understanding paganism and Christianity among the central European Slavs in the early Middle Ages." In *Europe's Centre around A.D. 1000,* ed. Alfried Wieczorek and Hans-Martin Hinz, 257–58. Stuttgart: Theiss.

Machilek, Franz, and Margarita Machilek. 2000. "St. Wenceslas: Cult and iconography."

In *Europe's Centre around A.D. 1000,* ed. Alfried Wieczorek and Hans-Martin Hinz, 589–93. Stuttgart: Theiss.

Madgearu, Alexandru. 2001. "The church organization at the lower Danube between 971 and 1020." *Etudes byzantines et post-byzantines* 4:71–85.

Madzharov, Mitko. 1995. "Early Christian cult buildings in the province of Thrace (IV–VI c.)." In *Akten des XII. internationalen Kongresses für christliche Archäologie, Bonn, 22.–28. September 1991,* ed. Ernst Dassmann and Josef Engemann, 2:993–96. Münster: Aschendorfsche Verlagsbuchhandlung.

Maksimović, Lj. 1992. "The Christianization of the Serbs and the Croats." In *The Legacy of Saints Cyril and Methodiu to Kiev and Moscow: Proceedings of the International Congress on the Millenium of the Conversion of Rus' to Christianity, Thessaloniki, 26–28 November 1988,* ed. A. E. Tachiaos, 167–84. Thessaloniki: Hellenic Association for Slavic Studies.

Malachowicz, Edmund. 2000. "Wrocław cathedral." In *Europe's Centre around A.D. 1000,* ed. Alfried Wieczorek and Hans-Martin Hinz, 328–29. Stuttgart: Theiss.

Malingoudis, Phaedon. 1994. "Aspects of early Slavic paganism: The evidence of Pseudo-Kaisarios." In *To Hellenikon: Studies in Honor of Speros Vryonis, Jr.,* ed. J. S. Allen, C. P. Joannides, J. S. Langdon, and S. W. Reinert, 2:77–86. New Rochelle, N.Y.: Caratzas.

Marsina, Richard. 1995. "Christianization of the Magyars and Hungary between the East and the West." *Studia Historica Slovaca* 19:37–52.

Mayr-Harting, Henry. 1992. "The church of Magdeburg: Its trade and its town in the tenth and early eleventh centuries." In *Church and City, 1000–1500: Essays in Honour of Christopher Brooke,* ed. David Abulafia, Michael J. Franklin, and Miri Rubin, 129–50. Cambridge: Cambridge University Press.

———. 1994. *Two Conversions to Christianity: The Bulgarians and the Anglo-Saxons.* Reading: University of Reading.

Moravcsik, Gyula. 1946. "Byzantine Christianity and the Magyars in the period of their migration." *American Slavic and East European Review* 5:29–45.

Morris, Rosemary. 1996. "The origins of Athos." In *Mount Athos and Byzantine Monasticism. Papers from the Twenty-Eighth Spring Symposium of Byzantine Studies, Birmingham, March 1994,* ed. Anthony Bryer and Mary Cunningham, 37–46. Aldershot/Brookfield: Variorum.

Mostert, Marco. 1997. "New perspectives for the study of East Central European Christianization? Christian behavior in Utrecht hagiography." In *Early Christianity in Central and Eastern Europe,* ed. Przemysław Urbańczyk, 175–86. Warsaw: Semper.

Müller, Heribert. 2000. "Archbishop Heribert of Cologne and 'the East.'" In *Europe's Centre around A.D. 1000,* ed. Alfried Wieczorek and Hans-Martin Hinz, 508–11. Stuttgart: Theiss.

Mussakova, Elisaveta. 1987. "The representation of the cross and the acceptance of Christian symbolism in Old Bulgarian culture." In *Das Christentum in Bulgarien und auf der übrigen Balkanhalbinsel in der Spätantike und im frühen Mittelalter,* ed. Vasil Giuzelev and Renate Pillinger, 313–20. Vienna: Verein "Freunde des Hauses Wittgenstein."

Mykula, W. 1988. "The Christianisation of Rus'-Ukraine and the development of Christianity in the Kyivan state." *Ukrainian Review* 36:14–21.

Noonan, Thomas S. 2000. "Why Orthodoxy did not spread among the Bulgars of the Crimea during the early medieval era: An early Byzantine conversion model." In

Christianizing Peoples and Converting Individuals, ed. Guyda Armstrong and Ian N. Wood, 15–24. Turnhout: Brepols.

Obelić, Bogomil, and Adela Sliepčević. 1999–2000. "Correction of radiocarbon age of wooden beams from St. Donat's church in Zadar by dendrochronological method." *Vjesnik Arheološkog Muzeja u Zagrebu* 32–33:197–206.

Olson, Lynette. 1996. "The conversion of the Visigoths and Bulgarians compared." In *Religious Change, Conversion, and Culture*, ed. Lynette Olson, 22–32. Sydney: Sydney Association for Studies and Culture.

Ovsiannikov, O. V. 1992. "The Gorodets sanctuary of the 6th–13th centuries on the lower Pechora River according to 1987–1989 excavations." In *Cultural Heritage of the Finno-Ugrians and Slavs: Papers Presented by the Participants in the Soviet-Finnish Archaeological Symposium, 10–16 May 1990 in Tallinn*, ed. V. Lang and J. Selirand, 171–79. Tallinn: Varrak.

Padberg, Lutz E.v. 2000. "Consolidation and expansion of Latin Christianity: The Ottonian mission to the western Slavs and Hungarians." In *Europe's Centre around A.D. 1000*, ed. Alfried Wieczorek and Hans-Martin Hinz, 439–42. Stuttgart: Theiss.

Petrukhin, V. Ia., and T. A. Pushkina. 1998. "Old Russia: The earliest stages of Christianisation." In *Rom und Byzanz im Norden: Mission und Glaubenwechsel im Ostseeraum während des 8.–14. Jahrhunderts; Internationale Fachkonferenz der Deutschen Forschungsgemeinschaft in Verbindung mit der Akademie der Wissenschaften und der Literatur, Mainz, Kiel, 18.–25. September 1994*, 247–58. Stuttgart: Steiner.

Pirivatrić, Srđan. 2002. "Between the East and the West. The Bulgarian Church in the Time of Samuilo (ca. 971–1018). Facts and interpretations." In *Srednovekovna khristianska Evropa: iztok i zapad. Cennosti, tradicii, obshtuvane*, ed. Vasil Giuzelev and Anisava Miltenova, 499–508. Sofia: Gutenberg.

Polek, Krzysztof. 1997. "The Great Moravian state and its participation in the Christianization of the western Slavs in recent studies." In *Early Christianity in Central and Eastern Europe*, ed. Przemysław Urbańczyk, 75–85. Warsaw: Semper.

Popescu, Emilian. 1986. "The city of Tomis as an autocephalous archbishopric of Scythia Minor (Dobrudja): Remarks on the chronology of Epiphanios' notitia." *Byzantiaka* 6:121–48.

Popović, Marko. 1997. "The early Byzantine basilica at Ras." *Starinar* 48:91–107.

Popović, Svetlana. 1998. "Prolegomena to early monasticism in the Balkans as documented in architecture." *Starinar* 49:131–44.

Poulter, Andrew G. 1994. "Churches in space: The early Byzantine city of Nicopolis." In *"Churches Built in Ancient Times": Recent Studies in Early Christian Archaeology*, ed. Kenneth Painter, 249–68. London: Society of Antiquaries.

Primov, Borislav. 1980. "Spread and influence of Bogomilism in Europe." *Byzantinobulgarica* 6:317–37.

Pritsak, Omeljan. 1978. "The Khazar kingdom's conversion to Judaism." *Harvard Ukrainian Studies* 2:261–81.

———. 1988–89. "Christianity in Rus' before 988." *Harvard Ukrainian Studies* 12–13: 87–113.

———. 1990. "At the dawn of Christianity in Rus': East meets West." In *Proceedings of the International Congress Commemorating the Millenium of Christianity in Rus'-Ukraine*, ed. Omeljan Pritsak, Ihor Sevcenko, and Miroslav Labunka, 87–113. Cambridge: Harvard University Press.

Reimitz, Helmut. 2001. "Conversion and control: The establishment of liturgical frontiers in Carolingian Pannonia." In *The Transformation of Frontiers from Late Antiquity to the Carolingians*, ed. Walter Pohl, Ian Wood, and Helmut Reimitz, 189–207. Leiden, Boston, and Cologne: Brill.

Roheim, Géza. 1951. "Hungarian shamanism." *Psychoanalysis and Social Sciences* 3:131–69.

Sanjek, Franjo. 1999. "Church and Christianity." In *Croatia in the Early Middle Ages: A Cultural Survey*, ed. Ivan Supičić, 217–36. London: Philip Wilson Publishers; Zagreb: AGM.

Sedov, V. V. 1980–81. "Pagan sanctuaries and idols of the eastern Slavs." *Slavica Gandensia* 7–8:69–85.

Ševčenko, Ihor. 1964. "Three paradoxes of the Cyrillomethodian mission." *Slavic Review* 23:226–32.

———. 1988–89. "Religious missions seen from Byzantium." *Harvard Ukrainian Studies* 12–13:7–27.

Shakhvoskoi, D. M. 1996. "The significance of the baptism of Rus' in the development of Russian culture." *Concilium* 6:1–9.

Shawarsky, Oleh. 1994. "Church and state in Kyyiv-Rus': 988–1240." Master's thesis, University of Manitoba.

Shchapov, Yaroslav N. 1993. *State and Church in Early Russia, 10th–13th Centuries*. New Rochelle, N.Y.: A. D. Caratzas.

Sheehan, Michael McMahon. 1991. "The bishop of Rome to a barbarian king on the rituals of marriage." In *In Iure Veritas: Studies in Canon Law in Memory of Schafer Williams*, ed. Steven B. Bowman and Blanche E. Cody, 187–99. Cincinnati: College of Law, University of Cincinnati.

Shepard, Jonathan. 1992. "Some remarks on the sources for the conversion of Rus'." In *Le origini e lo sviluppo della cristianità slavo-bizantina*, ed. S. W. Swierkosz-Lenárt, 76–77. Rome: Istituto storico italiano per il Medio Evo.

———. 1998. "The Khazars' formal adoption of Judaism and Byzantium's northern policy." *Oxford Slavonic Papers* 31:11–34.

Silagi, Gabriel. 2000. "Bishop Gerard (Gellért) of Csanád." In *Europe's Centre around A.D. 1000*, ed. Alfried Wieczorek and Hans-Martin Hinz, 417. Stuttgart: Theiss.

Simeonova, Liliana. 1998. *Diplomacy of the Letter and the Cross: Photios, Bulgaria, and the Papacy, 860s–880s*. Amsterdam: Hakkert.

Sluckii, A. S. 1993. "New evidence of the Slavonic liturgy of St. Peter." *Byzantinoslavica* 56:601–4.

Słupecki, Leszek Pawel. 1994. *Slavonic Pagan Sanctuaries*. Warsaw: Institute of Archaeology and Ethnology.

———. 1998. "Archaeological sources and written sources in studying symbolic culture (exemplified by research on the pre-Christian religion of the Slavs)." In *Theory and Practice of Archaeological Research*, ed. Witold Hensel, Stanisław Tabaczyński, and Przemysław Urbańczyk, 3:337–66. Warsaw: Scientia.

———. 2000. "The pagan religion of the western Slavs." In *Europe's Centre around A.D. 1000*, ed. Alfried Wieczorek and Hans-Martin Hinz, 157–65. Stuttgart: Theiss.

———. 2003. "Why Polish historiography has neglected the role of pagan Slavic mythology." In *Inventing the Pasts in North Central Europe. The National Perception of Early Medieval History and Archaeology*, ed. Matthias Hardt, Christian Lübke, and Dittmar Schorkowitz, 266–72. Bern, etc.: Peter Lang.

Smedovskii, Teodosii. 1977. "The Latin missions in Bulgaria in 866–870." *Palaeobulgarica* 2:39–55.

Smetánka, Zděnek, P. Chotebor, and M. Kostílkova. 1986. "Archaeological excavations in the chapel of St. Ludmila (St. George's basilical church, Prague Castle). A preliminary report." *Archaeologia historica* 11:283–93.

Smrzík, Stephen. 1959. *The Glagolitic or Roman-Slavonic Liturgy.* Cleveland: Slovak Institute.

Snively, Carolyn S. 1984. "Cemetery churches of the early Byzantine period in eastern Illyricum: Location and martyrs." *Greek Orthodox Theological Review* 29:117–24.

———. 1995. "Apsidal crypts in Macedonia: Possible places of pilgrimage." In *Akten des XII. internationalen Kongresses für christliche Archäologie, Bonn, 22.–28. September 1991,* ed. Ernst Dassmann and Josef Engemann, 2:1179–84. Münster: Aschendorfsche Verlagsbuchhandlung.

Sommer, Petr. 2000. "The Christianisation of Bohemia in the light of archaeological, art-historical, and written sources." In *Europe's Centre around A.D. 1000,* ed. Alfried Wieczorek and Hans-Martin Hinz, 255–56. Stuttgart: Theiss.

———. 2000. "The monastery of Břevnov." In *Europe's Centre around A.D. 1000,* ed. Alfried Wieczorek and Hans-Martin Hinz, 266. Stuttgart: Theiss.

——— 2000. "The monastery of Ostrov u Davle." In *Europe's Centre around A.D. 1000,* ed. Alfried Wieczorek and Hans-Martin Hinz, 267. Stuttgart: Theiss.

———. 2000. "The monastery of Sazava." In *Europe's Centre around A.D. 1000,* ed. Alfried Wieczorek and Hans-Martin Hinz, 268–69. Stuttgart: Theiss.

Staecker, Jörn. 2000. "The mission of the triangle: The Christianisation of the Saxons, west Slavs, and Danes in a comparative analysis." *Archaeological Review from Cambridge* 17:99–116.

Strzelcyzk, Jerzy. 2000. "The Christianisation of Poland in the light of written sources." In *Europe's Centre around A.D. 1000,* ed. Alfried Wieczorek and Hans-Martin Hinz, 314–16. Stuttgart: Theiss.

———. 2001. "The Church and Christianity about the year 1000 (the missionary aspect)." In *Europe around the Year 1000,* ed. Przemysław Urbańczyk, 41–67. Warsaw: Wydawnictwo DiG.

Sullivan, R. 1966. "Khan Boris and the conversion of Bulgaria: A case study of the impact of Christianity on a barbarian society." *Studies in Medieval and Renaissance History* 3:55–139.

Tachiaos, A. E. 2001. *Cyril and Methodius of Thessalonica: The Acculturation of the Slavs.* Crestwood: St. Vladimir's Seminary Press.

Takács, Imre. 2000. "Pannonhalma Abbey." In *Europe's Centre around A.D. 1000,* ed. Alfried Wieczorek and Hans-Martin Hinz, 405–6. Stuttgart: Theiss.

Tarnanidis, I. 1992. "Latin opposition to the missionary work of Cyril and Methodius." In *The Legacy of Saints Cyril and Methodius to Kiev and Moscow: Proceedings of the International Congress on the Millenium of the Conversion of Rus' to Christianity, Thessaloniki, 26–28 November 1988,* ed. A. E. Tachiaos, 49–62. Thessaloniki: Hellenic Association for Slavic Studies.

Tarnanidis, J. 1990. "Glagolitic canon to Saints Peter and Paul (Sin. slav. h.)." In *Filologia e letteratura nei paesi Slavi: Studi in onore di Sante Graciotti,* ed. Giovanna Brogi Bercoff, 91–108. Rome: Carucci.

Tashkovski, Dragan. 1972. "Macedonia: Cradle of Bogomil heresy." *Macedonian Review* 2:47–52.

Teteriatnikov, N. 1994. "Sanctuary design in the ninth- and tenth-century churches in Bulgaria: The question of origin." *Godishnik na Sofiiskiia Universitet "Kliment Ohridski": Istoricheski Fakultet* 84–85:197–209.

Thomson, Francis J. 1976. "Cosmas of Bulgaria and his discourse against the heresy of Bogomil." *Slavonic and East European Review* 54:263–69.

Tolochko, Petr Petrovich. 1988–89. "Volodimer Sviatoslavich's choice of religion: Fact or fiction?" *Harvard Ukrainian Studies* 12–13:816–29.

Topencharov, Vladimir. 1981. "Questions of Bogomilism." *Southeastern Europe* 8:48–63.

Tóth, Sándor László. 2000. "Veszprém cathedral." In *Europe's Centre around A.D. 1000*, ed. Alfried Wieczorek and Hans-Martin Hinz, 415–16. Stuttgart: Theiss.

Třeštík, Dušan. 1995. "The baptism of the Czech princes in 845 and the Christianization of the Slavs." *Historica* 32:7–59.

———. 2000. "The foundation of the Prague and Moravian bishoprics." In *Europe's Centre around A.D. 1000*, ed. Alfried Wieczorek and Hans-Martin Hinz, 259–61. Stuttgart: Theiss.

Urbańczyk, Przemysław. 1997. "The meaning of Christianization for medieval pagan societies." In *Early Christianity in Central and Eastern Europe*, ed. Przemysław Urbańczyk, 31–37. Warsaw: Semper.

———. 1997. "St. Adalbert-Vojtech, missionary and politician." In *Early Christianity in Central and Eastern Europe*, ed. Przemysław Urbańczyk, 155–62. Warsaw: Semper.

Vavřínek, Vladimír. 1964. "Study of the church architecture from the period of the Great Moravian Empire." *Byzantinoslavica* 25:288–301.

———. 1978. "The introduction of the Slavonic liturgy and the Byzantine missionary policy." In *Beiträge zur byzantinischen Geschichte im 9.–11. Jahrhundert: Akten des Colloquiums "Byzanz auf dem Höhepunkt seiner Macht," Liblice, 20.–23. September 1977*, ed. Vladimír Vavřínek, 255–82. Prague: Kabinet pro studia řecká, římská a latinská, Československé Akademie Věd.

———. 2000. "Missions to Moravia: Between the Latin West and Byzantium." In *Europe's Centre around A.D. 1000*, ed. Alfried Wieczorek and Hans-Martin Hinz, 196–99. Stuttgart: Theiss.

Vežić, Pavuša. 1996. "The early medieval phase of the episcopal complex in Zadar." *Hortus artium medievalium* 2:150–61.

Vincenz, André de. 1984. "The Moravian mission in Poland revisited." In *Okeanos: Essays Presented to Ihor Sevcenko on His Sixtieth Birthday by His Colleagues and Students*, ed. Cyril Mango, Omeljan Pritsak, and Uliana M. Pasicznyk, 639–54. Cambridge, Mass.: Ukrainian Research Institute.

Vlasto, A. P. 1970. *The Entry of the Slavs into Christendom: An Introduction to the Medieval History of the Slavs*. Cambridge: Cambridge University Press.

Ware, Kallistos. 1996. "St. Athanasios the Athonite: traditionalist or innovator?" In *Mount Athos and Byzantine Monasticism. Papers from the Twenty-Eighth Spring Symposium of Byzantine Studies, Birmingham, March 1994*, ed. Anthony Bryer and Mary Cunningham, 4–16. Aldershot/Brookfield: Variorum.

Wood, Ian. 2001. *Missionary Life: Saints and the Evangelization of Europe, 400–1050*. Harlow and New York: Longman.

Zguta, Russell. 1974. "The pagan priests of early Russia: Some new insights." *Slavic Review* 33:259–66.

Zubek, Theodoric J. 1987. "Great Moravia: The apostolic mission of Sts. Cyril and Methodius." In *Reflections on Slovak History (Conference on Slovak History in 1984*

Organized by the Slovak World Congress), ed. Stanislav J. Kirschbaum and Anne C. R. Roman, 21–36. Toronto: Slovak World Congress.

Zuckerman, Constantine. 1995. "On the date of the Khazars' conversion to Judaism and the chronology of the kings of the Rus, Oleg and Igor: A study of the anonymous Khazar letter from the Genizah of Cairo." *Revue des études byzantines* 53:237–70.

LITERARY PRODUCTION AND FINE ARTS

Antich, Vera. 1974. "Hrabar and his work 'On Letters.'" *Macedonian Review* 4:11–16.

Altbauer, Moshé. 1987. "Identification of newly discovered Slavic manuscripts in St. Catherine's monastery in Sinai." *Slovo* 37:35–40.

Badurina, Andelko. 1999. "Illuminated manuscripts." In *Croatia in the Early Middle Ages: A Cultural Survey,* ed. Ivan Supičić, 545–58. London: Philip Wilson Publishers; Zagreb: AGM.

Bazantová, Nina. 1990. "The tunic from the reliquary of Saint Ludmila." *Textile History* 21:3–12.

———. 1996. "Romanesque and early Gothic silk textiles from Czech sources." In *Ibrahim ibn Yakub al-Turtushi: Christianity, Islam, and Judaism meet in East-Central Europe, c. 800–1300 A.D.; Proceedings of the International Colloquy, 25–29 April 1994,* ed. Petr Charvát and Jiří Prosecký, 93–102. Prague: Oriental Institute, Academy of Sciences of the Czech Republic.

Bežić, Jerko. 1999. "Glagolitic chant." In *Croatia in the Early Middle Ages: A Cultural Survey,* ed. Ivan Supičić, 569–76. London: Philip Wilson Publishers; Zagreb: AGM.

Birnbaum, Henrik. 1985. "On the Eastern and Western components of the earliest Slavic liturgy: The evidence of the Euchologium Sinaiticum and related texts." In *Essays in the Area of Slavic Languages, Linguistic, and Byzantology: A Festschrift in Honor of Antonín Dostál on the Occasion of His Seventy-Fifth Birthday,* ed. Thomas G. Winner, 25–44. Irvine: Charles Schlacks Jr.

———. 1993. "The Lives of Sts. Constantine-Cyril and Methodius viewed against the background of Byzantine and early Slavic hagiography." In *To Hellenikon: Studies in Honor of Speros Vryonis, Jr.,* ed. Jelisaveta Stanojevich Allen, Christos P. Ioannides, John S. Langdon, and Stephen W. Reinert, 2:3–23. New Rochelle: Aristide D. Caratzas.

Brentjes, B. 1971. "On the prototype of the proto-Bulgarian temples at Pliska, Preslav, and Madara." *East and West* 21:213–16.

Capkova, Vera. 1987. "The Freising monuments." In *Irland und die Christenheit: Bibelstudien und Mission,* ed. Proinséas Ni Chathain and Michael Richter, 461–70. Stuttgart: Klett-Cotta.

Davidov, Angel. 1999. "Indices to the *Homily Against the Bogomils* by Cosmas the Priest." *Polata knigopisnaia* 30–31:3–18.

Dekan, Ján. 1980. *Moravia Magna: The Great Moravian Empire; Its Art and Times.* Bratislava: Tatran.

Dimitrova, Elizabeta. 1992–93. "The terracotta relief plaques from Vinica." *Starinar* 43–44:53–70.

Fisković, Igor. 1999. "Painting." In *Croatia in the Early Middle Ages: A Cultural Survey,* ed. Ivan Supičić, 493–509. London: Philip Wilson Publishers; Zagreb: AGM.

Georgiev, Emil I. 1976. "Bulgarian literature in the context of Slavic and European literatures." In *Bulgaria Past and Present: Studies in History, Literature, Economics, Music, Sociology, Folklore, and Linguistics; Proceedings of the First International Conference on Bulgarian Studies Held at the University of Wisconsin, Madison, May 3–5, 1973,* ed. Thomas Butler, 229–48. Columbus: American Association for the Advancement of Slavic Studies.

Golob, N. 2003. "Manuscripts and fragments: Slovenian territory in the Carolingian era." *Hortus artium medievalium* 8.

Goss, Vladimir P. 1987. *Early Croatian Architecture: A Study of the Pre-Romanesque.* London: Duckworth.

Gvozdanović, Vladimir. 1972. "Pre-Romanesque and early Romanesque architecture in Crotia." Ph.D. diss., Cornell University.

———. 1975–76. "Two early Croatian royal mausolea." *Peristil* 18–19:5–10.

———. 1978. "The southeastern border of the Carolingian architecture." *Cahiers archéologiques* 27:85–100.

Hannick, Christian. 1994. "Early Slavic liturgical hymns in musicological context." *Ricerche slavistiche* 41:9–29.

Havlík, Lubomír E. 1987. "On the dating of the Old Slav literary monuments and on the Primary Slav Chronology." *Studia zrodłoznawcze* 30:1–38.

Hayashi, Toshio. 2000. "East-West exchanges as seen through the dissemination of the griffin motif." In *Kontakte zwischen Iran, Byzanz und der Steppe im 6.–7. Jahrhundert,* ed. Csanád Bálint, 253–66. Budapest: Institut für Archäologie der Ungarischen Akademie der Wissenschaften.

Hensel, Witold. 1964. "Early Polish applied arts." *Zbornik* 4:197–99.

———. 1983. "How the statue of the Arkona Svatevit look like?" *Archaeologia Polona* 21–22:217–22.

Hoddinott, Ralph F. 1990. "Politics, liturgy, and architecture in Bulgaria during the second half of the ninth century." In *Harmos: Timetikos tomos ston kathegete N. K. Moutsopoulo gia ta 25 khronia pneumatikes tou prosphoras sto panepistemio,* 2:787–804. Thessaloniki: Aristoteleio Panepistemio Thessalonikes.

Ingham, Norman W. 1986. "The lost Church Slavonic 'Life of Saint Ludmila.'" In *Studia slavica mediaevalia et humanistica Riccardo Picchio dicata,* ed. Michele Colucci, Giuseppe Dell'Agata, and Harvey Goldblatt, 349–59. Rome: Edizioni dell'Ateneo.

———. 1993. "Sources on St. Ludmila, III. The homily and its 'echoes.'" In *American Contributions to the Eleventh International Congress of Slavists, Bratislava, August–September 1993: Literature, Linguistics, Poetics,* ed. Robert A. Maguire and Alan Timberlake, 65–73. Columbus, Ohio: Slavica.

Ivančević, Radovan. 1999. "The pre-Romanesque in Croatia: A question of interpretation." In *Croatia in the Early Middle Ages: A Cultural Survey,* ed. Ivan Supičić, 417–42. London: Philip Wilson Publishers; Zagreb: AGM.

Jakčić, Nikola. 1997. "Croatian art in the second half of the ninth century." *Hortium Artium Medievalium* 3:41–54.

———. 2003. "On the origin of the baptismal font with the name of Prince Višeslav." *Hortus artium medievalium* 8.

Jakobson, Roman. 1963. "St. Constantine's Prologue to the Gospel." *St. Vladimir's Seminary Quarterly* 7:14–19.

Kantor, Marvin. 1983. "The second Old Slavonic legend of St. Wenceslas: Problems of translation and dating." In *American Contributions to the Ninth International Congress of Slavists, Kiev, September 1983,* ed. Michael S. Flier and Paul Debreczeny, 2:147–59. Columbus, Ohio: Slavic Publishers.

Lamm, Jan Peder. 1991. "Ship or ducks? Comment on the picture-stone found at Grobin, Latvia." *Fornvännen* 86:9–10.

Leeming, Harry. 1987. "Early Slavonic translation technique: A contrast with Latin and Gothic." *Kirilo-metodievski studii* 4:180–91.

Marašović, Tomislav. 1999. "Pre-Romanesque architecture in Croatia." In *Croatia in the Early Middle Ages: A Cultural Survey,* ed. Ivan Supičić, 445–72. London: Philip Wilson Publishers; Zagreb: AGM.

Marosi, Ernö. 2000. "Christian architecture in Hungary." In *Europe's Centre around A.D. 1000,* ed. Alfried Wieczorek and Hans-Martin Hinz, 402–4. Stuttgart: Theiss.

Merhautová, Anežka, and Petr Sommer. 2000. "Christian art and architecture in the Bohemian state around AD 1000." In *Europe's Centre around A.D. 1000,* ed. Alfried Wieczorek and Hans-Martin Hinz, 262–65. Stuttgart: Theiss.

Miltenova, Anisava. 2002. "The source of one early Slavonic Eratopocriseis: Greek or Latin?" In *Srednovekovna khristianska Evropa: iztok i zapad. Cennosti, tradicii, obshtuvane,* ed. Vasil Giuzelev and Anisava Miltenova, 263–73. Sofia: Gutenberg.

Minaeva, Oksana. 1995. "The East and the formation of early medieval Bulgarian art, VIIth–Xth cc." *Bulgarian Historical Review* 23:91–105.

———. 1996. *From Paganism to Christianity: Formation of Medieval Bulgarian Art.* Frankfurt am Main and Berlin: Peter Lang.

Moss, Linda. 1984. "Some evidence for and causes of stylistic change at Pliska and Preslav." *Palaeobulgarica* 8:70–73.

Nickel, Heinrich L. 1982. *Medieval Architecture in Eastern Europe.* New York: Holmes and Meier.

Pejaković, Mladen. 1999. "The signs and their meanings in the Croatian pre-Romanesque art." In *Croatia in the Early Middle Ages: A Cultural Survey,* ed. Ivan Supičić, 513–42. London: Philip Wilson Publishers; Zagreb: AGM.

Petrenko, Valerii Petrovich. 1991. "A picture stone from Grobin (Latvia)." *Fornvännen* 86:1–9.

Petricioli, Ivo. 1999. "Sculpture from the 8th to the 11th century." In *Croatia in the Early Middle Ages: A Cultural Survey,* ed. Ivan Supičić, 475–91. London: Philip Wilson Publishers; Zagreb: AGM.

Picchio, Riccardo. 1982. "*VC* and *VM*s Pauline connotations of Cyril and Methodius' apostleship." *Palaeobulgarica* 6:112–18.

———. 1985. "Chapter 13 of *Vita Constantini:* Its text and contextual function." *Slavica Hierosolymitana* 7:133–52.

Schwartz, Ellen. 2001. "Reconsidering the Round Church of Symeon." *Palaeobulgarica* 25:3–15.

Ševčíková, Žužana. 1999. "The message of Byzantium in post-Greatmoravian picture of Slovakia (in architecture and arts)." In *Thessaloniki Magna Moravia,* 285–95. Thessaloniki: SS. Cyril and Methodios Center for Cultural Studies.

Sheppard, Carl D. 1984. "Pre-Romanesque sculpture: Evidence of the cultural evolution of the people of the Dalmatian coast." *Gesta* 23:7–16.

Tarnanidis, Ioannis C. 1988. *The Slavonic Manuscripts Discovered in 1975 at St. Catherine's Monastery on Mount Sinai.* Thessaloniki: Hellenic Association for Slavic Studies.

Thomson, F. J. 1998. "The Slavonic translation of the Old Testament." In *The Interpreta-*

tion of the Bible: The International Symposium in Slovenia, ed. Joze Krasovec, 605–920. Sheffield: Sheffield Academic Press.

———. 1999. "Has the Cyrillomethodian translation of the Bible survived?" In *Thessaloniki Magna Moravia,* 149–63. Thessaloniki: SS. Cyril and Methodios Center for Cultural Studies.

Tuksar, Stanislav. 1999. "The first centuries of Croatian music." In *Croatia in the Early Middle Ages: A Cultural Survey,* ed. Ivan Supičić, 561–67. London: Philip Wilson Publishers; Zagreb: AGM.

Ugrinova-Skalovska, Radmila. 1986. "Clement of Ohrid and the founding of the Ohrid literary school." *Macedonian Review* 16:258–62.

Urtans, Juris. 1993. "About a destroyed stone with signs on the Daugava River." *Journal of Baltic Studies* 24:385–88.

Veder, William R. 1999. *Utrum in Alterum Abiturum Erat? A Study of the Beginnings of Text Transmission in Church Slavic; The "Prologue" to the "Gospel Homiliary" by Constantine of Preslav; the Text "On the Script" and the Treatise "On the Letters" by Anonymous Authors.* Bloomington: Slavica.

Vicelja, Marina. 1993. "Centric compositional scheme of the early medieval slabs in Istria." In *Umjetnost na istočnoj obali Jadrana u kontekstu europeske tradicije: Zbornik radova za znanstevnog skupa u Opatiji u svibnju 1992; postvečenog djelu Prof. Dr. Radmile Matejčić,* ed. Nina Kudiš and Marina Vicelja, 165–75. Rijeka: Pedagoski fakultet Rijeka.

———. 1998. "The Justinianic sculpture at Pula: A reconsideration." In *Radovi XIII. Međunarodnog Kongresa za starokrščansku arheologiju, Split-Poreč (25.9.–1.10. 1994),* ed. Nenad Cambi and Emilio Marin, 2:1037–46. Vatican: Pontificio Istituto di Archeologia Cristiana; Split: Arheološki Muzej.

Zurowska, Klementyna. 2000. "Sacral architecture in Poland." In *Europe's Centre around A.D. 1000,* ed. Alfried Wieczorek and Hans-Martin Hinz, 325–27. Stuttgart: Theiss.

EARLY BYZANTINE BALKANS

Aleksova, Blaga. 1989. "Early Christian and Slav religious centres in Macedonia." In *Radovi XIII. Međunarodnog Kongresa za starokrščansku arheologiju, Split-Poreč (25.9.–1.10. 1994),* ed. Nenad Cambi and Emilio Marin, 3:7–28. Vatican: Pontificio Istituto di Archeologia Cristiana; Split: Arheološki Muzej.

Aleksova, Blaga, and Mango Cyril. 1971. "Bargala: A preliminary report." *Dumbarton Oaks Papers* 25:265–81.

Biernacka-Lubańska, Małgorzata. 1982. *The Roman and Early Byzantine Fortifications of Lower Moesia and Northern Thrace.* Wrocław, Warsaw, Cracow, Gdańsk, and Łódź: Zaklad Narodowy imenia Ossolińskich.

Biernacki, Andrzej Boleslaw. 1990. "Remarks on the basilica and episcopal residence at Novae." *Balcanica* 2:187–208.

Boer, J. G. de. 1988–89. "An early Byzantine fortress on the tell of Dyadovo." *Talanta* 20–21:7–15.

Bowden, William. 2001. "A new urban élite? Church builders and church building in late-antique Epirus." In *Recent Research in Late-Antique Urbanism,* ed. Luke Lavan, 57–68. Portsmouth: Journal of Roman Archaeology.

Bratož, Rajko. 1989. "The development of the early Christian research in Slovenia and

Istria between 1976 and 1986." In *Actes du XI-e Congrès international d'archéologie chrétienne, Lyon, Vienne, Grenoble, Genève et Aoste (21–28 septembre 1986)*, 3:2345–88. Rome: Ecole Française de Rome.

Cambi, Nenad. 1984. "Triconch churches on the eastern Adriatic." In *Actes du X-e Congrès international d'archéologie chrétienne, Thessalonique, 28 septembre–4 octobre 1980*, 2:45–54. Vatican: Pontificio Istituto di Archeologia Cristiana; Thessaloniki: Hetaireia Makedonikon Spoudon.

Ciglenečki, Slavko. 1999. "Results and problems in the archaeology of the late antiquity in Slovenia." *Arheološki vestnik* 50:287–309.

Croke, Brian. 1982. "The date of the Anastasian Long Wall." *Greek, Roman, and Byzantine Studies* 20:59–78.

Crow, James G. 1995. "The Long Walls of Thrace." In *Constantinople and Its Hinterland: Papers from the Twenty-Seventh Spring Symposium of Byzantine Studies, Oxford, April 1993*, ed. Cyril Mango and Gilbert Dagron, 110–19. Aldershot: Variorum.

———. 2001. "Fortifications and urbanism in late antiquity: Thessaloniki and other Eastern cities." In *Recent Research in Late-Antique Urbanism*, ed. Luke Lavan, 57–68. Portsmouth: Journal of Roman Archaeology.

Curta, Florin. 2001. "Peasants as 'makeshift soldiers for the occasion': Sixth-century settlement patterns in the Balkans." In *Urban Centers and Rural Contexts in Late Antiquity*, ed. Thomas S. Burns and John W. Eadie, 199–217. East Lansing: Michigan State University Press.

Davies, John Gordon. 1959. "The Arian and Orthodox baptiseries at Salona." *Antiquity* 33:57–60.

Dimitrov, Kamen. 1995. "Novae on the Lower Danube as an early Christian centre (5th–6th century AD)." In *Akten des XII. internationalen Kongresses für christliche Archäologie, Bonn, 22.–28. September 1991*, ed. Ernst Dassmann and Josef Engemann, 2:700–704. Münster: Aschendorfsche Verlagsbuchhandlung.

Dinchev, Vencislav. 1997. "Zikideva: An example of early Byzantine urbanism in the Balkans." *Archaeologia Bulgarica* 1:54–77.

———. 1999. "Classification of the late antique cities in the dioceses of Thracia and Dacia." *Archaeologia Bulgarica* 3:39–73.

———. 2000. "The limit of urban life in the late antique dioceses of Thracia and Dacia: The overestimated centers." *Archaeologia Bulgarica* 4:65–84.

Dunn, Archibald. 1994. "The transition from polis to kastron in the Balkans (III–VII cc.): General and regional perspectives." *Byzantine and Modern Greek Studies* 18: 60–80.

———. 1998. "Heraclius' 'reconstruction of cities' and their sixth-century Balkan antecedents." In *Radovi XIII. Međunarodnog Kongresa za starokšćansku arheologiju, Split-Poreč (25.9.–1.10. 1994)*, ed. Nenad Cambi and Emilio Marin, 2:795–806. Vatican: Pontificio Istituto di Archeologia Cristiana; Split: Arheološki Muzej.

Fisković, Igor. 1998. "Late antique buildings in Polače on the island of Mljet." In *Radovi XIII. Međunarodnog Kongresa za starokršćansku arheologiju, Split-Poreč (25.9.–1.10. 1994)*, ed. Nenad Cambi and Emilio Marin, 3:273–86. Vatican: Pontificio Istituto di Archeologia Cristiana; Split: Arheološki Muzej.

Giorgetti, D. 1983. "Ratiaria and its territory." In *Ancient Bulgaria: Papers Presented to the International Symposium on the Ancient History and Archaeology of Bulgaria, University of Nottingham, 1981*, ed. A. G. Poulter, 19–39. Nottingham: University of Nottingham.

Górecki, Danuta. 1989. "The Thrace of Ares during the sixth and seventh centuries." *Byzantinische Forschungen* 14:221–35.

Grabar, André, and William Emerson. 1946. "The basilica of Belovo." *Bulletin of the Byzantine Institute* 1:43–59.

Harrison, R. M. 1974. "To makron Teichos: The Long Wall in Thrace." In *Roman Frontier Studies, 1969: Eighth International Congress of Limesforschung,* ed. E. Birley, B. Dobson, and M. Jarrett, 244–48. Cardiff: University of Wales Press.

Hensel, Witold, and Jadwiga Rauhutowa. 1981. "Archaeological research at Debreŝte (Macedonia), 1974–1978." *Archaeologia Polona* 20:191–225.

Hoddinott, Ralph F. 1963. *Early Byzantine Churches in Macedonia and Southern Serbia: A Study of the Origins and the Initial Development of East Christian Art.* London: Macmillan.

———. 1975. *Bulgaria in Antiquity: An Archaeological Introduction.* New York: St. Martin's Press.

Hodges, R., G. Saraçi, W. Bowden, et al. 1997. "Late-antique and Byzantine Butrint: Interim report on the port and its hinterland (1994–1995)." *Journal of Roman Archaeology* 10:207–34.

Ivanov, Teofil, and Stoian Stoianov. 1985. *Abritus: Its History and Archaeology.* Razgrad: Cultural and Historical Heritage Directorate.

Jeličić-Radonić, Jasna. 1998. "The Salonitan cultural circle of Justinian's time." In *Radovi XIII. Međunarodnog Kongresa za starokršćansku arheologiju, Split-Poreč (25.9.–1.10. 1994),* ed. Nenad Cambi and Emilio Marin, 2:1023–36. Vatican: Pontificio Istituto di Archeologia Cristiana; Split: Arheološki Muzej.

Karać, Zlatko. 1998. "The problem of the exploration of 6th and 7th c. urban planning on Croatian soil within the context of general Byzantine urban studies." In *Radovi XIII. Međunarodnog Kongresa za starokršćansku arheologiju, Split-Poreč (25.9.–1.10. 1994),* ed. Nenad Cambi and Emilio Marin, 2:959–74. Vatican: Pontificio Istituto di Archeologia Cristiana; Split: Arheološki Muzej.

Karagiorgiou, Olga. 2001. "Demetrias and Thebes: The fortunes and misfortunes of two Thessalian port cities in late antiquity." In *Recent Research in Late-Antique Urbanism,* ed. Luke Lavan, 183–215. Portsmouth: Journal of Roman Archaeology.

Knific, Timotej. 1994. "Vranje near Sevnica: A Late Roman settlement in the light of certain pottery finds." *Arheološki vestnik* 45:211–37.

Korac, Miomir. 1996. "Late Roman and early Byzantine fort of Ljubičevac." In *Roman Limes on the Middle and Lower Danube,* ed. Petar Petrović, 105–9. Belgrade: Arheološki Institut.

Korkuti, Muzafer, and Karl M. Petruso. 1993. "Archaeology in Albania." *American Journal of Archaeology* 97:707–43.

Kuzmanov, Georgi. 2000. "A residence from the late antiquity in Ratiaria (Dacia Ripensis)." *Archaeologia Bulgarica* 4:27–343.

Lafontaine-Dosogne, Jacqueline. 1967. "Notes d'archéologie bulgare." *Cahiers archéologiques* 17:45–58.

Liebeschuetz, J. H. W. G. 2000. "The government of the late Roman city, with special reference to Thessaloniki." In *Byzantine Macedonia: Identity, Image, and History. Papers from the Melbourne Conference, July 1995,* ed. J. Burke and R. Scott, 116–27. Melbourne: Australian Association for Byzantine Studies.

Madgearu, Alexandru. 1996. "The province of Scythia and the Avaro-Slavic invasions." *Balkan Studies* 37:35–61.

————. 1997. "The downfall of the lower Danubian late Roman frontier." *Revue Roumaine d'Histoire* 36:315–36.

————. 2001. "The end of town-life in Scythia Minor." *Oxford Journal of Archaeology* 20:207–17.

Majewski, K. 1973. "Polish archaeological research at Novae (Bulgaria) in 1971." *Klio* 55:301–9.

Mcnally, Sheila. 1996. "Split in the Byzantine Empire: The archaeological evidence." In *Acts. XVIIIth International Congress of Byzantine Studies: Selected Papers; Moscow 1991*, ed. Ihor Ševčenko, G. G. Litavrin, and Walter Hanak, 2:250–64. Shepherdstown, W. V.: Byzantine Studies Press.

Milošević, Gordana. 1996. "Modular analysis of late Roman and early Byzantine fortifications in the Iron Gate area." In *Roman Limes on the Middle and Lower Danube*, ed. Petar Petrovic, 249–52. Belgrade: Arheološki Institut.

Parnicki-Pudelko, Stefan. 1983. "The early Christian episcopal basilica in Novae." *Archaeologia Polona* 21–22:241–70.

————. 1995. *The Episcopal Basilica in Novae: Archaeological Research, 1976–1990*. Poznan: Adam Mickiewicz University Press.

Poulter, Andrew G. 1981. "The end of Scythia Minor: The archaeological evidence." In *Byzantium and the Classical Tradition: University of Birmingham 13 Spring Symposium of Byzantine Studies, 1979*, ed. Margarett Mullett and Roger Scott, 198–204. Birmingham: Center for Byzantine Studies University of Birmingham.

————. 1983. "Town and country in Moesia Inferior." In *Ancient Bulgaria; Papers Presented to the International Symposium on the Ancient History and Archaeology of Bulgaria, University of Nottingham, 1981*, ed. A. G. Poulter, 74–118. Nottingham: Department of Classical and Archaeological Studies, University of Nottingham.

————. 1988. "Nicopolis and Istrum, Bulgaria: An interim report on the excavations, 1985–7." *Antiquaries Journal* 68:69–89.

————. 1992. "The use and abuse of urbanism in the Danubian provinces during the later Roman Empire." In *The City in Late Antiquity*, ed. John Rich, 99–135. New York: Routledge.

————. 1995. *Nicopolis ad Istrum: A Roman, late Roman, and early Byzantine City*. London: Society for the Promotion of Roman Studies.

————. 2000. "The Roman to Byzantine transition in the Balkans: Preliminary results in Nicopolis and its hinterland." *Journal of Roman Archaeology* 13:346–58.

Preshlenov, Hristo. 2001. "A late antique pattern of fortification in the eastern Stara Planina Mountain (the pass of Djulino)." *Archaeologia Bulgarica* 5:33–43.

Saradi, Helen. 1998. "Aspects of early Byzantine urbanism in Albania." In *Hoi Albanoi sto mesaiona*, ed. Charalambos Gasparis, 81–130. Athens: Institouto Byzantinon Ereunon.

Scorpan, C. 1974. "Sacidava: A New Roman fortress on the map of the Danube limes." In *Actes du IX-e Congrès international d'études sur les frontières romaines, Mamaia 6–13 sept. 1972*, ed. D. M. Pippidi, 109–16. Bucharest: Editura Academiei Republicii Socialiste Românîa; Cologne: Böhlau.

Snively, Carolyn S. 1982. "The sunken apse: A feature of early Byzantine churches in Macedonia." *American Journal of Archaeology* 86:284.

————. 1984. "Interrelated aspects of form and function in the early Christian churches of Stobi." In *Actes du X-e Congrès international d'archéologie chrétienne, Thessa-*

Ionique 28 septembre–4 octobre 1980, 2:521–33. Thessaloniki: Hetaireia makedonikon spoudon; Vatican City: Pontificio Istituto di Archeologia Cristiana.

Sotiroff, G. 1972. "Did Justinian do it? " *Anthropological Journal of Canada* 10:2–7.

Stevović, Ivan. 1991. "New cognizance on early Byzantine Dubrovnik in the 6th century." *Starinar* 42:141–51.

Tomičić, Željko. 1990. "Archaeological evidence of early Byzantine military building in the north Adriatic islands." *Prilozi Instituta az arheologiju u Zagrebu* 5–6:29–53.

Tomović, Miodrag. 1996. "Ravna: The Roman and early Byzantine fortification." In *Roman Limes on the Middle and Lower Danube*, ed. Petar Petrović, 73–80. Belgrade: Arheološki Institut.

Torbatov, Sergei. 1997. "Quaestura exercitus: Moesia Secunda and Scythia under Justinian." *Archaeologia Bulgarica* 1:78–87.

———. 2000. "Procop. *De Aedif.* IV,7,12–14 and the historical geography of Moesia Secunda." *Archaeologia Bulgarica* 4:58–77.

Vačić, Miloje. 1999. "Transdrobeta (Pontes) in the late antiquity." In *Der Limes an der unteren Donau von Diokletian bis Herakleios: Vorträge der internationalen Konferenz Svistov, Bulgarien (1–5 September 1998)*, ed. Gerda von Bülow and Alexandra Milcheva, 33–37. Sofia: NOUS.

Velkov, Ivan. 1946. "An early Christian basilica at Mesembria." *Bulletin of the Byzantine Institute* 1:61–70.

Velkov, Velizar. 1977. *Cities in Thrace and Dacia in Late Antiquity*. Amsterdam: Adolf M. Hakkert.

Velkov, Velizar, and Stefan Lisicov. 1994. "An early Byzantine and mediaeval fort in the Haemus with an inscription and grafitti of Emperor Anastasius." In *Sbornik v chest na akad. Dimităr Angelov*, ed. Velizar Velkov, Zhivko Aladzhov, Georgi Bakalov, et al., 257–65. Sofia: Izdatelstvo na Bălgarskata Akademiia na Naukite.

Werner, Michael. 1986. "The Moesian limes and the imperial mining districts." In *Studien zu den Militärgrenzen Roms III. 13. internationaler Limeskongreß Aalen 1983. Vorträge*, 561–64. Stuttgart: Konrad Theiss.

Whitby, Michael. 1985. "The Long Walls of Constantinople." *Byzantion* 55:560–83.

Wiseman, James R. 1984. "The city in Macedonia Secunda." In *Villes et peuplement dans l'Illyricum protobyzantin: Actes due colloque organisé par l'Ecole Française de Rome, Rome 12–14 mai 1982*, 289–314. Rome: Ecole Française de Rome.

Wozniak, F. E. 1982. "The Justinianic fortification of interior Illyricum." In *City, Town, and Countryside in the Early Byzantine Era*, ed. R. L. Hohlfelder, 199–209. New York: Columbia University Press.

Zahariade, Mihail, and Andrei Opaiţ. 1986. "A new late Roman fortification on the territory of Romania: The burgus at Topraichioi, Tulcea County." In *Studien zu den Militärgrenzen Roms III. 13. internationaler Limeskongreß Aealen 1983. Vorträge*, 565–72. Stuttgart: Konrad Theiss.

CHRONICLES OF ARCHAEOLOGICAL EXCAVATIONS

Baczyńska, Barbara. 1978. "Major results of 1977 excavations of early medieval sites in Poland." *Sprawozdania Archeologiczne* 30:271–74.

Bakirtzis, Ch. 1989. "Western Thrace in the early Christian and Byzantine periods:

Results of archaeological research and the prospects, 1973–1987." *Byzantinische Forschungen* 14:41–58.

Byzantine Thrace: A New Field Opened for Archaeological Research. 1994. Athens: Ministry of Culture.

Dąbrowska, Elżbieta. 1970. "Results of excavations carried out on early medieval sites in Poland in 1969." *Sprawozdania Archeologiczne* 22:311–15.

Tunia, Krzysztof. 1977. "Major results of 1976 excavations of early medieval sites in Poland." *Sprawozdania Archeologiczne* 29:199–203.

Zoll-Adamikowa, Helena. 1969. "Results of the 1968 excavations of early medieval sites in Poland." *Sprawozdania Archeologiczne* 21:385–90.

———. 1969. "Survey of the 1967 investigations of early medieval sites." *Sprawozdania Archeologiczne* 20:405–10.

———. 1971. "Results of 1970 excavations of early medieval sites in Poland." *Sprawozdania Archeologiczne* 23:207–13.

———. 1972. "Major results of 1971 excavations of early medieval sites in Poland." *Sprawozdania Archeologiczne* 24:321–26.

———. 1973. "Major results of the 1972 excavations of early medieval sites in Poland." *Sprawozdania Archeologiczne* 25:273–77.

———. 1976. "Major results of the 1975 excavations of early medieval sites in Poland." *Sprawozdania Archeologiczne* 28:277–81.

———. 1979. "Major results of 1978 excavations of early medieval sites in Poland." *Sprawozdania Archeologiczne* 31:281–84.

———. 1980. "Major results of the 1979 excavations of early medieval sites in Poland." *Sprawozdania Archeologiczne* 32:349–52.

———. 1981. "Major results of 1980 excavations of early medieval sites in Poland." *Sprawozdania Archeologiczne* 33:293–96.

———. 1982. "Major results of the 1981 excavations of early medieval sites in Poland." *Sprawozdania Archeologiczne* 34:315–17.

———. 1983. "Major results of the 1982 excavations of early medieval sites in Poland." *Sprawozdania Archeologiczne* 35:305–8.

———. 1984. "Major results of the 1983 excavations of early medieval sites in Poland." *Sprawozdania Archeologiczne* 36:329–32.

———. 1985. "Major results of the 1984 excavations of early medieval sites in Poland." *Sprawozdania Archeologiczne* 37:337–40.

———. 1986. "Major results of the 1985 excavations of early medieval sites in Poland." *Sprawozdania Archeologiczne* 38:387–90.

———. 1987. "Major results of the 1986 excavations of early medieval sites in Poland." *Sprawozdania Archeologiczne* 39:395–98.

———. 1988. "Major results of the 1987 excavations of early medieval sites in Poland." *Sprawozdania Archeologiczne* 40:405–7.

ARCHAEOLOGY OF RURAL SETTLEMENTS AND SETTLEMENT PATTERNS

Barford, Paul M., and E. Marczak. 1993. "The settlement complex at Podebłocie, gm. Trojanow: An interim report of investigations, 1981–1992." *Swiatowit* 37:147–67.

Čaplovič, Dušan. 1987. "New facts about the development of medieval rural house in East Slovakia." *Slovenská Archeológia* 35:7–18.

Čaplovič, Dušan, and Alojz Habovštiak. 1996. "The situation of the archaeological research of Middle Age agricultural settlement in the territory of Slovakia." *Ruralia* 1:269–76.

Dąbrowski, Krzysztof. 1975. "Archaeological investigations at Tumiany, near Olsztyn." *Archaeologia Polona* 16:179–97.

Dragotă, Aurel, C. M. Urian, I. Băbuț, et al. 2003. "Archaeological researches in Alba Iulia: 'Spitalul Veterinar' and 'Canton C.F.R.' (1961–1962)." In *In memoriam Radu Popa: Temeiuri ale civilizației românești în context european,* ed. Daniela Marcu Istrate, Angel Istrate, and Corneliu Gaiu, 207–16. Cluj-Napoca: Accent.

Frolík, Jan, and Jiří Sigl. 1995. "Development of early medieval settlement and related structural changes within the Chrudim region: A research contribution." *Památky Archeologické* 86:63–104.

Gojda, Martin. 1988. *The Development of the Settlement Pattern in the Basin of the Lower Vltava (Central Bohemia), 200–1200 A.D.* Oxford: British Archaeological Reports, International Series.

———. 1991. "Early medieval settlements at Roztoky: The 1986–1989 excavations." In *Archaeology in Bohemia, 1986–1990,* ed. Pavel Vařeka, 135 39. Prague: Institute of Archaeology of the Czechoslovak Academy of Sciences.

———. 1992. "Early medieval settlement study in Bohemia: Traditions and perspectives." *Památky Archeologické* 83:174–80.

Gojda, Martin, and Martin Kuna. 1986. "Roztoky—a newly discovered settlement area of the early Slavic period." In *Archaeology in Bohemia 1981–1985,* ed. Radomír Pleiner and Jiří Hrala, 175–83. Prague: Archaeological Institute of the Czechoslovak Academy of Sciences.

Iashaeva, T. I. 2003. "On the immediate hinterland of Cherson in Late Antiquity and early medieval times." *Ancient West and East* 2:117–33.

Kobyliński, Zbigniew. 1987. "The settlement structure and the settlement process: The identification of the continuity and change in a social-cultural system in time." *Archaeologia Polona* 25–26:121–55.

———. 1997. "Settlement structures in central Europe at the beginning of the Middle Ages." In *Origins of Central Europe,* ed. Przemysław Ubańczyk, 97–114. Warsaw: Scientific Society of Polish Archaeologists.

———. 2000. "Everyday life in a western Slav village around A.D. 1000." In *Europe's Centre around A.D. 1000,* ed. Alfried Wieczorek and Hans-Martin Hinz, 73–74. Stuttgart: Theiss.

Koledarov, P. S. 1969. "Settlement structure of the Bulgarian Slavs in their transition from a clan to a territorial community." *Byzantinobulgarica* 3:125–32.

Korošec, Paola. 1999. "Development of the early mediaeval Ptuj settlement." In *Istoriia i kul'tura drevnikh i srednevekovykh slavian,* ed. V. V. Sedov, 15–19. Moscow: Editorial URSS.

Kralovánszky, A. 1990. "The settlement history of Veszprém and Székesfehérvár in the Middle Ages." In *Towns in Medieval Hungary,* ed. L. Gerevich, 51–95. Highland Lakes: Atlantic Research and Publications.

Kurnatowski, Stanisław. 2000. "Settlement landscape, settlement, and economy among the western Slavs between the Oder and Vistula." In *Europe's Centre around A.D. 1000,* ed. Alfried Wieczorek and Hans-Martin Hinz, 61–64. Stuttgart: Theiss.

Lodowski, Jerzy. 1969. "Early medieval settlement complex near Sadowel, Gora district." *Archaeologia Polona* 11:227–43.

Marjanović-Vujović, Gordana. 1973. "Slavic Beograd." *Balcanoslavica* 2:9–16.

———. 1990. "Rural settlements in the 9th and 10th centuries in the Danube valley in Serbia." In *From the Baltic to the Black Sea: Studies in Medieval Archaeology*, ed. David Austin and Leslie Alcock, 236–47. London: Unwin Hyman.

Meduna, P. 1991. "On the early medieval settlement structure of NW Bohemia: Investigations of the drainage area of the Lomsky- and Loucensky-Potok." In *Archaeology in Bohemia, 1986–1990*, ed. Pavel Vařeka, 185–89. Prague: Institute of Archaeology of the Czechoslovak Academy of Sciences.

Meduna, P., and E. Cerna. 1991. "Settlement structure of the early Middle Ages in northwest Bohemia: Investigations of the Petipsy basin area." *Antiquity* 65:388–95.

Pleinerová, Ivana. 1986. "Březno: Experiments with building Old Slavic houses and living in them." *Památky Archeologické* 77:104–76.

Riabinin, E. A. 1992. "The ancient site of Unorozh, end of the first millenium A.D." In *Cultural Heritage of the Finno-Ugrians and Slavs: Papers Presented by the Participants in the Soviet-Finnish Archaeological Symposium, 10–16 May 1990 in Tallinn*, ed. V. Lang and J. Selirand, 122–34. Tallinn: Varrak.

Slabe, Marijan. 1987–89. "Settlement structure on the south-east pre-Alpine territory in the fifth and sixth centuries AD." *Balcanica* 18–19:195–201.

Torma, István. 1991. "Examples of continuity and discontinuity in the settlement history of the Vác area." *Antaeus* 19–20:159–68.

Walck, Christa Lynn. 1980. "Settlement patterns in Rostov-Suzdal' Rus', ninth through thirteenth centuries: Analysis of the material evidence for Slavic colonization and state formation in northeastern Rus'." Ph.D. diss., Harvard University.

Wolf, Mária. 1996. "Rural settlements." In *The Ancient Hungarians: Exhibition catalogue*, ed. István Fodor, 60–61. Budapest: Hungarian National Museum.

Zábojník, Jozef. 1988. "On the problems of settlements of the Avar khaganate period in Slovakia." *Archeologické rozhledy* 40:401–37.

STRONGHOLDS AND EMPORIA

Aladzhov, Dimităr. 2001. *Famous, Forgotten, Unknown Fortresses in the Region of Haskovo*. Haskovo: Klokotnica 96.

Avdusin, D. 1969. "Smolensk and the Varangians according to the archaeological data." *Norwegian Archaeological Review* 2:52–62.

———. 1970. "Material culture in the towns of ancient Rus' (in the light of the excavations at Novgorod)." In *Varangian Problems: Report on the First International Symposium on the Theme "The Eastern Connections of the Nordic Peoples in the Viking Period and Early Middle Ages," Moesgaard-University of Aarhus, October 7–11, 1968*, ed. Knud Hannestad, Knud Jordal, Ole Klindt-Jensen, et al., 95–120. Copenhague: Munksgaard.

Barford, Paul. 1995. "Early medieval earthwork settlement enclosures in northern Europe." In *Theory and Practice of Archaeological Excavation*, ed. Przemysław Urbańczyk, 2:191–212. Warsaw: Institute of Archaeology and Ethnology of the Polish Academy of Sciences.

Bartošková, Andrea. 2000. "Budeč." In *Europe's Centre around A.D. 1000*, ed. Alfried Wieczorek and Hans-Martin Hinz, 253–54. Stuttgart: Theiss.

———. 2000. "Stara Kouřim." In *Europe's Centre around A.D. 1000*, ed. Alfried Wieczorek and Hans-Martin Hinz, 202–3. Stuttgart: Theiss.

Bartošková, Andrea, and Jarmila Princová. 1994. "Budeč-Libice: Early medieval centres of Bohemia." In 25 Years of Archaeological Research in Bohemia, ed. Jan Fridrich, 185–200. Prague: Institute of Archaeology of the Czechoslovak Academy of Sciences.

Benkö, Elek. 2000. "Alba Iulia (Gyulafehérvár)." In Europe's Centre around A.D. 1000, ed. Alfried Wieczorek and Hans-Martin Hinz, 389–91. Stuttgart: Theiss.

————. 2000. "Mănăştur (Kolozsmonostor) near Cluj." In Europe's Centre around A.D. 1000, ed. Alfried Wieczorek and Hans-Martin Hinz, 392–93. Stuttgart: Theiss.

Bláha, Josef. 2000. "Olomouc." In Europe's Centre around A.D. 1000, ed. Alfried Wieczorek and Hans-Martin Hinz, 249–50. Stuttgart: Theiss.

Boháčová, I. 2000. "Stara Boleslav." In Europe's Centre around A.D. 1000, ed. Alfried Wieczorek and Hans-Martin Hinz, 247–48. Stuttgart: Theiss.

Boháčová, I., J. Frolík, L. Hrdlická, and Z. Smetánka. 1992. "Prague and Prague Castle, centre of the state of Bohemia in the 9th–13th centuries." In Medieval Europe 1992: Urbanism, 1:83–88. York: Medieval Europe.

Boháčová, I., J. Frolík, Z. Smetanka, et al. 1994. "Prague Castle, Vysehrad Castle, and the Prague agglomeration." In 25 Years of Archaeological Research in Bohemia, ed. Jan Fridrich, 153–84. Prague: Institute of Archaeology of the Czechoslovak Academy of Sciences.

Bortoli, Anne, and Michel Kazanski. 2002. "Kherson and its region." In The Economic History of Byzantium from the Seventh through the Fifteenth Century, ed. Angeliki E. Laiou, 659–65. Washington, D.C.: Dumbarton Oaks Research Library and Collection.

Brzostowicz, Michał. 2000. "Bruszczewo." In Europe's Centre around A.D. 1000, ed. Alfried Wieczorek and Hans-Martin Hinz, 172–73. Stuttgart: Theiss.

Bubeník, Jan. 1991. "Rubín Hill and its significance for early medieval settlement." In Archaeology in Bohemia, 1986–1990, ed. Pavel Vařeka, 233–36. Prague: Institute of Archaeology of the Czechoslovak Academy of Sciences.

Bubeník, Josef, Bořivoj Nechvatál, Ivana Pleinerová, et al. 1994. "From the emergence of hillforts to the beginning of the state: Research into the initial phase of the early Middle Ages in Bohemia." In 25 Years of Archaeological Research in Bohemia, ed. Jan Fridrich, 133–52. Prague: Institute of Archaeology of the Czechoslovak Academy of Sciences.

Buko, Andrzej. 1994. "Origins of towns in southern Poland: The example of medieval Sandomierz." Archaeologia Polona 32:171–84.

Callmer, Johan. 1981. "The archaeology of Kiev ca. AD 500–1000: A survey." In Les pays du Nord et Byzance (Scandinavie et Byzance): Actes du colloque nordique et international de byzantinologie tenu à Upsal 20–22 avril 1979, ed. R. Zeitler, 29–52. Uppsala: Almqvist and Wiksell International.

Carter, Francis W. 1983. "Cracow's early development." Slavonic and East European Review 61:197–225.

Čech, Petr. 2000. "Zatec." In Europe's Centre around A. D. 1000, ed. Alfried Wieczorek and Hans-Martin Hinz, 251. Stuttgart: Theiss.

Dąbrowski, Krzysztof. 1976. "Kalisz between the tenth and thirteenth centuries." In Medieval Settlement: Continuity and Change, ed. Peter H. Sawyer, 265–73. London: Edward Arnold.

Davidan, O. I. 1970. "Contacts between Staraja Ladoga and Scandinavia (on the evidence of archaeological material from Zemljanoe gorodišče)." In Varangian Problems: Report on the First International Symposium on the Theme "The Eastern Connections of the Nordic Peoples in the Viking Period and Early Middle Ages," Moesgaard-University of Aarhus, October 7–11, 1968, ed. Knud Hannestad, Knud Jordal, Ole Klindt-Jensen, et al., 79–94. Copenhague: Munksgaard.

Dimnik, Martin. 1979. "Kamenec." Russia mediaevalis 4:25–35.

Dulinicz, Marek. 1997. "The first dendrochronological dating of the strongholds of northern Mazovia." In Origins of Central Europe, ed. Przemysław Urbańczyk, 137–41. Warsaw: Scientific Society of Polish Archaeologists.

Dzieduszycki, Bożena. 1985. "Demographic and economic transformations in the area surrounding the early medieval Kruszwica." Archaeologia Polona 24:73–103.

Dzieduszycki, Bożena, and Wojciech Dzieduszycki. 1988. "Socio-economic and demographic transformations of early-urban Kruszwica and its subsidiaries." Slavia Antiqua 31:45–53.

Filipowiak, Władysław. 2000. "Wolin: An early medieval trading emporium on the Baltic." In Europe's Centre around A.D. 1000, ed. Alfried Wieczorek and Hans-Martin Hinz, 102–4. Stuttgart: Theiss.

Finley, John H. 1932. "Corinth in the Middle Ages." Speculum 7:477–99.

Frolík, Jan. 1991. "The most recent excavations and discoveries at Prague Castle." In Archaeology in Bohemia, 1986–1990, ed. Pavel Vařeka, 146–48. Prague: Institute of Archaeology of the Czechoslovak Academy of Sciences.

———. 1996. "Prague Castle: 70 years of archaeological excavations." In Frühmittelalterliche Machtzentren in Mitteleuropa: Mehrjährige Grabungen und ihre Auswertung; Symposion Mikulčice, 5.–9. September 1994, ed. Čenek Staňa and Lumír Poláček, 159–66. Brno: Archäologisches Institut der Akademie der Wissenschaften der Tschechischen Republik.

Frolík, Jan, and Milena Bravermanová. 2000. "Prague Castle." In Europe's Centre around A.D. 1000, ed. Alfried Wieczorek and Hans-Martin Hinz, 241–42. Stuttgart: Theiss.

Galuška, Ludek. 1993. "Staré Město, the Great Moravian centre of the 2nd half of the 9th century." In Actes du XII-e Congrès international des sciences préhistoriques et protohistoriques, Bratislava, 1–7 septembre 1991, ed. J. Pavuj, 4:96–102. Bratislava: Institut Archéologique de l'Académie Slovaque des Sciences.

———. 1996. "The question of evaluating and the present level of knowledge about the Great Moravian agglomeration of Staré Město–Uherské Hradište." In Frühmittelalterliche Machtzentren in Mitteleuropa: Mehrjährige Grabungen und ihre Auswertung: Symposion Mikulčice, 5.–9. September 1994, ed. Čenek Staňa and Lumír Poláček, 189–97. Brno: Archäologisches Institut der Akademie der Wissenschaften der Tschechischen Republik.

———. 2000. "Staré Město–Uherské Hradiste." In Europe's Centre around A.D. 1000, ed. Alfried Wieczorek and Hans-Martin Hinz, 206–7. Stuttgart: Theiss.

Górecki, Janusz. 2000. "Ostrów Lednicki: A stronghold centre of the early Piast rulers of Poland." In Europe's Centre around A.D. 1000, ed. Alfried Wieczorek and Hans-Martin Hinz, 301–3. Stuttgart: Theiss.

Hensel, Witold. 1988. "Archaeology on the origins of Polish towns." Slovenská Archeológia 36:77–84.

Hilczer-Kurnatowska, Zofia. 1962. "Early mediaeval fort in Bonikowo, district Kościan (Great Poland)." Archaeologia Polona 5:63–75.

Hrdlička, Ladislav. 1984. "Outline of development of the landscape of the Prague historical core in the Middle Ages." Archeologické rozhledy 36:638–52.

————. 2000. "Prague." In *Europe's Centre around A.D. 1000*, ed. Alfried Wieczorek and Hans-Martin Hinz, 239–40. Stuttgart: Theiss.

Huml, Vaclav. 1990. "Research in Prague: An historical and archaeological view of the development of Prague from the 9th century to the middle of the 14th century." In *From the Baltic to the Black Sea: Studies in Medieval Archaeology*, ed. David Austin and Leslie Alcock, 267–84. London: Unwin Hyman.

Ioannisyan, Oleg M. 1990. "Archaeological evidence for the development and urbanization of Kiev from the 8th to the 14th centuries." In *From the Baltic to the Black Sea: Studies in Medieval Archaeology*, ed. David Austin and Leslie Alcock, 285–312. London: Unwin Hyman.

Iordanov, Ivan. 2002. "Preslav." In *The Economic History of Byzantium from the Seventh through the Fifteenth Century*, ed. Angeliki E. Laiou, 669–71. Washington, D.C.: Dumbarton Oaks Research Library and Collection.

Iwanowska, Grazyna. 1991. "Excavations at the Jegliniec hillfort: Recent developments in Balt archaeology." *Antiquity* 65:684–95.

Jażdzewski, Konrad. 1975. "Ostrow Lednicki (the Isle of Lake Lednica): An early Polish prince's seat on a lake island." In *Recent Archaeological Excavations in Europe*, ed. Rupert Bruce-Mitford, 302–35. London: Routledge and Kegan Paul.

Justová, Jarmila. 1986. "Libice—a centre of the eastern domain of Bohemia. Excavation of the bailey." In *Archaeology in Bohemia 1981–1985*, ed. Radomír Pleiner and Jiři Hrala, 199–208. Prague: Archaeological Institute of the Czechoslovak Academy of Sciences.

————. 1991. "The bailey of the ducal residence at Libice-nad-Cidlinou and its hinterland." In *Archaeology in Bohemia, 1986–1990*, ed. Pavel Vareka, 140–45. Prague: Institute of Archaeology of the Czechoslovak Academy of Sciences.

Kajzer, Leszek. 1995. "Archaeological research into fortified buildings and architecture." *Slavia Antiqua* 36:19–27.

Kalligas, Haris. 2002. "Monemvasia, seventh–fifteenth centuries." In *The Economic History of Byzantium from the Seventh through the Fifteenth Century*, ed. Angeliki E. Laiou, 879–97. Washington, D.C.: Dumbarton Oaks Research Library and Collection.

Kara, Michał. 2000. "Poznań." In *Europe's Centre around A.D. 1000*, ed. Alfried Wieczorek and Hans-Martin Hinz, 306–8. Stuttgart: Theiss.

Kazanaki-Lappa, Maria. 2002. "Medieval Athens." In *The Economic History of Byzantium from the Seventh through the Fifteenth Century*, ed. Angeliki E. Laiou, 640–46. Washington, D.C.: Dumbarton Oaks Research Library and Collection.

Khoroshev, A. S. 1985. "The origins of Novgorod in Russian historiography." *Soviet Studies in History* 23:22–45.

Kivikoski, E. 1970. "Discussion continued from volume 2, Comments on Danill Avdusin: Smolensk and the Varangians according to the archaeological data." *Norwegian Archaeological Review* 3:115–17.

Kobyliński, Zbigniew. 1990. "Early medieval hillforts in Polish lands in the 6th to the 8th centuries: Problems of origins, function, and spatial organization." In *From the Baltic to the Black Sea: Studies in Medieval Archaeology*, ed. David Austin and Leslie Alcock, 147–56. London: Unwin Hyman.

Kountoura, Eleonora. 1997. "New fortresses and bishoprics in 8th century Thrace." *Revue des études byzantines* 55:279–89.

Krăndzhalov, Dimitar. 1966. "Is the fortress at Aboba identical with Pliska, the oldest capital of Bulgaria?" *Slavia Antiqua* 13:444–45.

Krąpiec, Marek. 1998. "Dendrochronological dating of early medieval fortified settlements in Poland." In *Frühmittelalterlicher Burgenbau in Mittel- und Osteuropa: Tagung, Nitra, vom 7. bis 10. Oktober 1996*, ed. Joachim Henning and Alexander T. Ruttkay, 257–67. Bonn: R. Habelt.

Krzystofiak, Teresa. 2000. "Giecz." In *Europe's Centre around A.D. 1000*, ed. Alfried Wieczorek and Hans-Martin Hinz, 299–300. Stuttgart: Theiss.

Kurnatowska, Zofia. 1995. "Ostrów Lednicki as an example of interdisciplinary regional research." *Slavia Antiqua* 36:39–48.

———. 2000. "Fortifications and the rise of tribal aristocracy among the Slavs in the period before the foundation of the Polish state." In *Europe's Centre around A.D. 1000*, ed. Alfried Wieczorek and Hans-Martin Hinz, 169–71. Stuttgart: Theiss.

Leciejewicz, Lech. 2000. "Kołobrzeg." In *Europe's Centre around A.D. 1000*, ed. Alfried Wieczorek and Hans-Martin Hinz, 109–10. Stuttgart: Theiss.

Losiński, Władysław. 2000. "Szczecin." In *Europe's Centre around A.D. 1000*, ed. Alfried Wieczorek and Hans-Martin Hinz, 105–6. Stuttgart: Theiss.

Macháček, Jiří. "Břeclav-Pohansko." In *Europe's Centre around A.D. 1000*, ed. Alfried Weiczorek and Hans-Martin Hinz, 210–11. Stuttgart: Theiss.

Maloney, Stephanie J. 1982. "The mediaeval fortress of Mietlica in Poland." *Archaeology* 35:26–32.

———. 1988. "Domestic construction at the early medieval fortress of Mietlica." *Slavia Antiqua* 31:233–55.

McGovern, Michéal. 1985. "Sarkel: A reflection of Byzantine power or weakness?" *Byzantinoslavica* 50:177–80.

Mezencev, Volodymyr I. 1986. "The emergence of the Podil and the genesis of the city of Kiev: Problems of dating." *Harvard Ukrainian Studies* 10:48–70.

———. 1989. "The territorial and demographic development of medieval Kiev and other major cities of Rus': A comparative analysis based on recent archaeological research." *Russian Review* 48:145–70.

Nosov, E. N. 1987. "New data on the Ryurik Gorodishche near Novgorod." *Fennoscandia archaeologica* 4:73–85.

———. 1992. "Ryurik Gorodishche and the settlements to the north of Lake Ilmen." In *The Archaeology of Novgorod, Russia: Recent Results from the Town and Its Hinterland*, ed. Mark A. Brisbane, 5–66. Lincoln: Society for Medieval Archaeology.

———. 1994. "The emergence and development of Russian towns: Some outline ideas." *Archaeologia Polona* 32:185–96.

Petrenko, V. P., and Juris Urtans. 1995. *The Archaeological Monuments of Grobina*. Stockholm/Riga: Museum of National Antiquities/Latvian Cultural Foundation.

Pianowski, Zbigniew. 2000. "Krakow." In *Europe's Centre around A.D. 1000*, ed. Alfried Wieczorek and Hans-Martin Hinz, 309–10. Stuttgart: Theiss.

Poláček, Lumír. 2000. "Hillforts, castles, and fortified towns in Moravia." In *Europe's Centre around A.D. 1000*, ed. Alfried Wieczorek and Hans-Martin Hinz, 186–88. Stuttgart: Theiss.

———. 2000. "Mikulčice." In *Europe's Centre around A.D. 1000*, ed. Alfried Wieczorek and Hans-Martin Hinz, 204–5. Stuttgart: Theiss.

———. 2000. "Moravian trade." In *Europe's Centre around A.D. 1000*, ed. Alfried Wieczorek and Hans-Martin Hinz, 97–98. Stuttgart: Theiss.

Poleski, Jacek. 2000. "Naszacowice." In *Europe's Centre around A.D. 1000*, ed. Alfried Wieczorek and Hans-Martin Hinz, 174–75. Stuttgart: Theiss.

Popović, Marko. 1991. *The Fortress of Belgrade*. Belgrade: Institute for the Protection of Cultural Monuments of Serbia.

Poulík, Josef. 1975. "Mikulčice: Capital of the lords of Great Moravia." In *Recent Archaeological Excavations in Europe*, ed. Rupert Bruce-Mitford, 1–31. London: Routledge and Kegan Paul.

Princová, Jarmila. 2000. "Libice." In *Europe's Centre around A.D. 1000*, ed. Alfried Wieczorek and Hans-Martin Hinz, 245–46. Stuttgart: Theiss.

Ruttkay, Alexander T. 2000. "Hillforts, castles, and fortified towns: Structures of power among the western Slavs in Slovakia." In *Europe's Centre around A.D. 1000*, ed. Alfried Wieczorek and Hans-Martin Hinz, 212–14. Stuttgart: Theiss.

———. 2000. "Nitra and Zobor." In *Europe's Centre around A.D. 1000*, ed. Alfried Wieczorek and Hans-Martin Hinz, 412–14. Stuttgart: Theiss.

Rzeznik, Pawel. 2000. "Wrocław." In *Europe's Centre around A.D. 1000*, ed. Alfried Wieczorek and Hans-Martin Hinz, 311–13. Stuttgart: Theiss.

Sanders, G. D. R. 2002. "Corinth." In *The Economic History of Byzantium from the Seventh through the Fifteenth Century*, ed. Angeliki E. Laiou, 647–54. Washington, D.C.: Dumbarton Oaks Research Library and Collection.

Sawicki, Tomasz. 2000. "Gniezno." In *Europe's Centre around A.D. 1000*, ed. Alfried Wieczorek and Hans-Martin Hinz, 304–5. Stuttgart: Theiss.

Sláma, Jiří. 2000. "Hillforts, castles, and fortified towns in Bohemia." In *Europe's Centre around A.D. 1000*, ed. Alfried Wieczorek and Hans-Martin Hinz, 184–85. Stuttgart: Theiss.

———. 2000. "Stary Plzenec." In *Europe's Centre around A.D. 1000*, ed. Alfried Wieczorek and Hans-Martin Hinz, 252. Stuttgart: Theiss.

Słupecki, Leszek Pawel. 2000. "Jómsvikingalog, Jómsvikings, Jomsborg/Wolin, and Danish circular strongholds." In *The Neighbors of Poland in the 10th Century*, ed. Przemysław Urbańczyk, 7–36. Warsaw: Institute of Archaeology and Ethnology.

Štefanovičová, Tatiana. 2000. "Devin and Bratislava: Two important early medieval castles on the middle Danube." In *Europe's Centre around A.D. 1000*, ed. Alfried Wieczorek and Hans-Martin Hinz, 208–9. Stuttgart: Theiss.

Szöke, Béla Miklós. 2000. "The Carolingian civitas Mosapurc (Zalavár)." In *Europe's Centre around A.D. 1000*, ed. Alfried Wieczorek and Hans-Martin Hinz, 140–42. Stuttgart: Theiss.

Szöke, Mátyás. 2000. "The medieval castle of Visegrad." In *Europe's Centre around A.D. 1000*, ed. Alfried Wieczorek and Hans-Martin Hinz, 383–84. Stuttgart: Theiss.

Tomková, Kateřina. 2000. "Levý Hradec." In *Europe's Centre around A.D. 1000*, ed. Alfried Wieczorek and Hans-Martin Hinz, 243–44. Stuttgart: Theiss.

Uino, Pirjo. 1988. "On the history of Staraia Ladoga." *Acta Archaeologica* 59:205–22.

Urbańczyk, Przemysław. 1994. "The origins of towns on the outskirts of medieval Europe: Poland, Norway, and Ireland." *Archaeologia Polona* 32:109–27.

Valić, Andrej. 1986. "Budeč: A ducal residence in the centre of Bohemia according to excavations in the latest years." In *Archaeology in Bohemia, 1981–1985*, ed. Radomír Pleiner and Jiři Hrala, 191–98. Prague: Archaeological Institute of the Czechoslovak Academy of Sciences.

Velímsky, T. 1992. "The typological development of the town of Most, Bohemia." In *Medieval Europe 1992: Urbanism*, 1:197–206. York: Medieval Europe.

Wolf, Mária. 1996. "Edelény-Borsod, earthen fort." In *The Ancient Hungarians: Exhibition Catalogue,* ed. István Fodor, 417–23. Budapest: Hungarian National Museum.

———. 2000. "Abaújvár." In *Europe's Centre around A.D. 1000,* ed. Alfried Wieczorek and Hans-Martin Hinz, 385–86. Stuttgart: Theiss.

———. 2000. "The hillfort of Borsod." In *Europe's Centre around A.D. 1000,* ed. Alfried Wieczorek and Hans-Martin Hinz, 387–88. Stuttgart: Theiss.

Zbierski, Andrzej. 1976. "Archaeology on spatial changes in Gdańsk." *Acta Poloniae Historica* 34:85–95.

———. 1985. "The development of the Gdańsk area from the ninth to the thirteenth century." In *The Comparative History of Urban Origins in Non-Roman Europe: Ireland, Wales, Denmark, Germany, Poland, and Russia from the Ninth to the Thirteenth Century,* ed. H. B. Clarke and Anngret Simms, 2:289–334. Oxford: British Archaeological Reports.

BURIALS AND MORTUARY ARCHAEOLOGY

Afanas'ev, Gennadii E. 1994. "System of socially marking grave goods in male burial complexes of the Alans of the Don." In *The Archaeology of the Steppes: Methods and Strategies. Papers from the International Symposium Held in Naples, 9–12 September 1992,* ed. Bruno Genito, 469–88. Naples: Istituto universitario orientale.

Avdusin, D. A. 1974. "Scandinavian graves in Gnezdovo." *Vestnik Moskovskogo universiteta, Seria VIII: Istoriia* 1:74–86.

Avdusin, D. A., and T. A. Pushkina. 1988. "Three chamber graves at Gniozdovo." *Fornvännen* 83:20–33.

Bárkoczi, L. 1968. "A 6th century cemetery from Keszthely-Fenékpuszta." *Acta Archaeologica Academiae Scientiarum Hungaricae* 20:275–311.

Brukner, Olga. 1982. "The sixth century necropolis at Vajska." In *Sirmium: Recherches archéologiques en Syrmie,* ed. Noël Duval, Edward L. Ochsenschlager, and Vladislav Popović, 4:29–40. Belgrade: Arheološki Institut; Rome: Ecole Française de Rome.

Bulkin, V. A. 1973. "On the classification and interpretation of archaeological material from Gnezdovo." *Norwegian Archaeological Review* 6:10–13.

Ercegović-Pavlović, Slavenka. 1982. "An eastern Germanic grave from Mačvanska Mitrovica." In *Sirmium: Recherches archéologiques en Syrmie,* ed. Noël Duval, Edward L. Ochsenschlager, and Vladislav Popović, 4:19–27. Belgrade: Institut Archéologique de Belgrade, Ecole Française de Rome, and Research Foundation of the City University of New York.

———. 1982. "An Avarian equestrian grave from Mandjelos." In *Sirmium: Recherches archéologiques en Syrmie,* ed. Noël Duval, Edward L. Ochsenschlager, and Vladislav Popović, 4:49–56. Belgrade: Institut Archéologique de Belgrade, Ecole Française de Rome, and Research Foundation of the City University of New York.

Evans, Huw M. A. 1989. *The Early Medieval Archaeology of Croatia, A.D. 600–900.* Oxford: British Archaeological Reports.

Fülöp, Gyula. 1990. "New research on finds of Avar chieftain-burial at Igar, Hungary." In *From the Baltic to the Black Sea: Studies in Medieval Archaeology,* ed. David Austin and Leslie Alcock, 138–46. London: Unwin Hyman.

Galuška, Luděk. 1996. "To the possibility of moving the dating of the material culture on the basis of the study of the graves from Staré Město und Uherské Hradiště-Sady." In

Ethnische und kulturelle Verhältnisse an der mittleren Donau vom 6. bis zum 11. Jahrhundert: Symposium Nitra 6. bis 10. November 1994, ed. D. Bialeková and J. Zábojník, 267–80. Bratislava: Verlag der Slowakischen Akademie der Wissenschaften.

Garam, Éva. 1975. "The Szebény I–III cemetery." In *Avar Finds in the Hungarian National Museum,* ed. Ilona Kovrig, 50–120. Budapest: Akadémiai Kiadó.

Gvozdanović-Goss, Vladimir. 1980. "Moravia's history reconsidered: The tomb of St. Methodius and the church of Our Lady at Morović (Yugoslavia)." *East European Quarterly* 14:487–98.

Hanáková, Hana, František Gabriel, and Luboš Vyhnánek. 1986. "Slavonic burial-ground in Litoměřice Plesivecká Street." *Sborník Narodního musea v Praže* 42:73–98.

Ivanov, V. A. 1993. "Statistical model of the funeral rites of Ugrians and Turks in east Eurasia during the Middle Ages." *Acta Archaeologica Academiae Scientiarum Hungaricae* 45:158–63.

Ivanov, Vladimir A., and Gennadii N. Garustovich. 1994. "The results of the statistical analyses of funeral rites of the nomads in the "Great steppe belt" in the 10th–11th centuries and their ethnic interpretation." In *The Archaeology of the Steppes: Methods and Strategies. Papers from the International Symposium Held in Naples, 9–12 September 1992,* ed. Bruno Genito, 573–89. Naples: Istituto universitario orientale.

Jeremić, Miroslav. 1994–95. "The Caričin Grad necropolis." *Starinar* 45–46:181–95.

Jovanović, Vojislav, and Ljiljana Vukšanović. 1973. "The Slavic necropolis at Matičane near Priština." In *Actes du VIII-e Congrès international des sciences préhistoriques et protohistoriques, Beograd 9–15 septembre 1971,* ed. Grga Novak, 3:370–80. Belgrade: Comité National d'Organisation.

Jovanović, Vojislav, Ljiljana Vukšanovič, and Nikola Berić. 1972. "New finds from the Slavic necropolis at Matičane near Priština." *Balcanoslavica* 1:107–11.

Kara, Michał. 1992. "The graves of armed Scandinavians from the middle and the younger Viking period from the territory of the first Piasts' state." In *Death and Burial: Pre-Printed Papers,* 4:167–77. York: Medieval Europe.

Kara, Michał, and Zofia Kurnatowska. 2000. "Christian burials." In *Europe's Centre around A.D. 1000,* ed. Alfried Wieczorek and Hans-Martin Hinz, 340–41. Stuttgart: Theiss.

Kiss, A. 1974. "Some archaeological finds of the Avar period in county Baranya." *Janus Pannonius Múzeum Évkönyve* 19:129–42.

———. 1977. *Avar Cemeteries in County Baranya.* Budapest: Akademiai Kiadó.

Kiss, A., and A. Bartha. 1970. "Graves from the age of the Hungarian conquest at Bana." *Acta Archaeologica Academiae Scientiarum Hungaricae* 22:219–60.

Kovrig, Ilona. 1975. "The Dévaványa cemetery." In *Avar Finds in the Hungarian National Museum,* ed. Ilona Kovrig, 122–55. Budapest: Akadémiai Kiadó.

———. 1975. "The Szob cemetery." In *Avar Finds in the Hungarian National Museum,* ed. Ilona Kovrig, 158–208. Budapest: Akadémiai Kiadó.

———. 1975. "The Tiszaderzs cemetery." In *Avar Finds in the Hungarian National Museum,* ed. Ilona Kovrig, 210–39. Budapest: Akadémiai Kiadó.

Lovag, Zsuzsa. 2000. "Christian burials." In *Europe's Centre around A.D. 1000,* ed. Alfried Wieczorek and Hans-Martin Hinz, 418–19. Stuttgart: Theiss.

Lutovský, Michal. 1996. "Between Sutton Hoo and Chernaya Mogila: Barrows in Eastern and Western early medieval Europe." *Antiquity* 70:671–76.

Madaras, László. 1995. *The Szeged-Fehértó A and B Cemeteries*. Debrecen and Budapest: Kapitalis.

Maneva, Elica. 1992. "Medieval necropolises in Macedonia." *Macedonian Review* 22:269–74.

Mesterházy, K., and N. Parádi. 1996. "Sály-Lator." In *The Ancient Hungarians: Exhibition Catalogue*, ed. István Fodor, 431–32. Budapest: Hungarian National Museum.

Mikić-Antonić, Br. 1988. "Bečej-Pionirska ulica: Early medieval cemetery." *Arheološki pregled*, 193–96.

Miljković-Pepek, Petar. 1995. "New evidence on the tombs of Sts. Cyril, St. Clement, and St. Naum." *Macedonian Review* 25:5–29.

Minić, Dušica. 1982. "The grave inventory from Stejanovci near Sremska Mitrovica." In *Sirmium*, 4:117–24. Belgrade: Arheološki Institut; Rome: Ecole Française de Rome.

Murasheva, Veronika, and Tamara Pushkina. 2002. "Excavations in Gnezdovo near Smolensk." In *Centre, Region, Periphery: Medieval Europe Basel 2002*, ed. Guido Helmig, Barbara Scholkmann, and Matthias Untermann. 1:329–32. Basel: Dr. G. Wesselkamp.

Pap, Livija. 1993. "Some ethnoarchaeological observations regarding an exceptional burial method in the early Middle Ages necropoleis in Vojvodina." In *Actes du XII-e Congrès international des sciences préhistoriques et protohistoriques, Bratislava, 1–7 septembre 1991*, ed. J. Pavuj, 4:60–65. Bratislava: Institut Archéologique de l'Académie Slovaque des Sciences.

Pásztor, A., and T. Vida. 1995. "Avar period cemetery at Budakalász: A preliminary archaeological report on the excavations of the Avar period cemetery of Budakalász-Dunapart." *Acta Archaeologica Academiae Scientiarum Hungaricae* 47:215–20.

Prikhodniuk, Oleg, and Viktor Fomenko. 2003. "Early medieval nomads' burials from the vicinity of the village of Hristoforovka, the district of Nikolaevo, Ukraine." *Archaeologia Bulgarica* 7:107–16.

Ricz, Péter. 1982–83. "Timber constructions in Avar graves: Contributions to the resolving of problems linked with burial of the Avars in North Backa." *Archaeologia Iugoslavica* 22–23:96–112.

Rusu, Mircea. 1962. "The prefeudal cemetery of Noşlac (VI–VIIth centuries)." *Dacia* 6: 269–92.

Salamon, Agnes. 1995. "The Szeged-Makkoserdö cemetery." In *Avar Corpus Füzetek*, 4: 109–207. Debrecen and Budapest: Kapitalis.

Salamon, Agnes, and Károlyi Cs Sebestyén. 1995. *The Szeged-Kundomb Cemetery*. Debrecen and Budapest: Kapitalis.

Sekeres, László. 1978. "Necropolis from the Avar period at Bačka Topola." In *Problemi seobe naroda u Karpatskoj kotlini: Saopštenja sa naučkog skupa 13.–16. decembre 1976*, ed. Danica Dimitrijević, Jovan Kovačević, and Zdenko Vinski, 157–61. Novi Sad: Matica Srpska.

Slabe, Marijan. 1973. "Dravlje: A cemetery from the time of the great migrations." In *Actes du VIII-e Congrès international des sciences préhistoriques et protohistoriques, Beograd 9–15 septembre 1971*, ed. Grga Novak, 3:325–32. Belgrade: Comité National d'Organisation.

Snively, Carolyn S. 1998. "Intramural burial in the cities of the late antique diocese of Macedonia." In *Radovi XIII. Međunarodnog Kongresa za starokršćansku arheologiju, Split-Poreč (25.9.–1.10. 1994)*, ed. Nenad Cambi and Emilio Marin, 2:491–98. Vatican: Pontificio Istituto di Archeologia Cristiana; Split: Arheološki Muzej.

Sommer, Petr. 2000. "Christian burials." In *Europe's Centre around A.D. 1000,* ed. Alfried Wieczorek and Hans-Martin Hinz, 272–73. Stuttgart: Theiss.

Sós, Agnés Cs., and Agnés Salamon. 1995. *Cemeteries of the Early Middle Ages (6th–9th Centuries A.D.) at Pókaszepetk.* Budapest: Akadémiai Kiadó.

Söyrinki-Harmo, Leena, and Pirjo Uino. 1998. "Problems concerning Iron Age cremation cemeteries in western and eastern Finland (Karelia)." In *Obshchestvo, ekonomika, kul'tura i isskusstvo slavian,* ed. V. V. Sedov, 356–61. Moscow: Institut Arkheologii Rossüskoi Akademii Nauk.

Szabó, János Györö. 1975. "The Pilismarót cemetery." In *Avar Finds in the Hungarian National Museum,* ed. Ilona Kovrig, 242–81. Budapest: Akadémiai Kiadó.

Török, Gyula. 1975. "The Kiskörös Cebe-puszta cemetery." In *Avar Finds in the Hungarian National Museum,* ed. Ilona Kovrig, 307–11. Budapest: Akadémiai Kiadó.

———. 1975. "The Kiskörös Pohibuj-Mackó dülö cemetery." In *Avar Finds in the Hungarian National Museum,* ed. Ilona Kovrig, 284–311. Budapest: Akadémiai Kiadó.

———. 1975. "The Kiskörös Szücsi-dülö cemetery." In *Avar Finds in the Hungarian National Museum,* ed. Ilona Kovrig, 315–20. Budapest: Akadémiai Kiadó.

———. 1975. "The Visznek cemetery." In *Avar Finds in the Hungarian National Museum,* ed. Ilona Kovrig, 322–45. Budapest: Akadémiai Kiadó.

———. 1995. "The Csengele-Feketehalom cemetery." In *Avar Corpus Füzetek,* 4:208–74. Debrecen and Budapest: Kapitalis.

Tóth, Elvira. 1972. "Preliminary account of the Avar princely find at Kunbábony." *Cumania* 1:143–60.

Trbuhović, Leposava. 1982. "Avar finds from Sirmium and the surrounding region." In *Sirmium: Recherches archéologiques en Syrmie,* ed. Noël Duval, Edward L. Ochsenschlager, and Vladislav Popović, 4:61–75. Belgrade: Institut Archéologique de Belgrade, Ecole Française de Rome, and Research Foundation of the City University of New York.

Valić, Andrej. 1980. "General issues of social structure studies of Old Slavic burials in Kranj." *Balcanoslavica* 9:51–58.

Vida, Tivadar. 1996. "Avar settlement remains and graves at the site of Gyoma 133." In *Cultural and Landscape Changes in South-East Hungary,* ed. Sándor Bököny, 323–64. Budapest: Archaeological Institute of the Hungarian Academy of Sciences.

Vuga, Davorin. 1973. "The early medieval necropolis at Roje pri Moravcah (Moravce pri Gabrovki) in Dolenjska, in the light of archaeological explorations up to the present time." *Balcanoslavica* 2:59–72.

———. 1980. "A study of burying methods in the period of the great migration (5th to 6th Century) in the south-eastern Alpine and Cisalpine world." *Balcanoslavica* 9: 17–25.

PHYSICAL ANTHROPOLOGY AND POPULATION STUDIES

Acsadi, G., L. Harsanyi, and J. Nemeskéri. 1962. "The population of Zalavár in the Middle Ages." *Acta Archaeologica Academiae Scientiarum Hungaricae* 14:113–41.

Bottyán, L. 1966. "Data to the anthropology of the Avar period population of Budapest." *Anthropologia Hungarica* 7:3–34.

Éry, Kinga. 1966. "The osteological data of the 9th century population of Artánd." *Anthropologia Hungarica* 7:85–114.

————. 1967–68. "Reconstruction of the tenth century population of Sárbogárd on the basis of archaeological and anthropological data." *Alba Regia* 8–9:93–147.

————. 1983. "Comparative statistical studies on the physical anthropology of the Carpathian Basin population between the 6–12th centuries A.D." *Alba Regia* 20: 89–141.

————. 1987. "Data on the physical anthropology of medieval Hungary." *Sborník Narodního musea v Praže* 43:118–21.

Ferencz, M. 1980–81. "Some data to the palaeoanthropology of the Avar period's population of Hungary." *Anthropologia Hungarica* 17:23–64.

Finnegan, Mike. 1993. "Biological distance during the Avar period based on non-metric cranial data." *Annales Historico-Naturales Musei Nationalis Hungarici* 85:181–202.

Grimes, Kenneth J. 1982. "An analysis of a human cranium from an Avar burial near Sirmium." In *Sirmium: Recherches archéologiques en Syrmie*, ed. Noël Duval, Edward L. Ochsenschlager, and Vladislav Popović, 4:57–59. Belgrade: Institut Archéologique de Belgrade, Ecole Française de Rome, and Research Foundation of the City University of New York.

Hanáková, Hana, and Milan Stloukal. 1987. "Health condition of the teeth in old Slavonic populations." *Sborník Narodního musea v Praže* 43:196–202.

Jakab, Julius. 1989. "The anthropological analysis of the differences among the early medieval sets of the territory of Slovakia on the basis of non-metrical skeletal traits." *Slovenská Archeológia* 37:105–50.

Kiszely, I. 1970. "On the peculiar custom of the artificial mutilation of the foramen occipitale magnum." *Acta Archaeologica Academiae Scientiarum Hungaricae* 22:301–21.

Koledarov, P. 1966. "On the toponymy and demography of south-east Dobroudja coast in the 6th and 7th centuries (Kroynioi=Karvuna=Kavarna)." *Byzantinobulgarica* 2: 323–28.

Kondova, Nelli, and Slavcho Cholakov. 1997. "Europeidity and mongoloidity on the territory of medieval Bulgaria." *Archaeologia Bulgarica* 1:88–96.

Lengyel, I. 1971. "Chemico-analytical aspects of human bone finds from the 6th century 'Pannonian' cemeteries." *Acta Archaeologica Academiae Scientiarum Hungaricae* 23:155–66.

Lipták, Pál. 1969. "The 'Avar period' mongoloids in Hungary." *Acta Archaeologica Academiae Scientiarum Hungaricae* 10:251–79.

————. 1983. *Avars and Ancient Hungarians*. Budapest: Akadémiai Kiadó.

Marcsik, Antónia. 1987. "Traumatic lesions (fractures) from the Avar period in Hungary." *Sborník Narodního musea v Praže* 43:186–87.

Nemeskeri, J., A. Kralovánszky, and L. Harsanyi. 1965. "Trephind skulls from the tenth century." *Acta Archaeologica Academiae Scientarium Hungaricae* 17:343–67.

Percac, H. 1981. "Pathological changes in the jaws of the early Middle Ages Slavic population." *Collegium Antropologicum* 5:101–4.

Piontek, Janusz, and Maria Kaczmarek. 1987. "Ethnogenesis and palaeodemography: Case of Slavonic populations." *Sborník Narodního musea v Praže* 43:171–77.

Russeva, Viktoria. 2003. "Mortality patterns and life expectancy in medieval skeleton populations from Bulgaria (VIII–X c. A.D.)." *Archaeologia Bulgarica* 7:77–84.

Soudský, Ondřej, and Milan Stloukal. 1987. "Computer comparison of several Old Slavonic populations." *Sborník Narodního musea v Praže* 43:122–30.

Stefančić, Marija. 1987. "Anthropological analysis of the Old Croat necropolis Nin-Zdrijać in reference to the Slav settlement in the Balkans." *Sborník Narodního musea v Praže* 43:131–39.

Stloukal, Milan. 1990. "The palaeodemography of medieval populations in Czechoslovakia." In *From the Baltic to the Black Sea: Studies in Medieval Archaeology*, ed. David Austin and Leslie Alcock, 209–15. London: Unwin Hyman.

Thurzo, Milan. 1987. "Anthropological evidence of the presence of Avars in Slovakia (Czechoslovakia) in the 7th–8th centuries A.D." *Sborník Narodního musea v Praže* 43:159.

Vlahović, P. 1972. "Current theories about the settlement of the Slavs in the contemporary Yugoslavian countries and their anthropological confirmation." *Ethnologia Slavica* 4:25–41.

ZOOARCHAEOLOGY

Bartosiewicz, L. 1995. "Animal remains from the Avar period cemetery of Budakalász-Dunapart." *Acta Archaeologica Academiae Scientiarum Hungaricae* 47:241–55.

———. 1995. "Archaeozoological studies from the Hahót basin, SW Hungary." *Antaeus* 22:307–67.

———. 1998. "Mobile pastoralism and meat consumption: An archaeozoological perspective." In *Tender Meat under the Saddle: Customs of Eating, Drinking, and Hospitality among Conquering Hungarians and Nomadic Peoples; In Memory of Gyula László (1910–1998)*, ed. József Lászlovszky, 157–78. Krems: Medium Aevum Quotidianum.

Bartosiewicz, L., and A. M. Choyke. 1991. "Animal remains from the 1970–1972 excavations of Iatrus (Krivina), Bulgaria." *Acta Archaeologica Academiae Scientiarum Hungaricae* 43:181–209.

ENVIRONMENTAL STUDIES

Avdusin, D. A. 1989. "Rivers, forests and the settlement pattern of the Eastern Slavs between the 6th and the 9th centuries." In *Montagnes, fleuves, forêts dans l'histoire: Barrières ou lignes de convergence? Travaux présentés au XVI–e Congrès international des sciences historiques, Stuttgart, août 1985*, ed. Jean-François Bergier, 135–46. St. Katharinen: Scripta Mercaturae.

Alsleben, Almuth, Ingmar Jansson, Thomas Hammar, et al. 1993. "Palaeobotanical studies on the Novgorod land, ca. 400–1200 AD." *Archäologisches Korrespondenzblatt* 23:527–35.

Björkman, Leif, Angelica Feurdean, and Barbara Wohlfarth. 2003. "Late-Glacial and Holocene forest dynamics at Steregoiu in Gutâiului Mountains, Northwest Romania." *Review of Palaeobotany and Palynology* 124:79–111.

Brazdil, Rudolf, and Oldrich Kotyza. 1995. *History of Weather and Climate in the Czech Lands*. Zurich: Eidgenössische Technische Hochschule, Geographisches Institut.

Gyulai, Ferenc. 1998. "Archaeobotanical sources in investigating the diet of conquering Hungarians." In *Tender Meat under the Saddle: Customs of Eating, Drinking, and Hospitality among Conquering Hungarians and Nomadic Peoples; In Memory of Gyula László (1910–1998)*, ed. József Lászlovszky, 120–56. Krems: Medium Aevum Quotidianum.

Hajnalová, Eva. 1981. "Cultivated plants at Pobedim, district Trenčin, in the 9th century AD." *Zeitschrift für Archäologie* 15:205–8.

———. 1985. "New palaeobotanical finds from medieval towns in Slovakia." *Slovenská Archeológia* 33:399–438.

Kosina, Romuald. 1981. "Cultivated plants, weeds, and wild plants from the early medieval granaries in Ostrów Tumski in Wrocław." *Zeitschrift für Archäologie* 15:177–90.

Krąpiec, Marek. 1998. "Oak dendrochronology of the neo-Holocene in Poland." *Folia quaternaria* 69:5–133.

Leciejewicz, Lech. 2002. "The European barbaricum in the early Middle Ages: ethnogeography and ecology." In *Centre, Region, Periphery: Medieval Europe Basel 2002,* ed. Guido Helmig, Barbara Scholkmann, and Matthias Untermann, 1:54–56. Basel: Dr. G. Wesselkamp.

Szydłowski, Jerzy, and Krystyna Wasylikowa. 1973. "Cereals from the early medieval fortified settlement in Lubomia, district Wodzisław Śląski, southern Poland." *Folia quaternaria* 42:37–93.

Tobolski, Każimierz. 2000. "The natural environment in central Greater Poland against the background of natural conditions in central Europe in the age of the Gniezno Congress." In *Europe's Centre around A.D. 1000,* ed. Alfried Wieczorek and Hans-Martin Hinz, 54–57. Stuttgart: Theiss.

Willis, K. J., P. Sümegi, M. Braun, et. al. 1998. "Prehistoric land degradation in Hungary: Who, how, and why?" *Antiquity* 72:101–13.

Zbierski, Andrzej. 1976. "Ichthyological studies in fishing in Gdańsk in the 9th–11th centuries based on archaeological materials from Pomerania." *Archaeologia Polona* 17: 247–55.

METAL ARTIFACTS

Andrási, Júlia. 1996. "A gold belt-end from the Ashmolean Museum, Oxford." In *Die Awaren am Rand der byzantinischen Welt: Studien zu Diplomatie, Handel und Technologietransfer im Frühmittelalter,* ed. Falko Daim, 67–76. Innsbruck: Wagner.

———. 2000. "The Berthier-Delagarde collection of Crimean jewellery: Difficulties with the documentation of an old collection." In *Les sites archéologiques en Crimée et au Caucase durant l'Antiquité tardive et le Haut Moyen Age,* ed. Michel Kazanski and Vanessa Soupault, 97–108. Leiden, Boston, and Cologne: Brill.

Atanasov, Georgi. 1999. "On the origin, function, and the owner of the adornments of the Preslav treasure from the 10th century." *Archaeologia Bulgarica* 3:81–94.

Bajalović-Hadži-Pešić, Marija. 1980–81. "Ugro-Finnic jewelry in the Museum of the city of Belgrade." *Archaeologia Iugoslavica* 20–21:158–61.

Bálint, Csanád. 2000. "Some Avar and Balkan connections of the Vrap treasure." In *From Attila to Charlemagne. Arts of the Early Medieval Period in the Metropolitan Museum of Art,* ed. Katharine Reynolds Brown, Dafydd Kidd, and Charles T. Little, 180–87. New York: Metropolitan Museum of Art/Yale University Press.

Bitner-Wróblewska, Anna. 1991. "Between Scania and Samland: From studies of stylistic links in the Baltic Basin during the early migration period." *Fornvännen* 86: 226–41.

———. 2001. *From Samland to Rogaland: East-West Connections in the Baltic Basin during the Early Migration Period.* Warsaw: Państwowe Muzeum Archeologiczne.

Curta, Florin. 1994. "On the dating of the 'Veţel-Coşoveni' group of curved fibulae." *Ephemeris Napocensis* 4:233–65.

———. 1997. "Blacksmiths, warriors, and tournaments of value: Dating and interpreting early medieval hoards of iron implements in Eastern Europe." *Ephemeris Napocensis* 7:211–68.

———. 1998–99. "Iron and potlatch: Early medieval hoards of implements and weapons in Eastern Europe." *Archivum Eurasiae Medii Aevi* 10:15–62.

Daim, Falko. 2001. "Byzantine belts and Avar birds: Diplomacy, trade, and cultural transfer in the eighth century." In *The Transformation of Frontiers: From Late Antiquity to the Carolingians*, ed. Walter Pohl, Ian Wood, and Helmut Reimitz, 143–88. Leiden, Boston, and Cologne: Brill.

Dalewski, Zbigniew. 2000. "The Holy Lance and the Polish insignia." In *Europe's Centre around A.D. 1000*, ed. Alfried Wieczorek and Hans-Martin Hinz, 602–5. Stuttgart: Theiss.

Damm, Inciser Gürçay. 2000. "Huns and Goths: Jewelry from the Ukraine and Southern Russia." In *From Attila to Charlemagne. Arts of the Early Medieval Period in the Metropolitan Museum of Art*, ed. Katharine Reynolds Brown, Dafydd Kidd, and Charles T. Little, 102–19. New York: Metropolitan Museum of Art/Yale University Press.

Duczko, Władysław. 1972. *Slavic Silver Jewellery from the Viking Period: An Analysis of Material from Gotland.* Uppsala: Uppsala Universitet.

———. 1995. "Contacts between Estonia and Scandinavia in the light of the 12th century hoard from Valbo." In *Archaeology East and West of the Baltic: Paper from the Second Estonian-Swedish Archaeological Symposium, Sigtuna, May 1991*, ed. Ingmar Jansson, 99–102. Stockholm: Department of Archaeology, Stockholm University.

Edgren, Torsten. 1988. "An engraved bronze bowl from Jarovščina on the Oyat River in the south-east coastal region of Lake Ladoga." In *Trade and Exchange in Prehistory: Studies in Honour of Berta Stjernquist*, ed. Birgitta Hårdh, 309–18. Lund: Lunds Universitets Historiska Museum.

Garam, Éva. 2000. "The Vrap treasure." In *From Attila to Charlemagne. Arts of the Early Medieval Period in the Metropolitan Museum of Art*, ed. Katharine Reynolds Brown, Dafydd Kidd, and Charles T. Little, 170–79. New York: Metropolitan Museum of Art/Yale University Press.

Garam, Éva, and Attila Kiss. 1992. *Gold Finds of the Migration Period in the Hungarian National Museum.* Milan: Electa; Budapest: Helikon.

Georgiev, Pavel. 1995. "The bronze rosette from Pliska: On decoding the runic inscriptions in Bulgaria." *Byzantinoslavica* 56:547–55.

Horníčková, Kateřina. 1999. "Byzantine reliquary pectoral crosses in central Europe." *Byzantinoslavica* 90:213–50.

Inkova, Mariela. 2003. "Duck image on a gilt silver strap end: On 'diffused' motifs of the early medieval Bulgarian culture." *Archaeologia Bulgarica* 7:83–96.

Jansson, Ingmar. 1992. "Scandinavian oval brooches found in Latvia." In *Die Kontakte zwischen Ostbaltikum und Skandinavien im frühen Mittelalter*, ed. Aleksander Loit, Evalds Mugurevics, and Andris Caune, 61–78. Stockholm: Almqvist & Wiksell International.

Kazakevičius, Vytautas. 1992. "The find of an East European sword quillon in a barrow in Visètiskès, Anyksčiai district, Lithuania." *Fornvännen* 87:175–79.

Kidd, Dafydd, and Ludmila Pekarskaya. 1995. "New insight into the hoard of 6th–7th century silver from Martynovka." In *La noblesse romaine et les chefs barbares du IIIe au VIIe siècle,* ed. Françoise Vallet and Michel Kazanski, 351–60. Saint-Germain-en-Laye: Association Française d'Archéologie Mérovingienne-Musée des Antiquités Nationales.

Kirpichnikov, A. N. 1970. "Connections between Russia and Scandinavia in the 9th and 10th centuries, as illustrated by weapon finds." In *Varangian Problems: Report on the First International Symposium on the Theme "The Eastern Connections of the Nordic Peoples in the Viking Period and Early Middle Ages," Moesgaard-University of Aarhus, October 7–11, 1968,* ed. Knud Hannestad, Knud Jordal, Ole Klindt-Jensen, et al. 50–78. Copenhague: Munksgaard.

Kiss, Attila. 1998. "The treasure of a Byzantine gold belt from the Sirmium region." *Acta Archaeologica Academiae Scientiarum Hungaricae* 50:251–58.

Kobyliński, Zbigniew, and Zdzisław Hensel. 1993. "Imports or local products? Trace elements analysis of copper-alloy artefacts from Haćki, Białystok Province, Poland." *Archaeologia Polona* 31:129–40.

Kóčka-Krenz, Hanna. 1982. "Some aspects of Polish early medieval metalworking." *Fornvännen* 77:38–47.

Kondakov, N. P. 1946. "The treasure of Nagy-Szent-Miklós." *Bulletin of the Byzantine Institute* 1:7–13.

Kouzov, Christo. 2000. "A find of medieval iron objects from the fortress near the village of Dolishte, Varna district (Bulgarian Black Sea coast)." *Archaeologia Bulgarica* 4:85–91.

Kovács, László. 2000. "The Holy Lance of Hungary." In *Europe's Centre around A.D. 1000,* ed. Alfried Wieczorek and Hans-Martin Hinz, 599. Stuttgart: Theiss.

Krumova, Teodora. 2001. "Secondary usage of Pecheneg bridle-bosses as dress decoration." *Archaeologia Bulgarica* 5:65–70.

Longauerová, Margita, and Jaroslav Kočich. 1993. "Structure of the early-medieval steel sickles from Pobedim and Šebastovce." In *Actes du XII-e Congrès international des sciences préhistoriques et protohistoriques, Bratislava, 1–7 septembre 1991,* ed. J. Pavuj, 1:254–59. Bratislava: Institut archéologique de l'Académie Slovaque des Sciences à Nitra.

Longauerová, Margita, Svätoboj Longauer, and Zlata Čilinská. 1991. "Structural analysis of ornaments and jewels from the 7.–8. century cemetery in Želovce." In *K problematike osídlenia stredodunajskej oblasti vo včasnom stredoveku,* ed. Z. Čilinská, 39–66. Nitra: Archeologický ústav Slovenskej akadémie vied.

———. 1993. "Structural analysis of the earrings from early medieval cemetery in Želovce." In *Actes du XII-e Congrès international des sciences préhistoriques et protohistoriques, Bratislava, 1–7 septembre 1991,* ed. J. Pavuj, 1:249–53. Bratislava: Institut archéologique de l'Académie Slovaque des Sciences à Nitra.

Lovag, Zsuzsa S. 1971. "Byzantine type reliquary pectoral crosses in the Hungarian National Museum." *Folia Archaeologica* 22:143–64.

Madgearu, Alexandru. 1998. "The Sucidava type of buckles and the relations between the late Roman Empire and the barbarians in the 6th century." *Arheologia Moldovei* 21:217–22.

Malmer, Brita. 1992. "On some Scandinavian elements in the Eversmuiza nad the Kolodezski hoards." In *Die Kontakte zwischen Ostbaltikum und Skandinavien im frühen Mittelalter,* ed. Aleksander Loit, Evalds Mugurevics, and Andris Caune, 115–23. Stockholm: Almqvist & Wiksell International.

Maneva, Elica. 1992. "Medieval jewellery of Macedonia." *Macedonian Review* 22:157–60.

Mihok, L'ubomir, Alojz Holy, and Zlata Čilinská. 1993. "Archaeometallurgy of Slav iron objects." In *Actes du XII-e Congrès international des sciences préhistoriques et protohistoriques, Bratislava, 1–7 septembre 1991,* ed. J. Pavuj, 1:232–37. Bratislava: Institut archéologique de l'Académie Slovaque des Sciences à Nitra.

Noonan, Thomas S. 1982. "Russia, the Near East, and the steppe in the early medieval period: An examination of the Sasanian and Byzantine finds from the Kama-Urals area." *Archivum Eurasiae Medii Aevi* 2:269–302.

Nosov, E. N. 1992. "A hoard of farm implements from the settlement Holopij Gorodok by the river Volkhov." In *Cultural Heritage of the Finno-Ugrians and Slavs: Papers Presented by the Participants in the Soviet-Finnish Archaeological Symposium, 10–16 May 1990 in Tallinn,* ed. V. Lang and J. Selirand, 135–41. Tallinn: Varrak.

Novikova, Galina L. 1992. "Iron neck-rings with Thor's hammers found in Eastern Europe." *Fornvännen* 87:73–89.

Ricz, Péter. 1983. "The weapons of the steppe nomads." *Balcanoslavica* 10:1–15.

Slabe, Marijan. 1980–81. "Something about the ear-rings from the cemetery at Sempeter (Ljubljana)." *Archaeologia Iugoslavica* 20–21:154–57.

Smetánka, Zdeněk, and Bohumil Stverák. 1992. "X-ray fluorescent analysis of gold and gilded jewels from the cemetery in Lumbe Gardens at Prague Castle." *Archeologické rozhledy* 44:418–30.

Somlosi, E. 1988. "Restoration of the Csolnok Avar iron sword." *Acta Archaeologica Academiae Scientiarum Hungaricae* 40:207–10.

Thunmark-Nylén, Lena. 1992. "Some comparative notes on Gotlandic and Livonian bead spacers of the Viking period." In *Contacts Across the Baltic Sea During the Late Iron Age (5th–12th Centuries). Baltic Sea Conference, Lund October 25–27, 1991,* ed. Birgitta Hårdh and Bożena Wyszomirska-Werbart, 109–14. Lund: Institute of Archaeology/Historical Museum.

Totev, Totiu Kosev. 1982. *The Preslav Gold Treasure.* Sofia: Septemvri.

———. 1993. *The Preslav Treasure.* Shumen: Altos.

Vagalinski, Liudmil, Georgi Atanassov, and Dimităr Dimitrov. 2000. "Eagle-head buckles from Bulgaria (6th–7th centuries)." *Archaeologia Bulgarica* 4:78–91.

Verna, A. C. 1994. "Bronze pectoral reliquary crosses: Objects from the Middle and Late Byzantine period." Master's thesis, George Washington University.

Vida, Tivadar. 1999. "Veil pin or dress pin. Data to the question of Avar period pin-wearing." In *Pannonia and Beyond. Studies in Honour of László Barkóczi,* ed. Andrea Vaday, 563–74 and 811–15. Budapest: Archaeological Institute of the Hungarian Academy of Sciences.

Zoll-Adamikowa, Helena, Maria Dekówkna, and Elżbieta Maria Nosek. 1999. *The Early Mediaeval Hoard from Zawada Lanckorońska (Upper Vistula River).* Warsaw: Institute of Archaeology and Ethnology.

NUMISMATICS AND SIGILLOGRAPHY

Adelson, Howard L. 1957. *Light Weight Solidi and Byzantine Trade during the Sixth and Seventh Centuries.* New York: American Numismatic Society.

Albrycht-Rapnicka, Danuta. 1960. "Italian coins in Polish medieval hoards." *Wiadomości Numizmatyczne* 5:99–110.

Anokhin, Vladilen Afanas'evich. 1980. *The Coinage of Chersonesus, IVth century B.C.–XII century A.D.* Oxford: British Archaeological Reports.

Bartczak, Andrzej. 1997. "Finds of dirhams in central Europe prior to the beginning of the 10th century A.D." In *Origins of Central Europe*, ed. Przemysław Urbańczyk, 227–38. Warsaw: Scientific Society of Polish Archaeologists.

———. 1997–98. "The early Abbasid dinars of the Petrovci hoard." *Vjesnik Arheološkog Muzeja u Zagrebu* 30–31:259–71.

Biró-Sey, Katalin. 1976. "Silver medal of Anastasius I in the Numismatic Collection of the Hungarian National Museum." *Folia Archaeologica* 27:121–27.

Blunt, C. E. 1943. "On a coin of the 'temple' type bearing the name of Aethelred, king of England." *Numismatic Chronicle* 3:101–2.

Boshkova, Bistra. 1984. "Coins from the excavations of the antique town Ratiaria." *Ratiariensia* 2:105–15.

Bykov, Alexi A. 1974. "Three notes on Islamic coins from hoards in the Soviet Union." In *Near Eastern Numismatics, Iconography, Epigraphy, and History: Studies in Honor of George C. Miles*, ed. Dickran K. Kouymjian, 203–10. Beirut: American University of Beirut.

Curta, Florin. 1996. "Invasion or inflation? Sixth- to seventh-century Byzantine coin hoards in Eastern and southeastern Europe." *Annali dell'Istituto Italiano di Numismatica* 43:65–224.

Czapkiewicz, Marek. 1980. "Some remarks on the imitations of Arabic dirhams from the 8th to the 10th century based on the examination of coin metal." In *Proceedings of the International Numismatic Symposium*, ed. István Gedai and Katalin Biró-Sey, 101–7. Budapest: Akadémiai Kiadó.

———. 1988. "The Arabic coins from Legnica." *Folia orientalia* 25:171–80.

Demo, Željko. 1994. *Ostrogothic Coinage from Collections in Croatia, Slovenia, and Bosnia and Herzegovina.* Ljubljana: Narodni Muzej.

Dimnik, Martin. 1993. "Oleg's status as a ruler of Tmutarakan': The sphragistic evidence." *Mediaeval Studies* 55:137–49.

Doimi De Frankopan, Peter. 1997. "The numismatic evidence from the Danube region, 971–1092." *Byzantine and Modern Greek Studies* 21:30–39.

Duncan, G. L. 1993. *Coin Circulation in the Danubian and Balkan Provinces of the Roman Empire, AD 294–578.* London: Royal Numismatic Society.

Fomin, A. V. and L. Kovács. 1987. *The 10th Century Maramaros County (Huszt) Dirham Hoards.* Budapest: Akademiai Kiadó.

Gaj-Popović, Dobrila. 1973. "The appearance of the barbarized folises (folles) in the 6th century in the Balkan Peninsula." *Balcanoslavica* 2:95–100.

Gaul, Jerzy. 1984. "The circulation of monetary and non-monetary currency in the West-Baltic zone in the 5th and 6th centuries AD." *Archaeologia Polona* 23:87–105.

Gedai, István. 1976. "Bavarian influence on the early coinage of the states in central Europe." In *Actes du 8-e Congrès international de numismatique, New York–Washington, septembre 1973*, ed. Herbert A. Cahn and Georges Le Rider, 415–21. Paris and Basel: Association internationale des numismates professionels.

———. 1985. "Italian coins in the 10th century Hungarian hoards." *Numismatica e antichità classiche* 14:343–58.

———. 1986. "Numismatic questions in the Carpathian Basin prior to the Magyar conquest." *Denárová mena na Morave:* 300–305.

———. 1988. "The coins of Berengar in a 10th century Hungarian grave." *Rivista italiana di numismatica e scienze affini* 90:457–68.

———. 1988. "The role of the Carpathian Basin in the Byzantine coinage of the 8th–11th centuries." In *Commentationes Numismaticae 1988: Festgabe für Gert und Vera Hatz zum 4. Januar 1988 dargebracht,* ed. Peter Berghaus, 29–36. Hamburg: Auktionshaus Tietjen.

———. 1991. "The influence of the Byzantine gold coins in the Carpathian Basin in the early Middle Ages." In *Ermanno A. Arslan studia dicata,* ed. Rodolfo Martini and Novella Vismara, 3:645–56. Milan: Edizioni Ennerre.

———. 1993. "The effect of Byzantine gold coins on the Hungarian coinage." In *Actes du XI-e Congrès International de Numismatique, organisé à l'occasion du 150-e anniversaire de la Société royale de numismatique de Belgique, Bruxelles, 8–13 septembre 1991,* ed. Tony Hackens and Ghislaine Moucharte, 3:191–94. Louvain-la-Neuve: Association Professeur Marcel Hoc pour l'encouragement des recherches numismatiques.

Gilevich, A. M. 1996. "Coin hoards of medieval Cherson." In *Acts. XVIIIth International Congress of Byzantine Studies: Selected papers; Moscow 1991,* ed. Ihor Sevcenko, Gennadi G. Litavrin, and Walter K. Hanak, 4:245–51. Shepherdstown, W.V.: Byzantine Studies Press.

Goldina, R. D., and A. B. Nikitin. 1997. "New finds of Sasanian, Central Asian, and Byzantine coins from the region of Perm', the Kama-Ural area." In *Studies in Silk Road Coins and Culture: Papers in Honour of Professor Ikuo Hirayama on His 65th Birthday,* ed. K. Tanabe, J. Cribb, and H. Wang, 111–25. Kamakura: Institute of Silk Road Studies.

Guest, Peter. 1999. "The Roman and Byzantine coins excavated at Nicopolis and Istrum and Gradishte, Bulgaria." *Numismatic Chronicle* 159:314–27.

Guruleva, V. V. 1996. "Coins of Constans II struck in Cherson." In *Acts. XVIIIth International Congress of Byzantine Studies: Selected Papers; Moscow 1991,* ed. Ihor Ševčenko, G. G. Litavrin, and Walter Hanak, 4:252–57. Shepherdstown, W.V.: Byzantine Studies Press.

Hahn, Wolfgang R. 1978. "The numismatic history of Cherson in early Byzantine times: A survey." *Numismatic Circular* 86:414–15, 471–72, 521–22.

Hásková, Jarmila. 2000. "Coinage and other forms of exchange in Bohemia." In *Europe's Centre around A.D. 1000,* ed. Alfred Wieczorek and Hans-Martin Hinz, 127. Stuttgart: Theiss.

Iordanov, Ivan. 1993. "Unpublished Byzantine seals from the village Zlati Voivoda (district of Sliven, Bulgaria)." *Studies in Byzantine Sigillography* 3:69–84.

———. 1995. "The Byzantine administration in Dobrudja (10th–12th century) according to sphragistic data." *Dobrudzha* 12:204–23.

———. 1995. "Medieval Plovdiv according to the sphragistic data." *Studies in Byzantine Sigillography* 4:111–38.

———. 1997. "Byzantine presence in Dobrudja from the seventh to the tenth centuries, according to sphragistic data." In *Von der Scythia zur Dobrudža,* ed. Khristo Kholiolchev, Renate Pillinger, and Reinhardt Harreither, 35–39. Vienna: Verein "Freunde des Hauses Wittgenstein."

Kierśnowski, Ryszard. 1960. "Coin finds and the problem of money hoarding in early medieval Poland." *Wiadomości Numizmatyczne* 5:35–56.

Kmiętowicz, Anna. 1972. "A hoard of dirhems from Szczecin-Niemierzyn." *Folia orientalia* 13:143–60.

———. 1995. "The dirham of the Arab emir of Crete in the Dzierznica II hoard." *Wiadomości Numizmatyczne* 39:21–28.

Kóčka-Krenz, Hanna. 2000. "Slav hoards." In *Europe's Centre around A.D. 1000*, ed. Alfried Wieczorek and Hans-Martin Hinz, 130–31. Stuttgart: Theiss.

Kondijanov, J. 1996. "The early Byzantine hoard from Novo Selo, near Strumica." *Makedonski numizmatichki glasnik* 2:95–104.

Koš, Peter. 1986. *The Monetary Circulation in the Southeastern Alpine Region ca. 300 BC–AD 1000*. Ljubljana: Narodni Muzej.

Kovács, László. 2000. "Coinage and other forms of currency in Hungary." In *Europe's Centre around A.D. 1000*, ed. Alfried Wieczorek and Hans-Martin Hinz, 125–26. Stuttgart: Theiss.

Kovalev, Roman K. 2002. "Dirham mint output of Samanid Samarqand and its connection to the beginnings of trade with northern Europe." *Histoire et Mesure* 17:197–216.

———. 2002–3. "The mint of al-Shash: The vehicle for the origins and continuation of trade relations between Viking-age northern Europe and Samanid Central Asia." *Archivum Eurasiae Medii Aevi* 12:47–79.

Kozub, Marcin. 1997. "The chronology of the inflow of Byzantine coins into the Avar khaganate." In *Origins of Central Europe*, ed. Przemysław Urbańczyk, 241–46. Warsaw: Scientific Society of Polish Archaeologists.

Leimus, Ivar, and Arkadi Molvögin. 2001. *Estonian Collections: Anglo-Saxon, Anglo-Norman, and Later British Coins*. Oxford: Oxford University Press; New York: Spink and Son.

Marović, Ivan. 1988. "A hoard of Byzantine gold coins from Narona." In *Studia Numismatica Labacensia: Alexandro Jeločnik oblata*, ed. Peter Koš and Željko Demo, 295–316. Ljubljana: Narodni Muzej.

Metcalf, David M. 1963. "The coinage of Thessaloniki, 829–1204, and its place in Balkan monetary history." *Balkan Studies* 4:277–88.

———. 1976. "Coinage and coin finds associated with a military presence in the medieval Balkans." In *Kovanje i kovnice antičkog i srednjovekovnog novca*, ed. Vladimir Kondić, 88–97. Belgrade: Arheološki Institut.

———. 1979. *Coinage of South-Eastern Europe, 820–1396*. London: Royal Numismatic Society.

———. 1981–82. "The copper coinage of Constantine VII with Zoe in the Balkans." *Buletinul Societății Numismatice Române* 75–76:253–55.

———. 1988. "The minting of gold coinage at Thessalonica in the fifth and sixth centuries and the gold currency of Illyricum and Dalmatia." In *Studies in Early Byzantine Gold Coinage*, ed. Wolfgang Hahn and William E. Metcalf, 65–109. New York: American Numismatic Society.

———. 1991. "Avar and Slav invasions into the Balkan Peninsula (c. 575–625): The nature of the numismatic evidence." *Journal of Roman Archaeology* 4:140–48.

Mikołajczyk, Andrzej. 1984–85. "Between Elbe and Vistula: The inflow of German coins into the west Slavonic lands in the 10th and 11th century." *Acta Praehistorica et Archaeologica* 16–17:183–201.

Mirnik, Ivan. 1981. *Coin Hoards in Yugoslavia*. Oxford: British Archaeological Reports.

Mirnik, Ivan, and Andrej Semrov. 1997–98. "Byzantine coins in the Zagreb Archaeological Museum Numismatic Collection: Anastasius I (A.D. 497–518)–Anastasius II (A.D. 713–715)." *Vjesnik Arheološkog Muzeja u Zagrebu* 30–31:129–258.

Noonan, Thomas S. 1979–80. "Monetary circulation in early medieval Rus': A study of the Volga Bulgar dirham finds." *Russian History* 7:294–311.

———. 1980. "When and how dirhams first reached Russia: A numismatic critique of the Pirenne theory." *Cahiers du monde russe et soviétique* 21:401–69.

———. 1981. "Ninth-century dirhem hoards from European Russia: A preliminary analysis." In *Viking-Age Coinage in the Northern Lands: The Sixth Oxford Symposium on Coinage and Monetary History*, ed. M. A. S. Blackburn and D. M. Metcalf, 47–117. Oxford: British Archaeological Reports.

——— 1982. "Did the Khazars possess a monetary economy? An analysis of the numismatic evidence." *Archivum Eurasiae Medii Aevi* 2:219–67.

———. 1982. "A ninth-century dirham hoard from Devista in southern Russia." *American Numismatic Society Museum Notes* 27:185–209.

———. 1982. "Ninth-century dirham hoards from northwestern Russia and the southeastern Baltic." *Journal of Baltic Studies* 13:220–44.

———. 1983. "A dirham hoard of the early eleventh century from northern Estonia and its importance for the routes by which dirhams reached Eastern Europe ca. 1000 AD." *Journal of Baltic Studies* 14:185–202.

———. 1983. "What does historical numismatics suggest about the history of Khazaria in the ninth century?" *Archivum Eurasiae Medii Aevi* 3:265–81.

———. 1984. "The regional composition of ninth-century dirham hoards from European Russia." *Numismatic Chronicle* 144:153–65.

———. 1984. "Why dirhems first reached Russia: The role of Arab-Khazar relations in the development of the earliest Islamic trade with Eastern Europe." *Archivum Eurasiae Medii Aevi* 4:151–282.

———. 1985. "The first major silver crisis in Russia and the Baltic, ca. 875–900." *Hikuin* 11:41–51.

———. 1986. "Khwarazmian coins of the eighth century from Eastern Europe: Post-Sassanian interlude in the relations between Central Asia and European Russia." *Archivum Eurasiae Medii Aevi* 6:243–58.

———. 1988. "The impact of the silver crisis in Islam upon Novgorod's trade with the Baltic." *Bericht der römisch-germanischen Kommission* 69:411–47.

———. 1990. "Dirham exports to the Baltic in the Viking age: Some preliminary observations." In *Sigtuna Papers: Proceedings of the Sigtuna Symposium on Viking-Age Coinage, 1–4 June 1989*, ed. Kenneth Jonsson and Brita Malmer, 251–57. Stockholm: Kungl. Vitterhets Historie och Antikvitets Akademien; London: Spink and Son.

———. 1992. "Dirham hoards from medieval Lithuania." *Journal of Baltic Studies* 23:395–413.

———. 1992. "Fluctuations in Islamic trade with Eastern Europe during the Viking Age." *Harvard Ukrainian Studies* 16:237–59.

———. 1998. *The Islamic World, Russia, and the Vikings, 750–900: The Numismatic Evidence*. Aldershot and Brookfield: Ashgate.

Oberländer-Târnoveanu, Ernest. 2000. "Coins and history: The case of the area of the Iron Gates of the Danube during the 10th–11th centuries." *Istros* 10:387–411.

————. 2001. "From the late antiquity to the early Middle Ages: The Byzantine coins in the territories of the Iron Gates of the Danube from the second half of the sixth century to the first half of the eighth century." *Etudes byzantines et post-byzantines* 4:29–69.

Pavlova, Elena. 1994. "The coinless period in the history of northeastern Rus': Historiography study." *Russian History* 21:375–92.

Penna, Vasso. 2002. "Numismatic circulation in Corinth from 976 to 1204." In *The Economic History of Byzantium from the Seventh through the Fifteenth Century,* ed. Angeliki E. Laiou, 655–58. Washington, D.C.: Dumbarton Oaks Research Library and Collection.

Perkowski, Jan L. 2000. "Linguistic history engraved in gold and silver: Legends on the coins of St. Vladimir." *Palaeoslavica* 8:1–17.

Petacki, D. 1996. "The early Byzantine hoard from the village of Orese." *Makedonski numizmatički glasnik* 2:87–93.

Preda, Constantin. 1975. "The Byzantine coins: An expression of the relations between the empire and the populations north of the Danube in the 6th–13th centuries." In *Relations between the Autochthonous Population and the Migratory Populations on the Territory of Romania,* ed. Miron Constantinescu, Ştefan Pascu, and Petre Diaconu, 219–29. Bucharest: Editura Academiei Republicü Socialiste România.

Rašković, D. 1997. "Findings of Roman and Byzantine coins in the National Museum in Kruševac, from the area of the Roman road—Via Publica." *Numizmatičar* 20:130.

Rispling, Gert. 1987. "Coins with crosses and bird heads: Christian imitations of Islamic coins?" *Fornvännen* 82:75–87.

————. 1990. "The Volga Bulgarian imitative coinage of al-Amir Yaltawar ('Barman') and Mikail b. Jafar." In *Sigtuna Papers: Proceedings of the Sigtuna Symposium on Viking-Age Coinage, 1–4 June 1989,* ed. Kenneth Jonsson and Brita Malmer, 275–82. Stockholm: Kungl. Vitterhets Historie och Antikvitets Akademien; London: Spink and Son.

————. 2001. "A list of coin finds relevant to the study of early Islamic type imitations." *Russian History* 28:327–38.

Salamon, M. 1996. "The Byzantine gold coin found at Żółków (southern Poland) and the problem of lightweight solidi in central Europe." *Notae numismaticae* 1:97–106.

Sejbal, Jiří. 1976. "The elements of medieval coinage in the territory of Great Moravia." In *Actes du 8-e Congrès international de numismatique, New York–Washington, septembre 1973,* ed. Herbert A. Cahn and Georges Le Rider, 473–76. Paris and Basel: Association internationale des numismates professionels.

Semenov, A. I. 1994. "New evidence on the Slavynsk (Anastasaiyevka) hoard of the 8th century and Byzantine Arab gold coins." In *New Archaeological Discoveries in Asiatic Russia and Central Asia,* 83–85. St. Petersburg: Institute of History of Material Culture.

Smedley, John. 1988. "Seventh-century Byzantine coins in southern Russia and the problem of light weight solidi." In *Studies in Early Byzantine Gold Coinage,* ed. Wolfgang Hahn and William E. Metcalf, 111–30. New York: American Numismatic Society.

Stepková, Jarmila. 1964. "The structure of finds of the Islamic silver coins in the territory of Czechoslovakia." *Annals of the Náprštek Muzeum* 3:113–28.

Stoliarik, Elena S. 1992. *Essays on Monetary Circulation in the North-Western Black Sea Region in the Late Roman and Byzantine Periods (Late 3rd Century–Early 13th Century AD).* Odessa: Polis.

————. 1996. "The problem of late Roman and Byzantine currency penetration into the northwestern Pontic region." In *Acts. XVIIIth International Congress of Byzantine Studies: Selected Papers; Moscow 1991*, ed. Ihor Ševčenko, G. G. Litavrin, and Walter Hanak, 4:262–67. Shepherdstown, W.V.: Byzantine Studies Press.

Suchodolski, Stanisław. 2000. "The earliest coinage of Poland." In *Europe's Centre around A.D. 1000*, ed. Alfried Wieczorek and Hans-Martin Hinz, 124. Stuttgart: Theiss.

————. 2001. "Change of transcontinental contacts as indicated by coins in the Baltic zone." In *Europe around the Year 1000*, ed. Przemysław Urbańczyk, 85–100. Warsaw: Wydawnictwo DiG.

Symons, David. 1993. "Medieval European coins in the Finney Collection. III: Central Europe." *Spink Numismatic Circular* 101:317.

Talvio, Tuukka. 1998. "Islamic coins found in Finland." In *Byzantium and Islam in Scandinavia: Acts of a Symposium at Uppsala University, June 15–16, 1996*, ed. Elisabeth Piltz, 77–84. Jonsered: Paul Åströms Förlag.

Teoklieva-Stoicheva, Evtelpa. 2001. *Mediaeval Coins from Mesemvria*. Sofia: Agathon.

Thompson, Margaret. 1940. "Some unpublished bronze money of the early eighth century." *Hesperia* 9:358–80.

Tomková, Kateřina. 1996. "Bohemian coins in tenth- to twelfth-century silver hoards." In *Ibrahim ibn Yakub al-Turtushi: Christianity, Islam, and Judaism meet in East-Central Europe, c. 800–1300 A.D.; Proceedings of the International Colloquy, 25–29 April 1994*, ed. Petr Charvát and Jiří Prosecký, 78–92. Prague: Oriental Institute, Academy of Sciences of the Czech Republic.

Wodak, E. 1958. "Anglo-Saxon coin design: Influence on early Bohemian coins." *South Australian Numismatic Journal* 9:1–2.

CERAMICS AND GLASS

Akrabova-Jandova, Ivanka. 1975. "Preslav inlaid ceramics." In *Studies in Memory of David Talbot Rice*, ed. G. Robertson and G. Henderson, 25–33. Edinburgh: Edinburgh University Press.

Balbolova-Ivanova, Maria. 2000. "A contribution to the research of the early medieval ceramics in Bulgaria." *Archaeologia Bulgarica* 4:73–85.

Balla, M. 1989. "Provenance studies of Avar ceramics by neutron activation analysis." *A Wosinszky Mór Múzeum Évkönyve* 15:131–33.

Barford, Paul, and Ewa Marczak. 1992. "Peasant households, potters, and phasing: Early medieval ceramics from Podebłocie, Poland." *Archaeologia Polona* 30:127–49.

Brather, Sebastian. 2000. "Western Slav pottery of the early and High Middle Ages." In *Europe's Centre around A.D. 1000*, ed. Alfried Wieczorek and Hans-Martin Hinz, 77–79. Stuttgart: Theiss.

Brusić, Zdenko. 1976. "Byzantine amphorae (9th to 12th century), from eastern Adriatic underwater sites." *Archaeologia Iugoslavica* 17:37–49.

Cvjetičanin, Tatjana. 1996. "Some observations about pottery evidence from Diana." In *Roman Limes on the Middle and Lower Danube*, ed. Petar Petrović, 93–99. Belgrade: Arheološki Institut.

Djingova, R., and I. Kuleff. 1992. "An archaeometric study of medieval glass from the first Bulgarian capital, Pliska (ninth to tenth century AD)." *Archaeometry* 34:53–61.

Dvoržak Schrunk, Ivančica. 1996. "Late Roman and early Byzantine ceramic trade in

Dalmatia: From the fourth to the eighth century." In *Acts. XVIIIth International Congress of Byzantine Studies: Selected Papers; Moscow 1991*, ed. Ihor Ševčenko, G. G. Litavrin, and Walter Hanak, 2:282–88. Shepherdstown, W.V.: Byzantine Studies Press.

Evans, Huw. 1988. "The potential for the analysis of early medieval pottery in Dalmatia." In *Recent Developments in Yugoslav Archaeology*, ed. J. C. Chapman, J. Bintliff, V. Gaffney, and B. Slapsak, 85–99. Oxford: British Archaeological Reports.

Franz, M. A. 1938. "Middle Byzantine pottery in Athens." *Hesperia* 7:429–67.

Gardawski, Aleksander. 1974. "The antique sources for the Slav ceramic ware (problematics concerning the so-called 'early Byzantine ceramic ware')." *Balcanoslavica* 3:1–12.

Janković, Milica. 1974. "The ceramic ware of the lower Danube basin culture in the 9th–11th century in the territory of Timočka Krajina." *Balcanoslavica* 3:75–87.

Klenina, Elena. 1999. "Table and cooking pottery of the IV–VI A.D. from the excavation of the episcopal residence at Novae." In *Der Limes an der unteren Donau von Diokletian bis Herakleios: Vorträge der internationalen Konferenz Svištov, Bulgarien (1–5 September 1998)*, ed. Gerda von Bülow and Alexandra Milcheva, 83–88. Sofia: NOUS.

Kontogiannis, Nikos D. 2002. "A fragment of a Chinese marbled ware bowl from Methoni, Greece." *Bizantinistica: Rivista di studi bizantini e slavi* 4:39–46.

Kurnatowska, Zofia. 1975. "On the development of the early mediaeval ceramics in Poland." In *Château Gaillard: Etudes de castellologie médiévale; Actes du colloque international tenu à Venlo (Pays-Bas), 4–9 septembre 1974*, ed. Michel de Brouard, 125–36. Caen: Centre de Recherches Archéologiques Médiévales de l'Université de Caen.

Minchev, A. 1983. "The late Roman fine ware import to the western Black Sea coast." In *Ancient Bulgaria: Papers Presented to the International Symposium on the Ancient History and Archaeology of Bulgaria, University of Nottingham, 1981*, ed. A. G. Poulter, 194–201. Nottingham: University of Nottingham.

Profantová, Nad'a. 1996. "On some Danubian influences in 8th–9th-century Bohemia: Particular pottery shapes." In *Ethnische und kulturelle Verhältnisse an der mittleren Donau vom 6. bis zum 11. Jahrhundert: Symposium Nitra 6. bis 10. November 1994*, ed. D. Bialeková and J. Zábojník, 227–44. Bratislava: Vydavatel'stvo Slovenskej Akadémie Vied.

Schwartz, Ellen C. 1982. "Medieval ceramic decoration in Bulgaria." *Byzantinoslavica* 43:45–50.

Šekelj-Ivančan, Tatiana. 2001. *Early Medieval Pottery in Northern Croatia. Typological and Chronological Pottery Analyses as Indicators of the Settlement of the Territory between the Rivers Drava and Sava from the 10th to 13th Centuries A.D.* Oxford: Archaeopress.

Takács, Miklós. 1996. "Pottery." In *The Ancient Hungarians: Exhibition Catalogue*, ed. István Fodor, 62–63. Budapest: Hungarian National Museum.

Teodor, Eugen S. 2003. "About some 'Slavic pottery' from Slovenia." *Studia antiqua et archaeologica* 9:399–410.

Tirpaková, Anna, Darina Bialeková, and Ivona Vlkolinská. 1989. "The application of some mathematic-statistical methods in solving the possibility of exploitation of Roman measures in manufacturing of Slavic axe-shaped currency bars and pottery." *Slovenská Archeológia* 37:427–50.

Tirpaková, Anna, and Ivona Vlkolinská. 1992. "The application of some mathematical-statistical methods for the analysis of Slavic pottery." In *Computer Applications and Quantitative Methods in Archaeology, 1991,* ed. Gary Lock and John Moffett, 183–86. Oxford.

Vlkolinská, Ivona. 1994. "Pottery from cemeteries of the 9th–10th centuries in the territory of Slovakia." In *Slawische Keramik in Mitteleuropa vom 8. bis zum 11. Jahrhundert: Kolloquium Mikulčice, 25.–27. Mai 1993,* ed. Čenek Staňa, 1:83–92. Brno: Archäologisches Institut der Akademie der Wissenschaften der Tschechischen Republick.

Zsolt, Visy. 2002. "Medieval pottery kilns in the Carpathian Basin." *European Journal of Archaeology* 5:309–42.

OTHER ARTIFACTS

Kolchin, B. A. 1989. *Wooden Artifacts from Medieval Novgorod.* Oxford: British Archaeological Reports.

Mitchell, John G., H. Askvik, and Heid Gjöstein Resi. 1984. "Potassium-argon of schist honestones from the Viking age sites at Kaupang (Norway), Aggersborg (Denmark), Hedeby (Schleswig-Holstein) and Wolin (Poland), and their archaeological implications." *Journal of Archaeological Science* 11:171–76.

Smirnova, Liuba. 2002. "Social hierarchy of early Novgorod on the evidence of an analysis of the 10th–11th century single-sided composite combs." In *Centre, Region, Periphery: Medieval Europe Basel 2002,* ed. Guido Helmig, Barbara Scholkmann, and Matthias Untermann, 1:552–65. Basel: Dr. G. Wesselkamp.

INSCRIPTIONS

Bozhilov, Ivan. 1973. "One of Omurtag's memorial inscriptions." *Bulgarian Historical Review* 1:72–76.

Delonga, Vedrana. 1996. *The Latin Epigraphic Monuments of Early Mediaeval Croatia.* Split: Museum of Croatian Archaeological Monuments.

Dobrev, Peter. 2003. "The inscriptions in Protobulgarian language discovered by Prof. V. Beshevliev and the origin of the Protobulgarians." In *Studia protobulgarica et mediaevalia europensia. V chest na profesor Veselin Beshevliev,* ed. Vasil Giuzelev, Kazimir Popkonstantinov, Georgi Bakalov, and Rosina Kostova, 385–90. Sofia: Centăr za izsledvaniia na bălgarite TANGRA TanNakRa IK.

Erdal, Marcel. 1988. "The Turkic Nagy-Szent-Miklós inscription in Greek letters." *Acta Orientalia Academiae Scientiarum Hungaricae* 42:221–34.

Fučić, Branko. 1999. "The Croatian Galgolitic and Cyrillic epigraphs." In *Croatia in the Early Middle Ages: A Cultural Survey,* ed. Ivan Supičić, 259–82. London: Philip Wilson Publishers; Zagreb: AGM.

Grigoriou-Ioannidou, M. 1997. *The Inscription of the "Madara Horseman": Remarks and Problems.* Athens: National Committee for South-Eastern European Studies.

Harmatta, János. 1995. "Sogdian inscriptions on Avar objects." *Acta Orientalia Academiae Scientiarum Hungaricae* 48:61–65.

———. 1996–97. "Turk and Avar runic inscriptions on metal belt-plates." *Acta Antiqua Academiae Scientiarum Hungaricae* 37:321–30.

Hercigonja, Eduard. 1999. "Glagolists and glagolism." In *Croatia in the Early Middle*

Ages: A Cultural Survey, ed. Ivan Supičić, 369–98. London: Philip Wilson Publishers; Zagreb: AGM.

Lunt, Horace G. 2000. "Thoughts, suggestions, and questions about the earliest Slavic writing systems." *Wiener slavistischer Jahrbuch* 46:271–86.

Kostova, Rossina. 1994–95. "Boot-graffiti from the monastery of Ravna, and early pilgrimage in Bulgaria." *Annual of the Medieval Studies at the CEU,* 1:140–65.

———. 1998. "A tenth-century graffito of St. Basil the Great in the light of his cult in eastern monasticism." *Palaeobulgarica* 22:75–95.

———. 1999. "Lust and piety: Graffiti from Bulgarian medieval monasteries." In *Disziplinierung im Alltag des Mittelalters und der frühen Neuzeit,* 233–54. Vienna: Verlag der Österreichischen Akademie der Wissenschaften.

Kyzlasov, Igor L. 1994. "Sphere of applications of the 8th–10th centuries steppe-runic alphabets." In *The Archaeology of the Steppes: Methods and Strategies. Papers from the International Symposium Held in Naples, 9–12 September 1992,* ed. Bruno Genito, 619–31. Naples: Istituto universitario orientale.

Liestøl, Aslak. 1970. "Runic inscriptions." In *Varangian Problems: Report on the First International Symposium on the Theme "The Eastern Connections of the Nordic Peoples in the Viking Period and Early Middle Ages," Moesgaard-University of Aarhus, October 7–11, 1968,* ed. Knud Hannestad, Knud Jordal, Ole Klindt-Jensen, et al., 121–32. Copenhague: Munksgaard.

Mathiesen, Robert. 1977. "The importance of the Bitolja inscription for Cyrillic palaeography." *Slavonic and East European Review* 21:1–2.

Matijević-Sokol, Mirjana. 1999. "Latin inscriptions." In *Croatia in the Early Middle Ages: A Cultural Survey,* ed. Ivan Supičić, 239–56. London: Philip Wilson Publishers; Zagreb: AGM.

Melnikova, Elena Aleksandrovna. 1981. "Scandinavian Runic inscriptions as a source for the history of Eastern Europe." In *Les pays du Nord et Byzance (Scandinavie et Byzance): Actes du colloque nordique et international de byzantinologie tenu à Upsal, 20–22 avril 1979,* ed. Rudolf Zeitler, 169–73. Uppsala: Almqvist and Wiksell.

Menges, Karl H. 1951. "Altaic elements in the proto-Bulgarian inscriptions." *Byzantion* 21:85–118.

———. 1958. "A note on the compound titles in the proto-Bulgarian inscriptions." *Byzantion* 28:441–53.

Minns, E. H. 1938. "The Greek inscription on nos. 9 and 10 of the Nagyszentmiklós treasure." In *Senatne un maksla,* ed. Francis Balodis and Ludolfs Liberst, 1:120–25. Riga: Valstpapiru spiestuve.

Nandriş, Grigore. 1960. "A spurious Slavonic inscription from the Danube Canal." *Slavonic and East European Review* 38:530–34.

Németh, J. 1971. "The runiform inscriptions from Nagyszentmiklós and the runiform scripts of Eastern Europe." *Acta Linguistica Academiae Scientiarum Hungarica* 21:1–52.

Orel, V. 1994. "Ancient Kievan graffiti: Linguistic and historical sources." *Palaeoslavica* 3:281–90.

———. 1996. "'Unofficial' Old Russian graffiti in Kiev." *Zeitschrift für Slawistik* 41:166–70.

Ovcharov, Dimităr. 1976. "A Cyrillic inscription of 931 in Preslav." *Bulgarian Historical Review* 4:71–75.

———. 1977. "Ship graffiti from medieval Bulgaria." *International Journal of Nautical Archaeology and Underwater Exploration* 6:59–61.

Riba, István. 2000. "Reading the runes: Evidence of the dual conquest." *Hungarian Quarterly* 41:80–84.

Róna-Tas, András. 1976. "A runic inscription in the Kujbyšev region." *Acta Orientalia Academiae Scientiarum Hungaricae* 30:267–71.

———. 1988. "Problems of the East European scripts with special regard to the newly found inscription of Szarvás." In *Popoli delle steppe: Unni, Avari, Ungari. Settimane di studio, Spoleto 23–29 aprile 1987*, 2:483–511. Spoleto: Presso la Sede del Centro.

Salamon, Maciej. 1971. "Some notes on a medieval inscription from Silistra (c. 976)." *Revue des études sud-est-européennes* 9:487–96.

Simpson, Catherine. 1992. "The Croats and the Glagolitic alphabet." *Medieval World* 7:17–23.

Stănciulescu-Bîrda, Alexandru N. 1986. "One hypothesis: The decipherment of the inscriptions from Murfatlar (Basarabi)." *Balkan Studies* 27:237–51.

Vasary, I. 1972. "Runiform signs on objects of the Avar period (6th–8th cc. A.D.)." *Acta Orientalia Academiae Scientiarum Hungaricae* 25:335–47.

LINGUISTICS

Baldwin, Barry. 1997. "'Torna, torna, phrater': What language?" *Byzantion* 67:264–67.

Benkö, Loránd. 2000. "The Hungarian language." In *Europe's Centre around A.D. 1000*, ed. Alfried Wieczorek and Hans-Martin Hinz, 368–69. Stuttgart: Theiss.

Birnbaum, Henrik. 1975. *Common Slavic: Progress and Problems in Its Reconstruction.* Columbus, Ohio: Slavica.

———. 1981. "Wie alt is das altertümlichste Sprachdenkmal? Weitere Erwägungen zur Herkunft der Kiewer Blätter und zu ihrem Platz in der Literatur des slawischen Mittelalters." *Welt der Slawen* 26:225–58.

———. 1982. "The Slavonic language community as a genetic and typological class." *Welt der Slawen* 27:5–43.

———. 1987. "On the genealogical and typological classification of Old Church Slavonic and its textual evidence." *Welt der Slawen* 32:362–407.

———. 1993. "On the ethnogenesis and protohome of the Slavs: The linguistic evidence." *Journal of Slavic Linguistics* 1:352–74.

Bubenik, Vit. 2001. *Morphological and Syntactic Change in Medieval Greek and South Slavic Languages.* Munich: Lincom Europa.

Chen, Sanping. 1998. "Some remarks on the Chinese 'Bulgar.'" *Acta Orientalia Academiae Scientiarum Hungaricae* 51:69–83.

Danylenko, Andrii. 2001. "The names of the Dnieper rapids in Constantine Porphyrogenitus revisited: An attempt at linguistic attribution." *Welt der Slawen* 46:43–62.

Dimitrov, S. 1994. "On the Proto-Bulgarian character of the toponym 'the mouth of Tiča.'" *Etudes Balkaniques* 30:102–8.

Duma, Jerzy. 1995. "The phonetic phenomena connected with the strengthening and weakening of sonants in Bulgarian and Macedonian dialects." In *Medieval Dialectology,* ed. Jacek Fisiak, 1–6. Berlin: Mouton de Gruyter.

Ekbo, Sven. 1981. "The etymology of Finnish Ruotsi 'Sweden.'" In *Les pays du Nord et Byzance (Scandinavie et Byzance): Actes du colloque nordique et international de byzantinologie tenu à Upsal, 20–22 avril 1979,* ed. Rudolf Zeitler, 143–45. Uppsala: Almqvist and Wiksell.

Galton, Herbert. 1988. "How the Czech language lost its correlation of palatalization: A case study of languages in context." *Folia linguistica* 22:161–78.

———. 1996. "After-effects of the Proto-Bulgarian language." *Zeitschrift für Balkanologie* 32:151–56.

Georgiev, Vl. 1981. "The genesis of the Bulgarian people and the origin of the Bulgarian language." *Palaeobulgarica* 5:16–20.

Gołab, Zbigniew. 1975. "Veneti/Venedi: The oldest name of the Slavs." *Journal of Indo-European Studies* 3:321–36.

———. 1983. "The ethnogenesis of the Slavs in the light of linguistics." In *American Contributions to the Ninth International Congress of Slavists,* ed. Michael S. Flier, 1:131–46. Columbus, Ohio: Slavica.

———. 1984. "Old Bulgarian Sever' (?) and Old Russian Severjane." *Wiener slavistischer Jahrbuch* 30:9–22.

———. 1992. *The Origins of the Slavs: A Linguist's View.* Columbus, Ohio: Slavica.

Habovštiak, Anton. 1992–93. "The ethnogenesis of the Slovaks from the linguistic aspect." *Ethnologia Slovaca et Slavica* 24–25:13–29.

Hamp, Eric P. 1970. "Early Slavic influence in Albanian." *Balkansko ezikoznanie* 14:11–17.

Ivić, Pavle. 1972. "Balkan Slavic migrations in the light of South Slavic dialectology." In *Aspects of the Balkans: Continuity and Change; Contributions to the International Balkan Conference held at UCLA, October 23–28, 1969,* ed. Henrik Birnbaum and Speros Vryonis Jr., 66–86. The Hague and Paris: Mouton.

Kaleta, Zofia. 1991. "The reconstruction of the earliest evolutionary stages of Slavic surnames in the context of European name-giving." In *Probleme der älteren Namenschichten: Leipziger Symposion, 21. bis 22. November 1989,* ed. Ernst Eichler, 223–36. Heidelberg: Carl Winter Universitätsverlag.

Kantor, Marvin. 1993. "A question of language: Church Slavonic and the west Slavs." In *American Contributions to the Eleventh International Congress of Slavists, Bratislava, August–September 1993: Literature, Linguistics, Poetics,* ed. Robert A. Maguire and Alan Timberlake, 320–29. Columbus, Ohio: Slavica.

Katičić, Radoslav. 1999. "Language and literacy." In *Croatia in the Early Middle Ages: A Cultural Survey,* ed. Ivan Supičić, 339–67. London: Philip Wilson Publishers; Zagreb: AGM.

Krajčović, Rudolf. 1988. "The language in Great Moravia and its continuity with Slovak." *Studia Historica Slovaca* 16:157–72.

Lozinski, Philip. 1964. "The name 'Slav.'" In *Essays in Russian History: A Collection Dedicated to George Vernadsky,* ed. Alan D. Ferguson and Alfred Levin, 19–32. Hamden, Conn.: Archon Books.

Lunt, Horace G. 1966. "Old Church Slavonic 'kralj.'" In *Orbis scriptus: Dmitrij Tschižewskij zum 70. Geburtstag,* ed. Gerhardt Dietrich, Wiktor Weintraub, and Hans-Jürgen Zum Winkel, 483–89. Munich: W. Fink.

———. 1975. "On the language of Old Rus: Some questions and suggestions." *Russian linguistics* 2:269–81.

———. 1984–85. "On Common Slavic." *Zbornik Matice sprske za filologiju i lingvistiku* 27–28:417–22.

———. 1985. "Slavs, Common Slavic, and Old Church Slavonic." In *Litterae Slavicae Medii Aevi: Francisco Venceslao Mares Sexagenario Oblatae,* ed. Johannes Reinhart, 185–204. Munich: Otto Sagner.

————. 1996. "Proto-Slavic or Common Slavic versus Pan-Slavic: Morpho-lexical puzzles of early Slavic written dialects." *International Journal of Slavic Linguistics and Poetics* 39–40:279–98.

Makkay, János. 1996. "Dating Hungarian." In *Az öshzaától Arpád honalapításáig*, ed. Kálmán Magyar, 271–92. Budapest: Magyar Nemzeti Történeti Társaság.

Mandoky Kongur, István. 1979. "Two Hungarian verbs of Old Turkic origin." *Acta Orientalia Academiae Scientiarum Hungaricae* 33:291–99.

Mihaljević, Milan. 1992. "The phonological system of the Croatian redaction of Church Slavonic." *Slavonic and East European Review* 36:1–16.

Petrucci, Peter R. 1995. "The historical development of the Rumanian /ɨ/." In *Contemporary Research in Romance Linguistics: Papers from the 22nd Linguistic Symposium on Romance Languages El Paso/Cd. Juárez, February 1992*, ed. Jon Amastae, Grant Goodall, Mario Montalbetti, and Marianne Phinney, 167–76. Amsterdam and Philadelphia: John Benjamins.

Popowska-Taborska, Hanna. 1997. "The Slavs in the early Middle Ages from the viewpoint of contemporary linguistics." In *Origins of Central Europe*, ed. Przemysław Urbańczyk, 91–96. Warsaw: Scientific Society of Polish Archaeologists.

Rudnyc'kyj, J. B. 1961. *The Origin of the Name "Slav."* Winnipeg: Ukrainian Free Academy of Sciences.

Rzetelska-Felesko, Ewa. 1995. "Slavonic Pomerania in the past: Its links with the neighboring areas and its internal division." In *Medieval Dialectology*, ed. Jacek Fisiak, 217–24. Berlin: Mouton de Gruyter.

Schaarschmidt, Gunter. 1992. "The northwest Slavic area umlaut i u: Chronology and conditions." *Canadian Slavonic Papers* 34:269–77.

Schenker, Alexander M. 1995. *The Dawn of Slavic: An Introduction to Slavic Philology.* New Haven and London: Yale University Press.

Schmidt, Knud Rahbek. 1970. "On the possible traces of Nordic influence in Russian place-names." In *Varangian Problems: Report on the First International Symposium on the Theme "The Eastern Connections of the Nordic Peoples in the Viking Period and Early Middle Ages," Moesgaard-University of Aarhus, October 7–11, 1968*, ed. Knud Hannestad, Knud Jordal, Ole Klindt-Jensen, et al., 143–48. Copenhague: Munksgaard.

Shapira, Dan. 1998–99. "Two names of the first Khazar Jewish beg." *Archivum Eurasiae Medii Aevi* 10:231–41.

Simeonova, Liliana. 1996. "Greek-Slavonic bilingualism in Bulgaria and Byzantine-Bulgarian relations, 860s–960s." In *Acts. XVIIIth International Congress of Byzantine Studies: Selected Papers; Moscow 1991*, ed. Ihor Sevcenko, G. G. Litavrin, and Walter Hanak, 2:96–109. Shepherdstown, W.V.: Byzantine Studies Press.

Simunović, Petar. 1999. "The evidence provided by proper names in the early centuries." In *Croatia in the Early Middle Ages: A Cultural Survey*, ed. Ivan Supičić, 401–12. London: Philip Wilson Publishers; Zagreb: AGM.

Szende, Tamás. 1994. "Do historical changes repeat themselves? (On historical "two-open syllable shortening" and present-day "fast-speech syllable elision" in Hungarian)." *Acta Linguistica Hungarica* 42:63–74.

Thulin, A. L. F. 1981. "The southern origin of the name *Rus'*: Some remarks." In *Les pays du Nord et Byzance (Scandinavie et Byzance): Actes du colloque nordique et international de byzantinologie tenu à Upsal, 20–22 avril 1979*, ed. Rudolf Zeitler, 175–83. Uppsala: Almqvist and Wiksell.

Trubachev, O. N. 1985. "Linguistics and ethnogenesis of the Slavs: The ancient Slavs as evidenced by etymology and onomastics." *Journal of Indo-European Studies* 13: 203–56.

Vlasto, A. P. 1986. *A Linguistic History of Russia to the End of the Eighteenth Century.* Oxford: Oxford University Press; New York: Clarendon Press.

Wedel, Alfred R., and Theodor Christchev. 1989. "The 'constative' and the 'complexive' aspects in Gothic and in the Old Bulgarian of the Zograph Codex." *Germano-Slavica* 6:195–208.

Wickman, Bo. 1984–86. "Old Hungarian from Arabic sources." *Orientalia Suecana* 33–35:475–77.

Contributors

PAUL M. BARFORD is a freelance British archaeologist living and working in Poland, specializing in early medieval archaeology, particularly of Poland and central Europe. He is the author of several articles on such diverse topics as early medieval ceramics, earthworks, and Marxism in Polish archaeology, as well as of *The Early Slavs: Culture and Society in Early Medieval Eastern Europe* (London and Ithaca, 2001). His current work concerns the origins of the Slavic-speaking populations of East Central Europe, but he also writes on heritage management.

ANDRZEJ BUKO is the director of the Early Medieval Archaeology Department of the Institute of Archaeology at the University of Warsaw and professor at the Institute of Archaeology and Ethnology of the Polish Academy of Sciences. He is the author of numerous articles and reviews concerning prehistoric and medieval archaeology, and with his *Introduction to the Study of Polish Medieval Pottery* (Warsaw 1997), he is a pioneer of systematic research on medieval ceramics. His fieldwork research was published in two monographs, *Kleczanów: Trial Excavations, 1989–1992* (Warsaw, 1998) and *The Beginnings of Sandomierz* (Warsaw, 2000). He is coauthor of *The Archaeology of Early Medieval Poland* and the editor of *Settlements and Architecture in the Polish Lands at the Time of the Gniezno Summit*, both volumes in preparation. His main research interests are the rise of the medieval state in Poland, medieval towns and rural archaeology, and pottery analysis.

FLORIN CURTA is an associate professor of medieval history and archaeology at the University of Florida. He received his Ph.D. in history from Western Michigan University (1998) and has published several studies on the archaeology, numismatics, and early medieval history of southeastern and Eastern Europe. His book *The Making of the Slavs: History and Archaeology of the Lower Danube Region, ca. 500–700* (Cambridge, 2001) received the Herbert Baxter Adams Award of the American Historical Association in 2002. Curta is currently working on a manuscript entitled *Southeast Europe in the Middle Ages, 500–1250*, to be published by Cambridge University Press, and on a collection of studies entitled *Borders, Barriers, and Ethnogenesis*, to be published by Brepols.

MÁRTA FONT is the head of the Department of Medieval and Early Modern History at the University of Pécs. She has taught medieval history in both Szeged and Pécs. She is the author of *Hungarians in the Kievan Chronicle* (Szeged, 1996), *Koloman the Learned, King of Hungary* (Szeged, 2001), and many articles on Arpadian Hungary and its relations to Kievan Rus'. She also coauthored *The History of Russia* (Szeged, 1996) and *The Ethnic and Demographic Situation of the Carpathian Basin during the Tenth to Seventeenth Centuries* (Szeged, 1998). Her work focusing on the medieval history of Hungarian-Russian cultural and political contacts was twice awarded the highest distinction of the Hungarian National Academy of Sciences (in 1997 and 2001).

JOACHIM HENNING is a professor of European archaeology at the Johann Wolfgang Goethe University in Frankfurt am Main. He has taught at both Free University and Humboldt University in Berlin. Specializing in the early medieval history of central and East Central Europe, he is the author of *Südosteuropa zwischen Antike und Mittelalter* (Berlin, 1987) and the editor of *Frühmittelalterlicher Burgenbau in Mittel- und Osteuropa* (Bonn, 1999) and *Europa im 10. Jahrhundert: Archäologie einer Aufbruchszeit* (Mainz, 2002), and he has authored many articles on the archaeology of the early Middle Ages and on new techniques of field research. He is also the director of the joint German-Bulgarian team responsible for archaeological excavations in Pliska. He was a visiting professor at the Universities of Sofia and Shumen (Bulgaria), an invited lecturer (2001) and visiting professor (2003) at Harvard University, and a Byzantine studies fellow at Dumbarton Oaks (2002). He currently conducts interdisciplinary research on the relationship between forms of agriculture and forms of political power.

ROMAN K. KOVALEV received his Ph.D. in Russian history from the University of Minnesota and is now an assistant professor of Russian history at the College of New Jersey. His specialty is early medieval Russia and its place in western and central Eurasian trade and cultural exchange. Among his main interests are Vikings in the East, Rus'-Byzantine trade relations, Novgorod's fur trade in the Middle Ages, the archaeological study of medieval Rus' birch-bark texts, and examination of deposits of medieval Islamic coin hoards for revelations about the patterns of trade relations between the Arab lands, Eastern Europe, and the Baltic. Some of his most recent studies have examined the mint outputs of medieval Islamic coins in Central Asia and the use of wooden tally sticks in credit operations and in the fur trade from Greenland to China. He is also a technical editor and a regular contributor of the journal *Archivum Eurasiae Medii Aevi.*

ALEXANDRU MADGEARU received his Ph.D. in history from the University of Bucharest (Romania) in 1997. Specializing in the late antique and early medieval history and archaeology of southeast Europe, he is the main researcher at the Institute for Defense Studies and Military History in Bucharest. He authored *The Romanians in the Work of the Hungarian Anonymous Notary* and *The Medieval Origins of the Balkan Conflict Areas* (both published in 2001) and was a Fulbright visiting scholar at the Ohio State University (2002–3).

NIKOLAI I. PETROV teaches archaeology in the Faculty of History at St. Petersburg State University. Among his current teaching interests are the archaeology of the Iron Age in northern Russia and the spread of Christianity in Rus'. He received his Ph.D. in archaeology from St. Petersburg State University (1997), with a dissertation on the *sopka* barrows of northwestern Russia between the eighth and the eleventh centuries. Petrov is the author of several studies on the mortuary assemblages of the early Middle Ages in the Novgorod region. He is the director of the Khvoshchinskaia Archaeological Expedition of St. Petersburg State University, which opened a number of excavations on several sites in the Mologa river basin of the Novgorod region, primarily in Bel'kovo and St'opanovo.

JONATHAN SHEPARD has taught Byzantine history for many years at Cambridge University. Together with Simon Franklin, he is coauthor of *The Emergence of Rus', 750–1200* (London, 1996) and coeditor of *Byzantine Diplomacy: Papers from the Twenty-Fourth Spring Symposium of Byzantine Studies* (Aldershot, 1992). He has published numerous studies pertaining to Byzantine, Balkan, and Rus' history, especially on relations between Byzantium and its "commonwealth." He is now working on a new book entitled *Byzantium between Barbarians, 812–1050,* to be published by Cambridge University Press.

TSVETELIN STEPANOV is a lecturer in history at the Center for Cultural Studies in the Faculty of Philosophy at the St. Kliment Ohridski University in Sofia. He is the author of *Power and Prestige in Early Medieval Bulgaria* (Sofia, 1999) and the editor of *Medieval Bulgarians: New Data, Interpretations, and Hypotheses* (Sofia, 2000) and *Bulgars and Khazars in the Early Middle Ages* (Sofia, 2003). He has also published numerous studies on the medieval history of Bulgaria and on the "steppe empires" of the Middle Ages. His main area of interest is power representation, as is illustrated by his most recent contributions to the periodicals *Early Medieval Europe* and *Byzantinoslavica*. He is also the editor of a collection of studies to be published in 2004 honoring the Bulgarian medievalist Georgi Bakalov.

PRZEMYSŁAW URBAŃCZYK is a professor of prehistory at the Podlaska Academy in Siedlce. He is the author of *Medieval Arctic Norway* (Warsaw, 1992), *Power and Politics in the Early Middle Ages* (Wrocław, 2000), and *The Year 1000* (Warsaw, 2001), and he edited numerous volumes dedicated to the medieval history of East Central Europe. His research interests range from the history of archaeology as an academic discipline to the medieval history of Central Europe and the North Atlantic region. A member of the European Science Foundation program "The Transformation of the Roman World," he has been engaged in an international project of multidisciplinary research on the earliest settlements in Iceland. He has given lectures at the Universities of Dublin, Tromsø, Lima, and Uppsala, as well as in the United States at Stanford and CUNY. A recipient of a Rockefeller Foundation grant as a resident of the Bellaggio Study Center in Italy, he was recently nominated the Polish representative on the standing committee for the humanities at the European Science Foundation.

Index